Moral Philosophy:
A Reader

Moral Philosophy:
A Reader

Third Edition

Edited, with Introduction, by
Louis P. Pojman

Hackett Publishing Company, Inc.
Indianapolis/Cambridge

This book is dedicated to the memory of the
Rev. Dr. Winfield and Mrs. Agnes Burggraaff
who lived the moral life
and showed others how to do so

Printed in the United States of America

09 08 07 06 05 04 03   1 2 3 4 5 6 7

For further information, please address:

Hackett Publishing Company, Inc.
P.O. Box 44937
Indianapolis, IN   46244-0937

www.hackettpublishing.com

Design by Dan Kirklin

Library of Congress Cataloging-in-Publication Data

Moral philosophy: a reader / edited, with introduction, by Louis P.
    Pojman.—3rd ed.
                                          p. cm.
    Includes bibliographical references.
    ISBN 0-87220-662-9 (cloth)—ISBN 0-87220-661-0 (paper)
      1. Ethics. I. Pojman, Louis P.

BJ1012.M6334 2003
170—dc21
                                                2002191910

Contents

Preface

Ethics courses are gaining new importance in universities and colleges. With the increased diversity and cultural pluralism in the West; the shrinking of the globe, so that we are increasingly all in one another's debt; the gradual erosion of traditional institutions, the family, and the church; and the dilemmas brought on by medical technology, a thoughtful examination of the foundations of morality has become an issue of the first magnitude. The undermining of older structures has resulted in a widespread uncritical acceptance of ethical relativism and egoism on our campuses. Yet, students are looking for guidance in solving moral dilemmas and resolving conflicts of interest. While moral philosophy does not by itself solve the world's problems, it sets them in a broader theoretical context, throws light on them, and gives us a conceptual apparatus that at least aids in achieving our moral goals. Furthermore, the subject, like any worthy pursuit, has intrinsic merit. It is inherently interesting. In light of this there is need of a short general reader in ethical theory to be used either on its own or together with a supporting single-authored text.

This work is an expansion of the core set of articles that I used in my 200-level ethical theory course for several years. It contains the classical readings in moral philosophy as well as leading contemporary expositions of perennial problems. I begin each part of the work with a classical selection, for the questions we ask have a perennial nature. Their classical rendition, as well as some of their classical solutions, have bearing on present-day understanding.

The book contains a general introduction to moral philosophy before the first reading and short abstracts and biographical sketches before the individual readings. The thirty readings are presented in a dialectical format (*pro-con*) and represent the most accessible readings I can find—without sacrificing argumentative cogency. Two of the readings have been commissioned specifically for this work.

Strategy of the Book

The user of this work may be interested in why I have arranged it the way I have. There is nothing sacred about this arrangement. The book can be used in many ways, but I have found the present structure optimal for teaching ethical theory.

First of all, you will find a lot of Plato in this work. Although Whitehead's dictum that the history of philosophy is merely a series of footnotes on Plato may be hyperbole, classical questions about the nature of morality are brilliantly discussed in Plato's work. It is here that the important questions are first raised in all their poignancy: Why should I be moral? (Glaucon and Gyges' Ring) What is morality? (*Republic* Book I) Does might make right? (Thrasymachus) Does God love the Good because it is good or is the Good good because God loves it? (Euthyphro) Are there objective values whose goodness is independent of whether we choose them? (Plato's notion of the Form of the Good) We may not accept all of his answers (though I think they have merit), but we cannot do better than begin with his questions.

Here is my suggestion on how to proceed in using the material in this book:

Weeks 1 and 2:

After a brief example of moral arguing over the meaning of justice or morality in *Republic* Book I, where Socrates rejects both common sense contractarianism and Thrasymachus's crude egoism, I like to confront the question of moral relativism. Between sixty and seventy percent of my students espouse some (usually crude) version of relativism or subjectivism. A basic understanding of these issues is necessary before we can go on to other matters.

Weeks 3 and 4:

I move on to the questions of morality and self-interest, including egoism, beginning with Glaucon's question to Socrates in *Republic* Book II, "Why should I be moral?" and moving on to Hobbes, where morality is linked with enlightened self-interest (in order to prevent a state of nature). I've used Rand's and Rachels's arguments with success and look forward to using the new article by Howard Kahane on sociobiology and egoism. Although I spend two weeks on this section, it could easily be expanded to take up three weeks.

I have on occasion discussed the material in Part VIII, the relationship between ethics and religion, before discussing the problems of self-interest and egoism, and if these are burning issues among your students, you may want to try this.

Week 5:

I usually spend one week on the nature of value, discussing whether there are things with intrinsic value and things that are objectively valuable. Again Plato is the locus classicus for this discussion, and Bentham provides the clearest example of hedonism, which is criticized by Robert Nozick and W. D. Ross. Ross provides a clear presentation of value pluralism, and Derek Parfit examines three theories of the good life in a way that is especially accessible to students.

Weeks 6–13:

In the central part of the course, I examine the three classical types of moral theories: utilitarianism, deontological (Kantian) ethics, and virtue ethics, emphasizing the first two. I am flexible in this part of the course, spending more or less time on the classics, depending on the abilities of the particular students in my course.

Weeks 6–9:

Utilitarianism (emphasizing Mill's *Utilitarianism*).

Midterm exam during week 8 or 9.

Weeks 10–12:

Deontological ethics (emphasizing Kant's *Grounding*).

Weeks 13:

Virtue ethics (emphasizing Aristotle's *Nicomachean Ethics*).

On occasion I spend week 14 on this part of the course.

Weeks 14–15:

Ethics and religion (emphasizing both the Euthyphro problem and the question of the relationship between secular and religious ethics). The Euthyphro problem has far-reaching implications, raising questions of value as well as of the nature of the relationship of religion to ethics. Bertrand Russell's "A Free Man's Worship" is an eloquent, if not slightly sad, rendition of secular stoicism. George Mavrodes' critique of secular morality is a worthy challenge to those who would build an adequate secular moral theory, and Kai Nielsen's attempt to meet that challenge presents strategies for building better secular systems of ethics.

To reiterate what I said earlier, some may want to use this part of the book (at least the Euthyphro question) earlier on, say after week 2 on moral relativism. One problem I have with placing this section last is that I often find myself taking more time than I anticipated (especially if I give more than one exam) and never get to the part on ethics and religion. In some places, however, the relationship between ethics and religion is not a burning issue, either because religion is not seen as crucial to ethics or because students already have a fairly sophisticated understanding of religion and its role in the moral life. Some philosophers cover this subject in philosophy of religion courses, so that there is less need to confront it in this course. In sum, Part VIII is the wild card in the pack and may play a role at different stages of the course for different teachers and students.

My students over a twenty-two-year period have been a source of enlightenment and inspiration in arranging this work. My wife, Trudy, has been for me the embodiment of moral virtue, and her (now deceased) parents, the Rev. Dr. Winfield and Mrs. Agnes Burggraaff, were two of the most

deeply moral, altruistic persons I've ever known, to whom I owe a tremendous debt. To their memory this book is dedicated.

Louis P. Pojman
United States Military Academy
West Point, New York
March 23, 1997

Statement on the Second Edition

I have made the following changes for this second edition. I have renamed Part II Moral Relativism and Moral Objectivism and have added Thomas Aquinas's classic discussion on Natural Law in which he justifies an objective and universal moral law based on reason and eternal law. I have also added my defense of moral objectivism, which includes a critique of moral relativism. In Part IV, on Value, I have added a section from Nietzsche's *Beyond Good and Evil*, on the transvaluation of values, as well as a section from Derek Parfit's *Reasons and Persons*, on the question of what gives human life value. I have added

Bernard Williams's provocative "Critique of Utilitarianism" to Part V, and Ross's classic discussion of moral rightness, especially the notion of prima facie duties, to Part VI. Part VII, on Virtue Ethics, has been enhanced by Alasdair MacIntyre's discussion of the nature of the virtues in *After Virtue*, and Jonathan Bennett's essay "The Conscience of Huckleberry Finn," in which he argues for the importance of moral sentiments. These additions should make this a more comprehensive work, filling in some of the gaps in the earlier edition.

Statement on the Third Edition

For this new edition I have added a section on Applied Ethics, including the following articles: Garrett Hardin, "Lifeboat Ethics"; Peter Singer, "Famine, Affluence, and Amorality"; John T. Noonan Jr. "Abortion is Morally Wrong," Mary Anne Warren: "The Personhood Argument in Favor of Abortion"; William James, "The Moral

Equivalent of War"; Michael Walzer, "Political Action: The Problem of Dirty Hands." These additions should enable students to apply ethical theory to actual moral problems, especially those of obligations to distant people, abortion, war, and the complex and ambiguous mixtures of good and evil in politics.

Acknowledgment

The editor gratefully acknowledges permission to reprint in this volume the following selections:

Excerpts from Plato, *Republic,* translated by G .M. A. Grube. Copyright © 1974 by Hackett Publishing Company, Inc. Reprinted by permission of the publisher.

Excerpt from A. Pegis, ed., *Basic Writings of St. Thomas Aquinas.* Copyright © 1948 A. C. Pegis. By permission of the A. C. Pegis Estate.

Excerpt from Ruth Benedict, "Anthropology and the Abnormal" in *The Journal of General Psychology* 10 (1934), 59–82. Published by Heldref Publications, 1319 Eighteenth Street, N.W., Washington, D.C. 20036-1802. Copyright © 1934. Reprinted by permission of the Helen Dwight Reid Educational Foundation.

Excerpt from Walter T. Stace, *The Concept of Morals.* Copyright © 1937 by Macmillan Publishing Company, © renewed 1965 by Walter T. Stace. Reprinted by permission of the publisher.

Excerpt from Ayn Rand, *Atlas Shrugged* (Random House, 1959). Reprinted by permission of the executor of the Estate of Ayn Rand.

Excerpt from James Rachels, *The Elements of Moral Philosophy.* Copyright © 1986. Reprinted by permission of the author and the publisher, McGraw-Hill.

Howard Kahane, "Sociobiology, Egoism and Reciprocity." Copyright © 1992 Howard Kahane. Reprinted by permission of the author.

Excerpt from *Anarchy, State and Utopia* by Robert Nozick. Copyright © 1974 by Basic Books, Inc. Reprinted by permission of Basic Books, a division of HarperCollins Publishers.

Excerpt from *The Right and the Good* by W. D. Ross. Copyright © 1930 by Oxford University Press. Reprinted by permission of the publisher.

Excerpt from Derek Parfit, *Reasons and Persons.* Copyright ©1984 Derek Parfit. Reprinted by permission of Oxford University Press.

Excerpt from Kai Nielsen, "Against Moral Conservatism" (*Ethics,* 82 [1972], pp. 113–24). Copyright © 1972. Reprinted by permission of the author and publisher.

Excerpt from John Hospers, *Human Conduct: Problems of Ethics* (Harcourt Brace Jovanovich, Inc. 1972). Copyright © 1972. Reprinted with permission.

Excerpt from Bernard Williams, *Utilitarianism: For and Against* by Bernard Williams and J. J. C. Smart. Copyright © 1973 Cambridge University Press. Reprinted by permission of Cambridge University Press.

Sterling Harwood, "Eleven Objections to Utilitarianism." Copyright © 1992 by Sterling Harwood. Reprinted by permission of the author.

Excerpt from Kant, *Grounding for the Metaphysics of Morals,* translated by James Ellington. Copyright © 1981 by Hackett Publishing Company, Inc. Reprinted by permission of the publisher.

Excerpt from Fred Feldman, *Introductory Ethics,* pp. 97–99, 101–17. Copyright © 1978. Reprinted by permission of the author and publisher, Prentice-Hall (Englewood Cliffs, New Jersey).

Excerpt from William Frankena, *Ethics* second edition, pp. 43–53, 63–71. Copyright © 1973. Reprinted by permission of the publisher, Prentice-Hall (Englewood Cliffs, New Jersey).

Excerpt from Aristotle, *Nicomachean Ethics,* translated by Terence Irwin. Copyright © 1985 by Terence Irwin. Reprinted by permission of the publisher, Hackett Publishing Company, Inc.

Excerpt from *Ethics and the Moral Life.* Copyright © 1958 by Bernard Mayo. Reprinted by permission of The Macmillan Press, Ltd.

Excerpt from Alasdair MacIntyre, *After Virtue.* Copyright © 1981 University of Notre Dame Press. Reprinted by permission of the University of Notre Dame Press and the author.

Jonathan Bennett, "The Conscience of Huckleberry Finn," from *Philosophy* 49 (1974). Copyright © 1974 Cambridge University Press. Reprinted by permission of Cambridge University Press and the author.

David L. Norton, "Moral Development and the Development of Character," from *Midwest Studies in Philosophy,* Volume XIII. Copyright © 1988 by the University of Notre Dame Press. Reprinted by permission.

Excerpt from Plato, *Euthyphro,* translated by G. M. A. Grube. Copyright © 1975 by Hackett Publishing Company, Inc. Reprinted by permission of the publisher.

Bertrand Russell, "A Free Man's Worship," from *The Basic Writings of Bertrand Russell,* edited by Robert Egner and Lester Denonn. Copyright © 1961 by Allen a Unwin. Reprinted by permission of Simon and Schuster.

George Mavrodes, "Religion and the Queerness of Mortality," in *Rationality, Religious Belief and Moral Commitment: New Essays in the Philosophy of Religion,* edited by Robert Audi and William J. Wainright. Copyright © 1986 by Cornell University. Reprinted by permission of the publisher, Cornell University Press.

Kai Nielsen, "Ethics without Religion," from *The Ohio University Review VI.* Copyright © 1964. Reprinted by permission of the publisher.

Excerpt from "The Case Against Helping the Poor," by Garrett Hardin, reprinted from *Psychology Today* (1974). Copyright © 1974 Sussex Publishers, Inc. Addendum Copyright © 1989. Reprinted by permission of *Psychology Today* magazine and the author.

Peter Singer, "Famine, Affluence, and Morality," reprinted from *Philosophy and Public Affairs* 1: 3 (1972). Copyright © 1972 Princeton University Press. Reprinted by permission of Princeton University Press.

Excerpt from *The Morality of Abortion: Legal and Historical Perspectives,* by John T. Noonan Jr. (Cambridge, MA: Harvard University Press). Copyright © 1970 by the President and Fellows of Harvard College. Reprinted by permission of Harvard University Press.

Excerpt from "On the Moral and Legal Status of Abortion," by Mary Anne Warren from *The Monist* 57: 1 (1973). Reprinted by permission of *The Monist.*

Michael Walzer, "Political Action: The Political Problem of Dirty Hands," from *Philosophy and Public Affairs* 2: 2 (1973). Copyright © 1973 Princeton University Press. Reprinted by permission of Princeton University Press.

General Introduction

What Is Moral Philosophy?

> We are discussing no small matter, but how we ought to live.
>
> (Socrates in Plato's *Republic*)

What is it to be a moral person? What is the nature of morality, and why do we need it? What is the good, and how shall I know it? Are moral principles absolute or simply relative to social groups or individual decision? Is it in my interest to be moral? Is it sometimes in my best interest to act immorally? How does one justify one's moral beliefs? What is the basis of morality? Which ethical theory provides the best justification and explanation of the moral life? What is the relationship between morality and religion?

These are some of the questions that we shall be looking at in this book. We want to understand the foundation and structure of morality. We want to know how we should live.

The terms 'moral' and 'ethics' come from Latin and Greek respectively (*mores* and *ethos*), deriving their meaning from the idea of custom. Although philosophers sometimes use these terms interchangeably, it is useful to have a clearer conceptual scheme. In this work I shall use 'morality' to refer to certain customs, precepts, and practices of people and cultures. This is sometimes referred to as 'positive morality.' I shall use 'moral philosophy' to refer to philosophical or theoretical reflection on morality. Specific moral theories issuing from such philosophical reflection I shall call 'ethical theories,' in line with a common practice. 'Ethics' I shall use to refer to the whole domain of morality and moral philosophy, since they have many features in common. For example, they both have to do with values, virtues, and principles and practices, though in different ways. I shall refer to specific moral theories as 'ethical theories,' in line with a common practice.

Moral philosophy is the systematic endeavor to understand moral concepts and justify moral principles and theories. It undertakes to analyze such concepts as 'right,' 'wrong,' 'permissible,' 'ought,' 'good,' and 'evil' in their moral contexts. Moral philosophy seeks to establish principles of right behavior that may serve as action guides for individuals and groups. It investigates which values and virtues are paramount to the worthwhile life or society. It builds and scrutinizes arguments in ethical theories, and it seeks to discover valid principles (e.g., 'Never kill innocent human beings') and the relationship between those principles (e.g., 'Does saving a life in some situations constitute a valid reason for breaking a promise?').

Morality as Compared with Other Normative Subjects

Moral precepts are concerned with norms; roughly speaking, they are concerned not with what is, but with what ought to be. How should I live my life? What is the right thing to do in this situation? Should one always tell the truth? Do I have a duty to report a coworker whom I have seen cheating our company? Should I tell my friend that his spouse is having an affair? Is premarital sex morally permissible? Ought a woman ever to have an abortion? Morality has a distinct action-guiding or *normative* aspect,[1] an aspect it shares with other practical institutions, such as religion, law, and etiquette.

Moral behavior, as defined by a given religion, is often held to be essential to the practice of that religion. But neither the practices nor precepts of morality should be identified with religion. The practice of morality need not be motivated by religious considerations. And moral precepts need not be grounded in revelation or divine authority—as religious teachings invariably are. The most salient characteristic of ethics—by which I mean both philosophical morality (or morality, as I will simply refer to it) and moral philosophy—is that it is grounded in reason and human experience.

To use a spatial metaphor, secular ethics are horizontal, omitting a vertical or transcendental dimension. Religious ethics have a vertical dimension, being grounded in revelation or divine authority, though generally using reason to supplement or complement revelation. These two differing orientations will often generate different moral principles and standards of evaluation, but they need not. Some versions of religious ethics, which posit God's revelation of the moral law in nature or conscience, hold that reason can discover what is right or wrong, even apart from divine revelation.

Morality also has much in common with law. And, not surprisingly perhaps, some people make the mistake of equating the two. After all, laws can promote well-being and social harmony, and can resolve conflicts of interest, just as morality can.

Yet there are crucial differences. Ethics may judge certain laws to be immoral without denying that they are valid laws. Laws may permit slavery, for example, or unjust discrimination. An anti-abortion advocate may believe laws permitting abortion to be immoral.

It is possible, too, that under some circumstances the requirements of law may be at odds with the requirements of ethics. Consider the reply given by a trial lawyer when asked what he would do if he discovered that a client had committed a murder some years back for which another man had been convicted and would soon be executed: The lawyer said it was his legal obligation to keep this information confidential and that, if he divulged it, he would be disbarred.[2] Might not a lawyer in this situation also have a moral obligation to save an innocent man from being executed? And might it not override a legal or moral obligation to preserve his client's confidentiality?

Not all aspects of morality are covered by law. While it is generally agreed, for example, that lying is usually immoral, there is no general law against it. (There are, to be sure, laws against lying in certain circumstances: while under oath, for example, or on an income-tax return.)

Sometimes college newspapers publish advertisements for "research assistance," where it is tacitly understood that the companies involved will aid and abet plagiarism. The publication of such ads is legal, but it is doubtful that it is morally correct.

In 1963, thirty-nine people in Queens, New York, watched from their apartments for some forty-five minutes while an assailant beat up and finally killed a woman, Kitty Genovese; they did nothing to intervene, not even calling the police. These people broke no law, but they were very likely morally culpable for not calling the police or otherwise coming to the aid of the victim.

Even if it were thought desirable to have laws which governed all aspects of morality, this would prove impractical. In 1351 King Edward III of England promulgated a law against treason that made it a crime merely to think homicidal thoughts about the king. For reasons easy to imagine, this law proved unenforceable. Once an act has been committed, of course, intention plays a crucial role in determining its legal character. But intention alone, intention that is not acted upon, remains outside the reach of law.

The mere fact that it is impractical to have laws against bad intentions, however, does not mean such intentions are not bad, are not morally wrong. Suppose I buy a gun with the intention of killing Uncle Charlie, but never get a chance to act on that intention (say, Uncle Charlie moves to Australia). Though I have committed no crime, I have committed a moral wrong.

How else does morality differ from law? To begin with, we might say that law is enforced by sanctions[3] that restrict a violator's liberty (for example, by imprisonment or fines), whereas morality does not rely on these sanctions. Morality does rely, however, on what we might call "moral sanctions," primarily those of conscience and reputation. (By morality, remember, we mean morality not motivated by religious considerations.)

Morality differs, too, from etiquette and custom, which concern form and style, rather than the essence of social existence. Etiquette determines what is polite behavior rather than what behavior is, in a deeper sense, right. Custom represents society's decision as to how we are to dress, greet one another, eat, celebrate festivals, dispose of the dead, and carry out social transactions.

Whether we greet others with a handshake, a bow, a hug, or a kiss on the cheek will differ in various cultures and social systems. People in England hold their fork in their right hand. In other countries, people hold a fork in their right hand or left hand or whichever hand a person feels like holding it. In India, people typically eat without a fork. They simply use the forefingers of the right hand.

None of these practices has any moral superiority. Etiquette helps social transactions flow smoothly, but it is not the substance of those transactions. The observance of custom graces our social existence, but it is not what social existence is about.

At the same time, it can be wrong to disregard etiquette and custom. A cultural crisis recently developed in India when some Americans went to the beaches clad in skimpy bathing suits. This was found highly offensive, though there is nothing intrinsically wrong with wearing skimpy bathing suits or, for that matter, with wearing none at all. Especially when one is a guest in someone else's home or country, however, ignoring or displaying contempt for such customs can be more than merely rude; it can be morally wrong. In the example just given, we might say it was not the wearing of the bathing suits but a kind of insensitivity that was wrong.

Law, etiquette and religion are all important institutions, but each has limitations. The limitation of the law is that we can not have a law against every social malady, nor can we enforce every desirable rule. The limitation of etiquette is that it does not get to the heart of what is of vital importance for personal and social existence. Whether or not one eats with one's fingers pales in significance compared with whether or not one is honest or trustworthy or just. Etiquette is a cultural *invention,* but morality claims to be a *discovery.*

The limitation of the religious injunction is that it rests on authority, and we are not always sure of or in agreement about the credentials of the authority or on how the authority would rule in ambiguous or new cases. Since religion is founded not on reason but on revelation, we cannot use reason to convince someone who does not share our religious views that our view is the right one. I hasten to add that when moral differences are caused by fundamental moral principles, it is unlikely that philosophical reasoning will settle the matter. Often, however, our moral differences turn out to be rooted in world views, not moral principles. For example, antiabortion and pro-choice advocates often agree that it is wrong to kill innocent persons, but differ on the facts. The antiabortion advocates may hold a religious view that states that the fetus has an eternal soul and thus possesses a right to life, while the pro-choice advocates may deny that anyone has a soul and hold that only self-conscious, rational beings have a right to life.

In summary, morality distinguishes itself from law and etiquette by going deeper into the essence of rational existence. It distinguishes itself from religion in that it seeks reasons, rather than authority, to justify its principles. The central purpose of moral philosophy is to secure valid principles of conduct and values that can be instrumental in guiding human actions and producing good character. As such, it is the most important activity known to humans, for it has to do with how we are to live.

Domains of Ethical Assessment

It might seem at this point that ethics concerns itself entirely with rules of conduct based solely on an evaluation of acts. However, the situation is more complicated than this. Most ethical analysis falls into one or some of the following four domains:

Domain	Evaluative terms	
1. Action (the act)	permissible	not permissible
	obligatory optional	wrong
	neutral supererogatory	
2. Consequences	good, bad, neutral	
3. Character	virtuous, vicious, neutral	
4. Motive	good, evil, neutral	

Let us examine each of these domains.

(1) *Action.* The most common classification of acts may be as obligatory, optional, or wrong.

(i) An obligatory act is an act morality requires you to do, an act it is not permissible for you to refrain from doing.

(ii) A wrong act is an act you have an obligation, or duty, to refrain from, an act you ought not to do, an act it is not permissible to do.

(iii) An optional act is an act which it is neither obligatory nor wrong to do. It is not your duty to do it; neither is it your duty to not to do it.

Theories which place the emphasis on the nature of the act are called 'deontological' (from the Greek word for "duty"). These theories hold that there is something inherently right or good about such acts as truth telling and promise keeping and something inherently wrong or bad about such acts as lying and promise breaking. The most famous of these systems is Kant's moral theory, which we shall study in Part VI.

(2) *Consequences.* We said above that lying is generally seen as wrong and telling the truth is generally seen as right. But consider this situation. You are hiding in your home an innocent woman named Laura, who is fleeing gangsters. Gangland Gus knocks on your door, and when you open it, he asks if Laura is in your house. What should you do? Should you tell the truth or lie? Those who say that morality has something to do with consequences of actions would prescribe lying as the morally right thing to do.

Those who deny that we should look at the consequences when considering what to do when there is a clear and absolute rule of action will say that we should either keep silent or tell the truth. When no other rule is at stake, of course, the rule-oriented ethicist will allow the foreseeable consequences to determine a course of action. Theories which focus primarily on consequences in determining moral rightness and wrongness are called 'teleological' ethical theories (from the Greek *telos,* meaning "goal-directed"). The most famous of these theories is utilitarianism, which we shall study in Part V.

(3) *Character.* While some ethical theories emphasize principles of action in themselves and some emphasize principles involving consequences of action, other theories, such as Aristotle's ethics, emphasize character or virtue. According to Aristotle, it is most important to develop virtuous character, for if and only if we have good people can we ensure habitual right action. Although the virtues are not central to other types of moral theories, most moral theories include the virtues as important. Most reasonable people, whatever their notions about ethics, would judge that the people who watched Kitty Genovese being assaulted lacked good character. Different moral systems emphasize different virtues, to varying degrees. We shall study virtue in Part VII.

(4) *Motive.* Finally, virtually all ethical systems, but especially Kant's, accept the relevance of motive. It is important to the full assessment of any action that the intention of the agent be

taken into account. Two acts may be identical, and one judged morally culpable, the other not. Consider John's pushing Joan off a ledge, causing her to break her leg. In situation (A) he is angry and intends to harm her. In situation (B) he sees a knife flying in her direction and intends to save her life. In (A), what he did was clearly wrong. In (B), he did the right thing.

By contrast, two acts may get opposite results and, on the basis of intention, be judged equally good. Imagine two soldiers trying to cross enemy lines in order to communicate with an ally. One is captured through no fault of his own, and the other succeeds. In a full moral description of any act, motive will be taken into consideration as a relevant factor.

In this work we will examine several fundamental questions in moral philosophy. In Part I, through Socrates' discussion with Polemarchus and Thrasymachus, we look at the question, "What is the morally right conduct?" In this classical discussion we find embedded many of the questions to be examined later in this book: "Is morality objectively valid?" "Why should I be moral?" "What is the nature of morality?"

In Part II we examine the question "Are moral principles valid relative to cultural or individual approval, or are they objectively and universally valid?" We begin with a classic example of cultural difference, Herodotus's account of the Callaticans and Greeks being offended by each other's burial rites. Ruth Benedict sets forth a defense of moral relativism, and Louis Pojman defends a form of moral objectivism.

In Part III we inquire into the relationship of morality to self-interest. Why should I be moral even when it is not in my interest to be so? Or is it really in my interest always to be moral? Or is morality simply enlightened self-interest, in a manner that precludes altruism? Our reading here from Plato's *Republic* picks up where we left off in I.1, discussing the issue of morality and self-interest. Then we turn to Hobbes's classic account of egoism as the basis for a contractual

morality. Ayn Rand defends a strong form of egoism, and James Rachels offers a comprehensive critique of ethical egoism. Howard Kahane argues for a type of morality that may be said to be based on rational self-interest, whose primary form is reciprocity.

In Part IV we examine the nature of value. Are there any intrinsic, objective values, or are all values subjective, simply objects of desire? Here we examine Platonic objectivism, Bentham's hedonism, Ross's value pluralism, and Parfit's objective theory of values.

In Part V we begin an examination of the three major ethical theories in the history of Western moral philosophy, looking first at utilitarianism. We will read part of John Stuart Mill's classic work *Utilitarianism,* as well as Kai Nielsen's act-utilitarianism and John Hospers's rule-utilitarianism, Bernard Williams's critique, concluding with a critical analysis by Sterling Harwood.

In Part VI we examine Kant's deontological ethics, reading a sizable portion from his *Grounding for the Metaphysics of Morals,* as well as an analysis by Fred Feldman. William Frankena concludes this section with an essay that attempts to reconcile utilitarianism with deontological ethics.

Part VII contains five important readings on virtue ethics, beginning with Aristotle's classic rendition in his *Nicomachean Ethics.* Bernard Mayo provides a contemporary interpretation of virtue ethics, and William Frankena criticizes this school of thought for failing to tie the virtues into stable principles. David Norton criticizes Urmson for not going far enough with his proposal and develops a fuller account of an ethics of character.

Finally, in Part VIII we turn to the relationship of ethics to religion. Are all moral principles based on divine commands, or are they autonomous, having independent validity? And, whatever our answer to that question, does secular morality have the resources sufficient to motivate compliance with moral reasons, or does morality need the support of divine sanctions? George Mavrodes argues that morality without a deeper metaphysical basis is impoverished, but Bertrand Russell and Kai Nielsen argue to the contrary, that morality can stand without the support of religion.

It is to be hoped that these readings will stimulate you to do your own thinging on each of the major questions raised in the study of moral philosophy. The challenge is as exciting as it is important, for, to quote Socrates, "We are discussing no small matter, but how we ought to live."

Notes

1. Webster's Collegiate Dictionary defines *normative* as "of, or relating or conforming to or prescribing norms or standards."

2. This question was asked, and this reply was given, in the television program *Ethics in America* (PBS, 1989).

3. A sanction is a mechanism for social control, used to enforce society's standards. It may consist of rewards or punishment, praise or blame, approbation or disapprobation.

4. Although Americans pride themselves on tolerance and awareness of other cultures, customs and etiquette can be a bone of contention. A friend of mine tells of an experience early in his marriage. John and his wife were hosting their first Thanksgiving meal. He had been used to small celebrations with his immediate family, whereas his wife had been used to grand celebrations. He writes, "I had been asked to carve, something I had never done before, but I was willing. I put on an apron, entered the kitchen, and attacked the bird with as much artistry as I could muster. And what reward did I get? [My wife] burst into tears. In *her* family the turkey is brought to the *table*, laid before the [father], grace is said, and *then* he carves! 'So I fail patriarchy,' I hollered later. 'What do you expect?'" (from John Buehrens and Forrester Church, *Our Chosen Faith* [Beacon Press, 1989], p. 140.)

PART I

What Is Morally Right Conduct?

Introduction: Plato's Moral Philosophy

Plato (427–347 B.C.) lived in Athens, the great Greek democratic city-state, in the aftermath of its glory under Pericles. He was Socrates' disciple and the founder of the first school of philosophy, the Academy. In his dialogues, and especially in the *Republic*, from which our first selection, as well as selections III.5 and IV.10, are taken, he sets forth and develops some of the ideas of his teacher, Socrates.

Socrates (470–399 B.C.) is the father of moral philosophy, the first philosopher in the Western tradition to raise fundamental questions about the nature of morality: "What is justice?" "What is virtue?" "Can virtue be taught?" "What is the good life?" "Why should I be moral?" "Is morality more than mere convention?" In our first two selections Socrates deals with two central questions, "What is justice or right conduct?" and "Why should I be moral (or just)?"

The *Republic* is a classic dialogue on political philosophy, centering on the nature of goodness and of the good life. Although the Greek idea of *justice* has some different connotations from our concept of morally right conduct, it is close enough to our concept to be serviceable in pro-

moting an understanding of the central features of moral philosophy.

The dialogue takes place around the year 422 B.C., in the Athenian home of Cephalus, an elderly, prosperous businessman. Socrates is in his 40s. Those present, besides Cephalus and his son, Polemarchus, include two of Plato's brothers, Glaucon and Adeimantus, and the sophist Thrasymachus. Socrates is the narrator.

In the initial discussion Cephalus defines justice or right conduct as telling the truth and paying back what one has borrowed. Socrates quickly dismisses this definition with a telling counterexample. Polemarchus then takes over from his father and, citing the poet Simonides, argues that right conduct is to give each man what is due him: doing good to one's friends and evil to one's enemies. This undergoes modifications under analysis but is finally rejected as inadequate. At this point Thrasymachus jumps in and vehemently argues that justice is that which promotes the interest of the stronger: Might makes right. As the argument proceeds, Thrasymachus changes his thesis to claim that injustice is more profitable than justice and is the way to happiness.

Reprinted from *Plato's Republic*, trans. G. M. A. Grube (Indianapolis: Hackett Publishing Company, 1974), by permission of the publisher.

1

What Is Right Conduct?

PLATO

So we went to the home of Polemarchus, and there we found Lysias and Euthydemus, the brothers of Polemarchus, also Thrasymachus of Chalcedon, Charmantides of Paiania, and Cleitophon the son of Aristonymus. Polemarchus's father Cephalus was also in the house. I thought he looked quite old, as I had not seen him for some time. He was sitting on a seat with a cushion, a wreath on his head, for he had been offering a sacrifice in the courtyard. There was a circle of seats there, and we sat down by him.

As soon as he saw me Cephalus welcomed me and said: Socrates, you don't often come down to the Piraeus to see us. You should. If it were still easy for me to walk to the city you would not need to come here, we would come to you, but now you should come more often. You should realize that, to the extent that my physical pleasures get feebler, my desire for conversation, and the pleasure I take in it, increase. So be sure to come more often and talk to these youngsters, as you would to good friends and relations.

I replied: Indeed, Cephalus, I do enjoy conversing with men of advanced years. As from those who have travelled along a road which we too will probably have to follow, we should enquire from them what kind of a road it is, whether rough and difficult or smooth and easy, and I should gladly learn from you what you think about this, as you have reached the point in life which the poets call "the threshold of old age,"[1] whether it is a difficult part of life, or how your experience would describe it to us.

Yes, by Zeus, Socrates, he said, I will tell you what I think of old age. A number of us who are more or less the same age often get together in accordance with the old adage.[2] When we meet, the majority of us bemoan their age: they miss the pleasures which were theirs in youth; they recall the pleasures of sex, drink, and feasts, and some other things that go with them, and they are angry as if they were deprived of important things, as if they then lived the good life and now were not living at all. Some others deplore the humiliations which old age suffers in the household, and because of this they repeat again and again that old age is the cause of many evils. However, Socrates, I do not think that they blame the real cause. For if old age were the cause, then I should have suffered in the same way, and so would all others who have reached my age. As it is, I have met other old men who do not feel like that, and indeed I was present at one time when someone asked the poet Sophocles: "How are you in regard to sex, Sophocles? Can you still make love to a woman?" "Hush man, the poet replied, I am very glad to have escaped from this, like a slave who has escaped from a mad and cruel master." I thought then that he was right, and I still think so, for a great peace and freedom from these things come with old age: after the tension of one's desires relaxes and ceases, then Sophocles' words certainly apply, it is an escape from many mad masters. As regards both sex and relations in the household there is one cause, Socrates, not old age but the manner of one's life: if it is moderate and contented, then old age too is but moderately burdensome; if it is not, then both old age and youth are hard to bear.

I wondered at his saying this and I wanted him to say more, so I urged him on by saying: Cephalus, when you say this, I don't think most people would agree with you; they think you endure old age easily not because of your manner of life but because you are wealthy, for the wealthy, they say, have many things to encourage them.

What you say is true, he said. They would not agree. And there is something in what they say, but not as much as they think. What Themistocles said is quite right: when a man from Seriphus[3] was insulting him by saying that his high reputation was due to his city and not to himself, he replied that, had he been a Seriphian, he would not be famous, but neither would the other had he been an Athenian. The same can be applied to those who are not rich and find old age hard to bear—namely, that a good man would not very easily bear old age in poverty, nor would a bad man, even if wealthy, be at peace with himself. . . .

It surely is, said I. Now tell me this much [, Cephalus], What is the greatest benefit you have received from the enjoyment of wealth?

I would probably not convince many people in saying this, Socrates, he said, but you must realize that when a man approaches the time when he thinks he will die, he becomes fearful and concerned about things which he did not fear before. It is then that the stories we are told about the underworld, which he ridiculed before—that the man who has sinned here will pay the penalty there—torture his mind lest they be true. Whether because of the weakness of old age, or because he is now closer to what happens there and has a clearer view, the man himself is filled with suspicion and fear, and he now takes account and examines whether he has wronged anyone. If he finds many sins in his own life, he awakes from sleep in terror, as children do, and he lives with the expectation of evil. However, the man who knows he has not sinned has a sweet and good hope as his constant companion, a nurse to his old age, as Pindar too puts it. The poet has expressed this charmingly, Socrates, that whoever lives a just and pious life

Sweet is the hope that nurtures his heart,
companion and nurse to his old age,
a hope which governs the rapidly changing
thoughts of mortals.

This is wonderfully well said. It is in this connection that I would say that wealth has its greatest value, not for everyone but for a good and well-balanced man. Not to have lied to or deceived anyone even unwillingly, not to depart yonder in fear, owing either sacrifices to a god or money to a man: to this wealth makes a great contribution. It has many other uses, but benefit for benefit I would say that its greatest usefulness lies in this for an intelligent man, Socrates.

Beautifully spoken, Cephalus, said I, but are we to say that justice or right[4] is simply to speak the truth and to pay back any debt one may have contracted? Or are these same actions sometimes right and sometimes wrong? I mean this sort of thing, for example: everyone would surely agree that if a friend has deposited weapons with you when he was sane, and he asks for them when he is out of his mind, you should not return them. The man who returns them is not doing right, nor is one who is willing to tell the whole truth to a man in such a state.

What you say is correct, he answered.

This then is not a definition of right or justice, namely, to tell the truth and pay one's debts.

It certainly is, said Polemarchus interrupting, if we are to put any trust in Simonides.

And now, said Cephalus, I leave the argument to you, for I must go back and look after the sacrifice.

Do I then inherit your role? asked Polemarchus.

You certainly do, said Cephalus laughing, and as he said it he went off to sacrifice.

Then do tell us, Polemarchus, said I, as the heir to the argument, what it is that Simonides stated about justice which you consider to be correct.

He stated, said he, that it is just to give to each what is owed to him, and I think he was right to say so.

Well now, I said, it is hard not to believe Simonides, for he is a wise and inspired man, but what does he mean? Perhaps you understand him, but I do not. Clearly he does not mean what we were saying just now, that anything he has deposited must be returned to a man who is not in his right mind; yet anything he has deposited is owing to him. Is that not so?—Yes.

But it is not to be returned to him at all if he is out of his mind when he asks for it?—That's true.

Certainly Simonides meant something different from this when he says that to return what is owed is just.

He did indeed mean something different, by Zeus, said he. He believes that one owes it to one's friends to do good to them, and not harm.

I understand, said I, that one does not give what is owed or due if one gives back gold to a depositor, when giving back and receiving are harmful, and the two are friends. Is that not what you say Simonides meant?—Quite.

Well then, should one give what is due to one's enemies?

By all means, said he, what is in fact due to them, and I believe that is what is properly due from an enemy to an enemy, namely, something harmful.

It seems, I said, that Simonides was suggesting the nature of the just poetically and in riddles. For he thought this to be just, to give to each man what is proper to him, and he called this what is due.—Surely.

Then by Zeus, I said, if someone asked him: "Simonides, what does the craft[5] which we call medicine give that is due, and to whom?" What do you think his answer would be?

Clearly, it is the craft which prescribes medicines and food and drink for our bodies.

And what does the craft which we call cooking give that is due and fitting, and to whom?—It adds flavor to food.

Very well. What, and to whom, does that craft give which we would call justice?

It must follow from what was said before, Socrates, that it is that which benefits one's friends and harms one's enemies.

He means then that to benefit one's friends and harm one's enemies is justice?—I think so.

And who is most capable of benefiting his friends and harming his enemies in matters of health and disease?—A physician.

And who can do so best when they are sailing and heading into a storm?—A pilot.

What about the just man? In what activity and what task is he most able to benefit his friends and harm his enemies?—In waging war and in alliances, I think.

Very well. Now when people are not ill, my dear Polemarchus, the physician is no use to them? —True.

Nor is the pilot when they are not sailing? —That is so.

So to people who are not fighting a war the just man is useless?—I do not think so at all.

Justice then is useful also in peace time?—It is.

And so is farming, is it not?—Yes.

For the producing of a harvest?—Yes.

And the cobbler's craft too?—Yes.

I think you would say for getting shoes?—Certainly.

Well then, what is it which justice helps one to use or acquire in peace time?—Contracts, Socrates.

By contracts you mean dealings between people, or something else?—That is what I mean.

Is the just man a good and useful associate in a game of checkers, or is the checkers player? —The checkers player.

And for putting together bricks and stones, is the just man a better and more useful associate than the builder?—Not at all.

In what kind of dealings then is the just man a better associate than the builder or the musician, as the musician is better than the just man in matters of music?—In money matters, I think.

Except perhaps, Polemarchus, when money is to be used, for whenever one needs to buy or sell a horse together, I think the horse breeder is a more useful associate. Is that not so?—Apparently.

And when one needs to buy a boat, the shipbuilder or the captain of a ship?—So it seems.

In what joint use of silver and gold is the just man a more useful associate than the others?

—Whenever one needs to deposit it and keep it safe.

You mean whenever there is no need to use it, but to keep it?—Quite so.

So it is whenever money is not being used that justice is useful?—I'm afraid so.

And whenever one needs to keep a pruning knife safe, but not to use it, justice is useful both in associations and in private. When you need to use it, however, it is the craft of vine dressing that is useful.—So it seems.

You will agree then that when one needs to keep a shield or a lyre safe and not use them, justice is a useful thing, but when you need to use them, it is the hoplite's or the musician's craft which is useful.—That necessarily follows.

So with all other things, justice is useless in their use, but useful when they are not in use.—I fear so.

In that case, my friend, justice is not a very important thing if it is only useful for things not in use. Let us, however, investigate the following point: is not the man most capable of landing a blow in a fight, be it boxing or any other kind, also the most capable of guarding against blows?—Certainly.

And the man most able to guard against disease is also the man most able to inflict it unnoticed?—So it seems.

Further, the same man is a good guardian of a camp who is also able to steal the plans of the enemy and be aware of their actions?—Quite so.

Whenever a man is a good guardian of anything, he is also a good thief of it.—Apparently.

If then the just man is good at guarding money, he is also good at stealing it.—So our argument shows.

The just man then has turned out to be a kind of thief. You may well have learned this from Homer, for he likes Odysseus's maternal grandfather Autolycus, and at the same time he says that he excelled all men in thieving and perjury. It follows that justice, according to you and Homer and Simonides, appears to be a craft of thieving, of course to the advantage of one's friends and to the harm of one's enemies. Is this not what you meant?

No, by Zeus, he said, I don't any longer know what I meant, but this I still believe to be true, that justice is to benefit one's friends and harm one's enemies.

When you say friends, do you mean those whom a man believes to be helpful to him, or those who are helpful even if they do not appear to be so, and so with enemies?

Probably, he said, one is fond of those whom one thinks to be good and helpful to one, and one hates those whom one considers bad and harmful.

Surely people make mistakes about this, and consider many to be helpful when they are not, and often make the opposite mistake about enemies?—They do.

Then good men are their enemies, and bad people their friends?—Quite so.

And so it is just and right for these mistaken people to benefit the bad and harm the good?—It seems so.

But the good are just and able to do no wrong?—True.

But according to your argument it is just to harm those who do no wrong.

Never, Socrates, he said. It is the argument that is wrong.

It is just to harm the wrongdoers and to benefit the just?

That statement, Socrates, seems much more attractive than the other.

Then, Polemarchus, for many who are mistaken in their judgment it follows that it is just to harm their friends, for these are bad, and to benefit their enemies, who are good, and so we come to a conclusion which is the opposite of what we said was the meaning of Simonides.

That certainly follows, he said, but let us change our assumption; we have probably not defined the friend and the enemy correctly.

Where were we mistaken, Polemarchus?

—When we said that a friend was one who was thought to be helpful.

How shall we change this now? I asked.

Let us state, he said, that a friend is one who is both thought to be helpful and also is; one who is thought to be, but is not, helpful is thought to be a friend but is not. And so also with the enemy.

According to this argument then, the good man will be a friend, and the bad man an enemy. —Yes.

You want us to add to what we said before about the just, namely, that it is just to benefit one's friend and harm one's enemy; to this you want us to make an addition and say that it is just to benefit the friend who is good and to harm the enemy who is bad?

Quite so, he said. This seems to me to be well said.

But, I said, is it the part of the just man to harm anyone at all?

Why certainly, he said, those who are bad and one's enemies.

Do horses become better or worse when they are harmed?—Worse.

Do they deteriorate in their excellence as dogs or as horses?—As horses.

And when dogs are harmed, they deteriorate in their excellence as dogs, not in that of horses? —Necessarily.

Shall we not say so about men too, that when they are harmed they deteriorate in their human excellence?—Quite so.

And is not justice a human excellence?—Of course.

Then men who are harmed, my friend, necessarily become more unjust.—So it appears.

Can musicians, by practising music, make men unmusical?—Not possibly.

Or can teachers of horsemanship, by the practice of their craft, make them into non-horsemen?—Impossible.

Well then, can the just, by the practice of justice, make men unjust? Or, in a word, can good men, by the practice of their virtue, make men bad?—They cannot.

It is not the function of heat to cool things, but the opposite?—Yes.

Nor of dryness to make things wet but the opposite?—Quite so.

And it is not the function of the good to harm people, but the opposite?—It seems so.

And the just man is good?—Certainly.

It is not then the function of the just man, Polemarchus, to do harm to a friend or anyone else, but it is that of his opposite, the unjust man?—I think that you are entirely right, Socrates.

If, then, anyone tells us that it is just to give everyone his due, and he means by this that from the just man harm is due to his enemies and benefit due to his friends—the man who says that is not wise, for it is not true. We have shown that it is never just to harm anyone.—I agree.

You and I, I said, will therefore together fight anyone who tells us that Simonides said this, or Bias or Pittacus or any other of our wise and blessed men.—Yes, and I am quite willing to join that fight. . . .

While we were speaking Thrasymachus often started to interrupt, but he was restrained by those who were sitting by him, for they wanted to hear the argument to the end. But when we paused after these last words of mine he could no longer keep quiet. He gathered himself together like a wild beast about to spring, and he came at us as if to tear us to pieces.

Polemarchus and I were afraid and flustered as he roared into the middle of our company: What nonsense have you two been talking, Socrates? Why do you play the fool in thus giving way to each other? If you really want to know what justice is, don't only ask questions and then score off anyone who answers, and refute him. You know very well that it is much easier to ask questions than to answer them. Give an answer yourself and tell us what you say justice is. And don't tell me that it is the needful, or the advantageous, or the beneficial, or the gainful, or the useful, but tell me clearly and precisely what you mean, for I will not accept it if you utter such rubbish.

His words startled me, and glancing at him I was afraid. I think if I had not looked at him before he looked at me, I should have been speechless. As it was I had glanced at him first when our discussion began to exasperate him, so I was able to answer him and I said, trembling: do not be hard on us, Thrasymachus, if we have erred in our investigation, he and I; be sore that we err unwillingly. You surely do not believe that if we were searching for gold we would be unwilling to give way to each other and thus destroy our chance of finding it, but that when searching for justice, a thing more precious than much gold, we mindlessly give way to one another, and that we are not thoroughly in earnest about finding it. You must believe that, my friend, for I think we could not do it. So it is much more seemly that you clever people should pity us than that you should be angry with us.

When he heard that he gave a loud and bitter laugh and said: By Heracles, that is just Socrates' usual irony. I knew this, and I warned these men here before that you would not be willing to answer any questions but would pretend ignorance, and that you would do anything rather than give an answer, if anyone questioned you.

You are clever, Thrasymachus, I said, for you knew very well that if you asked anyone how much is twelve, and as you asked him you warned him: "Do not, my man, say that twelve is twice six, or three times four, or six times two, or four times three, for I will not accept such nonsense," it would be quite clear to you that no one can answer a question asked in those terms. And if he said to you: "What do you mean, Thrasymachus? Am I not to give any of the answers you mention, not even, you strange man, if it happens to be one of those things, but am I to say something which is not the truth, or what do you mean?" What answer would you give him?

Well, he said, do you maintain that the two cases are alike?

They may well be, said I. Even if they are not, but the person you ask thinks they are, do you think him less likely to answer what he believes to be true, whether we forbid him or not?

And you will surely do the same, he said. Will you give one of the forbidden answers?

I shouldn't wonder, said I, if after investigation that was my opinion.

What, he said, if I show you a different answer about justice from all these and a better one? What penalty do you think you should pay then?

What else, said I, but what is proper for an ignorant man to pay? It is fitting for him to learn from one who knows. And that is what I believe I would deserve.

You amuse me, he said. You must not only learn but pay the fee.

Yes, when I have the money, I said.

We have the money, said Glaucon. If it is a matter of money, speak, Thrasymachus, for we shall all contribute for Socrates.

Quite so, said he, so that Socrates can carry on as usual: he gives no answer himself, and then, when someone else does give one, he takes up the argument and refutes it.

My dear man, I said, how could one answer, when in the first place he does not know and does not profess to know, and then, if he has an opinion, an eminent man forbids him to say what he believes? It is much more seemly for you to answer, since you say you know and have something to say. Please do so. Do me that favor, and do not begrudge your teaching to Glaucon and the others.

While I was saying this, Glaucon and the others begged him to speak. It was obvious that Thrasymachus was eager to do so and earn their admiration, and that he thought he had a beautiful answer, but he pretended that he wanted to win his point that I should be the one to answer. However, he agreed in the end, and then said: "There you have Socrates' wisdom; he himself is not willing to teach, but he goes around learning from others, and then he is not even grateful."

When you say that I learn from others you are right, Thrasymachus, said I, but when you say that I am not grateful, that is not true. I show what gratitude I can, but I can only give praise. I have no money, but how enthusiastically I praise when someone seems to me to speak well is something you will realize quite soon after you have given your answer, for I think you will speak well.

Listen then, said he. I say that the just is nothing else than the advantage of the stronger. Well, why don't you praise me? But you will not want to.

I must first understand your meaning, said I, for I do not know it yet. You say that the advantage of the stronger is just. What do you mean, Thrasymachus? Surely you do not mean such a thing as this: Poulydamas, the pancratist athlete, is stronger than we are; it is to his advantage to eat beef to build up his physical strength. Do you mean that this food is also advantageous and just for us who are weaker than he is?

You disgust me, Socrates, he said. Your trick is always to take up the argument at the point where you can damage it most.

Not at all, my dear sir, I said, but tell us more clearly what you mean.

Do you not know, he said, that some cities are ruled by a despot, others by the people, and others again by the artistocracy?—Of course.

And this element has the power and rules in every city?—Certainly.

Yes, and each government makes laws to its own advantage: democracy makes democratic laws, a despotism makes despotic laws, and so with the others, and when they have made these laws they declare this to be just for their subjects, that is, their own advantage, and they punish him who transgresses the laws as lawless and unjust. This then, my good man, is what I say justice is, the same in all cities, the advantage of the established government, and correct reasoning will conclude that the just is the same everywhere, the advantage of the stronger.

Now I see what you mean, I said. Whether it is true or not I will try to find out. But you too, Thrasymachus, have given as an answer that the just is the advantageous whereas you forbade that answer to me. True, you have added the words "of the stronger."

Perhaps, he said, you consider that an insignificant addition!

It is not clear yet whether or not it is significant. Obviously, we must investigate whether what you say is true. I agree that the just is some kind of advantage, but you add that it is the advantage of the stronger. I do not know. We must look into this.—Go on looking, he said.

We will do so, said I. Tell me, do you also say that obedience to the rulers is just?—I do.

And are the rulers in all cities infallible, or are they liable to error?—No doubt they are liable to error.

When they undertake to make laws, therefore, they make some correctly and make others incorrectly?—I think so.

"Correctly" means that they make laws to their own advantage, and "incorrectly" not to their own advantage. Or how would you put it?—As you do.

And whatever laws they make must be obeyed by their subjects, and this is just?—Of course.

Then, according to your argument, it is just to do not only what is to the advantage of the stronger, but also the opposite, what is not to their advantage.

What is that you are saying? he asked.

The same as you, I think, but let us examine it more fully. Have we not agreed that, in giving orders to their subjects, the rulers are sometimes in error as to what is best for themselves, yet it is just for their subjects to do whatever their rulers order. Is that much agreed?—I think so.

Think then also, said I, that you have agreed that it is just to do what is to the disadvantage of the rulers and the stronger whenever they unintentionally give orders which are bad for themselves, and you say it is just for the others to obey their given orders. Does it not of necessity follow, my wise Thrasymachus, that it is just to do the opposite of what you said? The weaker are then ordered to do what is to the disadvantage of the stronger.

Yes by Zeus, Socrates, said Polemarchus, that is quite clear.

Yes, if you bear witness for him, interrupted Cleitophon.

What need of a witness? said Polemarchus. Thrasymachus himself agrees that the rulers sometimes give orders that are bad for themselves, and that it is just to obey them.

Thrasymachus maintained that it is just to obey the orders of the rulers, Polemarchus.

He also said that the just was the advantage of the stronger, Cleitophon. Having established those two points, he went on to agree that the stronger sometimes ordered the weaker, their subjects, to do what was disadvantageous to themselves. From these agreed premises it follows that what is of advantage to the stronger is no more just than what is not.

But, Cleitophon replied, he said that the advantage of the stronger is what the stronger believes to be of advantage to him. This the weaker must do, and that is what he defined the just to be.

That is not how he stated it, said Polemarchus.

It makes no difference, Polemarchus, I said. If Thrasymachus now wants to put it that way, let us accept it. Tell me, Thrasymachus, was this what you intended to say justice is, namely, that which appears to the stronger to be to his advantage, whether it is so or not? Shall we say that this is what you mean?

Not in the least, said he. Do you think that I would call stronger a man who is in error at the time he errs?

I did think you meant that, said I, when you said that the rulers were not infallible but were liable to error.

You are being captious, Socrates, he said. Do you call a man a physician when he is in error in the treatment of patients, at the moment of, and in regard to this very error? Or would you call a man an accountant when he makes a miscalculation at the moment of, and with regard to this miscalculation? I think that we express ourselves in words which, taken literally, do say that the physician is in error, or the accountant, or the grammarian. But each of these, insofar as he is what we call him, never errs, so that, if you use language with precision—and you want to be precise—no practitioner of a craft ever errs. It is when the knowledge of his craft leaves him that he errs, and at that time he is not a practitioner of it. No craftsman, wise man, or ruler is in error at the time that he is a ruler in the precise sense. However, everyone will say that the physician or

the ruler is in error. Take it then that this is now my answer to you. To speak with precision, the ruler, insofar as he is a ruler, unerringly decrees what is best for himself, and this the subject must do. The just then is, as I said from the first, to do what is advantageous to the stronger.

Very well, Thrasymachus, said I. You think I am captious?

You certainly are, he said.

And you think that it was deliberate trickery on my part to ask you the questions I did ask?

I know it very well, he said, but it will not do you any good, for I would be well aware of your trickery; nor would you have the ability to force my agreement in open debate.

I would not even try, my good sir, I said, but in order to avoid a repetition of this, do define clearly whether it is the ruler in the ordinary or the precise sense whose advantage is to be pursued as that of the stronger.

I mean, he said, the ruler in the most exact sense. Now practice your trickery and your captiousness on this if you can, for I will not let any statement of yours pass, and you certainly won't be able to.

Do you think, I said, that I am crazy enough to try to shave a lion or trick Thrasymachus?

You certainly tried just now, he said, though you are no good at it.

Enough of this sort of thing, I said. But tell me: is the physician in the strict sense, whom you mentioned just now, a moneymaker or one who treats the sick? Tell me about the real physician.—He is one who treats the sick, said he.

What about the ship's captain? Is he, to speak correctly, a ruler of sailors or a sailor?—A ruler of sailors.

We should not, I think, take into account the fact that he sails in a ship, and we should not call him a sailor, for it is not on account of his sailing that he is called a ship's captain, but because of his craft and his authority over sailors.—True.

And there is something which is advantageous to each of these, that is: patients and sailors?—Certainly.

And is not the purpose of a craft's existence to

seek and secure the advantageous in each case? —That's right.

Now is there any other advantage to each craft, except that it be as perfect as possible?—What is the meaning of that question?

It is this, said I. If you asked me whether our body is sufficient unto itself, or has a further need I should answer: "It certainly has needs, and for this purpose the craft of medicine exists and has now been discovered, because the body is defective, not self-sufficient. So to provide it with things advantageous to it the craft of medicine has been developed." Do you think I am correct in saying this or not?—Correct.

Well then, is the craft of medicine itself defective, or is there any other craft which needs some further excellence—as the eyes are in need of sight, the ears of hearing, and, because of this need, they require some other craft to investigate and provide for this?—is there in the craft itself some defect, so that each craft requires another craft which will investigate what is beneficial to it, and then the investigating craft needs another such still, and so ad infinitum? Or does a craft investigate what is beneficial to it, or does it need neither itself nor any other to investigate what is required because of imperfections? There is in fact no defect or error of any kind in any craft, nor is it proper to any craft to seek what is to the advantage of anything but the object of its concern; it is itself pure and without fault, being itself correct, as long as it is wholly itself in the precise sense. Consider this with that preciseness of language which you mentioned. Is it so or otherwise?—It appears to be so.

The craft of medicine, I said, does not seek its own advantage but that of the body.—Yes.

Nor does horse breeding seek its own advantage but that of horses. Nor does any other craft seek its own advantage—it has no further need— but that of its object.—That seems to be the case.

And surely, Thrasymachus, the crafts govern and have power over their object.

He agreed, but with great reluctance at this point.

No science of any kind seeks or orders its own advantage, but that of the weaker which is subject to it and governed by it.

He tried to fight this conclusion, but he agreed to this too in the end. And after he had, I said: Surely no physician either, insofar as he is a physician, seeks or orders what is advantageous to himself, but to his patient? For we agreed that the physician in the strict sense of the word is a ruler over bodies and not a moneymaker. Was this not agreed?

He said yes.

So the ship's captain in the strict sense is a ruler over sailors, and not a sailor?—That has been agreed.

Does it not follow that the ship's captain and ruler will not seek and order what is advantageous to himself, but to the sailor, his subject.

He agreed, but barely.

So then, Thrasymachus, I said, no other ruler in any kind of government, insofar as he is a ruler, seeks what is to his own advantage or orders it, but that which is to the advantage of his subject who is the concern of his craft; it is this he keeps in view; all his words and actions are directed to this end.

When we reached this point in our argument and it was clear to all that the definition of justice had turned into its opposite, Thrasymachus, instead of answering, said: Tell me, Socrates, do you have a nanny?

What's this? said I. Had you not better answer than ask such questions?

Because, he said, she is letting you go around with a snotty nose and does not wipe it when she needs to, if she leaves you without any knowledge of sheep or shepherds.

What is the particular point of that remark? I asked.

You think, he said, that shepherds and cowherds seek the good of their sheep or cattle, whereas their sole purpose in fattening them and looking after them is their own good and that of their master. Moreover, you believe that rulers in the cities, true rulers that is, have a different attitude towards their subjects than one has towards sheep, and that they think of anything else, night and day, than their own advantage. You are so far from understanding the nature of justice and the just, of injustice and the unjust, that you do not realize that the just is really another's good, the advantage of the stronger and the ruler, but for the inferior who obeys it is a personal injury. Injustice on the other hand exercises its power over those who are truly naive and just, and those over whom it rules do what is of advantage to the other, the stronger, and, by obeying him, they make him happy, but themselves not in the least.

You must look at it in this way, my naive Socrates: the just is everywhere at a disadvantage compared with the unjust. First, in their contracts with one another: wherever two such men are associated you will never find, when the partnership ends, the just man to have more than the unjust, but less. Then, in their relation to the city: when taxes are to be paid, from the same income the just man pays more, the other less; but, when benefits are to be received, the one gets nothing while the other profits much; whenever each of them holds a public office, the just man, even if he is not penalized in other ways, finds that his private affairs deteriorate through neglect while he gets nothing from the public purse because he is just; moreover, he is disliked by his household and his acquaintances whenever he refuses them an unjust favor. The opposite is true of the unjust man in every respect. I repeat what I said before: the man of great power gets the better deal. Consider him if you want to decide how much more it benefits him privately to be unjust rather than just. You will see this most easily if you turn your thoughts to the most complete form of injustice which brings the greatest happiness to the wrongdoer, while it makes those whom he wronged, and who are not willing to do wrong, most wretched. This most complete form is depotism; it does not appropriate other people's property little by little, whether secretly or by force, whether public or private, whether sacred

objects or temple property, but appropriates it all at once.

When a wrongdoer is discovered in petty cases, he is punished and faces great opprobrium, for the perpetrators of these petty crimes are called temple robbers, kidnappers, housebreakers, robbers, and thieves, but when a man, besides appropriating the possessions of the citizens, manages to enslave the owners as well, then, instead of those ugly names he is called happy and blessed, not only by his fellow-citizens but by all others who learn that he has run through the whole gamut of injustice. Those who give injustice a bad name do so because they are afraid, not of practicing but of suffering injustice.

And so, Socrates, injustice, if it is on a large enough scale, is a stronger, freer, and more powerful thing than justice and, as I said from the first, the just is what is advantageous to the stronger, while the unjust is to one's own advantage and benefit.

Having said this and poured this mass of close-packed words into our ears as a bathman might a flood of water, Thrasymachus intended to leave, but those present did not let him, and made him stay for a discussion of his views. I too begged him to stay and I said: My dear Thrasymachus, after throwing such a speech at us, you want to leave before adequately instructing us or finding out whether you are right or not? Or do you think it a small thing to decide on a whole way of living, which, if each of us adopted it, would make him live the most profitable life?

Do I think differently? said Thrasymachus.

You seem to, said I, or else you care nothing for us nor worry whether we'll live better or worse, in ignorance of what you say you know. Do, my good sir, show some keenness to teach us. It will not be without value to you to be the benefactor of so many of us. For my own part, I tell you that I do not believe that injustice is more profitable than justice, not even if one gives it full scope and does not put obstacles in its way. No, my friend. Let us assume the existence of an unjust man with every opportunity to do wrong, either because his misdeeds remain secret or because he has the power to battle things through; nevertheless, he does not persuade me that injustice is more profitable than justice. Perhaps some other of us feels the same, and not only I. Come now, my good sir, really persuade us that we are wrong to esteem justice more highly than injustice in planning our life.

And how, said he, shall I persuade you, if you are not convinced by what I said just now? What more can I do? Am I to take my argument and pour it into your mind?

Zeus forbid! Don't you do that, but first stick to what you have said and, if you change your position, do so openly and do not deceive us. You see now, Thrasymachus—let us examine again what went before—that, while you first defined the true physician, you did not think it necessary later to observe the precise definition of the true shepherd, but you think that he fattens sheep, in so far as he is a shepherd, not with what is best for the sheep in mind, but like a guest about to be entertained at a feast, with a banquet in view, or again a sale, like a moneymaker, not a shepherd. The shepherd's craft is concerned only to provide what is best for the object of its care; as for the craft itself, it is sufficiently provided with all it needs to be at its best, as long as it does not fall short of being the craft of the shepherd. That is why I thought it necessary for us to agree just now that every kind of rule, as far as it truly rules, does not seek what is best for anything else than the subject of its rule and care, and this is true both of public and private kinds of rule. Do you think that those who rule over cities, the true rulers, rule willingly?—I don't think it, by Zeus, I know it, he said.

Well, but Thrasymachus, said I, do you not realize that in other kinds of rule no one is willing to rule, but they ask for pay, thinking that their rule will benefit not themselves but their subjects. Tell me, does not every craft differ from every other in that it has a different function? Please do not give an answer contrary to what you believe, so that we can come to some conclusion.

Yes, that is what makes it different, he said.

And each craft benefits us in its own particular way, different from the others. For example, medicine gives us health, navigation safety while sailing, and so with the others.—Quite so.

And the craft of earning pay gives us wages, for that is its function. Or would you call medicine the same craft as navigation? Or, if you wish to define with precision as you proposed, if the ship's captain becomes healthy because sailing benefits his health, would you for that reason call his craft medicine?—Not at all, he said.

Nor would you call wage-earning medicine if someone is healthy while earning wages?—Certainly not.

Nor would you call medicine wage-earning if someone earns pay while healing?—No.

So we agree that each craft brings its own benefit?—Be it so.

Whatever benefit all craftsmen receive in common must then result clearly from some craft which they pursue in common, and so are benefited by it.—It seems so.

We say then that if the practitioners of these crafts are benefited by earning a wage, this results from their practicing the wage-earning craft.

He reluctantly agreed.

So this benefit to each, the receiving pay, does not result from the practice of their own craft, but if we are to examine this precisely, medicine provides health while the craft of earning provides pay; house building provides a house, and the craft of earning which accompanies it provides a wage, and so with the other crafts; each fulfills its own function and benefits that with which it is concerned. If pay is not added, is there any benefit which the practitioner gets from his craft?—Apparently not.

Does he even provide a benefit when he works for nothing?—Yes, I think he does.

Is this not clear now, Thrasymachus, that no craft or rule provides its own advantage, but, as we have been saying for some time, it procures and orders what is of advantage to its subject; it aims at his advantage, that of the weaker, not of the stronger. That is why, my dear Thrasymachus, I said just now that no one willingly wants to rule, to handle and straighten out the affairs of others. They ask for pay because the man who intends to practice his craft well never does what is best for himself, nor, when he gives such orders, does he give them in accordance with his craft, but he pursues the advantage of his subject. For that reason, then, it seems one must provide remuneration if they are to be willing to rule, whether money or honor, or a penalty if he does not rule.

What do you mean, Socrates? said Glaucon. I understand the two kinds of remuneration, but I do not understand what kind of penalty you mean, which you mention under the heading of remuneration.

Then you do not understand the remuneration of the best men, I said, which makes them willing to rule. Do you not know that the love of honor and money are made a reproach, and rightly so? —I know that.

Therefore good men will not be willing to rule for the sake of either money or honor. They do not want to be called hirelings if they openly receive payment for ruling, nor, if they provide themselves with it secretly, to be called thieves. Nor will they do it for honor's sake, for they have no love for it. So, if they are to be willing to rule, some compulsion or punishment must be brought to bear on them. That is perhaps why to seek office willingly, before one must, is thought shameful. Now the greatest punishment is to be ruled by a worse man than oneself if one is not willing to rule. I think it is the fear of this which makes men of good character rule whenever they do. They approach office not as something good or something to be enjoyed, but as something necessary because they cannot entrust it to men better than, or even equal to, themselves. In a city of good men, if there were such, they would probably vie with each other in order not to rule, not, as now, in order to be rulers. There it would be quite clear that the nature of the true ruler is not to seek his own advantage but that of his subjects, and everyone, knowing this, would prefer to receive benefits rather than take the trouble to benefit others. In this matter I do not at all

agree with Thrasymachus that the just is the advantage of the stronger, but we will look into this matter another time. What seems to me of greater importance is what Thrasymachus is saying now, namely, that the life of the unjust man is to be preferred to that of the just. Which will you choose, Glaucon, and which of our views do you consider the more truly spoken?

I certainly think that the life of the just is more profitable.

You have heard, said I, all the blessings of the unjust life which Thrasymachus enumerated just now?

I heard, said he, but I am not convinced.

Do you want us to persuade him, if we could find the means to do so, that what he says is not true?

Of course I want it, he said.

If we were to oppose him, I said, with a parallel set speech on the blessings of the just life, then another speech from him in turn, then another from us, we should have to count and measure the blessings mentioned on each side, and we should need some judges to decide the case. If, on the other hand, we investigate the question, as we were doing, by seeking agreement with each other, then we can ourselves be both the judges and the advocates.—Quite so.

Which method do you prefer? I asked.—The second.

Come then, Thrasymachus, I said, answer us from the beginning. You say that complete injustice is more profitable than complete justice?

I certainly do say that, he said, and I have told you why.

Well then, what about this: you call one of the two a virtue and the other a vice?—Of course.

That is, you call justice a virtue, and injustice a vice?

Is that likely, my good man, said he, since I say that injustice is profitable, and justice is not?

What then?—The opposite.

Do you call being just a vice?—No, but certainly high-minded foolishness.

And you call being unjust low-minded?—No, I call it good judgment.

You consider the unjust then, Thrasymachus, to be good and knowledgeable?

Yes, he said, those who are able to carry injustice through to the end, who can bring cities and communities of men under their power. Perhaps you think I mean purse-snatchers? Not that those actions too are not profitable, if they are not found out, but they are not worth mentioning in comparison with what I am talking about.

I am not unaware of what you mean, I said, but this point astonishes me: do you include injustice under virtue and wisdom, and justice among their opposites?—I certainly do.

That makes it harder, my friend, and it is not easy now to know what to say. If you had declared that injustice was more profitable, but agreed that it was a vice or shameful as some others do, we could have discussed it along the lines of general opinion. Now, obviously, you will say that it is fine and strong, and apply to it all the attributes which we used to apply to justice, since you have been so bold as to include it under virtue and wisdom. —Your guess, he said, is quite right.

We must not, however, shrink from pursuing our argument and looking into this, so long as I am sure that you mean what you say. For I do not think you are joking now, Thrasymachus, but are saying what you believe to be true.

What difference, said he, does it make to you whether I believe it or not? Is it not my argument you are refuting?

No difference, said I, but try to answer this further question: do you think that the just man wants to get the better of the just?

Never, said he, for he would not then be well mannered and simple, as he is now.

Does he want to overreach a just action?[6]

Not a just action either, he said.

Would he want to get the better of an unjust man, and would he deem that just or not?

He would want to, he said, and he would deem it right, but he would not be able to.

That was not my question, said I, but whether the just man wants and deems it right to outdo not a just man, but an unjust one?—That is so.

What about the unjust man? Would he deem it right to outdo the just man and the just action?

Of course he does, he said, since he deems it right to get the better of everybody.

So the unjust man will get the better of another unjust man or an unjust action and he will strive to get all he can from everyone?—That is so.

Let us put it this way, I said. The just man does not try to get the better of one like him but of one unlike him, whereas the unjust man overreaches the like and the unlike?—Very well put.

The unjust man, I said, is knowledgeable and good, and the just man is neither?—That is well said too.

It follows, I said, that the unjust man is like the knowledgeable and the good, while the just man is unlike them?

Of course that will be so, he said, being such a man he will be like such men, while the other is not like them.

Good. Each of them has the qualities of those he is like?—Why not?

Very well, Thrasymachus. Now you speak of one man as musical, of another as unmusical?—I do indeed.

Which is knowledgeable and which is not?

Of course the musical man is knowledgeable, the unmusical is not.

What he has knowledge of he is good at,[7] and he who has no knowledge is bad?—Yes.

Is not the same true of the physician?—The same.

Do you think, my dear sir, that any musician, when tuning his lyre, desires, in the tightening and relaxing of the strings, to do better than another musician or deems it right to get the better of him?—I don't think so.

But he wants to do better than a nonmusician?—Necessarily.

What of a physician? When prescribing food or drink, does he want to do better than another medical man or action?—Certainly not.

But better than the nonmedical?—Yes.

In matters involving any kind of knowledge or

ignorance, do you think that any expert would wish to achieve more than any other expert would do or say, rather than, in respect to the same action, achieve the same as anyone like himself?—Well, perhaps it must be as you say.

What about the nonexpert? Does he not want to outdo the expert and the nonexpert equally?—Perhaps.

The man with knowledge is wise?—I agree.

And the wise is good?—I agree.

So the good and wise does not wish to get the better of one like himself, but of the unlike and opposite?—Apparently.

But the bad and ignorant would want to get the better of his like and his opposite?—So it appears.

Now Thrasymachus, I said, we found that the unjust man tries to get the better of both those like and those unlike him. Did you not say so?—I did.

Yes, and the just man will not get the better of his like, but of one unlike him?—Yes.

The just man then, I said, resembles the wise and good, while the unjust resembles the bad and ignorant?—It may be so.

Further, we agreed that each will be such as the man he resembles?—We did so agree.

So we find that the just man has turned out to be good and wise, and the unjust man ignorant and bad.

Thrasymachus agreed to all this, not easily as I am telling it, but reluctantly and after being pushed. It was summer and he was perspiring profusely. And then I saw something I had never seen before: Thrasymachus blushing. After we had agreed that justice was virtue and wisdom, and injustice vice and ignorance, I said: Very well, let us consider this as established, but we also said that injustice was powerful, or don't you remember, Thrasymachus?

I remember, he said, but then I am not satisfied with what you are now saying. I could make a speech about it, but if I should speak I know that you would say I am delivering a public oration. So either allow me to speak or, if you want to ask questions, ask them, and I will say "very well," and nod yes and no, as one does to old wives' tales.

Don't ever do that, I said, against your own opinion.

Just to please you, he said, since you won't let me speak. What else do you want?

Nothing at all, said I. If you will do this, do it. I will ask my questions.—Ask them then.

I am asking what I asked before, so that we may proceed with our argument about the relation of justice and injustice in an orderly way. It was said that injustice is more powerful and stronger than justice. But now, I said, since justice is wisdom and virtue, it will easily be shown to be also stronger than injustice which is ignorance; nobody could still not know that. However, I do not want to state this thus simply, Thrasymachus, but to look into it in some such way as this: would you say that it is unjust for a city to undertake to enslave other cities unjustly and hold them in subjection, having enslaved many cities to its power?

Of course, he said, this is what the best city will do, the most completely unjust.

I understand that this was your argument, I said, but let me examine this point: will the city which has become stronger than another achieve this power without justice, or must it do so with the help of justice?

If what you said just now stands—that justice is wisdom—with the help of justice, but if things are as I stated them, with injustice.

I am delighted, Thrasymachus, that you do not merely nod yes or no, but that you answer in a very fine manner.

I am doing it to please you, he said.

You are doing well. Now please me also by answering this question: do you think that a city, an army, a band of robbers or thieves, or any other body of men which engages unjustly upon a common course, could achieve anything if they wrong one another?—No indeed.

What if they do not wrong one another? Would they not achieve more?—Certainly.

Yes, for injustice, Thrasymachus, causes factions and hatreds and fights with one another, while justice brings a sense of common purpose and friendship. Is that not so?—Be it so, to agree with you.

You are doing well my good friend. Tell me this: if it is the result of injustice to bring hatred wherever it occurs, then its presence, whether among free men or slaves, will make them hate each other and quarrel, and be unable to achieve any common purpose?—Quite so.

What if it occurs between two men? Will they not be at odds, hate each other, and be hostile to each other as well as to the just?—They will be.

Does injustice, my good sir, lose this capacity for dissension when it occurs within one individual, or will it preserve it intact?

Let it be preserved intact, he said.

It seems to follow that injustice, wherever it occurs, be it in a city, a family, an army, or anything else results in making it incapable of achieving anything as a unit because of the dissensions and differences it creates, and, further, it makes that unit hostile to itself, to its every enemy, and to the just. Is that not so?—Quite.

Even in one individual it has the same effect, which follows from its nature. First, it makes that individual incapable of achievement because he is at odds with himself and not of one mind. It makes him his own enemy, as well as the enemy of the just, does it not?—It does.

The gods too, my friend, are just.—Be it so.

So the unjust man is also an enemy of the gods, while the just man is their friend.

Bravely enjoy your feast of words, he said. I will not oppose you, to avoid unpopularity in this company.

Come then, said I, complete the feast for me by answering as you are now doing. The just are shown to be wiser and more able in action, while the unjust are not even able to act together, for surely, when we speak of a powerful achievement by unjust men acting in common, we are altogether far from the truth. They could not have

kept their hands off each other if they had been completely bad, but clearly they had some justice which forbade them to wrong each other and their enemies at the same time. It was this which enabled them to do what they did. They started on their unjust course being half evil with injustice, for those who are completely evil and completely unjust are also completely incapable of achievement. I can see that this is so, and not as you at first assumed.

We must now examine whether the just also live a better life than the unjust and are happier, a point which we deferred for later investigation. I think it is clear even now that they are, yet we must look into this further, for the argument concerns no casual topic, but one's whole manner of living.—Look into it, then.

I am looking, said I. Do you think there is such a thing as the function of a horse?—I do.

And would you define the function of a horse, or of anything else, as to do that which can be done only, or be done best, by means of it?

I do not understand your question, he said.

Put it like this: is it possible to see by any other means than the eyes?—Certainly not.

Further, could you hear by any other means than the ears?—Not possibly.

Then we are right to say that these are the functions of eyes and ears?—Quite so.

Further, would you use a dagger or a carving knife to trim the branches of a vine, or many other instruments?—Of course.

But you would not do it as well with any other instrument as with a pruning knife which was made for the purpose?—That is true.

Then shall we put it that this is the function of a pruning knife?—We shall.

Now I think you will understand my recent question better, when I inquired whether the function of each thing is to do that which it alone can perform, or perform better than anything else could.—I understand, he said, and I think that is the function of each.

Very well, said I. Does each thing to which a

particular task is assigned also have its excellence? Let us go over the same ground again. We say that the eyes have a particular task?—Yes.

They also have their own excellence?—They have.

The ears, too, have a function?—Yes.

So they have their excellence?—That too.

Is that not the case with all other things?—It is.

Moreover, could the eyes perform their function well if they did not possess their own excellence or virtue, but their own vice instead?

How could they? he said. You mean blindness instead of sight?

Whatever their virtue is, for I am not now asking that, but whether any agent performs its function well by means of its own excellence or virtue, or badly through its own badness or vice. —What you say is true.

So the ears, too, deprived of their own virtue, would perform their function badly.—Quite so.

And we could say the same about all other things?—I think so.

Come now, consider this point next: There is a function of the soul which you could not fulfill by means of any other thing, as for example: to take care of things, to rule, to deliberate, and other things of the kind; could we entrust these things to any other agent than the soul and say that they belong to it?—To no other.

What of living? Is that not a function of the soul?—It most certainly is.

So there is also an excellence of the soul?—We say so.

And, Thrasymachus, will the soul ever fulfill its function well if it is deprived of its own particular excellence, or is this impossible?—Impossible.

It is therefore inevitable that the bad soul rules and looks after things badly and that the good soul does all these things well.—Inevitable.

Now we have agreed that justice is excellence of the soul, and that injustice is vice of soul?—We have so agreed.

The just soul and the just man, then, will live well, and the unjust man will live badly.—So it seems, according to your argument.

Surely the one who lives well is blessed and happy, and the one who does not is the opposite.—Of course.

So the just man is happy, and the unjust one is wretched.—So be it.

It profits no one to be wretched, but to be happy.—Of course.

And so, my good Thrasymachus, injustice is never more profitable than justice.

Let that be your banquet of words, he said, at the feast of Bendis, Socrates.

Given by you, Thrasymachus, I said, after you became gentle and ceased to be angry with me. Yet I have not had a good banquet, but that was my fault, not yours. I seem to have behaved as gluttons do, snatching at every dish that passes them and tasting it before they have reasonably enjoyed the one before. So I, before finding the answer to our first enquiry into the nature of justice, let that go and turned to investigate whether it was vice and ignorance or wisdom and virtue. Another argument came up after, that injustice was more profitable than justice, and I could not refrain from following this up and abandoning the previous one so that the result of our discussion for me is that I know nothing; for, when I do not know what justice is, I shall hardly know whether it is a kind of virtue or not, or whether the just man is unhappy or happy.

Notes

1. The phrase occurs several times in Homer (e.g., *Iliad* 22, 60). It refers to old age as the threshold on leaving life.

2. The old saying that like consorts with like.

3. Seriphus was a small island of little importance.

4. It should be kept in mind throughout the *Republic* that the Greek word *dikaios* and the noun *dikaiosyne* are often used, as here, in a much wider sense than our word "just" and "justice" by which we must usually translate them. They then mean "right" or "right-

eous," i.e., good conduct in relation to others, and the opposite, *adikia,* then has the general sense of wrong-doing.

5. By *technê,* here translated "craft," Socrates refers to any art or craft which requires special knowledge. The word "art" has been avoided in the translation because it implies for us other factors than knowledge, and it is knowledge alone which Socrates has in mind. He then proceeds to equate "justice" with such a *technê,* as implying the knowledge of how to behave, on the well-known Socratic belief that virtue is knowledge.

6. *pleon echein* or *pleonexia,* literally "to have more," comes to mean "to outdo, to overreach, to do better than." Now there is one right note to strike in music and the musician has the necessary knowledge to do so. He will want to do this, but he will not want to do

better than another musician with the same knowledge, which would be absurd. So the just man, if justice is a *technê,* a matter of knowledge, will have the knowledge to do the right thing, and cannot want to do better than that, so he will not desire to outdo another just man with the same knowledge.

7. As before, the craftsman with sufficient knowledge is good at his craft, and his virtue or excellence as a craftsman depends on, in a sense is, that knowledge. Socrates assumes throughout that *dikaiosyne* or "justice" in the sense it is here used is also a matter of knowledge, a *technê.* So the notion of "being good at one's craft" being a matter of knowledge is broadened to "being good is a matter of knowledge," i.e., the famous Socratic paradox that "virtue" *(aretê)* is knowledge.

PART II

Moral Relativism vs. Moral Objectivism

Introduction

Is morality completely relative solely to individual choice or cultural approval, or are there universally valid moral principles?

Ethical relativism maintains that all moral principles are valid relative to cultural or individual choice. It denies that there are any independently justified moral principles. It is to be distinguished from *moral skepticism,* the view that there are no valid moral principles at all (or at least none that we can be confident about). There are two forms of ethical relativism: (1) *subjectivism,* which views morality as a personal decision ("Morality is in the eyes of the beholder") and (2) *conventionalism,* which views moral validity in terms of social acceptance. Opposed to ethical relativism are various theories of *ethical objectivism.* All forms of objectivism affirm the universal validity of some moral principles. The strongest form, *moral absolutism,* holds that there is exactly one right answer to every question. "What should I do in situation *x*?" whatever that situation be, and that a moral principle can never be overridden—even by another moral principle. A weaker form of objectivism sees moral principles as universally valid but not always applicable. That is, moral principle A could be overridden by moral principle B in a given situation, and in other situations there might be no right answer. We turn to our readings. First we have the Greek historian Herodotus' classic description of cultural variation. After that we turn to St. Thomas Aquinas's classic defense of Natural Law, a universal law that is based on universal human nature to promote the common good. This law is eternal, ultimately based on the divine law, and is discoverable by reason. In turn, it constitutes the basis for civil law. Next we turn to Ruth Benedict's defense of moral relativism in which she argues that morality depends on the particular cultures and contexts in which people find themselves. Finally, Louis Pojman argues against moral relativism and in favor of moral objectivism.

2

Custom Is King

HERODOTUS

Herodotus (485–430 B.C.), a Greek, the first West-ern historian, in this brief passage from his Histo-ries *illustrates cultural relativism and may suggest that ethical relativism is the correct view ("culture is king").*

Thus it appears certain to me, by a great vari-ety of proofs, that Cambyses was raving mad; he would not else have set himself to make a mock of holy rites and long-established usages. For if one were to offer men to choose out of all the cus-toms in the world such as seemed to them the best, they would examine the whole number, and end by preferring their own; so convinced are they that their own usages far surpass those of all others. Unless, therefore, a man was mad, it is not likely that he would make sport of such mat-ters. That people have this feeling about their laws may be seen by very many proofs: among others, by the following. Darius, after he had got the kingdom, called into his presence certain Greeks who were at hand, and asked—"What he should pay them to eat the bodies of their fathers when they died?" To which they answered, that there was no sum that would tempt them to do such a thing. He then sent for certain Indians, of the race called Callatians, men who eat their fa-thers, and asked them, while the Greeks stood by, and knew by the help of an interpreter all that was said—"What he should give them to burn the bodies of their fathers at their decease?" The Indians exclaimed aloud, and bade him forbear such language. Such is men's wont herein; and Pindar was right, in my judgment, when he said, "Custom is the king o'er all."

Herodotus, *The Histories of Herodotus*, trans. George Rawlinson (New York: Appleton, 1859).

3

Natural Law

Thomas Aquinas

The Roman Catholic Dominican monk Thomas Aquinas (1225–1274) is considered by many to be one of the three or four greatest philosophers and the greatest philosopher of religion in Western thought. He was born near the Italian town of Aquino, the son of the Count Aquino. While at the University of Naples, much to the horror of his aristocratic parents, he decided to join the Dominicans, a mendicant (begging) order of monks, considered by many to be a hotbed of religious fanatics. Because he was stubborn, deliberate, methodical, slow and portly, his fellow students thought him stupid and unkindly gave him the nickname "The Dumb Ox." His teacher at the University of Cologne, Albertus Magnus, however, saw great promise in the youth and declared, "You call him a Dumb Ox; I tell you the Dumb Ox will bellow so loud his bellowing will fill the world." Among his great works are Summa Contra Gentiles *(On the Truth of the Catholic Faith against the Gentiles) and* Summa Theologica *(Summation of Theology) from which the present selection is taken.*

In this selection Aquinas argues that law, natural law, *is universal, morally binding on all human beings, because it is based on reason, which in turn participates in eternal law. It is unchangeable, possessed by all human beings, and the sole basis of all valid positive law, i.e., what legislatures enact. The purpose of this natural or* moral law *is to promote the common good. The first principle of natural law is that "good should be done and promoted, and evil is to be avoided." All other principles are based on this basic principle. Unjust positive "laws," being immoral, are not true laws, so that civil disobedience is warranted.*

Reprinted from A. Pegis, ed., *Basic Writings of Saint Thomas Aquinas* (New York: Random House, 1948), by permission.

The highly formal structure of the Summa Theologica *consists of a number of Questions, each divided into a number of Articles. An Article proceeds by (1) asking a question, (2) raising objections to the thesis Aquinas will argue for, (3) offering a general statement of Aquinas's position (beginning with the phrase "On the contrary" and "I answer," and finally (4) replying to the objections raised. When Aquinas refers to "the Philosopher," he means Aristotle; to "the Apostle," St. Paul.*

Question 90
On the Essence of Law

We have now to consider the extrinsic principle of acts. Now the extrinsic principles inclining to evil is the devil, of whose temptation we have spoken. But the extrinsic principle moving to good is God, Who both instructs us by means of His law, and assists us by His grace. Therefore, in the first place, we must speak of law; in the second place, of grace. Concerning law, we must consider (1) law itself in general; (2) its parts. Concerning law in general, three points offer themselves for our consideration: (1) its essence; (2) the different kinds of law; (3) the effects of law. Under the first head there are four points of inquiry: (1) Whether law is something pertaining to reason; (2) concerning the end of law; (3) its cause; (4) the promulgation of law.

First Article
Whether Law Is Something
Pertaining to Reason?

We proceed thus to the First Article:

Objection 2. In the reason there is nothing else but power, habit, and act. But law is not the power itself of reason. In like manner, neither is it a habit of reason, because the habits of reason are the intellectual virtues, of which we have spoken above. Nor again is it an act of reason, because then law would cease when the act of reason ceases; for instance, while we are asleep. Therefore law is nothing pertaining to reason.

Obj. 3. Further, the law moves those who are subject to it to act rightly. But it belongs properly to the will to move to act, as is evident from what has been said above. Therefore law pertains not to the reason but to the will, according to the words of the Jurist: *Whatsoever pleases the sovereign has the force of law.*

On the contrary, It belongs to the law to command and to forbid. But it belongs to reason to command, as was stated above. Therefore it is something pertaining to reason.

I answer that, Law is a rule and measure of acts whereby man is induced to act or is restrained from acting; for *lex* [law] is derived from *ligare* [to bind], because it binds one to act. Now the rule and measure of human acts is the reason, which is the first principle of human acts, as is evident from what has been stated above. For it belongs to the reason to direct to the end, which is the first principle of all matters of action, according to the Philosopher [Aristotle]. Now that which is the principle in any genus of numbers is the rule and measure of that genus: for instance, unity in the genus of numbers, and the first movement in the genus of movements. Consequently, it follows that law is something pertaining to reason.

Reply to Obj. 2. Just as, in external acts, we may consider the work and the work done—for instance, the work of building and the house built—so in the acts of reason we may consider the act itself of reason, i.e., to understand and to reason, and something produced by this act. With regard to the speculative reason, this is first of all the definitions; secondly, the proposition; thirdly, the syllogism or argument. And since the practical reason also makes use of the syllogism in operable matters, as we have stated above and as the philosopher teaches, hence we find in the . . . practical reason something that holds the same position in regard to operations, as, in the speculative reason, the proposition holds in regard to conclusions. Such universal propositions of the practical reason that are directed to operations have the nature of law. And these propositions sometimes are under our actual consideration, while sometimes they are retained in the reason by means of a habit.

Reply to Obj. 3. Reason has its power of moving from the will, as was stated above; for it is due to the fact that one wills the end, that the reason issues its commands as regards things ordained to the end. But in order that the volition of what is commanded may have the nature of law, it needs to be in accord with some rule of reason. It is in this sense that we should understand the saying that the will of the sovereign has the force of law; otherwise the sovereign's will would savor of lawlessness rather than of law.

Second Article
Whether Law Is Always Directed to the Common Good?

Objection 1. It would seem that law is not always directed to the common good as to its end. For it belongs to law to command and to forbid. But commands are directed to certain individual goods. Therefore the end of law is not always the common good.

Obj. 2. Further, law directs man in his actions. But human actions are concerned with particular matters. Therefore law is directed to some particular good.

Obj. 3. Further Isidore[1] says: *If law is based on reason, whatever is based on reason will be a law.* But reason is the foundation not only of what is ordained to the common good, but also of that which is directed to private good. Therefore law is not directed only to the good of all, but also to the private good of an individual.

On the contrary, Isidore says that *laws are enacted for no private profit, but for the common benefit of the citizens.*

I answer that, As we have stated above, law belongs to that which is a principle of human acts, because it is their rule and measure. Now as reason is a principle of human acts, so in reason itself there is something which is the principle of human acts, so in reason itself there is something which is the principle in respect of all the rest. Hence to this principle chiefly and mainly law must needs be referred. Now the first principle in practical matters, which are the object of the practical reason, is the last end: and the last end of human life is happiness or beatitude. Consequently, law must needs concern itself mainly with the order that is in beatitude. Moreover, since every part is ordained to the whole as the imperfect to the perfect, and since one man is a part of the perfect community, law must needs concern itself properly with the order directed to universal happiness. Therefore the Philosopher, in the above definition of legal matters, mentions both happiness and the body politic, since he says that we call those legal matters just *which are adapted to produce and preserve happiness and its parts for the body politic* [*Ethics* V.1]. For the state is a perfect community, as he says in the *Politics* I.

Now, in every genus, that which belongs to it chiefly is the principle of the others, and the others belong to that genus according to some order toward that thing. Thus fire, which is chief among hot things, is the cause of heat in mixed bodies, and these are said to be hot in so far as they have a share of fire. Consequently, since law is chiefly ordained to the common good, any other precept in regard to some individual work must needs be devoid of the nature of a law, save in so far as it regards the common good. Therefore every law is ordained to the common good.

Reply Obj. 1. A command denotes the application of a law to matters regulated by law. Now the order to the common good, at which law aims, is applicable to particular ends. And in this way commands are given even concerning particular matters.

Reply Obj. 2. Actions are indeed concerned with particular matters, but those particular matters are referable to the common good, not as to a common genus or species, but as to a common final cause, according as the common good is said to be the common end.

Reply Obj. 3. Just as nothing stands firm with regard to the speculative reason except that which is traced back to the first indemonstrable principles, so nothing stands firm with regard to the practical reason, unless it be directed to the law end which is the common good. Now whatever stands to reason in this sense has the nature of law.

Third Article
Whether the Reason of Any
Man Is Competent to Make Laws?

Obj. 1. It would seem that the reason of any man is competent to make laws. For the Apostle [Paul] says (Rom. 2:14) that *when the Gentiles, who have not the law, do by nature those things that are of the law, . . . they are a law to themselves.* Now he says this of all in general. Therefore anyone can make a law for himself.

Obj 2. Further, as the Philosopher says, *the intention of the lawgiver is to lead men to virtue.* But every man can lead another to virtue. Therefore the reason of any man is competent to make laws.

On the contrary, Isidore says, *A law is an ordinance of the people, whereby something is sanctioned by the Elders together with the Commonality.* Therefore not everyone can make laws.

I answer that, A law, properly speaking, regards first and foremost the order to the common good. Now to order anything to the common good belongs either to the whole people, or to someone who is the representative of the whole people. Hence the making of a law belongs either to the whole people or to a public person who has care of the whole people; for in all other matters the directing of anything to the end concerns him to whom the end belongs.

Reply Obj. 1. A law is in a person not only as in one who rules, but also, by participation, as in one that is ruled. In the latter way, each one is a law to himself, in so far as he shares the direction that he receives from one who rules him. Hence the same biblical text goes on: *Who show the work of the law written in their hearts (Rom. 2:15).*

Reply Obj. 2. A private person cannot lead another to virtue efficaciously, for he can only advise; and if his advice be not taken, it has no coercive power, such as the law should have in order to prove an efficacious inducement to virtue, as the philosopher says. But this coercive power is vested in the whole people or in some public person to whom it belongs to inflict penalties. Therefore the framing of laws belongs to him alone.

Question 91
On The Various Kinds of Law

First Article
Whether There Is an Eternal Law?

Objection 1. It would seem that there is no eternal law. For every law is imposed on someone. But there was not someone from eternity on whom a law could be imposed, since God alone was from eternity. Therefore no law is eternal.

Obj. 2. Further, promulgation is essential to law. But promulgation could not be from eternity. Therefore no law can be eternal.

On the contrary, Augustine says, *that Law which is the Supreme Reason cannot be understood to be otherwise than unchangeable and eternal.*

I answer that, Law is nothing else but a dictate of practical reason emanating from the ruler who governs a perfect community. Now it is evident, granted that the world is ruled by divine providence, that the whole community of the universe is governed by the divine reason. Therefore the very notion of the government of things in God, the ruler of the universe, has the nature of a law. And since the divine reason's conception of things is not subject to time, but is eternal, according to Prov. 8:23, therefore it is that this kind of law must be called eternal.

Reply Obj. 1. Those things that do not exist in themselves exist in God, inasmuch as they are known and preordained by Him, according to Rom. 4:17: *Who calls those things that are not, as those that are.* Accordingly, the eternal concept of the divine law bears the character of an eternal law in so far as it is ordained by God to the government of things foreknown by Him.

Reply Obj 2. Promulgation is made by word of mouth or in writing, and in both ways the eternal law is promulgated, because both the divine Word and the writing of the Book of Life are eternal. But the promulgation cannot be from eternity on the part of the creature that hears or reads.

Second Article
Whether There Is in Us a Natural Law?

Objection 1. It would seem that there is no natural law in us. For man is governed sufficiently by the eternal law, since Augustine says that *the eternal law is that by which it is right that all things should be most orderly.* But nature does not abound in superfluities, as neither does she fail in necessaries. Therefore man has no natural law.

Obj. 2. Further, by the law man is directed, in his acts, to the end, as was stated above. But the directing of human acts to their end is not a function of nature, as is the case in irrational creatures, which act for an end solely by their natural appetite; whereas man acts for an end by his reason and will. Therefore man has no natural law.

On the contrary, the Gloss on Rom. 2:14 *(When the Gentiles, who have not the law, do by nature those things that are of the law)* comments as follows: *Although they have no written law, yet they have the natural law, whereby each one knows, and is conscious of, what is good and what is evil. . . .* As we have stated above, law, being a rule and measure, can be in a person in two ways: in one way, as in him that rules and measures; in another way, as in that which is ruled and measured, since a thing is ruled and measured in so far as it partakes of the rule or measure. Therefore, since all things subject to divine providence are ruled and measured by the eternal law, as was stated above, it is evident that all things partake in some way in the eternal law, in so far as, namely, from its being imprinted on them, they derive their respective inclinations to their proper acts and ends. Now among all others, the rational creature is subject to divine providence in a more excellent way, in so far as it itself partakes of a share of providence, by being provident both for itself and for others. Therefore it has a share of the eternal reason, whereby it has a natural inclination to its proper act and end; and this participation of the eternal law in the rational creature is called the natural law. Hence the Psalmist, after saying (Ps. 4:5): *Offer up the sacrifice of justice,* and as though someone asked what the works of justice are, adds; *many say, Who shows us good things?* In answer to which question he says: *The light of Thy countenance, O Lord, is signed upon us.* He thus implies that the light of natural reason, whereby we discern what is good and what is evil, which is the function of the natural law, is nothing else than an imprint on us of the divine light. It is therefore evident that the natural law is nothing else than the rational creature's participation of the eternal law.

Reply Obj. 1. This argument would hold if the natural law were something different from the eternal law; whereas it is nothing but a participation thereof, as we have stated above.

Reply Obj. 2. Every act of reason and will in us is based on that which is according to nature, as was stated above. For every act of reasoning is based on principles that are known naturally, and every act of appetite in respect of the means is derived from the natural appetite in respect of the last end. Accordingly, the first direction of our acts of their end must needs be through the natural law.

Third Article
Whether There Is a Human Law?

Objection 1. It would seem that there is not a human law. For the natural law is a participation of the eternal law, as was stated above. Now through the eternal law *all things are most orderly,* as Augustine[2] states. Therefore the natural law suffices for the ordering of all human affairs. Consequently there is no need for a human law.

Obj. 2. Further, law has the character of a measure, as was stated above. But human reason is not a measure of things, but *vice versa,* as is stated in *Metaph.* x. Therefore no law can emanate from the human reason.

Obj. 3. Further, a measure should be most certain, as is stated in *Metaph.* x. But the dictates of the human reason in matters of conduct are uncertain, according to *Wis.* ix. 14: *The thoughts of mortal men are fearful, and our counsels uncertain.* Therefore no law can emanate from the human reason.

On the contrary, Augustine distinguishes two kinds of law, the one eternal, the other temporal, which he calls human.

I answer that, As we have stated above, a law is a dictate of the practical reason. Now it is to be observed that the same procedure takes place in the practical and in the speculative reason, for each proceeds from principles to conclusions, as was stated above. Accordingly, we conclude that, just as, in the speculative reason, from naturally known indemonstrable principles we draw the conclusions of the various sciences, the knowledge of which is not imparted to us by nature, but acquired by the efforts of reason, so too it is that from the precepts of the natural law, as from common and indemonstrable principles, the human reason needs to proceed to the more particular determination of certain matters. These particular determinations, devised by human reason, are called human laws, provided that the other essential conditions of law be observed, as was stated above. Therefore Tully[3] says in his *Rhetoric* that *justice has its source in nature; thence certain things came into custom by reason of their utility; afterwards these things which emanated from nature, and were approved by custom, were sanctioned by fear and reverence for the law.*

Reply Obj. 1. The human reason cannot have a full participation of the dictate of the divine reason, but according to its own mode, and imperfectly. Consequently, just as on the part of the speculative reason, by a natural participation of divine wisdom, there is in us the knowledge of certain common principles, but not a proper knowledge of each single truth such as that contained in the divine wisdom, so, too, on the part of the practical reason, man has a natural participation of the eternal law, according to certain common principles, but not as regards the particular determinations of individual cases, which are, however, contained in the eternal law. Hence the need for human reason to proceed further to sanction them by law.

Reply Obj. 2. Human reason is not, of itself, the rule of things. But the principles impressed on it by nature are the general rules and measures of all things relating to human conduct, of which the natural reason is the rule and measure, although it is not the measure of things that are from nature.

Reply Obj. 3. The practical reason is concerned with operable matters, which are singular and contingent, but not with necessary things, with which the speculative reason is concerned. Therefore human laws cannot have that inerrancy that belongs to the demonstrated conclusions of the sciences. Nor is it necessary for every measure to be altogether unerring and certain, but according as it is possible in its own particular genus.

Fourth Article
Whether There Was Any Need For a Divine Law?

We proceed thus to the Fourth Article:—

Objection 1. It would seem that there was no need for a divine law. For, as was stated above, the natural law is a participation in us of the eternal law. But the eternal law is the divine law, as was stated above. Therefore there is no need for a divine law in addition to the natural law and to human laws derived therefrom.

Obj. 2. Further, it is written (*Ecclus.* xv. 14) that *God left man in the hand of his own counsel.* Now counsel is an act of reason, as was stated above. Therefore man was left to the direction of his reason. But a dictate of human reason is a human law, as was stated above. Therefore there is no need for man to be governed also by a divine law. . . .

On the contrary, David prayed God to set His law before him, saying (*Ps.* cxix. 33): *Set before me for a law the way of Thy justifications, O Lord.*

I answer that, Besides the natural and the human law it was necessary for the directing of human conduct to have a divine law. And this for four reasons. First, because it is by law that man is directed how to perform his proper acts in view of his last end. Now if man were ordained to no other end than that which is proportionate to his natural ability, there would be no need for man to have any further direction, on the part of his reason, in addition to the natural law and humanly devised law which is derived from it. But since man is ordained to an end of eternal happiness which exceeds man's natural ability, as we have stated above, therefore it was necessary that, in addition to the natural and the human law, man should be directed to his end by a law given by God.

Secondly, because, by reason of the uncertainty of human judgment, especially on contingent and particular matters, different people form different judgments on human acts; whence also different and contrary laws result. In order, therefore, that man may know without any doubt what he ought to do and what he ought to avoid, it was necessary for man to be directed in his proper acts by a law given by God, for it is certain that such a law cannot err.

Thirdly, because man can make laws in those matters of which he is competent to judge. But man is not competent to judge of interior movements that are hidden, but only of exterior acts which are observable; and yet for the perfection of virtue it is necessary for man to conduct himself rightly in both kinds of acts. Consequently, human law could not sufficiently curb and direct interior acts, and it was necessary for this purpose that a divine law should supervene.

Fourthly, because, as Augustine says, human law cannot punish or forbid all evil deeds, since, while aiming at doing away with all evils, it would do away with many good things, and would hinder the advance of the common good, which is necessary for human living. In order, therefore, that no evil might remain unforbidden and unpunished, it was necessary for the divine law to supervene, whereby all sins are forbidden.

And these four causes are touched upon in *Ps.* cxix. 8, where it is said: *The law of the Lord is unspotted, i.e.,* allowing no foulness of sin; *converting souls,* because it directs not only exterior, but also interior, acts; *the testimony of the Lord is faithful,* because of the certainty of what is true and right; *giving wisdom to little ones,* by directing man to an end supernatural and divine.

Reply Obj. 1. By the natural law the eternal law is participated proportionately to the capacity of human nature. But to his supernatural end man needs to be directed in a yet higher way. Hence the additional law given by God whereby man shares more perfectly in the eternal law.

Reply Obj. 2. Counsel is a kind of inquiry, and hence must proceed from some principles. Nor is it enough for it to proceed from principles imparted by nature, which are the precepts of the natural law, for the reasons given above; but there is need for certain additional principles, namely, the precepts of the divine law. . . .

Question 94
The Natural Law

First Article
Whether the Natural Law Is a Habit?

We proceed thus to the First Article:—

Objection 1. It would seem that the natural law is a habit. For, as the Philosopher says, *there are three things in the soul—power, habit and passion.* But the natural law is not one of the soul's powers, nor is it one of the passions, as we may see by going through them one by one. Therefore the natural law is a habit.

Obj. 2. Further, Basil says that the *conscience or synderesis is the law of our mind,* which can apply only to the natural law. But *synderesis* is a habit, as was shown in the Fist Part. Therefore the natural law is a habit.

Obj. 3. Further, the natural law abides in man always, as will be shown further on. But man's reason, which the law regards, does not always think about the natural law. Therefore the natural law is not an act, but a habit.

On the contrary, Augustine says that *a habit is that whereby something is done when necessary.* But such is not the natural law, since it is in infants and in the damned who cannot act by it. Therefore the natural law is not a habit.

I answer that, A thing may be called a habit in two ways. First, properly and essentially, and thus the natural law is not a habit. For it has been stated above that the natural law is something appointed by reason, just as a proposition is a work of reason. Now that which a man does is not the same as that whereby he does it, for he makes a becoming speech by the habit of grammar. Since, then, a habit is that by which we act, a law cannot be a habit properly and essentially.

Secondly, the term habit may be applied to that which we hold by a habit. Thus *faith* may mean *that which we hold by faith.* Accordingly, since the precepts of the natural law are sometimes considered by reason actually, while sometimes they are in the reason only habitually, in this way the natural law may be called a habit. So, too, in speculative matters, the indemonstrable principles are not the habit itself whereby we hold these principles; they are rather the principles of which we possess the habit.

Reply Obj. 1. The Philosopher proposes there to discover the genus of virtue; and since it is evident that virtue is a principle of action, he mentions only those things which are principles of human acts, viz., powers, habits and passions. But there are other things in the soul besides these three: *e.g.,* acts, as *to will* is in the one that wills; again, there are things known in the knower; moreover, its own natural properties such as immortality and the like, are in the soul.

Reply Obj. 2. Synderesis is said to be the law of our intellect because it is a habit containing the precepts of the natural law, which are the first principles of human actions.

Reply Obj. 3. This argument proves that the natural law is held habitually; and this is granted.

To the argument advanced in the contrary sense we reply that sometimes a man is unable to make use of that which is in him habitually, because of some impediment. Thus, because of sleep, a man is unable to use the habit of science. In like manner, through the deficiency of his age, a child cannot use the habit of the understanding of principles, or the natural law, which is in him habitually.

Second Article
Whether the Natural Law Contains Several Precepts, or Only One?

We proceed thus to the Second Article:—

Objection 1. It would seem that the natural law contains, not several precepts, but only one. For law is a kind of precept, as was stated above. If therefore there were many precepts of the natural law, it would follow that there are also many natural laws.

Obj. 2. Further, the natural law is consequent upon human nature. But human nature, as a whole, is one; though, as to its parts, it is manifold. Therefore, either there is but one precept of the law of nature because of the unity of nature as a whole, or there are many by reason of the number of parts of human nature. The result would be that even things relating to the inclination of the concupiscible power would belong to the natural law.

Obj. 3. Further, law is something pertaining to reason, as was stated above. Now reason is but one in man. Therefore there is only one precept of the natural law.

On the contrary, The precepts of the natural law in man stand in relation to operable matters as first principles do to matters of demonstration. But there are several first indemonstrable principles. Therefore there are also several precepts of the natural law.

I answer that, As was stated above, the precepts of the natural law are to the practical reason what the first principles of demonstrations are to the speculative reason, because both are self-evident principles. Now a thing is said to be self-evident in two ways: first, in itself; secondly, in relation to us. Any proposition is said to be self-evident in it-self, if its predicate is contained in the notion of the subject; even though it may happen that to one who does not know the definition of the subject, such a proposition is not self-evident. For instance, this proposition, *Man is a rational being,* is, in its very nature, self-evident, since he who says *man says a rational being;* and yet to one who does not know what a man is, this proposition is not self-evident. Hence it is that, as Boethius says, certain axioms or propositions are universally self-evident to all; and such are the propositions whose terms are known to all, as, *Every whole is greater than its part,* and, *Things equal to one and the same are equal to one another.* But some propositions are self-evident only to the wise, who understand the meaning of the terms of such propositions. Thus to one who understands that an angel is not a body, it is self-evident that an angel is not circumscriptively in a place. But this is not evident to the unlearned, for they cannot grasp it.

Now a certain order is to be found in those things that are apprehended by men. For that which first falls under apprehension is *being,* the understanding of which is included in all things whatsoever a man apprehends. Therefore the first indemonstrable principle is that *the same thing cannot be affirmed and denied at the same time,* which is based on the notion of *being* and *not-being:* and on this principle all others are based, as is stated in *Metaph.* iv. Now as *being* is the first thing that falls under the apprehension absolutely, so *good* is the first thing that falls under the apprehension of the practical reason, which is directed to action (since every agent acts for an end, which has the nature of good.) Consequently, the first principle in the practical reason is one founded on the nature of good, viz., that *good is that which all things seek after.* Hence this is the first precept of law, that *good is to be done and promoted, and evil is to be avoided.* All other precepts of the natural law are based upon this; so that all the things which the practical reason naturally apprehends as man's good belong to the precepts of the natural law under the form of things to be done or avoided.

Since, however, good has the nature of an end, and evil, the nature of the contrary, hence it is that all those things to which man has a natural inclination are naturally apprehended by reason as being good, and consequently as objects of pursuit, and their contraries as evil, and objects of avoidance. Therefore, the order of the precepts of the natural law is according to the order of natural inclinations. For there is in man, first of all, an inclination to good in accordance with the nature which he has in common with all substances, inasmuch, namely, as every substance seeks the preservation of its own being, according to its nature; and by reason of this inclination, whatever is a means of preserving human life, and of warding off its obstacles, belongs to the natural law. Secondly, there is in man an inclination to things that pertain to him more specially, according to that nature which he has in common with other animals; and in virtue of this inclination, those things are said to belong to the natural law *which nature has taught to all animals,* such as sexual intercourse, the education of offspring, and so forth. Thirdly, there is in man an inclination to good according to the nature of his reason, which nature is proper to him. Thus man has a natural inclination to know the truth about God, and to live in society; and in this respect, whatever pertains to this inclination belongs to the natural law: *e.g.,* to shun ignorance, to avoid offending those among whom one has to live, and other such things regarding the above inclination.

Reply Obj. 1. All these precepts of the law of nature have the character of one natural law, inasmuch as they flow from one first precept.

Reply Obj. 2. All the inclinations of any parts whatsoever of human nature, *e.g.,* of the concupiscible and irascible parts, in so far as they are ruled by reason, belong to the natural law, and are reduced to one first precept, as was stated above. And thus the precepts of the natural law are many in themselves, but they are based on one common foundation.

Reply Obj. 3. Although reason is one in itself, yet it directs all things regarding man; so that

whatever can be ruled by reason is contained under the law of reason.

Fourth Article
Whether the Natural Law Is the Same in All Men?

We proceed thus to the Fourth Article:—

Objection 1. It would seem that the natural law is not the same in all. For it is stated in the *Decretals*[4] that *the natural law is that which is contained in the Law and the Gospel.* But this is not common to all men, because, as it is written (*Rom.* 10. 16), *all do not obey the gospel.* Therefore the natural law is not the same in all men.

Obj. 2. Further, *Things which are according to the law are said to be just,* as is stated in *Ethics* v. But it is stated in the same book that nothing is so just for all as not to be subject to change in regard to some men. Therefore even the natural law is not the same in all men.

Obj. 3. Further, as was stated above, to the natural law belongs everything to which a man is inclined according to his nature. Now different men are naturally inclined to different things—some to the desire of pleasures, others to the desire of honors, and other men to other things. Therefore, there is not one natural law for all.

On the contrary, Isidore says: *The natural law is common to all nations.*

I answer that, As we have stated above, to the natural law belong those things to which a man is inclined naturally; and among these it is proper to man to be inclined to act according to reason. Now it belongs to the reason to proceed from what is common to what is proper, as is stated in *Physics* i. The speculative reason, however, is differently situated, in this matter, from the practical reason. For, since the speculative reason is concerned chiefly with necessary things, which cannot be otherwise than they are, its proper conclusions, like the universal principles, contain the truth without fail. The practical reason, on the other hand, is concerned with contingent matters, which is the domain of human actions; and, consequently, although there is necessity in the common principles, the more we descend toward the particular, the more frequently we encounter defects. Accordingly, then, in speculative matters truth is the same in all men, both as to principles and as to conclusions; although the truth is not known to all as regards the conclusions, but only as regards the principles which are called *common notions*. But in matters of action, truth or practical rectitude is not the same for all as to what is particular, but only as to the common principles; and where there is the same rectitude in relation to particulars, it is not equally known to all.

It is therefore evident that, as regards the common principles whether of speculative or of practical reason, truth or rectitude is the same for all, and is equally known by all. But as to the proper conclusions of the speculative reason, the truth is the same for all, but it is not equally known to all. Thus, it is true for all that the three angles of a triangle are together equal to two right angles, although it is not known to all. But as to the proper conclusions of the practical reason, neither is the truth or rectitude the same for all; nor, where it is the same, is it equally known by all. Thus, it is right and true for all to act according to reason, and from this principle it follows, as a proper conclusion, that goods entrusted to another should be restored to their owner. Now this is true for the majority of cases. But it may happen in a particular case that it would be injurious, and therefore unreasonable, to restore goods held in trust; for instance, if they are claimed for the purpose of fighting against one's country. And this principle will be found to fail the more, according as we descend further toward the particular; *e.g.*, if one were to say that goods held in trust should be restored with such and such a guarantee, or in such and such a way; because the greater the number of conditions added, the greater the number of ways in which the principle may fail, so that it be not right to restore or not to restore.

Consequently, we must say that the natural law, as to the first common principles, is the same for all, both as to rectitude and as to knowledge. But

as to certain more particular aspects, which are conclusions, as it were, of those common principles, it is the same for all in the majority of cases, both as to rectitude and as to knowledge; and yet in some few cases it may fail, both as to rectitude, by reason of certain obstacles (just as natures subject to generation and corruption fail in some few cases because of some obstacle), and as to knowledge, since in some the reason is perverted by passion, or evil habit, or an evil disposition of nature. Thus at one time theft, although it is expressly contrary to the natural law, was not considered wrong among the Germans, as Julius Caesar relates.

Reply Obj. 1. The meaning of the sentence quoted is not that whatever is contained in the Law and the Gospel belongs to the natural law, since they contain many things that are above nature; but that whatever belongs to the natural law is fully contained in them. Therefore Gratian,[5] after saying that *the natural law is what is contained in the Law and the Gospel*, adds at once, by way of example, *by which everyone is commanded to do to others as he would be done by.*

Reply Obj. 2. The saying of the Philosopher is to be understood of things that are naturally just, not as common principles, but as conclusions drawn from them, having rectitude in the majority of cases, but failing in a few.

Reply Obj. 3. Just as in man reason rules and commands the other powers, so all the natural inclinations belonging to the other powers must needs be directed according to reason. Therefore it is universally right for all men that all their inclinations should be directed according to reason.

Fifth Article
Whether the Natural Law Can be Changed?

We proceed thus to the Fifth Article:—

Objection 1. It would seem that the natural law can be changed. For on *Ecclus*, xvii. 9 (*He gave them instructions, and the law of life*) the *Gloss* says: *He wished the law of the letter to be written, in order to correct the law of nature.* But that which is corrected is changed. Therefore the natural law can be changed.

Obj. 2. Further, the slaying of the innocent, adultery, and theft are against the natural law. But we find these things changed by God: as when God commanded Abraham to slay his innocent son (*Gen.* xxii. 2); and when He ordered the Jews to borrow and purloin the vessels of the Egyptians (*Exod.* xii. 35); and when He commanded Osee to take to himself *a wife of fornications* (*Osee* i. 2). Therefore the natural law can be changed.

Obj. 3. Further, Isidore says that *the possession of all things in common, and universal freedom, are matters of natural law.* But these things are seen to be changed by human laws. Therefore it seems that the natural law is subject to change.

On the contrary, It is said in the *Decretals: The natural law dates from the creation of the rational creature. It does not vary according to time, but remains unchangeable.*

I answer that, A change in the natural law may be understood in two ways. First, by way of addition. In this sense, nothing hinders the natural law from being changed, since many things for the benefit of human life have been added over and above the natural law, both by the divine law and by human laws.

Secondly, a change in the natural law may be understood by way of subtraction, so that what previously was according to the natural law ceases to be so. In this sense, the natural law is altogether unchangeable in its first principles. But in its secondary principles, which, as we have said, are certain detailed proximate conclusions drawn from the first principles, the natural law is not changed, so that what it prescribes be not right in most cases. But it may be changed in some particular cases of rare occurrence, through some special causes hindering the observance of such precepts, as was stated above.

Reply Obj. 1. The written law is said to be given for the correction of the natural law, either because it supplies what was wanting to the natural law, or because the natural law was so perverted in the hearts of some men, as to certain matters, that they esteemed those things good which are naturally evil; which perversion stood in need of correction.

Reply Obj. 2. All men alike, both guilty and innocent, die the death of nature; which death of nature is inflicted by the power of God because of original sin, according to *1 Kings* ii. 6: *The Lord killeth and maketh alive.* Consequently, by the command of God, death can be inflicted on any man, guilty or innocent, without any injustice whatever. In like manner, adultery is intercourse with another's wife, who is allotted to him by the law emanating from God. Consequently intercourse with any woman by the command of God is neither adultery nor fornication. The same applies to theft, which is the taking of another's property. For whatever is taken by the command of God, to Whom all things belong, is not taken against the will of its owner, whereas it is in this that theft consists. Nor is it only in human things that whatever is commanded by God is right; but also in natural things, whatever is done by God is, in some way, natural, as was stated in the First Part.

Reply Obj. 3. A thing is said to belong to the natural law in two ways. First, because nature inclines thereto: *e.g.,* that one should not do harm to another. Secondly, because nature did not bring with it the contrary. Thus, we might say that for man to be naked is of the natural law, because nature did not give him clothes, but art invented them. In this sense, *the possession of all things in common and universal freedom* are said to be the natural law, because, namely, the distinction of possessions and slavery were not brought in by nature, but devised by human reason for the benefit of human life. Accordingly, the law of nature was not changed in this respect, except by addition.

Notes

1. Isidore of Seville (ca. 560–636), Archbishop of Seville. He was the author of several theological works,

including *Sententiarum libri tres* and *De fide catholica*, which were highly influential in the Middle Ages.

2. Augustine: St. Augustine, Bishop of Hippo (354–430), one of the foremost Christian philosophers who taught that a divine illumination enlightened every soul with special knowledge of God. His most influential works are *Confessions* (400) and *On the City of God* (413–426).

3. Tully: Marcus Tullius Cicero (106–143 B.C.), Roman statesman, orator and Stoic philosopher, he set forth the early version of Natural Law.

4. Decretals: Papal epistles or decrees replying to some question on faith or authority.

5. Gratian (359–383), a Christian emperor who issued enactments against paganism.

A Defense of Ethical Relativism

RUTH BENEDICT

Ruth Benedict (1887–1948) was a foremost American anthropologist who taught at Columbia University. She is best known for her book Patterns of Culture *(1935). Benedict views social systems as communities with common beliefs and practices which have become more or less well integrated patterns of ideas and practices. Like a work of art, a social system chooses which theme of its repertoire of basic tendencies to emphasize and then goes about to produce a holistic grand design favoring those tendencies. The final systems differ from one another in striking ways, but there is no reason to say that one system is better than another. What is considered normal or abnormal behavior depends on the choices of these social systems, or what Benedict calls the "idea-practice pattern of the culture."*

Benedict views morality as dependent on the varying histories and environments of different cultures. In this essay she assembles an impressive amount of data from her anthropological research of tribal behavior on an island in northwest Melanesia, from which she draws her conclusion that moral relativism is the correct view of moral principles.

Modern social anthropology has become more and more a study of the varieties and common elements of cultural environment and the consequences of these in human behavior. For such a study of diverse social orders primitive peoples fortunately provide a laboratory not yet entirely vitiated by the spread of a standardized worldwide civilization. Dyaks and Hopis, Fijians and Yakuts are significant for psychological and sociological

From "Anthropology and the Abnormal," by Ruth Benedict, in *The Journal of General Psychology* 10 (1934): 59–82, a publication of the Helen Dwight Reid Educational Foundation. Reprinted by permission of Heldret Publications.

study because only among these simpler peoples has there been sufficient isolation to give opportunity for the development of localized social forms. In the higher cultures the standardization of custom and belief over a couple of continents has given a false sense of the inevitability of the particular forms that have gained currency, and we need to turn to a wider survey in order to check the conclusions we hastily base upon this near-universality of familiar customs. Most of the simpler cultures did not gain the wide currency of the one which, out of our experience, we identify with human nature, but this was for various historical reasons, and certainly not for any that gives us as its carriers a monopoly of social good or of social sanity. Modern civilization, from this point of view, becomes not a necessary pinnacle of human achievement but one entry in a long series of possible adjustments.

These adjustments, whether they are in mannerisms like the ways of showing anger, or joy, or grief in any society, or in major human drives like those of sex, prove to be far more variable than experience in any one culture would suggest. In certain fields, such as that of religion or of formal marriage arrangements, these wide limits of variability are well known and can be fairly described. In others it is not yet possible to give a generalized account, but that does not absolve us of the task of indicating the significance of the work that has been done and of the problems that have arisen.

One of these problems relates to the customary modern normal-abnormal categories and our conclusions regarding them. In how far are such categories culturally determined, or in how far can we with assurance regard them as absolute? In how far can we regard inability to function socially as diagnostic of abnormality, or in how far is it necessary to regard this as a function of the culture?

As a matter of fact, one of the most striking facts that emerge from a study of widely varying cultures is the ease with which our abnormals function in other cultures. It does not matter what kind of "abnormality" we choose for illustration, those which indicate extreme instability, or those which are more in the nature of character traits like sadism or delusions of grandeur or of persecution, there are well-described cultures in which these abnormals function at ease and with honor, and apparently without danger or difficulty to the society. . . .

The most notorious of these is trance and catalepsy. Even a very mild mystic is aberrant in our culture. But most people have regarded even extreme psychic manifestations not only as normal and desirable, but even as characteristic of highly valued and gifted individuals. This was true even in our own cultural background in that period when Catholicism made the ecstatic experience the mark of sainthood. It is hard for us, born and brought up in a culture that makes no use of the experience, to realize how important a role it may play and how many individuals are capable of it, once it has been given an honorable place in any society. . . .

Cataleptic and trance phenomena are, of course, only one illustration of the fact that those whom we regard as abnormals may function adequately in other cultures. Many of our culturally discarded traits are selected for elaboration in different societies. Homosexuality is an excellent example, for in this case our attention is not constantly diverted, as in the consideration of trance, to the interruption of routine activity which it implies. Homosexuality poses the problem very simply. A tendency toward this trait in our culture exposes an individual to all the conflicts to which all aberrants are always exposed, and we tend to identify the consequences of this conflict with homosexuality. But these consequences are obviously local and cultural. Homosexuals in many societies are not incompetent, but they may be such if the culture asks adjustments of them that would strain

any man's vitality. Wherever homosexuality has been given an honorable place in any society, those to whom it is congenial have filled adequately the honorable roles society assigns to them. Plato's *Republic* is, of course, the most convincing statement of such a reading of homosexuality. It is presented as one of the major means to the good life, and it was generally so regarded in Greece at that time.

The cultural attitude toward homosexuals has not always been on such a high ethical plane, but it has been very varied. Among many American Indian tribes there exists the institution of the *berdache,* as the French called them. These men-women were men who at puberty or thereafter took the dress and the occupations of women. Sometimes they married other men and lived with them. Sometimes they were men with no inversion, persons of weak sexual endowment who chose this role to avoid the jeers of the women. The berdaches were never regarded as of first-rate supernatural power, as similar men-women were in Siberia, but rather as leaders in women's occupations, good healers in certain diseases, or, among certain tribes, as the genial organizers of social affairs. In any case, they were socially placed. They were not left exposed to the conflicts that visit the deviant who is excluded from participation in the recognized patterns of his society.

The most spectacular illustrations of the extent to which normality may be culturally defined are those cultures where an abnormality of our culture is the cornerstone of their social structure. It is not possible to do justice to these possibilities in a short discussion. A recent study of an island of northwest Melanesia by Fortune describes a society built upon traits which we regard as beyond the border of paranoia. In this tribe the exogamic groups look upon each other as prime manipulators of black magic, so that one marries always into an enemy group which remains for life one's deadly and unappeasable foes. They look upon a good garden crop as a confession of theft, for everyone is engaged in making magic to induce into his garden the productiveness of his neighbors'; therefore no secrecy in the island is so rigidly insisted upon as the secrecy of a man's harvesting of his yams. Their polite phrase at the acceptance of a gift is, "And if you now poison me, how shall I repay you this present?" Their preoccupation with poisoning is constant; no woman ever leaves her cooking pot for a moment untended. Even the great affinal economic exchanges that are characteristic of this Melanesian culture area are quite altered in Dobu since they are incompatible with this fear and distrust that pervades the culture. They go farther and people the whole world outside their own quarters with such malignant spirits that all-night feasts and ceremonials simply do not occur here. They have even rigorous religiously enforced customs that forbid the sharing of seed even in one family group. Anyone else's food is deadly poison to you, so that communality of stores is out of the question. For some months before harvest the whole society is on the verge of starvation, but if one falls to the temptation and eats up one's seed yams, one is an outcast and a beachcomber for life. There is no coming back. It involves, as a matter of course, divorce and the breaking of all social ties.

Now in this society where no one may work with another and no one may share with another, Fortune describes the individual who was regarded by all his fellows as crazy. He was not one of those who periodically ran amok and, beside himself and frothing at the mouth, fell with a knife upon anyone he could reach. Such behavior they did not regard as putting anyone outside the pale. They did not even put the individuals who were known to be liable to these attacks under any kind of control. They merely fled when they saw the attack coming on and kept out of the way. "He would be all right tomorrow." But there was one man of sunny, kindly disposition who liked work and liked to be helpful. The compulsion was too strong for him to repress it in favor of the opposite tendencies of his culture. Men and women never spoke of him without laughing; he was silly and simple and definitely crazy. Nevertheless, to the ethnologist used to a culture that has, in

Christianity, made his type the model of all virtue, he seemed a pleasant fellow. . . .

. . . Among the Kwakiutl it did not matter whether a relative had died in bed of disease, or by the hand of an enemy, in either case death was an affront to be wiped out by the death of another person. The fact that one had been caused to mourn was proof that one had been put upon. A chief's sister and her daughter had gone up to Victoria, and either because they drank bad whiskey or because their boat capsized they never came back. The chief called together his warriors, "Now I ask you, tribes, who shall wail? Shall I do it or shall another?" The spokesman answered, of course, "Not you, Chief. Let some other of the tribes." Immediately they set up the war pole to announce their intention of wiping out the injury, and gathered a war party. They set out, and found seven men and two children asleep and killed them. "Then they felt good when they arrived at Sebaa in the evening."

The point which is of interest to us is that in our society those who on that occasion would feel good when they arrived at Sebaa that evening would be the definitely abnormal. There would be some, even in our society, but it is not a recognized and approved mood under the circumstances. On the Northwest Coast those are favored and fortunate to whom that mood under those circumstances is congenial, and those to whom it is repugnant are unlucky. This latter minority can register in their own culture only by doing violence to their congenial responses and acquiring others that are difficult for them. The person, for instance, who, like a Plains Indian whose wife has been taken from him, is too proud to fight, can deal with the Northwest Coast civilization only by ignoring its strongest bents. If he cannot achieve it, he is the deviant in that culture, their instance of abnormality.

This head-hunting that takes place on the Northwest Coast after a death is no matter of blood revenge or of organized vengeance. There is no effort to tie up the subsequent killing with any responsibility on the part of the victim for the death of the person who is being mourned. A chief whose son has died goes visiting wherever his fancy dictates, and he says to his host, "My prince has died today, and you go with him." Then he kills him. In this, according to their interpretation, he acts nobly because he has not been downed. He has thrust back in return. The whole procedure is meaningless without the fundamental paranoid reading of bereavement. Death, like all the other untoward accidents of existence, confounds man's pride and can only be handled in the category of insults.

Behavior honored upon the Northwest Coast is one which is recognized as abnormal in our civilization, and yet it is sufficiently close to the attitudes of our own culture to be intelligible to us and to have a definite vocabulary with which we may discuss it. The megalomaniac paranoid trend is a definite danger in our society. It is encouraged by some of our major preoccupations, and it confronts us with a choice of two possible attitudes. One is to brand it as abnormal and reprehensible, and is the attitude we have chosen in our civilization. The other is to make it an essential attribute of ideal man, and this is the solution in the culture of the Northwest Coast.

These illustrations, which it has been possible to indicate only in the briefest manner, force upon us the fact that normality is culturally defined. An adult shaped to the drives and standards of either of these cultures, if he were transported into our civilization, would fall into our categories of abnormality. He would be faced with the psychic dilemmas of the socially unavailable. In his own culture, however, he is the pillar of society, the end result of socially inculcated mores, and the problem of personal instability in his case simply does not arise.

No one civilization can possibly utilize in its mores the whole potential range of human behavior. Just as there are great numbers of possible phonetic articulations, and the possibility of language depends on a selection and standardization of a few of these in order that speech communication may be possible at all, so the possibility of organized behavior of every sort, from the fashions of local dress and houses to the dicta of a

people's ethics and religion, depends upon a similar selection among the possible behavior traits. In the field of recognized economic obligations or sex tabus this selection is as nonrational and subconscious a process as it is in the field of phonetics. It is a process which goes on in the group for long periods of time and is historically conditioned by innumerable accidents of isolation or of contact of peoples. In any comprehensive study of psychology, the selection that different cultures have made in the course of history within the great circumference of potential behavior is of great significance.

Every society, beginning with some slight inclination in one direction or another, carries its preference farther and farther, integrating itself more and more completely upon its chosen basis, and discarding those types of behavior that are uncongenial. Most of those organizations of personality that seem to us most uncontrovertibly abnormal have been used by different civilizations in the very foundations of their institutional life. Conversely the most valued traits of our normal individuals have been looked on in differently organized cultures as aberrant. Normality, in short, within a very wide range, is culturally defined. It is primarily a term for the socially elaborated segment of human behavior in any culture; and abnormality, a term for the segment that that particular civilization does not use. The very eyes with which we see the problem are conditioned by the long traditional habits of our own society.

It is a point that has been made more often in relation to ethics than in relation to psychiatry. We do not any longer make the mistake of deriving the morality of our locality and decade directly from the inevitable constitution of human nature. We do not elevate it to the dignity of a first principle. We recognize that morality differs in every society, and is a convenient term for socially approved habits. Mankind has always preferred to say, "It is a morally good," rather than "It is habitual," and the fact of this preference is matter enough for a critical science of ethics. But historically the two phrases are synonymous.

The concept of the normal is properly a variant

of the concept of the good. It is that which society has approved. A normal action is one which falls well within the limits of expected behavior for a particular society. Its variability among different peoples is essentially a function of the variability of the behavior patterns that different societies have created for themselves, and can never be wholly divorced from a consideration of culturally institutionalized types of behavior.

Each culture is a more or less elaborate working out of the potentialities of the segment it has chosen. In so far as a civilization is well integrated and consistent within itself, it will tend to carry farther and farther, according to its nature, its initial impulse toward a particular type of action, and from the point of view of any other culture those elaborations will include more and more extreme and aberrant traits.

Each of these traits, in proportion as it reinforces the chosen behavior patterns of that culture, is for that culture normal. Those individuals to whom it is congenial either congenitally, or as the result of childhood sets, are accorded prestige in that culture, and are not visited with the social contempt or disapproval which their traits would call down upon them in a society that was differently organized. On the other hand, those individuals whose characteristics are not congenial to the selected type of human behavior in that community are the deviants, no matter how valued their personality traits may be in a contrasted civilization.

The Dobuan who is not easily susceptible to fear of treachery, who enjoys work and likes to be helpful, is their neurotic and regarded as silly. On the Northwest Coast the person who finds it difficult to read life in terms of an insult contest will be the person upon whom fall all the difficulties of the culturally unprovided for. The person who does not find it easy to humiliate a neighbor, nor to see humiliation in his own experience, who is genial and loving, may, of course, find some unstandardized way of achieving satisfactions in his society, but not in the major patterned responses that his culture requires of him. If he is born to

play an important role in a family with many hereditary privileges, he can succeed only by doing violence to his whole personality. If he does not succeed, he has betrayed his culture; that is, he is abnormal.

I have spoken of individuals as having sets toward certain types of behavior, and of these sets as running sometimes counter to the types of behavior which are institutionalized in the culture to which they belong. From all that we know of contrasting cultures it seems clear that differences of temperament occur in every society. The matter has never been made the subject of investigation, but from the available material it would appear that these temperament types are very likely of universal recurrence. That is, there is an ascertainable range of human behavior that is found wherever a sufficiently large series of individuals is observed. But the proportion in which behavior types stand to one another in different societies is not universal. The vast majority of individuals in any group are shaped to the fashion of that culture. In other words, most individuals are plastic to the moulding force of the society into which they are born. In a society that values trance, as in India, they will have supernormal experience. In a society that institutionalizes homosexuality, they will be homosexual. In a society that sets the gathering of possessions as the chief human objective, they will amass property. The deviants, whatever the type of behavior the culture has institutionalized, will remain few in number, and there seems no more difficulty in moulding the vast malleable majority to the "normality" of what we consider an aberrant trait, such as delusions of reference, than to the normality of such accepted behavior patterns as acquisitiveness. The small proportion of the number of the deviants in any culture is not a function of the sure instinct with which that society has built itself upon the fundamental sanities, but of the universal fact that, happily, the majority of mankind quite readily take any shape that is presented to them. . . .

5

A Defense of Ethical Objectivism

LOUIS P. POJMAN

In this article I first analyze the structure of ethical relativism as constituted by two theses: the diversity thesis and the dependency thesis. Then I examine two types of ethical relativism: subjectivism and conventionalism, arguing that both types have serious problems. Next I indicate a way of taking into account the insights of relativism while maintaining an objectivist position. I outline two objectivist arguments. I conclude by suggesting some reasons why people have been misled by relativist arguments.

"Who's to Judge What's Right or Wrong?"

Like many people, I have always been instinctively a moral relativist. As far back as I can remember . . . it has always seemed to be obvious that the dictates of morality arise from some sort of convention or understanding among people, that different people arrive at different understandings, and that there are no basic moral demands that apply to everyone. This seemed so obvious to me I assumed it was everyone's instinctive view, or at least everyone who gave the matter any thought in this day and age.
—Gilbert Harman[1]

Ethical relativism is the doctrine that the moral rightness and wrongness of actions vary from society to society and that there are not absolute universal moral standards on all men at all times. Accordingly, it holds that whether or not it is right for an individual to act in a certain way depends on or is relative to the society to which he belongs.

—John Ladd[2]

Gilbert Harman's intuitions about the self-evidence of ethical relativism contrast strikingly with Plato's or Kant's equal certainty about the truth of objectivism, the doctrine that universally valid or true ethical principles exist.[3] "Two things fill the soul with ever new and increasing wonder and reverence the oftener and more fervently reflection ponders on it: the starry heavens above and the moral law within," wrote Kant. On the basis of polls taken in my ethics and introduction to philosophy classes over the past several years, Harman's views may signal a shift in contemporary society's moral understanding. The polls show a two-to-one ratio in favor of moral relativism over moral absolutism, with fewer than five percent of the respondents recognizing that a third position between these two polar opposites might exist. Of course, I'm not suggesting that all of these students had a clear understanding of what relativism entails, for many who said they were relativists also contended in the same polls that abortion except to save the mother's life is always wrong, that capital punishment is always wrong, or that suicide is never morally permissible.

Among my university colleagues, a growing number also seem to embrace moral relativism. Recently one of my nonphilosopher colleagues voted to turn down a doctoral dissertation proposal because the student assumed an objectivist position in ethics. (Ironically, I found in this same colleague's work rhetorical treatment of individual liberty that raised it to the level of a non-negotiable absolute.) But irony and inconsistency aside, many relativists are aware of the tension between their own subjective positions and their metatheory that entails relativism. I confess that I too am tempted by the allurements of this view and find some forms of it plausible and worthy of serious examination. However, I also find it deeply troubling.

In this essay I will examine the central notions of ethical relativism and look at the implications that seem to follow from it. Then I will present the outline of a very modest objectivism, one that takes into account many of the insights of relativism and yet stands as a viable option to it.

1. An Analysis of Relativism

Let us examine the theses contained in John Ladd's succinct statement on ethical (conventional) relativism that appears at the beginning of this essay. If we analyze it, we derive the following argument:

1. Moral rightness and wrongness of actions vary from society to society, so there are no universal moral standards held by all societies.
2. Whether or not it is right for individuals to act in a certain way depends on (or is relative to) the society to which they belong.
3. Therefore, there are no absolute or objective moral standards that apply to all people everywhere.

1. The first thesis, which may be called the *diversity thesis*, is simply a description that acknowledges the fact that moral rules differ from society to society. The Spartans of ancient Greece and the Dobu of New Guinea believe that stealing is morally right, but we believe it is wrong. The Roman father had the power of life and death (*just vitae necisque*) over his children, whereas we condemn parents for abusing their children. A tribe in East Africa once threw deformed infants to the hippopotamuses, and in ancient Greece and Rome infants were regularly exposed, while we abhor infanticide. Ruth Benedict describes a tribe in Melanesia that views cooperation and kindness as vices, whereas we see them as virtues. While in ancient Greece, Rome, China, and Korea parricide was condemned as "the most execrable of crimes," among Northern Indians aged persons, persons who were no longer capable of walking,

were left alone to starve. Among the California Gallinomero, when fathers became feeble, a burden to their sons, "the poor old wretch is not infrequently thrown down on his back and securely held while a stick is placed across his throat, and two of them seat themselves on the ends of it until he ceases to breathe."[4] Sexual practices vary over time and place. Some cultures permit homosexual behavior, while others condemn it. Some cultures practice polygamy, while others view it as immoral. Some cultures condone while others condemn premarital sex. Some cultures accept cannibalism, while the very idea revolts us. Some West African tribes perform clitoridectomies on girls, whereas we deplore such practices. Cultural relativism is well documented, and "custom is the king o'er all." There may or may not be moral principles that are held in common by every society, but if there are any, they seem to be few at best. Certainly it would be very difficult to derive any single "true" morality by observing various societies' moral standards.

2. The second thesis, the *dependency thesis*, asserts that individual acts are right or wrong depending on the nature of the society from which they emanate. Morality does not occur in a vacuum, and what is considered morally right or wrong must be seen in a context that depends on the goals, wants, beliefs, history, and environment of the society in question. As William G. Sumner says,

We learn the morals as unconsciously as we learn to walk and hear and breathe, and [we] never know any reason why the [morals] are what they are. The justification of them is that when we wake to consciousness of life we find them facts which already hold us in the bonds of tradition, custom, and habit.[5]

Trying to see things from an independent, noncultural point of view would be like taking out our eyes in order to examine their contours and qualities. There is no "innocent eye." We are simply culturally determined beings.

We could, of course, distinguish between a weak and a strong thesis of dependency, for the nonrelativist can accept a certain degree of relativity in the way moral principles are *applied* in various cultures, depending on beliefs, history, and environment. For example, Jewish men express reverence for God by covering their heads when entering places of worship, whereas Christian men uncover their heads when entering places of worship. Westerners shake hands upon greeting each other, whereas Hindus place their hands together and point them toward the person to be greeted. Both sides adhere to principles of reverence and respect but apply them differently. But the ethical relativist must maintain a stronger thesis, one that insists that the moral principles themselves are products of the cultures and may vary from society to society. The ethical relativist contends that even beyond environmental factors and differences in beliefs, a fundamental disagreement exists among societies. One way for the relativist to support this thesis is by appealing to an indeterminacy of translation thesis, which maintains that there is a conceptual relativity among language groups so that we cannot even translate into our language the worldviews of a culture with a radically different language.

In a sense we all live in radically different worlds. But the relativist wants to go further and maintain that there is something conventional about *any* morality, so that every morality really depends on a level of social acceptance. Not only do various societies adhere to different moral systems, but the very same society could (and often does) change its moral views over place and time. For example, the majority of people in the southern United States now view slavery as immoral, whereas one hundred and forty years ago they did not. Our society's views on divorce, sexuality, abortion, and assisted suicide have changed somewhat as well—and they are still changing.

3. The conclusion that there are no absolute or objective moral standards binding on all people follows from the first two propositions. Combining cultural relativism (*the diversity thesis*) with the *dependency thesis* yields ethical relativism in its classic form. If there are different moral principles from culture to culture and if all morality is rooted in culture, then it follows that there are no universal moral principles that are valid (or true) for all cultures and peoples at all times.

2. Subjectivism

Some people think that this conclusion is still too tame, and they maintain that morality is dependent not on the society but rather on the individual. As my students sometimes maintain, "Morality is in the eye of the beholder." They treat morality like taste or aesthetic judgments—person relative. This form of moral subjectivism has the sorry consequence that it makes morality a very useless concept, for, on its premises, little or no interpersonal criticism or judgment is logically possible. Suppose that you are repulsed by observing John torturing a child. You cannot condemn him if one of his principles is "torture little children for the fun of it." The only basis for judging him wrong might be that he was a hypocrite who condemned others for torturing. But suppose that another of his principles is that hypocrisy is morally permissible (for him); thus we cannot condemn him for condemning others for doing what he does.

On the basis of subjectivism Adolf Hitler and the serial murderer, Ted Bundy, could be considered as moral as Gandhi, so long as each lived by his own standards, whatever those might be. Witness the following paraphrase of a tape-recorded conversation between Ted Bundy and one of his victims in which Bundy justifies his murder:

Then I learned that all moral judgments are "value judgments," that all value judgments are subjective, and that none can be proved to be either 'right' or 'wrong.' I even read somewhere that the Chief Justice of the United States had written that the American Constitution expressed nothing more than collective value judgments. Believe it or not, I figured out for myself—what apparently the Chief Justice couldn't figure out for himself—that if the rationality of one value judgment was zero, multiplying it by millions would not make it one whit more rational. Nor is there any 'reason' to obey the law for anyone, like myself, who has the boldness and daring—the strength of character—to throw off its shackles. . . . I discovered that to become truly free, truly unfettered, I had to become truly uninhibited. And I quickly discovered that the greatest obstacle to my freedom, the greatest block and limitation to it, consists in the insupportable 'value judgment' that I was bound to respect the rights of others. I asked myself, who were these 'others'? Other human beings, with human rights? Why is it more wrong to kill a human animal than any other animal, a pig or a sheep or a steer? Is your life more to you than a hog's life to a hog? Why should I be willing to sacrifice my pleasure more for the one than for the other? Surely you would not, in this age of scientific enlightenment, declare that God or nature has marked some pleasures as 'moral' or 'good' and others as 'immoral' or 'bad'? In any case, let me assure you, my dear young lady, that there is absolutely no comparison between the pleasure I might take in eating ham and the pleasure I anticipate in raping and murdering you. That is the honest conclusion to which my education has led me—after the most conscientious examination of my spontaneous and uninhibited self.[6]

Notions of good and bad, or right and wrong, cease to have interpersonal evaluative meaning. We might be revulsed by the views of Ted Bundy, but that is just a matter of taste. A student might not like it when her teacher gives her an F on a test paper, while he gives another student an A for a similar paper, but there is no way to criticize him for injustice, because justice is not one of his chosen principles.

Absurd consequences follow from subjectivism. If it is correct, then morality reduces to aesthetic tastes about which there can be neither argument nor interpersonal judgment. Although many students say they espouse subjectivism, there is evidence that it conflicts with other of their moral views. They typically condemn Hitler as an evil man for his genocidal policies. A contradiction seems to exist between subjectivism and the very concept of morality, which it is supposed to characterize, for morality has to do with *proper* resolution of interpersonal conflict and the amelioration of the human predicament (both deontological and teleological systems do this, but in different ways—see Parts V and VI of this anthology). Whatever else it does, morality has a minimal aim of preventing a Hobbesian state of nature (see Part III), wherein life is "solitary, poor, nasty, brutish, and short." But if so, subjectivism is no help at all, for it rests neither on social agreement of principle (as the conventionalist maintains) nor on an objectively independent set of norms that bind all people for the common good. If there were only one person on earth, there would be no occasion for morality, because there wouldn't be any interpersonal conflicts to resolve or others whose suffering he or she would have a duty to ameliorate. Subjectivism implicitly assumes something of this solipsism, an atomism in which isolated individuals make up separate universes.

Subjectivism treats individuals like billiard balls on a societal pool table where they meet only in radical collisions, each aimed at his or her own goal and striving to do in the others before they themselves are done in. This atomistic view of personality is belied by the facts that we develop in families and mutually dependent communities in which we share a common language, common institutions, and similar rituals and habits, and that we often feel one another's joys and sorrows. As John Donne wrote, "No man is an island, entire of itself; every man is a piece of the continent."

Radical individualistic ethical relativism is incoherent. If so, it follows that the only plausible view of ethical relativism must be one that grounds morality in the group or culture. This form is called *conventionalism*.

3. Conventionalism

Conventional ethical relativism, the view that there are no objective moral principles but that all valid moral principles are justified (or are made true) by virtue of their cultural acceptance, recognizes the social nature of morality. That is precisely its power and virtue. It does not seem subject to the same absurd consequences which plague subjectivism. Recognizing the importance of our social environment in generating customs and beliefs, many people suppose that ethical relativism is the correct metaethical theory. Furthermore, they are drawn to it for its liberal philosophical stance. It seems to be an enlightened response to the sin of ethnocentricity, and it seems to entail or strongly imply an attitude of tolerance toward other cultures. Anthropologist Ruth Benedict says, that in recognizing ethical relativity, "We shall arrive at a more realistic social faith, accepting as grounds of hope and as new bases for tolerance the coexisting and equally valid patterns of life which mankind has created for itself from the raw materials of existence."[7] The most famous of those holding this position is the anthropologist Melville Herskovits, who argues even more explicitly than Benedict that ethical relativism entails intercultural tolerance.

(1) If morality is relative to its culture, then there is no independent basis for criticizing the morality of any other culture but one's own.
(2) If there is no independent way of criticizing any other culture, we ought to be *tolerant* of the moralities of other cultures.
(3) Morality is relative to its culture. Therefore,
(4) We ought to be *tolerant* of the moralities of other cultures.[8]

Tolerance is certainly a virtue, but is this a good argument for it? I think not. If morality simply is relative to each culture, then if the culture in question does not have a principle of tolerance, its members have no obligation to be tolerant. Herskovits seems to be treating the *principle of tolerance* as the one exception to his relativism. He seems to be treating it as an absolute moral principle. But from a relativistic point of view there is no more reason to be tolerant than to be intolerant and neither stance is objectively morally better than the other.

Not only do relativists fail to offer a basis for criticizing those who are intolerant, but they cannot rationally criticize anyone who espouses what they might regard as a heinous principle. If, as seems to be the case, valid criticism supposes an objective or impartial standard, relativists cannot morally criticize anyone outside their own culture. Adolf Hitler's genocidal actions, so long as they are culturally accepted, are as morally legitimate as Mother Teresa's works of mercy. If conventional relativism is accepted, racism, genocide of unpopular minorities, oppression of the poor, slavery, and even the advocacy of war for its own sake are as equally moral as their opposites. And if a subculture decided that starting a nuclear war was somehow morally acceptable, we could not morally criticize these people. Any actual morality, whatever its content, is as valid as every other, and more valid than ideal moralities—since the latter aren't adhered to by any culture.

There are other disturbing consequences of ethical relativism. It seems to entail that reformers are always (morally) wrong since they go against the tide of cultural standards. William Wilberforce was wrong in the eighteenth century to oppose slavery; the British were immoral in opposing *suttee* in India (the burning of widows, which is now illegal in India). The early Christians were wrong in refusing to serve in the Roman army or to bow down to Caesar, since the majority in the Roman Empire believed that these two acts were moral duties. In fact, Jesus himself was immoral in breaking the law of His day by healing on the Sabbath day and by advocating the principles of the Sermon on the Mount, since it is clear that few in His time (or in ours) accepted them.

Yet we normally feel just the opposite, that the reformer is a courageous innovator who is right, who has the truth, against the mindless majority. Sometimes the individual must stand alone with the truth, risking social censure and persecution.

As Dr. Stockman says in Ibsen's *Enemy of the People*, after he loses the battle to declare his town's profitable but polluted tourist spa unsanitary, "The most dangerous enemy of the truth and freedom among us—is the compact majority. Yes, the damned, compact and liberal majority. The majority has *might*—unfortunately—but *right* it is not. Right—are I and a few others." Yet if relativism is correct, the opposite is necessarily the case. Truth is with the crowd and error with the individual.

Similarly, conventional ethical relativism entails disturbing judgments about the law. Our normal view is that we have a prima facie duty to obey the law, because law, in general, promotes the human good. According to most objective systems, this obligation is not absolute but relative to the particular law's relation to a wider moral order. Civil disobedience is warranted in some cases where the law seems to be in serious conflict with morality. However, if moral relativism is true, then neither law nor civil disobedience has a firm foundation. On the one hand, from the side of the society at large, civil disobedience will be morally wrong, so long as the majority culture agrees with the law in question. On the other hand, if you belong to the relevant subculture which doesn't recognize the particular law in question (because it is unjust from your point of view), disobedience will be morally mandated. The Ku Klux Klan, which believes that Jews, Catholics, and Blacks are evil or undeserving of high regard, are, given conventionalism, morally permitted or required to break the laws which protect these endangered groups. Why should I obey a law that my group doesn't recognize as valid?

To sum up, unless we have an independent moral basis for law, it is hard to see why we have any general duty to obey it; and unless we recognize the priority of a universal moral law, we have no firm basis to justify our acts of civil disobedience against "unjust laws." Both the validity of law and morally motivated disobedience of unjust laws are annulled in favor of a power struggle.

There is an even more basic problem with the notion that morality is dependent on cultural acceptance for its validity. The problem is that the notion of a *culture* or *society* is notoriously difficult to define. This is especially so in a pluralistic society like our own where the notion seems to be vague with unclear boundary lines. One person may belong to several societies (subcultures) with different value emphases and arrangements of principles. A person may belong to the nation as a single society with certain values of patriotism, honor, courage, laws (including some which are controversial but have majority acceptance, such as the current law on abortion). But he or she may also belong to a church which opposes some of the laws of the state. He may also be an integral member of a socially mixed community where different principles hold sway, and he may belong to clubs and a family where still other rules are adhered to. Relativism would seem to tell us that where he is a member of societies with conflicting moralities, he must be judged both wrong and not-wrong whatever he does. For example, if Mary is a U.S. citizen and a member of the Roman Catholic Church, she is wrong (qua Catholic) if she chooses to have an abortion and not-wrong (qua citizen of the U.S.A.) if she acts against the teaching of the Church on abortion. As a member of a racist university fraternity, KKK, John has no obligation to treat his fellow Black student as an equal, but as a member of the university community itself (where the principle of equal rights is accepted) he does have the obligation; but as a member of the surrounding community (which may reject the principle of equal rights) he again has no such obligation; but then again as a member of the nation at large (which accepts the principle) he is obligated to treat his fellow with respect. What is the morally right thing for John to do? The question no longer makes much sense in this moral Babel. It has lost its action-guiding function.

Perhaps the relativist would adhere to a principle which says that in such cases the individual may choose which group to belong to as primary.

If Mary chooses to have an abortion, she is choosing to belong to the general society relative to that principle. And John must likewise choose among groups. The trouble with this option is that it seems to lead back to counter-intuitive results. If Murder Mike of Murder, Incorporated, feels like killing Bank President Ortcutt and wants to feel good about it, he identifies with the Murder, Incorporated society rather than the general public morality. Does this justify the killing? In fact, couldn't one justify anything simply by forming a small subculture that approved of it? Ted Bundy would be morally pure in raping and killing innocents simply by virtue of forming a little coterie. How large must the group be in order to be a legitimate subculture or society? Does it need ten or fifteen people? How about just three? Come to think about it, why can't my burglary partner and I found our own society with a morality of its own? Of course, if my partner dies, I could still claim that I was acting from an originally social set of norms. But why can't I dispense with the interpersonal agreements altogether and invent my own morality—since morality, on this view, is only an invention anyway? Conventionalist relativism seems to reduce to subjectivism. And subjectivism leads, as we have seen, to moral solipsism, to the demise of morality altogether.

Should one object that this is an instance of the *Slippery Slope Fallacy*,[9] let that person give an alternative analysis of what constitutes a viable social basis for generating valid (or true) moral principles. Perhaps we might agree (for the sake of argument, at least) that the very nature of morality entails two people making an agreement. This move saves the conventionalist from moral solipsism, but it still permits almost any principle at all to count as moral. And what's more, those principles can be thrown out and their contraries substituted for them as the need arises. If two or three people decide that they will make cheating on exams morally acceptable for themselves, via forming a fraternity "Cheaters Anonymous" at their university, then cheating becomes moral. Why not? Why not rape, as well?

However, I don't think you can stop the move from conventionalism to subjectivism. The essential force of the validity of the chosen moral principle is that it is dependent on *choice.* The conventionalist holds that it is the choice of the group, but why should I accept the group's silly choice, when my own is better (for me)? Why should anyone give such august authority to a culture of society? If this is all morality comes to, why not reject it altogether—even though one might want to adhere to its directives when others are looking in order to escape sanctions?

4. A Critique of Ethical Relativism

However, while we may fear the demise of morality, as we have known it, this in itself may not be a good reason for rejecting relativism. That is, for judging it false. Alas, truth may not always be edifying. But the consequences of this position are sufficiently alarming to prompt us to look carefully for some weakness in the relativist's argument. So let us examine the premises and conclusion listed at the beginning of this essay as the three theses of relativism.

1. *The Diversity Thesis.* What is considered morally right and wrong varies from society to society, so that there are no moral principles accepted by all societies.
2. *The Dependency Thesis.* All moral principles derive their validity from cultural acceptance.
3. *Ethical Relativism.* Therefore, there are no universally valid moral principles, objective standards which apply to all people everywhere and at all times.

Does any one of these seem problematic? Let us consider the first thesis, the diversity thesis, which we have also called cultural relativism. Perhaps there is not as much diversity as anthropologists like Sumner and Benedict suppose. One can also see great similarities between the moral codes of various cultures. E. O. Wilson has identified over a score of common features,[10] and before him

Clyde Kluckhohn has noted some significant common ground.

Every culture has a concept of murder, distinguishing this from execution, killing in war, and other "justifiable homicides." The notions of incest and other regulations upon sexual behavior, the prohibitions upon untruth under defined circumstances, of restitution and reciprocity, of mutual obligations between parents and children—these and many other moral concepts are altogether universal.[11]

Colin Turnbull's description of the sadistic, semidisplaced, disintegrating Ik tribe in Northern Uganda supports the view that a people without principles of kindness, loyalty, and cooperation will degenerate into a Hobbesian state of nature. But he has also produced evidence that underneath the surface of this dying society, there is a deeper moral code, from a time when the tribe flourished, which occasionally surfaces and shows its nobler face.

On the other hand, there is enormous cultural diversity, and many societies have radically different moral codes. Cultural relativism seems to be a fact, but even if it is, it does not by itself establish the truth of ethical relativism. Cultural diversity in itself is neutral between theories. For the objectivist could concede complete cultural relativism, but still defend a form of universalism; for he or she could argue that some cultures simply lack correct moral principles.[12]

On the other hand, a denial of complete cultural relativism (i.e., an admission of some universal principles) does not disprove ethical relativism. For even if we did find one or more universal principles, this would not prove that those principles had any objective status. We could still *imagine* a culture that was an exception to the rule and be unable to criticize it. So the first premise doesn't by itself imply ethical relativism, nor does its denial disprove ethical relativism.

We turn to the crucial second thesis, the dependency thesis. Morality does not occur in a vacuum; rather, what is considered morally right or wrong must be seen in a context, depending on the goals, wants, beliefs, history, and environment of the society in question. We distinguished a *weak* and a *strong* thesis of dependency. The weak thesis says that the application of principles depends on the particular cultural predicament, whereas the strong thesis affirms that the principles themselves depend on that predicament. The nonrelativist can accept a certain relativity in the way moral principles are *applied* in various cultures, depending on beliefs, history, and environment. For example, a raw environment with scarce natural resources may justify the Eskimos' brand of euthanasia to the objectivist, who in another environment would consistently reject that practice. The members of a tribe in the Sudan throw their deformed children into the river because of their belief that such infants *belong* to the hippopotamus, the god of the river. We believe that they have a false belief about this, but the point is that the same principles of respect for property and respect for human life are operative in these contrary practices. They differ with us only in belief, not in substantive moral principle. This is an illustration of how nonmoral beliefs (e.g., deformed children belong to the hippopotamus) when applied to common moral principles (e.g., give to each his due) generate different actions in different cultures. In our own culture the difference in the nonmoral belief about the status of a fetus generates opposite moral prescriptions. The major difference between pro-choicers and pro-lifers is not whether we should kill persons but whether fetuses are really persons. It is a debate about the facts of the matter, not the principle of killing innocent persons.

So the fact that moral principles are weakly dependent doesn't show that ethical relativism is valid. In spite of this weak dependency on nonmoral factors, there could still be a set of general moral norms applicable to all cultures and even recognized in most, which are disregarded at a culture's own expense.

What the relativist needs is a strong thesis of

dependency, that somehow all principles are essentially cultural inventions. But why should we choose to view morality this way? Is there anything to recommend the strong thesis over the weak thesis of dependency? The relativist may argue that in fact we don't have an obvious impartial standard from which to judge. "Who's to say which culture is right and which is wrong?" But this seems to be dubious. We can reason and perform thought experiments in order to make a case for one system over another. We may not be able to know with certainty that our moral beliefs are closer to the truth than those of another culture or those of others within our own culture, but we may be justified in believing that they are. If we can be closer to the truth regarding factual or scientific matters, why can't we be closer to the truth on moral matters? Why can't a culture be simply confused or wrong about its moral perceptions? Why can't we say that the society like the Ik which sees nothing wrong with enjoying watching its own children fall into fires is less moral in that regard than the culture that cherishes children and grants them protection and equal rights? To take such a stand is not to commit the fallacy of ethnocentricism, for we are seeking to derive principles through critical reason, not simply uncritical acceptance of one's own mores.

Many relativists embrace relativism as a default position. Objectivism makes no sense to them. I think this is Ladd and Harman's position, as the latter's quotation at the beginning of this article seems to indicate. Objectivism has insuperable problems, so the answer must be relativism. The only positive argument I know for the strong dependency thesis upon which ethical relativism rests is that of the indeterminacy of translation thesis. This theory, set forth by B. L. Whorf and W. V. Quine,[13] holds that languages are often so fundamentally different from one another that we cannot accurately translate concepts from one to another. But this thesis, while relatively true even within a language (each of us has an idiolect), seems falsified by experience. We do learn foreign languages and learn to translate across linguistic

frameworks. For example, people from a myriad of language groups come to the United States and learn English and communicate perfectly well. Rather than a complete hiatus, the interplay between these other cultures eventually enriches the English language with new concepts (for example, *forte/foible*, *taboo*, and *coup de grâce*), even as English has enriched (or "corrupted" as the French might argue) other languages. Even if it turns out that there is some indeterminacy of translation between language users, we should not infer from this that no translation or communication is possible. It seems reasonable to believe that general moral principles are precisely those things that can be communicated transculturally. The kind of common features that Kluckhohn and Wilson advance—duties of restitution and reciprocity, regulations on sexual behavior, obligations of parents to children, a no-unnecessary-harm principle, and a sense that the good should flourish and the guilty be punished—these and others constitute a common human experience, a common set of values within a common human predicament of struggling to survive and flourish in a world of scarce resources.[14] So it is possible to communicate cross-culturally and find that we agree on many of the important things in life. If this is so, then the indeterminacy of translation thesis, upon which relativism rests, must itself be relativized to the point where it is no objection to objective morality.

5. The Case for Moral Objectivism

If nonrelativists are to make their case, they will have to offer a better explanation of cultural diversity and why we should nevertheless adhere to moral objectivism. One way of doing this is to appeal to a divine law, and human sin, which causes deviation from that law. Although I think that human greed, selfishness, pride, self-deception, and other maladies have a great deal to do with moral differences and that religion may lend great support to morality, I don't think that a religious justification is necessary for the validity of moral principles. In any case, in this section I shall outline a modest nonreligious objectivism, first by appealing to our intuitions and secondly by giving a naturalist account of morality that transcends individual cultures.

First, I must make it clear that I am distinguishing moral *absolutism* from moral *objectivism*. The absolutist believes that there are nonoverrideable moral principles which ought never to be violated. Kant's system, or one version of it, is a good example. One ought never to break a promise, no matter what. Act utilitarianism also seems absolutist, for the principle, Do that act that has the most promise of yielding the most utility, is nonoverrideable. An objectivist need not posit any nonoverrideable principles, at least not in unqualified general form, and so need not be an absolutist. As Renford Bambrough put it,

To suggest that there is a *right* answer to a moral problem is at once to be accused of or credited with a belief in moral absolutes. But it is no more necessary to believe in moral absolutes in order to believe in moral objectivity than it is to believe in the existence of absolute space or absolute time in order to believe in the objectivity of temporal and spatial relations and of judgments about them.[15]

On the objectivist's account moral principles are what William Ross refers to as *prima facie* principles, valid rules of action which should generally be adhered to, but which may be overridden by another moral principle in cases of moral conflict. For example, while a principle of justice may generally outweigh a principle of benevolence, there are times when enormous good could be done by sacrificing a small amount of justice, so that an objectivist would be inclined to act according to the principle of benevolence. There may be some absolute or nonoverrideable principles, but there need not be many or any for objectivism to be true.[16]

If we can establish or show that it is reasonable to believe that there is at least one objective moral principle which is binding on all people every-

where in some ideal sense, we shall have shown that relativism is probably false and that a limited objectivism is true. Actually, I believe that there are many qualified general ethical principles which are binding on all rational beings, but one will suffice to refute relativism. The principle I've chosen is the following:

A. It is morally wrong to torture people for the fun of it.

I claim that this principle is binding on all rational agents, so that if some agent, S, rejects A, we should not let that affect our intuition that A is a true principle but rather try to explain S's behavior as perverse, ignorant, or irrational instead. For example, suppose Adolf Hitler doesn't accept A. Should that affect our confidence in the truth of A? Is it not more reasonable to infer that Adolf is morally deficient, morally blind, ignorant, or irrational than to suppose that his noncompliance is evidence against the truth of A?

Suppose further that there is a tribe of Hitlerites somewhere who enjoy torturing people. The whole culture accepts torturing others for the fun of it. Suppose that Mother Teresa or Gandhi tries unsuccessfully to convince them that they should stop torturing people altogether, and they respond by torturing the reformers. Should this affect our confidence in A? Would it not be more reasonable to look for some explanation of Hitlerite behavior? For example, we might hypothesize that this tribe lacked a developed sense of sympathetic imagination which is necessary for the moral life. Or we might theorize that this tribe was on a lower evolutionary level than most *Homo sapiens*. Or we might simply conclude that the tribe was closer to a Hobbesian state of nature than most societies, and as such probably would not survive. But we need not know the correct answer as to why the tribe was in such bad shape in order to maintain our confidence in A as a moral principle. If A is a basic or core belief for us, we will be more likely to doubt the Hitlerites' sanity or ability to think morally than to doubt the validity of A.

We can perhaps produce other candidates for membership in our minimally basic objective moral set. For example:

1. Do not kill innocent people.
2. Do not cause unnecessary pain or suffering.
3. Do not cheat or steal.
4. Keep your promises and honor your contracts.
5. Do not deprive another person of his or her freedom.
6. Do justice, treating equals equally and unequals unequally.
7. Tell the truth.
8. Help other people, at least when the cost to oneself is minimal.
9. Reciprocate (show gratitude for services rendered).
10. Obey just laws.

These ten principles are examples of the *core morality*, principles necessary for the good life. They are not arbitrary, for we can give reasons why they are necessary to social cohesion and human flourishing. Principles like the Golden Rule, not killing innocent people, treating equals equally, truth telling, promise keeping, and the like are central to the fluid progression of social interaction and the resolution of conflicts of which ethics are about (at least minimal morality is, even though there may be more to morality than simply these kinds of concerns). For example, language itself depends on a general and implicit commitment to the principle of truth telling. Accuracy of expression is a primitive form of truthfulness. Hence, every time we use words correctly we are telling the truth. Without this behavior, language wouldn't be possible. Likewise, without the recognition of a rule of promise keeping, contracts are of no avail and cooperation is less likely to occur. And without the protection of life and liberty, we could not secure our other goals.

A moral code or theory would be adequate if it contained a requisite set of these objective principles or the core morality, but there could be more than one adequate moral code or theory which contained different rankings of these principles and other principles consistent with *core morality*. That is, there may be a certain relativity to secondary principles (whether to opt for monogamy rather than polygamy, whether to include a principle of high altruism in the set of moral duties, whether to allocate more resources to medical care than to environmental concerns, whether to institute a law to drive on the left side of road or the right side of the road, and so forth), but in every morality a certain core will remain, though applied somewhat differently because of differences in environment, belief, tradition, and the like.

The core moral rules are analogous to the set of vitamins necessary for a healthy diet. We need an adequate amount of each vitamin—some humans more of one than another—but in prescribing a nutritional diet we don't have to set forth recipes, specific foods, place settings, or culinary habits. Gourmets will meet the requirements differently than ascetics and vegetarians, but the basic nutrients may be had by all without rigid regimentation or an absolute set of recipes.

Stated more positively, an objectivist who bases his or her moral system on a common human nature with common needs and desires might argue for objectivism somewhat in this manner:

1. Human nature is relatively similar in essential respects, having a common set of needs and interests.
2. Moral principles are functions of human needs and interests, instituted by reason in order to promote the most significant interests and needs of rational beings (and perhaps others).
3. Some moral principles will promote human interests and meet human needs better than others.
4. Those principles which will meet essential needs and promote the most significant interests of humans in optimal ways can be said to be objectively valid moral principles.
5. Therefore, since there is a common human nature, there is an objectively valid set of moral principles, applicable to all humanity.

This argument assumes that there is a common

human nature. In a sense, I accept a *strong dependency thesis*—morality *depends* on human nature and the needs and interests of humans in general, but not on any specific cultural choice. There is only one large human framework to which moral principles are relative.[17] I have considered the evidence for this claim toward the end of Section 4, but the relativist may object. I cannot defend it any further in this paper, but suppose we content ourselves with a less controversial first premise, stating that some principles will tend to promote the most significant interests of persons. The revised argument would go like this:

1. Objectively valid moral principles are those adherence to which meet the needs and promote the most significant interests of persons.
2. Some principles are such that adherence to them meets the needs and promotes the most significant interests of persons.
3. Therefore, there are some objectively valid moral principles.

Either argument would satisfy objectivism, but the former makes it clearer that it is our common human nature that generates the common principles.[18] However, as I mentioned, some philosophers might not like to be tied down to the concept of a common human nature, in which case the second version of the argument may be used. It has the advantage that even if it turned out that we did have somewhat different natures or that other creatures in the universe had somewhat different natures, some of the basic moral principles would still survive.

If this argument succeeds, there are ideal moralities (and not simply adequate ones). Of course, there could still be more than one ideal morality, from which presumably an ideal observer would choose under optimal conditions. The ideal observer may conclude that out of an infinite set of moralities two, three, or more combinations would tie for first place. One would expect that these would be similar, but there is every reason to believe that all of these would contain the set of core principles.

Of course, we don't know what an ideal observer would choose, but we can imagine that the conditions under which such an observer would choose would be conditions of maximal knowledge about the consequences of action-types and impartiality, second-order qualities which ensure that agents have the best chance of making the best decisions. If this is so, then the more we learn to judge impartially and the more we know about possible forms of life, the better chance we have to approximate an ideal moral system. And if there is the possibility of approximating ideal moral systems with an objective core and other objective components, then ethical relativism is certainly false. We can confidently dismiss it as an aberration and get on with the job of working out better moral systems.

Let me make the same point by appealing to your intuitions in another way. Imagine that you have been miraculously transported to the dark kingdom of hell, and there you get a glimpse of the sufferings of the damned. What is their punishment? Well, they have eternal back itches which ebb and flow constantly. But they cannot scratch their backs, for their arms are paralyzed in a frontal position, so they writhe with itchiness throughout eternity. But just as you are beginning to feel the itch in your own back, you are suddenly transported to heaven. What do you see in the kingdom of the blessed? Well, you see people with eternal back itches, who cannot scratch their own backs. But they are all smiling instead of writhing. Why? Because everyone has his or her arms stretched out to scratch someone else's back, and, so arranged in one big circle, a hell is turned into a heaven of ecstasy.

If we can imagine some states of affairs or cultures that are better than others in a way that depends on human action, we can ask what are those character traits that make them so. In our story people in heaven, but not in hell, cooperate for the amelioration of suffering and the production of pleasure. These are very primitive goods, not sufficient for a full-blown morality, but they give us a hint as to the objectivity of morality. Moral goodness has something to do with the ameliorating of suffering, the resolution of conflict, and the promotion of human flourishing. If our heaven is really better than the eternal itchiness of hell, then whatever makes it so is constitutively related to moral rightness.

6. An Explanation of the Attraction of Ethical Relativism

Why, then, is there such a strong inclination toward ethical relativism? I think that there are four reasons, which haven't been adequately emphasized. One is the fact that the options are usually presented as though absolutism and relativism were the only alternatives, so conventionalism wins out against an implausible competitor. At the beginning of this paper I referred to a student questionnaire that I have been giving for twenty years. It reads as follows: "Are there any ethical absolutes, moral duties binding on all persons at all times, or are moral duties relative to culture? Is there any alternative to these two positions?" Fewer than five percent suggest a third position and very few of them identify objectivism. Granted, it takes a little philosophical sophistication to make the crucial distinctions, and it is precisely for lack of this sophistication or reflection that relativism has procured its enormous prestige. But, as Ross and others have shown and as I have argued in this chapter, one can have an objective morality without being absolutist.

The second reason for an inclination toward ethical relativism is the confusion of moral objectivism with moral realism. A realist is a person who holds that moral values have independent existence, if only as emergent properties. The anti-realist claims that they do not have independent existence. But objectivism is compatible with either of these views. All it calls for is deep intersubjective agreement among humans because of a common nature and common goals and needs.

An example of a philosopher who confuses objectivity with realism is the late J. L. Mackie, who rejects objectivism because there are no good arguments for the independent existence of moral

values. He admits, however, that there is a great deal of intersubjectivity in ethics. "There could be agreement in valuing even if valuing is just something people do, even if this activity is not further validated. Subjective agreement would give intersubjective values, but intersubjectivity is not objectivity."[19] But Mackie fails to note that there are two kinds of intersubjectivity, and that one of them gives all that the objectivist wants for a moral theory. Consider the following situations of intersubjective agreement:

Set A

A1. All the children in first grade at School S would agree that playing in the mud is preferable to learning arithmetic.
A2. All the youth in the district would rather take drugs than go to school.
A3. All the people in Jonestown, British Guiana, agree that the Rev. Jones is a prophet from God, and they love him dearly.
A4. Almost all the people in community C voted for George Bush.

Set B

B1. All the thirsty desire water to quench their thirst.
B2. All humans (and animals) prefer pleasure to pain.
B3. Almost all people agree that living in society is more satisfying than living as hermits alone.

The naturalist contrasts these two sets of intersubjective agreements and says that the first set is accidental, not part of what it means to be a person, whereas the agreements in the second set are basic to being a person, basic to our nature. Agreement on the essence of morality, the core set, is the kind of intersubjective agreement more like the second kind, not the first. It is part of the essence of a human in community, part of what it means to flourish as a person, to agree and adhere to the moral code.

The third reason is that our recent sensitivity to cultural relativism and the evils of ethnocentricism, which have plagued the relations of Europeans and Americans with those of other cultures, has made us conscious of the frailty of many aspects of our moral repertoire, so that there is a tendency to wonder "Who's to judge what's really right or wrong?" However, the move from a reasonable cultural relativism, which rightly causes us to rethink our moral systems, to an ethical relativism, which causes us to give up the heart of morality altogether, is an instance of the fallacy of confusing factual or descriptive statements with normative ones. Cultural relativism doesn't entail ethical relativism. The very reason that we are against ethnocentricism constitutes the same basis for our being for an objective moral system: that impartial reason draws us to it.

We may well agree that cultures differ and that we ought to be cautious in condemning what we don't understand, but this in no way need imply that there are not better and worse ways of living. We can understand and excuse, to some degree at least, those who differ from our best notions of morality, without abdicating the notion that cultures without principles of justice or promise keeping or protection of the innocent are morally poorer for these omissions.

A fourth reason which has driven some to moral nihilism and others to relativism is the decline of religion in Western society. As one of Dostoevsky's characters has said, "If God is dead, all things are permitted." The person who has lost religious faith feels a deep vacuum and understandably confuses it with a moral vacuum, or he or she finally resigns to a form of secular conventionalism. Such people reason that if there is no God to guarantee the validity of the moral order, there must not be a universal moral order. There is just radical cultural diversity and death at the end. But even if there turns out to be no God and no immortality, we still will want to live happy, meaningful lives during our fourscore years on earth. If this is true, then it matters by which principles we live, and those which win

out in the test of time will be objectively valid principles.

In conclusion I have argued (1) that cultural relativism (the fact that there are cultural differences regarding moral principles) does not entail ethical relativism (the thesis that there are no objectively valid universal moral principles); (2) that the dependency thesis (that morality derives its legitimacy from individual cultural acceptance) is mistaken; and (3) that there are universal moral principles based on a common human nature and a need to solve conflicts of interest and flourish.

So "Who's to judge what's right or wrong?" We are. We are to do so on the basis of the best reasoning we can bring forth, and with sympathy and understanding.[20]

Notes

1. Gilbert Harman, "Is There a Single True Morality?" in *Morality, Reason and Truth*, eds. David Copp and David Zimmerman (Rowman & Allenheld, 1984).

2. John Ladd, *Ethical Relativism* (Wadsworth, 1973).

3. Lest I be misunderstood, in this essay I will generally be speaking about the validity rather than the truth of moral principles. Validity holds that they are proper guides to action, whereas truth presupposes something more. It presupposes Moral Realism, the theory that moral principles have special ontological status (see Part IX). Although this may be true, not all objectivists agree. R. M. Hare, for instance, argues that moral principles, while valid, do not have truth value. They are like imperatives which have practical application but cannot be said to be true. Also, I am mainly concerned with the status of *principles*, not theories themselves. There may be a plurality of valid moral theories, all containing the same objective principles. I am grateful to Edward Sherline for drawing this distinction to my attention.

4. Reported by the anthropologist Powers, *Tribes of California*, p. 178. Quoted in E. Westermarck, *Origin and Development of Moral Ideals* (London, 1906), p. 386. This work is a mine of examples of cultural diversity.

5. W. G. Sumner, *Folkways* (Ginn & Co., 1906), p. 76.

6. This is a paraphrased and rewritten statement of

Ted Bundy by Harry V. Jaffa, *Homosexuality and the Natural Law* (Claremont, CA: The Claremont Institute of the Study of Statesmanship and Political Philosophy, 1990), 3–4.

7. Ruth Benedict, *Patterns of Culture* (New American Library, 1934), p. 257.

8. Melville Herskovits, *Cultural Relativism* (Random House, 1972).

9. The fallacy of objecting to a proposition on the erroneous grounds that, if accepted, it will lead to a chain of states of affairs which are absurd or unacceptable.

10. E. O. Wilson, *On Human Nature* (Bantam Books, 1979), pp. 22–23.

11. Clyde Kluckhohn, "Ethical Relativity: Sic et Non," *Journal of Philosophy*, LII (1955).

12. Colin Turnbull, *The Mountain People* (New York: Simon & Schuster, 1972).

13. See Benjamin Whorf, *Language, Thought and Reality* (MIT Press, 1956); and W. V. Quine, *Word and Object* (MIT Press, 1960), and *Ontological Relativity* (Columbia University Press, 1969).

14. David Hume gave the classic expression to this idea of a common human nature when he wrote:

It is universally acknowledged that there is a great uniformity among the actions of men, in all nations and ages, and that human nature remains still the same, in its principles and operations. The same events follow from the same causes. Ambition, avarice, self-love, vanity, friendship, generosity, public spirit; these passions, mixed in various degrees, and distributed through society, have been, from the beginning of the world, and still are, the source of all the actions and enterprises which have ever been observed among mankind. Would you know the sentiments, inclinations, and course of life of the Greeks and Romans? Study well the temper and actions of the French and English: you cannot be much mistaken in transferring to the former most of the observations which you have made with regard to the latter. Mankind are so much the same, in all times and places, that history informs us of nothing new or strange in that particular. Its chief use is only to discover the constant and universal principles of human nature, by showing men in all varieties of circumstances and situations, and furnishing us with materials, from which we may form our observations, and become acquainted with the regular springs of human action and behavior. These records of wars, intrigues, factions, and revolutions, are so many collections of experiments by which the politician or moral philosopher fixes the principles of his science; in the same manner as the physician or natural philosopher becomes acquainted with the nature of plants, minerals, and other external objects, by the experiments which he forms concerning them. Nor are the earth, water, and other elements examined by Aristotle and Hippocrates more like to those which at present lie under our observation than the men described by Polybius and Tacitus are to those who now govern the world. *Essays, Moral, Political and Literary* (Longman, Green, 1875).

15. Renford Bambrough, *Moral Skepticism and Moral Knowledge* (London: Routledge & Kegan Paul, 1979), p. 33.

16. William Ross, *The Right and the Good* (Oxford University Press, 1931), p. 18f.

17. In his essay "Moral Relativism" in *Moral Relativism and Moral Objectivity* (Blackwell, 1996) by Gilbert Harman and Judith Jarvis Thomson, Harman defines moral relativism as the claim that "There is no single true morality. There are many different moral frameworks, none of which is more correct than the others." (p. 5) I hold that morality has a function of serving the needs and interests of human beings, so that some frameworks do this better than others. Essentially, all adequate theories will contain the principles I have identified in this essay.

18. I owe the reformulation of the argument to Bruce Russell. Edward Sherline has objected (in correspondence) that assuming a common human nature in the first argument begs the question against the relativist. You may be the judge.

19. J. L. Mackie, *Ethics: Inventing Right and Wrong* (Penguin, 1977), p. 22.

20. Bruce Russell, Morton Winston, Edward Sherline, and an anonymous reviewer made important criticisms on earlier versions of this article, issuing in this revision.

PART III

Ethics and Egoism

Introduction

Why should we be moral? That is, why should we be moral when it is in our self-interest to be immoral? Or is it always really in our interest to be moral, despite appearances to the contrary? Or is morality only generally in our best interest, so that we may have to decide whether to follow its commands when they become too burdensome?

Egoism is a challenge to morality. It comes in two main forms. The first form, call it "egoism proper," admits that morality consists of a set of objective, altruistic or other-regarding principles but simply denies that we ought always to be moral. If we have good reason to be selfish, we should be so. The egoist admits that sometimes it is in our interest to be moral but asks, "Why should I be moral when it is not in my interest to be so?" This is the kind of egoism with which

Thrasymachus seems to end up (reading I.1) and which Glaucon puts forth as the devil's advocate in our first selection.

The second form, call it "ethical egoism," *universalizes* the egoist principle, thus making it a moral principle: "Everyone ought always to act in his or her self-interest." In this way the question, "Why be moral?" does not arise. True morality is simply enlightened self-interest. Thomas Hobbes sets forth a contractual theory of ethical egoism in our second reading, and Ayn Rand espouses a more individualist version in our third reading. James Rachels sets out a comprehensive critique of ethical egoism in our fourth reading, and, finally, Howard Kahane develops a theory of egoism within the context of sociobiological thought, arguing for a morality based on reciprocity.

6

Why Should I Be Moral?

PLATO

Glaucon, Plato's older brother, uneasy with Socrates' reply to Thrasymachus (see reading I.1), asks Socrates whether justice is good in itself or only a necessary evil. Glaucon sets forth the hypothesis that egoistic power seeking and pleasure seeking con-

Reprinted from *Plato's Republic*, trans. G.M.A. Grube (Indianapolis: Hackett Publishing Company, 1974) by permission of the publisher.

stitute the ideally good life. However, the hypothesis continues, reason alerts us that others might seek the same power, which would greatly interfere with our freedom and result in a state of chaos in which no one was happy. Therefore, we must compromise our quest for power and unmitigated pleasure. Morality constitutes this compromise. As a mutually agreed-upon set of restrictions aimed at preventing others from prospering at our expense, morality has no intrinsic but only instrumental value.

To illustrate his hypothesis Glaucon relates a myth of Gyges, a sheperd who discovers a ring that enables him to become invisible. Gyges uses the ring to attain the highest reaches of power and pleasure. Glaucon asks whether it is not plausible to suppose that we all would do likewise? Then he offers a thought experiment that compares the life of the seemingly just (but unjust) man who is the epitome of success with that of the seemingly unjust (but just) man who is the epitome of failure. Which would we choose?

In the second part of this reading, we have highlights of Socrates' solution to this question, Why should I be moral?

We enter the dialogue where we left off in selection I.1. Socrates has just shown that the type of egoism advocated by Thrasymachus is contradictory. Socrates is speaking.

When I had said this I thought I had done with the discussion, but evidently this was only a prelude. Glaucon on this occasion too showed that boldness which is characteristic of him, and refused to accept Thrasymachus's abandoning the argument. He said: Do you, Socrates want to appear to have persuaded us, or do you want truly to convince us that it is better in every way to be just than unjust?

I would certainly wish to convince you truly, I said, if I could.

Well, he said, you are certainly not attaining your wish. Tell me, do you think there is a kind of good which we welcome not because we desire its consequences but for its own sake: joy, for example, and all the harmless pleasures which have no further consequences beyond the joy which one finds in them?

Certainly, said I, I think there is such a good.

Further, there is the good which we welcome for its own sake and also for its consequences, knowledge for example and sight and health. Such things we somehow welcome on both counts.

Yes, said I.

Are you also aware of a third kind, he asked, such as physical training, being treated when ill,

the practice of medicine, and other ways of making money? We should say that these are wearisome but beneficial to us; we should not want them for their own sake, but because of the rewards and other benefits which result from them.

There is certainly such a third kind, I said, but why do you ask?

Under which of these headings do you put justice? he asked.

I would myself put it in the finest class, I said, that which is to be welcomed both for itself and for its consequences by any man who is to be blessed with happiness.

That is not the opinion of the many, he said; they would put it in the wearisome class, to be pursued for the rewards and popularity which come from a good reputation, but to be avoided in itself as being difficult.

I know that is the general opinion, I said. Justice has now for some time been objected to by Thrasymachus on this score while injustice was extolled, but it seems I am a slow learner.

Come then, he said, listen to me also to see whether you are still of the same opinion, for I think that Thrasymachus gave up before he had to, charmed by you as by a snake charmer. I am not yet satisfied by the demonstration on either side. I am eager to hear the nature of each, of justice and injustice, and what effect its presence has upon the soul. I want to leave out of account the rewards and consequences of each. So, if you agree, I will do the following: I will renew the argument of Thrasymachus; I will first state what people consider the nature and origin of justice; secondly, that all who practice it do so unwillingly as being something necessary but not good; thirdly, that they have good reason to do so, for, according to what people say, the life of the unjust man is much better than that of the just.

It is not that I think so, Socrates, but I am perplexed and my ears are deafened listening to Thrasymachus and innumerable other speakers; I have never heard from anyone the sort of defense of justice that I want to hear, proving that it is better than injustice. I want to hear it praised for itself, and I think I am most likely to hear this from you. Therefore I am going to speak at length in praise of the unjust life, and in doing so I will show you the way I want to hear you denouncing injustice and praising justice. See whether you want to hear what I suggest.

I want it more than anything else, I said. Indeed, what subject would a man of sense talk and hear about more often with enjoyment?

Splendid, he said, then listen while I deal with the first subject I mentioned: the nature and origin of justice.

They say that to do wrong is naturally good, to be wronged is bad, but the suffering of injury so far exceeds in badness the good of inflicting it that when men have done wrong to each other and suffered it, and have had a taste of both, those who are unable to avoid the latter and practice the former decide that it is profitable to come to an agreement with each other neither to inflict injury nor to suffer it. As a result they begin to make laws and covenants, and the law's command they call lawful and just. This, they say, is the origin and essence of justice; it stands between the best and the worst, the best being to do wrong without paying the penalty and the worst to be wronged without the power of revenge. The just then is a mean between two extremes; it is welcomed and honored because of men's lack of the power to do wrong. The man who has that power, the real man, would not make a compact with anyone not to inflict injury or suffer it. For him that would be madness. This then, Socrates, is, according to their argument, the nature and origin of justice.

Even those who practice justice do so against their will because they lack the power to do wrong. This we could realize very clearly if we imagined ourselves granting to both the just and the unjust the freedom to do whatever they liked. We could then follow both of them and observe where their desires led them, and we would catch the just man redhanded traveling the same road as the unjust. The reason is the desire for undue gain which every organism by nature pursues as a good, but the law forcibly sidetracks him to honor equality. The freedom I just mentioned would most easily occur if these men had the power which they say the ancestor of the Lydian Gyges possessed. The story is that he was a shepherd in the service of the ruler of Lydia. There was a violent rainstorm and an earthquake which broke open the ground and created a chasm at the place where he was tending sheep. Seeing this and marvelling, he went down into it. He saw, besides many other wonders of which we are told, a hollow bronze horse. There were window-like openings in it; he climbed through them and caught sight of a corpse which seemed of more than human stature, wearing nothing but a ring of gold on its finger. This ring the shepherd put on and came out. He arrived at the usual monthly meeting which reported to the king on the state of the flocks, wearing the ring. As he was sitting among the others he happened to twist the hoop of the ring towards himself, to the inside of his hand, and as he did this he became invisible to those sitting near him and they went on talking as if he had gone. He marvelled at this and, fingering the ring, he turned the hoop outward again and became visible. Perceiving this, he tested whether the ring had this power and so it happened: if he turned the hoop inwards he became invisible, but was visible when he turned it outwards. When he realized this, he at once arranged to become one of the messengers to the king. He went, committed adultery with the king's wife, attacked the king with her help, killed him, and took over the kingdom.

Now if there were two such rings, one worn by the just man, the other by the unjust, no one, as these people think, would be so incorruptible that he would stay on the path of justice or bring himself to keep away from other people's property and not touch it, when he could with impunity take whatever he wanted from the market, go into houses and have sexual relations with anyone he wanted, kill anyone, free all those he wished from prison, and do the other things which would make him like a god among men. His actions would be in no way different from those of the other and they would both follow the same path. This, some would say, is a great proof that no one is just willingly but under compulsion, so that justice is not one's private good, since wherever either thought he could do wrong with impunity he would do so. Every man believes that injustice is much more profitable to himself than justice, and any exponent of this argument will say that he is right. The man who did not wish to do wrong with that opportunity, and did not touch other people's property, would be thought by those who knew it to be very foolish and miserable. They would praise him in public, thus deceiving one another, for fear of being wronged. So much for my second topic.

As for the choice between the lives we are discussing, we shall be able to make a correct judgment about it only if we put the most just man and the most unjust man face to face; otherwise we cannot do so. By face to face I mean this: let us grant to the unjust the fullest degree of injustice and to the just the fullest justice, each being perfect in his own pursuit. First, the unjust man will act as clever craftsmen do—a top navigator, for example, or physician distinguishes what his craft can do and what it cannot; the former he will undertake, the latter he will pass by, and when he slips he can put things right. So the unjust man's correct attempts at wrongdoing must remain secret; the one who is caught must be considered a poor performer, for the extreme of injustice is to have a reputation for justice, and our perfectly unjust man must be granted perfection in injustice. We must not take this from him, but we must allow that, while committing the greatest crimes, he has provided himself with the greatest reputation for justice; if he makes a slip he must be able to put it right; he must be a sufficiently persuasive speaker if some wrongdoing of his is made public; he must be able to use force, where force is needed, with the help of his courage, his strength, and the friends and wealth with which he has provided himself.

Having described such a man, let us now in our argument put beside him the just man, simple as he is and noble, who, as Aeschylus put it, does not wish to appear just but to be so. We must take away his reputation, for a reputation for justice would bring him honor and rewards, and it would then not be clear whether he is what he is for justice's sake or for the sake of rewards and honor. We must strip him of everything except justice and make him the complete opposite of the other. Though he does no wrong, he must have the greatest reputation for wrongdoing so that he may be tested for justice by not weakening under ill repute and its consequences. Let him go his incorruptible way until death with a reputation for injustice throughout his life, just though he is, so that our two men may reach the extremes, one of justice, the other of injustice, and let them be judged as to which of the two is the happier.

Whew! My dear Glaucon, I said, what a mighty scouring you have given those two characters, as if they were statues in a competition.

I do the best I can, he replied. The two being such as I have described, there should be no difficulty in following the argument through as to what kind of life awaits each of them, but it must be said. And if what I say sounds rather boorish, Socrates, realize that it is not I who speak, but those who praise injustice as preferable to justice. They will say that the just man in these circumstances will be whipped, stretched on the rack, imprisoned, have this eyes burnt out, and, after suffering every kind of evil, he will be impaled and realize that one should not want to be just but to appear so. Indeed, Aeschylus's words are far more correctly applied to the unjust than to the just, for we shall be told that the unjust man pursues a course which is based on truth and not on appearances; he does not want to appear but to be unjust:

> He harvests in his heart a deep furrow
> from which good counsels grow.

He rules his city because of his reputation for justice, he marries into any family he wants to, he gives his children in marriage to anyone he wishes, he has contractual and other associations with anyone he may desire, and, beside all these advantages, he benefits in the pursuit of gain because he does not scruple to practice injustice. In any contest, public or private, he is the winner, getting the better of his enemies and accumulating wealth; he benefits his friends and does harm to his enemies. To the gods he offers grand sacrifices and gifts which will satisfy them, he can serve the gods much better than the just man, and also such men as he wants to, with the result that he is likely to be dearer to the gods. This is what they say, Socrates, that both from gods and men the unjust man secures a better life than the just. . . .

The Socratic Solution to the Problem of Why Be Moral?

Socrates has argued that the soul is made up of three parts: a rational part, a spirited part, and an appetitive or passionate part. Justice is defined as a harmony of the soul when each part fulfills its proper function—reason ruling, the spirit courageously serving reason, and the appetites living in temperance, being guided by reason. We join Socrates as he is discussing the relationship of the spirited part to the reasoning part.

These two parts will also most effectively stand on guard on behalf of the whole soul and the body, the one by planning, the other by fighting, following its leader, and by its courage fulfilling his decisions.—That is so.

It is this part which causes us to call an individual brave, when his spirit preserves in the midst of pain and pleasure his belief in the declarations of reason as to what he should fear and what he should not.—Right.

And we shall call him wise because of that small part of himself which ruled in him and made those declarations, which possesses the knowledge of what is beneficial to each part, and of what is to the common advantage of all three.—Quite so.

Further, shall we not call him moderate because of the friendly and harmonious relations between these same parts, when the rulers and the ruled hold a common belief that reason should rule, and they do not rebel against it?—Moderation, he said, is surely just that, both in the individual and the city.

And he will be just in the way we have often described.—Necessarily.

Now, I said, has our notion of justice become at all indistinct? Does it appear to be something different from what it was seen to be in the city?—I do not think so.

If any part of our soul still disputes this, we could altogether confirm it by bringing up common arguments.—What are they?

For example, concerning the city and the man similar to it by nature and training, if we had to come to an agreement whether we think that this man has embezzled a deposit of gold and silver, who, do you think, would consider him to have done this rather than men of a different type?—No one would.

And he would have nothing to do with temple robberies, thefts, or betrayals, either of friends in his private life, or, in public life, of cities?—Nothing.

Further, he would be in no way untrustworthy in keeping an oath or any other agreement.—How could he be?

Adultery too, disrespect for parents, neglect of the gods would suit his character less than any other man's.—Much less.

And the reason for all this is that every part within him fulfills its own function, be that ruling or being ruled?—Certainly that, and nothing else.

Are you still looking for justice to be anything else than this power which produces such men and such cities as we have described?—By Zeus, he said, not I.

We have then completely realized the dream we had when we suspected that, by the grace of god, we came upon a principle and mold of justice right at the beginning of the founding of our city.—Very definitely.

Indeed, Glaucon—and this is why it is useful—it was a sort of image of justice, namely, that it was right for one who is by nature a cobbler to cobble and to do nothing else, and for the carpenter to carpenter, and so with the others.—Apparently.

And justice was in truth, it appears, something like this. It does not lie in a man's external actions, but in the way he acts within himself, really concerned with himself and his inner parts. He does not allow each part of himself to perform the work of another, or the sections of his soul to meddle with one another. He orders what are in the true sense of the word his own affairs well; he is master of himself, puts things in order, is his own friend, harmonizes the three parts like the limiting notes of a musical scale, the high, the low, and the middle, and any others there may be between. He binds them all together, and himself from a plurality becomes a unity. Being thus moderate and harmonious, he now performs any action, be it about the acquisition of wealth, the care of his body, some public actions, or private contract.[1] In all these fields he thinks the just and beautiful action, which he names as such, to be that which preserves this inner harmony and indeed helps to achieve it, wisdom to be the knowledge which oversees this action, an unjust action to be that which always destroys it, and ignorance the belief which oversees that.—Socrates you are altogether right.

Very well, I said, we would then not be thought to be lying if we claim that we have found the just man, the just city, and the justice that is in them.—No, by Zeus, we would not.

Shall we say so then?—Yes, let us.

Let that stand then, I said. After this we must, I think, look for injustice.—Obviously.

Surely it must be a kind of civil war between the three parts, a meddling and a doing of other people's task, a rebellion of one part against the whole soul in order to rule it, though this is not fitting, as the rebelling part is by nature fitted to serve, while the other part is by nature not fit to serve, for it is of the ruling kind. We shall say, I think, that such things, the turmoil and the stray-

ing, are injustice and license and cowardice and ignorance and, in a word, every kind of wickedness.—That is what they are.

If justice and injustice are now sufficiently clear to us, then so are unjust actions and wrongdoing on the one hand, just actions on the other, and all such things.—How so?

Because they are no different from healthy and diseased actions; what those are in the body, these are in the soul.—In what way?

Healthy actions produce health, diseased ones, disease.—Yes.

Therefore, just actions produce justice in a man, and unjust actions, injustice?—Inevitably.

To produce health in the body is to establish the parts of the body as ruler and ruled according to nature, while disease is that they rule and are ruled contrary to nature.—That is so.

Therefore, to produce justice is to establish the parts of the soul as ruler and ruled according to nature, while injustice means they rule and are ruled contrary to nature.—Most certainly.

Excellence then seems to be a kind of health and beauty and well-being of the soul, while vice is disease and ugliness and weakness.—That is so.

Then do not fine pursuits lead one to acquire virtue, ugly ones to acquire vice?—Of necessity.

It is left for us to enquire, it seems, if it is more profitable to act justly, to engage in fine pursuits and be just, whether one is known to be so or not, or to do wrong and be unjust, provided one does not pay the penalty and is not improved by punishment.

But Socrates, he said, this enquiry strikes me as becoming ridiculous now that justice and injustice have been shown to be such as we described. It is generally thought that life is not worth living when the body's nature is ruined, even if every kind of food and drink, every kind of wealth and power are available; yet we are to enquire whether life will be worth living when our soul, the very thing by which we live, is confused and ruined, if only one can do whatever one wishes, except that one cannot do what will free one from vice and injustice and make one acquire justice and virtue.

Ridiculous indeed. . . . Very well, I said. As we have come to this point in our discussion, let us take up again what was said at first, which has led us to this. It was said at some point that injustice was to the benefit of the completely unjust man who had a reputation for justice, was it not?—It certainly was.

Since we have fully agreed, I said, upon the effect of each, that is, of just and unjust behavior, let us now talk to the man who maintains this point of view.—How?

Let us in our argument fashion an image of the soul, so that he may understand the kind of thing he was saying.—What kind of image?

One of the kind that are told in ancient legends about creatures like the Chimera, Scylla, Cerberus, and many others in whose natures many different kinds had grown into one.—We are told of such creatures.

Fashion me then one kind of multiform beast with many heads, a ring of heads of both tame and wild animals, who is able to change these and grow them all out himself.

A work for a clever modeler, he said. However, as words are more malleable than wax and such things, take it as fashioned.

Then one other form, that of a lion, and another of a man, but the first form of all is much the largest, and the second, second.—That is easy and it is done.

Gather the three into one, so that they somehow grow together.—All right.

Model around them on the outside the appearance of being one, a man, so that anyone who cannot see what is inside but only the outside cover will think it is one creature, a man.—Done.

Let us now tell the one who maintains that injustice benefits this man, and that justice brings him no advantage, that his words simply mean that it benefits the man to feed the multiform beast well and make it strong, as well as the lion and all that pertains to him, but to starve and weaken the man within so that he is dragged along whithersoever one of the other two leads. He does not accustom one part to the other or make them friendly, but he leaves them alone to bite and fight and kill each other.—This is most certainly what one who praises injustice means.

On the other hand, one who maintains that justice is to our advantage would say that all our words and deeds would tend to make the man within the man the strongest. He would look after the many-headed beast as a farmer looks after his animals, fostering and domesticating the gentle heads and preventing the wild ones from growing. With the lion's nature as his ally, he will care for all of them and rear them by making them all friendly with each other and with himself.—This is most definitely the meaning of him who praises justice.

What is said of justice is true in every way, and what is said on the other side is false, whether one examines it from the point of view of pleasure, of good repute, or of advantage; whereas he who condemns justice has nothing sound to say, and he does not know what he is condemning.—I don't think he does at all.

Let us then gently persuade him—he is not willingly wrong—by asking him: "My good sir, should we not say that beautiful and ugly traditions have originated as follows: the beautiful are those which subordinate the beastlike parts of our nature to the human, or perhaps we should say to the divine, while the ugly enslaves the gentler side to the wilder?" Will he agree or what?— He will agree if he takes my advice.

Can it benefit anyone, I said, to acquire gold unjustly if when he takes the gold he enslaves the best part of himself to the most vicious part? Or, if by taking the gold he should make a slave of his son or daughter in the house of wild and evil men, it would certainly not benefit him to acquire even a great deal of gold on those terms.

If then he enslaves the most divine part of himself to the most ungodly and disgusting part and feels no pity for it, is he not wretched and is he not accepting a bribe of gold for a more terrible death than Eriphyle when she accepted the necklace for her husband's life?—Much more, said Glaucon. I will answer for him.

Then do you think that licentiousness has long been condemned because in a licentious man that terrible, that big, that multiform beast is let loose more than it should be?—Clearly.

Obstinacy and irritability are condemned whenever the lion and snakelike part is increased and stetched disproportionately?—Surely.

Are luxury and softness condemned because the slackening and looseness of this same part produce cowardice?—Of course.

And do not flattery and meanness come when this same spirited part is subordinated to the turbulent beast which accustoms it from youth to being abused for the sake of money and the beast's insatiability, and to become an ape instead of a lion?—Certainly.

Why do you think the mechanical work of one's own hands is subject to reproach? Shall we say that it is so only when the best part of one's soul is naturally weak and cannot rule the animals within but pampers them and can learn nothing except ways to flatter them.—That is likely.

Therefore, in order that such a man be ruled by a principle similar to that which rules the best man, we say he must be enslaved to the best man, who has a divine ruler within himself. It is not to harm the slave that we believe he must be ruled, as Thrasymachus thought subjects should be, but because it is better for everyone to be ruled by divine intelligence. It is best that he should have this within himself, but if he has not, then it must be imposed from outside, so that, as far as possible, we should all be alike and friendly and governed by the same principle.—Quite right.

This, I said, is clearly the aim of the law which is the ally of everyone in the city, and of our rule over children. We should not allow them to be free until we establish a government within them, as we did in the city, fostering the best in them with what is best in ourselves and securing

within the child a similar guardian and ruler, and then let him go free.—The law does make that clear.

How then and by what argument can we maintain, Glaucon, that injustice, licentiousness, and shameful actions are profitable, since they make a man more wicked, though he may acquire more riches or some other form of power?—We cannot.

Or that to do wrong without being discovered and not to pay the penalty is profitable? Does not one who remains undiscovered become even more vicious, whereas within the man who is discovered and punished the beast is calmed down and tamed; his whole soul, settling into its best nature, as it acquires moderation and justice together with wisdom, attains a more honored condition than a strong, beautiful, and healthy body, insofar as the soul is to be honoured more than the body.—Most certainly.

The man of sense then will direct all his efforts to this end; firstly, he will prize such studies as make his soul like this, and he will disregard the others.—Obviously.

Then, I said, he will see to his bodily condition and nurture it in such a way that he does not entrust it to the irrational pleasure of the beast, turn himself that way, and live on that level. It is not even health he aims at, nor does he consider it most important that he should be strong, healthy, or beautiful, unless he acquires moderation as a result, but he will cultivate harmony in his body for the sake of consonance in his soul.— That is altogether true, if he is truly to be a cultured man.

To the same end, there will be order and measure in his acquisition of wealth. He will not be panicked by the numbers of the crowd into accepting their idea of blessedness and increase his wealth without limit, and so have unlimited ills.— I do not think he will do so.

Looking to the government within, I said, he will guard against disturbances being caused there by too much wealth or too little, and he will direct, as far as he can, both the acquiring and spending of his possessions.—Very definitely.

He will have the same end in view as regards honors. He will share in, and willingly taste, those which he believes will make him a better man, but he will avoid both public and private honors which he believes will destroy the existing condition of his soul.

Note

1. Plato here seems to link his present more psychologically profound definition of justice and injustice as inner states of soul with the more external description of them in the first book. Clearly the unjust man who, in the argument with Thrasymachus, wanted to get the better of everybody is here the man whose appetitive part is out of control and rebels against the ruling reason. His antisocial conduct now follows from this.

7

Egoism as the Beginning of Morality

THOMAS HOBBES

Thomas Hobbes (1588–1679), the greatest English political philosopher, gave classic expression to the idea that morality and politics arise out of a social contract. The son of a clergyman, born in Gloucestershire during the approach of the Spanish Armada, he was educated at Oxford University and lived through an era of political revolutions as a scholar and tutor (he was tutor to Prince Charles II of England).

In the Leviathan *(1651), from which our selection is taken, he develops a moral and political theory based on psychological egoism. Hobbes believed that we always act in our own self-interest, to obtain gratification and to avoid harm. However, we cannot obtain any of the basic goods because of the inherent fear and insecurity in an unregulated "state of nature," in which life is "solitary, poor, nasty, brutish and short." Because of this "war of every man against every man," we cannot relax our guard. There is little time to build or to cultivate the earth or to enjoy life, since our neighbor may be plotting to undo us. In this state of anarchy the prudent person concludes that it really is in everyone's self-interest to make a contract to sustain a minimal morality of respecting human life, keeping covenants made, and obeying the laws of the society. This minimal morality, which Hobbes refers to as "The Laws of Nature," is nothing more than a set of maxims of prudence. To insure that we all obey this covenant Hobbes proposes a strong sovereign state, the "Leviathan," to impose severe penalties on those who disobey the laws, for "covenants without the sword are but words."*

From the *Leviathan* (1651), edited by Louis P. Pojham.

Of the Natural Condition of Mankind as Concerning Their Felicity, and Misery

Men by Nature Are Equal

Nature hath made men so equal, in the faculties of the body, and mind; so that though there be found one man sometimes manifestly stronger in body, or of quicker mind than another; yet when all is reckoned together, the difference between man, and man, is not so considerable, as that one man can thereupon claim to himself any benefit, to which another may not pretend, as well as he. For as to the strength of body, the weakest has strength enough to kill the strongest, either by secret machination, or by confederacy with others, that are in the same danger with himself.

And as to the faculties of the mind, setting aside the arts grounded upon words, and especially that skill of proceeding upon general, and infallible rules, called science; which very few have, and but in few things; as being not a native faculty, born with us; nor attained, as prudence, while we look after somewhat else, I find yet a greater equality amongst men, than that of strength. For prudence, is but experience; which equal time, equally bestows on all men, in those things they equally apply themselves unto. That which may perhaps make such equality incredible, is but a vain conceit of one's own wisdom, which almost all men think they have in a greater degree, than the vulgar; that is, than all men but themselves, and a few others, whom by fame, or for concurring with themselves, they approve. For such is the nature of men, that howsoever they may acknowledge many others to be more witty, or more eloquent, or more learned; yet they will hardly believe there be many so wise as themselves; for they see their own wit at hand, and other men's at a distance. But this proveth rather that men are in that point equal, than unequal. For there is not ordinarily a greater sign of the equal distribution of any thing, than that every man is contented with his share.

From Equality Proceeds Fear

From this equality of ability, arises equality of hope in the attaining of our ends. And therefore if any two men desire the same thing, which nevertheless they cannot both enjoy, they become enemies; and in the way to their end, which is principally their own preservation and sometimes their enjoyment only, endeavor to destroy, or subdue one another. And from hence it comes to pass, that where an invader hath no more to fear, than another man's single power; if one plant, sow, build, or possess a convenient seat, others may probably be expected to come prepared with forces united, to dispossess, and deprive him, not only of the fruit of his labor, but also of his life, or liberty. And the invader again is in the like danger of another.

From Fear Proceeds War

And from this fear of one another, there is no way for any man to secure himself, so reasonable, as anticipation; that is, by force, or wiles, to master the persons of all men he can, so long, till he see no other power great enough to endanger him: and this is no more than his own preservation requireth, and is generally allowed. Also because there be some, that taking pleasure in contemplating their own power in the acts of conquest, which they pursue farther than their security requires; if others, that otherwise would be glad to be at ease within modest bounds, should not by invasion increase their power, they would not be able, long time, by standing only on their defense, to subsist. And by consequence,

such increase of dominion over men being necessary to a man's preservation, it ought to be allowed him.

Again, men have no pleasure, but on the contrary a great deal of grief, in keeping company, where there is no power able to over-awe them all. For every man desires that his companion should value him, at the same rate he sets upon himself: and upon all signs of contempt, or undervaluing, naturally endeavors, as far as he dares, (which amongst them that have no common power to keep them in quiet, is far enough to make them destroy each other), to extort a greater value from his contemners, by damage; and from others, by the example.

So that in the nature of man, we find three principal causes of quarrel. First, competition; secondly, fear; thirdly, glory.

The first, maketh men invade for gain; the second, for safety; and the third, for reputation. The first use violence, to make themselves masters of other men's persons, wives, children, and cattle; the second, to defend them; the third, for trifles, as a word, a smile, a different option, and any other sign of undervalue, either direct in their persons, or by reflection in their kindred, their friends, their nation, their profession, or their name.

Out of Civil States There Is Always War of Everyone Against Everyone

Hereby it is manifest, that during the time men live without a common power to keep them all in awe, they are in that condition which is called war; and such a war, as is of every man, against every man. For war consists not in battle only or the act of fighting; but in a tract of time, wherein the will to contend by battle is sufficiently known: and therefore the notion of *time*, is to be considered in the nature of war; as it is in the nature of weather. For as the nature of foul weather, lies not in the shower or two of rain; but in an inclination thereto of many days together: so the nature of war, consists not in actual fighting; but in the known disposition thereto, during all the time there is no assurance to the contrary. All other time is PEACE.

The Problems and Inconvenience of Such a War

Whatsoever therefore occurs in a time of war, where every man is enemy to every man; the same occurs in the time, wherein men live without other security, than what their own strength, and their own invention shall furnish them withal. In such condition, there is no place for industry; because the fruit thereof is uncertain: and consequently no culture of the earth; no navigation, nor use of the commodities that may be imported by sea; no commodious building; no instruments of moving, and removing, such things as require much force; no knowledge of the face of the earth; no account of time; no arts; no letters; no society; and which is worst of all, continual fear, and danger of violent death; and the life of man solitary, poor, nasty, brutish, and short.

It may seem strange to some man, that has not well weighed these things; that nature should thus dissociate, and render men apt to invade, and destroy one another: and he may therefore, not trusting to this inference, made from the passions, desire perhaps to have the same confirmed by experience. Let him therefore consider with himself, when taking a journey, he arms himself, and seeks to go well accompanied; when going to sleep, he locks his doors; when even in his house he locks his chests; and this when he knows there be laws, and public officers, armed, to revenge all injuries shall be done him; what opinion he has of his fellow subjects, when he rides armed; of his fellow citizens, when he locks his doors; and of his children, and servants, when he locks his chests. Does he not there as much accuse mankind by his actions, as I do by my words? But neither of us accuse man's nature in it. The desires, and other passions of man, are in themselves no sin. No more are the actions, that proceed from those passions, till they know a law that forbids them: which till laws be made they cannot know: nor can any law be made, till they have agreed upon the person that shall make it.

It may perhaps be thought, there was never such a time, nor condition of war as this; and I believe it was never generally so, over all the world: but there are many places, where they live so now. For the savage people in many places of America, except the government of small families, the concord whereof depends on natural lust, have no government at all; and live at this day in that brutish manner, as I said before, Howsoever, it may be perceived what manner of life there would be, where there were no common power to fear, by the manner of life, which men that have formerly lived under a peaceful government, use to degenerate into, in a civil war.

But though there had never been any time, wherein particular men were in a condition of war one against another; yet in all times, kings, and persons of sovereign authority, because of their independency, are in continual jealousies, and in the state and posture of gladiators; having their weapons pointing, and their eyes fixed on one another; that is, their forts, garrisons, and guns upon the frontiers of their kingdoms; and continual spies upon their neighbors; which is a posture of war. But because they uphold thereby, the industry of their subjects; there does not follow from it, that misery, which accompanies the liberty of particular men.

In This State of War Nothing Is Unjust

To this war of every man, against every man, this also is a result; that nothing can be unjust. The notions of right and wrong, justice and injustice have there no place. Where there is no common power, there is no law: where no law, no injustice. Force, and fraud, are in war the two cardinal virtues. Justice, and injustice are none of the faculties neither of the body, nor mind. If they were, they might be in a man that were alone in the world, as well as his senses, and passions. They are qualities, that relate to men in society, not in solitude. It is consequent also to the same condition, that there be no property, no ownership, no *mine* and *thine* distinct; but only that to be every man's, that he can get; and for so long, as he can keep it. And thus much for the ill condition, which man be mere nature is actually placed in; though with a possibility to come out of it, consisting partly in the passions, partly in his reason.

The Passions Which Incline Men to Peace

The passions that incline men to peace are fear of death; desire of such things as are necessary to commodious living; and a hope by their industry to obtain them. And reason suggest convenient articles of peace, upon which men may be drawn to agreement. These articles, are they, which otherwise are called the Laws of Nature: whereof I shall speak more particularly, in the two following chapters.

Of the First and Second Natural Laws, and of Contracts

The Right of Nature

The Right of Nature, which writers commonly call *jus naturale*, is the liberty each man hath, to use his own power, as he will himself, for the preservation of his own nature; that is to say, of his own life; and consequently, of doing anything, which in his own judgment, and reason, he shall conceive to be the best means thereunto.

Liberty

By LIBERTY, is understood, according to the proper signification of the word, the absence of external impediments: which impediments, may oft take away part of a man's power to do what he would; but cannot hinder him from using the power left him, according as his judgment, and reason shall dictate to him.

A Law of Nature

A LAW OF NATURE, *lex naturalis*, is a precept or general rule, found out by reason, by which a man is forbidden to do that, which is destructive of his life, or taketh away the means of preserving the same; and to omit that, by which he thinketh it may be best preserved. For though they that speak of this subject, use to confound *jus*, and *lex*, *right* and *law:* yet they ought to be distinguished; because RIGHT, consisteth in liberty to do, or to forbear; whereas LAW, determines, and binds to one of them: so that law, and right, differ as much, as obligation and liberty; which in one and the same matter are inconsistent.

In the State of Nature Every Man Has a Right to Everything.

And because the condition of man, as has been shown in the precedent chapter, is a condition of war of every one against every one; in which case every one is governed by his own reason; and there is nothing he can make use of, that may not be a help unto him, in preserving his life against his enemies; it followeth, that in such a condition, every man has a right to every thing; even to one another's body. And therefore, as long as this natural right of every man to every thing endures, there can be no security to any man, how strong or wise soever he be, of living out the time, which nature ordinarily alloweth men to live. And consequently it is a precept, or general rule of reason, *that every man, ought to endeavor peace, as far as he has hope of obtaining it; and when he cannot obtain it, that he may seek, and use, all helps, and advantages, of war.* The first branch of which rule, contains the first, and fundamental law of nature; which is, *to seek peace, and follow it.* The second, the sum of the right of nature; which is, *by all means we can, to defend ourselves.*

The Second Law of Nature

From this fundamental law of nature, by which men are commanded to endeavor peace, is derived this second law; *that a man be willing, when others are so too, as far-forth, as for peace, and defense of himself he shall think it necessary, to lay down this right to all things; and be contented with so much liberty against other men, as he would allow other men against himself.* For as long as every man holds this right, of doing any thing he likes, so long are all men in the condition of war. But if other men will not lay down their right, as well as he; then there is no reason for any one, to divest himself of his: for that were to expose himself to prey, which no man is bound to, rather than to dispose himself to peace. This is that law of the Gospel; *whatsoever you require that others should do to you, that do ye to them.* And that law of all men, "What you do not want done to you, do not do to others."

Giving up a Right

To *lay down* a man's *right* to anything, is to *divest* himself of the *liberty,* of hindering another of the benefit of his own right to the same. For he that renounces, or passes away his right, gives not to any other man a right which he had not before; because there is nothing to which every man had not right by nature: but only stands out of his way, that he may enjoy his own original right, without hindrance from him; not without hindrance from another. So that the effect which redounds to one man, by another man's defect of right, is but so much diminution of impediments to the use of his own right original.

Right is laid aside, either by simply renouncing it; or by transferring it to another. By *simply* RENOUNCING; when he cares not to whom the benefit thereof redounds. By TRANSFERRING; when he intends the benefit thereof to some certain person, or persons. And when a man has in either manner abandoned, or granted away his right; then is he said to be OBLIGED, or BOUND, not to hinder those, to whom such right is granted, or abandoned, from the benefit of it: and that he *ought,* and it is his DUTY, not to make void that voluntary act of his own: and that such hin-

drance is INJUSTICE, and INJURY, as being "without right," the right being before renounced, or transferred. So that *injury,* or *injustice,* in the controversies of the world, is somewhat like to that, which in the disputations of scholars is called *absurdity.* For as it is there called an absurdity, to contradict what one maintained in the beginning: so in the world, it is called injustice, and injury, voluntarily to undo that, which from the beginning he had voluntarily done. The way by which a man either simply renounces, or transfers his right, is a declaration, or signification, by some voluntary and sufficient sign, or signs, that he does so renounce, or transfer; or has so renounced, or transferred the same, to him that accepts it. And these signs are either words only, or actions only; or, as it happens most often, both words, and actions. And the same are the BONDS, by which men are bound, and obliged: bonds, that have their strength, not from their own nature, for nothing is more easily broken than a man's word, but from fear of some evil consequence upon the rupture.

Some Rights Are Inalienable

Whensoever a man transfers his right, or renounces it; it is either in consideration of some right reciprocally transferred to himself; or for some other good he hopes for thereby. For it is a voluntary act: and of the voluntary acts of every man, the object is some *good to himself.* And therefore there be some rights, which no man can be understood by any words, or other signs, to have abandoned, or transferred. At first a man cannot lay down the right of resisting them, that assault him by force, to take away his life; because he cannot be understood to aim thereby, at any good to himself. The same may be said of wounds, and chains, and imprisonment; both because no benefit proceeds from such patience; as there is to the patience of suffering another to be wounded, or imprisoned: as also because a man cannot tell, when he seeth men proceed against him by violence, whether they intend his death or not. And lastly the motive, and end for which this renouncing, and transferring of right is introduced, is nothing else but the security of a man's person, in his life, and in the means of so preserving life, as not to be weary of it. And therefore if a man by words, or other signs, seem to despoil himself of the end, for which those signs were intended; he is not to be understood as if he meant it, or that it was his will; but that he was ignorant of how such words and actions were to be interpreted.

The Contract

The mutual transferring of right, is that which men call CONTRACT.

There is a different between transferring of right to the thing; and transferring, or tradition, that is delivery of the thing itself. For the thing may be delivered together with the translation of the right; as in buying and selling with ready-money; or exchange of goods, or lands: and it may be delivered some time after.

The Covenant

Again, one of the contractors, may deliver the thing contracted for on his part, and leave the other to perform his part as some determinate time after, and in the meantime be trusted; and then the contract on his part, is called PACT, or COVENANT: or both parts may contract now, to perform hereafter: in which cases, he that is to perform in time to come, being trusted, his performance is called *keeping of promise*, or faith; and the failing of performance, if it be voluntary, *violation of faith.*

When the transferring of right, is not mutual: but one of the parties transferreth, in hope to gain thereby friendship, or service from another, or from his friends; or in hope to gain the reputation of charity, or magnanimity; or to deliver his mind from the pain of compassion; or in hope of reward in heaven, this is not contract, but GIFT, FREE-GIFT, GRACE: which words signify one and the same thing.

Signs of contract, are either *express,* or *by inference.* Express, are words spoken with understanding of what they signify: and such words are either of the time *present,* or *past;* as, *I give, I grant, I have given, I have granted, I will that this be yours:* or of the future; as, *I will give, I will grant:* which words of the future are called PROMISE.

When Covenant of Mutual Trust Become Invalid

If a covenant be made, wherein neither of the parties perform presently, but trust one another; in the condition of mere nature, which is a condition of war of every man against every man, upon any reasonable suspicion, it is void: but if there be a common power set over them both, with right and force sufficient to compel performance, it is not void. For he that performs first, has no assurance the other will perform after; because the bonds of words are too weak to bridle men's ambition, avarice, anger, and other passions, without the fear of some coercive power; which in the condition of mere nature, where all men are equal, and judges of the justness of their own fears, cannot possibly be supposed. And therefore he which performs first, does but betray himself to his enemy; contrary to the right, he can never abandon, of defending his life, and means of living.

But in a civil estate, where there is a power set up to constrain those that would otherwise violate their faith, that fear is no more reasonable: and for that cause, he which by the covenant is to perform first, is obliged so to do.

The cause of fear, which maketh such a covenant invalid, must be always something arising after the covenant made; as some new fact, or other sign of the will not to perform: else it cannot make the covenant void. For that which could not hinder a man from promising, ought not to be admitted as a hindrance of performing.

Of Other Laws of Nature

The Third Law of Nature: Justice

From that law of nature, by which we are obliged to transfer to another, such rights, as being retained, hinder the peace of mankind, there followeth a third; which is this, *that men perform their covenants made:* without which, covenants are in vain, and but empty words; and the right of all men to all things remaining, we are still in the condition of war.

And in this law of nature, consists the fountain and origin of JUSTICE. For where no covenant has preceded, there has no right been transferred, and every man has right to everything; and consequently, no action can be unjust. But when a covenant is made, then to break it is *unjust:* and the definition of INJUSTICE is no other than *the not performance of covenant.* And whatsoever is not unjust, is *just.*

Justice and Injustice Come into Being with the Creation of the Commonwealth

But because covenants of mutual trust, where there is a fear of not performance on either part, as hath been said in the former chapter, are invalid; though the origin of justice be the making of covenants; yet injustice actually there can be none, till the cause of such fear be taken away; which while men are in the natural condition of war, cannot be done. Therefore before the names of just, and unjust can have place, there must be some coercive power, to compel men equally to the performance of their covenants, by the terror of some punishment, greater than the benefit they expect by the breach of their covenant; and to make good that propriety, which by mutual contract men acquire, in recompense of the universal right they abandon: and such power there is none before the erection of a commonwealth. And this is also to be gathered out of the ordinary definition of justice in the Schools: for they say, that *justice is the constant will of giving to every man his own,* and therefore where there is no *own,* that is, no property, there is no injustice; and where there is no coercive power erected, that is, where there is no commonwealth, there is no property; all men having right to all things: therefore where there is no commonwealth, there nothing is unjust. So that the nature of justice, consists in keeping of valid covenants: but the validity of covenants begins not but with the constitution of a civil power, sufficient to compel men to keep them: and then it is also that property begins. . . .

On the Duty to Submit to Arbitration

And because, though men be never so willing to observe these laws, there may nevertheless arise questions concerning a man's action; first, whether it were done, or not done; secondly, if done, whether against the law, or not against the law; the former whereof, is called a question *of fact;* the latter a question *of right,* therefore unless the parties to the question, covenant mutually to stand to the sentence of another, they are as far from peace as ever. This other to whose sentence they submit is called an ARBITRATOR. And therefore it is of the law of nature, *that they that are at controversy, submit their right to the judgment of an arbitrator.*

And seeing every man is presumed to do all things in order to his own benefit, no man is a fit arbitrator in his own cause; and if he were never so fit; yet equity allowing to each party equal benefit, if one be admitted to the judge, the other is to be admitted also; and so the controversy, that is, the cause of war, remains, against the law of nature.

For the same reason no man in any cause ought to be received for arbitrator, to whom greater profit, or honor, or pleasure apparently ariseth out of the victory of one party, than of the other: for he hath taken, though an unavoidable bribe, yet a bribe; and no man can be obliged to trust him. And thus also the controversy, and the condition of war remaineth, contrary to the law of nature.

And in a controversy of *fact*, the judge being to give no more credit to one, than to the other, if there be no other arguments, must give credit to a third; or to a third and fourth; or more: for else the question is undecided, and left to force, contrary to the law of nature.

These are the laws of nature, dictating peace, for a means of the conservation of men in multitudes; and which only concern the doctrine of civil society. There be other things tending to the destruction of particular men; as drunkenness, and all other parts of intemperance; which may therefore also be reckoned amongst those things which the law of nature hath forbidden; but are not necessary to be mentioned, nor are pertinent enough to this place.

A Rule by Which the Laws of Nature May Be Examined

And though this may seem too subtle a deduction of the laws of nature, to be taken notice of by all men; whereof the most part are too busy getting food, and the rest too negligent to understand; yet to leave all men inexcusable, they have been contracted into one easy sum, intelligible even to the meanest capacity; and that is, Do *not that to another, which thou wouldest not have done to thyself;* which shows him that he has no more to do in learning the laws of nature, but, when weighing the actions of other men with his own, they seem too heavy, to put them into the other part of the balance, and his own into their place, that his own passions, and selflove, may add nothing to the weight; and then there is none of these laws of nature that will not appear unto him very reasonable.

The Laws of Nature Oblige in Conscience Always, But in Effect Only When There is Security

The laws of nature oblige *in foro interno*, that is to say, they bind to a desire they should take place: but *in foro externo*, that is, to the putting them in

act, not always. For he that should be modest, and tractable, and perform all he promises, in such time, and place, where no man else should do so, should but make himself a prey to others, and procure his own certain ruin, contrary to the ground of all laws of nature, which tend to nature's preservation. And again, he that having sufficient security, that others shall observe the same laws towards him, observes them not himself, seeketh not peace, but war; and consequently the destruction of his nature by violence.

And whatsoever laws bind *in foro interno*, may be broken, not only by a fact contrary to the law, but also by a fact according to it, in case a man think it contrary. For though his action in this case, be according to the law; yet his purpose was against the law; which, where the obligation is *in foro interno*, is a breach.

The Laws of Nature Are Eternal

The laws of nature are immutable and eternal; for injustice, ingratitude, arrogance, pride, iniquity, acception of persons, and the rest, can never be made lawful. For it can never be that war shall preserve life, and peace destroy it.

The same laws, because they oblige only to a desire, and endeavor, I mean an unfeigned and constant endeavor, are easy to be observed. For in that they require nothing but endeavor, he that endeavoreth their performance, fulfilleth them; and he that fulfilleth the law, is just.

The Science of These Laws Is The True Moral Philosophy

And the science of them, is the true and only moral philosophy. For moral philosophy is nothing else but the science of what is *good*, and *evil*, in the conversation, and society of mankind. *Good*, and *evil*, are names that signify our appetites, and aversions; which in different tempers, customs, and doctrines of men, are different: and divers men, differ not only in their judgment, on the sense of what is pleasant, and unpleasant to the taste, smell, hearing, touch, and sight; but also of what is conformable, or disagreeable to reason, in the actions of common life. Nay, the same man, in divers times, differs from himself; and one time praises, that is, calls good, what another time he dispraises, and calls evil: from whence arise disputes, controversies, and at last war. And therefore so long as a man is in the condition of mere nature, which is a condition of war, as private appetite is the measure of good, and evil: and consequently all men agree on this, that peace is good, and therefore also the way, or means of peace, which, as I have showed before, are *justice, gratitude, modesty, equity, mercy*, and the rest of the laws of nature, are good; that is to say; *moral virtues;* and their contrary *vices*, evil. Now the science of virtue and vice, is moral philosophy; and therefore the true doctrine of the laws of nature, is the true moral philosophy. But the writers of moral philosophy, though they acknowledge the same virtues and vices; yet not seeing wherein consisted their goodness; nor that they come to be praised, as the means of peaceable, sociable, and comfortable living, place them in a mediocrity of passions: as if not the cause, but the degree of daring, made fortitude; or not the cause, but the quantity of a gift, made liberality.

These dictates of reason, men used to call by the name of laws, but improperly: for they are but conclusions, of theorems concerning what conduces to the conservation and defense of themselves; whereas law, properly, is the word of him, that by right hath command over others. But yet if we consider the same theorems, as delivered in the word of God, that by right commandeth all things; then are they properly called laws.

Of the Causes, Generation, and Definition of a Commonwealth

The final cause, end, or design of men, who naturally love liberty, and dominion over others, in the introduction of that restraint upon themselves, in which we see them live in commonwealths, is the foresight of their own preservation, and of a more contented life thereby; that is to say, of getting themselves out from that miserable condition of war, which is necessarily consequent, as has been shown, to the natural passions of men, when there is no visible power to keep them in awe, and tie them by fear of punishment to the performance of their covenants, and observation of those laws of nature set down in the fourteenth and fifteenth chapters.

For the laws of nature, as *justice, equity, modesty, mercy*, and, in sum, *doing to others, as we would be done to*, of themselves, without the terror of some power, to cause them to be observed, are contrary to our natural passions, that carry us to partiality, pride, revenge, and the like. And covenants, without the sword, are but words, and of no strength to secure a man at all. Therefore notwithstanding the laws of nature, which every one hath then kept, when he has the will to keep them, when he can do it safely, if there be no power erected, or not great enough for our security; every man will, and may lawfully rely on his own strength and art, for caution against all other men. And in all places, where men have lived by small families, to rob and spoil one another, has been a trade, and so far from being reputed against the law of nature, that the greater spoils they gained the greater was their honor; and men observed no other laws therein, but the laws of honor; that is, to abstain from cruelty, leaving to men their lives, and instruments of husbandry. And as small families did then; so now do cities and kingdoms which are but greater families, for their own security, enlarge their dominions, upon all pretenses of danger, and fear of invasion, or assistance that may be given to invaders, and endeavor as much as they can, to subdue, or weaken their neighbors, by open force, and secret arts, for want of other caution, justly; and are remembered for it in after ages with honor.

The only way to erect a common power, which may be able to defend men from invasion of foreigners, and the injuries of one another, and thereby to secure them in such fruits of the earth and enable them to live contentedly; is to confer all their power upon one man or upon one assembly of men, to bear in their person; and every one to own, and acknowledge himself to be author of whatsoever he that so beareth their person, shall act, or cause to be acted, in those things which concern the common peace and safety; and therein to submit their wills, every one to common peace and safety; and therein to submit their will, every one to his will, and their judgment to his judgment. This is more than consent or concord; it is a real unity of them all, in one and the same person, made by covenant of every man with every man, in such manner, as if every man should say to every man, *I authorize and give up my right of governing myself, to this man, or to this assembly of men, on this condition, that thou give up thy right to him, and authorize all his actions in like manner.* This done, the multitude so united in one person, is called a COMMONWEALTH, in Latin CIVITAS.

This is the generation of the great LEVIATHAN or rather, to speak more reverently, of that *mortal god,* to which we owe under the *immortal God,* our peace and defense. For by this authority, given him by every particular man in the commonwealth, he hath the use of so much power and strength conferred on him, that by terror thereof, he is enabled to perform the wills of them all, to peace at home, and mutual aid against their enemies abroad. And in him consists the essence of the commonwealth; which, to define it, is *one person, of whose acts a great multitude, by mutual covenants one with another, have made themselves every one the author, to the end he may use the strength and means of them all, as he shall think expedient, for their peace and common defense.*

And he that carries this person, is called SOVEREIGN, and said to have *sovereign* power; and every one besides, his SUBJECT.

8

A Defense of Ethical Egoism

AYN RAND

Ayn Rand (1908–1982) wrote several philosophical novels, including The Fountainhead *(1943) and* Atlas Shrugged *(1959), from which this selection is taken. Her work sets forth a version of ethical egoism that she called "objectivism," the theory that rational beings ought to pursue their own happiness and that altruism and self-sacrifice are incompatible with rational morality. In this selection she criticizes altruistic morality ("the morality of sacrifice") and praises the morality of selfishness.*

". . . Yes, this *is* an age of moral crisis. Yes, you *are* bearing punishment for your evil. But it is not man who is now on trial and it is not human nature that will take the blame. It is your moral code that's through, this time. Your moral code has reached its climax, the blind alley at the end of its course. And if you wish to go on living, what you now need is not to *return* to morality—you who have never known any—but to *discover* it.

"You have heard no concepts of morality but the mystical or the social. You have been taught that morality is a code of behavior imposed on you by whim, the whim of a supernatural power or the whim of society, to serve God's purpose or your neighbor's welfare, to please an authority beyond the grave or else next door—but not to serve *your* life or pleasure. Your pleasure, you have been taught, is to be found in immorality, your interests would best be served by evil, and any moral code must be designed not *for* you, but *against* you, not to further your life, but to drain it.

"For centuries, the battle of morality was fought

From *Atlas Shrugged* by Ayn Rand. Published by Random House, Inc. Reprinted by permission of the executor of the Estate of Ayn Rand.

between those who claimed that your life belongs to God and those who claimed that it belongs to your neighbors—between those who preached that the good is self-sacrifice for the sake of ghosts in heaven and those who preached that the good is self-sacrifice for the sake of incompetents on earth. And no one came to say that your life belongs to you and that the good is to live it.

"Both sides agreed that morality demands the surrender of your self-interest and of your mind, that the moral and the practical are opposites, that morality is not the province of reason, but the province of faith and force. Both sides agreed that no rational morality is possible, that there is no right or wrong in reason—that in reason there's no reason to be moral.

"Whatever else they fought about, it was against man's mind that all your moralists have stood united. It was man's mind that all their schemes and systems were intended to despoil and destroy. Now choose to perish or to learn that the anti-mind is the anti-life.

"Man's mind is his basic tool of survival. Life is given to him, survival is not. His body is given to him, its sustenance is not. His mind is given to him, its content is not. To remain alive, he must act, and before he can act he must know the nature and purpose of his action. He cannot obtain his food without a knowledge of food and of the way to obtain it. He cannot dig a ditch—or build a cyclotron—without a knowledge of his aim and of the means to achieve it. To remain alive, he must think.

"But to think is an act of choice. The key to what you so recklessly call 'human nature,' the open secret you live with, yet dread to name, is the fact that *man is a being of volitional consciousness*. Reason does not work automatically; thinking is not a mechanical process; the connections of logic are not made by instinct. The function of your stomach, lungs or heart is automatic; the function of your mind is not. In any hour and issue of your life, you are free to think or to evade that effort. But you are not free to escape from your nature, from the fact that *reason* is your means of survival—so that for *you*, who are a human being, the question 'to be or not to be' is the question 'to think or not to think.'

"A being of volitional consciousness has no automatic course of behavior. He needs a code of values to guide his actions. 'Value' is that which one acts to gain and keep, 'virtue' is the action by which one gains and keeps it. 'Value' presupposes an answer to the question: of value to whom and for what? 'Value' presupposes a standard, a purpose and the necessity of action in the face of an alternative. Where there are no alternatives, no values are possible.

"There is only one fundamental alternative in the universe: existence or non-existence—and it pertains to a single class of entities: to living organisms. The existence of inanimate matter is unconditional, the existence of life is not: it depends on a specific course of action. Matter is indestructible, it changes its forms, but it cannot cease to exist. It is only a living organism that faces a constant alternative: the issue of life or death. Life is a process of self-sustaining and self-generating action. If an organism fails in that action, it dies; its chemical elements remain, but its life goes out of existence. It is only the concept of 'Life' that makes the concept of 'Value' possible. It is only to a living entity that things can be good or evil.

"A plant must feed itself in order to live; the sunlight, the water, the chemicals it needs are the values its nature has set it to pursue; its life is the standard of value directing its actions. But a plant has no choice of action; there are alternatives in the conditions it encounters, but there is no alternative in its function: it acts automatically to further its life, it cannot act for its own destruction.

"An animal is equipped for sustaining its life; its senses provide it with an automatic code of action, an automatic knowledge of what is good for it or evil. It has no power to extend its knowledge or to evade it. In conditions where its knowledge proves inadequate, it dies. But so long as it lives, it acts on its knowledge, with automatic safety and no power of choice, it is unable to ignore its own good, unable to decide to choose the evil and act as its own destroyer.

"Man has no automatic code of survival. His particular distinction from all other living species is the necessity to act in the face of alternatives by means of *volitional choice*. He has no automatic knowledge of what is good for him or evil, what values his life depends on, what course of action it requires. Are you prattling about an instinct of self-preservation? An *instinct* of self-preservation is precisely what man does not possess. An 'instinct' is an unerring and automatic form of knowledge. A desire is not an instinct. A desire to live does not give you the knowledge required for living. And even man's desire to live is not automatic: your secret evil today is that *that* is the desire you do not hold. Your fear of death is not a love for life and will not give you the knowledge needed to keep it. Man must obtain his knowledge and choose his actions by a process of thinking, which nature will not force him to perform. Man has the power to act as his own destroyer—and that is the way he has acted through most of his history.

"A living entity that regarded its means of survival as evil, would not survive. A plant that struggled to mangle its roots, a bird that fought to break its wings would not remain for long in the existence they affronted. But the history of man has been a struggle to deny and to destroy his mind.

"Man has been called a rational being, but rationality is a matter of choice—and the alternative his nature offers him is: rational being or suicidal animal. Man has to be man—by choice; he has to hold his life as a value—by choice; he has to learn to sustain it—by choice; he has to discover the values it requires and practice his virtues—by choice.

"A code of values accepted by choice is a code of morality.

"Whoever you are, you who are hearing me now, I am speaking to whatever living remnant is left uncorrupted within you, to the remnant of the human, to your *mind,* and I say: There *is* a morality of reason, a morality proper to man, and *Man's Life* is its standard of value.

"All that which is proper to the life of a rational being is the good; all that which destroys it is the evil.

"Man's life, as required by his nature, is not the life of a mindless brute, of a looting thug or a mooching mystic, but the life of a thinking being—not life by means of force or fraud, but life by means of achievement—not survival at any price, since there's only one price that pays for man's survival: reason.

"Man's life is the *standard* of morality, but your own life is its *purpose.* If existence on earth is your goal, you must choose your actions and values by the standard of that which is proper to man—for the purpose of preserving, fulfilling and enjoying the irreplaceable value which is your life.

"Since life requires a specific course of action, any other course will destroy it. A being who does not hold his own life as the motive and goal of his actions is acting on the motive and standard of *death.* Such a being is a metaphysical monstrosity, struggling to oppose, negate, and contradict the fact of his own existence, running blindly amuck on a trail of destruction, capable of nothing but pain.

"Happiness is the successful state of life; pain is an agent of death. Happiness is that state of unconsciousness which proceeds from the achievement of one's values. A morality that dares to tell you to find happiness in the renunciation of your happiness—to value the failure of your values—is an insolent negation of morality. A doctrine that gives you, as an ideal, the role of a sacrificial animal seeking slaughter on the altars of others, is giving you *death* as your standard. By the grace

of reality and the nature of life, man—every man—is an end in himself, he exists for his own sake, and the achievement of his own happiness is his highest moral purpose.

"But neither life nor happiness can be achieved by the pursuit of irrational whims. Just as man is free to attempt to survive in any random manner, but will perish unless he lives as his nature requires, so he is free to seek his happiness in any mindless fraud, but the torture of frustration is all he will find, unless he seeks the happiness proper to man. The purpose of morality is to teach you, not to suffer and die, but to enjoy yourself and love.

"Sweep aside those parasites of subsidized classrooms, who live on the profits of the mind of others and proclaim that man needs no morality, no values, no code of behavior. They, who pose as scientists and claim that man is only an animal, do not grant him inclusion in the law of existence they have granted to the lowest of insects. They recognize that every living species has a way of survival demanded by its nature, they do not claim that a fish can live out of water or that a dog can live without its sense of smell—but man, they claim, the most complex of beings, man can survive in any way whatever, man has no identity, no nature, and there's no practical reason why he cannot live with his means of survival destroyed, with his mind throttled and placed at the disposal of any orders *they* might care to issue.

"Sweep aside those hatred-eaten mystics who pose as friends of humanity and preach that the highest virtue man can practice is to hold his own life as of no value. Do they tell you that the purpose of morality is to curb man's instinct of self-preservation? It is for the purpose of self-preservation that man needs a code of morality. The only man who desires to be moral is the man who desires to live.

"No, you do not have to live; it is your basic act of choice; but if you choose to live, you must live as a man—by the work and the judgment of your mind.

"No, you do not have to live as a man: it is an

act of moral choice. But you cannot live as anything else—and the alternative is that state of living death which you now see within you and around you, the state of a thing unfit for existence, no longer human and less than animal, a thing that knows nothing but pain and drags itself through its span of years in the agony of unthinking self-destruction.

"No, you do not have to think; it is an act of moral choice. But someone had to think to keep you alive; if you choose to default, you default on existence and you pass the deficit to some moral man, expecting him to sacrifice his good for the sake of letting you survive by your evil. . . .

"This much is true: the most *selfish* of all things is the independent mind that recognizes no authority higher than its own and no value higher than its judgment of truth. You are asked to sacrifice your intellectual integrity, your logic, your reason, your standard of truth—in favor of becoming a prostitute whose standard is the greatest good for the greatest number.

"If you search your code for guidance, for an answer to the question: 'What *is* the good?'—the only answer you will find is *'The good of others.'* The good is whatever others wish, whatever you feel they feel they wish, or whatever you feel they ought to feel. 'The good of others' is a magic formula that transforms anything into gold, a formula to be recited as a guarantee of moral glory and as a fumigator for any action, even the slaughter of a continent. Your standard of virtue is not an object, not an act, nor a principle, but an *intention*. You need no proof, no reasons, no success, you need not achieve *in fact* the good of others—all you need to know is that your motive was the good of others, *not* your own. Your only definition of the good is a negation: the good is the 'non-good for me.'

"Your code—which boasts that it upholds eternal, absolute, objective moral values and scorns the conditional, the relative and the subjective—your code hands out, as its version of the absolute, the following rule of moral conduct: If *you* wish it, it's evil; if others wish it, it's good; if the motive of your action is *your* welfare, don't do it;

if the motive is the welfare of others, then anything goes.

"As this double-jointed, double-standard morality splits you in half, so it splits mankind into two enemy camps: one is *you*, the other is all the rest of humanity. *You* are the only outcast who has no right to wish or live. *You* are the only servant, the rest are the masters, *you* are the only giver, the rest are the takers, *you* are the eternal debtor, the rest are the creditors never to be paid off. You must not question their right to your sacrifice, or the nature of their wishes and their needs: their right is conferred upon them by a negative, by the fact that they are 'non-you.'

"For those of you who might ask questions, your code provides a consolation prize and booby-trap: it is for your own happiness, it says, that you must serve the happiness of others, the only way to achieve your joy is to give it up to others, the only way to achieve your prosperity is to surrender your wealth to others, the only way to protect your life is to protect all men except yourself—and if you find no joy in this procedure, it is your own fault and the proof of your evil; if you were good, you would find your happiness in providing a banquet for others, and your dignity in existing on such crumbs as *they* might care to toss you.

"You who have no standard of self-esteem, accept the guilt and dare not ask the questions. But you know the unadmitted answer, refusing to acknowledge what you see, what hidden premise moves your world. You know it, not in honest statement, but as a dark uneasiness within you, while you flounder between guiltily cheating and grudgingly practicing a principle too vicious to name.

"I, who do not accept the unearned, neither in values nor in *guilt*, am here to ask the questions you evaded. Why is it moral to serve the happiness of others, but not your own? If enjoyment is a value, why is it moral when experienced by others, but immoral when experienced by you? If the sensation of eating a cake is a value, why is it an immoral indulgence in your stomach, but a moral goal for you to achieve in the stomach of others?

Why is it immoral for you to desire, but moral for others to do so? Why is it immoral to produce a value and keep it, but moral to give it away? And if it is not moral for you to keep a value, why is it moral for others to accept it? If you are selfless and virtuous when you give it, are they not selfish and vicious when they take it? Does virtue consist of serving vice? Is the moral purpose of those who are good, self-immolation for the sake of those who are evil? . . .

"Under a morality of sacrifice, the first value you sacrifice is morality; the next is self-esteem. When need is the standard, every man is both victim and parasite. As a victim, he must labor to fill the needs of others, leaving himself in the position of a parasite whose needs must be filled by others. He cannot approach his fellow men except in one of two disgraceful roles: he is both a beggar and a sucker.

"You fear the man who has a dollar less than you, that dollar is rightfully his, he makes you feel like a moral defrauder. You hate the man who has a dollar more than you, that dollar is rightfully yours, he makes you feel that you are morally defrauded. The man below is a source of your guilt, the man above is a source of your frustration. You do not know what to surrender or demand, when to give and when to grab, what pleasure in life is rightfully yours and what debt is still unpaid to others—you struggle to evade, as 'theory,' the knowledge that by the moral standard you've accepted you are guilty every moment of your life, there is no mouthful of food you swallow that is not *needed* by someone somewhere on earth—and you give up the problem in blind resentment, you conclude that moral perfection is not to be achieved *or desired*, that you will muddle through by snatching as snatch can and by avoiding the eyes of the young, of those who look at you as if self-esteem were possible and they expected you to have it. Guilt is all that you retain within your soul—and so does every other man, as he goes past, avoiding *your* eyes. Do you wonder why your morality has not achieved brotherhood on earth or the good will of man to man?

"The justification of sacrifice, that your moral-

ity propounds, is more corrupt than the corruption it purports to justify. The motive of your sacrifice, it tells you, should be *love*—the love you ought to feel for every man. A morality that professes the belief that the values of the spirit are more precious than matter, a morality that teaches you to scorn a whore who gives her body indiscriminately to all men—this same morality demands that you surrender your soul to promiscuous love for all comers.

"As there can be no causeless wealth, so there can be no causeless love or any sort of causeless emotion. An emotion is a response to a fact of reality, an estimate dictated by your standards. To love is to *value*. The man who tells you that it is possible to value without values, to love those whom you appraise as worthless, is the man who tells you that it is possible to grow rich by consuming without producing and that paper money is as valuable as gold.

"Observe that he does not expect you to feel a causeless fear. When his kind get into power, they are expert at contriving means of terror, at giving you ample cause to feel the fear by which they desire to rule you. But when it comes to love, the highest of emotions, you permit them to shriek at you accusingly that you are a moral delinquent if you're incapable of feeling causeless love. When a man feels fear without reason, you call him to the attention of a psychiatrist; you are not so careful to protect the meaning, the nature and the dignity of love.

"Love is the expression of one's values, the greatest reward you can earn for the moral qualities you have achieved in your character and person, the emotional price paid by one man for the joy he receives from the virtues of another. Your morality demands that you divorce your love from values and hand it down to any vagrant, not as response to his worth, but as response to his *need*, not as reward, but as alms, not as a payment for virtues, but as a blank check on vices. Your morality tells you that the purpose of love is to set you free of the bonds of morality, that love is superior to moral judgment, that true love transcends, forgives and survives every manner of evil in its object, and the greater the love the greater the depravity it permits to the loved. To love a man for his virtues is paltry and human, it tells you; to love him for his flaws is divine. To love those who are worthy of it is self-interest; to love the unworthy is sacrifice. You owe your love to those who don't deserve it, and the less they deserve it, the more love you owe them—the more loathsome the object, the nobler your love—the more unfastidious your love, the greater your virtue—and if you can bring your soul to the state of a dump heap that welcomes anything on equal terms, if you can cease to value moral values, you have achieved the state of moral perfection.

"Such is your morality of sacrifice and such are the twin ideals it offers: to refashion the life of your body in the image of a human stockyards, and the life of your spirit in the image of a dump. . . .

"Since childhood, you have been hiding the guilty secret that you feel no desire to be moral, no desire to seek self-immolation, that you dread and hate your code, but dare not say it even to yourself, that you're devoid of those moral 'instincts' which others profess to feel. The less you felt, the louder you proclaimed your selfless love and servitude to others, in dread of ever letting them discover your own self, the self that you betrayed, the self that you kept in concealment, like a skeleton in the closet of your body. And they, who were at once your dupes and your deceivers, they listened and voiced their loud approval, in dread of ever letting you discover that they were harboring the same unspoken secret. Existence among you is a giant pretense, an act you all perform for one another, each feeling that he is the only guilty freak, each placing his moral authority in the unknowable known only to others, each faking the reality he feels they expect him to fake, none having the courage to break the vicious circle.

"No matter what dishonorable compromise you've made with your impracticable creed, no matter what miserable balance, half-cynicism, half-superstition, you now manage to maintain, you still preserve the root, the lethal tenet: the belief that the moral and the practical are opposites. Since childhood, you have been running from the terror of a choice you have never dared fully to identify: If the *practical*, whatever you must practice to exist, whatever works, succeeds, achieves your purpose, whatever brings you food and joy, whatever profits you is evil—and if the good, the moral is the *impractical*, whatever fails, destroys, frustrates, whatever injures you and brings you loss or pain—then your choice is to be moral or to live.

"The sole result of that murderous doctrine was to remove morality from life. You grew up to believe that moral laws bear no relation to the job of living, except as an impediment and threat, that man's existence is an amoral jungle where anything goes and anything works. And in that fog of switching definitions which descends upon a frozen mind, you have forgotten that the evils damned by your creed were the virtues required for living, and you have come to believe that actual evils are the *practical* means of existence. Forgetting that the impractical 'good' was self-sacrifice, you believe that self-esteem is impractical; forgetting that the practical 'evil' was production, you believe that robbery is practical. . . .

"Accept the fact that the achievement of your happiness is the only *moral* purpose of your life, and that *happiness*—not pain or mindless self-indulgence—is the proof of your moral integrity, since it is the proof and the result of your loyalty to the achievement of your values. Happiness was the responsibility you dreaded, it required the kind of rational discipline you did not value yourself enough to assume—and the anxious staleness of your days is the monument to your evasion of the knowledge that there is no moral substitute for happiness, that there is no more despicable coward than the man who deserted the battle for his joy, fearing to assert his right to existence, lacking the courage and the loyalty to life of a bird or a flower reaching for the sun. Discard the protective rags of that vice which you called a virtue: humility—learn to value yourself, which means: to fight for your happiness—and when you learn that *pride* is the sum of all virtues, you will learn to live like a man.

"As a basic step of self-esteem, learn to treat as the mark of a cannibal any man's *demand* for your help. To demand it is to claim that your life is *his* property—and loathsome as such claim might be,

there's something still more loathsome: your agreement. Do you ask if it's ever proper to help another man? No—if he claims it as his right or as a moral duty that you owe him. Yes—if such is your own desire based on your own selfish pleasure in the value of his person and his struggle.

9

A Critique of Ethical Egoism

JAMES RACHELS

James Rachels is professor of philosophy at the University of Alabama and is the author of several articles in moral philosophy. He is the author of The End of Life: Euthanasia and Morality *and* The Elements of Moral Philosophy, *from which the present essay is taken. In this succinct essay Rachels first distinguishes ethical egoism, the doctrine that it is always our duty to act exclusively in our self-interest, from psychological egoism, the doctrine that people always act out of their own perceived self-interest. He examines three arguments in favor of ethical egoism showing that each fails to support its conclusion, and then examines three arguments against the doctrine. He argues that only one of these is sound, but it is enough to invalidate ethical egoism.*

Is There a Duty to Contribute for Famine Relief?

Each year millions of people die of malnutrition and related health problems. A common pattern among children in poor countries is death from dehydration caused by diarrhea brought on by malnutrition. James Grant, executive director of the United Nations Children's Fund (UNICEF), estimates that about 15,000 children die in this way *every day.* That comes to 5,475,000 children annually. Even if his estimate is too high, the number that die is staggering.

For those of us in the affluent countries, this poses an acute moral problem. We spend money on ourselves, not only for the necessities of life but for innumerable luxuries—for fine automobiles, fancy clothes, stereos, sports, movies, and

Reprinted from *The Elements of Moral Philosophy* (New York: Random House, 1986) by permission of McGraw-Hill Publishing Company and the author.

so on. In our country, even people with modest incomes enjoy such things. The problem is that we *could* forgo our luxuries and give the money for famine relief instead. The fact that we don't suggests that we regard our luxuries as more important than feeding the hungry.

Why do we allow people to starve to death when we could save them? Very few of us actually believe our luxuries are that important. Most of us, if asked the question directly, would probably be a bit embarrassed, and we would say that we probably should do more for famine relief. The explanation of why we do not is, at least in part, that we hardly ever think of the problem. Living our own comfortable lives, we are effectively insulated from it. The starving people are dying at some distance from us; we do not see them, and we can avoid even thinking of them. When we do think of them, it is only abstractly, as bloodless statistics. Unfortunately for the starving, statistics do not have much power to motivate action.

But leaving aside the question of *why* we behave as we do, what is our *duty*? What *should* we do? We might think of this as the "common-sense" view of the matter: morality requires that we balance our own interests against the interests of others. It is understandable, of course, that we look out for our own interests, and no one can be faulted for attending to his own basic needs. But at the same time the needs of others are also important, and when we can help others— especially at little cost to ourselves—we should do so. Suppose you are thinking of spending ten dollars on a trip to the movies, when you are reminded that ten dollars could buy food for a starving child. Thus you could do a great service for the child at little cost to yourself. Commonsense morality would say, then, that you should give the money for famine relief rather than spending it on the movies.

This way of thinking involves a general assumption about our moral duties: it is assumed that we have moral duties *to other people*—and not merely duties that we create, such as by making a promise or incurring a debt. We have "natural" duties to others *simply because they are people who could be helped or harmed by our actions.* If a certain action would benefit (or harm) other people, then that is a reason why we should (or should not) do that action. The common-sense assumption is that other people's interests *count,* for their own sakes, from a moral point of view.

But one person's common sense is another person's naive platitude. Some thinkers have maintained that, in fact, we have no "natural" duties to other people. *Ethical Egoism* is the idea that each person ought to pursue his or her own self-interest exclusively. It is different from Psychological Egoism, which is a theory of human nature concerned with how people *do* behave—Psychological Egoism says that people do in fact always pursue their own interests. Ethical Egoism, by contrast, is a normative theory—that is, a theory about how we *ought* to behave. Regardless of how we do behave, Ethical Egoism says we have no moral duty except to do what is best for ourselves.

It is a challenging theory. It contradicts some of our deepest moral beliefs—beliefs held by most of us, at any rate—but it is not easy to refute. We will examine the most important arguments for and against it. If it turns out to be true, then of course that is immensely important. But even if it turns out to be false, there is still much to be learned from examining it—we may, for example, gain some insight into the reasons why we *do* have obligations to other people.

But before looking at the arguments, we should be a little clearer about exactly what this theory says and what it does not say. In the first place, Ethical Egoism does not say that one should promote one's own interests *as well as* the interests of others. That would be an ordinary, unexceptional view. Ethical Egoism is the radical view that one's *only* duty is to promote one's own interests. According to Ethical Egoism, there is only one ultimate principle of conduct, the principle of self-interest, and this principle sums up *all* of one's natural duties and obligations.

However, Ethical Egoism does not say that you should *avoid* actions that help others, either. It may very well be that in many instances your interests coincide with the interests of others, so that in helping yourself you will be aiding others willy-nilly. Or it may happen that aiding others is an effective *means* for creating some benefit for yourself. Ethical Egoism does not forbid such actions; in fact, it may demand them. The theory insists only that in such cases the benefit to others is not what makes the act right. What makes the act right is, rather, the fact that it is to one's own advantage.

Finally, Ethical Egoism does not imply that in pursuing one's interests one ought always to do what one wants to do, or what gives one the most pleasure in the short run. Someone may want to do something that is not good for himself or that will eventually cause himself more grief than pleasure—he may want to drink a lot or smoke cigarettes or take drugs or waste his best years at the race track. Ethical Egoism would frown on all this, regardless of the momentary pleasure it affords. It says that a person ought to do what *really is* to his or her own best advantage, *over the long run.* It endorses selfishness but it doesn't endorse foolishness.

Three Arguments in Favor of Ethical Egoism

What reasons can be advanced to support this doctrine? Why should anyone think it is true? Unfortunately, the theory is asserted more often than it is argued for. Many of its supporters apparently think its truth is self-evident, so that arguments are not needed. When it *is* argued for, three lines of reasoning are most commonly used.

1. The first argument has several variations, each suggesting the same general point:

a. Each of us is intimately familiar with our own individual wants and needs. Moreover, each of us is uniquely placed to pursue those wants and needs effectively. At the same time, we know the desires and needs of other people only imperfectly, and we are not well situated to pursue them. Therefore, it is reasonable to believe that if we set out to be "our brother's keeper," we would often bungle the job and end up doing more mischief than good.

b. At the same time, the policy of "looking out for others" is an offensive intrusion into other people's privacy; it is essentially a policy of minding other people's business.

c. Making other people the object of one's "charity" is degrading to them; it robs them of their individual dignity and self-respect. The offer of charity says, in effect, that they are not competent to care for themselves; and the statement is self-fulfilling—they cease to be self-reliant and become passively dependent on others. That is why the recipients of "charity" are so often resentful rather than appreciative.

What this adds up to is that the policy of "looking out for others" is self-defeating. If we want to promote the best interests of everyone alike, we should *not* adopt so-called altruistic policies of behavior. On the contrary, if each person looks after his or her *own* interests, it is more likely that everyone will be better off, in terms of both physical and emotional well-being. Thus Robert G. Olson says in his book *The Morality of Self-Interest* (1965), "The individual is most likely to contribute to social betterment by rationally pursuing his own best long-range interests." Or as Alexander Pope said more poetically,

Thus God and nature formed the general frame
And bade self-love and social be the same.

It is possible to quarrel with this argument on a number of grounds. Of course no one favors bungling, butting in, or depriving people of their self-respect. But is this really what we are doing when we feed hungry children? Is the starving child in Ethiopia really harmed when we "intrude" into "her business" by supplying food? It hardly seems likely. Yet we can set this point aside, for considered as an argument for Ethical Egoism, this way of thinking has an even more serious defect.

The trouble is that it isn't really an argument *for Ethical Egoism* at all. The argument concludes that we should adopt certain policies of action; and on the surface they appear to be egoistic policies. However, the *reason* it is said we should adopt those policies is decidedly *un*egoistic. The reason is one that to an egoist shouldn't matter. It is said that we should adopt those policies because doing so will promote the "betterment of society"—but according to Ethical Egoism, that is something we should not be concerned about. Spelled out fully, with everything laid on the table, the argument says:

1. We ought to do whatever will promote the best interests of everyone alike.
2. The interests of everyone will best be promoted if each of us adopts the policy of pursuing our own interests exclusively.
3. Therefore, each of us should adopt the policy of pursuing our own interests exclusively.

If we accept this reasoning, then we are not ethical egoists at all. Even though we might end up *behaving* like egoists, our ultimate principle is one of beneficence—we are doing what we think will help everyone, not merely what we think will benefit ourselves. Rather than being egoists, we turn out to be altruists with a peculiar view of what in fact promotes the general welfare.

2. The second argument was put forward with some force by Ayn Rand, a writer little heeded by professional philosophers but who nevertheless was enormously popular on college campuses during the 1960s and 1970s. Ethical Egoism, in her view, is the only ethical philosophy that respects the integrity of the individual human life. She regarded the ethics of "altruism" as a totally destructive idea, both in society as a whole and in

the lives of individuals taken in by it. Altruism, to her way of thinking, leads to a denial of the value of the individual. It says to a person: *your* life is merely something that may be sacrificed. "If a man accepts the ethics of altruism," she writes, "his first concern is not how to live his life, but how to sacrifice it." Moreover, those who would *promote* this idea are beneath contempt—they are parasites who, rather than working to build and sustain their own lives, leech off those who do. Again, she writes:

Parasites, moochers, looters, brutes and thugs can be of no value to a human being—nor can he gain any benefit from living in a society geared to *their* needs, demands and protections, a society that treats him as a sacrificial animal and penalizes him for his virtues in order to reward *them* for their vices, which means: a society based on the ethics of altruism.

By "sacrificing one's life" Rand does not necessarily mean anything so dramatic as dying. A person's life consists (in part) of projects undertaken and goods earned and created. To demand that a person abandon his projects or give up his goods is also a clear effort to "sacrifice his life." Furthermore, throughout her writings Rand also suggests that there is a *metaphysical* basis for egoistic ethics. Somehow, it is the only ethics that takes seriously the *reality* of the individual person. She bemoans "the enormity of the extent to which altruism erodes men's capacity to grasp . . . the value of an individual life; it reveals a mind from which the reality of a human being has been wiped out."

What, then, of the starving people? It might be argued, in response, that Ethical Egoism "reveals a mind from which the reality of a human being has been wiped out"—namely, the human being who is starving. Rand quotes with approval the evasive answer given by one of her followers: "Once, when Barbara Brandon was asked by a student: 'What will happen to the poor . . . ?'—she answered: 'If *you* want to help them, you will not be stopped.'"

All these remarks are, I think, part of one continuous argument that can be summarized like this:

1. A person has only one life to live. If we place any value on the individual—that is, if the individual has any moral worth—then we must agree that this life is of supreme importance. After all, it is all one has, and all one is.
2. The ethics of altruism regards the life of the individual as something one must be ready to sacrifice for the good of others.
3. Therefore, the ethics of altruism does not take seriously the value of the human individual.
4. Ethical Egoism, which allows each person to view his or her own life as being of ultimate value, *does* take the human individual seriously—in fact, it is the only philosophy that does so.
5. Thus, Ethical Egoism is the philosophy that ought to be accepted.

The problem with this argument, as you may already have noticed, is that it relies on picturing the alternatives in such an extreme way. "The ethics of altruism" is taken to be such an extreme philosophy that *nobody,* with the possible exception of certain monks, would find it congenial. As Ayn Rand presents it, altruism implies that one's own interests have *no* value, and that *any* demand by others calls for sacrificing them. If that is the alternative, then any other view, including Ethical Egoism, will look good by comparison. But this is hardly a fair picture of the choices. What we called the common-sense view stands somewhere between the two extremes. It says that one's own interests and the interests of others are both important and must be balanced against one another. Sometimes, when the balancing is done, it will turn out that one should act in the interests of others; other times, it will turn out that one should take care of oneself. So even if the Randian argument refutes the extreme "ethics of altruism," it does not follow that one must accept the other extreme of Ethical Egoism.

3. The third line of reasoning takes a somewhat different approach. Ethical Egoism is usually presented as a *revisionist* moral philosophy, that is, as a philosophy that says our common-sense moral views are mistaken and need to be changed. It is possible, however, to interpret Ethical Egoism in a much less radical way, as a theory that *accepts* common-sense morality and offers a surprising account of its basis.

The less radical interpretation goes as follows. In everyday life, we assume that we are obliged to obey certain rules. We must avoid doing harm to others, speak the truth, keep our promises, and so on. At first glance, these duties appear to be very different from one another. They appear to have little in common. Yet from a theoretical point of view, we may wonder whether there is not some hidden *unity* underlying the hodge-podge of separate duties. Perhaps there is some small number of fundamental principles that explain all the rest, just as in physics there are basic principles that bring together and explain diverse phenomena. From a theoretical point of view, the smaller the number of basic principles, the better. Best of all would be *one* fundamental principle, from which all the rest could be derived. Ethical Egoism, then, would be the theory that all our duties are ultimately derived from the one fundamental principle of self-interest.

Taken in this way, Ethical Egoism is not such a radical doctrine. It does not challenge common-sense morality; it only tries to explain and systematize it. And it does a surprisingly successful job. It can provide plausible explanations of the duties mentioned above, and more:

a. If we make a habit of doing things that are harmful to other people, people will not be reluctant to do things that will harm *us*. We will be shunned and despised; others will not have us as friends and will not do us favors when we need them. If our offenses against others are serious enough, we may even end up in jail. Thus it is to our own advantage to avoid harming others.

b. If we lie to other people, we will suffer all the ill effects of a bad reputation. People will distrust us and avoid doing business with us. We will often need for people to be honest with us, but we can hardly expect them to feel much of an obligation to be honest with us if they know we have not been honest with them. Thus it is to our own advantage to be truthful.

c. It is to our own advantage to be able to enter into mutually beneficial arrangements with other people. To benefit from those arrangements, we need to be able to rely on others to keep their parts of the bargains we make with them—we need to be able to rely on them to keep their promises to us. But we can hardly expect others to keep their promises to us if we are not willing to keep our promises to them. Therefore, from the point of view of self-interest, we should keep our promises.

Pursuing this line of reasoning, Thomas Hobbes suggested that the principle of Ethical Egoism leads to nothing less than the Golden Rule: we should "do unto others" *because* if we do, others will be more likely to "do unto us."

Does this argument succeed in establishing Ethical Egoism as a viable theory of morality? It is, in my opinion at least, the best try. But there are two serious objections to it. In the first place, the argument does not prove quite as much as it needs to prove. At best, it shows only that *as a general rule* it is to one's own advantage to avoid harming others. It does not show that this is *always* so. And it could not show that, for even though it may usually be to one's advantage to avoid harming others, sometimes it is not. Sometimes one might even *gain* from treating another person badly. In that case, the obligation not to harm the other person could *not* be derived from the principle of Ethical Egoism. Thus it appears that not all our moral obligations can be explained as derivable from self-interest.

But set that point aside. There is still a more fundamental question to be asked about the proposed theory. Suppose it is true that, say, contributing money for famine relief is somehow to one's own advantage. It does not follow that this is the only reason, or even the most basic reason, why doing so is a morally good thing. (For example, the most basic reason might be *in order to help the starving people.* The fact that doing so is also to one's own advantage might be only a secondary, less important, consideration.) A demonstration that one could *derive* this duty from self-interest does not prove that self-interest is the *only reason* one has this duty. Only if you accept an additional proposition—namely, the proposition that there is no reason for giving *other than* self-interest—will you find Ethical Egoism a plausible theory.

Three Arguments against Ethical Egoism

Ethical Egoism has haunted twentieth-century moral philosophy. It has not been a popular doctrine; the most important philosophers have rejected it outright. But it has never been very far from their minds. Although no thinker of consequence has defended it, almost everyone has felt it necessary to explain why he was rejecting it—as though the very possibility that it might be correct was hanging in the air, threatening to smother their other ideas. As the merits of the various "refutations" have been debated, philosophers have returned to it again and again.

The following three arguments are typical of the refutations proposed by contemporary philosophers.

1. In his book *The Moral Point of View* (1958), Kurt Baier argues that Ethical Egoism cannot be correct because it cannot provide solutions for conflicts of interest. We need moral rules, he says, only because our interests sometimes come into conflict. (If they never conflicted, then there would be no problems to solve and hence no need for the kind of guidance that morality provides.) But Ethical Egoism does not help to resolve conflicts of interest; it only exacerbates them. Baier argues for this by introducing a fanciful example:

Let B and K be candidates for the presidency of a certain country and let it be granted that it is in the interest of either to be elected, but that only one can succeed. It would then be in the interest of B but against the interest of K if B were elected, and vice versa, and therefore in the interest of B but against the interest of K if K were liquidated, and vice versa. But from this it would follow that B ought to liquidate K, that it is wrong for B not to do so, that B has not "done his duty" until he has liquidated K; and vice versa. Similarly K, knowing that his own liquidation is in the interest of B and therefore, anticipating B's attempts to secure it, ought to take steps to foil B's endeavors. It would be wrong for him not to do so. He would "not have done his duty" until he had made sure of stopping B. . . .

This is obviously absurd. For morality is designed to apply in just such cases, namely, those where interests conflict. But if the point of view of morality were that of self-interest, then there could never be moral solutions of conflicts of interest.

Does this argument prove that Ethical Egoism is unacceptable? It does, *if* the conception of morality to which it appeals is accepted. The argument assumes that an adequate morality must provide solutions for conflicts of interest in such a way that everyone concerned can live together harmoniously. The conflict between B and K, for example, should be resolved so that they would no longer be at odds with one another. (One would not then have a duty to do something that the other has a duty to prevent.) Ethical Egoism does not do that, and if you think an ethical theory should, then you will not find Ethical Egoism acceptable.

But a defender of Ethical Egoism might reply that *he* does not accept this conception of morality. For him, life is essentially a long series of conflicts in which each person is struggling to come out on top; and the principle he accepts— the principle of Ethical Egoism—simply urges each one to do his or her best to win. On his view, the moralist is not like a courtroom judge, who resolves disputes. Instead, he is like the Commissioner of Boxing, who urges each fighter to do his best. So the conflict between B and K will be "resolved" not by the application of an ethical theory but by one or the other of them winning the struggle. The egoist will not be embarrassed by this—on the contary, he will think it no more than a realistic view of the nature of things.

2. Some philosophers, including Baier, have leveled an even more serious charge against Ethical Egoism. They have argued that it is a *logically inconsistent* doctrine—that is, they say it leads to logical contradictions. If this is true, then Ethical Egoism is indeed a mistaken theory, for no theory can be true if it is self-contradictory.

Consider B and K again. As Baier explains their predicament, it is in B's interest to kill K, and obviously it is in K's interest to prevent it. But, Baier says,

if K prevents B from liquidating him, his act must be said to be both wrong and not wrong—wrong because it is the prevention of what B ought to do, his duty, and wrong for B not to do it; not wrong because it is what K ought to do, his duty, and wrong for K not to do it. But one and the same act (logically) cannot be both morally wrong and not morally wrong.

Now, does *this* argument prove that Ethical Egoism is unacceptable? At first glance it seems persuasive. However, it is a complicated argument, so we need to set it out with each step individually identified. Then we will be in a better position to evaluate it. Spelled out fully, it looks like this:

1. Suppose it is each person's duty to do what is in his own best interests.
2. It is in B's best interest to liquidate K.
3. It is in K's best interest to prevent B from liquidating him.
4. Therefore B's duty is to liquidate K, and K's duty is to prevent B from doing it.
5. But it is wrong to prevent someone from doing his duty.
6. Therefore it is wrong for K to prevent B from liquidating him.
7. Therefore it is both wrong and not wrong for K to prevent B from liquidating him.
8. But no act can be both wrong and not wrong—that is a self-contradiction.
9. Therefore the assumption with which we started—that it is each person's duty to do what is in his own best interests—cannot be true.

When the argument is set out in this way, we can see its hidden flaw. The logical contradiction—that it is both wrong and not wrong for K to prevent B from liquidating him—does *not* follow simply from the principle of Ethical Egoism. It follows from that principle, *and* the additional premise expressed in step (5)—namely, that "it is wrong to prevent someone from doing his duty." Thus we are not compelled by the logic of the argument to reject Ethical Egoism. Instead, we could simply reject this additional premise, and the contradiction would be avoided. That is surely what the ethical egoist would want to do, for the ethical egoist would never say, without qualification, that it is always wrong to prevent someone from doing his duty. He would say, instead, that *whether one ought to prevent someone from doing his duty depends entirely on whether it would be to one's own advantage to do so.* Regardless of whether we think this is a correct view, it is, at the very least, a *consistent* view, and so this attempt to convict the egoist of self-contradiction fails.

3. Finally, we come to the argument that I think comes closest to an outright refutation of Ethical Egoism. It is also the most interesting of the arguments, because at the same time it provides the most insight into why the interests of other people *should* matter to a moral agent.

Before this argument is presented, we need to look briefly at a general point about moral values. So let us set Ethical Egoism aside for a moment and consider this related matter.

There is a whole family of moral views that have this in common: they all involve dividing people into groups and saying that the interests of some groups count for more than the interests of other groups. Racism is the most conspicuous example; it involves dividing people into groups according to race and assigning greater importance to the interests of one race than to others. The practical result is that members of the preferred race are to be *treated better* than the others. Anti-Semitism works the same way, and so can nationalism. People in the grip of such views will think, in effect: "*My* race counts for more," or "Those who believe in *my* religion count for more," or "*My* country counts for more," and so on.

Can such views be defended? Those who accept them are usually not much interested in argument—racists, for example, rarely try to offer rational grounds for their position. But suppose they did. What could they say?

There is a general principle that stands in the way of any such defense, namely: *We can justify treating people differently only if we can show that there is some factual difference between them that is relevant to justifying the difference in treatment.* For example, if one person is admitted to law school while another is rejected, this can be justified by pointing out that the first graduated from college with honors and scored well on the admissions test, while the second dropped out of college and never took the test. However, if *both* graduated with honors and did well on the entrance examination—in other words, if they are in all relevant respects equally well qualified—then it is merely arbitrary to admit one but not the other.

Can a racist point to any differences between, say, white people and black people that would justify treating them differently? In the past, racists have sometimes attempted to do this by picturing blacks as stupid, lacking in ambition, and the like. *If* this were true, then it might justify treating them differently, in at least some circumstances. (This is the deep purpose of racist stereotypes—to provide the "relevant differences" needed to justify differences in treatment.) But of course it is not true, and in fact there are no such general differences between the races. Thus racism is an *arbitrary* doctrine, in that it advocates treating some people differently even though there are no differences between them to justify it.

Ethical Egoism is a moral theory of the same type. It advocates that each of us divide the world into two categories of people—ourselves and all the rest—and that we regard the interests of those in the first group as more important than the interests of those in the second group. But each of us can ask, what is the difference between myself and others that justifies placing myself in this special category? Am I more intelligent? Do I

enjoy my life more? Are my accomplishments greater? Do I have needs or abilities that are so different from the needs or abilities of others? *What is it that makes me so special?* Failing an answer, it turns out that Ethical Egoism is an arbitrary doctrine, in the same way that racism is arbitrary.

The argument, then, is this:

1. Any moral doctrine that assigns greater importance to the interests of one group than to those of another is unacceptably arbitrary unless there is some difference between the members of the groups that justifies treating them differently.

2. Ethical Egoism would have each person assign greater importance to his or her own interests than to the interests of others. *But there is no general difference between oneself and others, to which each person can appeal, that justifies this difference in treatment.*

3. Therefore, Ethical Egoism is unacceptably arbitrary.

And this, in addition to arguing against Ethical Egoism, also sheds some light on the question of why we should care about others.

We should care about the interests of other people *for the very same reason we care about our own interests;* for their needs and desires are comparable to our own. Consider, one last time, the starving people we could feed by giving up some of our luxuries. Why should we care about them? We care about ourselves, of course—if *we* were starving, we would go to almost any lengths to get food. But what is the difference between us and them? Does hunger affect tham any less? Are they somehow less deserving than we? If we can find no relevant difference between us and them, then we must admit that if *our* needs should be met, so should *theirs*. It is this realization, that we are on a par with one another, that is the deepest reason why our morality must include some recognition of the needs of others, and why, then, Ethical Egoism fails as a moral theory.

10

Sociobiology, Egoism, and Reciprocity

HOWARD KAHANE

Howard Kahane, until his recent retirement, was professor of philosophy at the University of Maryland Baltimore County. He is the author of several works in philosophy, including Logic and Contemporary Rhetoric *and* Logic and Philosophy.

Egoists are right in insisting that it is rational to try to maximize one's own desires, but wrong in forgetting that most of us have strong desires favoring fair play, justice, and the like, whose satisfaction sometimes requires us to act contrary to egoistic principles. But when does this happen? And what are the principles of fair play and justice that we desire to satisfy? Recent sociobiological theories suggest answers to these questions based on ideas concerning reciprocal altruism and the evolution of moral and other regarding sentiments. Moral sentiments evolved, on this view, because of the tremendous benefits of cooperative behavior. That is why, for most of us, at any rate, playing the game fair and square means, roughly speaking, not taking advantage of others by making unfair agreements, and keeping (uncoerced) agreements, implicit as well as explicit, when others can be expected to do so in return. We see agreements as competitively fair *only if they treat all competitors in the same way and thus do not favor one party compared to others, and as* cooperatively fair *only if they distribute the benefits of cooperative ventures according to the time, wealth, effective effort, and so on, each party contributes. In addition, evolutionary forces have instilled in most of us a desire for retribution—a desire to strike back at those who betray us by failing to keep fair agreements—and sentiments of empathy, compassion, affection, and the like, that tend to motivate the keeping of fair agree-*

ments and the friendliness and trust that make for reasonably well functioning societies. Homo sapiens *having evolved as an in-group–out-group social animal.*

It must not be forgotten that although a high standard of morality gives but a slight or no advantage to each individual man and his children over the other men of the same tribe, yet that an increase in the number of well-endowed men and an advancement in the standard of morality will certainly give an immense advantage to one tribe over another. . . . [T]he standard of morality and the number of well-endowed men will thus everywhere tend to rise and increase.

—Charles Darwin

Crito, we owe a cock to Aesculapius. Pay it and do not neglect it.

—Last utterance of Socrates
(as reported by Plato)

There has been a controversy started of late . . . concerning the general foundation of Morals; whether they be derived from Reason, or from sentiment; whether we attain the knowledge of them by chain of argument and induction, or by an immediate feeling and finer internal sense; whether, like all sound judgment of truth and falsehood, they should be the same to every rational intelligent being, or whether, like the perception of beauty and deformity, they be founded entirely on the particular fabric and constitution of the human species.

—David Hume

1. Egoism

If, as Hume claimed, morals come down to a matter of internal sentiments—to desires, feelings, and the like—then why should we ever do anything other than what we feel like doing at any given moment? Why act unselfishly, or according to alleged moral principles foisted on us from the "outside"? Why not, in other words, adopt the extreme form of *egoism* that tells us to act so as to maximize strictly selfish immediate desires and goals?

The reason we should not is that rejecting externally grounded moral standards does not make it rational to always satisfy immediate selfish appetites. For one thing, rationality requires *prudence*. Unselfish actions engaged in now often have large selfish payoffs later. An enlightened egoistic theory thus will allow, for example, giving an expensive gift to one's boss in the expectation of large returns later. And for another, rationality requires that we take account of all of our motivating sentiments, including the *altruistic*, unselfish, ones directed towards friends, mates, and close kin, in particular, offspring. It is very human indeed to want to sacrifice for our own children, siblings, and dear friends. So if egoism is to be a sensible, rational, theory, it must permit a certain amount of altruistic, unselfish, behavior.

In fact, if there were no relevant human sentiments other than the ones just described, being an egoist and being rational would amount to pretty much the same thing. They do not because there is a particular type of nonegoistic sentiment that rationality requires us to weigh in the balance, namely, the kind that leads us to favor *justice, retribution, loyalty, fair play*, and that sort of thing. A truly egoistic theory, after all, has to counsel against giving in to sentiments of this kind.

Of course, saying that we have sentiments favoring justice, fair play, or whatever, is a far cry from spelling out what this means in practice. What are the principles of fair play that seem intuitively right to most of us? How do we feel about retribution? Do we really desire this kind of striking back at transgressors? Is retribution any different from nasty old revenge? What, if anything, makes, or ought to make, a person feel *obligated* to sacrifice for others? What, in other words, do these moral sentiments of ours tell us to *do*, or not do?

The history of philosophy is chock full of answers to these questions, but unfortunately, the answers given by one philosopher generally conflict with what many others have claimed to have proved beyond a shadow of a doubt. Utilitarians, such as John Stuart Mill, tie moral obligation to human happiness, pleasure, or satisfaction. Our duty, according to utilitarians, is to produce the greatest possible amount of these goods, irrespective of how they are distributed. Animal rights advocates insist we also need to take account of the welfare of other sentient beings. Kantians argue that morality requires us always to treat other human beings as ends, never as means. Others claim that morality requires us always to act out of love for all human beings. Which, if any, of these seekers-after-truth should we believe?

Clearly, introspection is not irrelevant to any investigation of these questions. If it feels radically wrong, or right, maybe it is wrong, or right. But human beings are notoriously self-deceivers. We tend, for example, to overestimate the strengths of our other-regarding, altruistic, sentiments and to think of ourselves as a good deal more high-minded than in fact we are. Looking into one's own psyche obviously needs to be complemented by other sorts of investigations. What, for instance (let's get to the point) does science have to say about the matter? Philosophers have always looked to the science of their day for guidance, and we are fortunate today in having the recently burgeoning science of evolutionary biology to consult. So before accepting any particular philosophical theory about the nature of human moral sentiments, not excluding the one to be presented here shortly, we ought at least to find out how it fits with what biologists tell is in the evolutionary cards. What could moral sentiments be like that have evolved in this world of tooth and claw?

2. Sociobiology and Reciprocity

To start with, we need to remember that *genes* are the basic units of natural selection, not species and certainly not individual organisms. Human beings, as all living things, thus can profitably be thought of as "gene survival machines."[1] Of course, genes do not produce behavior in any direct way; they just code for the production of complicated molecules in body cells, which in turn give us motivating interests (desires, perceived goals, and the like).

In everyday life, we often divide the actions typically engaged in by our fellows into those that are selfish—intended to benefit the actor—and those that are unselfish, designed to benefit others. Evolutionary biologists further divide the unselfish kind into those they call *kin altruistic*, intended to benefit close relatives, and those labeled *reciprocal altruistic*, designed to benefit others who can be expected to return the favor.

That we should be programmed to perform selfishly has an obvious evolutionary explanation. Gene survival machines need time to procreate, during which they have to survive and prosper. Similarly, that we engage in a great deal of kin altruism, in particular working hard to benefit our own children, makes good evolutionary sense. Close relatives harbor a nice portion of our own genes, and genetic success depends on our own genes being passed down through the next generation. Offspring well cared for obviously have a much better chance to win at the genetic game than those left to fend for themselves. The vital importance of kin altruism is the reason that the old saying about blood being thicker than water is so absolutely true.

But the widespread nature of reciprocal altruism in human populations needs a bit of explanation and discussion. In particular, why bother to reciprocate when we already have received our share of the benefits generated by a cooperative agreement? Why, to take a relatively trivial case, pay for goods already received, or for services already rendered? Where is the genetic payoff in this kind of honesty? Or, to put the question another way, how could moral sentiments motivating us to benefit nonkin, often at great sacrifice to ourselves, have evolved in this dog-eat-dog world? The answer is that they evolved because of the tremendous benefits of reciprocal altruistic behavior. Human beings are the cooperating animal par excellence,[2] and cooperation requires reciprocity. In most cases, two heads, or two pairs of hands, not to mention many, are much better than one. But scratching my back pays off for you, genetically speaking, only if I can be trusted to scratch your back in return. When cheating on reciprocal arrangements goes beyond a certain point, cooperative arrangements break down, and their vital benefits are lost. Morality is the oil that lubricates the machinery of cooperation, which makes possible the goods on which human life depends. The moral sentiments motivating us to keep bargains evolved because the actions they encourage have a greater average genetic payoff than behavior of the more selfish variety. In the long run, trustworthy cooperators win out in competition with those who cheat. (No wonder Socrates' last remark expressed his strong desire that a debt be repaid.)

Note, by the way, that cooperation pays off not just in the competitions that go on within societies but also with respect to conflicts between cultures. *Homo sapiens* has evolved as an in-group–out-group social animal. Victory in the genetic game depends not just on doing well within one's own society but also on the success of one's in-group vis-à-vis competing out-groups. It does a body little good to win out in competitions with compatriots if one's group as a whole loses out to other groups. Thus, to cite a famous case, the citizens of Carthage who were successful in competition with other Carthegenians became genetic losers when their whole society was wiped out by Roman legions.

So it isn't surprising that strong sentiments favoring group loyalty have evolved to the point, for instance, that individuals are willing to seriously risk their lives in time of war. Of course, risking life and limb in this way makes sense only when there is the morally required reciprocity of *trust*— when there is reasonable assurance that others also will do so. (Charles Darwin clearly understood this implication of his evolutionary theory; witness his remark that morality is an important element in the success of one tribe over others.)

We shouldn't forget, however, that the other human beings with whom we must cooperate in order to succeed in life are at the same time our most serious genetic competitors.[3] Indeed, this is very likely the most fundamental fact that needs to be kept in mind if we are to understand the human moral animal. *Success in life requires us to cooperate with our most serious genetic competitors!*

That is why, incidentally, it makes sense to speak of the *temptation* to sin. The cooperative side of our nature insists that we play the reciprocity game straight even when greater profits are to be made by cheating; the competitive side demands that we "defect" (a technical term) whenever doing so will maximize selfish interests. When (as in the case of saints) the cooperative side is totally in command, there is no temptation to cheat; when (as is regularly true only for sociopaths) the competitive side has exclusive sway, defection becomes automatic, temptation irrelevant.

Speaking of saints and sociopaths brings to mind the point that both, but especially saints, are bound to be rare in any human population. A society composed exclusively, or even on the whole, of one or the other cannot be *evolutionarily stable.* A group composed primarily of saints is bound to be invaded, sooner or later, by those programmed to clever cheating. A society made up chiefly of sinners will fail to hold its own against more diversely populated competing groups. Theory therefore suggests that most people in a society will fall somewhere in between these two extremes, an idea that is confirmed by even casual observations of *Homo sapiens* in action in everyday life. Virtually all of us are stocked with the stan-

dard sorts of sentiments, but we differ in their relative strengths—the reason, no doubt, some of us find it more difficult than do others to resist the temptation to renege on bargains when there is great profit to be had in doing so. (Because it is so important that our own reciprocal altruistic practices yield a satisfactory return on investment, one of life's chief tasks is to discover who among our fellows can be trusted and who cannot, so as to avoid dealings with the latter whenever possible. Finding a mate who will stick with us through thick and thin, and not be tempted away into greener pastures, is an important case in point. Betrayal of trust is one of life's most serious pitfalls.)

The point of all this talk about reciprocity and cooperation is that their evolution required a concurrent development of dispositions and sentiments making them viable. Sentiments do not evolve willy-nilly; they come into existence because animals stocked with them do better, genetically speaking, than those not so provisioned. The love and affection we feel for offspring, for example, make it more likely that we will engage in kin altruism when necessary rather than act selfishly.

What then are the chief sentiments associated with reciprocity and cooperation? Clearly, those such as affection, empathy, compassion, and the like, sentiments that tend to reduce the temptation to cheat on reciprocal arrangements. Fondness makes sacrifice easier, hate more difficult. Friends cooperate better, with less chicanery, than enemies, or even casual acquaintances. This is true, certainly, with respect to everyday cooperative agreements struck between in-group members; it is true in spades with respect to the societywide agreement, implied in group membership, not to betray one's fellows in conflicts with competing societies.

This brings to mind the point that evolutionary forces have produced not just specific sentiments, such as empathy and compassion, but also a general disposition to accept and find reasonable the customs and regulations of one's own in-group. Genetic success depends on working cohesively with one's compatriots, and it is difficult to do so with individuals who deviate greatly from accepted behavioral norms. Note, however, that this general disposition to conform often conflicts with specific sentiments favoring justice and fair play, not to mention those motivating us to seek personal gain.

Finally, before moving on to other matters, it needs to be noticed that in referring to theories of evolutionary biology we do not commit the fallacy David Hume railed against of inferring from what *is* the case—the way in which human beings in fact behave—to what *ought to be* the case, the way they ought to perform. The claim being made here is not that evolutionary theories *prove* anything about moral obligation but rather that they provide very good reasons for believing human beings on the whole are well supplied with sentiments tending to increase profitable cooperative activities, sentiments of the kind that have generally been regarded as moral. It would be a mistake to conclude after quick introspection, or without seriously considering the possibility of self-deception concerning one's true motives and intentions, that the cited biological theories are on the wrong track, just as it generally is a mistake to run afoul of theories confirmed by a great many diverse experiences in favor of conclusions that are more narrowly supported. Those who ignore what science tells us about human nature and adopt moral philosophies that fail to take appropriate account of what science says about our in-group–out-group nature, or that advocate unscientific, "goody-goody" theories obligating us to love and care for all of our fellows, do so at their peril. (We cannot, while hating the sin, love the sinner, nor do we genuinely wish to do so. Evolutionary forces have made sure of that.)

Even so, it would be a mistake to ignore everyday experiences, introspective or otherwise, that appear to contradict what science has to say. We need to weigh all of the evidence we can get on

the matter. Those who examine their own psyches and find little that conforms to what has been or is about to be said concerning fair play and moral sentiments will have good, although certainly not conclusive, reason to be skeptical. But the experiences of this writer, at any rate, lend support to the idea that most of us, when we face up to it, do indeed, with exceptions here and there, pretty much conform to what evolutionary theory suggests about the nature of human moral nature.[4]

3. Nature Versus Nurture

Underpinning the evolutionary theories appealed to in this essay is the idea that human behavior, like all animal behavior, has a strong genetic component. This does not mean, of course, that human behavior is "hard wired." In particular, it does not mean that genes provide us with a stock of moral sentiments of various strengths that we then carry around, unaltered, throughout our lives. Genes do determine certain physical characteristics, for instance eye color, once and for all. But they do not determine once and for all how we will act in the various sorts of situations encountered in everyday life. Rather, they establish a range of possible responses within which environmental factors—conditioning—play a role. The mix of moral sentiments and dispositions we have at a given time in life thus depends both on our genetic endowment, given to us at the moment of conception, and on the experiences we have had up to that time.

Unfortunately, scientific understanding of the ways in which these hereditary and environmental forces interact is still in its infancy. We know certain gross sorts of generalities, for instance, that being raised in a neglectful or abusive family tends to reduce the strengths of moral sentiments such as compassion and empathy, thus reducing the likelihood that those of us raised in this sort of inhospitable environment will play the game fair and square. But we also know that there are lots of exceptions to this general rule and that many individuals brought up in this way turn out to be kind, caring, upstanding members of society. Finer-tuned theories about how nature and nurture interact are needed, and no doubt will be supplied in the future.

But it is crystal clear now that evolutionary theories concerning human moral behavior cannot be rejected simply because we know that environmental factors influence behavior. We can be quite sure that, as stated before, environment influences behavior only within a range laid down by genetic factors that have evolved over long periods of time, factors that evolved because individuals stocked with certain combinations of genes have won out over competitors endowed with different genetic mixes.

In a great many cases, the genetic component of behavior is obvious. No one supposes, for instance, that we can shape randomly chosen individuals into athletic or aesthetic geniuses merely by providing them with the right sorts of environment, any more than that we can turn them into 100-meter-dash champions simply by having them step onto the track in a pair of Reeboks or Nikes. We all know that it takes both natural talent and intense practice to produce high-caliber performances of this kind. Similarly, although the languages individuals speak depend on where and by whom they are raised, no one supposes that we can teach, say, dogs to speak Chinese simply by having them raised in a Chinese-speaking family. Which language a person speaks depends on all sorts of environmental factors, but the ability to learn any languages at all requires the sort of genes that human beings have but dogs, alas, lack.

Why, then, suppose that moral dispositions and sentiments are any different? Even if we still do not completely understand how heredity and environment interact to generate particular responses to moral situations, we do understand why evolutionary forces have provisioned *Homo sapiens* with a moral dimension—to enable us to gain the advantages of cooperative behavior. And we know a

few modestly vague but still useful facts about the kinds of moral dispositions that evolutionary forces, shaped by environmental factors, are likely to produce in the general run of human beings. Philosophers ignore this knowledge at their peril.

4. Reciprocity and Morality: The Principles of Fair Play

Although sentiments such as affection and compassion certainly are important, perhaps even vital, to the evolution of complex reciprocal arrangements, they are not sufficient. What is required in addition is a general disposition, a genuine desire, to keep one's word—to be *trustable*. We can not be fond of everyone we deal with; bargains frequently need to be kept with people we hardly know, and even, sometimes, with enemies. A reciprocity of trust, generated in part by sentiments favoring the keeping of one's word, is required to get these sorts of arrangements off the ground.

But all agreements are not created equal. Some are a good deal fairer than others. We need to be able to tell, at least in some rough way, which bargains are *fair* and which are not. Fairness enters the picture because of the fact, insisted on before, that we have to cooperate so often with serious genetic rivals. (Bees, ants, and other social insects, cooperate with in-group members of the same caste without regard to fairness, but that is because, in effect, they are clones of each other and thus not genetic competitors.) Those who regularly get less than a fair share of the spoils of cooperative ventures, or do more than their share of service to the community as a whole, tend to be defeated by craftier competitors, and this is the reason we all have at least a modestly good sense of what counts as a *fair share* of the fruits of cooperative endeavors, or a fair share of our social duties, and why we usually try very hard not to get the short end of the stick. (Note, by the way, that even those intent on cheating need to know what constitutes a fair share. Most chicanery doesn't involve out-and-out thievery but rather just stacking the deck in one's favor.)

Life being as nasty as it is, however, we often need to take what we can get. Confronted with a choice, say, of less than a fair salary or none at all, prudence dictates knuckling under. But it always is better to garner a fair share if we can.

Of course, if a fair share is good, taking the whole pie would be even better, as would be doing less than one's share of community service. The genetic point behind the sentiments motivating us to resist this sort of temptation, moving us to settle for a fair share even when we might be able to get more, or to risk our necks in battle rather than letting buddies down, is the instability over very long periods of time of societies in which most people are motivated to cheat most of the time. Social life can and does limp along although we all cheat some of the time, and even though a few of us do most of the time, but it breaks down when most of us do so most of the time. Cooperation can stand only so much chicanery. Groups in which this sort of moral theft is more common tend, other things being equal, to lose out when competing with those in which it is less frequent. (Note that this is true with respect to private organizations and small groups as well as to whole societies.)

Most agreements are more or less of the explicit variety. The various parties indicate their acceptance of a contractual arrangement via the spoken or written word. But some are generated without explicit agreements being reached. Custom, for example, tends to generate agreements that are binding even though only implicit. Most everyday social obligations—to refrain from eating in certain public places, to give directions to strangers, to be civil when in public, and so on—very likely arose in this way and became explicitly voiced, those that have, only later.

Because cooperation takes place so often with genetic competitors, and because fair competition requires at least a modicum of cooperation (as it does, for example, in sporting competitions where all players must cooperate at least by conforming

to the agreed-upon rules of the game), to be completely fair an arrangement has to be both *competitively* and *cooperatively fair.*

An agreement is generally thought to be *competitively fair* only if the terms of the agreement do not favor a particular competitor over others—only if they do not provide an advantage to one party as compared to others. We see the rules, for instance, that assign greater weights to some horses than to others in a horse race as not fair to the horses themselves (as opposed to owners or wagerers) for that very reason. We do not mind being unfair to horses in this way, but certainly would not think an Olympic marathon fair if the rules required human competitors to be treated in this unequal manner.

Although our basic intuitions concerning competitive fairness given to us by evolutionary forces are reasonably clear, particular cases often are hard to decide. Nature wants us, whenever possible, to play games in which, at the very least, we are not at a disadvantage compared to genetic competitors. But when is this the case? Would a rule permitting insider stock trading, for instance, be fair because it allows everyone, whether an insider or outsider, to engage in this activity? The answer to this kind of question is that there is no automatic answer. It all depends on what sorts of competitive games we wish to play. We say, in fact, that insider trading is unfair because a rule that permitted it would give a tremendous advantage to some speculators (insiders) over others (outsiders) and thus would discourage most people from playing the game. But we could just as well say that a stock market competition allowing this practice is not unfair, because it allows everyone, outsiders as well as insiders, to engage in insider trading if they can. (The rules of bridge are thought to be fair in allowing all players to remember which cards have been played by whom, and in what order, even though lots of players are not up to this task.) We say, in fact, that having much greater wealth to wager than market competitors is not unfair, because it treats everyone in the same way (allowing everyone with any amount of money to play the game). But we could just as well say that allowing this kind of play, although desirable for practical reasons, is unfair, because it gives a tremendous advantage to fat cats. Either way of speaking can be correct; what counts is that we understand what has moved us to talk in one way rather than the other.[5]

It sometimes is argued that there is indeed an objective way to decide whether, say, a marketplace that permits stock competitions between rich and ordinary players is or is not fair. On this view, what counts is that the rules of the game tend to make victory go to those whose winning "talents" are internal to the players. Fair stock market rules, for instance, should on the whole produce winners who best understand the underlying forces that produce high, or low, stock prices, or perhaps who best understand the "true value" of stocks because they know about the competitive chances of the corporations whose issues are being traded. So some would argue against the fairness of trading rules that reward the external talent of having more venture capital than most other players. (Note that certain championship poker competitions are designed to assure complete competitive fairness by providing each player with the same number of startup chips.)

But this way of looking at the matter does not always work. Take the case of two males competing for the hand of the same female. We do not generally think that such a contest is unfair just because one of the factors tipping the scales is the greater wealth of the victorious suitor. We see the external talent of having lots of money as very relevant indeed to the game of choosing a mate wisely. (At this point, we again need to avoid the temptation to be goody-goody!) The point is that fairness or unfairness is determined at least in part by what sorts of games we wish to play, and this often has to do with practical considerations involving external talents, such as money or status.

What, then, about the other sort of fairness—the cooperative variety? What makes an agreement cooperatively fair? The answer reflects the fact that cooperators typically also are competi-

tors. A fair division of profits or duties, therefore, must not favor some cooperators over others, which means that profits must be parceled out so as to be commensurate with input. That is why an arrangement is generally thought to be *cooperatively fair* only when its fruits are divided according to the various amounts of time, wealth, effective effort, and so on, each participant contributes. Equal input merits equal share of profits, greater input a greater share. (Whatsoever ye sow, ye also *ought* to reap.) All other ways of dividing profits allow some competing cooperators to gain an advantage over others simply by entering into fair agreements with them, and not because they are superior competitors. To reduce this possibility to a minimum, nature has instilled in us a strong desire to gain at least a fair share, as just described, of the benefits of cooperative ventures.

It is important at this point to remember that the sentiments we have been discussing are *universal*. The peoples of all cultures are motivated by empathy, affection, compassion, and the like, as well as by a sense of fair play. Philosophers and social scientists often justify the contrary claim—that moral sentiments are shaped almost exclusively by environmental forces—by pointing to their great diversity from one culture to another. But this neglects the fact that amidst the diversity there is a common base—the sentiments we have concentrated on here.[6]

5. Retribution and Revenge

But the cooperative sentiments discussed so far are not quite the whole story. Another mechanism has evolved to increase the likelihood of successful cooperation, namely, a desire to strike back at those who do not play the game straight. This desire takes several different forms, which need to be distinguished.

One way to strike back is to refuse to play cooperative games with those who cheat, thus depriving them of the benefits cooperation tends to generate. Another is to return chicanery with chicanery—to fight fire with fire. (Only suckers feel obligated to be honest with those who are dishonest.) But a better way, perhaps, is to exact retribution—to punish those who cheat on contractual arrangements.

Unfortunately, everyday uses of the term "retribution" tend to be rather ambiguous, not to mention vague. And, indeed, retribution often is confused with its cousin, revenge. By *retribution* we mean here harming individuals because they have failed to play the game fairly, by *revenge,* harming someone in return for being harmed. The two concepts obviously overlap; some cases of revenge also constitute retribution. But revenge often has nothing to do with retribution, as in cases where guilty parties strike back at those who, with justification, exact retribution.

Sentiments favoring retribution evolved, no doubt, because of their deterrence value. When those who are cheated tend to strike back, crime is much less likely to pay. But deterrence is generally not the principal motive—certainly not the only one—pushing us into punishing guilty parties. Rather, it is the strong desire most of us have that "justice be done." This powerful sentiment favoring retribution is entirely separate from a desire to deter sin, even though, as just remarked, it no doubt evolved because of its deterrent value (just as, for instance, the desire for sexual intercourse is separate from a desire for offspring, although the desire for sex evolved without doubt because it increases the likelihood of reproduction). Deterrence is forward looking. When we punish the guilty in order to deter others from committing crimes, we try to influence what happens in the future. Retribution, by contrast, is backward looking. When we punish the guilty in order to gain retribution, we do so because of what they have done in the past, not in order to influence the future. Of course, we often punish for both of these reasons.

Unfortunately, retribution recently has had a rather poor press, perhaps because retribution usually also constitutes revenge, and nonretributive cases of revenge generally, and rightly, are seen to be odious. Negative feelings about these nonretributive instances tend to rub off onto retributive cases. Another reason may be that the desire for retribution, as for revenge, is seen as a holdover from our uncivilized past, when our distant ancestors were mere beasts. Of course, those who see it this way generally forget that this can be said about all human sentiments. (Note, again, the tendency towards the goody-goody, reinforced in this case, perhaps, by an inclination to deny the relationship between human beings and other animals, an inclination that to this day moves many people to reject the theory of evolution itself.)

In any case, theory suggests, and everyday experience confirms, that most of us do indeed harbor a rather strong desire that the guilty be punished in order to achieve justice. The fact that we expended a good deal of effort to punish the leaders of Germany and Japan after World War II, even though history attests to the unlikelihood that tyrants can be deterred in this way, supports theory on this point, as do the cathartic feelings generated when justice is done—when the guilty receive their due. (Note in this vein the Judeo-Christian doctrine of a "life for a life, eye for an eye, [and] tooth for a tooth.")

6. Degrees of Friendliness

The sentiments of empathy, compassion, affection, and the like, mentioned before, tend to generate *friendships* between individuals, in particular when they engage in various kinds of reciprocal activities. Friends form a kind of small in-group within or overlapping larger groups, including the primary ones that we think of as societies. In fact, societies can be thought of as very large groups of friends, although not on average nearly as *friendly* as close friends often are.

Other things being equal, friends tend to win out when competing with groups of people held together merely by the prospect of personal gain, and this, no doubt, is one reason for the evolution of the sentiments that make friendships endure.

Friends tend to be loyal to one another in much the same way as are citizens of the same society, and for many of the same reasons. Friendliness makes it more likely that citizens will hang together rather than separately.

The more important the kinds of cooperative behavior that individuals, whether true friends or not, engage in, the greater the *degree of friendliness* that holds between them. But no mere amount of cooperation is sufficient by itself to make an association into a friendship (or a group into a society). What is lacking in the case of cooperating nonfriends is a concern for the other fellow, feelings of affection that lead to an increase in trustworthiness, a decrease in advantage taking, and a willingness to come to one another's aid in time of need. Nonfriends cooperate primarily for their own advantage; friends are also motivated by a sense of concern and loyalty.

Friendships, nevertheless, are kept going because of mutual advantage. They are, after all, based pretty much on reciprocity, as are most human associations (including, it is important to remember, the association between mates). Of course, unlike the case of merely commercial relationships, the reciprocity books do not need to balance between friends, because of the concern, mentioned before, friends have for one another. But when ledgers becomes seriously unbalanced, friendships fade, as they also often do when friends compete with one another for positions or mates. (Recall Aristotle's remark: "Ah, my friends, there are no friends," intended to convey the point that friendships have their limits.)

In any case, friendliness needs to be kept separate in our minds from the related concept of fairness. A person can be scrupulously fair in dealings with others, be motivated by a high regard for fair play, and yet be completely lacking in the sentiments of affection and concern that characterize friendships. Even so, fair reciprocity is always more likely when a desire to play the game fairly is wedded to a concern for the other fellow. It is always easier to cheat enemies than friends.

In short, sentiments that tend to cement friendships, coupled with those that incline us to favor fair play, and reinforced by a strong desire to strike back at transgressors, constitute a large part of the winning biological package that has produced modern *Homo sapiens* and our cooperative ecological niche. The other part, of course, is the sentiments that guide the competitive side of human nature. These two sides of our psyches frequently are in harmony, but occasionally they clash, in which case the competitive side may win out over the cooperative, the reason all of us, at least now and then, give in to the temptation to sin—to take advantage of the trust of others.

7. Fair Group Decision Procedures

Unanimity is the only fair procedure for arriving at the terms of a two-party cooperative venture. Allowing one party greater say than the other clearly would not be competitively fair. Unanimity also is the most practical procedure when just two people are involved. But it becomes less and less practical as the number of potential cooperators becomes larger and larger. Practical considerations thus often force the choice of a different sort of procedure, such as majority rule.

But what makes a decision procedure fair is the same no matter how large the group in question happens to be. Nor does the nature of the group have any relevance. What counts is that the procedural rules followed do not favor one person, or group of persons, over others. (This is the crucial ingredient because coming to group-wide agreements is almost always a competitive activity.) Majority rule, and even plurality rule, are therefore usually just as fair as the decision procedure requiring unanimity.

It is true, of course, that a fair *procedure* does not guarantee a fair *outcome*. Mistakes are bound to be made, and, what's more, human beings are far from being governed solely by altruistic or fairminded motives. There is, in fact, no fair decision procedure that can guarantee fair outcomes, although clearly, unanimity makes it a good deal harder for unprincipled operators to tyrannize others. Nor does a fair outcome prove anything about the fairness of a procedure. Accidents will happen, and, anyway, despots do on occasion rule in the common interest.

Speaking of despots again brings to mind the fact that we all are members—citizens—of that special kind of organization anthropologists think of as an *in-group.* We are in our bones an in-group–out-group animal. During the vast sweep of human evolution, most of the cooperative behavior engaged in by *Homo sapiens* was of the in-group variety. Most moral strictures, requiring truth telling, forbidding certain kinds of killings, and so on, very likely got started as in-group agreements that applied, therefore, primarily to one's fellows and not necessarily to the people over on the next hill. Out-group relationships tended to be governed by different sorts of agreements reached by one group vis-à-vis another and were more easily broken when the situation warranted. Today, primary in-groups—nations—usually contain millions or even hundreds of millions of members, and things have changed somewhat for that reason as well as because of the vast amount of international trade that has generated complicated intergroup agreements. But the rules still are different for intragroup interactions than for the international variety, and many more agreements are struck, *and kept,* between citizens of the same society than of different societies. Fair play wins out more often when we deal with compatriots than with the peoples of other lands.

Although, as just mentioned, unanimity is not a viable option where large groups, in particular large in-groups, are concerned, these groups nevertheless can, and generally do, achieve a kind of "meta" unanimity via the implicit or explicit agreement of all members to accept and abide by group-wide decisions, however they happen to be reached. Indeed, the failure of a society to obtain this sort of overarching agreement from a large majority of its citizens tends to sound the death knell of an in-group (as the recent collapse of the Soviet Union illustrated all too well).

Finally, it is worth noting that the problems discussed before (in section 4) concerning relevant "talents" sometimes arise when we attempt to spell out fair group decision procedures. We want victory in the passing of legislation to be achieved by those with the most compelling reasons and arguments, not the largest bankrolls, biggest megaphones, or strongest goons. Merely requiring that everyone has just one vote thus is not sufficient. The problem is to specify the other ways in which voters must be equal if a decision procedure is to be completely fair, and there is no automatic, or easy, way in which this can be done.

8. Fair Play in the Real World

Moral theorists often neglect the fact, remarked on a while back, that sentiments favoring fair play do not always override the other springs to action. Practical considerations of various kinds sometimes are more pressing. In wartime, the *common good* requires some citizens to sacrifice while others gain more than a fair share of the benefits. When a government manipulates interest rates to stimulate the national economy, some profit while others lose. (Reducing interest rates, for instance, tends to benefit borrowers more than the general run of the population while harming those dependent on returns from savings.)

But there often are ways in which this kind of unfairness can be rectified. Having chosen a free market economic system for practical reasons (say, to maximize the production of goods), a fair-minded electorate can at least partially rectify any resulting unfair distributions of wealth (such as profits garnered by economic barons at the expense of ordinary workers) via high taxes for the rich, or by a negative income tax benefiting those at the bottom of the heap. And burdens usually can be passed around so that the same citizens do not always suffer.

The trouble is that remedies of this kind often are not forthcoming; the same groups tend to bear the burdens, or benefits, and, worse, governments controlled by foolish, ignorant, or corrupt politicians frequently mete out gratuitous harms of various kinds. In addition, honest citizens who obey laws at some expense to themselves frequently find themselves at a competitive disadvantage compared to less scrupulous compatriots.

Although resignation from an unfair or corrupt golf or chess club is a simple matter, and alternatives generally are readily available, resigning from one's primary in-group is usually fraught with difficulties and regrets, and becoming a member of another society is neither automatic nor always possible. Emigration is not like moving from one social club, or job, to another. What, then, is the morally right response of citizens, say, in a democracy where the laws of the land have been enacted by means of reasonably fair procedures, to the various kinds of social unfairness most of us are subjected to in everyday life?

What, for instance, about obedience to laws or customs that are widely flouted? In two-person agreements and similarly in agreements struck between several parties, it is clear that the noncompliance of one party releases the other or others from any obligations accrued under the agreements. Doesn't it follow, then, because laws are just agreements struck between much larger numbers of people, that when most citizens in a society violate a particular law, others tend to be absolved from strict obedience to that statute? Doesn't the fact (and it is a fact) that most taxpayers cheat on their income taxes constitute a very good reason for others to do so? Being moral does not entail being a patsy! Similarly, doesn't the fact that governments often discriminate in the enforcement of laws, as, for example, local governments tend to do with respect to real estate assessments, justify others in not being scrupulous, say, about notifying authorities concerning improvements that have increased the values of their properties? Doesn't it make sense that in these sorts of cases the implicit social agreement to obey the laws of the land can be disregarded?

Of course, even if the answer to these questions is *yes,* a principle of proportionality surely is

in order stating roughly that the greater the unfairness, the larger the justified deviation from scrupulous obedience. The greater the number of people who cheat on taxes, and the more serious their chicanery, the more justified others are in doing so, and on a larger scale. (It follows, by the way, that in extreme cases in which whole groups of citizens, for example, racial or caste minorities, find themselves repeatedly on the short end of the stick, the moral force of the general agreement to obey fairly enacted laws is seriously eroded.)

Laws proscribing behavior not harmful to others, for example, statutes forbidding the use of marijuana or the viewing of pornographic movies in the privacy of one's own home, provide another interesting kind of case. As in the others just considered, the fact of widespread disobedience tends to absolve others of a duty to compliance. But there is another reason often cited for noncompliance, namely, the essentially private nature of behavior that does no harm to anyone else. Forbidding cigarette smoking in public is one thing—others may be harmed, or annoyed, by the smoke produced; making it illegal when done in private is something else altogether. Wherein this difference?

Perhaps the chief difference has to do with social usefulness, or rather its lack. To take one example, when tax laws are fairly enacted and enforced, and not often infringed, no excuse exists for noncompliance. But even when all of this is true with respect to a law forbidding, say, the private consumption of alcohol, there still is a reason for imbibing anyway, namely, the lack of a socially useful purpose for the law requiring us to refrain. Cheating on taxes when others do not provides an unfair competitive advantage to those who do and a correlative disadvantage to citizens who do not; smoking tobacco at home harms the competitive chances of no one else. The thought that private behavior of this kind is no one else's business is firmly rooted in the fact that it *is* no one else's business! (The contrary argument, based on the idea that private behavior often has public consequences, is not well taken, in particular because the remedy then is to legislate against the public offense. Millions drink; only some drink and then drive. Wherein the justice in punishing those who drink responsibly because some drink irresponsibly? Note, by the way, that virtually all private behavior may, on occasion, have public consequences. Does it make sense, to take just one such case, to legislate against the rejection of one lover by another on grounds that this may, and indeed often does, have harmful public consequences?)

No doubt there are many who will find the idea quite shocking that it sometimes is rational, and not unfair, to violate fairly enacted legislation. But those who do might consider their thoughts about the many such laws passed at one time or another that discriminate against racial minorities, or against an entire sex (usually female). They might also think about laws that prohibit private fornication between unmarried adults, or those proscribing perfectly ordinary kinds of sexual intercourse performed by married couples in their own bedrooms. Those still shocked might dwell on the countless pieces of legislation enacted by reasonably fair procedures that have made it illegal to practice any but a preferred religion, and the favored religion only in an orthodox manner, or on laws *requiring* the practice of a favored religion, or barring those who do not at least pretend to accept the official doctrine from most positions of consequence in society.

9. Fair Play in the Marketplace

It's true, as they say, that we don't live by bread alone. But it is also true that we don't live without bread. Economic interactions thus are at least as important as any others. But we should expect intuitions concerning fair play in the marketplace to be rather vague, and even somewhat ambiguous, because they were designed by evolutionary forces to handle fairly simple kinds of transactions that are quite different from the complicated cooperative interactions characteristic of today's economic arenas.

As in the case of any other sorts of activities, to be competitively fair, the rules of an economic game must treat all players in the same way, and to be cooperatively fair, must return profits (and losses!) according to share of input. And economic activities, just as any others, can be more, or less, friendly. Generally, but not always, more means better (because unfriendly competitions tend to be less efficient, and because friendly competitors are more likely to play the game straight, thus producing larger long-term profits).

Also, as in the case of every other sort of competitive activity, whether or not economic practices fall within the limits of fair play depends on what games it is we wish to play—on how friendly we desire competitions to be—or, to put the matter another way, on what sorts of advantage takings, if any, we want to permit. Remember that a game can be competitively fair even though advantage takings are permitted, provided that all players are allowed them equally.

At one time or another, the rules of economic games have allowed competitors to take advantage of opponent ignorance, foolishness, stupidity, misfortune, and vulnerable economic condition, and have even permitted players to completely shut others out of the game. There never has been a marketplace in which all of these kinds of advantage takings have been forbidden, but markets that endure for very long generally devise ways to ensure a certain amount of friendliness and, in particular, have tried to assure the adherence to fair contracts that is at the heart of intuitions concerning fair play.

Happily, marketplaces these days tend to be somewhat friendlier than those in existence even a few years ago. The principle of *caveat emptor* (let the buyer beware) has been seriously eroded, insider trading is illegal on most exchanges, and so on. But free markets, at any rate, still allow players to take advantage of certain kinds of competitor ignorance and, especially, of competitor economic distress. Forbidding the latter sort of advantage taking, say, by making it illegal either to buy goods cheaply from those overstocked or to sell items in short supply at higher prices, would go a long way towards rescinding the law of supply and demand on which free markets depend. In any case, deciding which sorts of unfriendly behavior to permit, and which to proscribe, usually is decided as much on the basis of practical as on fair-play considerations, and is, in fact, one of the serious matters fought over (as it should be) in the sociopolitical arena.

This is true also with respect to quite a few issues concerning cooperative fairness. As stated before, intuitions on the matter tend to be clear only for the simplest sorts of cases in which all parties contribute equally, or at least make the same sorts of contributions (as when one person invests a hundred dollars and another five hundred, or one supplies one-fourth of an inventory and the other three-fourths). We do, however, have a few other extremely vague but nevertheless relevant sentiments to draw on. They tell us, most of us at any rate, that the more effective, dangerous, odious, tedious, skillful, or unhealthy labor happens to be, other things being equal, the greater the slice of profits it deserves, just as more venturesome capital deserves a more handsome return than investments that are safer.

But these intuitions are primarily qualitative. They do not tell us, for example, how much more remuneration dangerous employment deserves than the more prosaic variety, or how to compare one sort of skillful work with another. How can we compare the labor value of an engineer to that of a shop steward, or of an assembly line worker to a chief executive officer? What about the efforts of a waiter as compared to a college professor? How much more valuable is the labor of a Mozart than of a composer of pop tunes? Is there a way to compare invested capital with expended labor? We know that something is wrong when, for example, American CEOs earn on average seventeen times more than their Japanese counterparts and hundreds, sometimes thousands, of times more than the general run of their employees, or when junk bond entrepreneurs earn thousands of times as much as average workers by putting together deals that enrich a few while destroying once-sound corporations. But we don't

know what precise figures would make things right. We have comparative antennae that function somewhat, but lack intuitions concerning quantitative standards in most cases.

In any event, the problem is compounded by the fact that there is no such thing as *the* value of labor or capital, irrespective of particular human evaluations. Values do not exist independently of *valuers*. The value of labor to an employer (a buyer of labor) is in what it produces, whereas to a laborer (a seller of labor) it is in the time and effort expended, and, unfortunately, the two evaluations generally do not coincide. (Note that similar remarks apply to the value of commodities other than labor and capital.)

Suppose, however, we could determine that the labor of the president of a corporation produces, say, fifty times as much profit as the efforts of an average worker, thus being fifty times as valuable to the buyers of labor. It still would not follow that the CEO in question deserves fifty times the salary of an average employee. For one thing, no person is an island. What someone accomplishes is due in large part to the knowledge, training, and opportunity provided by society as a whole, and some receive much greater benefits of this kind than others. And for another thing, money is only one kind of payment for services rendered. In the case of truly outstanding producers—the Aristotles, Newtons, and Monets of the world—fame, honor, power, or in extreme cases even immortality, may well constitute the major portion of their just deserts. (It is interesting how much it bothers lots of people, including this writer, that a genius like Mozart should have died at an early age without an understanding of his place in history—uncertain as to how long his music would survive his own demise.) Note also that ordinary workers tend to value their own labor just as highly as do outstanding producers.

Of course, plenty of economists have argued that free markets provide the best guide to the value of capital, labor, and, indeed, of goods in general. Their view, no doubt, does have the merit that it ties value to what actual John Does or Mary Roes are willing to pay. The trouble, if we overlook the fact that no completely free markets have ever existed, is that marketplaces reward not just skill, insight, knowledge, perseverence, productivity, and other relevant talents, but also "talents" such as economic and political power, thus generally running counter to intuitions concerning fair wages and fair return on investment. (Note, by the way, that in actual marketplaces, the most odious jobs are among the lowest paying, while pop music phenoms whose products are quickly forgotten—for instance, New Kids on the Block—frequently earn a great deal more in one year than do the vast majority of great artists and thinkers in a lifetime.)

Of course, a fair-minded electorate might opt for a modestly free market economy anyway. For one thing, moral considerations do not necessarily take precedence over all others; and for another, as mentioned before, the unfairness of a free marketplace can be rectified to some extent by offsetting devices (such as negative income taxes). Nevertheless, it is important to remember the difficulty of obtaining true competitive fairness in a free-market economy, given the power of great wealth and the human tendencies towards nepotism that tilt socioeconomic playing fields in favor of the rich and their offspring.

10. Rights Talk

According to the contractual way of looking at things that is being championed here, it is agreements, promises, that *obligate* people to act in certain ways. On this view, therefore, *rights* are derivative from agreements: my promise to do something for you generates my obligation to perform as promised and your right to have me do so. Talk of rights divorced from agreements, implicit or explicit, makes no sense from this contractual point of view. Of course, only those of us with a high regard for keeping fair agreements have any *reason* to satisfy the rights of others generated by our promises.

In the history of philosophy, and in particular in the present day, a contrary view has often been championed, at least implicitly, according to which there are "natural rights" that we all are obligated to respect. But natural rights theorists are confronted with serious problems that advocates often neglect. How, for example, do these abstract objects, *natural* rights, come into existence? If we suppose that there are such things, why should anyone accept the burden of satisfying them? The contractual view has fairly simple answers to these questions. Rights come into existence via fair promises that generate obligations. It makes sense for those who are fair-minded to respect the rights of others precisely because they are fair-minded—precisely because they harbor strong sentiments favoring trust and fidelity. On this view, no appeal needs to be made to alleged objective "natural rights" that automatically adhere to "persons" by virtue of their humanity, or to sentient beings because of their capacity to experience, or to suffer.

11. The Good Person

The chief point of this essay has been to describe a particular sort of contractual theory of moral obligation and to support selection of that theory by appeal, in particular, to recent theories put forth by evolutionary biologists. According to these theories, moral sentiments generally evolved primarily because they tended to foster increasingly complicated and beneficial cooperative activities. The moral person, it has been implied, is someone who keeps fair bargains—whose word can be trusted.

But it should be noted that most philosophers have thought of morality in a somewhat wider sense. They often speak of a noncontractual obligation to be charitable, or compassionate, and generally claim that we have a special obligation to care for our own children. On the view being championed here, we only have obligations of this sort if we have agreed to them, either explicitly or implicitly, as, for example, when the citizens of a society decide that parents will take care of their own children (not a universal practice, by the way).

However, there is a good reason, at least in the eyes of this writer, for restricting the term "moral" in the way it has been here. For the moral obligation individuals have to keep bargains that *they* have entered into draws on actions *they* have performed. In demanding that these bargains be kept, others can appeal to these actions. Morality, in this sense, is self-imposed, in that it stems from one's own actions. Demanding, say, that others be charitable, in the absence of their agreement to act in this way, constitutes an attempt to impose obligations "from the outside."

Of course, there is nothing wrong in using the term "moral" in a wider sense than is employed here, provided we pay attention to relevant differences. Thus, those who extend the term to cover the treatment of offspring need to notice that the sentiments motivating most of us to care for our own children differ greatly from those leading us, say, to repay a debt to a bank. We sacrifice for offspring because we care about their welfare, whether or not we have agreed to do so. We pay back bank loans because, having agreed to do so, we feel obligated to hold up our end of the bargain (and also, of course, because we may be forced to anyway and don't want to ruin our credit rating), not because we have any great desire to increase the profits of the bank. Similarly, we are motivated to give street people money, those of us who are, by feelings of compassion and empathy, whether or not we have agreed to benefit them (say, via societywide legislation), but pay telephone bills because we have agreed to do so (and don't want service cut off), not because we have any great love for AT&T.

The point is that there are at least three different sorts of sentiments motivating altruistic behavior that need to be distinguished, one from another, namely, those favoring the keeping of fair bargains, those, such as compassion, leading us to care about the welfare of others, including non-kin, and those inclining us to desire the best for our own flesh and blood. The first evolved to foster reciprocal-altruistic practices, the third for kin-altruistic reasons, and the second to increase the likelihood both of reciprocal and of kin altruism.

But when we restrict the concept of moral obligation just to cases in which bargains have been made, as has been done in this essay, another term is needed to cover the wider sense often employed by other theorists. One way to do this is to say that being fair-minded, having a general disposition to make and keep fair contracts, is only part of what it takes to be a *good person*—to have the respect of one's fellows. The scrooges of the world may scrupulously obey the law and honor contracts and still be thought of as rather miserable human specimens. It is their unfriendly, mean-spirited natures—their lack of compassion or empathy for others—that makes others see them as *bad* individuals. (The evolutionary reason for our seeing things in this way no doubt is related to the value of compassion, empathy, and the like, in fostering both kin- and reciprocal-altruistic practices. Of course, this doesn't change the fact that we desire them for their own sake.)

But being a more or less good person is quite different from being goody-goody. Goody-goody tends to be a pose. We cannot just hate the sin while loving the sinner, as some moral philosophies require. Universal love and forgiveness are not in the cards for human beings. The reason, as insisted on before, is that the cooperation we all must engage in usually has to take place with our most serious genetic competitors. So the very activities that (biologically speaking) generate the other-regarding sentiments so favored by goody-goody philosophers also are responsible for the limits placed on these emotions. The typical reasonably good person is a full-blooded human animal, capable of anger and hatred as well as love, not a one-dimensional cardboard figure. Good individuals have an *appropriate* stock of other-regarding sentiments and do not need to deny feelings of contempt, disdain, or hatred felt for slippery, mean-spirited, or ungenerous characters.

This writer has lacked respect for most of the leaders of his native land during the second half of the twentieth century, not just because they have so often violated the principles of fair play, but also because they have been so lacking in empathy or compassion for those at the bottom of the pecking order. They have, in other words, not been good people. The reader is urged not to conclude that my intent in espousing a theory of contractual fair play has been to champion a victor/vanquished morality. My utopia, in which better competitors always emerge victorious, definitely is not one in which those who attain great success stand on a Neitzschean height and grind the rest of us into the dust.

Notes

1. This expression seems to have been introduced by Richard Dawkins. See his excellent book *The Selfish Gene* (Oxford and New York: Oxford University Press, 1976). Three other excellent books on the sociobiological approach are Robert Trivers's *Social Evolution* (Menlo Park, Calif., Benjamin/Cummings, 1985); E. O. Wilson's *On Human Nature* (Cambridge, Mass., Harvard University Press, 1978); and Robert Axelrod's *The Evolution of Cooperation* (New York: Basic Books, 1984), in particular the chapter by W. D. Hamilton.

2. Not counting animals, such as bees and ants, that do not reproduce bisexually. Interestingly, E. O. Wilson's pioneering evolutionary biology treatise, *Sociobiology: The New Synthesis* (Cambridge, Mass.: Harvard University Press, 1975), deals primarily with the social insects.

3. We pass over, because irrelevant to the topic of moral obligation, the ongoing competitions with viruses, bacteria, and fungi that need to be won in order to achieve genetic success.

4. The theories concerning reciprocal and kin altruism on which this account is based are not without their detractors. See in particular R. C. Lewontin, L. Kamin, and S. Rose: *Not in Our Genes* (New York: Pantheon, 1984). But in the opinion of this writer, the tide of research is going against the naysayers. See, for instance, Katherine Milton's fascinating article "Diet and Primary Evolution," (*Scientific American*, August, 1993), in which she convincingly ties the evolution of cooperation and fair play to diet problems encountered in an arboreal environment.

5. Note the connection to the age-old philosophical conundrum about whether, when we have had to replace every part of a ship over the years, the resulting vessel is or is not the same ship as the original. We answer one way or the other depending on other considerations, for example on whom we want to have title to the reconstructed item. There is no way to answer questions of this kind without bringing external interests to bear.

6. It may be thought that these sentiments are not universal on grounds that systems completely unfair to whole groups of people—women, slaves, untouchables—often gain general acceptance, being perceived as fair even by many of those who are given the short end of the stick. But anyone who is tempted to accept this line of reasoning should notice that, first, the general tendency to favor whatever system one grows into enables some of those tyrannized to overlook the unfairness of their situations (self-deception is quite valuable when nothing can be done to rectify matters); second, many of those persecuted understand the nature of their predicament very well indeed, in spite of the fact that the society as a whole sees their condition as fair; third, the more privileged members of disadvantaged groups, for example, educated slaves, generally look on their situations more favorably than those less privileged; and, fourth, human beings, as most social animals, tend, rightly or wrongly (and no doubt very often wrongly), to see the dominance of some members of their in-group over others as justified by the superior qualities or performance of the privileged members. The point is that the acceptance, or pretense of acceptance, of unfair social arrangements as fair by large numbers of the oppressed merely proves their gullibility, or self-deception, or ignorance of nonmoral facts, not their lack of a sense of fairness of the kind discussed here, a point reinforced by the well-known fact that members of oppressed classes are notoriously picky about minor sorts of unfairnesses in their relationships with others who belong to oppressed classes. (That those who gain by unfair social arrangements so often tend to think their good fortune justified—even Aristotle tried to justify slavery—should produce no surprise. There is, after all, an evolutionary benefit in being able to justify a double standard when there is personal profit in doing so.)

PART IV

Value: What Is the Good?

Introduction

Morality is said to aim at the good, whether it is defined in terms of motives, actions, character, or consequences. This leads to an inquiry into Value.

What sort of things are valuable? The term 'value' (from the Latin *valere,* meaning "to be of worth") is highly elastic, being used sometimes narrowly as a synonym for 'good' or 'valuable' and sometimes broadly for the whole scope of evaluative terms, ranging from the highest good through the indifferent to the worst evil, comprising positive neutral as well as negative "values." In the narrow sense the opposite of 'value' is 'evil' or 'disvalue.' In a comprehensive value theory (sometimes referred to as *axiology*) the broader meaning of the word is used.

What Kinds of Goods Are There?

In reading III.6 (Plato's "Why Should I Be Moral?"), Socrates distinguishes three kinds of goods: (1) purely intrinsic good (of which simple joys are an example); (2) purely instrumental good (of which medicine and making money are examples); and (3) combination goods (such as knowledge, sight, and health), which are good in themselves and good as a means to further goods.

The essential difference is between intrinsic and instrumental goods. We consider some things good or worthy of desire (desirable) in themselves and other things good or desirable only because of their consequences. Intrinsic goods are good because of their nature—they are not derived from other goods; whereas instrumental goods are worthy of desire because they are effective means in reaching our intrinsic goods.

Money is the other example of an instrumental value. Few if any of us really value money for its own sake, but almost all of us value it for what it can buy. When we ask, What is money for? we arrive at such goods as food and clothing, shelter and automobiles, entertainment and education. But are any of these really intrinsic goods, or are they all themselves instrumental goods? When we ask, for example, What is entertainment for? what answer do we come up with? Most of us will come up with the answer of enjoyment or pleasure—Socrates' example of an intrinsic good. Can we further ask, What is enjoyment or pleasure for?

Are there any intrinsic values? Are there any entities whose values are not derived from anything else, which are sought after for their own sake, that are just good in themselves? Or are all values relative to desirers, instrumental to goals which are the creation of choosers? Those who espouse the notion of intrinsic value usually argue that pleasure is an example of an intrinsic value and that pain is an example of an intrinsic disvalue. It is just good to experience pleasure and bad to experience pain. Naturally, these philosophers admit that individual experiences of pleasure can be bad (because they result in some other disvalue—like a hangover after a drinking spree) and individual painful experiences can be valuable (e.g., having a painful operation to save one's life). The intrinsicalist affirms that pleasure just is better than pain. We can see this straight off. We don't need any arguments to convince us that pleasure is good or that gratuitous pain is intrinsically bad. Suppose we see a man torturing a child and order him to stop it at once. If he replies, "I agree that the child is experiencing great pain, but why should I stop torturing her?" we would suspect some mental aberration on his part.

The nonintrinsicalist denies that the above arguments have any force. The notion that the experience itself has any value is unclear. It is only by our choosing pleasure over pain that the notion of value gets off the ground. In a sense, all value is extrinsic or a product of choosing. Many existentialists, most notably Jean-Paul Sartre, believe that we invent our values by arbitrary choice. The freedom to create our values and so define ourselves is godlike and, at the same time, deeply frightening, for we have no one to blame for our failures but ourselves. "We are condemned to freedom." "Value is nothing else but the meaning that you choose. One may choose anything so long as it is done from the ground of freedom."[1]

What Things Are Good?

Philosophers divide into two broad camps: those of *hedonists* and *nonhedonists*. The hedonist (being derived from *hedon*, the Greek word for 'pleasure') asserts that all pleasure is good, that pleasure is the only thing good in itself, and that all other goodness is derived from this value. An experience is good in itself if and only if it provides some pleasure and to the extent that it provides pleasure. Sometimes this definition is widened to include the amelioration of pain, pain being seen as the only thing bad in itself. For simplicity's sake we will use the former definition, realizing that it may need to be supplemented by reference to pain.

Hedonists subdivide into (a) *sensualists* and (b) *satisfactionists*, the former equating all pleasure with sensual titillation and the latter with satisfaction or enjoyment, which may not involve sensuality. It is a pleasurable state of consciousness, such as one we experience after accomplishing a successful venture or receiving a gift. The opposite of (a), sensual enjoyment, is physical pain. The opposite of (b), satisfaction, is displeasure or dissatisfaction.

The Greek philosopher Aristippus (c. 435–356 B.C.) and his school, the Cyrenaics, espoused the sensualist position—that the only (or primary) good was sensual pleasure and that this goodness was defined in terms of its intensity.

Most hedonists since the third century B.C. fol-

low Epicurus (342–270 B.C.), who had a broader view of pleasure:

It is not continuous drinkings and revellings, nor the satisfaction of lusts, nor the enjoyment of fish and other luxuries of the wealthy table, which produce a happy life, but sober reasoning, searching out the motives for all choice and avoidance, and banishing mere opinions, to which are due the greatest disturbance of the spirit.[2]

The distinction between pleasure as satisfaction and as sensation is important, and failure to recognize it results in confusion and paradox. One example of this is the paradox of masochism. How can it be that the masochist enjoys (i.e., takes pleasure in) pain, which is the opposite of pleasure? "Well," the hedonist responds, "because of certain psychological aberrations, the masochist enjoys (qua *satisfaction*) what is painful (qua *sensation*)." He or she does not enjoy (qua *sensation*) what is painful (qua *sensation*). It could also be the case that there is a two-level analysis available to explain the masochist's behavior. On a lower or basic level he is experiencing either pain or dissatisfaction, but on a higher level he approves and finds satisfaction from that pain or dissatisfaction.

Nonhedonists divide into two camps: *monists* and *pluralists*. Monists believe that there is a single intrinsic value but that it is not pleasure. Perhaps it is a transcendent value, 'the Good,' which we do not fully comprehend but which is the basis of all our other values. This seems to be Plato's view. Pluralist nonhedonists generally admit that pleasure or enjoyment is an intrinsic good but add that there are other intrinsic goods as well, such as knowledge, friendship, freedom, love, conscientiousness, and life itself.

A hedonist like Jeremy Bentham (1748–1832) in our second reading argues that while these qualities are good, their goodness is derived from the fact that they bring pleasure or satisfaction. Such hedonists ask of each of the above-mentioned values, What is it for? What is knowledge for? If it gave no one any satisfaction or enjoyment, would it really be good? Why do we feel there is a significant difference between knowing how many stairs there are in New York City and whether or not there is life after death? We do not normally value knowledge of the first kind, but knowledge of the second kind is relevant for our enjoyment.

What are friendship and love for? the hedonist asks. If we were made differently and did not get any satisfaction out of love and friendship, would they still be valuable? Are they not highly valuable, significant instrumental goods because they bring enormous satisfaction?

Even moral commitment or conscientiousness is not good in itself, avers the hedonist. Morality is not intrinsically valuable but is meant to serve human need, which in turn has to do with bringing about satisfaction.

According to the hedonist, life is not intrinsically good. It is quality that counts. An ameoba or a permanently comatose patient has life but no intrinsic value. Only when consciousness appears does the possibility for value arrive. Consciousness is a necessary but not a sufficient condition for satisfaction.

The nonhedonist responds that this is counterintuitive. In our fourth reading Robert Nozick challenges those who would identify value with simple states like pleasure or satisfying experience. In our fifth reading W. D. Ross argues against hedonism and for value pluralism.

In our third reading Friedrich Nietzsche posits the will to power as the dominant value that humans, like all creatures caught up in the evolutionary struggle for survival, desire most. Genuine morality is based on the will to power, but there is a constant tendency on the part of the mediocre ("the herd") to invert morality and promulgate the passive virtues of self-denial, humility, tolerance, resignation, and pity.

In our final reading Derek Parfit explores three theories of "the good life": hedonism, desire for fulfillment, and objective lists. He illustrates the problems in each of these theories and suggests that the best life may consist in a combination of hedonism and objective lists.

Are Values Objective or Subjective?

Do we desire the Good because it is good or is the Good good because we desire it?

The objectivist holds that values are worthy of desire whether or not anyone actually desires them. They are somehow independent of us. The subjectivist holds, to the contrary, that values are dependent on desirers, relative to desirers.

The classic objectivist view on values (the absolutist version) is given by Plato (in our first reading), who taught that the Good was the highest form, ineffable, godlike, independent, and knowable only after a protracted education in philosophy. We desire the Good because it is good. The allegory of the cave gives us a picture of Plato's ideas.

Philosophers in the Platonic tradition like G. E. Moore hold to the independent existence of values apart from human or rational interest. Moore claims that the Good is a simple, unanalyzable quality like the color yellow, but one which must be known through the intuitions. Moore believes that a world with beauty is more valuable than one that is a garbage dump, regardless of whether there are conscious beings in those worlds. "Let us imagine one world exceedingly beautiful. Imagine it as beautiful as you can . . . and then imagine the ugliest world you can possibly conceive. Imagine it simply one heap of filth."[3] Moore asks us, even if there were no conscious being, no one who might derive pleasure or pain, in either world, wouldn't we want the first world to exist rather than the second?

Subjectivism treats values as merely products of conscious desire. A value is simply the object of interest. Values are created by desires, and they are valuable only to that degree to which they are desired: the stronger the desire, the greater the value. The difference between the subjectivist and the weak objectivist position (or mixed view) is simply that the subjectivist makes no normative claims about "proper desiring," judging all desires equal. Anything one happens to desire is, by definition, a value, a Good.

The objectivist responds that we can separate

the Good from what one desires. We can say, for example, Joan desires more than anything else to get into the Pleasure Machine, where she will experience unmitigated but mindless pleasures, but it is not good; or John desires more than anything else to join the Ku Klux Klan, but it is not good (not even for John). There is something just plain bad about the Pleasure Machine and the Klan even if Joan and John never experience any dissatisfaction on account of them.

On the other hand, suppose Joan does not want to have any friends and John does not want to know any history or science (beyond that which is necessary for his needs as a mud-wrestler). The objectivist would reply that it really would be an objectively good thing if Joan did have friends and

that John knew something about history and science.

Is there a way to adjudicate the disagreement between the subjectivist and the objectivist?

We turn to Plato's vision of the Good as a transcendent reality.

Notes

1. Jean-Paul Sartre, *Existentialism and Human Emotions,* trans. Bernard Frechtman (Philosophical Library, 1957), pp. 23, 48f. "Value is nothing else but the meaning that you choose. . . . One may choose anything if it is on the grounds of free involvement."
2. Epicurus, "Letter to Manoeceus," C. Bailey (trans.), in W. J. Oates, ed., *The Stoics and Epicurean Philosophers* (Random House, 1940, p. 32).
3. G. E. Moore, *Principia Ethica* (Cambridge, 1903).

11

The Good and the Allegory of the Cave

PLATO

For Plato, values are objective realities that exist independently of knowers. We become good by knowing the Good. In a sense virtue is knowledge and vice is ignorance. No rational person would willingly do evil, for evil corrupts the soul. The Good is good for us, so we must know the Good if we would be happy. What is knowledge for Plato? To know, rather than merely to believe, is to apprehend eternal forms or ideas. The forms are objective, eternal, intangible, unchangeable, transcendent, universal, and absolute realities. To know that some particular object is beautiful is to understand the absolute form of beauty. There is a form or idea of justice, the form of

equality, the form of courage, and so on. The highest form of all is the form of the Good in which all of the other forms participate. The task of each person or "soul," as Plato calls our inner person, is to perfect our selves by philosophical education to the point where we grasp the eternal forms.

In this classic passage from the Republic *Socrates argues that all of the moral and political virtues are centered in the Good and that only by knowing the Good can we achieve political harmony and harmony in the soul. He compares the Good to the sun, and then, using an allegory of the cave, argues that becoming virtuous consists in the soul's turning from looking at appearances to studying the eternal ideas.*

We join Socrates in the midst of a discussion of the virtues with Plato's brothers, Adeimantus and Glaucon.

Reprinted from *Plato's Republic,* trans. G. M. A. Grube (Indianapolis: Hackett Publishing Company, 1974) by permission of the publisher.

Socrates, said Adeimantus, are these virtues not the most important subject of study? Is there anything still more important than justice, courage, self-control, and wisdom?

There is, I said, the Form of the Good is the greatest object of study, and that it is by their relation to it that just actions and the other things become useful and beneficial. You probably knew that I was about to say this and, besides, that our knowledge of it is inadequate. If we do not know the Good, even the fullest possible knowledge of others things is no help to us, any more than if we acquire any possession without the Good. Do you think there is any advantage to have acquired every kind of possession, if it is not good, or to have every kind of knowledge without that of the Good, thus knowing nothing beautiful or good? —No, by Zeus, I do not.

Furthermore, you certainly know that most people believe that pleasure is the Good, while the more enlightened believe it is knowledge. —Of course.

What about those who define the Good as pleasure? Are they less confused than others? Are not even they compelled to admit that there are bad pleasures?—Definitely

So then this is a subject of great and frequent controversies?—It is.

Further, is it not clear that in the case of just and beautiful things, many are content with what seems so, even if it is not, yet they act, acquire, and think on that basis; but when it comes to good things nobody is satisfied to acquire what seems to be so, but they seek things that really are good, and everybody in this case disdains appearances.—Quite so.

Every soul pursues the Good, and all its actions are done for its sake. The soul divines that it is something but is perplexed and cannot adequately grasp what it is, nor does it have about this the firm opinion which it has about other things, and because of this it misses the benefits, if any, even of those other things. Should we say that even the best men in the city to whom we entrust everything must remain in such darkness

about so great and so important a subject? —Least of all.

If people do not recognize the Good, they are not likely to find a guardian who is able to recognize what is right and desirable in institutions and customs.—No doubt.

Our society will only be perfectly governed when such a man who knows the Good looks after it.

Necessarily, Adeimantus replied, but, Socrates, what is your own view of the Good? Is it knowledge, or pleasure, or something else?

What a man! I said. I knew all along that you would not be content with the views of the masses.

Well, Socrates, he said, it does not seem right to me to be able to tell the opinions of others and not one's own, especially for a man who has spent so much time as you have occupying himself with this subject.

Why? said I. Do you think it right to talk about things one does not know as if one knew them? Have you never noticed that opinions not based on knowledge are ugly things? The best of them are blind; or do you think that those who express a true opinion without knowledge are any different from blind people who yet follow the right road?—They are not different.

Do you want to contemplate ugly, blind, and crooked things when you can hear bright and beautiful things from others?

Here Glaucon broke in. By Zeus, Socrates, you must not give up now that you are in sight of the goal. We shall be satisfied if you discuss the Good in the same fashion as you did justice, moderation, and the other virtues.

I would like to do that, but I fear I shall not be able to do so, and that in my eagerness I shall disgrace myself and make myself ridiculous, but I am willing to tell you what appears to be the offspring of the Good and most like it, if that is agreeable to you.—Tell us.

We were speak of many beautiful things and many good things, and we define them in speech. —We do.

And beauty itself and Goodness itself, and so with all the things which we then classed as many; we now class them again according to one Form of each, which is one and which we in each case call that which is.—That is so.

And we say that the many things are the objects of sight but not of thought, while the Forms are the objects of thought but not of sight. —Altogether true.

With what part of ourselves do we see the objects that are seen?—With our sight.

And so things heard are heard by our hearing, and all that is perceived is perceived by our other senses?—Quite so.

Have you considered how very lavishly the maker of our senses made the faculty of seeing and being seen?—I cannot say I have.

Look at it this way: do hearing and sound need another kind of thing for the former to hear and the latter to be heard, and in the absence of this third element the one will not hear and the other not be heard?—No, they need nothing else.

Neither do many other senses, if indeed any, need any such other thing, or can you mention one?—Not I.

But do you not realize that the sense of sight and that which is seen do have such a need? —How so?

Sight may be in the eyes, and the man who has it may try to use it, and colours may be present in the objects, but unless a third kind of thing is present, which is by nature designed for this very purpose, you know that sight will see nothing and the colours remain unseen.—What is this third kind of thing?

What you call light, I said.—Right.

So to no small extent the sense of sight and the power of being seen are yoked together by a more honorable yoke than other things which are yoked together, unless light is held in no honor.—That is far from being the case.

Which of the gods in the heavens can you hold responsible for this, whose light causes our sight to see as beautifully as possible, and the objects of

sight to be seen?—The same as you would, he said, and as others would; obviously the answer to your question is the sun.

And is not sight naturally related to the sun in this way?—Which way?

Sight is not the sun, neither itself nor that in which it occurs which we call the eye.—No indeed.

But I think it is the most sunlike of the organs of sense.—Very much so.

And it receives from the sun the capacity to see as a kind of outflow.—Quite so.

The sun is not sight, but is it not the cause of it, and is also seen by it?—Yes.

Say then, I said, that it is the sun which I called the offspring of the Good, which the Good begot as analogous to itself. What the Good itself is in the world of thought in relation to the intelligence and things known, the sun is in the visible world, in relation to sight and things seen.—How? Explain further.

You know, I said, that when one turns one's eyes to those objects of which the colors are no longer in the light of day but in the dimness of the night, the eyes are dimmed and seem nearly blind, as if clear vision was no longer in them. —Quite so.

Yet whenever one's eyes are turned upon objects brightened by sunshine, they see clearly, and clear vision appears in those very same eyes? —Yes indeed.

So too understand the eye of the soul: whenever it is fixed upon that upon which truth and reality shine, it understands and knows and seems to have intelligence, but whenever it is fixed upon what is mixed with darkness—that which is subject to birth and destruction—it opines and is dimmed, changes its opinions this way and that, and seems to have no intelligence.—That is so.

Say that what gives truth to the objects of knowledge, and to the knowing mind the power to know, is the Form of Good. As it is the cause of knowledge and truth, think of it also as being the object of knowledge. Both knowledge and truth are beautiful, but you will be right to think of the Good as other and more beautiful than they. As in the visible world light and sight are rightly considered sunlike, but it is wrong to think of them as the sun, so here it is right to think of knowledge and truth as Goodlike, but wrong to think of either as the Good, for the Good must be honored even more than they.

This is an extraordinary beauty you mention, he said, if it provides knowledge and truth and is itself superior to them in beauty. You surely do not mean this to be pleasure!

Hush! said I, rather examine the image of it in this way.—How?

You will say, I think, that the sun not only gives to the objects of sight the capacity to be seen, but also that it provides for their generation, increase, and nurture, though it is not itself the process of generation.—How could it be?

And say that as for the objects of knowledge, not only is their being known due to the Good, but also their reality being, though the Good is not being but superior to and beyond being in dignity and power. . . .

Next, I said, compare the effect of education and the lack of it upon our human nature to a situation like this: imagine men to be living in an underground cavelike dwelling place, which has a way up to the light along its whole width, but the entrance is a long way up. The men have been there from childhood, with their neck and legs in fetters, so that they remain in the same place and can only see ahead of them, as their bonds prevent them turning their heads. Light is provided by a fire burning some way behind and above them. Between the fire and the prisoners, some way behind them and on a higher ground, there is a path across the cave and along this a low wall has been built, like the screen at a puppet show in front of the performers who show their puppets above it.—I see it.

See then also men carrying along that wall, so that they overtop it, all kinds of artifacts, statues of men, reproductions of other animals in stone or wood fashioned in all sorts of ways, and, as is likely, some of the carriers are talking while others are silent.—This is a strange picture, and strange prisoners.

They are like us, I said. Do you think, in the first place, that such men could see anything of themselves and each other except the shadows which the fire casts upon the wall of the cave in front of them?—How could they, if they have to keep their heads still throughout life?

And is not the same true of the objects carried along the wall?—Quite.

If they could converse with one another, do you not think that they would consider these shadows to be the real things?—Necessarily.

What if their prison had an echo which reached them from in front of them? Whenever one of the carriers passing behind the wall spoke, would they not think that it was the shadow passing in front of them which was talking? Do you agree? —By Zeus I do.

Altogether then, I said, such men would believe the truth to be nothing else than the shadows of the artifacts?—They must believe that.

Consider then what deliverance from their bonds and the curing of their ignorance would be if something like this naturally happened to them. Whenever one of them was freed, had to stand up suddenly, turn his head, walk, and look up toward the light, doing all that would give him pain, the flash of the fire would make it impossible for him to see the objects of which he had earlier seen the shadows. What do you think he would say if he was told that what he saw then was foolishness, that he was now somewhat closer to reality and turned to things that existed more fully, that he saw more correctly? If one then pointed to each of the objects passing by, asked him what each was, and forced him to answer, do you not think he would be at a loss and believe that the things which he saw earlier were truer than the things now pointed out to him?—Much truer.

If one then compelled him to look at the fire itself, his eyes would hurt, he would turn round and flee toward those things which he could see, and think that they were in fact clearer than those now shown to him.—Quite so.

And if one were to drag him thence by force up the rough and steep path, and did not let him go before he was dragged into the sunlight, would he not be in physical pain and angry as he was dragged along? When he came into the light, with the sunlight filling his eyes, he would not be able to see a single one of the things which are now said to be true.—Not at once, certainly.

I think he would need time to get adjusted before he could see things in the world above; at first he would see shadows most easily, then reflections of men and other things in water, then the things themselves. After this he would see objects in the sky and the sky itself more easily at night, the light of the stars and the moon more easily than the sun and the light of the sun during the day.—Of course.

Then, at last, he would be able to see the sun, not images of it in water or in some alien place, but the sun itself in its own place, and be able to contemplate it.—That must be so.

After this he would reflect that it is the sun which provides the seasons and the years, which governs everything in the visible world, and is also in some way the cause of those other things which he used to see.—Clearly that would be the next stage.

What then? As he reminds himself of his first dwelling place, of the wisdom there and of his fellow prisoners, would he not reckon himself happy for the change, and pity them?—Surely.

And if the men below had praise and honors from each other, and prizes for the man who saw most clearly the shadows that passed before them, and who could best remember which usually came earlier and which later, and which came together and thus could most ably prophesy the future, do you think our man would desire those rewards and envy those who were honored and held power among the prisoners, or would he feel, as Homer put it, that he certainly wished to be "serf to another man without possessions upon the earth"[1] and go through any suffering, rather than share their opinions and live as they do?—Quite so, he said, I think he would rather suffer anything.

Reflect on this too, I said. If this man went down into the cave again and sat down in the same seat, would his eyes not be filled with darkness, coming suddenly out of the sunlight?—They certainly would.

And if he had to contend again with those who had remained prisoners in recognizing those shadows while his sight was affected and his eyes had not settled down—and the time for this adjustment would not be short—would he not be ridiculed? Would it not be said that he had returned from his upward journey with his eyesight spoiled, and that it was not worthwhile even to attempt to travel upward? As for the man who tried to free them and lead them upward, if they could somehow lay their hands on him and kill him, they would do so.—They certainly would.

This whole image, my dear Glaucon, I said, must be related to what we said before. The realm of the visible should be compared to the prison dwelling, and the fire inside it to the power of the sun. If you interpret the upward journey and the contemplation of things above as the upward journey of the soul to the intelligible realm, you will grasp what I surmise since you were keen to hear it. Whether it is true or not only the god knows, but this is how I see it, namely, that in the intelligible world the Form of the Good is the last to be seen, and with difficulty; when seen it must be reckoned to be for all the cause of all that is right and beautiful, to have produced in the visible world both light and the fount of light, while in the intelligible world it is itself that which produces and controls truth and intelligence, and he who is to act intelligently in public or in private must see it.—I share your thought as far as I am able.

Come then, share with me this thought also: do not be surprised that those who have reached this point are unwilling to occupy themselves with human affairs, and that their souls are always pressing upward to spend their time there, for this is natural if things are as our parable indicates.—That is very likely.

Further, I said, do you think it at all surprising that anyone coming to the evils of human life from the contemplation of the divine behaves awkwardly and appears very ridiculous while his eyes are still dazzled and before he is sufficiently adjusted to the darkness around him, if he is compelled to contend in court or some other place about the shadows of justice or the objects of which they are shadows, and to carry through the contest about these in the way these things are understood by those who have never seen Justice itself?—That is not surprising at all.

Anyone with intelligence, I said, would remember that the eyes may be confused in two ways and from two causes, coming from light into darkness as well as from darkness into light. Realizing that the same applies to the soul, whenever he sees a soul disturbed and unable to see something, he will not laugh mindlessly but will consider whether it has come from a brighter life and is dimmed because unadjusted, or has come from greater ignorance into greater light and is filled with a brighter dazzlement. The former he would declare happy in its life and experience, the latter he would pity, and if he should wish to laugh at it, his laughter would be less ridiculous than if he laughed at a soul that has come from the light above.—What you say is very reasonable.

We must then, I said, if these things are true, think something like this about them, namely, that education is not what some declare it to be; they say that knowledge is not present in the soul and that they put it in, like putting sight into blind eyes.—They surely say that.

Our present argument shows, I said, that the capacity to learn and the organ with which to do so are present in every person's soul. It is as if it were not possible to turn the eye from darkness to light without turning the whole body; so one must turn one's whole soul from the world of

becoming until it can endure to contemplate reality, and the brightest of realities, which we say is the Good.—Yes.

Education then is the art of doing this very thing, this turning around, the knowledge of how the soul can most easily and most effectively be turned around; it is not the art of putting the capacity of sight into the soul; the soul possesses that already but it is not turned the right way or looking where it should. This is what education has to deal with.—That seems likely.

Now the other so-called virtues of the soul seem to be very close to those of the body—they really do not exist before and are added later by habit and practice—but the virtue of intelligence belongs above all to something more divine, it seems, which never loses its capacity but, according to which way it is turned, becomes useful and beneficial or useless and harmful. Have you ever noticed in men who are said to be wicked but clever, how sharply their little soul looks into things to which it turns its attention? Its capacity for sight is not inferior, but it is compelled to serve evil ends, so that the more sharply it looks the more evils it works.—Quite so.

Yet if a soul of this kind had been hammered at from childhood and those excrescences had been knocked off it which belong to the world of becoming and have been fastened upon it by feasting, gluttony, and similar pleasures, and which like leaden weights draw the soul to look downward—if, being rid of these, it turned to look at things that are true, then the same soul of the same man would see these just as sharply as it now sees the things towards which it is directed. —That seems likely.

Notes

1. *Odyssey* 11, 489–90, where Achilles says to Odysseus, on the latter's visit to the underworld, that he would rather be a servant to a poor man on earth than king among the dead.

12

Classical Hedonism

Jeremy Bentham

Jeremy Bentham (1748–1832) was a British utili-tarian (see Part V) and legal reformer. In this essay from An Introduction to the Principles of Morals and Legislation, *he argues that pleasure is the only intrinsic value and pain the only intrinsic evil. All other goods and evils derive from these two qualities. Moral rightness and wrongness are defined in terms of his hedonistic calculus, according to their conse-quences in producing pleasure and pain.*

Of the Principle of Utility

I. Nature has placed mankind under the gover-nance of two sovereign masters, *pain* and *pleasure.* It is for them alone to point out what we ought to do, as well as to determine what we shall do. On the one hand the standard of right and wrong, on the other the chain of causes and effects, are fastened to their throne. They govern us in all we do, in all we say, in all we think: every effort we can make to throw off our subjection, will serve but to demonstrate and confirm it. In words a man may pretend to abjure their empire: but in reality he will remain subject to it all the while. The *principle of utility* recognizes this subjection, and assumes it for the foundation of that system, the object of which is to rear the fabric of felicity by the hands of reason and of law. Systems which attempt to question it, deal in sounds instead of sense, in caprice instead of reason, in darkness instead of light.

But enough of metaphor and declamation: it is not by such means that moral science is to be improved.

II. The principle of utility is the foundation of

Excerpted from *An Introduction to the Principles of Morals and Legislation* (1789).

the present work: it will be proper therefore at the outset to give an explicit and determinate ac-count of what is meant by it. By the principle of utility is meant that principle which approves or disapproves of every action whatsoever, according to the tendency which it appears to have to aug-ment or diminish the happiness of the party whose interest is in question: or, what is the same thing in other words, to promote or to oppose that happiness. I say of every action whatsoever; and therefore not only of every action of a private individual, but of every measure of government.

III. By utility is meant that property in any object, whereby it tends to produce benefit, ad-vantage, pleasure, good, or happiness, (all this in the present case comes to the same thing) or (what comes again to the same thing) to prevent the happening of mischief, pain, evil, or unhappi-ness to the party whose interest is considered: if that party be the community in general, then the happiness of the community: if a particular indi-vidual, then the happiness of that individual.

Value of a Lot of Pleasure or Pain, How to Be Measured

I. Pleasures then, and the avoidance of pains, are the *ends* which the legislator has in view: it be-hoves him therefore to understand their *value.* Pleasures and pains are the *instruments* he has to work with: it behoves him therefore to under-stand their *force,* which is again, in other words, their value.

II. To a person considered *by himself,* the value of a pleasure or pain considered *by itself,* will be greater or less, according to the four following circumstances:

1. Its *intensity.*
2. Its *duration.*
3. Its *certainty* or *uncertainty.*
4. Its *propinquity* or *remoteness.*

III. These are the circumstances which are to be considered in estimating a pleasure or a pain considered each of them by itself. But when the value of any pleasure or pain is considered for the purpose of estimating the tendency of any *act* by which it is produced, there are two other circumstances to be taken into the account; these are,

5. Its *fecundity,* or the chance it has of being followed by sensations of the *same* kind: that is, pleasures, if it be a pleasure: pains, if it be a pain.

6. Its *purity,* or the chance it has of *not* being followed by sensations of the *opposite* kind: that is, pains, if it be a pleasure: pleasures, if it be a pain.

These two last, however, are in strictness scarcely to be deemed properties of the pleasure or the pain itself; they are not, therefore, in strictness to be taken into the account of the value of that pleasure or that pain. They are in strictness to be deemed properties only of the act, or other event, by which such pleasure or pain has been produced; and accordingly are only to be taken into the account of the tendency of such act or such event.

IV. To a *number* of persons, with reference to each of whom the value of a pleasure or a pain is considered, it will be greater or less, according to seven circumstances: to wit, the six preceding ones; *viz.*

1. Its *intensity.*
2. Its *duration.*
3. Its *certainty* or *uncertainty.*
4. Its *propinquity* or *remoteness.*
5. Its *fecundity.*
6. Its *purity.*

And one other; to wit:

7. Its *extent*; that is, the number of persons to whom it *extends*; or (in other words) who are affected by it.

V. To take an exact account then of the general tendency of any act, by which the interests of a community are affected, proceed as follows. Be-gin with any one person of those whose interests seem most immediately to be affected by it: and take an account,

1. Of the value of each distinguishable *pleasure* which appears to be produced by it in the *first* instance.

2. Of the value of each *pain* which appears to be produced by it in the *first* instance.

3. Of the value of each pleasure which appears to be produced by it *after* the first. This constitutes the *fecundity* of the first *pleasure* and the *impurity* of the first *pain.*

4. Of the value of each *pain* which appears to be produced by it after the first. This constitutes the *fecundity* of the first *pain,* and the *impurity* of the first pleasure.

5. Sum up all the values of all the *pleasures* on the one side, and those of all the pains on the other. The balance, if it be on the side of pleasure, will give the *good* tendency of the act upon the whole, with respect to the interests of that *individual* person; if on the side of pain, the *bad* tendency of it upon the whole.

6. Take an account of the *number* of persons whose interests appear to be concerned; and repeat the above process with respect to each. *Sum up* the numbers expressive of the degrees of *good* tendency, which the act has, with respect to each individual, in regard to whom the tendency of it is *good* upon the whole: do this again with respect to each individual, in regard to whom the tendency of it is *good* upon the whole: do this again with respect to each individual, in regard to whom the tendency of it is *bad* upon the whole. Take the *balance*; which, if on the side of *pleasure,* will give the general *good tendency* of the act, with respect to the total number or community of individuals concerned; if on the side of pain, the general *evil tendency,* with respect to the same community.

VI. It is not to be expected that this process should be strictly pursued previously to every moral judgment, or to every legislative or judicial operation. It may, however, be always kept in view: and as near as the process actually pursued on these occasions approaches to it, so near will such process approach to the character of an exact one.

VII. The same process is alike applicable to pleasure and pain, in whatever shape they appear: and by whatever denomination they are distinguished: to pleasure, whether it be called *good* (which is properly the cause or instrument of pleasure) or *profit* (which is distant pleasure, or the cause or instrument of distant pleasure,) or *convenience*, or *advantage, benefit, emolument, happiness*, and so forth: to pain, whether it be called *evil*, (which corresponds to *good*) or *mischief*, or *inconvenience*, or *disadvantage*, or *loss*, or *unhappiness*, and so forth.

VIII. Nor is this a novel and unwarranted, any more than it is a useless theory. In all this there is nothing but what the practice of mankind, wheresoever they have a clear view of their own interest, is perfectly comfortable to. An article of property, an estate in land, for instance, is valuable, on what account? On account of the pleasures of all kinds which it enables a man to produce, and what comes to the same thing the pains of all kinds which it enables him to avert. But the value of such an article of property is universally understood to rise or fall according to the length or shortness of the time which a man had in it: the certainty or uncertainty of its coming into possession: and the nearness or remoteness of the time at which, if at all, it is to come into possession. As to the *intensity* of the pleasures which a man may derive from it, this is never thought of, because it depends upon the use which each particular person may come to make of it; which cannot be estimated till the particular pleasures he may come to derive from it, or the particular pains he may come to exclude by means of it, are brought to view. For the same reason, neither does he think of the *fecundity* or *purity* of those pleasures.

Thus much for pleasure and pain, happiness and unhappiness, in *general*.

13

Beyond Good and Evil

FRIEDRICH NIETZSCHE

Friedrich Nietzsche (1844–1900) was a German philosopher and a forerunner of Existentialism. Descended through both of his parents from Lutheran ministers, Nietzsche was raised in a devout Christian home and was known as "the little Jesus" by his schoolmates. He studied theology at the University of Bonn and philology at Leipzig, becoming an atheist in the process. At the age of twenty-four he was appointed professor of classical philology at the University of Basel in Switzerland, where he taught for ten years until forced by ill health to retire. Eventually he became mentally ill. He died on August 25, 1900.

Nietzsche believes that the fundamental creative force that motivates all creation is the will to power. We all seek, not happiness, but to affirm ourselves, to flourish and dominate. Since we are essentially unequal in ability, intelligence, and imagination, it follows that the fittest will survive and be victorious in the contest with the weaker and the baser. Great beauty inheres in the struggle of the noble spirit ascending to his pinnacle on the trunks of lesser beings, including lesser human beings. But this process is hampered by Judeo-Christian morality, which Nietzsche labels "slave morality." Slave morality, which is the invention of the jealous priests, envious and resentful of the power and excellence of the noble spirit, makes us become meek and mild, so that we believe the lie that all humans have equal worth. He sometimes, as in our reading, refers to this as the ethics of "resentment."

Nietzsche's idea of an inegalitarian aesthetic-ethic assumes the thesis that "God is dead." God plays no vital role in our culture—except as a protector of the slave morality, including the idea of the equal worth of all persons. If we recognize that there is no rational basis for believing in God, we will see that the whole edifice of slave morality must crumble and with it the notion of equal worth. In its place will arise the morality of the noble person based on the virtues of high courage, disciplined passion, pride, and intelligence, in the pursuit of affirmation and excellence.

We begin this section with Nietzsche's famous description of the madman who announces the death of God; we then turn to selections from Beyond Good and Evil, The Genealogy of Morals *and* The Twilight of the Idols.

The Madman and the Death of God

Have you ever heard of the madman who on a bright morning lighted a lantern and ran to the marketplace calling out unceasingly, "I seek God! I seek God!"—As there were many people standing about who did not believe in God, he caused a great deal of amusement. Why! Is he lost? Said one. Has he strayed away like a child? said another. Or does he keep himself hidden? Is he afraid of us? Has he taken a sea-voyage? Has he emigrated?—the people cried out laughingly, all in a hubbub. The insane man jumped into their midst and transfixed them with his glances. "Where is God gone?" he called out. "I mean to tell you! *We have killed him,*—you and I! We are all his murderers! But how have we done it? How were we able to drink up the sea? Who gave us the sponge to wipe away the whole horizon? What did we do when we loosened this earth from its sun? Whither does it now move? Whither do we move? Away from all suns? Do we not dash on unceasingly? Backwards, sideways, forwards, in all directions? Is there still an above and below? Do we not stray, as through infinite nothingness? Does not empty space breathe upon us? Has it not become colder? Does not night come on continu-

Reprinted from *The Complete Works of Nietzsche,* ed. Oscar Levy, vols. 10 and 11 (New York: T. Foulis, 1910).

ally, darker and darker? Shall we not have to light
lanterns in the morning? Do we not hear the noise
of the grave-diggers who are burying God? Do we
not smell the divine putrefaction?—for even
Gods putrefy! God is dead! God remains dead!
And we have killed him! How shall we console
ourselves, the most murderous of all murderers?
The holiest and the mightiest that the world has
hitherto possessed has bled to death under our
knife,—who will wipe the blood from us? With
what water could we cleanse ourselves? What lus-
trums, what sacred games shall we have to devise?
Is not the magnitude of this deed too great for us?
Shall we not ourselves have to become gods,
merely to seem worthy of it? There never was a
greater event,—and on account of it, all who are
born after us belong to a higher history than any
history hitherto!"—Here the madman was silent
and looked again at his hearers; they also were
silent and looked at him in surprise. At last he
threw his lantern on the ground, so that it broke
in pieces and was extinguished. "I come too
early," he then said, "I am not yet at the right
time. This prodigious event is still on its way, and
is travelling,—it has not yet reached men's ears.
Lightning and thunder need time, the light of the
stars needs time, deeds need time, even after they
are done, to be seen and heard. This deed is as yet
further from them than the furthest star,—*and
yet they have done it!*"—It is further stated that
the madman made his way into different churches
on the same day, and there intoned his *Requiem
aeternam deo*. When led out and called to account,
he always gave the reply: "What are these
churches now, if they are not the tombs and mon-
uments of God?"— . . .

What Is Noble?

Every elevation of the type "man" has hitherto
been the work of an aristocratic society and so it
will always be—a society believing in a long scale
of gradations of rank and differences of worth
among human beings, and requiring slavery in
some form or other. Without the *pathos of dis-*

tance, such as grows out of the incarnated difference of classes, out of the constant outlooking and
downlooking of the ruling caste on subordinates
and instruments, and out of their equally constant
practice of obeying and commanding, of keeping
down and keeping at a distance—that other more
mysterious pathos could never have arisen, the
longing for an ever new widening of distance
within the soul itself, the formation of ever
higher, rarer, further, more extended, more comprehensive states, in short, just the elevation of
the type "man," the continued "self-surmounting
of man," to use a moral formula in a supermoral
sense. To be sure, one must not resign oneself to
any humanitarian illusions about the history of
the origin of an aristocratic society (that is to say,
of the preliminary condition for the elevation of
the type "man"): the truth is hard. Let us acknowledge unprejudicedly how ever higher civilisation hitherto has *originated!* Men with a still
natural nature, barbarians in every terrible sense
of the word, men of prey, still in possession of un-
broken strength of will and desire for power,
threw themselves upon weaker, more moral, more
peaceful races (perhaps trading or cattle-rearing
communities), or upon old mellow civilisations in
which the final vital force was flickering out in
brilliant fireworks of wit and depravity. At the
commencement, the noble caste was always the
barbarian caste: their superiority did not consist
first of all in their physical, but in their psychical
power—they were more *complete* men (which at
every point also implies the same as "more complete beasts").

Corruption—as the indication that anarchy
threatens to break out among the instincts, and
that the foundation of the emotions, called "life,"
is convulsed—is something radically different according to the organisation in which it manifests
itself. When, for instance, an aristocracy like that
of France at the beginning of the Revolution,
flung away its privileges with sublime disgust and
sacrificed itself to an excess of its moral sentiments, it was corruption:—it was really only the
closing act of the corruption which had existed

for centuries, by virtue of which that aristocracy had abdicated step by step its lordly prerogatives and lowered itself to a *function* of royalty (in the end even to its decoration and parade-dress). The essential thing, however, in a good and healthy aristocracy is that it should *not* regard itself as a function either of the kingship or the commonwealth, but as the *significance* and highest justification thereof—that it should therefore accept with a good conscience the sacrifice of a lesion of individuals, who, *for its sake,* must be suppressed and reduced to imperfect men, to slaves and instruments. Its fundamental belief must be precisely that society is *not* allowed to exist for its own sake, but only as a foundation and scaffolding, by means of which a select class of beings may be able to elevate themselves to their higher duties, and in general to a higher *existence:* like those sun-seeking climbing plants in Java—they are called *Sipo Matador,*—which encircle an oak so long and so often with their arms, until at last, high above it, but supported by it, they can unfold their tops in the open light, and exhibit their happiness.

To refrain mutually from injury, from violence, from exploitation, and put one's will on a par with that of others: this may result in a certain rough sense in good conduct among individuals when the necessary conditions are given (namely, the actual similarity of the individuals in amount of force and degree of worth, and their co-relation within one organisation). As soon, however, as one wished to take this principle more generally, and if possible even as *the fundamental principle of society,* it would immediately disclose what it really is—namely, a Will to the *denial* of life, a principle of dissolution and decay. Here one must think profoundly to the very basis and resist all sentimental weakness: life itself is *essentially* appropriation, injury, conquest of the strange and weak, suppression, severity, obtrusion of peculiar forms, incorporation, and at the least, putting it mildest, exploitation;—but why should one for ever use precisely these words on which for ages a disparaging purpose has been stamped? Even the organisation within which, as was previously sup-posed, the individuals treat each other as equal— it takes place in every healthy aristocracy—must itself, if it be a living and not a dying organisation, do all that towards other bodies, which the individuals within it refrain from doing to each other: it will have to be the incarnated Will to Power, it will endeavour to grow, to gain ground, attract to itself and acquire ascendancy—not owing to any morality or immorality, but because it *lives,* and because life *is* precisely Will to Power. On no point, however, is the ordinary consciousness of Europeans more unwilling to be corrected than on this matter; people now rave everywhere, even under the guise of science, about coming conditions of society in which "the exploiting character" is to be absent:—that sounds to my ears as if they promised to invent a mode of life which should refrain from all organic functions. "Exploitation" does not belong to a depraved, or imperfect and primitive society: it belongs to the *nature* of the living being as a primary organic function; it is a consequence of the intrinsic Will to Power, which is precisely the Will to Life.— Granting that as a theory this is a novelty—as a reality it is the *fundamental fact* of all history: let us be so far honest toward ourselves!

Master and Slave Morality

In a tour through the many finer and coarser moralities which have hitherto prevailed or still prevail on the earth, I found certain traits recurring regularly together, and connected with one another, until finally two primary types revealed themselves to me, and a radical distinction was brought to light. There is *master-morality* and *slave-morality;*—I would at once add, however, that in all higher and mixed civilisations, there are also attempts at the reconciliation of the two moralities; but one finds still oftener the confusion and mutual misunderstanding of them, indeed, sometimes their close juxtaposition—even in the same man, within one soul. The distinctions of moral values have originated either in a ruling caste, pleasantly conscious of being different from the ruled—or among the ruled class, the slaves and dependents of all sorts. In the first case, when it is the rulers who determine the conception "good," it is the exalted, proud disposition which is regarded as the distinguishing feature, and that which determines the order of rank. The noble type of man separates from himself the beings in whom the opposite of this exalted, proud disposition displays itself: he despises them. Let it at once be noted that in this first kind of morality the antithesis "good" and "bad" means practically the same as "noble" and "despicable";—the antithesis "good" and "*evil*" is of a different origin. The cowardly, the timid, the insignificant, and those thinking merely of narrow utility are despised; moreover, also, the distrustful, with their constrained glances, the self-abasing, the doglike kind of men who let themselves be abused, the mendicant flatterers, and above all the liars:—it is a fundamental belief of all aristocrats that the common people are untruthful. "We truthful ones"—the nobility in ancient Greece called themselves. It is obvious that everywhere the designations of moral value were at first applied to *men,* and were only derivatively and at a later period applied to *actions;* it is a gross mistake, therefore, when historians of morals start with questions like, "Why have sympathetic actions been praised?" The noble type of man regards *himself* as a determiner of values; he does not require to be approved of; he passes the judgment: "What is injurious to me is injurious in itself"; he knows that it is he himself only who confers honour on things; he is a *creator of values.* He honours whatever he recognises in himself: such morality is self-glorification. In the foreground there is the feeling of plenitude, of power, which seeks to overflow, the happiness of high tension, the consciousness of a wealth which would fain give and bestow:—the noble man also helps the unfortunate, but not—or scarcely—out of pity, but rather from an impulse generated by the superabundance of power. The noble man honours in himself the powerful one, him also who has power over himself, who knows how to speak and

how to keep silence, who takes pleasure in subjecting himself to severity and hardness, and has reverence for all that is severe and hard. "Wotan placed a hard heart in my breast," says an old Scandinavian Saga: it is thus rightly expressed from the soul of a proud Viking. Such a type of man is even proud of *not* being made for sympathy; the hero of the Saga therefore adds warningly "He who has not a hard heart when young, will never have one." The noble and brave who think thus are the furthest removed from the morality which sees precisely in sympathy, or in acting for the good of others, or in *désintéressement,* the characteristic of the moral; faith in oneself, pride in oneself, a radical enmity and irony toward "selflessness," belong as definitely to noble morality, as do a careless scorn and precaution in presence of sympathy and the "warm heart."—It is the powerful who *know* how to honour, it is their art, their doman for invention. The profound reverence for age and for tradition—all law rests on this double reverence,—the belief and prejudice in favour of ancestors and unfavourable to newcomers, is typical in the morality of the powerful; and if, reversely, men of "modern ideas" believe almost instinctively in "progress" and the "future," and are more and more lacking in respect for old age, the ignoble origin of these "ideas" has complacently betrayed itself thereby. A morality of the ruling class, however, is more especially foreign and irritating to present-day taste in the sternness of its principle that one has duties only to one's equals; that one may act toward beings of a lower rank, toward all that is foreign, just as seems good to one, or "as the heart desires," and in any case "beyond good and evil": it is here that sympathy and similar sentiments can have a place. The ability and obligation to exercise prolonged gratitude and prolonged revenge—both only within the circle of equals,—artfulness in retaliation, *raffinement* of the idea in friendship, a certain necessity to have enemies (as outlets for the emotions of envy, quarrelsomeness, arrogance—in fact, in order to be a good *friend*): all these are typical characteristics of the noble morality, which, as has been pointed out, is not the morality of "modern ideas," and is therefore at present difficult to realise and also to unearth and disclose.—It is otherwise with the second type of morality, *slave-morality*. Supposing that the abused, the oppressed, the suffering, the unemancipated, the weary, and those uncertain of themselves, should moralise, what will be the common element in their moral estimates? Probably a pessimistic suspicion with regard to the entire situation of man will find expression, perhaps a condemnation of man, together with his situation. The slave has an unfavourable eye for the virtues of the powerful; he has a skepticism and distrust, a *refinement* of distrust of everything "good" that is there honoured—he would fain persuade himself that the very happiness there is not genuine. On the other hand, *those* qualities which serve to alleviate the existence of sufferers are brought into prominence and flooded with light; it is here that sympathy, the kind, helping hand, the warm heart, patience, diligence, humility, and friendliness attain to honour; for here these are the most useful qualities, and almost the only means of supporting the burden of existence. Slave-morality is essentially the morality of utility. Here is the seat of the origin of the famous antithesis "good" and "evil":—power and dangerousness are assumed to reside in the evil, a certain dreadfulness, subtlety, and strength, which do not admit of being despised. According to slave-morality, therefore, the "evil" man arouses fear; according to master-morality, it is precisely the "good" man who arouses fear and seeks to arouse it, while the bad man is regarded as the despicable being. The contrast attains its maximum when, in accordance with the logical consequences of slave-morality, a shade of depreciation—it may be slight and well-intentioned—at last attaches itself to the "good" man of this morality; because, according to the servile mode of thought, the good man must in any case be the *safe* man: he is good-natured, easily deceived, perhaps a little stupid, *un bonhomme.* Everywhere that slave-morality gains the ascendancy, language shows a tendency to approximate the significations of the words "good" and "stupid."—A last fundamental difference: the desire for *freedom,* the instinct for happiness and the refinements of the feeling of liberty belong as necessarily to slave-morals and morality, as artifice and enthusiasm in reverence and devotion are the regular symptoms of an aristocratic mode of thinking and estimating.— Hence we can understand without further detail why love *as a passion*—it is our European specialty—must absolutely be of noble origin; as is well known, its invention is due to the Provençal poet-cavaliers, those brilliant, ingenious men of the *"gai saber,"* to whom Europe owes so much, and almost owes itself. . . .

There is an *instinct for rank,* which more than anything else is already the sign of a *high* rank; there is a *delight* in the *nuances* of reverence which leads one to infer noble origin and habits. The refinement, goodness, and loftiness of a soul are put to a perilous test when something passes by that is of the highest rank, but is not yet protected by the awe of authority from obtrusive touches and incivilities: something that goes its way like a living touchstone, undistinguished, undiscovered, and tentative, perhaps voluntarily veiled and disguised. He whose task and practice it is to investigate souls, will avail himself of many varieties of this very art to determine the ultimate value of a soul, the unalterable, innate order of rank to which it belongs; he will test it by its *instinct for reverence. Difference engendre haine* [Difference engenders hate.—ED.]: the vulgarity of many a nature spurts up suddenly like dirty water, when any holy vessel, any jewel from closed shrines, any book bearing the marks of great destiny, is brought before it; while on the other hand, there is an involuntary silence, a hesitation of the eye, a cessation of all gestures, by which *it* is indicated that a soul *feels* the nearness of what is worthiest of respect. . . .

The revolt of the slaves in morals begins in the very principle of *resentment* becoming creative and giving birth to values—a resentment experienced by creatures who, deprived as they are of the proper outlet of action, are forced to find their compensation in an imaginary revenge. While every aristocratic morality springs from a triumphant affirmation of its own demands, the slave morality says "no" from the very outset to what is "outside itself," "different from itself," and "not itself": and this "no" is its creative deed. This reversal of the valuing standpoint—this *inevitable* gravitation to the objective instead of back to the subjective—is typical of "resentment": the slave-morality requires as the condition of its existence an external and objective world, to employ physiological terminology, it requires objective stimuli to be capable of action at all—its action is fundamentally a reaction. The contrary is the case when we come to the aristocrat's system of values: it acts and grows spontaneously, it merely seeks its antithesis in order to pronounce a more grateful and exultant "yes" to its own self;—its negative conception, "low," "vulgar," "bad," is merely a pale late-born foil in comparison with its positive and fundamental conception (saturated as it is with life and passion), of "we aristocrats, we good ones, we beautiful ones, we happy ones."

When the aristocratic morality goes astray and commits sacrilege on reality, this is limited to that particular sphere with which it is *not* sufficiently acquainted—a sphere, in fact, from the real knowledge of which it disdainfully defends itself. It misjudges, in some cases, the sphere which it despises, the sphere of the common vulgar man and the low people: on the other hand, due weight should be given to the consideration that in any case the mood of contempt, of disdain, of superciliousness, even on the supposition that it *falsely* portrays the object of its contempt, will always be far removed from that degree of falsity which will always characterise the attacks—in effigy, of course—of the vindictive hatred and revengefulness of the weak in onslaughts on their enemies. In point of fact, there is in contempt too strong an admixture of nonchalance, of casualness, of boredom, of impatience, even of personal exultation, for it to be capable of distorting its victim into a real caricature or a real monstrosity. Attention again should be paid to the almost benevolent *nuances* which, for instance, the Greek nobility imports into all the words by which it distinguishes the common people from itself; note how continuously a kind of pity, care, and consideration imparts its honeyed *flavour*, until at last almost all the words which are applied to the vulgar man survive finally as expressions for "unhappy," "worthy of pity" . . .—and how, conversely, "bad," "low," "unhappy" have never ceased to ring in the Greek ear with a tone in which "unhappy" is the predominant note: this is a heritage of the old noble aristocratic morality, which remains true to itself even in contempt. . . . The "well-born" simply *felt* themselves the "happy"; they did not have to manufacture their happiness artificially through looking at their enemies, or in cases to talk and lie themselves into happiness (as is the custom with all resentful men); and similarly, complete men as they were, exuberant with strength, and consequently *necessarily* energetic, they were too wise to dissociate happiness from action—activity becomes in their minds necessarily counted as happiness (that is the etymology of εὐ πράττειν)—all in sharp contrast to the "happiness" of the weak and the oppressed, with their festering venom and malignity, among whom happiness appears essentially as a narcotic, a deadening, a quietude, a peace, a "Sabbath," an enervation of the mind and relaxation of the limbs,—in short, a purely *passive* phenomenon. While the aristocratic man lived in confidence and openness with himself (γεν–ναῖος, "noble-born," emphasises the nuance "sincere," and perhaps also "naïf"), the resentful man, on the other hand, is neither sincere nor naïf, nor honest and candid with himself. His soul *squints;* his mind loves hidden crannies, tortuous paths and back doors, everything secret appeals to him as *his* world, *his* safety, *his* balm; he is past master in silence, in not forgetting, in waiting, in provisional self-deprecation and self-abasement. A race of such *resentful* men will of necessity eventually prove more *prudent* than any aristocratic race, it will honour prudence on quite a distinct scale, as, in fact, a paramount condition of existence, while prudence among aristocratic men is apt to be tinged with a delicate flavour of luxury and refinement; so among them it plays nothing like so integral a part as that complete certainty of function of the governing *unconscious* instincts, or as indeed a certain lack of prudence, such as a vehement and valiant charge, whether against danger or the enemy, or as those ecstatic bursts of rage, love, reverence, gratitude, by which at all times noble souls have recognised each other. When the resentment of the aristocratic man manifests itself, it fulfills and exhausts itself in an immediate reaction, and consequently instills no *venom:* on the other hand, it never manifests itself at all in countless instances, when in the case of the feeble and weak it would be inevitable. An inability to take seriously for any length of time their enemies, their disasters, their *misdeeds*—that is the sign of the full strong natures who possess a superfluity of moulding plastic force, that heals completely and produces forgetfulness: a good example of this in the modern world is Mirabeau, who had no memory for any insults and meannesses which were practised on him, and who was only incapable of forgiving because he forgot. Such a man indeed shakes off with a shrug many a worm which would have buried itself in another; it is only in characters like these that we see the possibility (supposing, of course, that there is such a possibility in the world) of the real "*love* of one's enemies." What respect for his enemies is found, forsooth, in an aristocratic man—and such a reverence is already a bridge to love! He insists on having his enemy to himself as his distinction. He tolerates no other enemy but a man in whose character there is nothing to despise and *much* to honour! On the other hand, imagine the "enemy" as the resentful man conceives him—and it is here exactly that we see his work, his creativeness; he has conceived "the evil enemy," the "evil one," and indeed that is the root idea from which he now evolves as a contrasting and corresponding figure a "good one," himself—his very self!

The method of this man is quite contrary to that of the aristocratic man, who conceives the root idea "good" spontaneously and straight away, that is to say, out of himself, and from that material then creates for himself a concept of "bad"! This "bad" of aristocratic origin and that "evil" out of the cauldron of unsatisfied hatred—the former an imitation, an "extra," and additional nuance; the latter, on the other hand, the original, the beginning, the essential act in the conception of a slave-morality—these two words "bad" and "evil," how great a difference do they mark, in spite of the fact that they have an identical contrary in the idea "good." But the idea "good" is *not* the same: much rather let the question be asked, "Who is really evil according to the meaning of the morality of resentment?" In all sternness let it be answered thus:—*just* the good man of the other morality, just the aristocrat, the powerful one, one who rules, but who is distorted by the venomous eye of resentfulness, into a new colour, a new signification, a new appearance. This particular point we would be the last to deny: the man who learnt to know those "good" ones only as enemies, learnt at the same time not to know them only as *"evil enemies"* and the same men who . . . were kept so rigorously in bounds through convention, respect, custom, and gratitude, though much more through mutual vigilance and jealousy, . . . these men who in their relations with each other find so many new ways of manifesting consideration, self-control, delicacy, loyalty, pride, and friendship, these men are in reference to what is outside their circle (where the foreign element, a *foreign* country, begins), not much better than beasts of prey, which have been let loose. They enjoy there freedom from all social control, they feel that in the wilderness they can give vent with impunity to that tension which is produced by enclosure and imprisonment in the peace of society, they *revert* to the innocence of the beast-of-prey conscience, like jubilant monsters, who perhaps come from a ghostly bout of murder, arson, rape, and torture, with bravado and a moral equanimity, as though merely some wild student's prank had been played, perfectly convinced that the poets have now an ample theme to sing and celebrate. It is impossible not to recognise at the core of all these aristocratic races the beast of prey; the magnificent *blonde brute*, avidly rampant for spoil and victory; this hidden core needed an outlet from time to time, the beast must get loose again, must return into the wilderness—the Roman, Arabic, German, and Japanese nobility, the Homeric heroes, the Scandinavian Vikings, are all alike in this need. It is the aristocratic races who have left the idea "Barbarian" on all the tracks in which they have marched; nay, a consciousness of this very barbarianism, and even a pride in it, manifests itself even in their highest civilisation (for example, when Pericles says to his Athenians in that celebrated funeral oration, "Our audacity has forced a way over every land and sea, rearing everywhere imperishable memorials of self for *good* and for *evil*"). This audacity of aristocratic races, mad, absurd, and spasmodic as may be its expression; the incalculable and fantastic nature of their enterprises, . . . their nonchalance and contempt for safety, body, life, and comfort, their awful joy and intense delight in all destruction, in all the ecstasies of victory and cruelty,—all these features become crystallised, for those who suffered thereby in the picture of the "barbarian," of the "evil enemy," perhaps of the "Goth" and of the "Vandal." The profound, icy mistrust which the German provokes, as soon as he arrives at power,—even at the present time,—is always still an aftermath of that inextinguishable horror with which for whole centuries Europe has regarded the wrath of the blonde Teuton beast. . . .

. . . One may be perfectly justified in being always afraid of the blonde beast that lies at the core of all aristocratic races, and in being on one's guard: but who would not a hundred times prefer to be afraid, when one at the same time admires, than to be immune from fear, at the cost of being perpetually obsessed with the loathsome spectacle of the distorted, the dwarfed, the stunted, the envenomed? And is that not our fate? What produces today our repulsion towards "man"?—for we *suffer* from "man," there is no doubt about it. It is not fear; it is rather that we have nothing more to fear from men; it is that the worm "man" is in the foreground and pullulates; it is that the "tame man," the wretched mediocre and unedifying creature, has learnt to consider himself a goal and a pinnacle, an inner meaning, an historic principle, a "higher man"; yes, it is that he has a certain right so to consider himself, in so far as he feels that in contrast to that excess of deformity, disease, exhaustion, and effeteness whose odour is beginning to pollute present-day Europe, he at any rate has achieved a relative success, he at any rate still says "yes" to life.

Goodness and the Will to Power

What is good?—All that enhances the feeling of power, the Will to Power, and the power itself in man. What is bad?—All that proceeds from weakness. What is happiness?—The feeling that power is increasing—that resistance has been overcome.

Not contentment, but more power; not peace at any price but war; not virtue, but competence (virtue in the Renaissance sense, *virtu*, free from all moralistic acid). The first principle of our humanism: The weak and the failures shall perish. They ought even to be helped to perish.

What is more harmful than any vice?—Practical sympathy and pity for all the failures and all the weak: Christianity.

Christianity is the religion of pity. Pity opposes the noble passions which heighten our vitality. It has a depressing effect, depriving us of strength. As we multiply the instances of pity we gradually lose our strength of nobility. Pity makes suffering contagious and under certain conditions it may cause a total loss of life and vitality out of all proportion to the magnitude of the cause. . . . Pity is the practice of nihilism.

14

The Experience Machine

ROBERT NOZICK

Robert Nozick is Professor of Philosophy at Harvard University and the author of several important works in philosophy, especially Anarchy, State and Utopia, *from which the present selection is taken. Nozick argues against hedonism. If pleasure were the only intrinsic value, we would have an overriding reason to be hooked up to a machine which would produce favorable sensations. Nozick discusses the reasons for rejecting the experience machine and, with it, hedonism.*

There are also substantial puzzles when we ask what matters other than how *people's* experiences feel "from the inside." Suppose there were an experience machine that would give you any experience you desired. Superduper neuropsychologists could stimulate your brain so that you would think and feel you were writing a great novel, or making a friend, or reading an interesting book. All the time you would be floating in a tank, with electrodes attached to your brain. Should you plug into this machine for life, preprogramming your life's experiences? If you are worried about missing out on desirable experiences, we can suppose that business enterprises have researched thoroughly the lives of many others. You can pick and choose from their large library or smorgasbord of such experiences, selecting your life's experiences for, say, the next two years. After two years have passed, you will have ten minutes or ten hours out of the tank, to select the experiences of your *next* two years. Of course, while in the tank you won't know that you're there; you'll think it's all actually happening. Others can also plug in to have the experiences they want, so there's no need

Reprinted from *Anarchy, State and Utopia* (Harvard University Press, 1973) by permission of the publisher.

to stay unplugged to serve them. (Ignore problems such as who will service the machines if everyone plugs in.) Would you plug in? *What else can matter to us, other than how our lives feel from the inside?* Nor should you refrain because of the few moments of distress between the moment you've decided and the moment you're plugged. What's a few moments of distress compared to a lifetime of bliss (if that's what you choose), and why feel any distress at all if your decision *is* the best one?

What does matter to us in addition to our experiences? First, we want to *do* certain things, and not just have the experience of doing them. In the case of certain experiences, it is only because first we want to do the actions that we want the experiences of doing them or thinking we've done them. (But *why* do we want to do the activities rather than merely to experience them?) A second reason for not plugging in is that we want to *be* a certain way, to be a certain sort of person. Someone floating in a tank is an indeterminate blob. There is no answer to the question of what a person is like who has long been in the tank. Is he courageous, kind, intelligent, witty, loving? It's not merely that it's difficult to tell; there's no way he is. Plugging into the machine is a kind of suicide. It will seem to some, trapped by a picture, that nothing about what we are like can matter except as it gets reflected in our experiences. But should it be surprising that what *we are* is important to us? Why should we be concerned only with how our time is filled, but not with what we are?

Thirdly, plugging into an experience machine limits us to a man-made reality, to a world no deeper or more important than that which people can construct. There is no *actual* contact with any deeper reality, though the experience of it can be simulated. Many persons desire to leave themselves open to such contact and to a plumbing of deeper significance.[1] This clarifies the intensity of the conflict over psychoactive drugs, which some view as mere local experience machines, and others view as avenues to a deeper reality; what some view as equivalent to surrender to the experience machine, others view as following one of the reasons *not* to surrender!

We learn that something matters to us in addition to experience by imagining an experience machine and then realizing that we would not use it. We can continue to imagine a sequence of machines each designed to fill lacks suggested for the earlier machines. For example, since the experience machine doesn't meet our desire to *be* a certain way, imagine a transformation machine which transforms us into whatever sort of person we'd like to be (compatible with our staying us). Surely one would not use the transformation machine to become as one would wish, and thereupon plug into the experience machine![2] So something matters in addition to one's experiences *and* what one is like. Nor is the reason merely that one's experiences are unconnected with what one is like. For the experience machine might be limited to provide only experiences possible to the sort of person plugged in. Is it that we want to make a difference in the world? Consider then the result machine, which produces in the world any result you would produce and injects your vector input into any joint activity. We shall not pursue here the fascinating details of these or other machines. What is most disturbing about them is their living of our lives for us. Is it misguided to search for *particular* additional functions beyond the competence of machines to do for us? Perhaps what we desire is to live (an active verb) ourselves, in contact with reality. (And this,

machines cannot do *for* us.) Without elaborating on the implications of this, which I believe connect surprisingly with issues about free will and causal accounts of knowledge, we need merely note the intricacy of the question of what matters *for people* other than their experiences. Until one finds a satisfactory answer, and determines that this answer does not *also* apply to animals, one cannot reasonably claim that only the felt experiences of animals limit what we may do to them.

Notes

1. Traditional religious views differ on the *point* of contact with a transcendent reality. Some say that contact yields eternal bliss or Nirvana, but they have not distinguished this sufficiently from merely a *very* long run on the experience machine. Others think it is intrinsically desirable to do the will of a higher being which created us all, though presumably no one would think this if we discovered we had been created as an object of amusement by some superpowerful child from another galaxy or dimension. Still others imagine an eventual merging with a higher reality, leaving unclear its desirability, or where that merging leaves *us*.

2. Some wouldn't use the transformation machine at all; it seems like *cheating*. But the one-time use of the transformation machine would not remove all challenges; there would still be obstacles for the new us to overcome, a new plateau from which to strive even higher. And is this plateau any the less earned or deserved than that provided by genetic endowment and early childhood environment? But if the transformation machine could be used indefinitely often, so that we could accomplish anything by pushing a button to transform ourselves into someone who could do it easily, there would remain no limits we *need* to strain against or try to transcend. Would there be anything left *to do*? Do some theological views place God outside of time because an omniscient omnipotent being couldn't fill up his days?

15

Value Pluralism

W. D. ROSS

Sir William David Ross (1877–1971) was provost of Oriel College, Oxford University. His book The Right and the Good *(1930), from which the present selection is taken, is a classic treatise in ethical intuitionism. Ross agrees with Bentham that pleasure is intrinsically good but argues that other things are also good in themselves. In this selection he identifies four intrinsic goods and shows how they make up other complex values.*

What Things Are Good?

Our next step is to inquire what kinds of thing are intrinsically good. (1) The first thing for which I would claim that it is intrinsically good is virtuous disposition and action, i.e., action, or disposition to act, from any one of certain motives, of which at all events the most notable are the desire to do one's duty, the desire to bring into being something that is good, and the desire to give pleasure or save pain to others. It seems clear that we regard all such actions and dispositions as having value in themselves apart from any consequence. And if anyone is inclined to doubt this and to think that, say, pleasure alone is intrinsically good, it seems to me enough to ask the question whether, of two states of the universe holding equal amounts of pleasure, we should really think no better of one in which the actions and dispositions of all the persons in it were thoroughly virtuous than of one in which they were highly vicious. To this there can be only one answer. Most hedonists would shrink from giving the plainly false answer which their theory re-

Reprinted from W. D. Ross, *The Right and the Good*, first published by The Clarendon Press, Oxford, 1930, by permission of Hackett Publishing Company.

quires, and would take refuge in saying that the question rests on a false abstraction. Since virtue, as they conceive it, is a disposition to do just the acts which will produce most pleasure, a universe full of virtuous persons would be bound, they might say, to contain more pleasure than a universe full of vicious persons. To this two answers may be made. (*a*) Much pleasure, and much pain, do not spring from virtuous or vicious actions at all but from the operation of natural laws. Thus even if a universe filled with virtuous persons were bound to contain more of the pleasure and less of the pain that springs from human action than a universe filled with vicious persons would, that inequality of pleasantness might easily be supposed to be precisely counteracted by, for instance, a much greater incidence of disease. The two states of affairs would then, on balance, be equally pleasant; would they be equally good? And (*b*) even if we could not imagine any circumstances in which two states of the universe equal in pleasantness but unequal in virtue could exist, the supposition is a legitimate one, since it is only intended to bring before us in a vivid way what is really self-evident, that virtue is good apart from its consequences.

(2) It seems at first sight equally clear that pleasure is good in itself. Some will perhaps be helped to realize this if they make the corresponding supposition to that we have just made; if they suppose two states of the universe including equal amounts of virtue but the one including also widespread and intense pleasure and the other widespread and intense pain. Here too it might be objected that the supposition is an impossible one, since virtue always tends to promote general pleasure, and vice to promote general misery. But this objection may be answered just as we have answered the corresponding objection above.

Apart from this, however, there are two ways in which even the most austere moralists and the most antihedonistic philosophers are apt to betray the conviction that pleasure is good in itself. (*a*) One is the attitude which they, like all other normal human beings, take towards kindness and towards cruelty. If the desire to give pleasure to others is approved, and the desire to inflict pain on others condemned, this seems to imply the conviction that pleasure is good and pain bad. Some may think, no doubt, that the mere thought that a certain state of affairs would be *painful* for another person is enough to account for our conviction that the desire to produce it is bad. But I am inclined to think that there is involved the further thought that a state of affairs in virtue of being painful is *prima facie* (i.e., where other considerations do not enter into the case) one that a rational spectator would not approve, i.e., is *bad*; and that similarly our attitude towards kindness involves the thought that pleasure is good. (*b*) The other is the insistence, which we find in the most austere moralists as in other people, on the conception of merit. If virtue deserves to be rewarded by happiness (whether or not vice also deserves to be rewarded by unhappiness), this seems at first sight to imply that happiness and unhappiness are not in themselves things indifferent, but are good and bad respectively.

Kant's view on this question is not as clear as might be wished. He points out that the Latin *bonum* covers two notions, distinguished in German as *das Gute* (the good) and *das Wohl* (well-being, i.e., pleasure or happiness); and he speaks of 'good' as being properly applied only to actions,[1] i.e., he treats 'good' as equivalent to 'morally good,' and by implication denies that pleasure (even deserved pleasure) is good. It might seem then that when he speaks of the union of virtue with the happiness it deserves as the *bonum consummatum* he is not thinking of deserved happiness as good but only as *das Wohl*, a source of satisfaction to the person who has it. But if this exhausted his meaning, he would have no right to speak of virtue, as he repeatedly does, as *das oberste*

Gut; he should call it simply *das Gute*, and happiness, *das Wohl.* Further, he describes the union of virtue with happiness not merely as 'the object of the desires of rational finite beings,' but adds that it approves itself 'even in the judgment of an impartial reason' as 'the whole and perfect good,' rather than virtue alone. And he adds that 'happiness, while it is pleasant to the possessor of it, is not of itself absolutely and in all respects good, but always presupposes morally right behavior as its condition'; which implies that *when* that condition is fulfilled, happiness *is* good.[2] All this seems to point to the conclusion that in the end he had to recognize that while virtue alone is morally good, deserved happiness also is not merely a source of satisfaction to its possessor, but objectively good.

But reflection on the conception of merit does not support the view that pleasure is always good in itself and pain always bad in itself. For while this conception implies the conviction that pleasure when deserved is good, and pain when undeserved bad, it also suggests strongly that pleasure when undeserved is bad and pain when deserved good.

There is also another set of facts which casts doubt on the view that pleasure is always good and pain always bad. We have a decided conviction that there are bad pleasures and (though this is less obvious) that there are good pains. We think that the pleasure taken either by the agent or by a spectator in, for instance, a lustful or cruel action is bad; and we think it a good thing that people should be pained rather than pleased by contemplating vice or misery.

Thus the view that pleasure is always good and pain always bad, while it seems to be strongly supported by some of our convictions, seems to be equally strongly opposed by others. The difficulty can, I think, be removed by ceasing to speak simply of pleasure and pain as good or bad, and by asking more carefully what it is that we mean. Consideration of the question is aided if we adopt the view (tentatively adopted already)[3] that what is good or bad is always something properly expressed by a that-clause, i.e., an objective, or as I should prefer to call it, a *fact*. If we look at the matter thus, I think we can agree that the fact that a sentient being is in a state of pleasure is always in itself good, and the fact that a sentient being is in a state of pain always in itself bad, when this fact is not an element in a more complex fact having some other characteristic relevant to goodness or badness. And where considerations of desert or of moral good or evil do not enter, i.e., in the case of animals, the fact that a sentient being is feeling pleasure or pain is the whole fact (or the fact sufficiently described to enable us to judge of its goodness or badness), and we need not hesitate to say that the pleasure of animals is always good, and the pain of animals always bad, in itself and apart from its consequences. But when a moral being is feeling a pleasure or pain that is deserved or undeserved, or a pleasure or pain that implies a good or a bad disposition, the total fact is quite inadequately described if we say 'a sentient being is feeling pleasure, or pain.' The total fact may be that 'a sentient and moral being is feeling a pleasure that is undeserved, or that is the realization of a vicious disposition,' and though the fact included in this, that 'a sentient being is feeling pleasure' would be good if it stood alone, that creates only a presumption that the total fact is good, and a presumption that is outweighed by the other element in the total fact.

Pleasure seems, indeed, to have a property analogous to that which we have previously recognized under the name of conditional or *prima facie* rightness. An act of promise-keeping has the property, not necessarily of being right but of being something that is right if the act has no other morally significant characteristic (such as that of causing much pain to another person). And similarly a state of pleasure has the property, not necessarily of being good, but of being something that is good if the state has no other characteristic that prevents it from being good. The two characteristics that may interfere with its being good are (*a*) that of being contrary to desert, and

(*b*) that of being a state which is the realization of a bad disposition. Thus the pleasures of which we can say without doubt that they are good are (i) the pleasures of nonmoral beings (animals), (ii) the pleasures of moral beings that are deserved and are either realizations of good moral dispositions or realizations of neutral capacities (such as the pleasures of the senses).

Insofar as the goodness or badness of a particular pleasure depends on its being the realization of a virtuous or vicious disposition, this has been allowed for by our recognition of virtue as a thing good in itself. But the mere recognition of virtue as a thing good in itself, and of pleasure as a thing *prima facie* good in itself, does not do justice to the conception of merit. If we compare two imaginary states of the universe, alike in the total amounts of virtue and vice and of pleasure and pain present in the two, but in one of which the virtuous were all happy and the vicious miserable, while in the other the virtuous were miserable and the vicious happy, very few people would hesitate to say that the first was a much better state of the universe than the second. It would seem then that, besides virtue and pleasure, we must recognize (3), as a third independent good, the apportionment of pleasure and pain to the virtuous and the vicious respectively. And it is on the recognition of this as a separate good that the recognition of the duty of justice, in distinction from fidelity to promises on the one hand and from beneficence on the other, rests.

(4) It seems clear that knowledge, and in a less degree what we may for the present call 'right opinion,' are states of mind good in themselves. Here too we may, if we please, help ourselves to realize the fact by supposing two states of the universe equal in respect of virtue and of pleasure and of the allocation of pleasure to the virtuous, but such that the persons in the one had a far greater understanding of the nature and laws of the universe than those in the other. Can anyone doubt that the first would be a better state of the universe?

From one point of view it seems doubtful

whether knowledge and right opinion, no matter what it is of or about, should be considered good. Knowledge of mere matters of fact (say, of the number of stories in a building), without knowledge of their relation to other facts, might seem to be worthless; it certainly seems to be worth much less than the knowledge of general principles, or of facts as depending on general principles—what we might call insight or understanding as opposed to mere knowledge. But on reflection it seems clear that even about matters of fact right opinion is in itself a better state of mind to be in than wrong, and knowledge than right opinion.

There is another objection which may naturally be made to the view that knowledge is as such good. There are many pieces of knowledge which we in fact think it well for people *not* to have; e.g., we may think it a bad thing for a sick man to know how ill he is, or for a vicious man to know how he may most conveniently indulge his vicious tendencies. But its seems that in such cases it is not the knowledge but the consequences in the way of pain or of vicious action that we think bad.

It might perhaps be objected that knowledge is not a better state than right opinion, but merely a source of greater satisfaction to its possessor. It no doubt is a source of greater satisfaction. Curiosity is the desire to *know,* and is never really satisfied by mere opinion. Yet there are two facts which seem to show that this is not the whole truth. (*a*) While opinion recognized to be such is never thoroughly satisfactory to its possessor, there is another state of mind which is not knowledge—which may even be mistaken—yet which through lack of reflection is not distinguished from knowledge by its possessor, the state of mind which Professor Cook Wilson has called 'that of being under the impression that so-and-so is the case.'[4] Such a state of mind may be as great a source of satisfaction to its possessor as knowledge, yet we should all think it to be an inferior state of mind to knowledge. This surely points to a recognition by us that knowledge has a worth other than that of being a source of satisfaction

to its possessor. (*b*) Wrong opinion, so long as its wrongness is not discovered, may be as great a source of satisfaction as right. Yet we should agree that it is an inferior state of mind, because it is to a less extent founded on knowledge and is itself a less close approximation to knowledge; which again seems to point to our recognizing knowledge as something good in itself.

Four things, then, seem to be intrinsically good—virtue, pleasure, the allocation of pleasure to the virtuous, and knowledge (and in a less degree right opinion). And I am unable to discover anything that is intrinsically good, which is not either one of these or a combination of two or more of them. And while this list of goods has been arrived at on its own merits, by reflection on what we really think to be good, it perhaps derives some support from the fact that it harmonizes with a widely accepted classification of the elements in the life of the soul. It is usual to enumerate these as cognition, feeling, and conation. Now knowledge is the ideal state of the mind, and right opinion an approximation to the ideal, on the cognitive or intellectual side; pleasure is its ideal state on the side of feeling; and virtue is its ideal state on the side of conation; while the allocation of happiness to virtue is a good which we recognize when we reflect on the ideal relation between the conative side and the side of feeling. It might of course be objected that there are or may be intrinsic goods that are not states of mind or relations between states of mind at all, but in this suggestion I can find no plausibility. Contemplate any imaginary universe from which you suppose mind entirely absent, and you will fail to find anything in it that you can call good in itself. That is not to say, of course, that the existence of a material universe may not be a necessary condition for the existence of many things that are good in themselves. Our knowledge and our true opinions are to a large extent about the material world, and to that extent could not exist unless it existed. Our pleasures are to a large extent derived from material objects. Virtue owes many of its opportunities to the existence of material conditions of good and material hindrances to good. But the value of material things appears to be purely instrumental, not intrinsic.

Of the three elements virtue, knowledge, and pleasure are compounded all the complex states of mind that we think good in themselves. Aesthetic enjoyment, for example, seems to be a blend of pleasure with insight into the nature of the object that inspires it. Mutual love seems to be a blend of virtuous disposition of two minds towards each other, with the knowledge which each has of the character and disposition of the other, and with the pleasure which arises from such disposition and knowledge. And a similar analysis may probably be applied to all other complex goods.

Notes

1. *Kritik der pr. Vernunft*, pp. 59–60 (Akad. Ausgabe, vol. v), pp. 150–51 (Abbott's Trans., ed. 6).

2. Ibid., pp. 110–11 (Akad. Ausgabe), 206–7 (Abbott).

3. Ibid., pp. 111–13.

4. *Statement and Inference*, 1: 113.

16

What Makes Someone's Life Go Best?

Derek Parfit

Derek Parfit (1942–   ) is a Research Fellow at All Souls College, Oxford. He is the author of numerous articles on personal identity, population problems, and ethical theory. His book Reasons and Persons, *from which this selection is taken, has been hailed as one of the most original and important works in contemporary moral philosophy. In it he develops his views on personal identity and their consequences for ethical theory.*

In this essay Parfit compares three theories of the good life: hedonism, desire-fulfillment, *and* objective-list. *Hedonism, such as Bentham's and Mill's theories, is centered in the idea that pleasure or happiness is what makes life go best. Desire-fulfillment theories hold that the good life is centered in actual or possible desires being satisfied. Objective list theories hold that certain good things are necessary for the good life: knowledge, rational activity, mutual love, and awareness of beauty. Parfit examines several versions of these theories and concludes by suggesting that the good life consists in a combination of a type of hedonism and the good things identified in the objective list theories.*

What would be best for someone, or would be most in this person's interests, or would make this person's life go, for him, as well as possible? Answers to this question I call *theories about self-interest*. There are three kinds of theory. On *Hedonistic Theories*, what would be best for someone is what would make his life happiest. On *Desire-Fulfillment Theories*, what would be best for someone is what, throughout his life, would best fulfill his desires. On *Objective List Theories*, certain things are good or bad for us, whether or not we want to have the good things, or to avoid the bad things.

Narrow Hedonists assume, falsely, that pleasure and pain are two distinctive kinds of experience. Compare the pleasures of satisfying an intense thirst or lust, listening to music, solving an intellectual problem, reading a tragedy, and knowing that one's child is happy. These various experiences do not contain any distinctive common quality.

What pains and pleasures have in common are their relations to our desires. On the use of 'pain' which has rational and moral significance, all pains are when experienced unwanted, and a pain is worse or greater the more it is unwanted. Similarly, all pleasures are when experienced wanted, and they are better or greater the more they are wanted. These are the claims of *Preference-Hedonism*. On this view, one of two experiences is more pleasant if it is preferred.

This theory need not follow the ordinary uses of the words 'pain' and 'pleasure.' Suppose that I could go to a party to enjoy the various pleasures of eating, drinking, laughing, dancing, and talking to my friends. I could instead stay at home and read *King Lear*. Knowing what both alternatives would be like, I prefer to read *King Lear*. It extends the ordinary use to say that this would give me more pleasure. But on Preference-Hedonism, if we add some further assumptions given below, reading *King Lear* would give me a better evening. Griffin cites a more extreme case. Near the end of his life Freud refused pain-killing drugs, preferring to think in torment than to be confusedly euphoric. Of these two mental states, euphoria is more pleasant. But on Preference-Hedonism, thinking in torment was, for Freud, a better mental state. It is clearer here not to stretch the meaning of the word 'pleasant.' A Preference-Hedonist should merely claim that, since Freud preferred to think clearly though in torment, his life went better if it went as he preferred.

Consider next Desire-Fulfillment Theories. The simplest is the *Unrestricted Theory*. This claims that what is best for someone is what would best fulfill *all* of his desires, throughout his life. Suppose that I meet a stranger who has what is believed to be a fatal disease. My sympathy is aroused, and I strongly want this stranger to be cured. Much later, when I have forgotten our meeting, the stranger is cured. On the Unrestricted Desire-Fulfillment Theory, this event is good for me, and makes my life go better. This is not plausible. We should reject this theory.

Another theory appeals only to someone's desires about his own life. I call this the *Success Theory*. This theory differs from Preference-Hedonism in only one way. The Success Theory appeals to all of our preferences about our own lives. A Preference-Hedonist appeals only to preferences about those present features of our lives that are introspectively discernible. Suppose that I strongly want not to be deceived by other people. On Preference-Hedonism it would be better for me if I believe that I am not being deceived. It would be irrelevant if my belief is false, since this makes no difference to my state of mind. On the Success Theory, it would be worse for me if my belief is false. I have a strong desire about my own life—that I should not be deceived in this way. It is bad for me if this desire is not fulfilled, even if I falsely believe that it is.

When this theory appeals only to desires that are about our own lives, it may be unclear what this excludes. Suppose that I want my life to be such that all of my desires, whatever their objects, are fulfilled. This may seem to make the Success Theory, when applied to me, coincide with the Unrestricted Desire-Fulfillment Theory. But a Success Theorist should claim that this desire is not really about my own life. This is like the distinction between a real change in some object, and a so-called *Cambridge-change*. An object undergoes a Cambridge-change if there is any change in the true statements that can be made

about this object. Suppose that I cut my cheek while shaving. This causes a real change in me. It also causes a change in Confucius. It becomes true, of Confucius, that he lived on a planet in which later one more cheek was cut. This is merely a Cambridge-change.

Suppose that I am an exile, and cannot communicate with my children. I want their lives to go well. I might claim that I want to live the life of someone whose children's lives go well. A Success Theorist should again claim that this is not really a desire about my own life. If unknown to me one of my children is killed by an avalanche, this is not bad for me, and does not make my life go worse.

A Success Theorist *would* count some similar desires. Suppose that I try to give my children a good start in life. I try to give them the right education, good habits, and psychological strength. Once again, I am now an exile, and will never be able to learn what happens to my children. Suppose that, unknown to me, my children's lives go badly. One finds that the education that I gave him makes him unemployable, another has a mental breakdown, another becomes a petty thief. If my children's lives fail in these ways, and these failures are in part the result of mistakes I made as their parent, these failures in my children's lives would be judged to be bad for me on the Success Theory. One of my strongest desires was to be a successful parent. What is now happening to my children, though it is unknown to me, shows that this desire is not fulfilled. My life failed in one of the ways in which I most wanted it to succeed. Though I do not know this fact, it is bad for me, and makes it true that I have had a worse life. This is like the case where I strongly want not to be deceived. Even if I never know, it is bad for me both if I am deceived and if I turn out to be an unsuccessful parent. These are not introspectively discernible differences in my conscious life. On Preference-Hedonism, these events are not bad for me. On the Success Theory, they are.

Because they are thought by some to need special treatment, I mention next the desires that people have about what happens after they are dead. For a Preference-Hedonist, once I am dead, nothing bad can happen to me. A Success Theorist should deny this. Return to the case where all my children have wretched lives because of the mistakes I made as their parent. Suppose that my children's lives all go badly only after I am dead. My life turns out to have been a failure, in the one of the ways I cared about most. A Success Theorist should claim that, here too, this makes it true that I had a worse life.

Some Success Theorists would reject this claim. Their theory ignores the desires of the dead. I believe this theory to be indefensible. Suppose that I was asked, 'Do you want it to be true that you were a successful parent even after you are dead?' I would answer 'Yes.' It is irrelevant to my desire whether it is fulfilled before or after I am dead. These Success Theorists count it as bad for me if my desire is not fulfilled, even if, because I am an exile, I never know this. How then can it matter whether, when my desire is not fulfilled, I am dead? All that my death does is to *ensure* that I will never know this. If we think it irrelevant that I never know about the nonfulfillment of my desire, we cannot defensibly claim that my death makes a difference.

I turn now to questions and objections which arise for both Preference-Hedonism and the Success Theory.

Should we appeal only to the desires and preferences that someone actually has? Return to my choice between going to a party or staying at home to read *King Lear*. Suppose that, knowing what both alternatives would be like, I choose to stay at home. And suppose that I never later regret this choice. On one theory, this shows that staying at home to read *King Lear* gave me a better evening. This is a mistake. It might be true that, if I had chosen to go to the party, I would never have regretted that choice. According to this theory, this would have shown that going to the party gave me a better evening. This theory thus implies that each alternative would have been better than the other. Since this theory implies such contradictions, it must be revised. The

obvious revision is to appeal not only to my actual preferences, in the alternative I choose, but also to the preferences that I would have had if I had chosen otherwise.

In this example, whichever alternative I choose, I would never regret this choice. If this is true, can we still claim that one of the alternatives would give me a better evening? On some theories, when in two alternatives I would have such contrary preferences, neither alternative is better or worse for me. This is not plausible when one of my contrary preferences would have been much stronger. Suppose that, if I choose to go to the party, I shall be only mildly glad that I made this choice, but that, if I choose to stay and read *King Lear*, I shall be extremely glad. If this is true, reading *King Lear* gives me a better evening.

Whether we appeal to Preference-Hedonism or the Success Theory, we should not appeal only to the desires or preferences that I actually have. We should also appeal to the desires and preferences that I would have had, in the various alternatives that were, at different times, open to me. One of these alternatives would be best for me if it is the one in which I would have the strongest desires and preferences fulfilled. This allows us to claim that some alternative life would have been better for me, even if throughout my actual life I am glad that I chose this life rather than this alternative.

There is another distinction which applies both to Preference-Hedonism and to the Success Theory. These theories are *Summative* if they appeal to all of someone's desires, actual and hypothetical, about his own life. In deciding which alternative would produce the greatest total net sum of desire-fulfillment, we assign some positive number to each desire that is fulfilled, and some negative number to each desire that is not fulfilled. How great these numbers are depends on the intensity of the desires in question. (In the case of the Success Theory, which appeals to past desires, it may also depend on how long these desires were had. [. . .] this may be a weakness in this theory. The issue does not arise for Preference-Hedonism, which appeals only to desires about one's present state of mind.) The total net sum of desire-fulfillment is the sum of the positive numbers minus the negative numbers. Provided that we can compare the relative strength of different desires, this calculation could in theory be performed. The choice of a unit for the numbers makes no difference to the result.

Another version of both theories does not appeal, in this way, to all of a person's desires and preferences about his own life. It appeals only to *global* rather than *local* desires and preferences. A preference is global if it is about some part of one's life considered as a whole, or is about one's whole life. The *Global* versions of these theories I believe to be more plausible.

Consider this example. Knowing that you accept a Summative theory, I tell you that I am about to make your life go better. I shall inject you with an addictive drug. From now on, you will wake each morning with an extremely strong desire to have another injection of this drug. Having this desire will be in itself neither pleasant nor painful, but if the desire is not fulfilled within an hour it would then become extremely painful. This is no cause for concern, since I shall give you ample supplies of this drug. Every morning, you will be able at once to fulfill this desire. The injection, and its after-effects, would also be neither pleasant nor painful. You will spend the rest of your days as you do now.

What would the Summative theories imply about this case? We can plausibly suppose that you would not welcome my proposal. You would prefer not to become addicted to this drug, even though I assure you that you will never lack supplies. We can also plausibly suppose that, if I go ahead, you will always regret that you became addicted to this drug. But it is likely that your initial desire not to become addicted, and your later regrets that you did, would not be as strong as the desires you have each morning for another injection. Given the facts as I described them, your reason to prefer not to become addicted would

not be very strong. You might dislike the thought of being addicted to anything. And you would regret the minor inconvenience that would be involved in remembering always to carry with you, like a diabetic, sufficient supplies. But these desires might be far weaker than the desires you would have each morning for a fresh injection.

On the Summative Theories, if I make you an addict, I would be increasing the sum-total of your desire-fulfillment. I would be causing one of your desires not to be fulfilled: your desire not to become an addict, which, after my act, becomes a desire to be cured. But I would also be giving you an indefinite series of extremely strong desires, one each morning, all of which you can fulfill. The fulfillment of all these desires would outweigh the nonfulfillment of your desires not to become an addict, and to be cured. On the Summative Theories, by making you an addict, I would be benefiting you—making your life go better.

This conclusion is not plausible. Having these desires, and having them fulfilled, are neither pleasant nor painful. We need not be Hedonists to believe, more plausibly, that it is in no way better for you to have and to fulfill this series of strong desires.

Could the Summative Theories be revised, so as to meet this objection? Is there some feature of the addictive desires which would justify the claim that we should ignore them when we calculate the sum total of your desire-fulfillment? We might claim that they can be ignored because they are desires that you would prefer not to have. But this is not an acceptable revision. Suppose that you are in great pain. You now have a very strong desire not to be in the state that you are in. On our revised theory, a desire does not count if you would prefer not to have this desire. This must apply to your intense desire not to be in the state you are in. You would prefer not to have this desire. If you did not dislike the state you are in, it would not be painful. Since our revised theory does not count desires that you would prefer not to have, it implies, absurdly, that it cannot be bad for you to be in great pain.

There may be other revisions which could meet these objections. But it is simpler to appeal to the Global versions of both Preference-Hedonism and the Success Theory. These appeal only to someone's desires about some part of his life, considered as a whole, or about his whole life. The Global Theories give us the right answer in the case where I make you an addict. You would prefer not to become addicted, and you would later prefer to cease to be addicted. These are the only preferences to which the Global Theories appeal. They ignore your particular desires each morning for a fresh injection. This is because you have yourself taken these desires into account in forming your Global preference.

This imagined case of addiction is in its essentials similar to countless other cases. There are countless cases in which it is true both (1) that, if someone's life goes in one of two ways, this would increase the sum total of his local desire-fulfillment, but (2) that the other alternative is what he would globally prefer, *whichever* way his actual life goes.

Rather than describing another of the countless actual cases, I shall mention an imaginary case. . . . Suppose that I could have either fifty of years of life of an extremely high quality, or an indefinite number of years that are barely worth living. In the first alternative, my fifty years would, on any theory, go extremely well. I would be very happy, would achieve great things, do much good, and love and be loved by many people. In the second alternative my life would always be, though not by much, worth living. There would be nothing bad about this life, and it would each day contain a few small pleasures.

On the Summative Theories, if the second life was long enough, it would be better for me. In each day within this life I have some desires about my life that are fulfilled. In the fifty years of the first alternative, there would be a very great sum of local desire-fulfillment. But this would be a fi-

nite sum, and in the end it would be outweighed by the sum of desire-fulfillment in my indefinitely long second alternative. A simpler way to put this point is this. The first alternative would be good. In the second alternative, since my life is worth living, living each extra day is good for me. If we merely add together whatever is good for me, some number of these extra days would produce the greatest total sum.

I do not believe that the second alternative would give me a better life. I therefore reject the Summative Theories. It is likely that, in both alternatives, I would globally prefer the first. Since the Global Theories would then imply that the first alternative gives me a better life, these theories seem to me more plausible.

Turn now to the third kind of Theory that I mentioned: the *Objective List Theory*. According to this theory, certain things are good or bad for people, whether or not these people would want to have the good things, or to avoid the bad things. The good things might include moral goodness, rational activity, the development of one's abilities, having children and being a good parent, knowledge, and the awareness of true beauty. The bad things might include being betrayed, manipulated, slandered, deceived, being deprived of liberty or dignity, and enjoying either sadistic pleasure, or aesthetic pleasure in what is in fact ugly.

An Objective List Theorist might claim that his theory coincides with the Global version of the Success Theory. On this theory, what would make my life go best depends on what I would prefer, now and in the various alternatives, if I knew all of the relevant facts about these alternatives. An Objective List Theorist might say that the most relevant facts are what his theory claims—what would in fact be good or bad for me. And he might claim that anyone who knew these facts would want what is truly good for him, and want to avoid what would be bad for him.

If this was true, though the Objective List Theory would coincide with the Success Theory, the two theories would remain distinct. A Success Theorist would reject this description of the coincidence. On his theory, nothing is good or bad for people, whatever their preferences are. Something is bad for someone only if, knowing the facts, he wants to avoid it. And the relevant facts do not include the alleged facts cited by the Objective List Theorist. On the Success Theory it is, for instance, bad for someone to be deceived if and because this is not what he wants. The Objective List Theorist makes the reverse claim. People want not to be deceived because this is bad for them.

As these remarks imply, there is one important difference between on the one hand Preference-Hedonism and the Success Theory, and on the other hand the Objective List Theory. The first two kinds of theory give an account of self-interest which is entirely factual, or which does not appeal to facts about value. The account appeals to what a person does and would prefer, given full knowledge of the purely nonevaluative facts about the alternatives. In contrast, the Objective List Theory appeals directly to facts about value.

In choosing between these theories, we must decide how much weight to give to imagined cases in which someone's fully informed preferences would be bizarre. If we can appeal to these cases, they cast doubt on both Preference-Hedonism and the Success Theory. Consider the man that Rawls imagined who wants to spend his life counting the numbers of blades of grass in different lawns. Suppose that this man knows that he could achieve great progress if instead he worked in some especially useful part of Applied Mathematics. Though he could achieve such significant results, he prefers to go on counting blades of grass. On the Success Theory, if we allow this theory to cover all imaginable cases, it could be better for this person if he counts his blades of grass rather than achieves great and beneficial results in Mathematics.

The counterexample might be more offensive.

Suppose that what someone would most prefer, knowing the alternatives, is a life in which, without being detected, he causes as much pain as he can to other people. On the Success Theory, such a life would be what is best for this person.

We may be unable to accept these conclusions. Ought we therefore to abandon this theory? This is what Sidgwick did, though those who quote him seldom notice this. He suggests that 'a man's future good on the whole is what he would now desire and seek on the whole if all the consequences of all the different lines of conduct open to him were accurately foreseen and adequately realised in imagination at the present point of time.' As he comments: 'The notion of "Good" thus attained has an ideal element: it is something that *is* not always actually desired and aimed at by human beings: but the ideal element is entirely interpretable in terms of *fact*, actual or hypothetical, and does not introduce any judgment of value.' Sidgwick then rejects this account, claiming that what is ultimately good for someone is what this person *would* desire if his desires were in harmony with reason. This last phrase is needed, Sidgwick thought, to exclude the cases where someone's desires are irrational. He assumes that there are some things that we have good reason to desire, and others that we have good reason not to desire. These might be the things which are held to be good or bad for us by Objective List Theories.

Suppose we agree that, in some imagined cases, what someone would most want both now and later, fully knowing about the alternatives, would *not* be what would be best for him. If we accept this conclusion, it may seem that we must reject both Preference-Hedonism and the Success Theory. Perhaps, like Sidgwick, we must put constraints on what can be rationally desired.

It might be claimed instead that we can dismiss the appeal to such imagined cases. It might be claimed that what people would in fact prefer, if they knew the relevant facts, would always be something that we could accept as what is really good for them. Is this a good reply? If we agree that in the imagined cases what someone would prefer might be something that is bad for him, in these cases we have abandoned our theory. If this is so, can we defend our theory by saying that, in the actual cases, it would not go astray? I believe that this is not an adequate defence. But I shall not pursue this question here.

This objection may apply with less force to Preference-Hedonism. On this theory, what can be good or bad for someone can only be discernible features of his conscious life. These are the features that, at the time, he either wants or does not want. I asked above whether it is bad for people to be deceived because they prefer not to be, or whether they prefer not to be deceived because this is bad for them. Consider the comparable question with respect to pain. Some have claimed that pain is intrinsically bad and that this is why we dislike it. As I have suggested, I doubt this claim. After taking certain kinds of drug, people claim that the quality of their sensations has not altered, but they no longer dislike these sensations. We would regard such drugs as effective analgesics. This suggests that the badness of a pain consists in its being disliked, and that it is not disliked because it is bad. The disagreement between these views would need much more discussion. But, if the second view is better, it is more plausible to claim that whatever someone wants or does not want to experience—however bizarre we find his desires—should be counted as being for this person truly pleasant or painful, and as being for that reason good or bad for him. There may still be cases where it is plausible to claim that it would be bad for someone if he enjoys certain kinds of pleasure. This might be claimed, for instance, about sadistic pleasure. But there may be few such cases.

If instead we appeal to the Success Theory, we are not concerned only with the experienced quality of our conscious life. We are concerned with such things as whether we are achieving what we are trying to achieve, whether we are be-

ing deceived, and the like. When considering this theory, we can more often plausibly claim that, even if someone knew the facts, his preferences might go astray, and fail to correspond to what would be good or bad for him.

Which of these different theories should we accept? I shall not attempt an answer here. But I shall end by mentioning another theory, which might be claimed to combine what is most plausible in these conflicting theories. It is a striking fact that those who have addressed this question have disagreed so fundamentally. Many philosophers have been convinced Hedonists; many others have been as much convinced that Hedonism is a gross mistake.

Some Hedonists have reached their view as follows. They consider an opposing view, such as that which claims that what is good for someone is to have knowledge, to engage in rational activity, and to be aware of true beauty. These Hedonists ask, 'Would these states of mind be good, if they brought no enjoyment, and if the person in these states of mind had not the slightest desire that they continue?' Since they answer No, they conclude that the value of these states of mind must lie in their being liked, and in their arousing a desire that they continue.

This reasoning assumes that the value of a whole is just the sum of the value of its parts. If we remove the part to which the Hedonist appeals, what is left seems to have no value, hence Hedonism is the truth.

Suppose instead that we claim that the value of a whole may not be a mere sum of the value of its parts. We might then claim that what is best for people is a composite. It is not just their being in the conscious states that they want to be in. Nor is it just their having knowledge, engaging in rational activity, being aware of true beauty, and the like. What is good for someone is neither just what Hedonists claim, nor just what is claimed by Objective List Theorists. We might believe that if we had *either* of these, *without the other*, what we had would have little or no value. We might claim, for example, that what is good or bad for someone is to have knowledge, to be engaged in rational activity, to experience mutual love, and to be aware of beauty, while strongly wanting just these things. On this view, each side in this disagreement saw only half of the truth. Each put forward as sufficient something that was only necessary.

Pleasure with many other kinds of object has no value. And, if they are entirely devoid of pleasure, there is no value in knowledge, rational activity, love, or the awareness of beauty. What is of value, or is good for someone, is to have both; to be engaged in these activities, and to be strongly wanting to be so engaged.

PART V

Utilitarian Ethics

Introduction: "The Greatest Happiness for the Greatest Number"

Traditionally, two major types of ethical systems have dominated the field, one in which the locus of value is the act or kind of act, the other in which the locus of value is the outcome or consequences of the act. The former type of theory is called "deontological" (from the Greek *deon* which means "duty") and the latter is called "teleological" (from the Greek *telos* which means "end" or "goal"). Whereas teleological systems see the ultimate criterion of morality in some nonmoral value that results from acts, deontological systems see certain features in the act itself as having intrinsic value. For example, a teleologist would judge whether lying was morally right or wrong by the consequences it produced, but a deontologist would see something intrinsically wrong in the very act of lying. In this section we shall consider teleological ethical theories and in Part VI we shall study deontological theories.

In order to get to the heart of this type of theory, let us begin with an oft-used example. Suppose there is a raft floating in the Pacific Ocean. On the raft are two men who are starving to death. One day they discover some food in an inner compartment of a box on the raft. They have reason to believe that the food will be sufficient to keep one of them alive until the raft reaches a certain island where help is available, but that if they share the food, both will most likely die. Now, one of these men is a brilliant scientist who has in his mind the cure for cancer. The other man is undistinguished. Otherwise there is no relevant difference between the two men. What is the morally right thing to do? Share the food and hope against the odds for a miracle? Flip a coin in order to see which man gets the food? Give the food to the scientist?

If you voted to flip a coin or share the food, you sided with the deontologist, but if you voted to give the food to the scientist, then you sided with the teleologist, the utilitarian, who would calculate that there would be greater good accomplished as a result of the scientist getting the food and living than in any of the other likely outcomes.

There are two main features of utilitarianism: (1) the consequentialist principle (its teleological aspect), and (2) the utility principle (its hedonic aspect). The consequentialist principle states that the rightness or wrongness of an act is determined by the results that flow from it. The utility principle states that the only thing that is good in itself is some specific type of state (e.g., pleasure, happiness, welfare, fulfillment). Hedonistic utilitarianism views pleasure as the sole good and pain as the only evil. To quote the English philosopher Jeremy Bentham (reading IV), the first one to systematize classical utilitarianism, "Nature has placed mankind under the governance of two sovereign masters, pain and pleasure. It is for them alone to point out what we ought to do, as well as what we shall do."

Bentham's philosophy has often been criticized for being too simplistic. Pleasure seems either too sensuous or too ambiguous a notion. In fact, Bentham's version was in his own day referred to as the "Pig-philosophy," since a pig enjoying his life would constitute a higher moral state than a slightly dissatisfied human being. For this reason John Stuart Mill, in our first reading, sought to distinguish happiness from mere sensual pleasure "A being of higher faculties requires more to make him happy, is capable probably of more acute suffering, and certainly accessible to it at more points, than one of an inferior type," but still he is qualitatively better off than the person without these higher faculties. "It is better to be a human being dissatisfied than a pig satisfied; better to be Socrates dissatisfied than a fool satisfied." Mill's version of utilitarianism has been called 'eudaimonistic utilitarianism' (*eudaimonia* is the Greek for "happiness") in order to distinguish it from Bentham's hedonistic utilitarianism.

Utilitarians can be divided into two types: '*act*' and '*rule.*' That is, in applying the principle of utility, act-utilitarians say that we ought ideally apply the principle to all of the alternatives open to us at any given moment. Of course, we cannot do this for each possible act, for often we must act spontaneously and quickly. So rules of thumb (e.g., in general, do not lie, keep your promises) are of practical importance. However, the right act is still that alternative which will result in the most utility.

Rule-utilitarians, by contrast, state that an act is right if it conforms to a valid rule within a system of rules that, if followed, will result in the best possible state of affairs (or least bad state of affairs, if it is a question of all the alternatives being bad). The rule-utilitarian resembles the rule-deontologist (a deontologist who holds that we ought always act according to principle rather than according to our intuition at the moment, a position to be discussed in Part VI) in that both emphasize the importance of following specific principles that are public and universal. The difference is that the deontologist sees the principles as having intrinsic value, whereas the utilitarian sees the principles as having only instrumental value. Nonetheless, it is arguable that they could have identical principles for different reasons. John Hospers defends rule-utilitarianism in our third reading.

It is a subject of keen debate whether John Stuart Mill was a rule- or an act-utilitarian. He does not seem to have noticed the difference, and there seem to be aspects of both theories in his work. But our second reading, Kai Nielsen's "Against Moral Conservatism" seems a clearer example of act-utilitarianism. Nielsen defines 'moral conservativism' as "a normative ethical theory which maintains that there is a privileged moral principle or cluster of moral principles, prescribing determinate actions, with which it would always be

wrong not to act in accordance no matter what the consequences." For Nielsen, no rules are sacrosanct, but differing situations call forth different actions, and potentially, any rule could be overridden (though in fact we may need to retreat some as absolutes for the good of society).

Nielsen's argument in favor of utilitarianism makes strong use of the notion of *negative responsibility.* That is, we are not only responsible for the consequences of our actions, but we are also responsible for the consequences of our nonactions. Suppose that you are the driver of a trolley, and suddenly, you discover that your brakes have failed. You are just about to run over five workmen on the tract ahead of you. However, if you quickly turn the steering wheel you will cause the trolley to turn onto a side track where only one man is working. What should you do? One who makes a strong distinction between active and passive evil (allowing versus doing evil) would argue that you should do nothing and merely allow the trolley to kill the five men, but one who denies that this is an absolute distinction would prescribe that we do something positive in order to minimize evil. Negative responsibility means that we are going to be responsible for someone's death in either case. Doing the right thing, the utilitarian urges us, means minimizing the amount of evil. So we should actively cause the one to die in order to save the five.

In our fourth reading, "A Critique of Utilitarianism," Bernard Williams argues that utilitarianism violates personal integrity by commanding that we violate those principles that are central and deepest in our lives. "How can a man, as a utilitarian agent, come to regard as one satisfaction among others, and a dispensable one, a project or attitude round which he has built his life, just because someone else's projects have so structured the causal scene that that is how the utilitarian scheme comes out?" His conclusion is that utilitarianism leads to personal alienation and so is deeply flawed.

Our final reading by Sterling Harwood discusses eleven criticisms of utilitarianism.

17

Utilitarianism

JOHN STUART MILL

John Stuart Mill (1806–73) was one of the most important British philosophers in the nineteenth century, one who made a significant contribution to logic, philosophy of science, political theory, and ethics. The present essay contains parts of chapters 2 and 4 of his Utilitarianism. *Mill seeks to distinguish happiness from mere sensual pleasure. "A being of higher faculties requires more to make him happy, is capable probably of more acute suffering, and certainly accessible to it at more points, than one of an inferior type," but still he is qualitatively better off than the person without these higher faculties. "It is better to be a human being dissatisfied than a pig satisfied; better to be Socrates dissatisfied than a fool satisfied." Mill's version of utilitarianism has been called 'eudaimonistic utilitarianism' (eudaimonia is the Greek for "happiness") to distinguish it from Bentham's hedonistic utilitarianism (see reading IV.12).*

What Utilitarianism Is

. . . The creed which accepts as the foundation of morals, Utility, or the Greatest Happiness Principle, holds that actions are right in proportion as they tend to promote happiness, wrong as they tend to produce the reverse of happiness. By happiness is intended pleasure, and the absence of pain; by unhappiness, pain, and the privation of pleasure. To give a clear view of the moral standard set up by the theory, much more requires to be said; in particular, what things it includes in the ideas of pain and pleasure; and to what extent this is left an open question. But these supplementary explanations do not affect the theory of life on which this theory of morality is grounded—namely, that pleasure, and freedom from pain, are

From John Stuart Mill, *Utilitarianism* (1861), chapters 2 and 4.

the only things desirable as ends; and that all desirable things (which are as numerous in the utilitarian as in any other scheme) are desirable either for the pleasure inherent in themselves, or as a means to the promotion of pleasure and the prevention of pain.

Now, such a theory of life excites in many minds, and among them in some of the most estimable in feeling and purpose, inveterate dislike. To suppose that life has (as they express it) no higher end than pleasure—no better and nobler object of desire and pursuit—they designate as utterly mean and groveling; as a doctrine worthy only of swine, to whom the followers of Epicurus were, at a very early period, contemptuously likened; and modern holders of the doctrine are occasionally made the subject of equally polite comparisons by its German, French, and English assailants.

When thus attacked, the Epicureans have always answered, that it is not they, but their accusers, who represent human nature in a degrading light; since the accusation supposes human beings to be capable of no pleasures except those of which swine are capable. If this supposition were true, the charge could not be gainsaid, but would then be no longer an imputation; for if the sources of pleasure were precisely the same to human beings and to swine, the rule of life which is good enough for the one would be good enough for the other. The comparison of the Epicurean life to that of beasts is felt as degrading, precisely because a beast's pleasures do not satisfy a human being's conception of happiness. Human beings have faculties more elevated than the animal appetites, and when once made conscious of them, do not regard anything as happiness which does not include their gratification. I do not, indeed, consider the Epicureans to have been by any means faultless in drawing out their scheme of consequences from the utilitarian principle. To do this in any sufficient manner, many Stoic, as well as Christian elements require to be included. But there is no known Epicurean theory of life which does not assign to the pleasures of the intellect, of the feelings and imagination, and of the moral sentiments, a much higher value as pleasures than to those of mere sensation. It must be admitted, however, that utilitarian writers in general have placed the superiority of mental over bodily pleasures chiefly in the greater permanency, safety, uncostliness, etc., of the former—that is, in their circumstantial advantages rather than in their intrinsic nature. And on all these points utilitarians have fully proved their case; but they might have taken the other, and, as it may be called, higher ground, with entire consistency. It is quite compatible with the principle of utility to recognize the fact, that some *kinds* of pleasure are more desirable and more valuable than others. It would be absurd that while, in estimating all other things, quality is considered as well as quantity, the estimation of pleasures should be supposed to depend on quantity alone.

If I am asked, what I mean by difference of quality in pleasures, or what makes one pleasure more valuable than another, merely as a pleasure, except its being greater in amount, there is but one possible answer. Of two pleasures, if there be one which all or almost all who have experience of both give a decided preference, irrespective of any feeling of moral obligation to prefer it, that is the more desirable pleasure. If one of the two is, by those who are competently acquainted with both, placed so far above the other that they prefer it, even though knowing it to be attended with a great amount of discontent, and would not resign it for any quantity of the other pleasure which their nature is capable of, we are justified in ascribing to the preferred enjoyment a superiority in quality, so far out-weighing quantity as to render it, in comparison, of small account.

Now it is an unquestionable fact that those who are equally acquainted with, and equally capable of appreciating and enjoying, both, do give a most marked preference to the manner of existence which employs their higher faculties. Few human creatures would consent to be changed into any of the lower animals, for a promise of the fullest allowance of a beast's pleasures; no intelligent human being would consent to be a fool, no instructed person would be an ignoramus, no person of feeling and conscience would be selfish and base, even though they should be persuaded that the fool, the dunce, or the rascal is better satisfied with his lot than they are with theirs. They would not resign what they possess more than he for the most complete satisfaction of all the desires which they have in common with him. If they ever fancy they would, it is only in cases of unhappiness so extreme, that to escape from it they would exchange their lot for almost any other, however undesirable in their own eyes. A being of higher faculties requires more to make him happy, is capable probably of more acute suffering, and certainly accessible to it at more points, than one of an inferior type; but in spite of these liabilities, he can never really wish to sink into what he feels to be a lower grade of existence. We may give what explanation we please of this unwillingness; we may attribute it to pride, a name which is given indiscriminately to some of the most and to some of the least estimable feelings of which mankind are capable; we may refer it to the love of liberty and personal independence, an appeal to which was with the Stoics one of the most effective means for the inculcation of it; to the love of power, or to the love of excitement, both of which do really enter into and contribute to it: but its most appropriate appellation is a sense of dignity, which all human beings possess in one form or another, and in some, though by no means in exact, proportion to their higher faculties, and which is so essential a part of the happiness of those in whom it is strong, that nothing which conflicts with it could be, otherwise than momentarily, an object of desire to them. Whoever supposes that this preference takes place at a sacrifice of happiness—that the superior being, in anything like equal circumstances, is not happier than the inferior—confounds the two very different ideas, of happiness, and content. It is indisputable that the being whose capacities of enjoyment are low, has the greatest chance of having them fully satisfied; and a highly endowed being will always feel that any happiness which he can look for, as the world is constituted, is imperfect. But he can learn to bear its imperfections, if they are at all bearable; and they will not make him envy the being who is indeed unconscious of the imperfections, but only because he feels not at all the good which those imperfections qualify. It is better to be a human being dissatisfied than a pig satisfied; better to be Socrates dissatisfied than a fool satisfied. And if the fool, or the pig, are of a different opinion, it is because they only know their own side of the question. The other party to the comparison knows both sides.

It may be objected, that many who are capable of the higher pleasures, occasionally, under the influence of temptation, postpone them to the lower. But this is quite compatible with a full appreciation of the intrinsic superiority of the higher. Men often, from infirmity of character, make their election for the nearer good, though they know it to be the less valuable; and this no less when the choice is between two bodily pleasures, than when it is between bodily and mental. They pursue sensual indulgences to the injury of health, though perfectly aware that health is the greater good. It may be further objected, that many who begin with youthful enthusiasm for everything noble, as they advance in years sink into indolence and selfishness. But I do not believe that those who undergo this very common change, voluntarily choose the lower description of pleasures in preference to the higher. I believe that before they devote themselves exclusively to the one, they have already become incapable of the other. Capacity for the nobler feelings is in most natures a very tender plant, easily killed, not only by hostile influences, but by mere want of sustenance; and in the majority of young persons it speedily dies away if the occupations to which their position in life has devoted them, and the society into which it has thrown them, are not favorable to keeping that higher capacity in exercise. Men lose their high aspirations as they lose their intellectual tastes, because they have not time or opportunity for indulging them; and they addict themselves to inferior pleasures, not because they deliberately prefer them, but because they are either the only ones to which they have access, or the only ones which they are any longer capable of enjoying. It may be questioned whether any one who has remained equally susceptible to both classes of pleasures, ever knowingly and calmly preferred the lower; though many, in all ages, have broken down in an ineffectual attempt to combine both.

From this verdict of the only competent judges, I apprehend there can be no appeal. On a question which is the best worth having of two pleasures, or which of two modes of existence is the most grateful to the feelings, apart from its moral attributes and from its consequences, the judgment of those who are qualified by knowledge of both, or, if they differ, that of the majority among them, must be admitted as final. And there needs to be the less hesitation to accept this judgment respecting the quality of pleasures, since there is no other tribunal to be referred to even on the question of quantity. What means are there of determining which is the acutest of two pains, or the intensest of two pleasurable sensations, except the general suffrage of those who are familiar with both? Neither pains nor pleasures are homogeneous, and pain is always heterogeneous with pleasure. What is there to decide whether a particular pleasure is worth purchasing at the cost of a particular pain, except the feelings and judgment of the experienced? When, therefore, those feelings and judgment declare the pleasures derived from the higher faculties to be preferable *in kind,* apart from the question of intensity, to those of which the animal nature, disjoined from the higher faculties, is susceptible, they are entitled on this subject to the same regard.

I have dwelt on this point, as being a necessary part of a perfectly just conception of Utility or Happiness, considered as the directive rule of human conduct. But it is by no means an indispensable condition to the acceptance of the utilitarian standard; for that standard is not the agent's own greatest happiness, but the greatest amount of happiness altogether; and if it may possibly be doubted whether a noble character is always the happier for its nobleness, there can be no doubt that it makes other people happier, and that the world in general is immensely a gainer by it. Utilitarianism, therefore, could only attain its end by the general cultivation of nobleness of character, even if each individual were only benefited by the nobleness of others, and his own, so far as happiness is concerned, were a sheer deduction from the benefit. But the bare enunciation of such an absurdity as this last, renders refutation superfluous.

According to the Greatest Happiness Principle, as above explained, the ultimate end, with reference to and for the sake of which all other things are desirable (whether we are considering our own good or that of other people), is an existence exempt as far as possible from pain, and as rich as possible in enjoyments, both in point of quantity and quality; the test of quality, and the rule for measuring it against quantity, being the preference felt by those who in their opportunities of experience, to which must be added their habits of self-consciousness and self-observation, are best furnished with the means of comparison. This, being, according to the utilitarian opinion, the end of human action, is necessarily also the standard of morality; which may accordingly be defined, the rules and precepts for human conduct, by the observance of which an existence such as has been described might be, to the greatest extent possible, secured to all mankind; and not to them only, but, so far as the nature of things admits, to the whole sentient creation. . . .

The objectors to utilitarianism cannot always be charged with representing it in a discreditable light. On the contrary, those among them who entertain anything like a just idea of its disinterested character, sometimes find fault with its standard as being too high for humanity. They say it is exacting too much to require that people shall always act from the inducement of promoting the general interests of society. But this is to mistake the very meaning of a standard of morals, and confound the rule of action with the motive of it. It is the business of ethics to tell us what are our duties, or by what test we may know them; but no system of ethics requires that the sole motive of all we do shall be a feeling of duty; on the contrary, ninety-nine hundredths of all our actions are done from other motives, and rightly so done, if the rule of duty does not condemn them. It is the more unjust to utilitarianism that this particular misapprehension should be made a ground of objection to it, inasmuch as utilitarian moralists have gone beyond almost all others in affirming that the motive has nothing to do with the morality of the action, though much with the worth of the agent. He who saves a fellow-creature from drowning does what is morally right, whether his motive be duty, or the hope of being paid for his trouble; he who betrays the friend that trusts him, is guilty of a crime, even if his object be to serve another friend to whom he is under greater obligation. But to speak only of actions done from the motive of duty, and in direct obedience to principle: it is a misapprehension of the utilitarian mode of thought, to conceive it as implying that people should fix their minds upon so wide a generality as the world, or society at large. The great majority of good actions are intended not for the benefit of the world, but for that of individuals, of which the good of the world is made up; and the thoughts of the most virtuous man need not on these occasions travel beyond the particular persons concerned, except so far as is necessary to assure himself that in benefiting them he is not violating the rights, that is, the legitimate and authorised expectations, of any one else. The multiplication of happiness is, according to the utilitarian ethics, the object of virtue: the occasions on which any person (except one in a thousand) has it in his power to do this on an extended scale, in other words to be a public benefactor, are but exceptional; and on these occasions alone is he called on to consider public utility; in every other case, private utility, the interest or happiness of some few persons, is all he has to attend to. Those alone the influence of whose actions extends to society in general, need concern themselves habitually about so large an object. In the case of abstinences indeed—of things which people forbear to do from moral considerations, though the consequences in the particular case might be beneficial—it would be unworthy of an intelligent agent not to be consciously aware that the action is of a class which, if practiced generally, would be generally injurious, and that this is the ground of the obligation to abstain from it. The amount of regard for the public interest implied in this recognition, is no greater than is demanded by every system of morals, for they all enjoin to abstain from whatever is manifestly pernicious to society. . . .

Chapter IV   Of What Sort of Proof the Principle of Utility Is Susceptible

It has already been remarked, that questions of ultimate ends do not admit of proof, in the ordinary acceptation of the term. To be incapable of proof by reasoning is common to all first principles; to the first premises of our knowledge, as well as to those of our conduct. But the former, being matters of fact, may be the subject of a direct appeal to the faculties which judge of fact—namely, our senses, and our internal consciousness. Can an appeal be made to the same faculties on questions of practical ends? Or by what other faculty is cognizance taken of them?

Questions abouts ends are, in other words, questions about what things are desirable. The utilitarian doctrine is, that happiness is desirable, and the only thing desirable, as an end; all other things being only desirable as means to that end. What ought to be required of this doctrine—what conditions is it to requisite that the doctrine

should fulfil—to make good its claim to be believed?

The only proof capable of being given that an object is visible, is that people actually see it. The only proof that a sound is audible, is that people hear it: and so of the other sources of our experience. In like manner, I apprehend, the sole evidence it is possible to produce that anything is desirable, is that people do actually desire it. If the end which the utilitarian doctrine proposes to itself were not, in theory and in practice, acknowledged to be an end, nothing could ever convince any person that it was so. No reason can be given why the general happiness is desirable, except that each person, so far as he believes it to be attainable, desires his own happiness. This, however, being a fact, we have not only all the proof which the case admits of, but all which it is possible to require, that happiness is a good: that each person's happiness is a good to that person, and the general happiness, therefore, a good to the aggregate of all persons. Happiness has made out its title as *one* of the ends of conduct, and consequently one of the criteria of morality.

But it has not, by this alone, proved itself to be the sole criterion. To do that, it would seem, by the same rule, necessary to show, not only that people desire happiness, but that they never desire anything else. . . .

We have now, then, an answer to the question, of what sort of proof the principle of utility is susceptible. If the opinion which I have now stated is psychologically true—if human nature is so constituted as to desire nothing which is not either a part of happiness or a means of happiness, we can have no other proof, and we require no other, that these are the only things desirable. If so, happiness is the sole end of human action, and the promotion of it the test by which to judge of all human conduct; from whence it necessarily follows that it must be the criterion of morality, since a part is included in the whole.

And now to decide whether this is really so; whether mankind do desire nothing for itself but that which is a pleasure to them, or of which the absence is a pain; we have evidently arrived at a question of fact and experience, dependent, like all similar questions, upon evidence. It can only be determined by practised self-consciousness and self-observation, assisted by observation of others. I believe that these sources of evidence, impartially consulted, will declare that desiring a thing and finding it pleasant, aversion to it and thinking of it as painful, are phenomena entirely inseparable, or rather two parts of the same phenomenon; in strictness of language, two different modes of naming the same psychological fact: that to think of an object as desirable (unless for the sake of its consequences), and to think of it as pleasant, are one and the same thing; and that to desire anything, except in proportion as the idea of it is pleasant, is a physical and metaphysical impossibility.

18

Against Moral Conservatism

KAI NIELSEN

Kai Nielsen is professor of philosophy at Calgary University and has written important works in philosophy of religion and political theory as well as in ethics. This essay is a clear example of act-utilitarianism. Nielsen defines 'moral conservativism' as "a normative ethical theory which maintains that there is a privileged moral principle or cluster of moral principles, prescribing determinate actions, with which it would always be wrong not to act in accordance no matter what the consequences." For Nielsen, no rules are sacrosanct, but differing situations call forth different actions, and potentially any rule could be overridden (though in fact we may need to treat some as absolutes for the good of society).

Nielsen's argument in favor of utilitarianism makes strong use of the notion of negative responsibility. *That is, we are responsible not only for the consequences of our actions, but also for the consequences of our nonactions.*

I

It is sometimes claimed that any consequentialist view of ethics has monstrous implications which make such a conception of morality untenable. What we must do—so the claim goes—is reject all forms of consequentialism and accept what has been labeled 'conservatism' or 'moral absolutism.' By 'conservatism' is meant, here, a normative ethical theory which maintains that there is a privileged moral principle or cluster of moral principles, prescribing determinate actions, with which it would always be wrong not to act in accordance no matter what the consequences. A key example

From *Ethics* 82 (1972): 113–24. Reprinted with permission of The University of Chicago Press and the author.

of such a principle is the claim that it is always wrong to kill an innocent human, whatever the consequences of not doing so.

I will argue that such moral conservatism is itself unjustified and, indeed, has morally unacceptable consequences, while consequentialism does not have implications which are morally monstrous and does not contain evident moral mistakes.

A consequentialist maintains that actions, rules, policies, practices, and moral principles are ultimately to be judged by certain consequences: to wit (for a very influential kind of consequentialism), by whether doing them more than, or at least as much as doing anything else, or acting in accordance with them more than or at least as much as acting in accordance with alternative policies, practices, rules or principles, tends, on the whole, and for *everyone* involved, to maximize satisfaction and minimize dissatisfaction. The states of affairs to be sought are those which maximize these things to the greatest extent possible for all mankind. But while this all sounds very humane and humanitarian, when its implications are thought through, it has been forcefully argued, it will be seen actually to have inhumane and morally intolerable implications. Circumstances could arise in which one holding such a view would have to assert that one was justified in punishing, killing, torturing, or deliberately harming the innocent, and such a consequence is, morally speaking, unacceptable.[1] As Anscombe has put it, anyone who "really thinks, *in advance,* that it is open to question whether such an action as procuring the judicial execution of the innocent should be quite excluded from consideration—I do not want to argue with him; he shows a corrupt mind."[2]

At the risk of being thought to exhibit a corrupt mind and a shallow consequentialist morality, I should like to argue that things are not as simple and straightforward as Anscombe seems to believe.

Surely, every moral man must be appalled at the judicial execution of the innocent or at the punishment, torture, and killing of the innocent. Indeed, being appalled by such behavior partially defines what it is to be a moral agent. And a consequentialist has very good utilitarian grounds for being so appalled, namely, that it is always wrong to inflict pain for its own sake. But this does not get to the core considerations which divide a conservative position such as Anscombe's from a consequentialist view. There are a series of tough cases that need to be taken to heart and their implications thought through by any reflective person, be he a conservative or a consequentialist. By doing this, we can get to the heart of the issue between conservatism and consequentialism. Consider this clash between conservatism and consequentialism arising over the problem of a 'just war.'

If we deliberately bomb civilian targets, we do not pretend that civilians are combatants in any simple fashion, but argue that this bombing will terminate hostilities more quickly, and will minimize all around suffering. It is hard to see how any brand of utilitarian will escape Miss Anscombe's objections. We are certainly killing the innocent . . . we are not killing them for the sake of killing them, but to save the lives of other innocent persons. Utilitarians, I think, grit their teeth and put up with this as part of the logic of total war; Miss Anscombe and anyone who thinks like her surely has to either redescribe the situation to ascribe guilt to the civilians or else she has to refuse to accept this sort of military tactics as simply wrong.[3]

It is indeed true that we cannot but feel the force of Anscombe's objections here. But is it the case that anyone shows a corrupt mind if he defends such bombing when, horrible as it is, it will quite definitely lessen appreciably the total amount of suffering and death in the long run, and if he is sufficiently nonevasive not to rationalize such a bombing of civilians into a situation in which all the putatively innocent people—children and all—are somehow in some measure judged guilty? Must such a man exhibit a corrupt moral sense if he refuses to hold that such military tactics are never morally justified? Must this be the monstrous view of a fanatical man devoid of any proper moral awareness? It is difficult for me to believe that this must be so.

Consider the quite parallel actions of guerrilla fighters and terrorists in wars of national liberation. In certain almost unavoidable circumstances, they must deliberately kill the innocent. We need to see some cases in detail here to get the necessary contextual background, and for this reason the motion picture *The Battle of Algiers* can be taken as a convenient point of reference. There we saw Algerian women—gentle, kindly women with children of their own and plainly people of moral sensitivity—with evident heaviness of heart, plant bombs which they had every good reason to believe would kill innocent people, including children; and we also saw a French general, also a human being of moral fiber and integrity, order the torture of Arab terrorists and threaten the bombing of houses in which terrorists were concealed but which also contained innocent people, including children. There are indeed many people involved in such activities who are cruel, sadistic beasts, or simply morally indifferent or, in important ways, morally uncomprehending. But the characters I have referred to from *The Battle of Algiers* were not of that stamp. They were plainly moral agents of a high degree of sensitivity, and yet they deliberately killed or were prepared to kill the innocent. And, with inessential variations, this is a recurrent phenomenon of human living in extreme situations. Such cases are by no means desert-island or esoteric cases.

It is indeed arguable whether such actions are always morally wrong—whether anyone should ever act as the Arab women or French general acted. But what could not be reasonably maintained, *pace* Anscombe, by any stretch of the imagination, is that the characters I described from *The Battle of Algiers* exhibited corrupt minds. Possibly morally mistaken, yes; guilty of moral corruption, no.

Dropping the charge of moral corruption but sticking with the moral issue about what actions are right, is it not the case that my consequentialist position logically forces me to conclude that under some circumstances—where the good to be achieved is great enough—I must not only countenance but actually advocate such violence toward the innocent? But is it not always, no matter what the circumstances or consequences, wrong to countenance, advocate, or engage in such violence? To answer such a question affirmatively is to commit oneself to the kind of moral absolutism or conservatism which Anscombe advocates. But, given the alternatives, should not one be such a conservative or at least hold that certain deontological principles must never be overridden?

I will take, so to speak, the papal bull by the horns and answer that there are circumstances when such violence must be reluctantly assented to or even taken to be something that one, morally speaking, must do. But, *pace* Anscombe, this very much needs arguing, and I shall argue it; but first I would like to set out some further but simpler cases which have a similar bearing. They are, by contrast, artificial cases. I use them because, in their greater simplicity, by contrast with my above examples, there are fewer variables to control and I can more conveniently make the essential conceptual and moral points. But, if my argument is correct for these simpler cases, the line of reasoning employed is intended to be applicable to those more complex cases as well.

II

Consider the following cases embedded in their exemplary tales:

1. The Case of the Innocent Fat Man

Consider the story (well known to philosophers) of the fat man stuck in the mouth of a cave on a coast. He was leading a group of people out of the cave when he got stuck in the mouth of the cave and in a very short time high tide will be upon them, and unless he is promptly unstuck, they all will be drowned except the fat man, whose head is out of the cave. But, fortunately or unfortunately, someone has with him a stick of dynamite. The short of the matter is, either they use the dynamite and blast the poor innocent fat man out of the mouth of the cave or everyone else drowns. Either one life or many lives. Our conservative presumably would take the attitude that it is all in God's hands and say that he ought never to blast the fat man out, for it is always wrong to kill the innocent. Must or should a moral man come to that conclusion? I shall argue that he should not.

My first exemplary tale was designed to show that our normal, immediate, rather absolutistic, moral reactions need to be questioned along with such principles as 'The direct intention of the death of an innocent person is never justifiable.' I have hinted (and later shall argue) that we should *beware* of our moral outrage here—our naturally conservative and unreflective moral reactions— for here the consequentialist has a strong case for what I shall call 'moral radicalism.' But, before turning to a defense of that, I want to tell another story taken from Phillipa Foot but used for my own purposes.[4] This tale, I shall argue, has a different import than our previous tale. Here our unrehearsed, commonsense moral reactions will stand up under moral scrutiny. But, I shall also argue when I consider them in section III, that our commonsense moral reactions here, initial expectations to the contrary not withstanding, can be shown to be justified on consequentialist grounds. The thrust of my argument for this case is that we are not justified in opting for a theistic and/or deontological absolutism or in rejecting consequentialism.

2. *The Magistrate and the Threatening Mob*

A magistrate or judge is faced with a very real threat from a large and uncontrollable mob of rioters demanding a culprit for a crime. Unless the criminal is produced, promptly tried, and executed, they will take their own bloody revenge on a much smaller and quite vulnerable section of the community (a kind of frenzied pogrom). The judge knows that the real culprit is unknown and that the authorities do not even have a good clue as to who he may be. But he also knows that there is within easy reach a disreputable, thoroughly disliked, and useless man, who, though innocent, could easily be framed so that the mob would be quite convinced that he was guilty and would be pacified if he were promptly executed. Recognizing that he can prevent the occurrence of extensive carnage only by framing some innocent person, the magistrate has him framed, goes through the mockery of a trial, and has him executed. Most of us regard such a framing and execution of such a man in such circumstances as totally unacceptable.[5] There are some who would say that it is categorically wrong—morally inexcusable—*whatever the circumstances.* Indeed, such a case remains a problem for the consequentialist, but here again, I shall argue, one can consistently remain a conesquentialist and continue to accept commonsense moral convictions about such matters.

My storytelling is at an end. The job is to see what the stories imply. We must try to determine whether thinking through their implications should lead a clearheaded and morally sensitive man to abandon consequentialism and to adopt some form of theistic absolutism and/or deontological absolutism. I shall argue that it does not.

III

I shall consider the last case first because there are good reasons why the consequentialist should stick with commonsense moral convictions for such cases. I shall start by giving my rationale for that claim. If the magistrate were a tough-minded but morally conscientious consequentialist, he could still, on straightforward consequentalist grounds, refuse to frame and execute the innocent man, even knowing that this would unleash the mob and cause much suffering and many deaths. The rationale for his particular moral stand would be that, by so framing and then executing such an innocent man, he would, in the long run, cause still more suffering through the resultant corrupting effect on the institution of justice. That is, in a case involving such extensive general interest in the issue—without that, there would be no problem about preventing the carnage or call for such extreme measures—knowledge that the man was framed, that the law had prostituted itself, would, surely, eventually leak out. This would encourage mob action in other circumstances, would lead to an increased skepticism about the incorruptibility or even the reliability of the judicial process, and would set a dangerous precedent for less clearheaded or less scrupulously humane magistrates. Given such a potential for the corruption of justice, a utilitarian or consequentialist judge or magistrate could, on good utilitarian or consequentialist grounds, argue that it was morally wrong to frame an innocent man. If the mob must rampage if such a sacrificial lamb is not provided, then the mob must rampage.

Must a utilitarian or consequentialist come to such a conclusion? The answer is no. It is the conclusion which is, as things stand, the most reasonable conclusion, but that he *must* come to it is far too strong a claim. A consequentialist could *consistently*—I did not say successfully—argue that, in taking the above tough-minded utilitarian position, we have overestimated the corrupting effects of such judicial railroading. His circumstance was an extreme one: a situation not often to be repeated even if, instead of acting as he did, he had set a precedent by such an act of judicial murder. A utilitarian rather more skeptical than most utilitarians about the claims of commonsense morality might reason that the lesser evil here is the judicial murder of an innocent man, vile as it is. He would persist in his moral iconoclasm by standing on the consequentialist rock that the lesser evil is always to be preferred to the greater evil.

The short of it is that utilitarians could disagree, as other consequentialists could disagree, about what is morally required of us in that case. The disagreement here between utilitarians or consequentialists of the same type is not one concerning fundamental moral principles but a disagreement about the empirical facts, about what course of action would in the long run produce the least suffering and the most happiness for *everyone* involved.[6]

However, considering the effect advocating the deliberate judicial killing of an innocent man would have on the reliance people put on commonsense moral beliefs of such a ubiquitous sort as the belief that the innocent must not be harmed, a utilitarian who defended the centrality of commonsense moral beliefs would indeed have a strong utilitarian case here. But the most crucial thing to recognize is that, to regard such judicial bowing to such a threatening mob as unqualifiedly wrong, as morally intolerable, one need not reject utilitarianism and accept some form of theistic or deontological absolutism.

It has been argued, however, that, in taking such a stance, I still have not squarely faced the moral conservative's central objection to the judicial railroading of the innocent. I allow, as a consequentialist, that there could be circumstances, at least as far as logical possibilities are concerned, in which such a railroading would be justified but that, as things actually go, it is not and probably never in fact will be justified. But the conservative's point is that in *no circumstances, either actual or conceivable, would it be justified*. No matter what the consequences, it is unqualifiedly unjustified. To say, as I do, that the situations in which it might be justified are desert-island, esoteric cases which do not occur in life, is not to the point, for,

as Alan Donagan argues, "Moral theory is *a priori*, as clear-headed utilitarians like Henry Sidgwick recognized. It is, as Leibniz would say, 'true of all possible worlds.'"[7] Thus, to argue as I have and as others have that the counterexamples directed against the consequentialist's appeal to conditions which are never in fact fulfilled or are unlikely to be fulfilled is beside the point.[8] Whether "a moral theory is true or false depends on whether its implications for all possible worlds are true. Hence, whether utilitarianism (or consequentialism) is true or false cannot depend on how the actual world is."[9] It is possible to specify logically conceivable situations in which consequentialism would have implications which are monstrous—for example, certain beneficial judicial murders of the innocent (whether they are even remotely likely to obtain is irrelevant)—hence consequentialism must be false.

We should not take such a short way with consequentialists, for what is true in Donagan's claim about moral theory's being a priori will not refute or even render implausible consequentialism, and what would undermine it in such a claim about the a priori nature of moral theory and presumably moral claims is not true.

To say that moral theory is a priori is probably correct if that means that categorical moral claims—fundamental moral statements—cannot be deduced from empirical statements or nonmoral theological statements, such that it is a contradiction to assert the empirical and/or nonmoral theological statements and deny the categorical moral claims or vice versa.[10] In that fundamental sense, it is reasonable and, I believe, justifiable to maintain that moral theory is autonomous and a priori. It is also a priori in the sense that moral statements are not themselves a kind of empirical statement. That is, if I assert 'One ought never to torture any sentient creature' or 'One ought never to kill an innocent man,' I am not trying to predict or describe what people do or are likely to do but am asserting what they are *to do*. It is also true that, if a moral statement is true, it holds for all possible worlds *in which sit-*

uations are exactly the sort characterized in the statement obtain. If it is true for one, it is true for all. You cannot consistently say that *A* ought to do *B* in situation *Y* and deny that someone exactly like *A* in a situation exactly like *Y* ought to do *B.*

In these ways, moral claims and indeed moral theory are a priori. But it is also evident that none of these ways will touch the consequentialist or utilitarian arguments. After all, the consequentialist need not be, and typically has not been, an ethical naturalist—he need not think moral claims are derivable from factual claims or that moral claims are a subspecies of empirical statement and he could accept—indeed, he must accept— what is an important truism anyway, that you cannot consistently say that *A* ought to do *B* in situation *Y* and deny that someone exactly like *A* in a situation exactly like *Y* ought to do *B.* But he could and should deny that moral claims are a priori in the sense that rational men must or even will make them without regard for the context, the situation, in which they are made. We say people ought not to drive way over the speed limit, or speed on icy roads, or throw knives at each other. But, if human beings had a kind of metallic exoskeleton and would not be hurt, disfigured, or seriously inconvenienced by knives sticking in them or by automobile crashes, we would not—so evidently at least—have good grounds for saying such speeding or knife throwing is wrong. It would not be so obvious that it was unreasonable and immoral to do these things if these conditions obtained.

In the very way we choose to describe the situation when we make ethical remarks, it is important in making this choice that we know what the world is like and what human beings are like. Our understanding of the situation, our understanding of human nature and motivation cannot but effect our structuring of the moral case. The consequentialist is saying that, as the world goes, there are good grounds for holding that judicial killings are morally intolerable, though he would have to admit that if the world (including human beings) were very different, such killings could

be something that ought to be done. But, in holding this, he is not committed to denying the universalizability of moral judgments, for, where he would reverse or qualify the moral judgment, the situation must be different. He is only committed to claiming that, where the situation is the same or relevantly similar and the persons are relevantly similar, they must, if they are to act morally, do the same thing. However, he is claiming both (1) that, as things stand, judicial killing of the innocent is always wrong and (2) that it is an irrational moral judgment to assert of reasonably determinate actions (e.g., killing an innocent man) that they are unjustifiable and morally unacceptable in all *possible* worlds, whatever the situation and whatever the consequences.

Donagan's claims about the a priori nature of moral theories do not show such a consequentialist claim to be mistaken or even give us the slightest reason for thinking that it is mistaken. What is brutal and vile, for example, throwing a knife at a human being just for the fun of it, would not be so, if human beings were invulnerable to harm from such a direction because they had a metallic exoskeleton. Similarly, what is, as things are, morally intolerable, for example, the judicial killing of the innocent, need not be morally intolerable in all conceivable circumstances.

Such considerations support the utilitarian or consequentialist skeptical of simply taking the claims of our commonsense morality as a rock-bottom ground of appeal for moral theorizing. Yet it may also well be the case—given our extensive cruelty anyway—that, if we ever start sanctioning such behavior, an even greater callousness toward life than the very extensive callousness extant now will, as a matter of fact, develop. Given a normative ethical theory which sanctions, *under certain circumstances,* such judicial murders, there may occur an undermining of our moral disapproval of killing and our absolutely essential moral principle that all human beings, great and small, are deserving of respect. This is surely enough, together with the not unimportant weight of even our unrehearsed moral feelings, to give strong utilitarian weight *here* to the dictates of our commonsense morality. Yet, I think I have also said enough to show that someone who questions their 'unquestionableness' in such a context does not thereby exhibit a 'corrupt mind' and that it is an open question whether he must be conceptually confused or morally mistaken over this matter.

IV

So far, I have tried to show with reference to the case of the magistrate and the threatening mob how conseqentialists can reasonably square their normative ethical theories with an important range of commonsense moral convictions. Now, I wish by reference to the case of the innocent fat man to establish that there is at least a serious question concerning whether such fundamental commonsense moral convictions should always function as 'moral facts' or a kind of moral ground to test the adequacy of normative ethical theories or positions. I want to establish that careful attention to such cases shows that we are not justified in taking the principles embodied in our commonsense moral reasoning about such cases as normative for all moral decisions. That a normative ethical theory is incompatible with some of our 'moral intuitions' (moral feelings or convictions) does not refute the normative ethical theory. What I will try to do here is to establish that this case, no more than the case examined in section III, gives us adequate grounds for abandoning consequentialism and for adopting moral conservativism.

Forget the levity of the example and consider the case of the innocent fat man. If there really is no other way of unsticking our fat man and if plainly, without blasting him out, everyone in the cave will drown, then, innocent or not, he should be blasted out. This indeed overrides the principle that the innocent should never be deliberately killed, but it does not reveal a callousness toward life, for the people involved are caught in a desperate situation in which, if such extreme action is not taken, many lives will be lost and far greater misery will obtain. Moreover, the people who do such a horrible thing or acquiesce in the doing of it are not likely to be rendered more callous about human life and human suffering as a result. Its occurrence will haunt them for the rest of their lives and is as likely as not to make them more rather than less morally sensitive. It is not even correct to say that such a desperate act shows a lack of respect for persons. We are not treating the fat man merely as a means. The fat man's person—his interests and rights—are not ignored. Killing him is something which is undertaken with the greatest reluctance. It is only when it is quite certain that there is no other way to save the lives of the others that such a violent course of action is justifiably undertaken.

Alan Donagan, arguing rather as Anscombe argues, maintains that "to use any innocent man ill for the sake of some public good is directly to degrade him to being a mere means" and to do this is of course to violate a principle essential to morality, that is, that human beings should never merely be treated as means but should be treated as ends in themselves (as persons worthy of respect).[11] But, as in my above remarks show, it need not be the case, and in the above situation it is not the case, that in killing such an innocent man we are treating him *merely* as a means. The action is universalizable, all alternative actions which would save his life are duly considered, the blasting out is done only as a last and desperate resort with the minimum of harshness and indifference to his suffering and the like. It indeed sounds ironical to talk this way, given what is done to him. But if such a terrible situation were to arise, there would always be more or less humane ways of going about one's grim task. And in acting in the more humane ways toward the fat man, as we do what we must do and would have done to ourselves were the roles reversed, we show a respect for his person.[12]

In so treating the fat man—not just to further the public good but to prevent the certain death of a whole group of people (that is to prevent an even greater evil than his being killed in this way)—the claims of justice are not overridden either, for each individual involved, if he is reasoning correctly, should realize that if he were so stuck rather than the fat man, he should in such situations be blasted out. Thus, there is no question of being unfair. Surely we must choose between evils here, but is there anything more reasonable, more morally appropriate, than choosing the lesser evil when doing or allowing some evil cannot be avoided? That is, where there is no avoiding both and where our actions can determine whether a greater or lesser evil obtains, should we not plainly always opt for the lesser evil? And is it not obviously a greater evil that all those other innocent people should suffer and die than that the fat man should suffer and die? Blowing up the fat man is indeed monstrous. But letting him remain stuck while the whole group drowns is still more monstrous.

The consequentialist is on strong moral ground here, and, if his reflective moral convictions do not square either with certain unrehearsed or with certain reflective particular moral convictions of human beings, so much the worse for such commonsense moral convictions. One could even usefully and relevantly adapt here—though for a quite different purpose—an argument of Donagan's. Consequentialism of the kind I have been arguing for provides so persuasive "a theoretical basis for common morality that when it contradicts some moral intuition, it is natural to suspect that intuition, not theory, is corrupt."[13] Given the comprehensiveness, plausibility, and overall rationality of consequentialism, it is not unreasonable to override even a deeply felt moral conviction if it does not square with such a theory, though, if it made no sense or overrode the bulk of or even a great many of our considered moral convictions, that would be another matter indeed.

Anticonsequentialists often point to the inhumanity of people who will sanction such killing of the innocent, but cannot the compliment be returned by speaking of the even greater inhumanity, conjoined with evasiveness, of those who will allow even more death and far greater misery and then excuse themselves on the ground that they did not intend the death and misery but merely forbore to prevent it? In such a context, such reasoning and such forbearing to prevent seems to me to constitute a moral evasion. I say it is evasive because rather than steeling himself to do what in normal circumstances would be a horrible and vile act but in this circumstance is a harsh moral necessity, he allows, when he has the power to prevent it, a situation which is still many times worse. He tries to keep his 'moral purity' and avoid 'dirty hands' at the price of utter moral failure and what Kierkegaard called 'double-mindedness.' It is understandable that people should act in this morally evasive way but this does not make it right.

My consequentialist reasoning about such cases as the case of the innocent fat man is very often resisted on the grounds that it starts a very dangerous precedent. People rationalize wildly and irrationally in their own favor in such situations. To avoid such rationalization, we must stubbornly stick to our deontological principles and recognize as well that very frequently, if people will put their wits to work or just endure, such admittedly monstrous actions done to prevent still greater evils will turn out to be unnecessary.

The general moral principles surrounding bans on killing the innocent are strong and play such a crucial role in the ever-floundering effort to humanize the savage mind—savage as a primitive and savage again as a contemporary in industrial society—that it is of the utmost social utility, it can be argued, that such bans against killing the innocent not be called into question in any practical manner by consequentialist reasoning.

However, in arguing in this way, the moral conservative has plainly shifted his ground, and he is himself arguing on consequentialist grounds that we must treat certain nonconsequentialist moral principles as absolute (as principles which can never *in fact*, from a reasonable moral point of view, be overridden, for it would be just too disastrous to do so).[14] But now he is on my home court, and my reply is that there is no good evidence at all that in the circumstances I characterized, overriding these deontological principles would have this disastrous effect. I am aware that a bad precedent could be set. Such judgments must not be made for more doubtful cases. But my telling my two stories in some detail, and my contrasting them, was done in order to make evident the type of situation, with its attendant rationale, in which the overriding of those deontological principles can be seen clearly to be justified and the situations in which this does obtain and why. My point was to specify the situations in which we ought to override our commonsense moral convictions about those matters, and the contexts in which we are not so justified or at least in which it is not clear which course of action is justified.[15]

If people are able to be sufficiently clearheaded about these matters, they can see that there are relevant differences between the two sorts of cases. But I was also carefully guarding against extending such 'moral radicalism'—if such it should be called—to other and more doubtful cases. Unless solid empirical evidence can be given that such a 'moral radicalism' would—if it were to gain a toehold in the community—overflow destructively and inhumanely into the other doubtful and positively unjustifiable situations, nothing has been said to undermine the correctness of my consequentialist defense of 'moral radicalism' in the contexts in which I defended it.[16]

Notes

1. Alan Donagan, "Is There a Credible Form of Utilitarianism?" and H. J. McCloskey, "A Non-Utilitarian Approach to Punishment," both in Michael D. Bayles, ed. *Contemporary Utilitarianism* (Garden City, N.Y.: Doubleday, 1968).

2. Elizabeth Anscombe, "Modern Moral Philosophy," *Philosophy* 23 (January 1957): 16–17.

3. Alan Ryan, "Review of Jan Narveson's *Morality and Utility*," *Philosophical Books* 9, no. 3 (October 1958): 14.

4. Phillipa Foot, "The Problem of Abortion and the Doctrine of the Double Effect," *Oxford Review*, no. 5 (1967): 5–15.

5. Later, I shall show that there are desert-island circumstances—i.e., highly improbable situations—in which such judicial railroading might be a moral necessity. But I also show what little force desert-island cases have in the articulation and defense of a normative ethical theory.

6. 'Everyone' here is used distributively; i.e., I am talking about the interests of each and every one. In that sense, everyone's interests need to be considered.

7. Donagan, *op. cit.*, p. 189.

8. T. L. S. Sprigge argues in such a manner in his "A Utilitarian Reply to Dr. McCloskey," in Michael D. Bayles, ed. *Contemporary Utilitarianism* (Garden City, N.Y.: Doubleday, 1968).

9. Donagan, *op. cit.*, p. 194.

10. There is considerable recent literature about whether it is possible to derive moral claims from nonmoral claims. See W. D. Hudson, ed., *The Is-Ought Question: A Collection of Papers on the Central Problem in Moral Philosophy* (New York: St. Martin's Press, 1969).

11. Donagan, *op. cit.*, pp. 199–200.

12. Again, I am not asserting that we would have enough fortitude to assent to it were the roles actually reversed. I am making a conceptual remark about what as moral beings we must try to do and not a psychological observation about what we can do.

13. Donagan, *op. cit.*, p. 198.

14. Jonathan Bennett, "Whatever the Consequences," *Analysis* 26 (1966), has shown that this is a very common equivocation for the conservative and makes, when unnoticed, his position seem more plausible than it actually is.

15. I have spoken, conceding this to the Christian absolutist for the sake of the discussion, as if (1) it is fairly evident what our commonsense moral convictions are here and (2) that they are deontological principles taken to hold no matter what the consequences. But that either (1) or (2) is clearly so seems to me very much open to question.

16. I do not mean to suggest that I am giving a blanket defense to our commonsense morality; that is one of the last things I would want to do. Much of what we or any other tribe take to be commonsense morality is

little better than a set of magical charms to deal with our social environment. But I was defending the importance of such cross-culturally ubiquitous moral principles as that one ought not to harm the innocent or that promises ought to be kept. However, against Christian absolutists of the type I have been discussing, I take them to be prima facie obligations. This means that they always hold *ceteris paribus;* but the *ceteris paribus* qualification implies that they can be overridden on occasion. On my account, appeal to consequences and considerations about justice and respect for persons determines when they should on a given occasion be overridden.

19

Rule-Utilitarianism

JOHN HOSPERS

John Hospers (b. 1918) is the director of the School of Philosophy at the University of Southern California and the author of several works in philosophy, most notably Libertarianism and Human Conduct: An Introduction to Ethics, *from which the present selection is taken. In 1972 he ran for president of the United States on the Libertarian party ticket.*

With the use of counterexamples, Hospers rejects the act-utilitarianism defended by Bentham, Nielsen, and, perhaps, Mill. We need rules without being rigidly rule-bound or forgetting the consequentialist point of morality. Hence, Hospers opts for a version of utilitarianism that is centered in rules, which he and others have called "rule-utilitarianism."

1. In order to receive a high enough grade average to be admitted to medical school, a certain student must receive either an A or a B in one of my courses. After his final examination is in, I find, on averaging his grades, that his grade for the course comes out to a C. The student comes into my office and begs me to change the grade, on the ground that I have not read his paper carefully enough. So I reread his final exam paper, as well as some of the other papers in the class in order to get a better sense of comparison; the rechecking convinces me that his grade should be no higher than the one I have given him—if anything, it should be lower. I inform him of my opinion and he still pleads with me to change the grade, but for a different reason. "I know I didn't deserve more than a C, but I

appeal to you as a human being to change my grade, because without it I can't get into medical school, which naturally means a great deal to me." I inform him that grades are supposed to be based on achievement in the course, not on intentions or need or the worthiness of one's plans. But he pleads: "I know it's unethical to change a grade when the student doesn't deserve a higher one, but can't you please make an exception to the rule just this once?" And before I can reply, he sharpens his plea: "I appeal to you as a utilitarian. Your goal is the greatest happiness of everyone concerned, isn't it? If you give me only the grade I deserve, who will be happier? Not I, that's sure. Perhaps you will for a little while, but you have hundreds of students and you'll soon forget about it; and I will be ever so much happier for being admitted into a school that will train me for the profession I have always desired. It's true that I didn't work as hard in your course as I should have, but I realize my mistake and I wouldn't waste so much time if I had it to do over again. Anyway, you should be forward-looking rather than backward-looking in your moral judgments, and there is no doubt whatever that much more happiness will be caused (and unhappiness prevented) by your giving me the higher grade even though I fully admit that I don't deserve it."

After pondering the matter, I persist in believing that it would not be right to change the grade under these circumstances. Perhaps you agree with my decision and perhaps you don't, but *if* you agree that I should not have changed the grade, and *if* you are also a utilitarian, how are you going to reconcile such a decision with utilitarianism? *Ex hypothesi*, the greatest amount of happiness will be brought about by my changing the grade, so why shouldn't I change it?

Of course, if I changed the grade and went around telling people about it, my action would tend to have an adverse effect on the whole system of grading—and this system is useful to graduate schools and future employers to give some indication of the student's achievement in his various courses. But of course if I tell no one, nobody will know, and my action cannot set a bad example to others. This in turn raises an interesting question: If it is wrong for me to do the act publicly, is it any the less wrong for me to do it secretly?

2. A man is guilty of petty theft and is sentenced to a year in prison. Suppose he can prove to the judge's satisfaction that he would be happier out of jail, that his wife and family would too (they depend on his support), that the state wouldn't have the expense of his upkeep if he were freed, and that people won't hear about it because his case didn't hit the papers and nobody even knows that he was arrested—in short, everyone concerned would be happier and nobody would be harmed by his release. And yet, we feel, or at least many people would, that to release him would be a mistake. The sentence imposed on him is the minimum permitted by law for his offense, and he should serve out his term in accordance with the law.

3. A district attorney who has prosecuted a man for robbery chances upon information which shows conclusively that the man he has prosecuted is innocent of the crime for which he has just been sentenced. The man is a wastrel who, if permitted to go free, would almost certainly commit other crimes. Moreover, the district attorney has fairly conclusive evidence of the man's guilt in prior crimes, for which, however, the jury has failed to convict him. Should he, therefore, "sit on the evidence" and let the conviction go through in this case, in which he knows the man to be innocent? We may not be able to articulate exactly *why*, but we feel strongly that the district attorney should not sit on the evidence but that he should reveal every scrap of evidence he knows, even though the revelation means releasing the pris-

oner (now known to be innocent) to do more crimes and be convicted for them later.

X: It seems to me that some acts are right or wrong, not *regardless* of the consequences they produce, but *over and above* the consequences they produce. We would all agree, I suppose, that you should break a promise to save a life but not that you should break it whenever you considered it probable (even with good reason) that more good effects will come about through breaking it. Suppose you had promised someone you would do something and you didn't do it. When asked why, you replied, "Because I thought breaking it would have better results." Wouldn't the promisee condemn you for your action, and rightly? This example is quite analogous, I think, to the example of the district attorney; the district attorney might argue that more total good will be produced by keeping the prisoner's innocence secret. Besides, if he is released, people may read about it in the newspaper and say, "You see, you can get by with anything these days" and may be encouraged to violate the law themselves as a result. Still, even though it would do more total good if the man were to remain convicted, wouldn't it be wrong to do so in view of the fact that he is definitely innocent of *this* crime? The law punishes a man, not necessarily because the most good will be achieved that way, but because he has committed a crime; if we don't approve of the law, we can do our best to have it changed, but meanwhile aren't we bound to follow it? Those who execute the law are sworn to obey it; they are *not* sworn to produce certain consequences.

Y: Yes, but remember that the facts *might* always come out after their concealment and that we can never be sure they won't. If they do, keeping the man in prison will be far worse than letting the man go; it will result in a great public distrust for the law itself; nothing is more demoralizing than corruption of the law by its own supposed enforcers. Better let a hundred human derelicts go free than risk that! You see, *one* of the consequences you always have to consider is the effect of *this* action on the *general practice* of law-breaking itself; and when you bring in *this* consequence, it will surely weigh the balance in favor of divulging the information that will release the innocent man. So utilitarianism will still account quite satisfactorily for this case. I agree that the man should be released, but I do so on utilitarian grounds; I needn't abandon my utilitarianism at all to take care of this case.

X: But your view is open to one fatal objection. You say that one never can be sure that the news *won't* leak out. Perhaps so. But suppose that in a given case one *could* be sure; would that really make any difference? Suppose you are the only person that knows and you destroy the only existing evidence. Since you are not going to talk, there is simply no chance that the news will leak out, with consequent damage to public morale. Then is it all right to withhold the information? You see, I hold that if it's wrong not to reveal the truth when others might find out, then it's equally wrong not to reveal it when *nobody* will find out. You utilitarians are involved in the fatal error of making the rightness or wrongness of an act depend on whether performing it will ever be publicized. And I hold that it is immoral even to consider this condition; the district attorney should reveal the truth regardless of whether his concealing it would ever be known.

Y: But surely you aren't saying that one should *never* conceal the truth? not even if your country is at war against a totalitarian enemy and revealing truths to the people would also mean revealing them to the enemy?

X: Of course I'm not saying that—don't change the subject. I am saying that *if* in situation S it is wrong to convict an innocent man, then it is equally wrong whether or not the public knows that it is wrong; the public's knowledge will certainly have bad consequences, but the conviction would be wrong anyway even *without* these bad consequences; so you can't appeal to the consequences of the conviction's becoming public as grounds for saying that the conviction is wrong. I think that you utilitarians are really stuck here. For you, the consideration "but nobody is ever

going to know about it anyway" is a relevant consideration. It has to be; for the rightness of an act (according to you) is estimated in terms of its total consequences, and its total consequences, of course, include its effects (or lack of effects) on other acts of the same kind, and there won't be any such effects if the act is kept absolutely secret. You have to consider *all* the consequences relevant; the matter of keeping the thing quiet is one consequence; so you have to consider this one relevant too. Yet I submit to you that it isn't relevant; the suggestion "but nobody is going to know about it anyway" is not one that will help make the act permissible if it wasn't before. If anything, it's the other way round: something bad that's done publicly and openly is not as bad as if it's done secretly so as to escape detection; secret sins are the worst. . . .

Y: I deny what you say. It seems to me worse to betray a trust in public, where it may set an example to others, than to do so in secret, where it can have no bad effects on others.

X: And I submit that you would never say that if you weren't already committed to the utilitarian position. Here is a situation where you and practically everyone else would not hesitate to say that an act done in secret is no less wrong than when done in public, were it not that it flies in the face of a doctrine to which you have already committed yourself on the basis of quite different examples.

4. Here is a still different kind of example. We consider it our duty in a democracy to vote and to do so wisely and intelligently as possible, for only if we vote wisely can a democracy work successfully. But in a national election my vote is only one out of millions, and it is more and more improbable that *my* vote will have any effect upon the outcome. Nor is my failure to vote going to affect other people much, if at all. Couldn't a utilitarian argue this way: "My vote will have no effect at all—at least far, far less than other things I could be doing instead. Therefore, I shall not vote." Each and every would-be voter could argue in exactly the same way. The result would be that

nobody would vote, and the entire democratic process would be destroyed.

What conclusion emerges from these examples? If the examples point at all in the right direction, they indicate that there are some acts which it is right to perform, even though by themselves they will not have good consequences (such as my voting), and that there are some acts which it is wrong to perform, even though by themselves they would have good consequences (such as sitting on the evidence). But this conclusion is opposed to utilitarianism as we have considered it thus far. . . .

Rule-Utilitarianism and Objections to It

The batter swings, the ball flies past, the umpire yells "Strike three!" The disappointed batter pleads with the umpire, "Can't I have four strikes just this once?" We all recognize the absurdity of this example. Even if the batter could prove to the umpire's satisfaction that he would be happier for having four strikes this time, that the spectators would be happier for it (since most of the spectators are on his side), that there would be little dissatisfaction on the side of the opposition (who might have the game clinched anyway), and that there would be no effect on future baseball games, we would still consider his plea absurd. We might think, "Perhaps baseball would be a better game— i.e., contribute to the greatest total enjoyment of all concerned—if four strikes were permitted. If so, we should change the rules of the game. But until that time, we must play baseball according to the rules which are now the accepted rules of the game."

This example, though only an analogy, gives us a clue to the kind of view we are about to consider— let us call it *rule-utilitarianism*. Briefly stated (we shall amplify it gradually), rule-utilitarianism comes to this: Each act, in the moral life, falls under a *rule*; and we are to judge the rightness or wrongness of the act, not by *its* consequences, but by the consequences of its universalization—that is, by the consequences of the adoption of the *rule* under which this act falls. This . . . interpretation of Kant's categorical imperative . . . differs from Kant in being concerned with consequences, but retains the main feature which Kant introduced, that of universalizability.

Thus: The district attorney may do more good in a particular case by sitting on the evidence, but even if this case has no consequences for future cases because nobody ever finds out, still, the general policy or *practice* of doing this kind of thing is a very bad one; it uproots one of the basic premises of our legal system, namely, that an innocent person should not be condemned. Our persistent conviction that it would be wrong for him to conceal the evidence in this case comes *not* from the conviction that concealing the evidence will produce less good—we may be satisfied that it will produce more good in this case— but from the conviction that the *practice* of doing this kind of thing will have very bad consequences. In other words, "Conceal the evidence when you think that it will produce more happiness" would be a bad rule to follow, and it is because this *rule* (if adopted) would have bad consequences, not because *this* act itself has bad consequences, that we condemn the act.

The same applies in other situations: . . . perhaps I can achieve more good, in this instance, by changing the student's grade, but the consequences of the general practice of changing students' grades for such reasons as these would be very bad indeed; a graduate school or a future employer would no longer have reason to believe that the grade-transcript of the student had any reference to his real achievement in his courses; he would wonder how many of the high grades resulted from personal factors like pity, need, and irrelevant appeals by the student to the teacher. The same considerations apply also to the voting example: if Mr. Smith can reason that his vote won't make any difference to the outcome, so can Mr. Jones and Mr. Robinson and every other would-be voter; but if everyone reasoned in this way, no one would vote, and this *would* have bad effects. It is considered one's duty to vote, not because the consequences of one's not doing so are bad, but because the consequences of the general practice of not doing so are bad. To put it in Kantian language, the maxim of the action, if universalized, would have bad consequences. But the individual act of *your* not voting on a specific occasion—or of any *one* person's not voting, as long as *others* continued to vote—would probably have no bad consequences.

There are many other examples of the same kind of thing. If during a water shortage there is a regulation that water should not be used to take baths every day or to water gardens, there will be virtually no bad consequences if only *I* violate the rule. Since there will be no discernible difference to the city water supply and since my plants will remain green and fresh and pleasant to look at, why shouldn't I water my plants? But if everyone watered his plants, there would not be enough water left to drink. My act is judged wrong, not because of *its* consequences, but because the consequences of everyone doing so would be bad. If I walk on the grass where the sign says, "Do not walk on the grass," there will be no ill effects; but if everyone did so it would destroy the grass. There are some kinds of act which have little or no effect if any one person (or two, or three) does them but which have very considerable effects if everyone (or even just a large number) does them. Rule-utilitarianism is designed to take care of just such situations.

Rule-utilitarianism also takes care of situations which are puzzling in traditional utilitarianism, . . . namely, the secrecy with which an act is performed. "But no one will ever know, so my act won't have any consequences for future acts of the same kind," the utilitarian argued; and we felt that he was being somehow irrelevant, even immoral: that if something is wrong when people know about it, it is just as wrong when done in secret. Yet this condition *is* relevant according to traditional utilitarianism, for if some act with bad consequences is never known to anyone, this ignorance does mitigate the bad consequences, for it undeniably keeps the act from setting an example (except, of course, that it may start a habit

in the agent himself). Rule-utilitarianism solves this difficulty. If I change the student's grade in secret, my act is wrong, in spite of its having almost no consequences (and never being known to anyone else), because if I change the grade and don't tell anyone, how do I know how many other teachers are changing their students' grades without telling anybody? It is the result of the *practice* which is bad, not the result of my single action. The result of the practice is bad whether the act is done in secret or not: the result of the practice of changing grades in secret is just as bad as the results of the practice done in full knowledge of everyone; it would be equally deleterious to the grading system, equally a bad index of a student's actual achievement. In fact, if changing grades is done in secret, this in one way is worse; for prospective employers will not know, as they surely ought to know in evaluating their prospective employees, that their grades are not based on achievement but on other factors such as poverty, extra-curricular work load, and persuasive appeal.

Rule utilitarianism is a distinctively twentieth-century amendment of the utilitarianism of Bentham and Mill, often called *act-utilitarianism*. . . . Since this pair of labels is brief and indicates clearly the contents of the theories referred to, we prefer these terms to a second pair of labels, which are sometimes used for the same theories: *restricted utilitarianism* as opposed to *unrestricted* (or extreme, or *traditional*) *utilitarianism*. (Whether or not Mill's theory is strictly act-utilitarianism is a matter of dispute. Mill never made the distinction between act-utilitarianism and rule-utilitarianism. . . . Some of Mill's examples, however, have to do not with individual acts but with general principles and rules of conduct. Mill and Bentham were both legislators, interested in amending the laws of England into greater conformity to the utilitarian principle; and to the extent that Mill was interested in providing a criterion of judging rules of conduct rather than individual acts, he may be said to have been a rule-utilitarian.)

Much more must be said before the full nature of the rule-utilitarian theory becomes clear. To understand it better, we shall consider some possible questions, comments, and objections that can be put to the theory as thus far stated.

1. Doesn't the . . . problem arise here . . . of *what* precisely we are to universalize? Every act can be put into a vast variety of classes of acts; or, in our present terminology, every act can be made to fall under many different general rules. Which rule among this vast variety are we to select? We can pose our problem by means of an imaginary dialogue referring back to Kant's ethics and connecting it with rule-utilitarianism:

A: Whatever may be said for Kant's ethics in general, there is one principle of fundamental importance which must be an indispensable part of every ethics—the principle of universalizability. If some act is right for me to do, it would be right for all rational beings to do it; and if it is wrong for them to do it, it would be wrong for me too.

B: If this principle simply means that nobody should make an exception in his own favor, the principle is undoubtedly true and is psychologically important in view of the fact that people constantly do make exceptions in their own favor. But as it stands I can't follow you in agreeing with Kant's principle. Do you mean that if it is wrong for Smith to get a divorce, it is also wrong for Jones to do so? But this isn't so. Smith may be hopelessly incompatible with his wife, and they may be far better off apart, whereas Jones may be reconcilable with his wife (with some mutal effort) and a divorce in his case would be a mistake. Each case must be judged on its own merits.

A: The principle doesn't mean that if it's right for one person, A, to do it, it is therefore right for B and C and D to do it. It means that if it's right for one person to do it, it is right for anyone *in those circumstances* to do it. And Jones isn't in the same circumstances as Smith. Smith and his wife would be better off apart, and Jones and his wife would be better off together.

B: I see. Do you mean *exactly* the same circumstances or *roughly* the same (similar) circumstances?

A: I think I would have to mean exactly the

same circumstances for if the circumstances were not quite alike, that little difference might make the difference between a right act (done by Smith) and a wrong act (done by Jones). For instance, if in Smith's case there are no children and in Jone's case there are, this fact may make a difference.

B: Right. But I must urge you to go even further. Two men might be in exactly the same *external* circumstances, but owing to their *internal constitution* what would be right for one of them wouldn't be for the other. Jones may have the ability to be patient, impartial, and approach problems rationally, and Smith may not have this ability; here again is a relevant difference between them, although not a difference in their external circumstances. Or: Smith, after he reaches a certain point of fatigue, would do well to go fishing for a few days—this would refresh and relax him as nothing else could. But Jones dislikes fishing; it tries and irritates and bores him; so even if he were equally tired and had an equally responsible position, he would not be well advised to go fishing. Or again: handling explosives might be all right for a trained intelligent person, but not for an ignorant blunderbuss. In the light of such examples as these, you see that under the "same circumstances" you'll have to include not only the external circumstances in which they find themselves but their own internal character.

A: I grant this. So what?

B: But now your universalizability principle becomes useless. For two people never *are* in exactly the same circumstances. Nor can they be: if Smith were in exactly the same circumstances as Jones, including all his traits of character, his idiosyncracies, and his brain cells, he would *be* Jones. You see, your universalizability principle is inapplicable. It would become applicable only under conditions (two people being the same person) which are self-contradictory—and even if not self-contradictory, you'll have to admit that two exactly identical situations never occur; so once again the rule is inapplicable.

A: I see your point; but I don't think I need go along with your conclusion. Smith and Jones should do the same thing only if their situation or circumstances are the same in certain *relevant respects.* The fact that Jones is wearing a white shirt and Smith a blue one, is a difference of circumstances, but, surely, an *irrelevant* difference, a difference that for moral purposes can be ignored. But the fact that Smith and his wife are emotionally irreconcilable while Jones and his wife could work things out, would be a morally relevant circumstance.

B: Possibly. But how are you going to determine which differences are relevant and which are not?

Kant . . . never solved this problem. He assumed that "telling a lie" was morally relevant but that "telling a lie to save a life" was not; but he gave no reason for making this distinction. The rule-utilitarian has an answer.

Suppose that a red-headed man with one eye and a wart on his right cheek tells a lie on a Tuesday. What rule are we to derive from this event? Red-headed men should not tell lies? People shouldn't lie on Tuesdays? Men with warts on their cheeks shouldn't tell lies on Tuesdays? These rules seem absurd, for it seems so obvious that whether it's Tuesday or not, whether the man has a wart on his cheek or not, has nothing whatever to do with the rightness of his action—these circumstances are just *irrelevant.* But this is the problem: how are we going to establish this irrelevance? What is to be our criterion?

The criterion we tried to apply . . . was to make the rule more *specific*: instead of saying, "This is a lie and is therefore wrong," . . . we made it more specific and said, "This is a lie told to save a life and is therefore right." We could make the rule more specific still, involving the precise circumstances in which this lie is told, other than the fact that it is told to save a life. But, now it seems the use of greater specificity will not always work: instead of "Don't tell lies," suppose we say, "Don't tell lies on Tuesdays." The second is certainly more specific than the first, but is it a better rule? It seems plain that it is not—that its being a Tuesday is, in fact, wholly irrelevant. Why?

"Because," says the rule-utilitarian, "there is no difference between the effects of lies told on Tuesdays and the effects of lies told on any other day. This is simply an empirical fact, and because of this empirical fact, bringing in Tuesday is irrelevant. If lies told on Tuesdays always had good consequences and lies told on other days were disastrous, then a lie's being told on a Tuesday would be relevant to the moral estimation of the act; but in fact this is not true. Thus there is no advantage in specifying the subclass of lies, 'lies told on Tuesdays.' The same is true of 'lies told by redheads' and 'lies told by persons with warts on their cheeks.' The class of lies can be made more specific—that is no problem—but not more *relevantly* specific, at least not in the direction of Tuesdays and redheads. (However, the class can be made more relevantly specific considering certain other aspects of the situation, such as whether the lie was told to produce a good result that could not have been brought about otherwise.)"

Consider by contrast a situation in which the class of acts can easily be made relevantly more specific. A pacifist might argue as follows: "I should never use physical violence in any form against another human being, since if everyone refrained from violence, we would have a warless world." There are aspects of this example that we cannot discuss now, but our present concern with it is as follows. We can break down violence into more specific types such as violence which is unprovoked, violence in defense of one's life against attack by another, violence by a policeman in catching a lawbreaker, violence by a drunkard in response to an imaginary affront. The effects of these subclasses of violence do differ greatly in their effects upon society. Violence used by a policeman in apprehending a lawbreaker (at least under some circumstances, which could be spelled out) and violence used in preventing a would-be murderer from killing you, do on the whole have good effects; but the unprovoked violence of an aggressor or a drunkard does not. Since these subclasses do have different effects, therefore, it *is* relevant to consider them. Indeed, it is imperative to do so: the pacifist who condemns *all* violence would probably, if he thought about it, not wish to condemn the policeman who uses violent means to prevent an armed madman from killing a dozen people. In any event, the effects of the two subclasses of acts are vastly different; and, the rule-utilitarian would say, it is accordingly very important for us to consider them—to break down the general class of violent acts into more specific classes and consider separately the effects of each one until we have arrived at subclasses which cannot *relevantly* be made more specific.

How specific shall we be? Won't we get down to "acts of violence to prevent aggression, performed on Tuesdays at 11:30 P.M. in hot weather" and subclasses of that sort? And aren't these again plainly irrelevant? Of course they are, and the reason has already been given: acts of violence performed on Tuesdays, or at 11:30 P.M., or by people with blue suits, are no different in their effects from acts-of-violence-to-prevent-aggression done in circumstances other than these; and therefore these circumstances, though more specific, are not relevantly more specific. When the consequences of these more specific classes of acts differ from the consequences of the more general class, it is this specific class which should be considered; but when the consequences of the specific classes are not different from those of the more general class, the greater specificity is irrelevant and can be ignored.

The rule, then, is this: we should consider the consequences of the general performance of certain classes of actions only if that class contains within itself no subclasses, the consequences of the general practice of which would be either better or worse than the consequences of the class itself.

Let us take an actual example of how this rule applies. Many people, including Kant, have taken the principle "Thou shalt not kill" as admitting of no exceptions. But as we have just seen, such principles can be relevantly made more specific. Killing for fun is one thing, killing in self-defense another. Suppose, then, that we try to arrive at a general rule on which to base our actions in this

regard. We shall try to arrive at that rule the general following of which will have the best results. Not to kill an armed bandit who is about to shoot you if you don't shoot him first, would appear to be a bad rule by utilitarian standards; for it would tend to eliminate the good people and preserve the bad ones; moreover, if nobody resisted aggressors, the aggressors, knowing this, would go hog-wild and commit indiscriminate murder, rape, and plunder. Therefore, "Don't kill except in self-defense" (though we might improve this rule too) would be a better rule than "Never kill." But "Don't kill unless you feel angry at the victim" would be a bad rule, because the adoption of this rule would lead to no end of indiscriminate killing for no good reason. The trick is to arrive at the rule which, if adopted, would have the very best possible consequences (which includes, of course, the absolute minimum of bad consequences). Usually no simple or easily statable rule will do this, the world being as complex as it is. There will usually be subclasses of classes-of-acts which are relevantly more specific than the simple, general class with which we began. And even when we think we have arrived at a satisfactory rule, there always remains the possibility that it can relevantly be made more specific, and thus amended, with an increase in accuracy but a consequent decrease in simplicity.

To a considerable extent most people recognize this complexity. Very few people would accept the rule against killing without some qualifications. However much they may preach and invoke the rule "Thou shall not kill" in situations where it happens to suit them, they would never recommend its adoption in all circumstances: when one is defending himself against an armed killer, almost everyone would agree that killing is permissible, although he may not have formulated any theory from which this exception follows as a logical consequence. Our practical rule against killing contains within itself (often not explicitly stated) certain *classes of exceptions:* "Don't kill *except* in self-defense, in war against an aggressor nation, in carrying out the verdict of a jury recommending capital punishment." This would be a far better rule—judged by its consequences—than any simple one-line rule on the subject. Each of the classes of exceptions could be argued pro and con, of course. But such arguments would be empirical ones, hinging on whether or not the adoption of such classes of exceptions into the rule would have the maximum results in intrinsic good. (Many would argue, for example, that capital punishment achieves no good effects; on the other hand, few would contend that the man who pulls the switch at Sing Sing is committing a crime in carrying out the orders of the legal representatives of the state.) And there may always be other kinds of situations that we have not previously thought of, situations which, if incorporated into the rule, would improve the rule—that is, make it have better consequences; and thus the rule remains always open, always subject to further qualification if the addition of such qualification would improve the rule.

These qualifications of the rule are not, strictly speaking, *exceptions to* the rule. According to rule-utilitarianism, the rule, once fully stated, admits of no exceptions; but there may be, and indeed there usually are, numerous classes of exceptions *built into the* rule; a simple rule becomes through qualification a more complex rule. Thus, if a man kills someone in self-defense and we do not consider his act wrong, we are not making him an exception to the rule. Rather, his act *falls under* the rule—the rule that includes killing in self-defense as one of the classes of acts which is permissible (or, if you prefer, the rule that includes self-defense as one of the circumstances in which the rule against killing does not apply). Similarly, if a man parks in a prohibited area and the judge does not fine him because he is a physician making a professional call, the judge is not extending any favoritism to the physician; he is not making the physician an exception to the rule; rather, the rule (though it may not always be written out in black and white) includes within itself this recognized class of exceptions—or, more accurately still, the rule includes within itself a reference to just this kind of situation, so that the action of the judge in exonerating the physician is just as much an application of the rule (not an exception to it) as another act of the same judge in imposing a fine on someone else for the same offense.

We can now see how our previous remarks about acts committed in secret fit into the rule-utilitarian scheme. On the one hand, the rule "Don't break a promise except (1) under extreme duress and (2) to promote some very great good" is admittedly somewhat vague, and perhaps it could be improved by still further qualification; but at least it is much better than the simple rule "Never break promises." On the other hand, the rule "Don't break a promise except when nobody will know about it" is a bad rule: there are many situations in which keeping promises is important . . . situations in which promises could not be relied on if this rule were adopted. That is why, among the circumstances which excuse you from keeping your word, the fact that it was broken in secret is not one of them—and for a very good reason: if this class of exceptions were incorporated into the rule, the rule's adoption would have far worse effects than if it did not contain such a clause. . . .

Rule-utilitarianism and act-utilitarianism are alike with regard to relativism. They are *not* relativistic in that they have one standard, one "rule of rules," one supreme norm, applicable to all times and situations: "Perform that act which will produce the most intrinsic good" (act-utilitarianism), "Act according to the rule whose adoption will produce the most intrinsic good" (rule-utilitarianism). But within the scope of that one standard, the recommended rules of conduct may well vary greatly from place to place. . . . In a desert area the act of wasting water will cause much harm and is therefore wrong, but it is not wrong in a region where water is plentiful. In a society where men and women are approximately equal in number, it will be best for a husband to have only one wife; but in a society in which there is great numerical disparity between the two, this arrangement may no longer be wise. So much for act-utilitarianism; the same goes for rule-utilitarianism. The rule "Never waste water" is a good rule, indeed an indispensable rule, in a desert region but not in a well-watered region. Monogamy seems to be the best possible marital system in our society but not necessarily in all societies—it depends on the conditions. What are the best acts and the best rules at a given time and place, then, depends on the special circumstances of that time and place. Some conditions, of course, are so general that the rules will be much the same everywhere: a rule against killing (at least within the society) is an indispensable condition of security and survival and therefore must be preserved in all societies.

The situation, then, is this: Rule or Act A is right in circumstances C_1, and Rule or Act B is right in circumstances C_2. In X-land circumstances C_1 prevail, so A is right; and in Y-land circumstances C_2 prevail, so B is right. Perhaps this is all the relativism that ethical relativists will demand.

4. Can't there be, in rule-utilitarianism, a conflict of rules? Suppose you have to choose between breaking a promise and allowing a human life to be lost. . . . What would the rule-utilitarian say? Which rule are we to go by?

No rule-utilitarian would hold such a rule as "Never break a promise" or "Never take a human life." Following such rigid, unqualified rules would certainly not lead to the best consequences—for example, taking Hitler's life would have had better consequences than sparing him. Since such simple rules would never be incorporated into rule-utilitarian ethics to begin with, there would be no conflict between these rules. The rule-utilitarian's rule on taking human life would be of the form, "Do not take human life except in circumstances of types A, B, C . . ." and these circumstances would be those in which taking human life *would* have the best consequences. And the same with breaking promises. Thus, when the rules in question are fully spelled out, there would be no conflict.

In any event, if there were a conflict between rules, there would have to be a second-order rule to tell us which first-order rule to adopt in cases of conflict. Only with such a rule would our rule-utilitarian ethics be *complete*, i.e., made to cover every situation that might arise. But again such a second-order rule would seldom be simple. It would not say, "In cases of conflict between preserving a life and keeping a promise, always preserve the life." For there might always be kinds of cases in which this policy would not produce the best consequences: a president who has promised something to a whole nation or who has signed a treaty with other nations which depend on that treaty being kept and base their own national policies upon it, would not be well advised to say simply, "In cases of conflict, always break your word rather than lose one human life." In cases of this kind, keeping the promise would probably produce the best results, though the particular instance would have to be decided empirically. We would have to go through a detailed empirical examination to discover which rule, among all the rules we might adopt on the matter, would have the best consequences if adopted.

5. Well, then, why not just make the whole thing simple and say, "Always keep your promises except when breaking them will produce the most good," "Always conserve human life except when taking it will produce the most good"? In other words, "In every case do what will have the best consequences"—why not make this the Rule of Rules? To do so is to have act-utilitarianism with us once again; but why not? Is there anything more obvious in ethics than that we should always try to produce the most good possible?

"No," says the rule-utilitarian, "not if this rule means that we should always do the individual *act* that produces the most good possible. We must clearly distinguish rules from acts. 'Adopt the rule which will have the best consequences' is different from 'Do the act which will have the best consequences.' (When you say, 'Always do the most good,' this is ambiguous—it could mean either one.)" The rule-utilitarian, of course, recommends the former in preference to the latter;

for if everyone were to do acts which (taken individually) had the best consequences, the result would *not* in every case be a policy having the best consequences. For example, my not voting but doing something else instead may produce better consequences than my voting (my voting may have no effect at all); your not voting will do the same; and so on for every individual, as long as most *other* people vote. But the results would be very bad, for if each individual adopted the policy of not voting, nobody would vote. In other words, the rule "Vote, except in situations where not voting will do more good" is a rule which, if followed, would *not* produce the best consequences.

Another example: The rule "Don't kill except where killing will do the most good"—which the act-utilitarian would accept—is not, the rule-utilitarian would say, as good a rule to follow as "Don't kill except in self-defense . . ." (and other classes of acts which we discussed earlier). That is, the rule to prohibit killing except under special kinds of conditions specified in advance would do more good, if followed, than the rule simply to refrain except when not refraining will do more

good. The former is better, not just because people will rationalize themselves into believing that what they want to do will produce the most good in a particular situation (though this is very important), but also because when there are certain standard classes of exceptions built into the rule, there will be a greater *predictability* of the results of such actions; the criminal will know what will happen if he is caught. If the law said, "Killing is prohibited except when it will do the most good," what could you expect? Every would-be killer would think it would do the most good in his specific situation. And would you, a potential victim, feel more secure or less secure, if such a law were enacted? Every criminal would think that he would be exonerated even if he were caught, and every victim (or would-be victim) would fear that this would be so. The effects of having such a rule, then, would be far worse than the effects of having a general rule prohibiting killing, with certain classes of qualifications built into the rule.

There is, then, it would seem, a considerable difference between act-utilitarianism and rule-utilitarianism.

20

A Critique of Utilitarianism

Bernard Williams

Bernard Williams (b. 1929) is Professor of Philosophy at Oxford University and the University of California at Berkeley. He has made important contributions to philosophy of mind, as well as to moral philosophy. In this essay he argues that utilitarianism violates personal integrity by commanding that we violate those principles that are central and deepest in our lives. That is, utilitarianism often calls on us to reject conscience and compunctions and do the "lesser of evils"—even when it is loathsome to do so. He illustrates this by two examples. In one, an unemployed scientist, George, is offered a job doing research in biological warfare, to which he is opposed. Yet it turns out that on utilitarian grounds he would be obligated to take this job, for it would be even worse if an unscrupulous scientist were involved in the research. In the second example, a soldier will shoot twenty innocent Indians unless Jim, an unlucky tourist, shoots them. If Jim kills one, the rest of the Indians will be freed. Jim finds killing abhorrent. Williams examines these cases carefully and argues that because the precepts of utilitarianism cause deep alienation, utilitarianism should be rejected as a moral theory.

Negative Responsibility: And Two Examples

Consequentialism is basically indifferent to whether a state of affairs consists in what I do, or is produced by what I do, where that notion is itself wide enough to include, for instance, situations in which other people do things which I

Reprinted with permission from *Utilitarianism: For and Against*, by Bernard Williams and J.J.C. Smart (Cambridge University Press, 1973), pp. 97–99; 101–3; 108–9; 112–16.

have made them do, or allowed them to do, or encouraged them to do, or given them a chance to do. All that consequentialism is interested in is the idea of these doings being *consequences* of what I do, and that is a relation broad enough to include the relations just mentioned, and many others.

Just what the relation is, is a different question, and at least as obscure as the nature of its relative, cause and effect. It is not a question I shall try to pursue; I will rely on cases where I suppose that any consequentialist would be bound to regard the situations in question as consequences of what the agent does. There are cases where the supposed consequences stand in a rather remote relation to the action, cases which are sometimes difficult to assess from a practical point of view, but which raise no very interesting question for the present enquiry. The more interesting points about consequentialism lie rather elsewhere. There are certain situations in which the causation of the situation, the relation it has to what I do, is in no way remote or problematic in itself, and entirely justifies the claim that the situation is a consequence of what I do: for instance, it is quite clear, or reasonably clear, that if I do a certain thing, this situation will come about, and if I do not, it will not. So from a consequentialist point of view it goes into the calculation of consequences along with any other state of affairs accessible to me. Yet from some, at least, non-consequentialist points of view, there is a vital difference between some such situations and others: namely, that in some a vital link in the production of the eventual outcome is provided by *someone else's* doing something. But for consequentialism, all causal connexions are on the same level, and it makes no difference, so far as that goes, whether the causation of a given state of affairs lies through another agent, or not.

Correspondingly, there is no relevant difference which consists *just* in one state of affairs being brought about by me, without intervention of other agents, and another being brought about through the intervention of other agents; although some genuinely causal differences involving a difference of value may correspond to that (as when, for instance, the other agents derive pleasure or pain from the transaction), that kind of difference will already be included in the specification of the state of affairs to be produced. Granted that the states of affairs have been adequately described in causally and evaluatively relevant terms, it makes no further comprehensible difference who produces them. It is because consequentialism attaches value ultimately to states of affairs, and its concern is with what states of affairs the world contains, that it essentially involves the notion of *negative responsibility:* that if I am ever responsible for anything, then I must be just as much responsible for things that I allow or fail to prevent, as I am for things that I myself, in the more everyday restricted sense, bring about. Those things also must enter my deliberations, as a responsible moral agent, on the same footing. What matters is what states of affairs the world contains, and so what matters with respect to a given action is what comes about if it is done, and what comes about if it is not done, and those are questions not intrinsically affected by the nature of the causal linkage, in particular by whether the outcome is partly produced by other agents.

The strong doctrine of negative responsibility flows directly from consequentialism's assignment of ultimate value to states of affairs. Looked at from another point of view, it can be seen also as a special application of something that is favoured in many moral outlooks not themselves consequentialist—something which, indeed, some thinkers have been disposed to regard as the essense of morality itself: a principle of impartiality. Such a principle will claim that there can be no relevant difference from a moral point of view which consists just in the fact, not further explicable in general terms, that benefits or harms accrue to one person rather than to another—'it's me' can never in itself be a morally comprehensible reason. [By] this principle, familiar with regard to the reception of harms and benefits, we can see consequentialism as extending to their production: from the moral point of view, there is no comprehensible difference which consists just in my bringing about a certain outcome rather than someone else's producing it. That the doctrine of negative responsibility represents in this way the extreme of impartiality, and abstracts from the identity of the agent, leaving just a locus of causal intervention in the world—that fact is not merely a surface paradox. It helps to explain why consequentialism can seem to some to express a more serious attitude than nonconsequentialist views, why part of its appeal is to a certain kind of high-mindedness. Indeed, that is part of what is wrong with it.

For a lot of the time so far we have been operating at an exceedingly abstract level. This has been necessary in order to get clearer in general terms about the differences between consequentialist and other outlooks, an aim which is important if we want to know what features of them lead to what results for our thought. Now, however, let us look more concretely at two examples, to see what utilitarianism might say about them, what we might say about utilitarianism and, most importantly of all, what would be implied by certain ways of thinking about the situations. The examples are inevitably schematized, and they are open to the objection that they beg as many questions as they illuminate. There are two ways in particular in which examples in moral philosophy tend to beg important questions. One is that, as presented, they arbitrarily cut off and restrict the range of alternative courses of action—this objection might particularly be made against the first of my two examples. The second is that they inevitably present one with the situation as a going concern, and cut off questions about how the agent got into it, and correspondingly about moral considerations which might flow from that: this objection might perhaps specially arise with regard to the second of my two situations. These difficulties, however, just have to be accepted, and if anyone finds these examples cripplingly defective in this sort of respect, then he must in his own thought rework them in richer and less question-begging form. If he feels that no presentation of any imagined situation can ever be other than misleading in morality, and that there can never be any substitute for the concrete experienced complexity of actual moral situations, then this discussion, with him, must certainly grind to a halt: but then one may legitimately wonder whether every discussion with him about conduct will not grind to a halt, including any discussion about the actual situations, since discussion about how one would think and feel about situations somewhat different from the actual (that is to say, situations to that extent imaginary) plays an important role in discussion of the actual.

(1) George, who has just taken his Ph.D. in chemistry, finds it extremely difficult to get a job. He is not very robust in health, which cuts down the number of jobs he might be able to do satisfactorily. His wife has to go out to work to keep them, which itself causes a great deal of strain, since they have small children and there are severe problems about looking after them. The results of all this, especially on the children, are damaging. An older chemist who knows about this situation says that he can get George a decently paid job in a certain laboratory which pursues research into chemical and biological warfare. George says that he cannot accept this, since he is opposed to chemical and biological warfare. The older man replies that he is not too keen on it himself, come to that, but after all George's refusal is not going to make the job or the laboratory go away; what is more, he happens to know that if George refuses the job, it will certainly go to a contemporary of George's who is not inhibited by any such scruples and is likely if appointed to push along the research with greater zeal than George would. Indeed, it is not merely concern

for George and his family, but (to speak frankly and in confidence) some alarm about this other man's excess of zeal which has led the older man to offer to use his influence to get George the job. . . . George's wife, to whom he is deeply attached, has views (the details of which need not concern us) from which it follows that at least there is nothing particularly wrong with research into CBW. What should he do?

(2) Jim finds himself in the central square of a small South American town. Tied up against the wall are a row of twenty Indians, most terrified, a few defiant, in front of them several armed men in uniform. A heavy man in a sweat-stained khaki shirt turns out to be the captain in charge and, after a good deal of questioning of Jim which establishes that he got there by accident while on a botanical expedition, explains that the Indians are a random group of the inhabitants who, after recent acts of protest against the government, are just about to be killed to remind other possible protestors of the advantages of not protesting. However, since Jim is an honoured visitor from another land, the captain is happy to offer him a guest's privilege of killing one of the Indians himself. If Jim accepts, then as a special mark of the occasion, the other Indians will be let off. Of course, if Jim refuses, then there is no special occasion, and Pedro here will do what he was about to do when Jim arrived, and kill them all. Jim, with some desperate recollection of schoolboy fiction, wonders whether if he got hold of a gun, he could hold the captain, Pedro and the rest of the soldiers to threat, but it is quite clear from the set-up that nothing of that kind is going to work: any attempt at that sort of thing will mean that all the Indians will be killed, and himself. The men against the wall, and the other villagers, understand the situation, and are obviously begging him to accept. What should he do?

To these dilemmas, it seems to me that utilitarianism replies, in the first case, that George should accept the job, and in the second, that Jim should kill the Indian. Not only does utilitarianism give these answers but, if the situations are essentially as described and there are no further special factors, it regards them, it seems to me, as *obviously* the right answers. But many of us would certainly wonder whether, in (1), that could possibly be the right answer at all; and in the case of (2), even one who came to think that perhaps that was the answer, might well wonder whether it was obviously the answer. Nor is it just a question of the rightness or obviousness of these answers. It is also a question of what sort of considerations come into finding the answer. A feature of utilitarianism is that it cuts out a kind of consideration which for some others makes a difference to what they feel about such cases: a consideration involving the idea, as we might first and very simply put it, that each of us is specially responsible for what *he* does, rather than for what other people do. This is an idea closely connected with the value of integrity. It is often suspected that utilitarianism, at least in its direct forms, makes integrity as a value more or less unintelligible. I shall try to show that this suspicion is correct. Of course, even if that is correct, it would not necessarily follow that we should reject utilitarianism; perhaps, as utilitarians sometimes suggest, we should just forget about integrity, in favour of such things as a concern for the general good. However, if I am right, we cannot merely do that, since the reason why utilitarianism cannot understand integrity is that it cannot coherently describe the relations between a man's projects and his actions.

Two Kinds of Remoter Effect

A lot of what we have to say about this question will be about the relations between my projects and other people's projects. But before we get on to that, we should first ask whether we are assuming too hastily what the utilitarian answers to the dilemmas will be. In terms of more direct effects of the possible decisions, there does not indeed seem much doubt about the answer in either case; but it might be said that in terms of more remote or less evident effects counterweights might be found to enter the utilitarian scales. Thus the ef-

fect on George of a decision to take the job might be invoked, or its effect on others who might know of his decision. The possibility of there being more beneficent labours in the future from which he might be barred or disqualified might be mentioned; and so forth. Such effects—in particular, possible effects on the agent's character, and effects on the public at large—are often invoked by utilitarian writers dealing with problems about lying or promise-breaking, and some similar considerations might be invoked here.

There is one very general remark that is worth making about arguments of this sort. The certainty that attaches to these hypotheses about possible effects is usually pretty low; in some cases, indeed, the hypothesis invoked is so implausible that it would scarcely pass if it were not being used to deliver the respectable moral answer, as in the standard fantasy that one of the effects of one's telling a particular lie is to weaken the disposition of the world at large to tell the truth. The demands on the certainty or probability of these beliefs as beliefs about particular actions are much milder than they would be on beliefs favouring the unconventional course. It may be said that this is as it should be, since the presumption must be in favour of the conventional course: but that scarcely seems a *utilitarian* answer, unless utilitarianism has already taken off in the direction of not applying the consequences to the particular act at all.

Leaving aside that very general point, I want to consider now two types of effect that are often invoked by utilitarians, and which might be invoked in connexion with these imaginary cases. The attitude or tone involved in invoking these effects may sometimes seem peculiar; but that sort of peculiarity soon becomes familiar in utilitarian discussions, and indeed it can be something of an achievement to retain a sense of it.

First, there is the psychological effect on the agent. Our descriptions of these situations have not so far taken account of how George or Jim will be after they have taken the one course or the other; and it might be said that if they take the course which seemed at first the utilitarian one, the effects on them will be in fact bad enough and extensive enough to cancel out the initial utilitarian advantages of that course. Now there is one version of this effect in which, for a utilitarian, some confusion must be involved, namely that in which the agent feels bad, his subsequent conduct and relations are crippled and so on, *because he thinks that he has done the wrong thing*—for if the balance of outcomes was as it appeared to be *before* invoking this effect, then he has not (from the utilitarian point of view) done the wrong thing. So that version of the effect, for a rational and utilitarian agent, could not possibly make any difference to the assessment of right and wrong. However, perhaps he is not a thoroughly rational agent, and is disposed to have bad feelings whichever he decided to do. Now such feelings, which are from a strictly utilitarian point of view irrational—nothing, a utilitarian can point out, is advanced by having them—cannot, consistently, have any great weight in a utilitarian calculation. I shall consider in a moment an argument to suggest that they should have no weight at all in it. But short of that, the utilitarian could reasonably say that such feelings should not be encouraged, even if we accept their existence, and that to give them a lot of weight is to encourage them. Or, at the very best, even if they are straightforwardly and without any discount to be put into the calculation, their weight must be small: they are after all (and at best) one man's feelings.

That consideration might seem to have particular force in Jim's case. In George's case, his feelings represent a larger proportion of what is to be weighed, and are more commensurate in character with other items in the calculation. In Jim's case, however, his feelings might seem to be of very little weight compared with other things that are at stake. There is a powerful and recognizable appeal that can be made on this point: as that a refusal by Jim to do what he has been invited to do would be a kind of self-indulgent squeamishness. That is an appeal which can be made by other than utilitarians—indeed, there are some uses of

it which cannot be consistently made by utilitarians, as when it essentially involves the idea that there is something dishonourable about such self-indulgence. But in some versions it is a familiar, and it must be said a powerful, weapon of utilitarianism. One must be clear, though, about what it can and cannot accomplish. The most it can do, so far as I can see, is to invite one to consider how seriously, and for what reasons, one feels that what one is invited to do is (in these circumstances) wrong, and in particular, to consider that question from the utilitarian point of view. When the agent is not seeing the situation from a utilitarian point of view, the appeal cannot force him to do so; and if he does come round to seeing it from a utilitarian point of view, there is virtually nothing left for the appeal to do. If he does not see it from a utilitarian point of view, he will not see his resistance to the invitation, and the unpleasant feelings he associates with accepting it, *just* as disagreeable experiences of his; they figure rather as emotional expressions of a thought that to accept would be wrong. He may be asked, as by the appeal, to consider whether he is right, and indeed whether he is fully serious, in thinking that. But the assertion of the appeal, that he is being self-indulgently squeamish, will not itself answer that question, or even help to answer it, since it essentially tells him to regard his feelings just as unpleasant experiences of his, and he cannot, by doing that, answer the question they pose when they are precisely not so regarded, but are regarded as indications of what he thinks is right and wrong. If he does come round fully to the utilitarian point of view, then of course he will regard these feelings just as unpleasant experiences of his. And once Jim—at least—has come to see them in that light, there is nothing left for the appeal to do, since *of course* his feelings, so regarded, are of virtually no weight at all in relation to the other things at stake. The 'squeamishness' appeal is not an argument which adds in a hitherto neglected consideration. Rather, it is an invitation to consider the situation, and one's own feelings, from a utilitarian point of view.

The reason why the squeamishness appeal can be very unsettling, and one can be unnerved by the suggestion of self-indulgence in going against utilitarian considerations, is not that we are utilitarians who are uncertain what utilitarian value to attach to our moral feelings, but that we are partially at least not utilitarians, and cannot regard our moral feelings merely as objects of utilitarian value. Because our moral relation to the world is partly given by such feelings, and by a sense of what we can or cannot 'live with,' to come to regard those feelings from a purely utilitarian point of view, that is to say, as happenings outside one's moral self, is to lose a sense of one's moral identity; to lose, in the most literal way, one's integrity. At this point utilitarianism alienates one from one's moral feelings; we shall see a little later how, more basically, it alienates one from one's actions as well.

If, then, one is really going to regard one's feelings from a strictly utilitarian point of view, Jim should give very little weight at all to his; it seems almost indecent, in fact, once one has taken that point of view, to suppose that he should give any at all. In George's case one might feel that things were slightly different. It is interesting, though, that one reason why one might think that—namely that one person principally affected is his wife—is very dubiously available to a utilitarian. George's wife has some reason to be interested in George's integrity and his sense of it; the Indians, quite properly, have no interest in Jim's. But it is not at all clear how utilitarianism would describe that difference.

There is an argument, and a strong one, that a strict utilitarian should give not merely small extra weight, in calculations of right and wrong, to feelings of this kind, but that he should give absolutely no weight to them at all. This is based on the point, which we have already seen, that if a course of action is, before taking these sorts of feelings into account, utilitarianly preferable, then bad feelings about that kind of action will be from a utilitarian point of view irrational. Now it might be thought that even if that is so, it would

not mean that in a utilitarian calculation such feelings should not be taken into account; it is after all a well-known boast of utilitarianism that it is a realistic outlook which seeks the best in the world as it is, and takes any form of happiness or unhappiness into account. While a utilitarian will no doubt seek to diminish the incidence of feelings which are utilitarianly irrational—or at least of disagreeable feelings which are so—he might be expected to take them into account while they exist. This is without doubt classical utilitarian doctrine, but there is good reason to think that utilitarianism cannot stick to it without embracing results which are startlingly unacceptable and perhaps self-defeating.

Suppose that there is in a certain society a racial minority. Considering merely the ordinary interests of the other citizens, as opposed to their sentiments, this minority does no particular harm; we may suppose that it does not confer any very great benefits either. Its presence is in those terms neutral or mildly beneficial. However, the other citizens have such prejudices that they find the sight of this group, even the knowledge of its presence, very disagreeable. Proposals are made for removing in some way this minority. If we assume various quite plausible things (as that programmes to change the majority sentiment are likely to be protracted and ineffective) then even if the removal would be unpleasant for the minority, a utilitarian calculation might well end up favouring this step, especially if the minority were a rather small minority and the majority were very severely prejudiced, that is to say, were made very severely uncomfortable by the presence of the minority.

A utilitarian might find that conclusion embarrassing; and not merely because of its nature, but because of the grounds on which it is reached. While a utilitarian might be expected to take into account certain other sorts of consequences of the prejudice, as that a majority prejudice is likely to be displayed in conduct disagreeable to the minority, and so forth, he might be made to wonder whether the unpleasant experiences of the prejudiced people should be allowed, *merely as such,* to count. If he does count them, merely as such, then he has once more separated himself from a body of ordinary moral thought which he might have hoped to accommodate; he may also have started on the path of defeating his own view of things. For one feature of these sentiments is that they are from the utilitarian point of view itself irrational, and a thoroughly utilitarian person would either not have them, or if he found that he did tend to have them, would himself seek to discount them. Since the sentiments in question are such that a rational utilitarian would discount them in himself, it is reasonable to suppose that he should discount them in his calculations about society; it does seem quite unreasonable for him to give just as much weight to feelings—considered just in themselves, one must recall, as experiences of those that have them—which are essentially based on views which are from a utilitarian point of view irrational, as to those which accord with utilitarian principles. Granted this idea, it seems reasonable for him to rejoin a body of moral thought in other respects congenial to him, and discount those sentiments, just considered in themselves, totally, on the principle that no pains or discomforts are to count in the utilitarian sum which their subjects have just because they hold views which are by utilitarian standards irrational. But if he accepts that, then in the cases we are at present considering no extra weight at all can be put in for bad feelings of George or Jim about their choices, if those choices are, leaving out those feelings, on the first round utilitarianly rational.

Integrity

The [two] situations have in common that if the agent does not do a certain disagreeable thing someone else will, and in Jim's situation at least the result, the state of affairs after the other man has acted, if he does, will be worse than after Jim has acted, if Jim does. The same, on a smaller scale, is true of George's case. I have already sug-

gested that it is inherent in consequentialism that it offers a strong doctrine of negative responsibility: if I know that if I do X, O_1 will eventuate, and if I refrain from doing X, O_2 will, and that O_2 is worse than O_1, then I am responsible for O_2 if I refrain voluntarily from doing X. 'You could have prevented it,' as will be said, and truly, to Jim, if he refuses, by the relatives of the other Indians.

In the present cases, the situation of O_2 includes another agent bringing about results worse than O_1. So far as O_2 has been identified up to this point—merely as the worse outcome which will eventuate if I refrain from doing X—we might equally have said that what that other brings about is O_2; but that would be to underdescribe the situation. For what occurs if Jim refrains from action is not solely twenty Indians dead, but *Pedro's killing twenty Indians,* and that is not a result which Pedro brings about, though the death of the Indians is. We can say: what one does is not included in the outcome of what one does, while what another does can be included in the outcome of what one does. For that to be so, as the terms are now being used, only a very weak condition has to be satisfied: for Pedro's killing the Indians to be the outcome of Jim's refusal, it only has to be causally true that if Jim had not refused, Pedro would not have done it.

That may be enough for us to speak, in some sense, of Jim's responsibility for that outcome, if it occurs; but it is certainly not enough, it is worth noticing, for us to speak of Jim's *making* those things happen. For granted this way of their coming about, he could have made them happen only by making Pedro shoot, and there is no acceptable sense in which his refusal makes Pedro shoot. If the captain had said on Jim's refusal, 'you leave me with no alternative' he would have been lying, like most who use that phrase. While the deaths, and the killing, may be the outcome of Jim's refusal, it is misleading to think, in such a case, of Jim having an *effect* on the world through the medium (as it happens) of Pedro's acts; for this is to leave Pedro out of the picture in his essential role of one who has intentions and projects, projects for realizing which Jim's refusal would leave an opportunity. Instead of thinking in terms of supposed effects of Jim's projects on Pedro, it is more revealing to think in terms of the effects of Pedro's projects on Jim's decision.

Utilitarianism would do well then to acknowledge the evident fact that among the things that make people happy is not only making other people happy, but being taken up or involved in any of a vast range of projects, or—if we waive the evangelical and moralizing associations of the word—commitments. One can be committed to such things as a person, a cause, an institution, a career, one's own genius, or the pursuit of danger.

Now none of these is itself the *pursuit of happiness:* by an exceedingly ancient platitude, it is not at all clear that there could be anything which was just that, or at least anything that had the slightest chance of being successful. Happiness, rather, requires being involved in, or at least content with, something else. It is not impossible for utilitarianism to accept that point: it does not have to be saddled with a naïve and absurd philosophy of mind about the relation between desire and happiness. What it does have to say is that if such commitments are worthwhile, then pursuing the projects that flow from them, and realizing some of those projects, will make the person for whom they are worthwhile, happy. It may be that to claim that is still wrong: it may well be that a commitment can make sense to a man (can make sense of his life) without his supposing that it will make him *happy*. But that is not the present point, let us grant to utilitarianism that all worthwhile human projects must conduce, one way or another, to happiness. The point is that even if that is true, it does not follow, nor could it possibly be true, that those projects are themselves projects of pursuing happiness. One has to believe in, or at least want, or quite minimally be content with, other things for there to be anywhere that happiness can come from.

Utilitarianism, then, should be willing to agree that its general aim of maximizing happiness does not imply that what everyone is doing is just pursuing happiness. On the contrary, people have to be pursuing other things. What those other things may be, utilitarianism, sticking to its professed empirical stance, should be prepared just to find out. No doubt some possible projects it will want to discourage, on the grounds that their being pursued involves a negative balance of happiness to others: though even there, the unblinking accountant's eye of the strict utilitarian will have something to put in the positive column, the satisfactions of the destructive agent. Beyond that, there will be a vast variety of generally beneficent or at least harmless projects; and some no doubt will take the form not just of tastes or fancies, but of what I have called 'commitments.' It may even be that the utilitarian researcher will find that many of those with commitments, who have really identified themselves with objects outside themselves, who are thoroughly involved with other persons or institutions or activities or causes, are actually happier than those whose projects and wants are not like that. If so, that is an important piece of utilitarian empirical love.

When I say 'happier' here, I have in mind the sort of consideration which any utilitarian would be committed to accepting: as for instance that such people are less likely to have a breakdown or commit suicide. Of course that is not all that is actually involved, but the point in this argument is to use to the maximum degree utilitarian notions in order to locate a breaking point in utilitarian thought. In appealing to this strictly utilitarian notion, I am being more consistent with utilitarianism than Smart is. In his struggles with the problem of the brain-electrode man, Smart commends the idea that 'happy' is a partly evaluative term, in the sense that we call 'happiness' those kinds of satisfaction which, as things are, we approve of. But *by what standard* is this surplus element of approval supposed, from a utilitarian point of view, to be allocated? There is no source for it, on a strictly utilitarian view, except further degrees of satisfaction, but there are none of those available, or the problem would not arise. Nor does it help to appeal to the fact that we dislike in prospect things which we like when we get there, for from a utilitarian point of view it would seem that the original dislike was merely irrational or based on an error. Smart's argument at this point seems to be embarrassed by a well-known utilitarian uneasiness which comes from a feeling that it is not respectable to ignore the 'deep,' while not having anywhere left in human life to locate it.

Let us now go back to the agent as utilitarian, and his higher-order project of maximizing desirable outcomes. At this level, he is committed only to that: what the outcome will actually consist of will depend entirely on the facts, on what persons with what projects and what potential satisfactions there are within calculable reach of the causal levers near which he finds himself. His own substantial projects and commitments come into it, but only as one lot among others—they potentially provide one set of satisfactions among those which he may be able to assist from where he happens to be. He is the agent of the satisfaction system who happens to be at a particular point at a particular time: in Jim's case, our man in South America. His own decisions as a utilitarian agent are a function of all the satisfactions which he can effect from where he is: and this means that the projects of others, to an indeterminately great extent, determine his decision.

This may be so either positively or negatively. It will be so positively if agents within the causal field of his decision have projects which are at any rate harmless, and so should be assisted. It will equally be so, but negatively, if there is an agent within the causal field whose projects are harmful, and have to be frustrated to maximize desirable outcomes. So it is with Jim and the soldier Pedro. On the utilitarian view, the undesirable projects of other people as much determine, in this negative way, one's decisions as the desirable ones do positively: if those people were not there, or had different projects, the causal nexus would be different, and it is the actual state of the causal nexus which determines the decision. The determination to an indefinite degree of my decisions

by other people's projects is just another aspect of my unlimited responsibility to act for the best in a causal framework formed to a considerable extent by their projects.

The decision so determined is, for utilitarianism, the right decision. But what if it conflicts with some project of mine? This, the utilitarian will say, has already been dealt with: the satisfaction to you of fulfilling your project, and any satisfactions to others of your so doing, have already been through the calculating device and have been found inadequate. Now in the case of many sorts of projects, that is a perfectly reasonable sort of answer. But in the case of projects of the sort I have called 'commitments,' those with which one is more deeply and extensively involved and identified, this cannot just by itself be an adequate answer, and there may be no adequate answer at all. For, to take the extreme sort of case, how can a man, as a utilitarian agent, come to regard as one satisfaction among others, and a dispensable one, a project or attitude round which he has built his life, just because someone else's projects have so structured the causal scene that that is how the utilitarian sum comes out?

The point here is not, as utilitarians may hasten to say, that if the project or attitude is that central to his life, then to abandon it will be very disagreeable to him and great loss of utility will be involved. I have already argued in section 4* that it is not like that; on the contrary, once he is prepared to look at it like that, the argument in any serious case is over anyway. The point is that he is identified with his actions as flowing from projects and attitudes which in some cases he takes seriously at the deepest level, as what his life is about (or, in some cases, this section of his life—seriousness is not necessarily the same as persistence). It is absurd to demand of such a man, when the sums come in from the utility network which the projects of others have in part determined, that he should just step aside from his own project and decision and acknowledge the decision which utilitarian calculation requires. It is to alienate him in a real sense from his actions and

*Not included in this selection—Editor.

the source of his action in his own convictions. It is to make him into a channel between the input of everyone's projects, including his own, and an output of optimistic decision; but this is to neglect the extent to which *his* actions and his decisions have to be seen as the actions and decisions which flow from the projects and attitudes with which he is most closely identified. It is thus, in the most literal sense, an attack on his integrity.

These sorts of considerations do not in themselves give solutions to practical dilemmas such as those provided by our examples; but I hope they help to provide other ways of thinking about them. In fact, it is not hard to see that in George's case, viewed from this perspective, the utilitarian solution would be wrong. Jim's case is different, and harder. But if (as I suppose) the utilitarian is probably right in this case, that is not to be found out just by asking the utilitarian's questions. Discussions of it—and I am not going to try to carry it further here—will have to take seriously the distinction between my killing someone, and its coming about because of what I do that someone else kills them: a distinction based, not so much on the distinction between action and inaction, as on the distinction between my projects and someone else's projects. At least it will have to start by taking that seriously, as utilitarianism does not; but then it will have to build out from there by asking why that distinction seems to have less, or a different, force in this case than it has in George's. One question here would be how far one's powerful objection to killing people just is, in fact, an application of a powerful objection to their being killed. Another dimension of that is the issue of how much it matters that the people at risk are actual, and there, as opposed to hypothetical, or future, or merely elsewhere.

There are many other considerations that could come into such a question, but the immediate point of all this is to draw one particular contrast with utilitarianism: that to reach a grounded decision in such a case should not be regarded as a matter of just discounting one's reactions, impulses and deeply held projects in the face of the

pattern of utilities, nor yet merely adding them in—but in the first instance of trying to understand them.

Of course, time and circumstances are unlikely to make a grounded decision, in Jim's case at least, possible. It might not even be decent. Instead of thinking in a rational and systematic way either about utilities or about the value of human life, the relevance of the people at risk being present, and so forth, the presence of the people at risk may just have its effect. The significance of the immediate should not be underestimated. Philosophers, not only utilitarian ones, repeatedly urge one to view the world *sub specie aeternitatis*, but for most human purposes that is not a good *species* to view it under. If we are not agents of the universal satisfaction system, we are not primarily janitors of any system of values, even our own: very often, we just act, as a possibly confused result of the situation in which we are engaged. That, I suspect, is very often an exceedingly good thing.

Utilitarianism is in more than one way an important subject; at least I hope it is, or these words, and this book, will have been wasted. One important feature of it, which I have tried to bring out, is the number of dimensions in which it runs against the complexities of moral thought: in some part because of its consequentialism, in some part because of its view of happiness, and so forth. A common element in utilitarianism's showing in all these respects, I think, is its great simple-mindedness. This is not at all the same thing as lack of intellectual sophistication: utilitarianism, both in theory and in practice, is alarmingly good at combining technical complexity with simple-mindedness. Nor is it the same as simple-heartedness, which it is at least possible (with something of an effort and in private connexions) to regard as a virtue. Simple-mindedness consists in having too few thoughts and feelings to match the world as it really is. In private life and the field of personal morality it is often possible to survive in that state—indeed, the very statement of the problem for that case is over-simple, since the question of what moral demands life makes is not independent of what one's morality demands of it. But the demands of political reality and the complexities of political thought are obstinately what they are, and in face of them the simple-mindedness of utilitarianism disqualifies it totally.

The important issues that utilitarianism raises should be discussed in contexts more rewarding than that of utilitarianism itself. The day cannot be too far off in which we hear no more of it.

21

Eleven Objections to Utilitarianism

STERLING HARWOOD

Sterling Harwood received his Ph.D. from Cornell University and is Assistant Professor of Philosophy at San Jose State University.

In this essay Harwood examines eleven criticisms of various forms of utilitarianism (he mentions twelve forms), arguing that the most plausible form of utilitarianism is act-utilitarianism (see reading V.17), as opposed to rule-utilitarianism (see reading V.1). However, act-utilitarianism is still subject to severe criticisms, including the criticisms that utilitarianism is unjust, fails to grant sufficient weight to promise keeping, enjoins going into an experience machine (see reading IV.14), and gives undue weight to animals.

A. Introduction

I will discuss eleven significant objections to utilitarianism, though I will not accept all eleven. My purpose is not to bury utilitarianism once and for all but to survey a large number of objections and provoke further discussion, although I may perhaps put a few more nails in utilitarianism's coffin. I start by trying to clarify the nature of utilitarianism since it has so many versions both drawing criticism and developing as responses to criticism. Here is a list of twelve versions I will at least mention below (though some of these can be combined to form still more versions): motive-utilitarianism, act-utilitarianism, rule-utilitarianism, average utilitarianism, total utilitarianism, hedonistic utilitarianism, eudaimonistic utilitarianism, negative utilitarianism, welfare-utilitarianism, preference-satisfaction utilitarianism, felt-satisfaction utilitarianism, and ideal utilitarianism. Of course these twelve versions of utilitarianism do not correspond to the eleven

objections to utilitarianism I consider, but many of these versions were developed to deal with objections to other versions of utilitarianism. Indeed, many critics who thought they had finally driven a stake through the heart of utilitarianism have only seen utilitarianism live on by being transformed into another version.

Utilitarianism is a consequentialist (that is, teleological) moral principle. As a moral principle, utilitarianism tells us how we should act. Consequentialism is not itself a moral principle but a category into which some moral principles fit. Consequentialism insists that an act is determined to be morally right (or morally wrong) exclusively by particular consequences of doing that act. (Consequentialism and utilitarianism can go beyond acts to include evaluations of institutions, policies, motives, and persons, but for simplicity I shall focus on acts and deemphasize versions of utilitarianism such as motive-utilitarianism.) Some include the maximizing theory of the right as a definition of consequentialism, but this would make the definition of consequentialism underinclusive because we can imagine moral principles that value consequences alone but do not require maximizing good consequences (because, for example, there could be two different kinds of consequences to maximize and no rule for trading off between them). The particular consequences determining the rightness (or wrongness) of the act in question are specified not by consequentialism itself but by a particular consequentialist principle. Utilitarianism is the particular consequentialist principle that specifically concerns utility. Utility is psychological satisfaction (for example, pleasure, happiness, and well-being). Since utility is utilitarianism's only value, utilitarianism is a monistic rather than a pluralistic moral principle. And it is utilitarianism's monism rather than its consequentialism that explains why utilitarianism requires maximizing utility. Because utility is the only value, there is no other value to check or limit the logical approach of requiring the gain of more and more of the only value.

Many versions of utilitarianism differ primarily according to which psychological satisfaction they emphasize. For example, hedonistic utilitarianism stresses pleasure; preference-satisfaction utilitarianism stresses satisfaction of preferences; ideal utilitarianism stresses what would be desired under ideal conditions; negative utilitarianism stresses that avoiding dissatisfaction is more important than gaining satisfaction; and welfare-utilitarianism stresses what is in the best interests of those whose well-being is in question. And of course, many of these psychological satisfactions interrelate and overlap with one another. Disutility—psychological dissatisfaction (for example, pain and unhappiness)—is the opposite of utility.

Utilitarianism essentially specifies that the consequences that determine an act's rightness (or wrongness) are the psychological satisfactions that the act causes. Utilitarianism is a monistic moral principle, since it implies that there is only one thing that has moral value, namely, psychological satisfaction. Since there is no other moral value to check or limit the value of psychological satisfaction, utilitarianism says an act is right only to the extent that it maximizes these satisfactions, that is, produces the greatest balance of satisfaction over dissatisfaction for all in the long run. If only dissatisfaction is available, then utilitarianism says an act is right to the extent that it minimizes dissatisfaction. This is not a second or separate value in utilitarianism; for we can represent utilitarianism as claiming that an act is right to the extent that its expected consequences fall as far to the right as possible on the following scale. The far left ranges to an infinite amount of dissatisfaction, the 0 represents where the amount

of satisfaction equals the amount of dissatisfaction, and the far right ranges to an infinite amount of satisfaction.

$$\longleftarrow\!\!\!\!\!\!\!\!\!\!\!\longleftarrow\!\!\!\!\!\!\!-\!\!0\!\!-\!\!\!\!\!\!\!\longrightarrow\!\!\!\!\!\!\!\!\!\!\!\longrightarrow$$

The left and right directions on the scale should not be confused with the political left or political right. Indeed, utilitarians have historically promoted governmental reforms, (for example, abolishing slavery, improving prisons, and feeding, clothing, and housing the poor) that the political left has also endorsed.

B. The Eleven Objections

1. *Utilitarianism Is Overly Demanding*

Perhaps the first objection that occurs to students is that utilitarianism appears to demand an extreme amount of self-sacrifice from us. This stems from utilitarianism's monism, its insistence that only one thing has moral value, and its insistence that we obtain more and more of that thing without limit; for there is no other value to counterbalance or limit it. Must we really sell all of our nonessential material goods (for example, musical recordings and baseball cards) and give the money to worthy charitable causes (for example, relief of famine)? Further, must we be ready to sacrifice friends and loved ones by acting impartially to maximize satisfaction? Bentham stated the utilitarian formula "Everybody to count for one, and nobody for more than one."[1] Utilitarianism's impartiality stems from its counting everyone's satisfaction as equally valuable (so long as the amount of the satisfaction is the same). Later, we will see that eudaimonistic utilitarianism seems to depart from Bentham's statement, and we will see an objection to the statement from those who believe that interpersonal comparisons of utility are impossible. Alleged counterexamples often hurled at utilitarianism include: 1) the instance where utilitarianism requires that the least useful person in a lifeboat lost at sea be killed and eaten whenever necessary to keep the other persons in the lifeboat alive long enough to be rescued; and 2) the instance where a healthy and innocent person comes in for a checkup, but his doctor can maximize satisfaction by killing him and using his organs to save the lives of five or more other people. Indeed, if the person in charge of the lifeboat or the doctor, respectively, can make these facts clear enough to us, then utilitarianism requires us to submit to being killed rather than to resist.

So we can see why a version of Objection 1, called the "objection from integrity," says that utilitarianism requires us to have a psychologically impossible (or nearly impossible) impartiality and detachment from our own lives, projects, friends, and loved ones. Of course, utilitarianism scarcely requires us to attempt the impossible, since that would be futile and would fail to maximize *expected* satisfaction; for the satisfaction expected from an act known to be impossible must be nil. The objection thus seems to be merely a complaint that morality is sometimes or oftentimes difficult to live up to. But this is hardly a conclusive objection. Nobody ever said it was going to be easy to be moral. Indeed, all or almost all moral principles require us to give up our lives under some scenarios. Even the most self-centered of moral principles, ethical egoism, which commands each person to maximize his or her own satisfaction, requires us to commit suicide the moment when the satisfaction we can expect in the rest of our lives is outweighed—even slightly—by the dissatisfaction we can expect in the rest of our lives. Every moral principle seems to require extreme actions under some scenario or other. And it would also be extreme to require this alternative: "*Never* do any extreme acts." So the objection that utilitarianism sometimes leads to extreme self-sacrifice or extreme acts is inconclusive.

Moreover, I suspect that utilitarianism is not as extremely demanding in everyday life as many think. Here is how a utilitarian could argue that utilitarianism is easy enough to pursue in every-

day life. All indications are that overpopulation and depletion of needed natural resources will get worse. Therefore, rather than give almost all of one's wealth away now, one ought to invest one's wealth wisely, probably making more wealth, and hold one's wealth in reserve for these more troubled times ahead, when charity will be needed more than ever and when the stakes will be even greater. In the meantime, one can gain satisfaction from the security of having wise investments and from the knowledge that one is self-sufficient and not a charity case oneself. Indeed, some investment activities (for example, following the business news) and investments (for example, collectibles such as baseball cards, rare musical recordings, and other art) are intrinsically satisfying for many investors. As long as the population explosion continues and needed natural resources continue to be depleted faster than they are replaced, one can maximize satisfaction by wisely investing his or her wealth to make more wealth and by holding it in reserve to help with the greater calamity likely to occur in the foreseeable future. If these trends continue through the rest of one's life, with a greater calamity always likely to occur in the foreseeable future, then one can then leave all of his or her amassed wealth to the charity one believes will maximize satisfaction. One's leaving wealth to others at one's death is no personal sacrifice at all, since "you can't take it with you when you die." But one's legal will must sacrifice some satisfaction of one's relatives if they are not needy enough. Some critics of utilitarianism will doubtless say, "How convenient!" But that misses the point here, which is that at least utilitarianism would dodge Objection 1, which claims utilitarianism is not convenient for individuals but overly demanding.

Finally, in case one thinks that utilitarianism will still be overly demanding in too many cases, consider these two arguments by Kurt Baier:

Surely, in the absence of any *special* reasons for preferring someone else's interests, *everyone's* interests are best served if *everyone* puts his own interests first. For, by and large, everyone is himself the best judge of what is in his own best interests, since everyone usually knows best what his plans, aims, ambitions, or aspirations are. Moreover, everyone is more diligent in the promotion of his own interests than that of others.[2]

2. Utilitarianism Eliminates Supererogation

Some have argued that since utilitarianism leaves no room for supererogation (that is, self-sacrifice above and beyond the call of duty), utilitarianism objectionably flies in the face of commonsense morality, which recognizes supererogation. For example, during a hasty retreat a soldier might stop to pick up and carry a fellow soldier many hazardous yards to safety, and endure being wounded. There seems to be nothing *above* or *beyond* the call of utilitarian duty, since utilitarianism says our duty is to *maximize* satisfaction. Of course, one cannot cause an amount of satisfaction above or beyond the maximum amount. So we seem to face a dilemma. Either we reject utilitarianism, or else we reject supererogation.

But this is a false dilemma, since ties are overlooked. Utilitarianism allows that the expected satisfaction of two (or even more) alternatives can be tied for the maximal amount. One of these alternatives can involve more sacrifice (dissatisfaction) for us than that expected from the other alternatives tied for the maximal amount of satisfaction. Utilitarianism cannot *require* us to make this sacrifice by choosing this alternative among those that are tied, since all of those alternatives are equally acceptable, but utilitarianism *permits* us to choose the alternative that sacrifices more of our satisfaction than the other alternatives do. So utilitarianism does allow for moral self-sacrifice that is not morally required (that is, moral self-sacrifice beyond the call of duty).

One may object that ties are so uncommon that utilitarianism still leaves too little room for supererogation, which is the main point of Objection 2. But ties are probably more common than

many of us think. For example, Raymond D. Gastil interprets James Q. Wilson's research as pointing out:

that almost all recent major American studies testing hypotheses that major long-term behavior changes result from particular social policy or educational inputs have provided inconclusive or negative findings. Thus, studies have shown that the type of school or educational method makes no difference (Coleman report). . . . [Wilson] suggests, and it is probably true, that in real-life situations there is too much going on, too many cycles of reinforcement stretched over too many years, for particular interventions to get up out of the noise.[3]

This feature of ties is notorious in the so-called dismal science, economics, the social science utilitarianism has perhaps influenced most. Some joke that one can lay all the economists from end to end and never reach a definite conclusion. And some joke that the search continues for the one-armed economist, the one who cannot say "On the other hand. . . ." The serious undertone to these jokes is that utilitarianism all too often has us consider two or more alternatives which, as far as we can tell, are tied in the amount of satisfaction they will produce. Perhaps this is why some joke that economists know the price of everything but the value of nothing.

3. Utilitarianism Is Unjust

Utilitarianism is often criticized for failing to treat retributive justice (giving the guilty and only the guilty the punishment they deserve in fair proportion to the severity of their respective crimes) as having intrinsic moral importance. Familiar counterexamples to utilitarianism here include: 1) a case where a scientific genius murders his wife just as he is about to develop a cure for cancer, and giving him the punishment he justly deserves will delay the development of the cure for years or decades; 2) a case (such as that discussed by Kai Nielsen in reading V.18) involving racial violence, where a local woman has been raped and murdered, and angry mobs are about to take the law into their own hands by executing people of the opposite race whom they suspect of being involved in the crime. The sheriff can easily prevent all this violence, which is likely to kill innocent people, by framing the useless town drunk who remembers nothing about the night in question and who has no alibi. The sheriff alone knows that he is innocent because he locked the drunk up for public drunkenness at the same time the crime was committed in the middle of the night; and 3) a case where parking offenders (or other minor offenders) are punished way out of proportion to the severity of their offenses whenever the deterrent effect of the unjustly severe punishment produces so much satisfaction from a nearly perfectly obeyed law that it maximizes satisfaction even while leading to the torture and execution of that one driver in a million or more who is foolish enough to break the law. Critics object that utilitarianism would unjustly: 1) fail to give the scientist the severe punishment he deserves; 2) frame the innocent town drunk; and 3) sometimes torture and execute people for merely parking illegally.

Critics also charge that utilitarianism violates distributive justice (giving each person his or her fair share of benefits and burdens in society). Familiar counterexamples to utilitarianism here include: 1) the case where, instead of fairly and randomly determining who should bear the burden of dying by casting lots, the occupants of a lifeboat lost at sea kill and eat the least useful occupant as a last resort to keep all others alive long enough to be rescued; 2) a case of secretly killing a healthy man just in for a routine checkup in order to maximize satisfaction by using his various organs in a number of life-saving operations; and 3) a case of neglecting to give ordinary people their fair share of benefits and instead indulging so-called utility monsters, people with nearly insatiable appetites for wealth and for whom the general economic law of diminishing margi-

nal utility of wealth does not apply because they are so miserly and greedy that each new unit of wealth obtained causes far more satisfaction for the utility monster than it would for those with normal human psychologies.

Utilitarians often dismiss such examples as unrealistic and thus irrelevant to our real world of troubles. Utilitarians say they have done enough to develop a moral principle that deals with the problems of real life, and need not develop a moral principle that covers every imaginable problem in every fantasy land. But the utilitarian defense that these cases are unrealistic misses the point. How realistic or unrealistic a case is surely is a matter of degree. These cases are realistic enough that some of them can and will eventually occur in real life, and when they do utilitarianism will be refuted, a refutation we can know in advance by thinking ahead.

Indeed, there have been, after all, some lifeboat cases where cannibalism has been a last resort to survive. And there have been some awfully greedy people in the history of the world. Perhaps they were utility monsters. And some would say that at least one of these situations recently occurred in California, and even one of these counterexamples is enough to refute utilitarianism. The nearly all-white jury that acquitted the police officers of nearly all criminal charges in the famous videotaped beating of motorist Rodney King has been called the jury from another planet! But of course it was a real jury. Suppose you were one of these jurors who believed there was a reasonable doubt on almost all the charges against the policemen but who also predicted, as many others did, that rioting would occur if almost all the policemen were acquitted of these charges. So, you could realistically change your vote from "not guilty beyond a reasonable doubt" to "guilty beyond a reasonable doubt" on every charge and create a mistrial, preventing the policemen from being acquitted on any charge, allowing a new trial, and probably preventing enough violence to maximize satisfaction with your vote of "guilty beyond a reasonable doubt."

I conclude that at least some of these counter-examples concerning retributive and distributive justice seem realistic enough to refute utilitarianism, especially since truth is often stranger than fiction.

4. Utilitarianism Fails to Take Promises Seriously Enough

Utilitarianism implies that keeping one's promises has no intrinsic moral value apart from any satisfaction it causes but has only instrumental and contingent moral value. Objection 4 pits utilitarianism squarely against commonsense morality, which recognizes the intrinsic moral importance of keeping promises. For example, one promises his or her dying mother to beautify her grave by always putting fresh and gorgeous flowers on her grave when her birthday arrives each year. But since an afterlife with a dissatisfied mother is unexpected, utilitarianism requires one to completely discount one's solemn pledge. After all, she will never know the difference. So utilitarianism emphasizes that life is for the living, and that one should spend his or her time, energy, and money, not putting flowers on a grave, but doing what will maximize satisfaction.

Utilitarians reply that we should not uncritically accept whatever commonsense morality dictates. Sometimes commonsense morality is wrong (for example, racist and sexist views that used to be considered commonsensical). But this reply will go only so far; for the commonsense belief in the intrinsic importance of keeping promises survives critical scrutiny that racist and sexist views cannot.

The example also seems to commit the appeal to pity. It is surely pitiful that the dying mother has such a son. But the mere fact that something is pitiful is not a conclusive reason against it. For example, it is pitiful to amputate a child's leg, but this is all too often medically necessary and for the best.

Further, some forms of utilitarianism would count the mother's preference as something to satisfy. Felt-satisfaction utilitarianism would not count her preference, since she will never feel the satisfaction. But preference-satisfaction utilitarianism can count it. Yet as Robert E. Goodin has said in objecting to a somewhat different form of utilitarianism, the closer a version of utilitarianism comes to embracing an "aesthetic ideal regardless of whether or not that is good for any living being, the less credible this analysis is as an ethical theory."[4] Keeping the promise to beautify one's mother's grave each year does seem to be a matter of aesthetics, which is presumably distinct from ethics.

There is a further problem with this type of utilitarian defense. Where do we draw the line in respecting the preferences of the dead? It seems arbitrary to limit it to those covered by promises. The other preferences were just as real and important to those now dead. Sometimes it is a fluke that one preference was covered by a promise and another was not. For example, suppose our mother is struck by lightning before we can make another promise to her. But surely we cannot cater to all the preferences the dead had. We cannot cater to all the preferences that those now dead had to live longer. Otherwise, we might have to exhaust our resources trying to put them in cryogenic freeze so that they can be thawed later when science might be able to revive them. But this seems absurd. Drawing the line at death, when preferences and satisfactions and all other psychological states presumably cease, seems less arbitrary than trying to distinguish between which preferences of the dead we will try to satisfy.

Utilitarianism cannot completely dismiss Objection 4 as requiring the impossible, namely, the satisfaction of a dead person's preference. One might think that death prevents the preference from being satisfied. But this is to assume that felt-satisfactions are the only satisfactions, which seems false. For example, a man prefers that his wife not commit adultery. But his wife is clever and decides while he is on submarine duty for months to have a secret affair with a sexually inexperienced bookworm who is a leading specialist in prevention of sexually transmitted diseases and who shyly wants only a few months more of secret sexual experience. The wife rightly expects, let us suppose, that her husband will never know the difference. He will have no felt-dissatisfaction of his preference that she not commit adultery.

Felt-satisfaction utilitarianism requires the wife to have the affair she and the bookworm want, but preference-satisfaction utilitarianism would at least count her husband's preference that she not do so (though whether there is an affair or not will make no difference to how he feels). Some critics charge that this is enough to refute felt-satisfaction utilitarianism. But again we should be concerned about whether the alleged counterexample commits the fallacy of appealing to pity. It may seem a pity that this dutiful submariner is deceived by his wife, who has broken her marriage vows (that is, promises). But mere pity is not decisive.

The error utilitarianism makes about promises is exposed by another example, though. You promise to meet me for an ordinary lunch. On your way to meet me you spot victims just emerging from a car accident in a remote area. They need your medical help immediately. So you stop to help them at the cost of making me dissatisfied with your lateness to lunch. Utilitarianism clearly requires this, and so does commonsense morality. Where they differ is in the reply you give when you come to lunch late. Commonsense morality implies, rightly I think, that you *owe* me an explanation and an expression of regret that you were sidetracked. A utilitarian cannot *simply* express sincere regret here. Once your dissatisfaction was outweighed by the prevention of more serious dissatisfaction for the accident victims, there was either nothing to be regretted or at least the expression of regret is viewed as a completely separate act, whose rightness or wrongness is determined exclusively by a separate calculation of its consequences rather than on a backward-looking expression of a genuinely felt emotion. Utilitarianism's unnecessarily complex conceptual separation of these conceptually, emotionally, and simply linked acts seems mistaken.

5. Average and Total Utilitarianism Produce Absurdities

Average utilitarianism states that an act is morally right only to the extent that it maximizes the amount of satisfaction per person in existence (that is, maximizes the mean of utility). Total utilitarianism states that an act is morally right only to the extent that it maximizes the aggregate amount of satisfaction (that is, maximizes the sum of satisfaction). These two forms of utilitarianism lead to different results only when population policy is involved; for, if the population is held constant, then average satisfaction and total satisfaction must rise or fall together.

Critics charge that average utilitarianism degenerates into number worship that squanders satisfaction, whereas total utilitarianism will lead us to reduce the standard of living too much and make the world barely livable. Either way, utilitarianism seems objectionable.

First, here is a counterexample to average utilitarianism. Suppose we have a person who is quite satisfied in his life but whose level of satisfaction is always consistently and predictably below the average amount of satisfaction people have. And suppose that from our experience trying to help him we know that there is no way to raise his level of satisfaction without lowering the overall average amount of satisfaction. Now, if we can raise the average of satisfaction for all by painlessly killing and disposing of this fellow who is below average, then average utilitarianism requires us to do so. But this seems absurd and contrary to a key point of utilitarianism, which is that satisfaction is the only value. Here, average utilitarianism requires us to squander an amount of net satisfaction just to raise a mere number, an average level of satisfaction. We can suppose that not one more unit of satisfaction is gained, but that the average is raised only by subtracting the below-average fellow from the population. (This would be a rather extreme case of what baseball genius Branch Rickey called "addition by subtraction"!). So average utilitarianism seems unacceptable, even to many utilitarians.

But total utilitarianism seems to err on an even more massive scale; for it requires us to bring more and more people into the world—even if this lowers the average level of satisfaction—so long as adding another person to the world adds more net satisfaction to the world than any other alternative. The worry here is that total utilitarianism will be too tolerant of the population explosion and will lead to a world where standards of living are drastically lowered and almost all of us eke out a life just barely worth living because our planet is filled to capacity. Because there will be so many of us, this will make up for the extremely low average satisfaction we will have and will maximize total satisfaction. Total satisfaction is figured by adding the amount of satisfaction each person has. Making the world barely satisfactory for everyone seems to miss a key point of utilitarianism, which is that we should try to improve the lives of everyone as much as possible. So total utilitarianism seems unacceptable, even to many utilitarians.

Since utilitarianism must take a stand on population policy, and since both its alternatives—average and total utilitarianism—seem absurd, is utilitarianism *obviously* unacceptable here? No, because total utilitarianism *might* survive. In real life, we cannot jam the planet full of people and expect to retain enough control of the situation to maximize total satisfaction. First, the more people there are to satisfy, the harder it is likely to be to satisfy them. Second, a world where everyone ekes out a life barely worth living is likely to be unstable, presenting a great danger of disease and a chain reaction of catastrophes going through the population. Given these empirically contingent facts, it is unlikely that pushing population to such extreme limits will maximize expected total satisfaction, since the catastrophes would involve so much dissatisfaction and since the chances of them occurring would be so high.

In conclusion, utilitarianism's best prospect for surviving Objection 5 is the endorsement of total utilitarianism and the rejection of average utilitarianism. But even this strategy will probably fail,

since we saw in the previous section (section 4) that utilitarianism should avoid overreliance on contingent empirical facts and avoid dismissal of hypothetical counterexamples. A world where we can maximize total satisfaction by increasing the population explosion and lowering average satisfaction is possible. It might be, for example, that our technology will improve to allow us to control the weather and the entire planet and that the more people we have the more labor power we have to enable us to keep the low average satisfaction stable and to avoid catastrophes. So utilitarianism seems unacceptable because it is woefully unprepared for this eventuality. It will yield unacceptable requirements whenever that day arrives. But we are entitled to think ahead and find utilitarianism unacceptable now.

6. *Rule-Utilitarianism Is Incoherent or Redundant*

Rule-utilitarianism (sometimes called restricted or indirect utilitarianism) is often distinguished from act-utilitarianism (sometimes called extreme or direct utilitarianism). R. M. Hare says:

Act-utilitarianism is the view that we have to apply the so-called 'principle of utility' [that is, maximize satisfaction] directly to individual acts. . . . Rule-utilitarianism . . . is the view that this test is not to be applied to individual actions, but to *kinds* of action. . . . Actions are to be assessed by asking whether they are forbidden or enjoined by certain moral rules or principles; and it is only when we start to ask which moral rules or principles we are to adopt for assessing actions, that we apply the utilitarian test.[5]

Rule-utilitarianism was developed to try to save utilitarianism from the sort of counterexamples we have seen from commonsense morality (for example, "do not hang the innocent," and "keep promises"). Utilitarianism recognizes that commonsense moral rules such as "Keep promises" and "do not kill" are generally useful in gaining satisfaction.

Jonathan Harrison, however, gives at least three good reasons for rejecting rule-utilitarianism. First, "It is not the case that I ought to obey a rule which has good consequences, however bad the consequences of my obeying it are."[6] For example, "Do not steal" is a rule which, if generally adopted, would seem to maximize satisfaction, but we can easily imagine a scenario where stealing a radio is necessary to warn people to evacuate before a dam bursts and kills thousands of people. If the rule-utilitarian makes an exception to the rules to cover such cases, then rule-utilitarianism would seem redundant; for it would contain rules such as "Do not kill, except to maximize satisfaction"; "Do not steal, except to maximize satisfaction"; and "Keep promises, but only if it maximizes satisfaction." These rules tell us nothing more than utilitarianism's fundamental rule "maximize satisfaction for all in the long run."

Second, following J. J. C. Smart, Harrison argues that "rule-utilitarianism is a manifestation of rule-worship."[7] Act-utilitarianism and rule-utilitarianism lead to different conclusions only if rule-utilitarianism sometimes forbids us from breaking a rule by doing an act that maximizes satisfaction. So rule-utilitarianism seems more a form of rule-worship than a form of utilitarianism, which says satisfaction—not rule following—is the only value.

Third, rule-utilitarians fail to distinguish three types of rule: 1) an actually operating social rule; 2) "a general moral *belief*, which most people in most societies have, *about* this (social) rule, to the effect that it usually or always ought to be acted upon"; and 3) "the *fact* about the social rule that it ought usually to be obeyed, whether most members of the society which has it think that it ought to be obeyed or not."[8] If rule-utilitarianism means (1) then it is still subject to the other objections above, but at least it is coherent. But if rule-utilitarianism means either (2) or (3), then it will end up referring to itself—for it is also a rule—in such a viciously circular way that it will be incoherent.

Finally, there is a fourth objection to rule-utilitarianism that Harrison does not explore. This objection uses the concept of *extensional equivalence.* Two moralities are extensionally equivalent if they always agree about what we should do in any case. Some critics argue that rule-utilitarianism is extensionally equivalent to act-utilitarianism and thus cannot coherently defend utilitarianism from familiar objections using plausible examples from commonsense morality (for example, "Do not hang the innocent") as counterexamples to utilitarianism.[9] As R. M. Hare says, "The merit of rule-utilitarianism has been said to be that it is more in accord with our common moral beliefs than is act-utilitarianism. . . ."[10] But if the two are extensionally equivalent, then rule-utilitarianism has no more merit than act-utilitarianism. Act- and rule-utilitarianism do seem to be extensionally equivalent, because if rule-utilitarianism ever disagreed with act-utilitarianism and required us to follow a rule by doing an act that failed to maximize satisfaction, then rule-utilitarianism would be rejecting the lone value of utilitarianism, satisfaction (not mere obedience to rules). Further, act- and rule-utilitarianism seem to agree and converge because the adoption of a rule is itself an act. So if a rule really were so useful that its adoption would maximize satisfaction, then act-utilitarianism would require us to do the act of adopting that rule and taking that rule to heart.

In conclusion, the best prospect for utilitarianism's surviving Objection 6 is to reject rule-utilitarianism and emphasize the strength and flexibility of act-utilitarianism, which still has its own problems, as we have seen.

7. *Utilitarianism Requires Us to Enter the Experience Machine*

I suspect that all of us are intrigued by the experimental new technology called *virtual reality.* Some models are already used as flight simulators to train pilots. But imagine programming one's own artificial universe! What wonders would it contain?! With utilitarianism, however, it seems we will be forced to have too much of a good thing here. Robert Nozick has theorized about what he calls the *experience machine,* which resembles virtual reality, though he fails to apply his example of the experience machine directly to refuting utilitarianism (see reading IV.12 in the text).[11]

We can use the experience machine to object to utilitarianism because utilitarianism will require us to spend our entire lives in the machine if that will maximize satisfaction, as it might very well do. A life spent inside the experience machine seems like one of mental masturbation, an unreal and degraded life unworthy of us, though it will seem perfectly real and satisfying to us as long as we stay inside the machine. Utilitarianism's monism, its insistence that satisfaction is the only moral value, prevents utilitarians from placing greater moral value on genuine, veridical experiences than on artificial yet credible simulations. Utilitarianism is objectionable because its monism leaves no room to place any intrinsic value on truth, knowledge, or reality, with which we lose touch once we enter the experience machine. Moreover, independent of utilitarianism's monism, utilitarianism is also objectionable because the subjective character of what utilitarianism counts as valuable—namely, the subjects' feelings or satisfactions—allows value to be radically and objectionably disconnected from how things are in the world external to the subjects.

8. Utilitarianism Wildly Overstates Our Duties to Animals

One might conceive of Objection 8 as a version of Objection 1, since animals (I use 'animals' to mean 'nonhuman animals') outnumber humans by so much that humans will be swamped with duties to maximize the satisfactions animals are psychologically capable of having. (Of course, some living things evidently have no psychology.) But Objection 8 can be made by those who refuse to object to utilitarianism as overly demanding; for they can object that what is wrong with utili-

tarianism here is not how much it demands but what utilitarianism is demanding of us, namely, the satisfaction of mere nonhuman animals. Utilitarians from Bentham to Mill to Singer have insisted on considering animals in moral deliberations. But critics charge that utilitarianism will all too often require debased or beastly satisfaction. The critics charge that utilitarianism implies that it is better to be a pig satisfied than to be Socrates dissatisfied.

In response to such criticisms, John Stuart Mill tried to develop eudaimonistic utilitarianism, which would distinguish qualities of happiness, with some types of satisfaction having more moral value than other types present in the same quantity but of lower quality. But eudaimonistic utilitarianism is incompatible with utilitarianism's monism. Since utilitarianism insists that there is only one moral value, satisfaction, there is no other value to which a utilitarian can consistently appeal in claiming that one type of satisfaction is morally better than another type of satisfaction.[12]

9. Utilitarianism Panders to Bigots and Sadists

Critics charge that utilitarianism is fundamentally mistaken in treating racist, sexist, bigoted, and sadistic satisfaction as intrinsically valuable. Since satisfaction is utilitarianism's only value, utilitarianism has no other value enabling the utilitarian to distinguish between better and worse satisfactions. Only the amount of satisfaction (or dissatisfaction) caused makes an act right (or wrong), not whether the satisfaction is noble or unbiased. Critics charge that some motivations ought not to be satisfied because they are intrinsically wrong and their satisfaction is morally bankrupt and completely without value.

But Tom L. Beauchamp and LeRoy Walters suggest that utilitarianism can dodge this objection. They say:

because 'perverse' [for example, extremely sadistic] desires have been determined on the basis of past experience to cut against the objectives of utilitarianism by creating conditions productive of unhappiness, the desires (preferences) could never even be permitted to count. We discount preferences to rape children. . . . Preferences that serve merely to frustrate the preferences of others are thus ruled out by the goal of utilitarianism. As Mill himself argued, the cultivation of certain kinds of desires is built into the 'ideal' of utilitarianism.[13]

But this defense of utilitarianism is unconvincing, since we saw in section 8 that Mill's eudaimonistic utilitarianism was developed to handle similar objections to the kinds of satisfactions utilitarianism would respect, and we saw that eudaimonistic utilitarianism seems inconsistent because it abandons utilitarianism's monism, its insistence that there is only one value, namely, satisfaction. As Hare suggested, "Mill's mistake was perhaps to try to incorporate ideals into a utilitarian theory, which cannot really absorb them."[14] Utilitarianism's single-minded pursuit of the maximization of only one value leaves no room for other ideals. Further, unfortunately some preferences to rape children do not serve merely to frustrate the preferences of others but also serve to satisfy the rapists. The problem for utilitarianism is not the general prohibition of rape; it surely does condemn almost all rapes. Rather, Objection 9 claims utilitarianism is pandering to sadists and bigots by counting their sadistic and bigoted satisfactions as morally valuable *at all*—even if their satisfactions are readily overridden by the dissatisfactions of others.

10. Utilitarianism Makes Interpersonal Comparisons of Utility

I am a child.
I last awhile.
You can't conceive of the pleasure in my smile.
  —The Buffalo Springfield (1967)[15]

Utilitarianism requires interpersonal comparisons of utility (that is, satisfaction) because it re-

quires us to maximize satisfaction for all in the long run. Thus, we must consider trade-offs, promoting the satisfaction of some at the expense of allowing the dissatisfaction of others in order to maximize the net satisfaction for everyone over the long haul. But how can we compare one person's pleasure, for example, with another's pain? Are not pleasure and pain subjective experiences? Are not thresholds and tolerances for pain highly idiosyncratic and unpredictable? Being stuck with a needle, for example, seems to bother some people much more than others. And even though sugar presumably tastes the same to everyone, some seem to have more of a sweet tooth than others and enjoy sweets immeasurably more than others. After all, critics charge, it is a well-recognized maxim that there is no accounting for or disputing matters of taste (that is, *De gustibus non est disputandum*).

Objection 10 is flashy, but there is less here than meets the eye. Objection 10 relies on what it takes to be commonsensical, namely, that people enjoy and value the same psychological experiences differently. This is true even for basic psychological experiences such as pain. Masochists sometimes seem to enjoy significant levels of pain. But there is an equivocation in Objection 10 that is illustrated by the following joke: A masochist goes up to a sadist and says, "Hit me"; the sadist prepares to hit the masochist but then, realizing the masochist will enjoy being hit, says, "No." These mind games take some surprising twists and turns for which human psychology is notorious. But the point is that pain or sweet taste should not be equated with satisfaction. Utilitarianism is fully capable of allowing individual differences in what brings about satisfaction. The bottom line is to maximize the satisfaction, not any particular experience we might misidentify as satisfaction.

Moreover, we commonsensically make interpersonal comparisons every day. For example, we build freeways even though we know that it is just a matter of time before an innocent baby who would not have died nearly so soon had the free-

way never been built gets crushed in an automobile accident on the freeway. But the great
convenience of the freeway and the other lives
saved by allowing ambulances and other emergency vehicles to use the new freeway to speed to
emergencies outweighs the harm caused to the
crushed baby. So, whatever plausibility Objection 10 gains by relying on common sense is
blunted by the commonsensical way we make interpersonal comparisons of satisfaction everyday.

Further, *inter*personal comparisons of satisfaction seem no more problematic than *intra*personal comparisons of satisfaction. All the same arguments for Objection 10 could be made against
intrapersonal comparisons of satisfaction. After
all, Objection 10 must allow that I might become
a masochist or an old man with satisfactions incommensurable with those I can now have. Yet we
still think that it makes good common sense to
trade off some satisfaction at one stage of life (for
example, exercising hard rather than enjoying
more sleep) for more satisfaction later in life (for
example, living longer and with fewer illnesses).

Furthermore, Objection 10 strikes me as being
mathematically suspect. Even if satisfaction was
as wildly unpredictable from person to person as
Objection 10 states, which I doubt, would it not
minimize our margin of error if we assumed that
each person's satisfactions were comparable? It
seems so. For if we started giving preference or
extra weight to persons whose satisfaction was
assumed to be weightier, then the wildly unpredictable nature of satisfaction, which Objection 10 insists upon, would imply that we are as
apt to be preferring and weighting the satisfactions of the right persons (those whose satisfaction is more satisfying than others' satisfactions)
as those of the wrong persons. If we chose the
wrong person and thus gave extra weight, in deciding what to do, to the satisfactions of a person
whose satisfactions are actually *less* satisfying
than the satisfactions of others, then we have
compounded any mistake we would have made
considering all satisfactions comparable, and we
have extended the margin of error further than it
was. For example, suppose we expect to get ten

percent more satisfaction by satisfying Pojman
slightly than by satisfying Harwood slightly, but
Pojman actually gets ten percent less satisfaction
from being slightly satisfied than Harwood does
from being slightly satisfied. Our margin of error
is then twenty percent rather than the ten percent margin of error present in treating the satisfactions of Harwood and Pojman as comparable,
only to learn that we could have obtained ten
percent more satisfaction by satisfying Harwood
slightly rather than satisfying Pojman slightly.

Finally, how can Objection 10 make sense of
its claims such as, "Interpersonal comparisons of
satisfaction are impossible because a slightly satisfied Harwood has immeasurably more satisfaction than a very satisfied Pojman. That's just the
kind of guy Harwood is." How could we ever
know such a thing unless interpersonal comparisons of satisfaction were not only possible but
actually known? This very claim seems to make
an interpersonal comparison of the satisfactions
of Harwood and Pojman. The contradiction in
claiming to know that interpersonal comparisons
of satisfaction are impossible is similar to that of
claiming, "My experience was impossible to describe; it was simply indescribable." Our making
this very claim describes the experience. In calling our satisfactions incommensurable we make a
comparison among them, namely, that they all
have in common the feature for which we lack a
scale by which we can accurately measure them
all in the same units. But—and this is my main
point—this common lack of a scale would also
prevent anyone from knowing if we made a mistake in treating the satisfactions as comparable.

I conclude that rough-and-ready, short-and-
snappy interpersonal comparisons of satisfaction
are justified enough. Some interpersonal comparisons of utility are clearly much more plausible
and defensible than others. For example, do we
really have any doubt that the following claim is
false: "Each time I lose a penny from my pocket
change it causes me more dissatisfaction than all
the dissatisfactions in human history combined"?
The implications of Objection 10 are too extreme and absurd to accept.

11. *Utilitarianism Is Too Secretive, Undemocratic, and Elitist*

Since moral principles conceptually must concern how each person should live, we might think that any acceptable moral principle must be public and available for all to use in our thinking. But utilitarians often think that it would be a mistake to let most or all people directly pursue maximizing satisfaction, since too many will show bias or incompetence in calculating what will maximize satisfaction, thereby leading to too much dissatisfaction. Many critics find utilitarianism's restriction of the direct pursuit of maximizing satisfaction to a trusted utilitarian elite objectionably secretive, undemocratic, and elitist.

Utilitarians might reply that rule-utilitarianism can be more public than act-utilitarianism, since the people can be trusted as competent to follow basic and straightforward rules such as "Do not kill" and "Keep your promises." But we have already seen (in section 6) numerous reasons to doubt that rule-utilitarianism can ultimately remain distinct enough from act-utilitarianism, or to doubt that rule-utilitarianism is acceptable.

But Objection 11 fails because it accepts too uncritically the commonsense morality of public notification and use of moral rules. Indeed, it seems uncertain whether this is a requirement of commonsense morality at all. No less a champion of democracy than Winston Churchill insisted that "democracy is the worst form of Government except all those other forms that have been tried from time to time."[16] And Churchill's wisdom here is commonly quoted and accepted. So perhaps a utilitarian form of government would improve upon democracy and all the other forms of government tried so far.

C. Conclusion

In conclusion, though I reject some of the objections to utilitarianism that I still found to be worth presenting (Objections 1, 2, 10, and 11), the remaining objections collectively have enough force to convince me and many others to reject utilitarianism. But I can hardly rule out the development of a new version of utilitarianism that will dodge or withstand any silver bullets fired at utilitarianism here. I encourage those who wish to try to develop a new and improved utilitarianism.[17]

Notes

1. Quoted in J. S. Mill, *Utilitarianism* (many editions), chapter 5.

2. Kurt Baier, *The Moral Point Of View: A Rational Basis of Ethics*, abr. ed. (New York: Random House, 1965), p. 147; unabridged edition (Ithaca, N.Y.: Cornell University Press, 1958), p. 307.

3. Raymond D. Gastil, "The Moral Right Of The Majority To Restrict Obscenity And Pornography Through Law," 86 *Ethics* (1976): 231–40, pp. 235–36; reprinted in John Arthur and William H. Shaw, eds., *Readings In Philosophy Of Law* (Englewood Cliffs, N.J.: Prentice-Hall, 1984), p. 572.

4. Robert E. Goodin, "Utility And The Good," in Peter Singer, ed., *A Companion To Ethics* (Oxford: Basil Blackwell, 1991), p. 243.

5. Richard Mervyn Hare, *Freedom And Reason* (Oxford: Oxford University Press, 1963), p. 130.

6. Jonathan Harrison, "Rule Utilitarianism and Cumulative-Effect Utilitarianism," in Wesley E. Cooper, Kai Nielsen, and Steven C. Patten, eds., *New Essays on John Stuart Mill and Utilitarianism* (Guelph, Ont.: Canadian Association For Publishing In Philosophy, 1979), p. 22.

7. Harrison, "Rule-Utilitarianism and Cumulative-Effect Utilitarianism," p. 24.

8. Ibid., p. 25.

9. Hare was apparently the first in print to argue that act- and rule-utilitarianism are extensionally equivalent, though David Lyons shortly thereafter published a similar argument with much more detail and logical rigor. See, Hare, *Freedom and Reason*, p. 131 and David Lyons, *The Forms And Limits Of Utilitarianism* (Oxford: Oxford University Press, 1965).

10. Hare, *Freedom and Reason*, p. 130.

11. Robert Nozick, *Anarchy, State & Utopia* (Cambridge: Harvard University Press, 1974), pp. 42–45. Compare the idea of the experience machine with Woody Allen's 'orgasmitron' in his film "Sleeper" from

1973 and with the 'Holodeck' on the current television program "Star Trek: The Next Generation."

12. For a recent attempt to rescue Mill's utilitarianism from this type of objection, see David O. Brink, "Mill's Deliberative Utilitarianism," *Philosophy & Public Affairs* 21 (1992): 67–103.

13. Tom L. Beauchamp and LeRoy Walters, eds., *Contemporary Issues In Bioethics*, 2d ed. (Belmont, Calif.: Wadsworth Publishing Co., 1982), p. 15.

14. Hare, *Freedom and Reason*, p. 121.

15. From "I Am A Child," written by Neil Young for The Buffalo Springfield. Springalo Toones/Cotillion Music, Inc.—BMI (Atco Records, 1967).

16. Winston Churchill, quoted in *The Oxford Dictionary Of Quotations*, 3d ed., s. v. "Winston Churchill."

17. I thank Louis Pojman and an anonymous reviewer for comments on this paper.

PART VI

Deontological Ethics

Introduction

Whereas teleological systems place the ultimate of criterion of morality in some nonmoral value such as pleasure or happiness, that results from acts, deontological systems assert that certain features in the act itself have intrinsic value. For example, there is something inherently right about truth telling and acting justly, even when so acting may bring about harmful consequences. Likewise, there is something inherently wrong about lying and injustice, even if they may produce good consequences. One ought to aim at doing what is morally right without concerning oneself with the possible consequences of doing so.

Two main types of deontological theories exist: *intuitionism* and *rationalism*. Intuitionists claim that moral principles are self-evident on reflection, so that we can discover our duty by consulting these rules. The Oxford University philosopher W. D. Ross (1877–1971), in our third reading, held that our moral principles or duties had objective, though not absolute validity. Ross lists six types of *prima facie* duties: (1) duties of fidelity (such as promise keeping); (2) duties of gratitude; (3) duties of justice; (4) duties of beneficence; (5) duties of self-improvement; and (6) duties of nonmaleficence. These duties have prima facie validity. They have presumptive force, so that if no other duty conflicts with a prima facie rule, the prima facie duty becomes our *actual* or absolute duty. But one prima facie duty can override another. For example, although we have a duty to keep our promises, our higher duty to save a life would normally override such a duty when we can only satisfy one of these duties. We discover which prima facie duties override which other ones by again consulting our intuitions.

Intuitionism has been sharply criticized. For one thing, it seems to preclude rational discussion of principles. If all we have to go on is our introspective deliberations, we cannot reason with one another about our duties. Since different people seem to have different intuitions, and since the kinds of intuitions we hold seem to be accounted for by our cultural upbringing, intuitionism tends towards a crude ethical relativism.

But whatever its merits, the major type of deontological theory has been rationalism, in which some second-order principle is used to generate a set of first-order principles. The classic example of such a rationalist theory is Kant's theory of the moral law in which he sets forth three versions of the *categorical imperative*. Our first reading is from his classic work, *Grounding for the Metaphysics of Morals* (1785), in which he outlines such a rational system.

Kant is concerned to reject those ethical theories, such as the theory of moral sentiments set forth by Scottish moralists Francis Hutcheson (1694–1746) and David Hume (1711-76), in which morality is contingent and hypothetical. The moral-sentiment view is contingent in that it is based on human nature and, in particular, on our feelings or sentiments. Had we been created differently, we would have a different nature and, hence, different moral duties. Duties in the moral-sentiment view are hypothetical in that they depend on our desires for their realization. For example, we should obey "Be honest" because it is good for business.

Kant rejects this naturalistic account of ethics. Ethics is not contingent but absolute, and its duties or imperatives are not hypothetical but categorical (nonconditional). Ethics is based not on feeling but on reason. It is because we are rational beings that we are valuable and are capable of discovering moral laws binding on all persons at all times. Thus, our moral duties are dependent not on feelings but on reason. Those duties are unconditional, universally valid, and necessary, regardless of the possible consequences or opposition to our inclinations.

Kant's first formulation of his categorical imperative is: "Act only on that maxim whereby thou canst at the same time will that it would become a universal law." This imperative is given as the criterion (or second-order principle) by which to judge all other principles. If we could consistently will that everyone would do some type of action, then there is an application of the categorical imperative enjoining that type of action. If we cannot consistently will that everyone would do some type of action, then that type of action is morally wrong. Kant argues, for example, that we cannot consistently will that everyone make lying-promises, for the very institution of promising entails or depends on general adher-

ence to keeping the promise or an intention to do so.

Kant offers a second formulation of the categorical imperative: "So act as to treat humanity, whether in your own person or in that of any other, in every case as an end and never as merely a means only." Each person, by virtue of his or her reason, has dignity and profound worth, which entails that he or she must never be exploited or manipulated or merely used as a means to our idea of what is for the general good. A third form of the categorical imperative has to do with our being universal legislators.

In our third reading Fred Feldman submits Kant's theory to a close critical scrutiny. Our final reading is an attempt by William Frankena to offset some criticisms of deontological systems by incorporating a strong consequentialist element into his system, so that the principle of beneficence supplements the principle of justice.

22

The Foundations of Ethics

IMMANUEL KANT

Immanuel Kant (1724–1804), who was born in a deeply pietistic Lutheran family in Konigsberg, Germany, lived in that town his entire life and taught at the University of Konigsberg. He lived a duty-bound, methodical life, so regular that citizens were said to have set their clocks by his walks. Kant is one of the premier philosophers in the Western tradition. In his monumental work The Critique of Pure Reason *(1781) he inaugurated the equivalent of a Copernican revolution in the theory of knowledge.*

Excerpt from Kant, *Grounding for the Metaphysics of Morals*, translated by James Ellington. Copyright © 1981 by Hackett Publishing Company, Inc. Reprinted by permission of the publisher.

This selection is from his classic work Grounding for the Metaphysics of Morals *(1785), in which he outlines a rationalist ethical system centered in the notion of the* categorical imperative *as the fundamental principle of action.*

After a brief preface in which he eschews any appeal to empirical considerations, he begins his treatise by arguing that only the good will, a will to act out of a sense of duty, has unqualified moral worth.

Preface

Since I am here primarily concerned with moral philosophy, the foregoing question will be limited to a consideration of whether or not there is the utmost necessity for working out for once a pure moral philosophy that is wholly cleared of everything which can only be empirical and can only belong to anthropology. That there must be such a philosophy is evident from the common idea of duty and of moral laws. Everyone must admit that if a law is to be morally valid, i.e., is to be valid as a ground of obligation, then it must carry with it absolute necessity. He must admit that the command, "Thou shalt not lie," does not hold only for men, as if other rational beings had no need to abide by it, and so with all the other moral laws properly so called. And he must concede that the ground of obligation here must therefore be sought not in the nature of man nor in the circumstances of the world in which man is placed, but must be sought a priori solely in the concepts of pure reason; he must grant that every other precept which is founded on principles of mere experience—even a precept that may in certain respects be universal—insofar as it rests in the least on empirical grounds—perhaps only in its motive—can indeed be called a practical rule, but never a moral law.

Thus not only are moral laws together with their principles essentially different from every kind of practical cognition in which there is anything empirical, but all moral philosophy rests entirely on its pure part. When applied to man, it does not in the least borrow from acquaintance with him (anthropology) but gives a priori laws to him as a rational being. To be sure, these laws require, furthermore, a power of judgment sharpened by experience, partly in order to distinguish in what cases they are applicable, and partly to gain for them access to the human will as well as influence for putting them into practice. For man is affected by so many inclinations that, even though he is indeed capable of the idea of a pure practical reason, he is not so easily able to make that idea effective *in concreto* in the conduct of his life.

A metaphysics of morals is thus indispensably necessary, not merely because of motives of spec-

ulation regarding the source of practical principles which are present a priori in our reason, but because morals themselves are liable to all kinds of corruption as long as the guide and supreme norm for correctly estimating them are missing. For in the case of what is to be morally good, that it conforms to the moral law is not enough; it must also be done for the sake of the moral law. Otherwise that conformity is only very contingent and uncertain, since the nonmoral ground may now and then produce actions that conform with the law but quite often produces actions that are contrary to the law. Now the moral law in its purity and genuineness (which is of the utmost concern in the practical realm) can be sought nowhere but in a pure philosophy. Therefore, pure philosophy (metaphysics) must precede; without it there can be no moral philosophy at all. That philosophy which mixes pure principles with empirical ones does not deserve the name of philosophy (for philosophy is distinguished from ordinary rational knowledge by its treatment in a separate science of what the latter comprehends only confusedly). Still less does it deserve the name of moral philosophy, since by this very confusion it spoils even the purity of morals and counteracts its own end.

First Section

Transition From the Ordinary Rational Knowledge of Morality to the Philosophical

The Good Will

There is no possibility of thinking of anything at all in the world, or even out of it, which can be regarded as good without qualification, except a *good will*. Intelligence, wit, judgment, and whatever talents of the mind one might want to name are doubtless in many respects good and desirable, as are such qualities of temperament as courage, resolution, perseverance. But they can also become extremely bad and harmful if the will, which is to make use of these gifts of nature and which in its special constitution is called character, is not good. The same holds with gifts of fortune; power, riches, honor, even health, and that complete well-being and contentment with one's condition which is called happiness make for pride and often hereby even arrogance, unless there is a good will to correct their influence on the mind and herewith also to rectify the whole principle of action and make it universally conformable to its end. The sight of a being who is not graced by any touch of a pure and good will but who yet enjoys an uninterrupted prosperity can never delight a rational and impartial spectator. Thus a good will seems to constitute the indispensable condition of being even worthy of happiness.

Some qualities are even conducive to this good will itself and can facilitate its work. Nevertheless, they have no intrinsic unconditional worth; but they always presuppose, rather, a good will, which restricts the high esteem in which they are otherwise rightly held, and does not permit them to be regarded as absolutely good. Moderation in emotions and passions, self-control, and calm deliberation are not only good in many respects but even seem to constitute part of the intrinsic worth of a person. But they are far from being rightly called good without qualification (however unconditionally they were commended by the ancients). For without the principles of a good will, they can become extremely bad; the coolness of a villain makes him not only much more dangerous but also immediately more abominable in our eyes than he would have been regarded by us without it.

A good will is good not because of what it effects or accomplishes, nor because of its fitness to attain some proposed end; it is good only through its willing, i.e., it is good in itself. When it is considered in itself, then it is to be esteemed very much higher than anything which it might ever bring about merely in order to favor some inclination, or even the sum total of all inclinations. Even if, by some especially unfortunate fate or by the niggardly provision of stepmotherly nature, this will should be wholly lacking in the

power to accomplish its purpose; if with the greatest effort it should yet achieve nothing, and only the good will should remain (not, to be sure, as a mere wish but as the summoning of all the means in our power), yet would it, like a jewel, still shine by its own light as something which has its full value in itself. Its usefulness or fruitlessness can neither augment nor diminish this value. Its usefulness would be, as it were, only the setting to enable us to handle it in ordinary dealings or to attract to it the attention of those who are not yet experts, but not to recommend it to real experts or to determine its value.

Nature's Purpose in Making Reason the Guide of the Will

But there is something so strange in this idea of the absolute value of a mere will, in which no account is taken of any useful results, that in spite of all the agreement received even from ordinary reason, yet there must arise the suspicion that such an idea may perhaps have as its hidden basis merely some high-flown fancy, and that we may have misunderstood the purpose of nature in assigning to reason the governing of our will. Therefore, this idea will be examined from this point of view.

In the natural constitution of an organized being, i.e., one suitably adapted to the purpose of life, let there be taken as a principle that in such a being no organ is to be found for any end unless it be the most fit and the best adapted for that end. Now if that being's preservation, welfare, or in a word its happiness, were the real end of nature in the case of a being having reason and will, then nature would have hit upon a very poor arrangement in having the reason of the creature carry out this purpose. For all the actions which such a creature has to perform with this purpose in view, and the whole rule of his conduct would have been prescribed much more exactly by instinct; and the purpose in question could have been attained much more certainly by instinct than it ever can be by reason. And if in addition reason had been imparted to this favored creature, then it would have had to serve him only to contemplate the happy constitution of his nature, to admire that nature, to rejoice in it, and to feel grateful to the cause that bestowed it; but reason would not have served him to subject his faculty of desire to its weak and delusive guidance nor would it have served him to meddle incompetently with the purpose of nature. In a word, nature would have taken care that reason did not strike out into a practical use nor presume, with its weak insight, to think out for itself a plan for happiness and the means for attaining it. Nature would have taken upon herself not only the choice of ends but also that of the means, and would with wise foresight have entrusted both to instinct alone.

And, in fact, we find that the more a cultivated reason devotes itself to the aim of enjoying life and happiness, the further does man get away from true contentment. Because of this there arises in many persons, if only they are candid enough to admit it, a certain degree of misology, i.e., hatred of reason. This is especially so in the case of those who are the most experienced in the use of reason, because after calculating all the advantages they derive, I say not from the invention of all the arts of common luxury, but even from the sciences (which in the end seem to them to be also a luxury of the understanding), they yet find that they have in fact only brought more trouble on their heads than they have gained in happiness. Therefore, they come to envy, rather than despise, the more common run of men who are closer to the guidance of mere natural instinct and who do not allow their reason much influence on their conduct. And we must admit that the judgment of those who would temper, or even reduce below zero, the boastful eulogies on behalf of the advantages which reason is supposed to provide as regards the happiness and contentment of life is by no means morose or ungrateful to the goodness with which the world is governed: There lies at the root of such judgments, rather, the idea that existence has another and much more worthy purpose, for which, and

not for happiness, reason is quite properly intended, and which must, therefore, be regarded as the supreme condition to which the private purpose of men must, for the most part, defer.

Reason, however, is not competent enough to guide the will safely as regards its objects and the satisfaction of all our needs (which it in part even multiplies); to this end would an implanted natural instinct have led much more certainly. But inasmuch as reason has been imparted to us as a practical faculty, i.e., as one which is to have influence on the will, its true function must be to produce a will which is not merely good as a means to some further end, but is good in itself. To produce a will good in itself reason was absolutely necessary, inasmuch as nature in distributing her capacities has everywhere gone to work in a purposive manner. While such a will may not indeed be the sole and complete good, it must, nevertheless, be the highest good and the condition of all the rest, even of the desire for happiness. In this case there is nothing inconsistent with the wisdom of nature that the cultivation of reason, which is requisite for the first and unconditioned purpose, may in many ways restrict, at least in this life, the attainment of the second purpose, viz., happiness, which is always conditioned. Indeed happiness can even be reduced to less than nothing, without nature's failing thereby in her purpose; for reason recognizes as its highest practical function the establishment of a good will, whereby in the attainment of this end reason is capable only of its own kind of satisfaction, viz., that of fulfilling a purpose which is in turn determined only by reason, even though such fulfilment were often to interfere with the purposes of inclination.

The First Proposition: An Act Must Be Done from a Sense of Duty to Have Moral Worth

The concept of a will estimable in itself and good without regard to any further end must now be developed. This concept already dwells in the natural sound understanding and needs not so much to be taught as merely to be elucidated. It always holds first place in estimating the total worth of our actions and constitutes the condition of all the rest. Therefore, we shall take up the concept of *duty,* which includes that of a good will, though with certain subjective restrictions and hindrances, which far from hiding a good will or rendering it unrecognizable, rather bring it out by contrast and make it shine forth more brightly.

I here omit all actions already recognized as contrary to duty, even though they may be useful for this or that end; for in the case of these the question does not arise at all as to whether they might be done from duty, since they even conflict with duty. I also set aside those actions which are really in accordance with duty, yet to which men have no immediate inclination, but perform them because they are impelled thereto by some other inclination. For in this [second] case to decide whether the action which is in accord with duty has been done from duty or from some selfish purpose is easy. This difference is far more difficult to note in the [third] case where the action accords with duty and the subject has in addition an immediate inclination to do the action. For example, that a dealer should not overcharge an inexperienced purchaser certainly accords with duty; and where there is much commerce, the prudent merchant does not overcharge but keeps to a fixed price for everyone in general, so that a child may buy from him just as well as everyone else may. Thus customers are honestly served, but this is not nearly enough for making us believe that the merchant has acted this way from duty and from principles of honesty; his own advantage required him to do it. He cannot, however, be assumed to have in addition [as in the third case] an immediate inclination toward his buyers, causing him, as it were, out of love to give no one as far as price is concerned any advantage over another. Hence the action was done neither from duty nor from immediate inclination, but merely for a selfish purpose.

On the other hand, to preserve one's life is a duty; and, furthermore, everyone has also an immediate inclination to do so. But on this account the often anxious care taken by most men for it has no intrinsic worth, and the maxim of their action has no moral content. They preserve their lives, to be sure, in accordance with duty, but not from duty. On the other hand, if adversity and hopeless sorrow have completely taken away the taste for life, if an unfortunate man, strong in soul and more indignant at his fate than despondent or dejected, wishes for death and yet preserves his life without loving it—not from inclination or fear, but from duty—then his maxim indeed has a moral content.

To be beneficent where one can is a duty; and besides this, there are many persons who are so sympathetically constituted that, without any further motive of vanity or self-interest, they find an inner pleasure in spreading joy around them and can rejoice in the satisfaction of others as their own work. But I maintain that in such a case an action of this kind, however dutiful and amiable it may be, has nevertheless no true moral worth. It is on a level with such actions as arise from other inclinations, e.g., the inclination for honor, which if fortunately directed to what is in fact beneficial and accords with duty and is thus honorable, deserves praise and encouragement, but not esteem; for its maxim lacks the moral content of an action done not from inclination but from duty. Suppose then the mind of this friend of mankind to be clouded over with his own sorrow so that all sympathy with the lot of others is extinguished, and suppose him still to have the power to benefit others in distress, even though he is not touched by their trouble because he is sufficiently absorbed with his own; and now suppose that, even though no inclination moves him any longer, he nevertheless tears himself from this deadly insensibility and performs the action without any inclination at all, but solely from duty—then for the first time his action has genuine moral worth. Further still, if nature has put little sympathy in this or that man's heart, if (while being an honest man in other respects) he is by temperament cold and indifferent to the sufferings of others, perhaps because as regards his own sufferings he is endowed with the special gift of patience and fortitude and expects or even requires that others should have the same; if such a man (who would truly not be nature's worst product) had not been exactly fashioned by her to be a philanthropist, would he not yet find in himself a source from which he might give himself a worth far higher than any that a good-natured temperament might have? By all means, because just here does the worth of the character come out; this worth is moral and incomparably the highest of all, viz., that he is beneficent, not from inclination, but from duty.

To secure one's own happiness is a duty (at least indirectly); for discontent with one's condition under many pressing cares and amid unsatisfied wants might easily become a great temptation to transgress one's duties. But here also do men of themselves already have, irrespective of duty, the strongest and deepest inclination toward happiness, because just in this idea are all inclinations combined into a sum total. But the precept of happiness is often so constituted as greatly to interfere with some inclinations, and yet men cannot form any definite and certain concept of the sum of satisfaction of all inclinations that is called happiness. Hence there is no wonder that a single inclination which is determinate both as to what it promises and as to the time within which it can be satisfied may outweigh a fluctuating idea; and there is no wonder that a man, e.g., a gouty patient, can choose to enjoy what he likes and to suffer what he may, since by his calculation he has here at least not sacrificed the enjoyment of the present moment to some possibly groundless expectations of the good fortune that is supposed to be found in health. But even in this case, if the universal inclination to happiness did not determine his will and if health, at least for him, did not figure as so necessary an element in his calculations; there still remains here, as in all other cases, a law, viz., that he should promote his happiness not from inclination but from duty, and thereby for the first time does his conduct have real moral worth.

Undoubtedly in this way also are to be understood those passages of Scripture which command us to love our neighbor and even our enemy. For love as an inclination cannot be commanded; but beneficence from duty, when no inclination impels us and even when a natural and unconquerable aversion opposes such beneficence, is practical, and not pathological, love. Such love resides in the will and not in the propensities of feeling, in principles of action and not in tender sympathy; and only this practical love can be commanded.

The Second Proposition of Morality

The second proposition is this: An action done from duty has its moral worth, not in the purpose that is to be attained by it, but in the maxim according to which the action is determined. The moral worth depends, therefore, not on the realization of the object of the action, but merely on the principle of volition according to which, without regard to any objects of the faculty of desire, the action has been done. From what has gone before it is clear that the purposes which we may have in our actions, as well as their effects regarded as ends and incentives of the will, cannot give to actions any unconditioned and moral worth. Where, then, can this worth lie if it is not to be found in the will's relation to the expected effect? Nowhere but in the principle of the will, with no regard to the ends that can be brought about through such action. For the will stands, as it were, at a crossroads between its a priori principle, which is formal, and its a posteriori incentive, which is material; and since it must be determined by something, it must be determined by the formal principle of volition, if the action is done from duty—and in that case every material principle is taken away from it.

The Third Proposition of Morality

The third proposition, which follows from the other two, can be expressed thus: Duty is the necessity of an action done out of respect for the law. I can indeed have an inclination for an object as the effect of my proposed action; but I can never have respect for such an object, just because it is merely an effect and is not an activity of the will. Similarly, I can have no respect for inclination as such, whether my own or that of another. I can at most, if my own inclination, approve it; and, if that of another, even love it, i.e., consider it to be favorable to my own advantage. An object of respect can only be what is connected with my will solely as ground and never as effect—something that does not serve my inclination but, rather, outweighs it, or at least excludes it from consideration when some choice is made—in other words, only the law itself can be an object of respect and hence can be a command. Now an action done from duty must altogether exclude the influence of inclination and therewith every object of the will. Hence, there is nothing left which can determine the will except objectively the law and subjectively pure respect for this practical law, i.e., the will can be subjectively determined by the maxim[1] that I should follow such a law even if all my inclinations are thereby thwarted.

Thus, the moral worth of an action does not lie in the effect expected from it nor in any principle of action that needs to borrow its motive from this expected effect. For all these effects (agreeableness of one's condition and even the furtherance of other people's happiness) could have been brought about also through other causes and would not have required the will of a rational being, in which the highest and unconditioned good can alone be found. Therefore, the preeminent good which is called moral can consist in nothing but the representation of the law in itself, and such a representation can admittedly be found only in a rational being insofar as this representation, and not some expected effect, is the determining ground of will. This good is already present in the person who acts according to this representation, and such good need not be awaited merely from the effect.

The Supreme Principle of Morality: The Categorical Imperative

But what sort of law can that be the thought of which must determine the will without reference to any expected effect, so that the will can be

called absolutely good without qualification? Since I have deprived the will of every impulse that might arise for it from obeying any particular law, there is nothing left to serve the will as principle except the universal conformity of its actions to law as such, i.e., I should never act except in such a way that I can also will that my maxim should become a universal law. Here mere conformity to law as such (without having as its basis any law determining particular actions) serves the will as principle and must so serve it if duty is not to be a vain delusion and a chimerical concept. The ordinary reason of mankind in its practical judgments agrees completely with this, and always has in view the aforementioned principle.

For example, take this question. When I am in distress, may I make a promise with the intention of not keeping it? I readily distinguish here the two meanings which the question may have; whether making a false promise conforms with prudence or with duty. Doubtless the former can often be the case. Indeed, I clearly see that escape from some present difficulty by means of such a promise is not enough. In addition I must carefully consider whether from this lie there may later arise far greater inconvenience for me than from what I now try to escape. Furthermore, the consequences of my false promise are not easy to foresee, even with all my supposed cunning; loss of confidence in me might prove to be far more disadvantageous than the misfortune which I now try to avoid. The more prudent way might be to act according to a universal maxim and to make it a habit not to promise anything without intending to keep it. But that such a maxim is, nevertheless, always based on nothing but a fear of consequences becomes clear to me at once. To be truthful from duty is, however, quite different from being truthful from fear of disadvantageous consequences; in the first case the concept of the action itself contains a law for me, while in the second I must first look around elsewhere to see what are the results for me that might be connected with the action. For to deviate from the principle of duty is quite certainly bad; but to abandon my maxim of prudence can often be very advantageous for me, though to abide by it is certainly safer. The most direct and infallible way, however, to answer the question as to whether a lying promise accords with duty is to ask myself whether I would really be content if my maxim (of extricating myself from difficulty by means of a false promise) were to hold as a universal law for myself as well as for others, and could I really say to myself that everyone may promise falsely when he finds himself in a difficulty from which he can find no other way to extricate himself. Then I immediately become aware that I can indeed will the lie but can not at all will a universal law to lie. For by such a law there would really be no promises at all, since in vain would my willing future actions be professed to other people who would not believe what I professed, or if they overhastily did believe, then they would pay me back in like coin. Therefore, my maxim would necessarily destroy itself just as soon as it was made a universal law.

Therefore, I need no far-reaching acuteness to discern what I have to do in order that my will may be morally good. Inexperienced in the course of the world and incapable of being prepared for all its contingencies, I only ask myself whether I can also will that my maxim should become a universal law. If not, then the maxim must be rejected, not because of any disadvantage accruing to me or even to others, but because it cannot be fitting as a principle in a possible legislation of universal law, and reason exacts from me immediate respect for such legislation. Indeed, I have as yet no insight into the grounds of such respect (which the philosopher may investigate). But I at least understand that respect is an estimation of a worth that far outweighs any worth of what is recommended by inclination, and that the necessity of acting from pure respect for the practical law is what constitutes duty, to which every other motive must give way because duty is the condition of a will good in itself, whose worth is above all else.

Thus, within the moral cognition of ordinary human reason we have arrived at its principle. To be sure, such reason does not think of this principle abstractly in its universal form, but does always have it actually in view and does use it as the standard of judgment. . . .

Second Section

Transition From Popular Moral Philosophy to a Metaphysics of Morals

If we have so far drawn our concept of duty from the ordinary use of our practical reason, one is by no means to infer that we have treated it as a concept of experience. On the contrary, when we pay attention to our experience of the way human beings act, we meet frequent and—as we ourselves admit—justified complaints that there cannot be cited a single certain example of the disposition to act from pure duty; and we meet complaints that although much may be done that is in accordance with what duty commands, yet there are always doubts as to whether what occurs has really been done from duty and so has moral worth. Hence there have always been philosophers who have absolutely denied the reality of this disposition in human actions and have ascribed everything to a more or less refined self-love. Yet in so doing they have not cast doubt upon the rightness of the concept of morality. Rather, they have spoken with sincere regret as to the frailty and impurity of human nature, which they think is noble enough to take as its precept an idea so worthy of respect but yet is too weak to follow this idea: reason, which should legislate for human nature, is used only to look after the interest of inclinations, whether singly or, at best, in their greatest possible harmony with one another.

In fact there is absolutely no possibility by means of experience to make out with complete certainty a single case in which the maxim of an action that may in other respects conform to duty has rested solely on moral grounds and on the representation of one's duty. It is indeed sometimes the case that after the keenest self-examination we can find nothing except the moral ground of duty that could have been strong enough to move us to this or that good action and to such great sacrifice. But there cannot with certainty be at all inferred from this that some secret impulse of self-love, merely appearing as the idea of duty, was not the actual determining cause of the will. We like to flatter ourselves with the false claim to a more noble motive; but in fact we can never, even by the strictest examination, completely plumb the depths of the secret incentives of our actions. For when moral value is being considered, the concern is not with the actions, which are seen, but rather with their inner principles, which are not seen.

Moreover, one cannot better serve the wishes of those who ridicule all morality as being a mere phantom of human imagination getting above itself because of self-conceit than by conceding to them that the concepts of duty must be drawn solely from experience (just as from indolence one willingly persuades himself that such is the case as regards all other concepts as well). For by so conceding, one prepares for them a sure triumph. I am willing to admit out of love for humanity that most of our actions are in accordance with duty; but if we look more closely at our planning and striving, we everywhere come upon the dear self, which is always turning up, and upon which the intent of our actions is based rather than upon the strict command of duty (which would often require self-denial). One need not be exactly an enemy of virtue, but only a cool observer who does not take the liveliest wish for the good to be straight off its realization, in order to become doubtful at times whether any true virtue is actually to be found in the world. Such is especially the case when years increase and one's power of judgment is made shrewder by experience and keener in observation. Because of these things nothing can protect us from a complete falling away from our ideas of duty and preserve in the soul a well-grounded respect for duty's law except the clear conviction that, even if there never have been actions springing from such pure sources, the question at issue here is not whether this or that has happened but that reason of itself and independently of all experi-

ence commands what ought to happen. Consequently, reason unrelentingly commands actions of which the world has perhaps hitherto never provided an example and whose feasibility might well be doubted by one who bases everything upon experience; for instance, even though there might never yet have been a sincere friend, still pure sincerity in friendship is nonetheless required of every man, because this duty, prior to all experience, is contained as duty in general in the idea of a reason that determines the will by means of a priori grounds.

There may be noted further that unless we want to deny to the concept of morality all truth and all reference to a possible object, we cannot but admit that the moral law is of such widespread significance that it must hold not merely for men but for all rational beings generally, and that it must be valid not merely under contingent conditions and with exceptions but must be absolutely necessary. Clearly, therefore, no experience can give occasion for inferring even the possibility of such apodictic laws. For with what right could we bring into unlimited respect as a universal precept for every rational nature what is perhaps valid only under the contingent conditions of humanity? And how could laws for the determination of our will be regarded as laws for the determination of a rational being in general and of ourselves only insofar as we are rational beings, if these laws were merely empirical and did not have their source completely a priori in pure, but practical, reason?

Moreover, worse service cannot be rendered morality than that an attempt be made to derive it from examples. For every example of morality presented to me must itself first be judged according to principles of morality in order to see whether it is fit to serve as an original example, i.e., as a model. But in no way can it authoritatively furnish the concept of morality. Even the Holy One of the gospel must first be compared with our ideal of moral perfection before he is recognized as such. Even he says of himself, "Why do you call me (whom you see) good? None is good (the archetype of the good) except God only (whom you do not see)." But whence have we the concept of God as the highest good? Solely from the idea of moral perfection, which reason frames a priori and connects inseparably with the concept of a free will. *Imitation* has no place at all in moral matters. And examples serve only for encouragement, i.e., they put beyond doubt the feasibility of what the law commands and they make visible what the practical rule expresses more generally. But examples can never justify us in setting aside their true original, which lies in reason, and letting ourselves be guided by them.

If there is then no genuine supreme principle of morality that must rest merely on pure reason, independently of all experience, I think it is unnecessary even to ask whether it is a good thing to exhibit these concepts generally (*in abstracto*), which, along with the principles that belong to them, hold a priori, so far as the knowledge involved is to be distinguished from ordinary knowledge and is to be called philosophical. But in our times it may well be necessary to do so. For if one were to take a vote as to whether pure rational knowledge separated from everything empirical, i.e., metaphysics of morals, or whether popular practical philosophy is to be preferred, one can easily guess which side would be preponderant.

This descent to popular thought is certainly very commendable once the ascent to the principles of pure reason has occurred and has been satisfactorily accomplished. That would mean that the doctrine of morals has first been grounded on metaphysics and that subsequently acceptance for morals has been won by giving it a popular character after it has been firmly established. But it is quite absurd to try for popularity in the first inquiry, upon which depends the total correctness of the principles. . . .

Imperatives: Hypothetical and Categorical

Everything in nature works according to laws. Only a rational being has the power to act according to his conception of laws, i.e., according

to principles, and thereby has he a will. Since the derivation of actions from laws requires reason, the will is nothing but practical reason. If reason infallibly determines the will, then in the case of such a being actions which are recognized to be objectively necessary are also subjectively necessary, i.e., the will is a faculty of choosing only that which reason, independently of inclination, recognizes as being practically necessary, i.e., as good. But if reason of itself does not sufficiently determine the will, and if the will submits also to subjective conditions (certain incentives) which do not always agree with objective conditions; in a word, if the will does not in itself completely accord with reason (as is actually the case with men), then actions which are recognized as objectively necessary are subjectively contingent, and the determination of such a will according to objective laws is necessitation. That is to say that the relation of objective laws to a will not thoroughly good is represented as the determination of the will of a rational being by principles of reason which the will does not necessarily follow because of its own nature.

The representation of an objective principle insofar as it necessitates the will is called a *command* (of reason), and the formula of the command is called an *imperative.*

All imperatives are expressed by an *ought* and thereby indicate the relation of an objective law of reason to a will that is not necessarily determined by this law because of its subjective constitution (the relation of necessitation). Imperatives say that something would be good to do or to refrain from doing, but they say it to a will that does not always therefore do something simply because it has been represented to the will as something good to do. That is practically good which determines the will by means of representations of reason and hence not by subjective causes, but objectively, i.e., on grounds valid for every rational being as such. It is distinguished from the pleasant as that which influences the will only by means of sensation from merely subjective causes, which hold only for this or that person's senses but do not hold as a principle of reason valid for everyone.

A perfectly good will would thus be quite as much subject to objective laws (of the good), but could not be conceived as thereby necessitated to act in conformity with law, inasmuch as it can of itself, according to its subjective constitution, be determined only by the representation of the good. Therefore no imperatives hold for the divine will, and in general for a holy will; the *ought* is here out of place, because the *would* is already of itself necessarily in agreement with the law. Consequently, imperatives are only formulas for expressing the relation of objective laws of willing in general to the subjective imperfection of the will of this or that rational being, e.g., the human will.

Now, all imperatives command either hypothetically or categorically. The former represent the practical necessity of a possible action as a means for attaining something else that one wants (or may possibly want). The categorical imperative would be one which represented an action as objectively necessary in itself, without reference to another end.

Every practical law represents a possible action as good and hence as necessary for a subject who is practically determinable by reason; therefore all imperatives are formulas for determining an action which is necessary according to the principle of a will that is good in some way. Now, if the action would be good merely as a means to something else, so is the imperative hypothetical. But if the action is represented as good in itself, and hence as necessary in a will which of itself conforms to reason as the principle of the will, then the imperative is categorical.

An imperative thus says what action possible by me would be good, and it presents the practical rule in relation to a will which does not forthwith perform an action simply because it is good, partly because the subject does not always know that the action is good and partly because (even if he does know it is good) his maxims might yet be opposed to the objective principles of practical reason.

A hypothetical imperative thus says only that an action is good for some purpose, either possible or actual. In the first case it is a problematic practical principle; in the second case an assertoric one. A categorical imperative, which declares an action to be of itself objectively necessary without reference to any purpose, i.e., without any other end, holds as an apodictic practical principle. . . .

The Rational Ground of the Categorical Imperative

. . . the question as to how the imperative of morality is possible is undoubtedly the only one requiring a solution. For it is not at all hypothetical; and hence the objective necessity which it presents cannot be based on any presupposition, as was the case with the hypothetical imperatives. Only there must never here be forgotten that no example can show, i.e., empirically, whether there is any such imperative at all. Rather, care must be taken lest all imperatives which are seemingly categorical may nevertheless be covertly hypothetical. For instance, when it is said that you should not make a false promise, the assumption is that the necessity of this avoidance is no mere advice for escaping some other evil, so that it might be said that you should not make a false promise lest you ruin your credit when the falsity comes to light. But when it is asserted that an action of this kind must be regarded as bad in itself, then the imperative of prohibition is therefore categorical. Nevertheless, it cannot with certainty be shown by means of an example that the will is here determined solely by the law without any other incentive, even though such may seem to be the case. For it is always possible that secretly there is fear of disgrace and perhaps also obscure dread of other dangers; such fear and dread may have influenced the will. Who can prove by experience that a cause is not present? Experience only shows that a cause is not perceived. But in such a case the so-called moral imperative, which as such appears to be categorical and unconditioned, would actually be only a pragmatic precept which makes us pay attention to our own advantage and merely teaches us to take such advantage into consideration.

We shall, therefore, have to investigate the possibility of a categorical imperative entirely a priori, inasmuch as we do not here have the advantage of having its reality given in experience and consequently of thus being obligated merely to explain its possibility rather than to establish it. In the meantime so much can be seen for now: the categorical imperative alone purports to be a practical law, while all the others may be called principles of the will but not laws. The reason for this is that whatever is necessary merely in order to attain some arbitrary purpose can be regarded as in itself contingent, and the precept can always be ignored once the purpose is abandoned. Contrariwise, an unconditioned command does not leave the will free to choose the opposite at its own liking. Consequently, only such a command carries with it that necessity which is demanded from a law.

Secondly, in the case of this categorical imperative, or law of morality, the reason for the difficulty (of discerning its possibility) is quite serious. The categorical imperative is an a priori synthetic practical proposition, and since discerning the possibility of propositions of this sort involves so much difficulty in theoretic knowledge, there may readily be gathered that there will be no less difficulty in practical knowledge.

First Formulation of the Categorical Imperative: Universal Law

In solving this problem, we want first to inquire whether perhaps the mere concept of a categorical imperative may not also supply us with the formula containing the proposition that can alone be a categorical imperative. For even when we know the purport of such an absolute command, the question as to how it is possible will still require a special and difficult effort, which we postpone to the last section.

If I think of a hypothetical imperative in general, I do not know beforehand what it will contain until its condition is given. But if I think of a categorical imperative, I know immediately what it contains. For since, besides the law, the imperative contains only the necessity that the maxim[2] should accord with this law, while the law contains no condition to restrict it, there remains nothing but the universality of a law as such with which the maxim of the action should conform. This conformity alone is properly what is represented as necessary by the imperative.

Hence there is only one categorical imperative and it is this: Act only according to that maxim whereby you can at the same time will that it should become a universal law.[3]

Now if all imperatives of duty can be derived from this one imperative as their principle, then there can at least be shown what is understood by the concept of duty and what it means, even though there is left undecided whether what is called duty may not be an empty concept.

The universality of law according to which effects are produced constitutes what is properly called nature in the most general sense (as to form), i.e., the existence of things as far as determined by universal laws. Accordingly, the universal imperative of duty may be expressed thus: Act as if the maxim of your action were to become through your will a universal law of nature.[4]

We shall now enumerate some duties, following the usual division of them into duties to ourselves and to others and into perfect and imperfect duties.[5]

1. A man reduced to despair by a series of misfortunes feels sick of life but is still so far in possession of his reason that he can ask himself whether taking his own life would not be contrary to his duty to himself.[6] Now he asks whether the maxim of his action could become a universal law of nature. But his maxim is this: from self-love I make as my principle to shorten my life when its continued duration threatens more evil than it promises satisfaction. There only remains the question as to whether this principle of self-love can become a universal law of nature. One sees at once a contradiction in a system of nature whose law would destroy life by means of the very same

feeling that acts so as to stimulate the furtherance of life, and hence there could be no existence as a system of nature. Therefore, such a maxim cannot possibly hold as a universal law of nature and is, consequently, wholly opposed to the supreme principle of all duty.

2. Another man in need finds himself forced to borrow money. He knows well that he won't be able to repay it, but he sees also that he will not get any loan unless he firmly promises to repay it within a fixed time. He wants to make such a promise, but he still has conscience enough to ask himself whether it is not permissible and is contrary to duty to get out of difficulty in this way. Suppose, however, that he decides to do so. The maxim of his action would then be expressed as follows: when I believe myself to be in need of money, I will borrow money and promise to pay it back, although I know that I can never do so. Now this principle of self-love or personal advantage may perhaps be quite compatible with one's entire future welfare, but the question is now whether it is right.[7] I then transform the requirement of self-love into a universal law and put the question thus: how would things stand if my maxim were to become a universal law? He then sees at once that such a maxim could never hold as a universal law of nature and be consistent with itself, but must necessarily be self-contradictory. For the universality of a law which says that anyone believing himself to be in difficulty could promise whatever he pleases with the intention of not keeping it would make promising itself and the end to be attained thereby quite impossible, inasmuch as no one would believe what was promised him but would merely laugh at all such utterances as being vain pretenses.

3. A third finds in himself a talent whose cultivation could make him a man useful in many respects. But he finds himself in comfortable circumstances and prefers to indulge in pleasure rather than to bother himself about broadening and improving his fortunate natural aptitudes. But he asks himself further whether his maxim of neglecting his natural gifts, besides agreeing of itself with his propensity to indulgence, might agree also with what is called duty.[8] He then sees that a system of nature could indeed always subsist according to such a universal law, even though every man (like South Sea Islanders) should let his talents rust and resolve to devote his life entirely to idleness, indulgence, propagation, and, in a word, to enjoyment. But he cannot possibly will that this should become a universal law of nature or be implanted in us as such a law by a natural instinct. For as a rational being he necessarily wills that all his faculties should be developed, inasmuch as they are given him for all sorts of possible purposes.

4. A fourth man finds things going well for himself but sees others (whom he could help) struggling with great hardships; and he thinks: what does it matter to me? Let everybody be as happy as Heaven wills or as he can make himself; I shall take nothing from him nor even envy him; but I have no desire to contribute anything to his well-being or to his assistance when in need. If such a way of thinking were to become a universal law of nature, the human race admittedly could very well subsist and doubtless could subsist even better than when everyone prates about sympathy and benevolence, and even on occasion exerts himself to practice them but, on the other hand, also cheats when he can, betrays the rights of man, or otherwise violates them. But even though it is possible that a universal law of nature could subsist in accordance with that maxim, still it is impossible to will that such a principle should hold everywhere as a law of nature.[9] For a will which resolved in this way would contradict itself, inasmuch as cases might often arise in which one would have need of the love and sympathy of others and in which he would deprive himself, by such a law of nature springing from his own will, of all hope of the aid he wants for himself.

These are some of the many actual duties, or at least what are taken to be such, whose derivation from the single principle cited above is clear. We must be able to will that a maxim of our action become a universal law; this is the canon for morally estimating any of our actions. Some actions are so constituted that their maxims cannot without contradiction even be thought as a universal law of nature, much less be willed as what should become one. In the case of others this internal impossibility is indeed not found, but there is still no possibility of willing that their maxim should be raised to the universality of a law of nature, because such a will would contradict itself. There is no difficulty in seeing that the former kind of action conflicts with strict or narrow [perfect] (irremissible) duty, while the second kind conflicts only with broad [imperfect] (meritorious) duty. By means of these examples there has thus been fully set forth how all duties depend as regards the kind of obligation (not the object of their action) upon the one principle.

If we now attend to ourselves in any transgression of a duty, we find that we actually do not will that our maxim should become a universal law— because this is impossible for us—but rather that the opposite of this maxim should remain a law universally.[10] We only take the liberty of making an exception to the law for ourselves (or just for this one time) to the advantage of our inclination. Consequently, if we weighed up everything from one and the same standpoint, namely, that of reason, we would find a contradiction in our own will, viz., that a certain principle be objectively necessary as a universal law and yet subjectively not hold universally but should admit of exceptions. But since we at one moment regard our action from the standpoint of a will wholly in accord with reason and then at another moment regard the very same action from the standpoint of a will affected by inclination, there is really no contradiction here. Rather, there is an opposition of inclination to the precept of reason, whereby the universality of the principle is changed into a mere generality so that the practical principle of reason may meet the maxim halfway. Although this procedure cannot be justified in our own im-

partial judgment, yet it does show that we actually acknowledge the validity of the categorical imperative and (with all respect for it) merely allow ourselves a few exceptions which, as they seem to us, are unimportant and forced upon us.

The Need for an A Priori Proof
for the Categorical Imperative

We have thus at least shown that if duty is a concept which is to have significance and real legislative authority for our actions, then such duty can be expressed only in categorical imperatives but not at all in hypothetical ones. We have also—and this is already a great deal—exhibited clearly and definitely for every application what is the content of the categorical imperative, which must contain the principle of all duty (if there is such a thing at all). But we have not yet advanced far enough to prove a priori that there actually is an imperative of this kind, that there is a practical law which of itself commands absolutely and without any incentives, and that following this law is duty.

In order to attain this proof there is the utmost importance in being warned that we must not take it into our mind to derive the reality of this principle from the special characteristics of human nature. For duty has to be a practical, unconditioned necessity of action; hence it must hold for all rational beings (to whom alone an imperative is at all applicable) and for this reason only can it also be a law for all human wills. On the other hand, whatever is derived from the special natural condition of humanity, from certain feelings and propensities, or even, if such were possible, from some special tendency peculiar to human reason and not holding necessarily for the will of every rational being—all of this can indeed yield a maxim valid for us, but not a law. This is to say that such can yield a subjective principle according to which we might act if we happen to have the propensity and inclination, but cannot yield an objective principle according to which we would be directed to act even though our every propensity, inclination, and natural tendency were opposed to it. In fact, the sublimity and inner worth of the command are so much the more evident in a duty, the fewer subjective causes there are for it and the more they oppose it; such causes do not in the least weaken the necessitation exerted by the law or take away anything from its validity.

Here philosophy is seen in fact to be put in a precarious position, which should be firm even though there is neither in heaven nor on earth anything upon which it depends or is based. Here philosophy must show its purity as author of its laws, and not as the herald of such laws as are whispered to it by an implanted sense or by who knows what tutelary nature. Such laws may be better than nothing at all, but they can never give us principles dictated by reason. These principles must have an origin that is completely a priori and must at the same time derive from such origin their authority to command. They expect nothing from the inclination of men but, rather, expect everything from the supremacy of the law and from the respect owed to the law. Without the latter expectation, these principles condemn man to self-contempt and inward abhorrence.

Hence, everything empirical is not only quite unsuitable as a contribution to the principle of morality, but is even highly detrimental to the purity of morals. For the proper and inestimable worth of an absolutely good will consists precisely in the fact that the principle of action is free of all influences from contingent grounds, which only experience can furnish. This lax or even mean way of thinking which seeks its principle among empirical motives and laws cannot too much or too often be warned against, for human reason in its weariness is glad to rest upon this pillow. In a dream of sweet illusions (in which not Juno but a cloud is embraced) there is substituted for morality some bastard patched up from limbs of quite varied ancestry and looking like anything one wants to see in it but not looking like virtue to him who has once beheld her in her true form.[11]

Therefore, the question is this: is it a necessary law for all rational beings always to judge their actions according to such maxims as they can themselves will that such should serve as universal laws? If there is such a law, then it must already be connected (completely a priori) with the concept of a rational being in general. But in order to discover this connection we must, however reluctantly, take a step into metaphysics, although into a region of it different from speculative philosophy, i.e., we must enter the metaphysics of morals. In practical philosophy the concern is not with accepting grounds for what happens but with accepting laws of what ought to happen, even though it never does happen—that is, the concern is with objectively practical laws. Here there is no need to inquire into the grounds as to why something pleases or displeases, how the pleasure of mere sensation differs from taste, and whether taste differs from a general satisfaction of reason, upon what does the feeling of pleasure and displeasure rest, and how from this feeling desires and inclinations arise, and how, finally, from these there arise maxims through the cooperation of reason. All of this belongs to an empirical psychology, which would constitute the second part of the doctrine of nature, if this doctrine is regarded as the philosophy of nature insofar as this philosophy is grounded on empirical laws. But here the concern is with objectively practical laws, and hence with the relation of a will to itself insofar as it is determined solely by reason. In this case everything related to what is empirical falls away of itself, because if reason entirely by itself determines conduct (and the possibility of such determination we now wish to investigate), then reason must necessarily do so a priori.

Second Formulation of the Categorical Imperative: Humanity as an End in Itself

The will is thought of as a faculty of determining itself to action in accordance with the representation of certain laws, and such a faculty can be found only in rational beings. Now what serves the will as the objective ground of its self-determination is an end; and if this end is given by reason alone, then it must be equally valid for all rational beings. On the other hand, what contains merely the ground of the possibility of the action, whose effect is an end, is called the means. The subjective ground of desire is the incentive; the objective ground of volition is the motive. Hence, there arises the distinction between subjective ends, which rest on incentives, and objective ends, which depend on motives valid for every rational being. Practical principles are formal when they abstract from all subjective ends; they are material, however, when they are founded upon subjective ends, and hence upon certain incentives. The ends which a rational being arbitrarily proposes to himself as effects of this action (material ends) are all merely relative, for only their relation to a specially constituted faculty of desire in the subject gives them their worth. Consequently, such worth cannot provide any universal principles, which are valid and necessary for all rational beings and, furthermore, are valid for every volition, i.e., cannot provide any practical laws. Therefore, all such relative ends can be grounds only for hypothetical imperatives.

But let us suppose that there were something whose existence has in itself an absolute worth, something which as an end in itself could be a ground of determinate laws. In it, and in it alone, would there be the ground of a possible categorical imperative, i.e., of a practical law.

Now I say that man, and in general every rational being, exists as an end in himself and not merely as a means to be arbitrarily used by this or that will. He must in all his actions, whether directed to himself or to other rational beings, always be regarded at the same time as an end. All the objects of inclinations have only a conditioned value; for if there were not these inclinations and the needs founded on them, then their object would be without value. But the inclinations themselves, being sources of needs, are so far from having an absolute value such as to render them desirable for their own sake that the universal wish of every rational being must be, rather, to be wholly free from them. Accordingly, the value of any object obtainable by our action is always conditioned. Beings whose existence depends not on our will but on nature have, nevertheless, if they are not rational beings, only a relative value as means and are therefore called things. On the other hand, rational beings are called persons inasmuch as their nature already marks them out as ends in themselves, i.e., as something which is not to be used merely as means, and hence, there is imposed thereby a limit on all arbitrary use of such beings, which are thus objects of respect. Persons are, therefore, not merely subjective ends, whose existence as an effect of our actions has a value for us; but such beings are objective ends, i.e., exist as ends in themselves. Such an end is one for which there can be substituted no other end to which such beings should serve merely as means, for otherwise nothing at all of absolute value would be found anywhere. But if all value were conditioned and hence contingent, then no supreme practical principle could be found for reason at all.

If then there is to be a supreme practical principle and, as far as the human will is concerned, a categorical imperative, then it must be such that from the conception of what is necessarily an end for everyone because this end is an end in itself it constitutes an objective principle of the will and can hence serve as a practical law. The ground of such a principle is this: rational nature exists as an end in itself. In this way man necessarily thinks of his own existence; thus far is it a subjective principle of human actions. But in this way also does every other rational being think of his existence on the same rational ground that holds also for me; hence it is at the same time an objective principle, from which, as a supreme practical ground, all laws of the will must be able to be derived. The practical imperative will therefore be the following: Act in such a way that you treat humanity, whether in your own person or in the person of another, always at the same time as an end and never simply as a means. . . .

The Third Formulation of the Categorical Imperative: The Autonomy of the Will as Universal Legislator

This principle of humanity and of every rational nature generally as an end in itself is the supreme limiting condition of every man's freedom of action. This principle is not borrowed from experience, first, because of its universality, inasmuch as it applies to all rational beings generally, and no experience is capable of determining anything about them; and, secondly, because in experience (subjectively) humanity is not thought of as the end of men, i.e., as an object that we of ourselves actually make our end which as a law ought to constitute the supreme limiting condition of all subjective ends (whatever they may be); and hence this principle must arise from pure reason [and not from experience]. That is to say that the ground of all practical legislation lies objectively in the rule and in the form of universality, which (according to the first principle) makes the rule capable of being a law (say, for example, a law of nature). Subjectively, however, the ground of all practical legislation lies in the end; but (according to the second principle) the subject of all ends is every rational being as an end in himself. From this there now follows the third practical principle of the will as the supreme condition of the will's conformity with universal practical reason, viz., the idea of the will of every rational being as a will that legislates universal law.

According to this principle all maxims are rejected which are not consistent with the will's own legislation of universal law. The will is thus not merely subject to the law but is subject to the law in such a way that it must be regarded also as legislating for itself and only on this account as being subject to the law (of which it can regard itself as the author).

In the previous formulations of imperatives, viz., that based on the conception of the confor-

mity of actions to universal law in a way similar to a natural order and that based on the universal prerogative of rational beings as ends in themselves, these imperatives just because they were thought of as categorical excluded from their legislative authority all admixture of any interest as an incentive. They were, however, only assumed to be categorical because such an assumption had to be made if the concept of duty was to be explained. But that there were practical propositions which commanded categorically could not itself be proved, nor can it be proved anywhere in this section. But one thing could have been done, viz., to indicate that in willing from duty the renunciation of all interest is the specific mark distinguishing a categorical imperative from a hypothetical one and that such renunciation was expressed in the imperative itself by means of some determination contained in it. This is done in the present (third) formulation of the principle, namely, in the idea of the will of every rational being as a will that legislates universal law.

When such a will is thought of, then even though a will which is subject to law may be bound to this law by means of some interest, nevertheless a will that is itself a supreme lawgiver is not able as such to depend on any interest. For a will which is so dependent would itself require yet another law restricting the interest of its self-love to the condition that such interest should itself be valid as a universal law.

Thus the principle that every human will is a will that legislates universal law in all its maxims, provided it is otherwise correct, would be well suited to being a categorical imperative in the following respect: just because of the idea of legislating universal law such an imperative is not based on any interest, and therefore it alone of all possible imperatives can be unconditional. Or still better, the proposition being converted, if there is a categorical imperative (i.e., a law for the will of every rational being), then it can only command that everything be done from the maxim of such a will as could at the same time have as its object only itself regarded as legislating universal law.

For only then are the practical principle and the imperative which the will obeys unconditional, inasmuch as the will can be based on no interest at all.

When we look back upon all previous attempts that have been made to discover the principle of morality, there is no reason now to wonder why they one and all had to fail. Man was viewed as bound to laws by his duty; but it was not seen that man is subject only to his own, yet universal, legislation and that he is bound only to act in accordance with his own will, which is, however, a will purposed by nature to legislate universal laws. For when man is thought as being merely subject to a law (whatever it might be), then the law had to carry with it some interest functioning as an attracting stimulus or as a constraining force for obedience, inasmuch as the law did not arise as a law from his own will. Rather, in order that his will conform with law, it had to be necessitated by something else to act in a certain way. By this absolutely necessary conclusion, however, all the labor spent in finding a supreme ground for duty was irretrievably lost; duty was never discovered, but only the necessity of acting from a certain interest. This might be either one's own interest or another's, but either way the imperative had to be always conditional and could never possibly serve as a moral command. I want, therefore, to call my principle the principle of the autonomy of the will, in contrast with every other principle, which I accordingly count under heteronomy.

The Kingdom of Ends

The concept of every rational being as one who must regard himself as legislating universal law by all his will's maxims, so that he may judge himself and his actions from this point of view, leads to another very fruitful concept, which depends on the aforementioned one, viz., that of a kingdom of ends.

By "kingdom" I understand a systematic union of different rational beings through common laws. Now laws determine ends as regards their universal validity; therefore, if one abstracts from the personal differences of rational beings and also from all content of their private ends, then it will be possible to think of a whole of all ends in systematic connection (a whole both of rational being as ends in themselves and also of the particular ends which each may set for himself); that is, one can think of a kingdom of ends that is possible on the aforesaid principles.

For all rational beings stand under the law that each of them should treat himself and all others never merely as means but always at the same time as an end in himself. Hereby arises a systematic union of rational beings through common objective laws, i.e., a kingdom that may be called a kingdom of ends (certainly only an ideal), inasmuch as these laws have in view the very relation of such beings to one another as ends and means.

A rational being belongs to the kingdom of ends as a member when he legislates in it universal laws while also being himself subject to these laws. He belongs to it as sovereign, when as legislator he is himself subject to the will of no other.

A rational being must always regard himself as legislator in a kingdom of ends rendered possible by freedom of the will, whether as member or as sovereign. The position of the latter can be maintained not merely through the maxims of his will but only if he is a completely independent being without needs and with unlimited power adequate to his will.

Hence, morality consists in the relation of all action to that legislation whereby alone a kingdom of ends is possible. This legislation must be found in every rational being and must be able to arise from his will, whose principle then is never to act on any maxim except such as can also be a universal law and hence such as the will can thereby regard itself as at the same time the legislator of universal law. If now the maxims do not by their very nature already necessarily conform with this objective principle of rational beings as legislating universal laws, then the necessity of acting on that principle is called practical necessitation, i.e., duty. Duty does not apply to the sovereign in the kingdom of ends, but it does apply to every member and to each in the same degree.

The practical necessity of acting according to this principle, i.e., duty, does not rest at all on feelings, impulses, and inclinations, but only on the relation of rational beings to one another, a relation in which the will of a rational being must always be regarded at the same time as legislative, because otherwise he could not be thought of as an end in himself. Reason, therefore, relates every maxim of the will as legislating universal laws to every other will and also to every action toward oneself; it does so not on account of any other practical motive or future advantage but rather from the idea of the dignity of a rational being who obeys no law except what he at the same time enacts himself.

In the kingdom of ends everything has either a price or a dignity. Whatever has a price can be replaced by something else as its equivalent; on the other hand, whatever is above all price, and therefore admits of no equivalent, has a dignity.

Whatever has reference to general human inclinations and needs has a market price; whatever, without presupposing any need, accords with a certain taste, i.e., a delight in the mere unpurposive play of our mental powers, has an affective price; but that which constitutes the condition under which alone something can be an end in itself has not merely a relative worth, i.e., a price, but has an intrinsic worth, i.e., dignity.

Now morality is the condition under which alone a rational being can be an end in himself, for only thereby can he be a legislating member in the kingdom of ends. Hence morality and humanity, insofar as it is capable of morality, alone have dignity. Skill and diligence in work have a market price; wit, lively imagination, and humor have an affective price; but fidelity to promises and benevolence based on principles (not on instinct) have intrinsic worth. Neither nature nor art contain anything which in default of these could be put in their place; for their worth consists, not in the effects which arise from them, nor in the advantage and profit which they pro-

vide, but in mental dispositions, i.e., in the maxims of the will which are ready in this way to manifest themselves in action, even if they are not favored with success. Such actions also need no recommendation from any subjective disposition or taste so as to meet with immediate favor and delight; there is no need of any immediate propensity or feeling toward them. They exhibit the will performing them as an object of immediate respect; and nothing but reason is required to impose them upon the will, which is not to be cajoled into them, since in the case of duties such cajoling would be a contradiction. This estimation, therefore, lets the worth of such a disposition be recognized as dignity and puts it infinitely beyond all price, with which it cannot in the least be brought into competition or comparison without, as it were, violating its *sanctity.*

What then is it that entitles the morally good disposition, or virtue, to make such lofty claims? It is nothing less than the share which such a disposition affords the rational being of legislating universal laws, so that he is fit to be a member in a possible kingdom of ends, for which his own nature has already determined him as an end in himself and therefore as a legislator in the kingdom of ends. Thereby is he free as regards all laws of nature, and he obeys only those laws which he gives to himself. Accordingly, his maxims can belong to a universal legislation to which he at the same time subjects himself. For nothing can have any worth other than what the law determines. But the legislation itself which determines all worth must for that very reason have dignity, i.e., unconditional and incomparable worth; and the word *respect* alone provides a suitable expression for the esteem which a rational being must have for it. Hence autonomy is the ground of the dignity of human nature and of every rational nature. . . .

Notes

1. A maxim is the subjective principle of volition. The objective principle (i.e., on which would serve all rational beings also subjectively as a practical principle if

reason had full control over the faculty of desire) is the practical law.

2. A maxim is the subjective principle of acting and must be distinguished from the objective principle, viz., the practical law. A maxim contains the practical rule which reason determines in accordance with the conditions of the subject (often his ignorance or his inclinations) and is thus the principle according to which the subject does act. But the law is the objective principle valid for every rational being, and it is the principle according to which he ought to act, i.e., an imperative.

3. [This formulation of the categorical imperative is often referred to as the formula of universal law.]

4. [This is often called the formula of the law of nature.]

5. There should be noted here that I reserve the division of duties for a future *Metaphysics of Morals* [in Part II of the *Metaphysics of Morals*, entitled *The Metaphysical Principles of Virtue*, Ak. 417–474]. The division presented here stands as merely an arbitrary one (in order to arrange my examples). For the rest, I understand here by a perfect duty one which permits no exception in the interest of inclination. Accordingly, I have perfect duties which are external [to others], while other ones are internal [to oneself]. This classification runs contrary to the accepted usage of the schools, but I do not intend to justify it here, since there is no difference for my purpose whether this classification is accepted or not.

6. [Not committing suicide is an example of a perfect duty to oneself.]

7. [Keeping promises is an example of a perfect duty to others.]

8. [Cultivating one's talents is an example of an imperfect duty to oneself.]

9. [Benefiting others is an example of an imperfect duty to others.]

10. [This is to say, for example, that when you tell a lie, you do so on the condition that others are truthful and believe that what you are saying is true, because otherwise your lie will never work to get you what you want. When you tell a lie, you simply take exception to the general rule that says everyone should always tell the truth.]

11. To behold virtue in her proper form is nothing other than to present morality stripped of all admixture of what is sensuous and of every spurious adornment of reward or self-love. How much she then eclipses all else that appears attractive to the inclinations can be easily seen by everyone with the least effort of his reason, if it be not entirely ruined for all abstraction.

23

An Examination of Kantian Ethics

FRED FELDMAN

Fred Feldman is professor of philosophy at the University of Massachusetts and the author of several works in philosophy, including Introductory Ethics, *from which this essay is taken. Feldman analyzes the central concepts and arguments of Kant's moral philosophy.*

Sometimes our moral thinking takes a decidedly nonutilitarian turn. That is, we often seem to appeal to a principle that is inconsistent with the whole utilitarian standpoint. One case in which this occurs clearly enough is the familiar tax-cheat case. A person decides to cheat on his income tax, rationalizing his misbehavior as follows: "The government will not be injured by the absence of my tax money. After all, compared with the enormous total they take in, my share is really a negligible sum. On the other hand, I will be happier if I have the use of the money. Hence, no one will be injured by my cheating, and one person will be better off. Thus, it is better for me to cheat than it is for me to pay."

In response to this sort of reasoning, we may be inclined to say something like this: "Perhaps you are right in thinking that you will be better off if you cheat. And perhaps you are right in thinking that the government won't even know the difference. Nevertheless, your act would be wrong. For if everyone were to cheat on his income taxes, the government would soon go broke. Surely you can see that you wouldn't want others to act in the way you propose to act. So you shouldn't act in that way." While it may not be clear that this sort of response would be decisive,

From *Introductory Ethics* (Prentice-Hall, 1978), © 1978. Reprinted by permission of the author and Prentice-Hall, Englewood Cliffs, New Jersey.

it should be clear that this is an example of a sort of response that is often given.

There are several things to notice about this response. For one, it is not based on the view that the example of the tax cheat will provoke everyone else to cheat too. If that were the point of the response, then the response might be explained on the basis of utilitarian considerations. We could understand the responder to be saying that the tax cheater has miscalculated his utilities. Whereas he thinks his act of cheating has high utility, in fact it has low utility because it will eventually result in the collapse of the government. It is important to recognize that the response presented above is not based upon any such utilitarian considerations. This can be seen by reflecting on the fact that the point could just as easily have been made in this way: "Of course, very few other people will know about your cheating, and so your behavior will not constitute an example to others. Thus, it will not provoke others to cheat. Nevertheless, your act is wrong. For if everyone were to cheat as you propose to do, then the government would collapse. Since you wouldn't want others to behave in the way you propose to behave, you should not behave in that way. It would be wrong to cheat."

Another thing to notice about the response in this case is that the responder has not simply said, "What you propose to do would be cheating; hence, it is wrong." The principle in question is not simply the principle that cheating is wrong. Rather, the responder has appealed to a much more general principle, which seems to be something like this: If you wouldn't want everyone else to act in a certain way, then you shouldn't act in that way yourself.

This sort of general principle is in fact used

quite widely in our moral reasoning. If someone proposes to remove the pollution-control devices from his automobile, his friends are sure to say "What if everyone did that?" They would have in mind some dire consequences for the quality of the air, but their point would not be that the removal of the pollution-control device by one person will in fact cause others to remove theirs, and will thus eventually lead to the destruction of the environment. Their point, rather, is that if their friend would not want others to act in the way he proposes to act, then it would be wrong for him to act in that way. This principle is also used against the person who refrains from giving to charity; the person who evades the draft in time of national emergency; the person who tells a lie in order to get out of a bad spot; and even the person who walks across a patch of newly seeded grass. In all such cases, we feel that the person acts wrongly not because his actions will have bad results, but because he wouldn't want others to behave in the way he behaves.

A highly refined version of this nonutilitarian principle is the heart of the moral theory of Immanuel Kant.[1] In his *Groundwork of the Metaphysic of Morals,*[2] Kant presents, develops, and defends the thesis that something like this principle is the "supreme principle of morality." Kant's presentation is rather complex; in parts, it is very hard to follow. Part of the trouble arises from his use of a rather unfamiliar technical vocabulary. Another source of trouble is that Kant is concerned with establishing a variety of other points in this little book, and some of these involve fairly complex issues in metaphysics and epistemology. Since our aim here is simply to present a clear, concise account of Kant's basic moral doctrine, we will have to ignore quite a bit of what he says in the book.

Kant formulates his main principle in a variety of different ways. All of the members of the following set of formulations seem to have a lot in common:

I ought never to act except in such a way that my maxim should become a universal law.[3]

Act only on that maxim through which you can at the same time will that it should become a universal law.[4]

Act as if the maxim of your action were to become through your will a universal law of nature.[5]

We must be able to will that a maxim of our action should become a universal law—this is the general canon for all moral judgment of action.[6]

Before we can evaluate this principle, which Kant calls the *categorical imperative,* we have to devote some attention to figuring out what it is supposed to mean. To do this, we must answer a variety of questions. What is a maxim? What is meant by "universal law"? What does Kant mean by "will"? Let us consider these questions in turn.

Maxims

In a footnote, Kant defines *maxim* as "a subjective principle of volition."[7] This definition is hardly helpful. Perhaps we can do better. First, however, a little background.

Kant apparently believes that when a person engages in genuine action, he always acts on some sort of general principle. The general principle will explain what the person takes himself to be doing and the circumstances in which he takes himself to be doing it. For example, if I need money, and can get some only by borrowing it, even though I know I won't be able to repay it, I might proceed to borrow some from a friend. My maxim in performing this act might be, "Whenever I need money and can get it by borrowing it, then I will borrow it, even if I know I won't be able to repay it."

Notice that this maxim is *general.* If I adopt it, I commit myself to behaving in the described way *whenever* I need money and the other conditions are satisfied. In this respect, the maxim serves to formulate a general principle of action rather than just some narrow reason applicable in just one case.[8] So a maxim must describe some general sort of situation, and then propose some form of action for the situation. To adopt a maxim is to commit yourself to acting in the described way whenever the situation in question arises.

It seems clear that Kant holds that every action has a maxim, although he does not explicitly state this view. When we speak of an action here, we mean a concrete, particular action, or *act-token*, rather than an *act-type*. Furthermore, we must distinguish between genuine actions and what we may call "mere bodily movements." It would be absurd to maintain that a man who scratches himself in his sleep is acting on the maxim "When I itch, I shall scratch." His scratching is a mere bodily movement, and has no maxim. A man who deliberately sets out to borrow some money from a friend, on the other hand, does perform an action. And according to our interpretation of Kant, his action must have a maxim.

It would be implausible to maintain that before we act, we always consciously formulate the maxim of our action. Most of the time we simply go ahead and perform the action without giving any conscious thought to what we're doing, or what our situation is. We're usually too intent on getting the job done. Nevertheless, if we are asked after the fact, we often recognize that we actually were acting on a general policy, or maxim. For example, if you are taking a test, and you set about to answer each question correctly, you probably won't give any conscious thought to your maxim. You will be too busy thinking about the test. But if someone were to ask you to explain what you are doing and to explain the policy upon which you are doing it, you might then realize that in fact you have been acting a maxim. Your maxim might be, "Whenever I am taking an academic test, and I believe I know the correct answers, I shall give what I take to be the correct answers." So a person may act on a maxim even though she hasn't consciously entertained it.

In one respect, the maxim of an action may be inaccurate: it does not so much represent the actual situation of the action as it does the situation the agent takes himself to be in. Suppose, for example, that I have a lot of money in my savings

account but I have forgotten all about it. I take myself to be broke. When I go out to borrow some money from a friend, my maxim might be, "When I am broke and can get money in no other way, I shall borrow some from a friend." In this case, my maxim does not apply to my actual situation. For my actual situation is not one in which I am broke. Yet the maxim does apply to the situation I take myself to be in. For I believe that I am broke, and I believe that I can get money in no other way. So it is important to recognize that a maxim is a general policy statement that describes the sort of situation the agent takes himself to be in when he performs an action, and the sort of action he takes himself to be performing. In fact, both the situation and the action may be different from what the agent takes them to be.

Another point about maxims that should be recognized is this. Externally similar actions may in fact have radically different maxims. Here is an elaborated version of an example given by Kant that illustrates this point.[9] Suppose there are two grocers, Mr. Grimbley and Mr. Hughes. Mr. Grimbley's main goal in life is to get rich. After careful consideration, he has decided that in the long run he'll make more money if he gains a reputation for treating his customers fairly. In other words, he believes that "honesty is the best policy—because it pays." Hence, Mr. Grimbley scrupulously sees to it that every customer gets the correct change. When Mr. Grimbley gives correct change to a customer, he acts on this maxim:

M_1: When I can gain a good business reputation by giving correct change, I shall give correct change.

Mr. Hughes, on the other hand, has decided that it would be morally wrong to cheat his customers. This decision has moved him to adopt the policy of always giving the correct change. He doesn't care whether his honest dealings will in the long run contribute to an increase in sales. Even if he were to discover that honesty in business dealings does *not* pay, he would still treat his customers honestly. So Mr. Hughes apparently acts on some maxim such as this:

M₂: When I can perform a morally right act by giving correct change, I shall give correct change.

Mr. Grimbley's overt act of giving correct change to a customer looks just like Mr. Hughes's overt act of giving correct change to a customer. Their customers cannot tell, no matter how closely they observe the behavior of Mr. Grimbley and Mr. Hughes, what their maxims are. However, as we have seen, the actions of Mr. Grimbley are associated with a maxim radically different from that associated with the actions of Mr. Hughes.

For our purposes, it will be useful to introduce a concept that Kant does not employ. This is the concept of the *generalized form* of a maxim. Suppose I decide to go to sleep one night and my maxim in performing this act is this:

M₃: Whenever I am tired, I shall sleep.

My maxim is stated in such a way as to contain explicit references to me. It contains two occurrences of the word "I." The generalized form of my maxim is the principle we would get if we were to revise my maxim so as to make it applicable to everyone. Thus, the generalized form of my maxim is this:

GM₃: Whenever anyone is tired, he will sleep.

In general, then, we can represent the form of a maxim in this way:

M: Whenever I am ⸺, I shall ⸺.

Actual maxims have descriptions of situations in the first blank and descriptions of actions in the second blank. The generalized form of a maxim can be represented in this way:

GM: Whenever anyone is ⸺, she will ⸺.

So much, then, for maxims. Let us turn to our second question, "What is meant by universal law?"

Universal Law

When, in the formulation of the categorical imperative, Kant speaks of "universal law," he seems to have one or the other of two things in mind. Sometimes he seems to be thinking of a *universal law of nature*, and sometimes he seems to be thinking of a *universal law of freedom*.

A *law of nature* is a fully general statement that describes not only how things are, but how things always *must* be. Consider this example: If the temperature of a gas in an enclosed container is increased, then the pressure will increase too. This statement accurately describes the behavior of gases in enclosed containers. Beyond this, however, it describes behavior that is, in a certain sense, necessary. The pressure not only *does* increase, but it *must* increase if the volume remains the same and the temperature is increased. This "must" expresses not logical or moral necessity, but "physical necessity." Thus, a law of nature is a fully general statement that expresses a physical necessity.

A *universal law of freedom* is a universal principle describing how all people ought to act in a certain circumstance. It does not have to be a legal enactment—it needn't be passed by Congress or signed by the president. Furthermore, some universal laws of freedom are not always followed—although they should be. If in fact it is true that all promises ought to be kept, then this principle is a universal law of freedom: If anyone has made a promise, he keeps it. The "must" in a statement such as "If you have made a promise, then you must keep it" does not express logical or physical necessity. It may be said to express moral necessity. Using this concept of moral necessity, we can say that a universal law of freedom is a fully general statement that expresses a moral necessity.

Sometimes Kant's categorical imperative is stated in terms of universal laws of nature, and sometimes in terms of universal laws of freedom. We will consider the "law of nature" version, since Kant appeals to it in discussing some fairly important examples.

Willing

To will that something be the case is more than to merely wish for it to be the case. A person might wish that there would be peace everywhere in the world. Yet knowing that it is not within his power to bring about this wished-for state of affairs, he might refrain from willing that there be peace everywhere in the world. It is not easy to say just what a person does when he wills that something be the case. According to one view, willing that something be the case is something like commanding yourself to make it be the case. So if I will my arm to go up, that would be something like commanding myself to raise my arm. The Kantian concept of willing is a bit more complicated, however. According to Kant, it makes sense to speak of willing something to happen, even if that something is not an action. For example, we can speak of someone willing that everyone keep their promises.

Some states of affairs are impossible. They simply cannot occur. For example, consider the state of affairs of your jumping up and down while remaining perfectly motionless. It simply cannot be done. Yet a sufficiently foolish or irrational person might will that such a state of affairs occur. That would be as absurd as commanding someone else to jump up and down while remaining motionless. Kant would say of a person who has willed in this way that his will has "contradicted itself." We can also put the point by saying that the person has willed inconsistently.

Inconsistency in willing can arise in another, somewhat less obvious way. Suppose a person has already willed that he remain motionless. He does not change this volition, but persists in willing that he remain motionless. At the same time, however, he begins to will that he jump up and down. Although each volition is self-consistent, it is inconsistent to will both of them at the same

time. This is a second way in which inconsistency in willing can arise.

It may be the case that there are certain things that everyone must always will. For example, we may have to will that we avoid intense pain. Anyone who wills something that is inconsistent with something everyone must will, thereby wills inconsistently.

Some of Kant's examples suggest that he held that inconsistency in willing can arise in a third way. This form of inconsistency is a bit more complex to describe. Suppose a person wills to be in Boston on Monday and also wills to be in San Francisco on Tuesday. Suppose, furthermore, that because of certain foul-ups at the airport it will be impossible for her to get from Boston to San Francisco on Tuesday. In this case, Kant would perhaps say that the person has willed inconsistently.

In general, we can say that a person wills inconsistently if he wills that p be the case and he wills that q be the case and it is impossible for p and q to be the case together.

The Categorical Imperative

With all this as background, we may be in a position to interpret the first version of Kant's categorical imperative. Our interpretation is this:

CI_1: An act is morally right if and only if the agent of the act can consistently will that the generalized form of the maxim of the act can be a law of nature.

We can simplify our formulation slightly by introducing a widely used technical term. We can say that a maxim is *universalizable* if and only if the agent who acts upon it can consistently will that its generalized form be a law of nature. Making use of this new term, we can restate our first version of the categorical imperative as follows:

CI_1': An act is morally right if and only if its maxim is universalizable.

As formulated here, the categorical imperative is a statement of necessary and sufficient conditions for the moral rightness of actions. Some commentators have claimed that Kant did not intend his principle to be understood in this way. They have suggested that Kant meant it to be understood merely as a necessary but not sufficient condition for morally right action. Thus, they would prefer to formulate the imperative in some way such as this:

CI₁'': An act is morally right only if its maxim is universalizable.

Understood in this way, the categorical imperative points out one thing to avoid in action. That is, it tells us to avoid actions whose maxims cannot be universalized. But it does not tell us the distinguishing feature of the actions we should perform. Thus, it does not provide us with a criterion of morally right action. Since Kant explicitly affirms that his principle is "the supreme principle of morality," it is reasonable to suppose that he intended it to be taken as a statement of necessary and sufficient conditions for morally right action. In any case, we will take the first version of the categorical imperative to be CI₁, rather than CI₁''.

It is interesting to note that other commentators have claimed that the categorical imperative isn't a criterion of right action at all. They have claimed that it was intended to be understood as a criterion of correctness for *maxims*.[10] These commentators might formulate the principle in this way:

CI₁''': A maxim is normally acceptable if and only if it is universalizable.

This interpretation is open to a variety of objections. In the first place, it is not supported by the text. Kant repeatedly states that the categorical imperative is the basic principle by which we are to evaluate actions.[11] Furthermore, when he presents his formulations of the categorical imperative, he generally states it as a principle about the moral rightness of action. Finally, it is some-

what hard to see why we should be interested in a principle such as CI₁'''. For it does not constitute a theory about right action, or good persons, or anything else that has traditionally been a subject of moral enquiry. CI₁, on the other hand, competes directly with act-utilitarianism, rule-utilitarianism, and other classical moral theories.

In order to gain a better insight into the workings of the categorical imperative, it may be worthwhile to compare it with a doctrine with which it is sometimes confused—the golden rule. The golden rule has been formulated in a wide variety of ways.[12] Generally, however, it looks something like this:

GR: An act is morally right if and only if, in performing it, the agent refrains from treating others in ways in which he would not want the others to treat him.

According to GR, then, if you wouldn't want others to lie to you, it is wrong to lie to them. If you would want others to treat you with respect, then it is right to treat others with respect.

Kant explicitly rejects the view that his categorical imperative is equivalent to the golden rule.[13] He points out a number of respects in which the two doctrines differ. For one, GR is not applicable to cases in which only one person is involved. Consider suicide. When a person commits suicide, he does not "treat others" in any way; he only "treats himself." Hence, when a person commits suicide, he does not treat others in ways in which he would not want the others to treat him. Therefore, under GR, anyone who commits suicide performs a morally right act. CI₁, on the other hand, may not yield this result. For if a person commits suicide, he does so on a maxim, whether other people are involved or not. Either his maxim is universalizable, or it is not. If it is not, CI₁ entails that his action is not right. If it is, CI₁ entails that his action is right. In this respect, CI₁ is clearly distinct from GR.

Kant also hints at another respect in which the two doctrines differ. Suppose a person considers herself to be utterly self-sufficient. She feels that she has no need of aid from others. GR then has nothing to say against her refraining from extending any kindness to others. After all, she has no objection to being treated in this unkind way by them. So GR entails that her behavior is morally right. CI_1, on the other hand, has no such consequence. Whether this person is willing to be mistreated by others or not, it may still be irrational of her to will that it be a law of nature that no one help anyone else. If so, CI_1 rules out uncharitableness, whether the agent likes it or not.

Similar considerations apply to masochists, whose behavior is not adequately guided by GR. After all, we surely don't want to allow the masochist to torture others simply on the grounds that he wouldn't object to being tortured by them! The unusual desires of masochists do not pose any special threat to CI_1.

So the main difference between GR and CI_1 seems to be this: According to GR, what makes an act right is the fact that the agent would not object to "having it done to himself." This opens the door to incorrect results in cases in which the agent, for some unexpected reason, would not object to being mistreated. According to CI_1, what makes an act right is the fact that the agent's maxim in performing it can be universalized. Thus, even if he would not object to being mistreated by others, his mistreatment of them may be wrong simply because it would be *irrational* to will that everyone should mistreat others in the same way.

Kant's Four Examples

In a very famous passage in chapter 2 of the *Groundwork*, Kant presents four illustrations of the application of the categorical imperative.[14] In each case, in Kant's opinion, the act is morally wrong and the maxim is not universalizable. Thus, Kant holds that his theory implies that each of these acts is wrong. If Kant is right about this, then he has given us four positive instances of his theory. That is, he has given us four cases in which his theory yields correct results. Un-

fortunately, the illustrations are not entirely persuasive.

Kant distinguishes between "duties to self" and "duties to others." He also distinguishes between "perfect" and "imperfect" duties. This gives him four categories of duty: "perfect to self," "perfect to others," "imperfect to self," and "imperfect to others." Kant gives one example of each type of duty. By "perfect duty," Kant says he means a duty "which admits of no exception in the interests of inclination."[15] Kant seems to have in mind something like this: If a person has a perfect duty to perform a certain kind of action, then he must *always* do that kind of action when the opportunity arises. For example, Kant apparently holds that we must always perform the (negative) action of refraining from committing suicide. This would be a perfect duty. On the other hand, if a person has an imperfect duty to do a kind of action, then he must at least *sometimes* perform an action of that kind when the opportunity arises. For example, Kant maintains that we have an imperfect duty to help others in distress. We should devote at least some of our time to charitable activities, but we are under no obligation to give all of our time to such work.

The perfect/imperfect distinction has been drawn in a variety of ways—none of them entirely clear. Some commentators have said that if a person has a perfect duty to do a certain action, *a*, then there must be someone else who has a corresponding right to demand that *a* be done. This seems to be the case in Kant's second example, but not in his first example. Thus, it isn't clear that we should understand the concept of perfect duty in this way. Although the perfect/imperfect distinction is fairly interesting in itself, it does not play a major role in Kant's theory. Kant introduces the distinction primarily to insure that his examples will illustrate different kinds of duty.

Kant's first example illustrates the application of CI_1 to a case of perfect duty to oneself—the alleged duty to refrain from committing suicide. Kant describes the miserable state of the person contemplating suicide, and tries to show that his categorical imperative entails that the person should not take his own life. In order to simplify our discussion, let us use the abbreviation "a_1" to refer to the act of suicide the man would commit, if he were to commit suicide. According to Kant, every act must have a maxim. Kant tells us the maxim of a_1: "From self-love I make it my principle to shorten my life if its continuance threatens more evil than it promises pleasure."[16] Let us simplify and clarify this maxim, understanding it as follows:

M(a_1): When continuing to live will bring me more pain than pleasure, I shall commit suicide out of self-love.

The generalized form of this maxim is as follows:

GM(a_1): Whenever continuing to live will bring anyone more pain than pleasure, he will commit suicide out of self-love.

Since Kant believes that suicide is wrong, he attempts to show that his moral principle, the categorical imperative, entails that a_1 is wrong. To do this, of course, he needs to show that the agent of a_1 cannot consistently will that GM(a_1) be a law of nature. Kant tries to show this in the following passage:

. . . a system of nature by whose law the very same feeling whose function is to stimulate the furtherance of life should actually destroy life would contradict itself and consequently could not subsist as a system of nature. Hence this maxim cannot possibly hold as a universal law of nature and is therefore entirely opposed to the supreme principle of all duty.[17]

The general outline of Kant's argument is clear enough:

Suicide Example

1. GM(a_1) cannot be a law of nature.
2. If GM(a_1) cannot be a law of nature, then the agent of a_1 cannot consistently will that GM(a_1) be a law of nature.
3. a_1 is morally right if and only if the agent of a_1 can consistently will that GM(a_1) be a law of nature.
4. Therefore, a_1 is not morally right.

In order to determine whether Kant really has shown that his theory entails that a_1 is not right, let us look at this argument more closely. First of all, for our purposes we can agree that the argument is valid. If all the premises are true, then the argument shows that the imagined act of suicide would not be right. CI_1, here being used as premise (3), would thus be shown to imply that a_1 is not right.

Since we are now interested primarily in seeing how Kant makes use of CI_1, we can withhold judgment on the merits of it for the time being.

The second premise seems fairly plausible. For although an irrational person could probably will almost anything, it surely would be difficult for a perfectly rational person to will that something be a law of nature if that thing could not be a law of nature. Let us grant, then, that it would not be possible for the agent to consistently will that GM(a_1) be a law of nature if in fact GM(a_1) could not be a law of nature.

The first premise is the most troublesome. Kant apparently assumes that "self-love" has as its function, the stimulation of the furtherance of life. Given this, he seems to reason that self-love cannot also contribute sometimes to the destruction of life. Perhaps Kant assumes that a given feeling cannot have two "opposite" functions. However, if GM(a_1) were a law of nature, self-love would have to contribute toward self-destruction in some cases. Hence, Kant seems to conclude, GM(a_1) cannot be a law of nature. And so we have our first premise.

If this is Kant's reasoning, it is not very impressive. In the first place, it is not clear why we should suppose that self-love has the function of stimulating the furtherance of life. Indeed, it is not clear why we should suppose that self-love has any function at all! Second, it is hard to see why self-love can't serve two "opposite" functions. Perhaps self-love motivates us to stay alive when continued life would be pleasant, but motivates us to stop living when continued life would be unpleasant. Why should we hold this to be impossible?

So it appears that Kant's first illustration is not entirely successful. Before we turn to the second illustration, however, a few further comments may be in order. First, some philosophers would say that it is better that Kant's argument failed here. Many moralists would take the following position: Kant's view about suicide is wrong. The act of suicide out of self-love, a_1, is morally blameless. In certain circumstances suicide is each person's "own business." Thus, these moralists would say that if the categorical imperative did imply that a_1 is morally wrong, as Kant tries to show, then Kant's theory would be defective. But since Kant was not entirely successful in showing that his theory had this implication, the theory has not been shown to have any incorrect results.

A second point to notice about the suicide example is its scope. It is important to recognize that in this passage Kant has not attempted to show that suicide is always wrong. Perhaps Kant's personal view is that it is never right to commit suicide. However, in the passage in question he attempts to show only that a certain act of suicide, one based on a certain maxim, would be wrong. For all Kant has said here, other acts of suicide, done according to other maxims, might be permitted by the categorical imperative.

Let us turn now to the second illustration. Suppose I find myself hard-pressed financially and I decide that the only way in which I can get some money is by borrowing it from a friend. I realize that I will have to promise to repay the money, even though I won't in fact be able to do so. For I foresee that my financial situation will be even worse later on than it is at present. If I perform this action, a_2, of borrowing money on a false promise, I will perform it on this maxim:

$M(a_2)$: When I need money and can get some by borrowing it on a false promise, then I shall borrow the money and promise to repay, even though I know that I won't be able to repay.

The generalized form of my maxim is this:

$GM(a_2)$: Whenever anyone needs money and can get some by borrowing it on a false promise, then he will borrow the money and promise to repay, even though he knows that he won't be able to repay.

Kant's view is that I cannot consistently will that $GM(a_2)$ be a law of nature. This view emerges clearly in the following passage:

. . . I can by no means will a universal law of lying; for by such a law there could properly be no promises at all, since it would be futile to profess will for future action to others who would not believe my profession or who, if they did so overhastily, would pay me back in like coin; and consequently my maxim, as soon as it was made a universal law, would be bound to annul itself.[18]

It is important to be clear about what Kant is saying here. He is not arguing against lying on the grounds that if I lie, others will soon lose confidence in me and eventually won't believe my promises. Nor is he arguing against lying on the grounds that my lie will contribute to a general practice of lying, which in turn will lead to a breakdown of trust and the destruction of the practice of promising. These considerations are basically utilitarian. Kant's point is more subtle. He is saying that there is something covertly self-contradictory about the state of affairs in which, as a law of nature, everyone makes a false promise when in need of a loan. Perhaps Kant's point is this: Such a state of affairs is self-contradictory because, on the one hand, in such a state of affairs everyone in need would borrow money on a false promise, and yet, on the other hand, in that state of affairs no one could borrow money on a false promise—for if promises were always violated, who would be silly enough to loan any money?

Since the state of affairs in which everyone in need borrows money on a false promise is covertly self-contradictory, it is irrational to will it to occur. No one can consistently will that this state of affairs should occur. But for me to will that $GM(a_2)$ be a law of nature is just for me to will that this impossible state of affairs occur. Hence, I cannot consistently will that the generalized form of my maxim be a law of nature. According to CI_1, my act is not right unless I can consistently will that the generalized form of its maxim be a law of nature. Hence, according to CI_1, my act of borrowing the money on the false promise is not morally right.

We can restate the essentials of this argument much more succinctly:

Lying-Promise Example

1. $GM(a_2)$ cannot be a law of nature.
2. If $GM(a_2)$ cannot be a law of nature, then I cannot consistently will that $GM(a_2)$ be a law of nature.
3. a_2 is morally right if and only if I can consistently will that $GM(a_2)$ be a law of nature.
4. Therefore, a_2 is not morally right.

The first premise is based upon the view that it would somehow be self-contradictory for it to be a law of nature that everyone in need makes a lying promise. For in that (allegedly impossible) state of affairs there would be promises, since those in need would make them, and there would also not be promises, since no one would believe that anyone was really committing himself to future payment by the use of the words "I promise." So, as Kant says, the generalized form of the maxim "annuls itself." It cannot be a law of nature.

The second premise is just like the second premise in the previous example. It is based on the idea that it is somehow irrational to will that something be the case if in fact it is impossible

for it to be the case. So if it really is impossible for $GM(a_2)$ to be a law of nature, then it would be irrational of me to will that it be so. Hence, I cannot consistently will that the generalized form of my maxim be a law of nature. In other words, I cannot consistently will that it be a law of nature that whenever anyone needs money and can get some on a false promise, then he will borrow some and promise to repay, even though he knows that he won't be able to repay.

The third premise of the argument is the categorical imperative. If the rest of the argument is acceptable, then the argument as a whole shows that the categorical imperative, together with these other facts, implies that my lying promise would not be morally right. This would seem to be a reasonable result.

Some readers have apparently taken this example to show that according to Kantianism, it is always wrong to make a false promise. Indeed, Kant himself may have come to this conclusion. Yet if we reflect on the argument for a moment, we will see that the view of these readers is surely not the case. At best, the argument shows only that one specific act of making a false promise would be wrong. That one act is judged to be wrong because its maxim allegedly cannot be universalized. Other acts of making false promises would have to be evaluated independently. Perhaps it will turn out that every act of making a false promise has a maxim that cannnot be universalized. If so, CI_1 would imply that they are all wrong. So far, however, we have been given no reason to suppose that this is the case.

Other critics would insist that Kant hasn't even succeeded in showing that a_2 is morally wrong. They would claim that the first premise of the argument is false. Surely it could be a law of nature that everyone will make a false promise when in need of money, they would say. If people borrowed money on false promises rarely enough, and kept their word on other promises, then no contradiction would arise. There would then be no reason to support that "no one would believe he was being promised anything, but would laugh at utterances of this kind as empty shams."[19]

Let us turn, then, to the third example. Kant now illustrates the application of the categorical imperative to a case of imperfect duty to oneself. The action in question is the "neglect of natural talents." Kant apparently holds that it is wrong for a person to let all of his natural talents go to waste. Of course, if a person has several natural talents, he is not required to develop all of them. Perhaps Kant considers this to be an imperfect duty partly because a person has the freedom to select which talents he will develop and which he will allow to rust.

Kant imagines the case of someone who is comfortable as he is and who, out of laziness, contemplates performing that act, a_3, or letting all his talents rust. His maxim in doing this would be:

$M(a_3)$: When I am comfortable as I am, I shall let my talents rust.

When generalized, the maxim becomes:

$GM(a_3)$: Whenever anyone is comfortable as he is, he will let his talents rust.

Kant admits that $GM(a_3)$ could be a law of nature. Thus, his argument in this case differs from the arguments he produced in the first two cases. Kant proceeds to outline the reasoning by which the agent would come to see that it would be wrong to perform a_3:

He then sees that a system of nature could indeed always subsist under such a universal law, although (like the South Sea Islanders) every man should let his talents rust and should be bent on devoting his life solely to idleness, indulgence, procreation, and, in a word, to enjoyment. Only he cannot possibly *will* that this should become a universal law of nature or should be implanted in us as such a law by a natural instinct. For as a rational being he necessarily wills that all his powers should be developed, since they serve him, and are given him, for all sorts of possible ends.[20]

Once again, Kant's argument seems to be based on a rather dubious appeal to natural purposes. Allegedly, nature implanted our talents in us for all sorts of purposes. Hence, we necessarily will to develop them. If we also will to let them rust, we are willing both to develop them (as we must) and to refrain from developing them. Anyone who wills both of these things obviously wills inconsistently. Hence, the agent cannot consistently will that his talents rust. This, together with the categorical imperative, implies that it would be wrong to perform the act, a_3, of letting one's talents rust.

The argument can be put as follows:

Rusting-Talents Example

1. Everyone necessarily wills that all his talents be developed.
2. If everyone necessarily wills that all his talents be developed, then the agent of a_3 cannot consistently will that $GM(a_3)$ be a law of nature.
3. a_3 is morally right if and only if the agent of a_3 can consistently will that $GM(a_3)$ be a law of nature.
4. Therefore a_3 is not morally right.

This argument seems even less persuasive than the others. In the quoted passage Kant himself presents a counterexample to the first premise. The South Sea Islanders, according to Kant, do not will to develop their talents. This fact, if it is one, is surely inconsistent with the claim that we all necessarily will that all our talents be developed. Even if Kant is wrong about the South Sea Islanders, his first premise is still extremely implausible. Couldn't there be a rational person who, out of idleness, simply does not will to develop his talents? If there could not be such a person, then what is the point of trying to show that we are under some specifically moral obligation to develop all our talents?

Once again, however, some philosophers may feel that Kant would have been worse off if his example had succeeded. These philosophers would hold that we in fact have no moral obligation to develop our talents. If Kant's theory had entailed that we have such an obligation, they would insist, then that would have shown that Kant's theory is defective.

In Kant's fourth illustration the categorical imperative is applied to an imperfect duty to others—the duty to help others who are in distress. Kant describes a man who is flourishing and who contemplates performing the act, a_4, of giving nothing to charity. His maxim is not stated by Kant in this passage, but it can probably be formulated as follows:

$M(a_4)$: When I'm flourishing and others are in distress, I shall give nothing to charity.

When generalized, this maxim becomes:

$GM(a_4)$: Whenever anyone is flourishing and others are in distress, he will give nothing to charity.

As in the other example of imperfect duty, Kant acknowledges that $GM(a_4)$ could be a law of nature. Yet he claims once again that the agent cannot consistently will that it be a law of nature. He explains this by arguing as follows:

For a will which decided in this way would be in conflict with itself, since many a situation might arise in which the man needed love and sympathy from others, and in which, by such a law of nature sprung from his own will, he would rob himself of all hope of the help he wants for himself.[21]

Kant's point here seems to be this: The day may come when the agent is no longer flourishing. He may need charity from others. If that day does come, then he will find that he wills that others give him such aid. However, in willing that $GM(a_4)$ be a law of nature, he has already willed that no one should give charitable aid to anyone. Hence, on that dark day, his will will contradict itself. Thus, he cannot consistently will that $GM(a_4)$ be a law of nature. This being so, the categorical imperative entails that a_4 is not right.

If this is Kant's reasoning, then his reasoning is defective. For we cannot infer from the fact that the person *may* someday want aid from others, that he in fact already is willing inconsistently when he wills today that no one should give aid to anyone. The main reason for this is that that dark day may not come, in which case no conflict will arise. Furthermore, as is pretty obvious upon reflection, even if that dark day does arrive, the agent may steadfastly stick to his general policy. He may say, "I didn't help others when they were in need, and now that I'm in need I don't want any help from them." In this way, he would avoid having inconsistent policies. Unless this attitude is irrational, which it does not seem to be, Kant's fourth example is unsuccessful.

More Examples

It should be clear, then, that Kant has not provided us with a clear, persuasive example of the application of the categorical imperative. In light of this, some may feel that the categorical imperative is a worthless doctrine. Such a harsh judgment would probably be premature. For in the first place, Kant surely would have been worse off if he had succeeded in showing that suicide, or letting your talents rust, are invariably wrong. The normative status of these acts is hardly as obvious as Kant suggests. In the second place, the failure of Kant's illustrations may be due in part to his choice of some rather strange maxims, and to the fact that he presupposed some questionable views about the purposes of nature. Let us attempt to develop a more plausible illustration of the application of the categorical imperative.

In attempting to develop such an example, we should turn to the sort of case in which the categorical imperative stands the greatest chance of working correctly. This would be a case in which an agent proposes to take unfair advantage of his neighbors. It would be a case in which others, out of regard for the common good, have generously refrained from performing a certain kind of act, even though many of them might like to do such an act. Our agent, however, finds that he can get away with the act. The crucial feature of this case is that the agent cannot consistently will that the others act in the way he proposes to act. For if they all were to try to act in this way, that would destroy his opportunity for so acting.

Here is a good example of this sort of case. Primarily out of laziness, Miss Perkins, a college student, buys a term paper for her ethics course and submits it as her own work. Miss Perkins deals with a skillful term paper manufacturer, so she is assured of getting a very high grade. There is no chance that she will be found out. Most of us would say that regardless of its utility, Miss Perkins's act is morally wrong. She should not deceive her instructor and take advantage of her fellow students in this way. What does the categorical imperative say?

Let us call Miss Perkins's act of submitting the phoney term paper "a_5," and let us suppose that her maxim in performing a_5 is:

$M(a_5)$: When I need a term paper for a course and don't feel like writing one, I shall buy a term paper and submit it as my own work.

The generalized form of her maxim is:

$GM(a_5)$: Whenever anyone needs a term paper for a course and doesn't feel like writing one, she will buy one and submit it as her own work.

According to Kant's doctrine, a_5 is morally right only if Miss Perkins can consistently will that $GM(a_5)$ be a law of nature. So to see if a_5 is right, we must determine whether Miss Perkins can consistently will that everyone needing a term paper but not feeling like writing one should submit a store-bought one.

It is reasonable to suppose that Miss Perkins cannot will that $GM(a_5)$ be a law of nature. For consider what would happen if $GM(a_5)$ were a law of nature, and everyone needing a term paper but not feeling like writing one were therefore to submit a store-bought one. Clearly, college instructors would soon realize that they were reading work not produced by their students. The instruc-

tors would have to deal with the problem—perhaps by resorting to a system under which each student would be required to take a final oral exam instead of submitting a term paper. If some such alteration in the course requirements were instituted, Miss Perkins would lose her opportunity to get a good grade by cheating. Thus, she surely does not will that any such change in the system should occur. She prefers to have the system remain as it is. Since it is clear that some such change would occur if $GM(a_5)$ were a law of nature, Miss Perkins cannot consistently will that $GM(a_5)$ be a law of nature. Thus, according to CI_1, her act is not right.

The essentials of this example are simple. Miss Perkins wills that the system remain as it is—thus providing her with the opportunity to take advantage of her instructor and her fellow students. She recognizes that if everyone were to submit a store-bought term paper, the system would be changed. Hence, she cannot consistently will that everyone should submit a store-bought term paper. In other words, she cannot consistently will that $GM(a_5)$ be a law of nature. CI_1, together with this fact, entails that a_5 is morally wrong.

One of the most troubling aspects of this example is that it is pretty easy to see how the categorical imperative can be short-circuited. That is, it is pretty easy to see how Miss Perkins can make Kant's doctrine yield the result that her act is morally right. She needs only to change her maxim in a fairly trivial way:

$M(a_6)$: When I need a term paper for a course, and I don't feel like writing one, and no change in the system will occur if I submit a store-bought one, then I shall buy a term paper and submit it as my own work.

$M(a_6)$ differs from $M(a_5)$ in only one respect. $M(a_6)$ contains the extra phrase "and no change in the system will occur if I submit a store-bought one." But this little addition makes a big difference to the argument. We found that Miss Perkins could not consistently will that $GM(a_5)$ be a law of nature. For if she willed that $GM(a_5)$

be a law of nature, she would, indirectly, will that the system be changed. But she already willed that the system remain as it is. However, no such argument applies to $GM(a_6)$. For it appears that if $GM(a_6)$ were a law of nature, the system would not be changed. Apparently, then, Miss Perkins can consistently will that $GM(a_6)$ be a law of nature. Hence, according to CI_1, her act of submitting a store-bought term paper, if performed under $M(a_6)$ rather than under $M(a_5)$, would be morally acceptable. This seems wrong.

The categorical imperative, interpreted as CI_1, yields incorrect results in another sort of case too. Consider a man who has a large amount of money in a savings account. He decides that he will wait until the Stock Market Index reaches 1000 and then take all of his money out of the bank. This act seems quite acceptable from the moral point of view. However, it seems that CI_1 yields the odd result that the act is morally wrong. Let us consider why this is so.

We can call the man's act of removing his money from the bank "a_7." The maxim of a_7 is:

$M(a_7)$: When the Stock Market Index reaches 1000, I shall withdraw all my money from the bank.

The generalized form of $M(a_7)$ is:

$GM(a_7)$: Whenever the Stock Market Index reaches 1000, everyone shall withdraw all of their money from the bank.

It should be clear that the man cannot consistently will that $GM(a_7)$ be a law of nature. For banks have loaned out most of the money deposited in them. If everyone came to withdraw their savings from their bank, banks would soon run out of money. Not everyone can withdraw simultaneously. Hence, $GM(a_7)$ cannot be a law of nature. Thus, the agent cannot consistently will that it be so. CI_1 entails, together with this fact, that it would not be right for the man to withdraw his own money under this maxim. Surely, there is something wrong with a moral theory that has this result.

This same problem arises in any number of cases. Whenever, for some irrelevant reason, an otherwise innocent maxim cannot be universalized, CI_1 yields the result that the act is wrong. So if a person acts on the maxim, for example, of not becoming a doctor, he acts wrongly. For he surely could not will that *everyone* should refrain from becoming a doctor. As a rational being, he recognizes that there must be some doctors. Similarly, if a person acts on the maxim of always using adequate contraceptive devices when engaging in sexual intercourse, she acts wrongly, according to this interpretation of CI_1. For if everyone were to do what she does, there would soon be no human race at all. This, Kant would think, is something no rational agent can consistently will.

These absurd results show that there is a very deep problem with CI_1. The problem in general, is that there are many different reasons why a maxim may fail to be universalizable. Some of these reasons have nothing whatever to do with morality. Yet, as far as can be discerned from the text of the *Groundwork*, Kant nowhere attempts to distinguish between innocent-but-nonuniversalizable maxims, on the one hand, and evil-and-nonuniversalizable ones, on the other. Without such a distinction, CI_1 yields obviously incorrect results in innumerable cases.

So we can conclude that there are very serious problems with CI_1. Perhaps CI_1 is not an adequate interpretation of Kant's categorical imperative. Perhaps a more adequate version of that doctrine would not have these unsatisfactory results. However, if CI_1 is not Kant's theory, then it is very hard to see what Kant's theory might be.

Notes

1. Immanuel Kant (1724–1804) is one of the greatest Continental philosophers. He produced quite a few philosophical works of major importance. The *Critique of Pure Reason* (1781) is perhaps his most famous work.
2. Kant's *Grundlegung zur Metaphysik der Sitten* (1785) has been translated into English many times. All refer-

ences here are to Immanuel Kant, *Groundwork of the Metaphysic of Morals,* translated and analysed by H. J. Paton (New York: Harper & Row, 1964).

3. Kant, *Groundwork,* p. 70.

4. *Ibid.,* p. 88.

5. *Ibid.,* p. 89.

6. *Ibid.,* p. 91.

7. *Ibid.,* p. 69n.

8. In some unusual cases, it may accidentally happen that the situation to which the maxim applies can occur only once, as, for example, in the case of successful suicide. Nevertheless, the maxim is general in form.

9. Kant, *Groundwork,* p. 65.

10. See, for example, Robert Paul Wolff, *The Autonomy of Reason* (New York: Harper & Row, 1973), p. 163.

11. This is stated especially clearly on p. 107 of the *Groundwork.*

12. For an interesting discussion of various formulations of the golden rule, see Marcus Singer, "The Golden Rule," in Paul Edwards, ed. *The Encyclopedia of Philosophy* (New York: Macmillan; Free Press, 1967), Vol. 3, pp. 365–67.

13. Kant, *Groundwork,* p. 97n.

14. *Ibid.,* p. 89–91.

15. *Ibid.,* p. 89n.

16. *Ibid.,* p. 89.

17. *Ibid.*

18. *Ibid.,* p. 71.

19. *Ibid.*

20. *Ibid.*

21. *Ibid.,* p. 91.

24

What Makes Right Acts Right?

W. D. ROSS

A biographical sketch of W. D. Ross appears at the beginning of selection 15. Ross argues against utilitarianism, asserting that optimal consequences have nothing to do with moral rightness or wrongness. We have intuitive knowledge of rightness and wrongness in terms of action-guiding principles, such as to keep promises made, to promote justice, to show gratitude for benefits rendered, and to refrain from harming others. Unlike Kant's principles, however, these principles are not absolutes, that is, duties that must never be overridden. On the contrary, putative moral duties may be overridden by more binding moral duties. Moral principles are prima facie duties. That is, while their intrinsic value is not dependent on circumstances, their application is. They can be overridden by other prima facie duties. So, for example, our prima facie duty to tell the truth will be overridden by another prima facie duty to save an innocent life in a situation in which a murderer asks us where his intended victim is hiding. Essentially, these principles are the outcomes of generations of reflection, and their holistic schema has been internalized within us, so that ultimately, as Aristotle said, the "decision lies in the perception."

. . . A . . . theory has been put forward by Professor Moore that what makes actions right is that they are productive of more *good* than could have been produced by any other action open to the agent.

This theory is in fact the culmination of all the attempts to base rightness on productivity of some sort of result. The first form this attempt takes is the attempt to base rightness on condu-

Reprinted by permission of Hackett Publishing Company from W. D. Ross, *The Right and the Good*, first published by The Clarendon Press, Oxford, 1930.

civeness to the advantage or pleasure of the agent. This theory comes to grief over the fact, which stares us in the face, that a great part of duty consists in an observance of the rights and a furtherance of the interests of others, whatever the cost to ourselves may be. Plato and others may be right in holding that a regard for the rights of others never in the long run involves a loss of happiness for the agent, that 'the just life profits a man.' But this, even if true, is irrelevant to the rightness of the act. As soon as a man does an action *because* he thinks he will promote his own interests thereby, he is acting not from a sense of its rightness but from self-interest.

To the egoistic theory hedonistic utilitarianism supplies a much-needed amendment. It points out correctly that the fact that a certain pleasure will be enjoyed by the agent is no reason why he *ought* to bring it into being, rather than an equal or greater pleasure to be enjoyed by another, though, human nature being what it is, it makes it not unlikely that he *will* try to bring it into being. But hedonistic utilitarianism in its turn needs a correction. On reflection it seems clear that pleasure is not the only thing in life that we think good in itself, that for instance we think the possession of a good character, or an intelligent understanding of the world, as good or better. A great advance is made by the substitution of 'productive of the greatest good' for 'productive of the greatest pleasure.'

Not only is this theory more attractive than hedonistic utilitarianism, but its logical relation to that theory is such that the latter could not be true unless *it* were true, while it might be true though hedonistic utilitarianism were not. It is in fact one of the logical bases of hedonistic utilitarianism. For the view that what produces the maximum pleasure is right has for its bases the views (1) that what produces the maximum good is right, and (2) that pleasure is the only thing good in itself. If they were not assuming that what produces the maximum *good* is right, the utilitarians' attempt to show that pleasure is the only thing good in itself, which is in fact the point they take most pains to establish, would have been quite irrelevant to their attempt to prove that only what produces the maximum *pleasure* is right. If, therefore, it can be shown that productivity of the maximum good is not what makes all right actions right, we shall *a fortiori* have refuted hedonistic utilitarianism.

When a plain man fulfills a promise because he thinks he ought to do so, it seems clear that he does so with no thought of its total consequences, still less with any opinion that these are likely to be the best possible. He thinks in fact much more of the past than of the future. What makes him think it right to act in a certain way is the fact that he has promised to do so—that and, usually, nothing more. That his act will produce the best possible consequences is not his reason for calling it right. What lends colour to the theory we are examining, then, is not the actions (which form probably a great majority of our actions) in which some such reflection as 'I have promised' is the only reason we give ourselves for thinking a certain action right, but the exceptional cases in which the consequences of fulfilling a promise (for instance) would be so disastrous to others that we judge it right not to do so. It must of course be admitted that such cases exist. If I have promised to meet a friend at a particular time for some trivial purpose, I should certainly think myself justified in breaking my engagement if by doing so I could prevent a serious accident or bring relief to the victims of one. And the supporters of the view we are examining hold that my thinking so is due to my thinking that I shall bring more good into existence by the one action than by the other. A different account may, however, be given of the matter, an account which will, I believe, show itself to be the true one. It may be said

that besides the duty of fulfilling promises, I have and recognize a duty of relieving distress,[1] and that when I think it right to do the latter at the cost of not doing the former, it is not because I think I shall produce more good thereby but because I think it the duty which is in the circumstances more of a duty. This account surely corresponds much more closely with what we really think in such a situation. If, so far as I can see, I could bring equal amounts of good into being by fulfilling my promise and by helping someone to whom I had made no promise, I should not hesitate to regard the former as my duty. Yet on the view that what is right is right because it is productive of the most good I should not so regard it.

There are two theories, each in its way simple, that offer a solution of such cases of conscience. One is the view of Kant, that there are certain duties of perfect obligation, such as those of fulfilling promises, of paying debts, of telling the truth, which admit of no exception whatever in favour of duties of imperfect obligation, such as that of relieving distress. The other is the view of, for instance, Professor Moore and Dr. Rashdall, that there is only the duty of producing good, and that all 'conflicts of duties' should be resolved by asking 'By which action will most good be produced?' But it is more important that our theory fit the facts than that it be simple, and the account we have given above corresponds (it seems to me) better than either of the simpler theories with what we really think, viz. that normally promise-keeping, for example, should come before benevolence, but that when and only when the good to be produced by the benevolent act is very great and the promise comparatively trivial, the act of benevolence becomes our duty.

In fact the theory of 'ideal utilitarianism' if I may for brevity refer so to the theory of Professor Moore, seems to simplify unduly our relations to our fellows It says, in effect, that the only morally significant relation in which my neighbours stand to me is that of being possible beneficiaries by my action.[2] They do stand in this relation to me, and this relation is morally significant. But they may also stand to me in the relation of promisee to promiser, of creditor to debtor, of wife to husband, of child to parent, of friend to friend, of fellow countryman to fellow countryman, and the like; and each of these relations is the foundation of a *prima facie* duty which is more or less incumbent on me according to the circumstances of the case. When I am in a situation, as perhaps I always am, in which more than one of these *prima facie* duties is incumbent on me, what I have to do is to study the situation as fully as I can until I form the considered opinion (it is never more) that in the circumstances one of them is more incumbent than any other; then I am bound to think that to do this *prima facie* duty is my duty *sans phrase* in the situation.

I suggest '*prima facie* duty' or 'conditional duty' as a brief way of referring to the characteristic (quite distinct from that of being a duty proper) which an act has, in virtue of being of a certain kind (e.g., the keeping of a promise), of being an act which would be a duty proper if it were not at the same time of another kind which is morally significant. Whether an act is a duty proper or actual duty depends on *all* the morally significant kinds it is an instance of. The phrase '*prima facie* duty' must be apologized for, since (1) it suggests that what we are speaking of is a certain kind of duty, whereas it is in fact not a duty but something related in a special way to duty. Strictly speaking, we want not a phrase in which duty is qualified by an adjective, but a separate noun. (2) '*Prima' facie* suggests that one is speaking only of an appearance which a moral situation presents at first sight, and which may turn out to be illusory; whereas what I am speaking of is an objective fact involved in the nature of the situation, or more strictly in an element of its nature, though not, as duty proper does, arising from its *whole* nature. I can, however, think of no term which fully meets the case. 'Claim' has been suggested by Professor Prichard. The word 'claim' has the advantage of being quite a familiar one in

this connexion, and it seems to cover much of the ground. It would be quite natural to say, 'a person to whom I have made a promise has a claim on me,' and also, 'a person whose distress I could relieve (at the cost of breaking the promise) has a claim on me.' But (1) while 'claim' is appropriate from *their* point of view, we want a word to express the corresponding fact from the agent's point of view—the fact of his being subject to claims that can be made against him; and ordinary language provides us with no such correlative to 'claim.' And (2) (what is more important) 'claim' seems inevitably to suggest two persons, one of whom might make a claim on the other; and while this covers the ground of social duty, it is inappropriate in the case of that important part of duty which is the duty of cultivating a certain kind of character in oneself. It would be artificial, I think, and at any rate metaphorical, to say that one's character has a claim on oneself.

There is nothing arbitrary about these *prima facie* duties. Each rests on a definite circumstance which cannot seriously be held to be without moral significance. Of *prima facie* duties I suggest, without claiming completeness or finality for it, the following division.[3]

(1) Some duties rest on previous acts of my own. These duties seem to include two kinds, (*a*) those resting on a promise or what may fairly be called an implicit promise, such as the implicit undertaking not to tell lies which seems to be implied in the act of entering into conversation (at any rate by civilized men), or of writing books that purport to be history and not fiction. These may be called the duties of fidelity. (*b*) Those resting on a previous wrongful act. These may be called the duties of reparation. (2) Some rest on previous acts of other men, i.e. services done by them to me. These may be loosely described as the duties of gratitude. (3) Some rest on the fact or possibility of a distribution of pleasure or happiness (or of the means thereto) which is not in accordance with the merit of the persons concerned; in such cases there arises a duty to upset

or prevent such a distribution. These are the duties of justice. (4) Some rest on the mere fact that there are other beings in the world whose condition we can make better in respect of virtue, or of intelligence, or of pleasure. These are the duties of beneficence. (5) Some rest on the fact that we can improve our own condition in respect of virtue or of intelligence. These are the duties of self-improvement. (6) I think that we should distinguish from (4) the duties that may be summed up under the title of 'not injuring others.' No doubt to injure others is incidentally to fail to do them good; but it seems to me clear that non-maleficence is apprehended as a duty distinct from that of beneficence, and as a duty of a more stringent character. It will be noticed that this alone among the types of duty has been stated in a negative way. An attempt might no doubt be made to state this duty, like the others, in a positive way. It might be said that it is really the duty to prevent ourselves from acting either from an inclination to harm others or from an inclination to seek our own pleasure, in doing which we should incidentally harm them. But on reflection it seems clear that the primary duty here is the duty not to harm others, this being a duty whether or not we have an inclination that if followed would lead to our harming them; and that when we have such an inclination the primary duty not to harm others gives rise to a consequential duty to resist the inclination. The recognition of this duty of non-maleficence is the first step on the way to the recognition of the duty of beneficence; and that accounts for the prominence of the commands 'thou shalt not kill,' 'thou shalt not commit adultery,' 'thou shalt not steal,' 'thou shalt not bear false witness,' in so early a code as the Decalogue. But even when we have come to recognize the duty of beneficence, it appears to me that the duty of non-maleficence is recognized as a distinct one, and as *prima facie* more binding. We should not in general consider it justifiable to kill one person in order to keep another alive, or to steal from one in order to give alms to another.

The essential defect of the 'ideal utilitarian' theory is that it ignores, or at least does not do full justice to, the highly personal character of duty. If the only duty is to produce the maximum of good, the question who is to have the good—whether it is myself, or my benefactor, or a person to whom I have made a promise to confer that good on him, or a mere fellow man to whom I stand in no such special relation—should make no difference to my having a duty to produce that good. But we are all in fact sure that it makes a vast difference.

One or two other comments must be made on this provisional list of the divisions of duty. (1) The nomenclature is not strictly correct. For by 'fidelity' or 'gratitude' we mean, strictly, certain states of motivation; and, as I have urged, it is not our duty to have certain motives, but to do certain acts. By 'fidelity,' for instance, is meant, strictly, the disposition to fulfill promises and implicit promises *because we have made them*. We have no general word to cover the actual fulfillment of promises and implicit promises *irrespective of motive;* and I use 'fidelity,' loosely but perhaps conveniently, to fill this gap. So too I use 'gratitude' for the returning of services, irrespective of motive. The term 'justice' is not so much confined, in ordinary usage, to a certain state of motivation, for we should often talk of a man as acting justly even when we did not think his motive was the wish to do what was just simply for the sake of doing so. Less apology is therefore needed for our use of 'justice' in this sense. And I have used the word 'beneficence' rather than 'benevolence,' in order to emphasize the fact that it is our duty to do certain things, and not to do them from certain motives.

(2) If the objection be made that this catalogue of the main types of duty is an unsystematic one resting on no logical principle, it may be replied, first, that it makes no claim to being ultimate. It is a *prima facie* classification of the duties which reflection on our moral convictions seems actually to reveal. And if these convictions are, as I would

claim that they are, of the nature of knowledge, and if I have not misstated them, the list will be a list of authentic conditional duties, correct as far as it goes though not necessarily complete. The list of *goods* put forward by the rival theory is reached by exactly the same method—the only sound one in the circumstances—viz. that of direct reflection on what we really think. Loyalty to the facts is worth more than a symmetrical architectonic or a hastily reached simplicity. If further reflection discovers a perfect logical basis for this or for a better classification, so much the better.

(3) It may, again, be objected that our theory that there are these various and often conflicting types of *prima facie* duty leaves us with no principle upon which to discern what is our actual duty in particular circumstances. But this objection is not one which the rival theory is in a position to bring forward. For when we have to choose between the production of two heterogeneous goods, say knowledge and pleasure, the 'ideal utilitarian' theory can only fall back on an opinion, for which no logical basis can be offered, that one of the goods is the greater; and this is no better than a similar opinion that one of two duties is the more urgent. And again, when we consider the infinite variety of the effects of our actions in a way of pleasure, it must surely be admitted that the claim which *hedonism* sometimes makes, that it offers a readily applicable criterion of right conduct, is quite illusory.

I am unwilling, however, to content myself with an *argumentum ad hominem,* and I would contend that in principle there is no reason to anticipate that every act that is our duty is so for one and the same reason. Why should two sets of circumstances, or one set of circumstances, *not* possess different characteristics, any one of which makes a certain act our *prima facie* duty? When I ask what it is that makes me in certain cases sure that I have a *prima facie* duty to do so and so, I find that it lies in the fact that I have made a promise; when I ask the same question in another case, I find the answer lies in the fact that I have done a wrong.

And if on reflection I find (as I think I do) that neither of these reasons is reducible to the other, I must not on any *a priori* ground assume that such a reduction is possible.

It is necessary to say something by way of clearing up the relation between *prima facie* duties and the actual or absolute duty to do one particular act in particular circumstances. If, as almost all moralists except Kant are agreed and as most plain men think, it is sometimes right to tell a lie or to break a promise, it must be maintained that there is a difference between *prima facie* duty and actual or absolute duty. When we think ourselves justified in breaking, and indeed morally obliged to break, a promise in order to relieve someone's distress, we do not for a moment cease to recognize a *prima facie* duty to keep our promise, and this leads us to feel, not indeed shame or repentance, but certainly compunction, for behaving as we do; we recognize, further, that it is our duty to make up somehow to the promise for the breaking of the promise. We have to distinguish from the characteristic of being our duty that of tending to be our duty. Any act that we do contains various elements in virtue of which it falls under various categories. In virtue of being the breaking of a promise, for instance, it tends to be wrong; in virtue of being an instance of relieving distress it tends to be right. Tendency to be one's duty may be called a parti-resultant attribute, i.e. one which belongs to an act in virtue of some one component in its nature. *Being* one's duty is a toti-resultant attribute, one which belongs to an act in virtue of its whole nature and of nothing less than this.

Something should be said of the relation between our apprehension of the *prima facie* rightness of certain types of acts and our mental attitude toward particular acts. It is proper to use the word 'apprehension' in the former case and not in the latter. That an act, *qua* fulfilling a promise, or *qua* effecting a just distribution of good, or *qua* returning services rendered, or *qua* promoting the good of others, or *qua* promoting the virtue or insight of the agent, is *prima facie* right, is self-evident; not in the sense that it is evident from the beginning of our lives, or as soon as we attend to the proposition for the first time, but in the sense that when we have reached sufficient mental maturity and have given sufficient attention to the proposition it is evident without any need of proof, or of evidence beyond itself. It is self-evident, just as a mathematical axiom, or the validity of a form of inference, is evident. The moral order expressed in these propositions is just as much part of the fundamental nature of the universe (and, we may add, of any possible universe in which there were moral agents at all) as is the spatial or numerical structure expressed in the axioms of geometry or arithmetic. In our confidence that these propositions are true there is involved the same trust in our reason that is involved in our confidence in mathematics; and we should have no justification for trusting it in the latter sphere and distrusting it in the former. In both cases we are dealing with propositions that cannot be proved, but that just as certainly need no proof.

Supposing it to be agreed, as I think on reflection it must, that no one *means* by 'right' just 'productive of the best possible consequences,' or 'optimific,' the attributes 'right' and 'optimific' might stand in either of two kinds of relation to each other. (1) They might be so related that we could apprehend *a priori*, either immediately or deductively, that any act that is optimific is right and any act that is right is optimific, as we can apprehend that any triangle that is equilateral is equiangular and *vice versa*. Professor Moore's view is, I think, that the coextensiveness of 'right' and 'optimific' is apprehended immediately.[4] He rejects the possibility of any proof of it. Or (2) the two attributes might be such that the question whether they are invariably connected had to be answered by means of an inductive inquiry. Now at first sight it might seem as if the constant connexion of the two attributes could be immediately apprehended. It might seem absurd to suggest that it could be right for anyone to do an act which would produce consequences less good than those which would be produced by some other act in his power. Yet a little thought will convince us that this is not absurd. The type of case in which it is easiest to see that this is so is, perhaps, that in which one has made a promise. In such a case we all think that *prima facie* it is our duty to fulfill the promise irrespective of the precise goodness of the total consequences. And though we do not think it is necessarily our actual or absolute duty to do so, we are far from thinking that any, even the slightest, gain in the value of the total consequences will necessarily justify us in doing something else instead. Suppose, to simplify the case by abstraction, that the fulfillment of a promise to A would produce 1,000 units of good[5] for him, but that by doing some other act I could produce 1,001 units of good for B, to whom I have made no promise, the other consequences of the two acts being of equal value; should we really think it self-evident that it was our duty to do the second act and not the first? I think not. We should, I fancy, hold that only a much greater disparity of value between the total consequences would justify us in failing to discharge our *prima facie* duty to A. After all, a promise is a promise, and is not to be treated so lightly as the theory we are examining would imply. What, exactly, a promise is, is not so easy to determine, but we are surely agreed that it constitutes a serious moral limitation to our freedom of action. To produce the 1,001 units of good for B rather than fulfill our promise to A would be to take, not perhaps our duty as philanthropists too seriously, but certainly our duty as makers of promises too lightly.

Or consider another phase of the same problem. If I have promised to confer on A a particular benefit containing 1,000 units of good, is it self-evident that if by doing some different act I could produce 1,001 units of good for A himself (the other consequences of the two acts being supposed equal in value), it would be right for me to do so? Again, I think not. Apart from my general *prima facie* duty to do *A* what good I can, I have another *prima facie* duty to do him the particular service I have promised to do him, and this is not to be set aside in consequence of a disparity of good of the order of 1,001 to 1,000, though a much greater disparity might justify me in so doing.

Or again, suppose that *A* is a very good and *B* a very bad man, should I then, even when I have made no promise, think it self-evidently right to produce 1,001 units of good for *B* rather than 1,000 for *A*? Surely not. I should be sensible of a *prima facie* duty of justice, i.e., of producing a distribution of goods in proportion to merit, which is not outweighed by such a slight disparity in the total goods to be produced.

Such instances—and they might easily be added to—make it clear that there is no self-evident connexion between the attributes 'right' and 'optimific.' The theory we are examining has a certain attractiveness when applied to our decision that a particular act is our duty (though I have tried to show that it does not agree with our actual moral judgments even here). But it is not even plausible when applied to our recognition of *prima facie* duty. For if it were self-evident that the right coincides with the optimific, it should be self-evident that what is *prima facie* right is *prima facie* optimific. But whereas we are certain that keeping a promise is *prima facie* right, we are not certain that it is *prima facie* optimific (though we are perhaps certain that it is *prima facie* bonific). Our certainty that it is *prima facie* right depends not on its consequences but on its being the fulfillment of a promise. The theory we are examining involves too much difference between the evident ground of our conviction about *prima facie* duty and the alleged ground of our conviction about actual duty.

The coextensiveness of the right and the optimific is, then, not self-evident. And I can see no way of proving it deductively; nor, so far as I know, has anyone tried to do so. There remains the question whether it can be established inductively. Such an inquiry, to be conclusive, would

have to be very thorough and extensive. We should have to take a large variety of the acts which we, to the best of our ability, judge to be right. We should have to trace as far as possible their consequences, not only for the persons directly affected but also for those indirectly affected, and to these no limit can be set. To make our inquiry thoroughly conclusive, we should have to do what we cannot do, viz. trace these consequences into an unending future. And even to make it reasonably conclusive, we should have to trace them far into the future. It is clear that the most we could possibly say is that a large variety of typical acts that are judged right appear, so far as we can trace their consequences, to produce more good than any other acts possible to the agents in the circumstances. And such a result falls far short of proving the constant connexion of the two attributes. But it is surely clear that no inductive inquiry justifying even this result has ever been carried through. The advocates of utilitarian systems have been so much persuaded either of the identity or of the self-evident connexion of the attributes 'right' and 'optimific' (or 'felicific') that they have not attempted even such an inductive inquiry as is possible. And in view of the enormous complexity of the task and the inevitable inconclusiveness of the result, it is worth no one's while to make the attempt. What, after all, would be gained by it? If, as I have tried to show, for an act to be right and to be optimific are not the same thing, and an act's being optimific is not even the ground of its being right, then if we could ask ourselves (though the question is really unmeaning) which we ought to do, right acts because they are right or optimific acts because they are optimific, our answer must be 'the former.' If they are optimific as well as right, that is interesting but not morally important; if not, we still ought to do them (which is only another way of saying that they *are* the right acts), and the question whether they are optimific has no importance for moral theory.

There is one direction in which a fairly serious attempt has been made to show the connexion of the attributes 'right' and 'optimific.' One of the most evident facts of our moral consciousness is the sense which we have of the sanctity of promises, a sense which does not, on the face of it, involve the thought that one will be bringing more good into existence by fulfilling the promise than by breaking it. It is plain, I think, that in our normal thought we consider that the fact that we have made a promise is in itself sufficient to create a duty of keeping it, the sense of duty resting on remembrance of the past promise and not on thoughts of the future consequences of its fulfillment. Utilitarianism tries to show that this is not so, that the sanctity of promises rests on the good consequences of the fulfillment of them and the bad consequences of their nonfulfillment. It does so in this way: it points out that when you break a promise you not only fail to confer a certain advantage on your promise but you diminish his confidence, and indirectly the confidence of others, in the fulfillment of promises. You thus strike a blow at one of the devices that have been found most useful in the relations between man and man—the device on which, for example, the whole system of commercial credit rests—and you tend to bring about a state of things wherein each man, being entirely unable to rely on the keeping of promises by others, will have to do everything for himself, to the enormous impoverishment of human well-being.

To put the matter otherwise, utilitarians say that when a promise ought to be kept it is because the total good to be produced by keeping it is greater than the total good to be produced by breaking it, the former including as its main element the maintenance and strengthening of general mutual confidence, and the latter being greatly diminished by a weakening of this confidence. They say, in fact, that the case I put some pages back never arises—the case in which by fulfilling a promise I shall bring into being 1,000 units of good for my promisee, and by breaking it 1,001 units of good for someone else, the other effects of the two acts being of equal value. The other effects, they say, never are of equal value. By

keeping my promise I am helping to strengthen the system of mutual confidence; by breaking it I am helping to weaken this; so that really the first act produces $1,000 + x$ units of good, and the second $1,001 - y$ units, and the difference between $+x$ and $-y$ is enough to outweigh the slight superiority in the immediate effects of the second act. In answer to this it may be pointed out that there must be *some* amount of good that exceeds the difference between $+x$ and $-y$ (i.e. exceeds $x + y$); say, $x + y + z$. Let us suppose the *immediate* good effects of the second act to be assessed not at 1,001 but at $1,000 + x + y + z$. Then its *net* good effects are $1,000 + x + z$, i.e. greater than those of the fulfillment of the promise; and the utilitarian is bound to say forthwith that the promise should be broken. Now, we may ask whether that is really the way we think about promises. Do we really think that the production of the slightest balance of good, no matter who will enjoy it, by the breach of a promise frees us from the obligation to keep our promise? We need not doubt that a system by which promises are made and kept is one that has great advantages for the general well-being. But that is not the whole truth. To make a promise is not merely to adapt an ingenious device for promoting the general well-being; it is to put oneself in a new relation to one person in particular, a relation which creates a specifically new *prima facie* duty to him, not reducible to the duty of promoting the general well-being of society. By all means let us try to foresee the net good effects of keeping one's promise and the net good effects of breaking it, but even if we assess the first at $1,000 + x$ and the second at $1,000 + x + z$, the question still remains whether it is not our duty to fulfill the promise. It may be suspected, too, that the effect of a single keeping or breaking of a promise in strengthening or weakening the fabric of mutual confidence is greatly exaggerated by the theory we are examining. And if we suppose two men dying together alone, do we think that the duty of one to fulfill before he dies a promise he has made to the other would be extinguished by the fact that neither act would have any effect on the general confidence? Anyone who holds this may be suspected of not having reflected on what a promise is.

I conclude that the attributes 'right' and 'optimific' are not identical, and that we do not know either by intuition, by deduction, or by induction that they coincide in their application, still less that the latter is the foundation of the former. It must be added, however, that if we are ever under no special obligation such as that of fidelity to a promisee or of gratitude to a benefactor, we ought to do what will produce most good; and that even when we are under a special obligation the tendency of acts to promote general good is one of the main factors in determining whether they are right.

In what has preceded, a good deal of use has been made of 'what we really think' about moral questions; a certain theory has been rejected because it does not agree with what we really think. It might be said that this is in principle wrong; that we should not be content to expound what our present moral consciousness tells us but should aim at a criticism of our existing moral consciousness in the light of theory. Now I do not doubt that the moral consciousness of men has in detail undergone a good deal of modification as regards the things we think right, at the hands of moral theory. But if we are told, for instance, that we should give up our view that there is a special obligatoriness attaching to the keeping of promises because it is self-evident that the only duty is to produce as much good as possible, we have to ask ourselves whether we really, when we reflect, *are* convinced that this is self-evident, and whether we really *can* get rid of our view that promise-keeping has a bindingness independent of productiveness of maximum good. In my own experience I find that I cannot, in spite of a very genuine attempt to do so; and I venture to think that most people will find the same, and that just because they cannot lose the sense of special obligation, they cannot accept as self-evident, or even as true, the theory which would require

them to do so. In fact it seems, on reflection, self-evident that a promise, simply as such, is something that *prima facie* ought to be kept, and it does *not,* on reflection, seem self-evident that production of maximum good is the only thing that makes an act obligatory. And to ask us to give up at the bidding of a theory our actual apprehension of what is right and what is wrong seems like asking people to repudiate their actual experience of beauty, at the bidding of a theory which says 'only that which satisfies such and such conditions can be beautiful.' If what I have called our actual apprehension is (as I would maintain that it is) truly an apprehension, i.e. an instance of knowledge, the request is nothing less than absurd.

I would maintain, in fact, that what we are apt to describe as 'what we think' about moral questions contains a considerable amount that we do not think but know, and that this forms the standard by reference to which the truth of any moral theory has to be tested, instead of having itself to be tested by reference to any theory. I hope that I have in what precedes indicated what in my view these elements of knowledge are that are involved in our ordinary moral consciousness.

It would be a mistake to found a natural science on 'what we really think,' i.e. on what reasonably thoughtful and well-educated people think about the subjects of the science before they have studied them scientifically. For such opinions are interpretations, and often misinterpretations, of sense-experience; and the man of science must appeal from these to sense-experience itself, which furnishes his real data. In ethics no such appeal is possible. We have no more direct way of access to the facts about rightness and goodness and about what things are right or good, than by thinking about them; the moral convictions of thoughtful and well-educated people are the data of ethics just as sense-perceptions are the data of a natural science. Just as some of the latter have to be rejected as illusory, so have some of the former; but as the latter are rejected only when they are in conflict with other more accurate sense-perceptions, the former are rejected only when they are in conflict with other convictions which stand better the test of reflection. The existing body of moral convictions of the best people is the cumulative product of the moral reflection of many generations, which has developed an extremely delicate power of appreciation of moral distinctions; and this the theorist cannot afford to treat with anything other than the greatest respect. The verdicts of the moral consciousness of the best people are the foundation on which he must build; though he must first compare them with one another and eliminate any contradictions they may contain.

25

A Reconciliation of Ethical Theories

WILLIAM FRANKENA

William Frankena was, until his recent retirement, professor of philosophy at the University of Michigan, where he distinguished himself as one of the premier moral philosophers in the nation. He is the author of several works in ethical theory, including Ethics *(1963), from which the following reading is taken.*

Frankena argues that both utilitarianism and deontological ethics have strengths and weaknesses. Utilitarianism, among other problems, makes the mistake of not respecting rights or giving adequate weight to the principle of justice. Deontological theories often fail to see that "morality is made for man, not man for morality," and becomes rigidly rule bound. Frankena opts for a compromise system with two principles: beneficence and justice, thus producing a system that is essentially deontological but preserving what is valuble in utilitarianism.

I. My Proposed Theory of Obligation

So far in this chapter I have been trying to show that we cannot be satisfied with the principle of utility as our sole basic standard of right and wrong in morality, whether it is applied in AU, GU, or RU* style. In particular, I have contended that we should recognize a principle of justice to guide our distribution of good and evil that is independent of any principle about maximizing the balance of good over evil in the world. It may still be, of course, that we should recognize other independent principles as well, as deontologists like Ross think, e.g., that of keeping promises.

From *Ethics*, Second Edition (Prentice-Hall, 1973), © 1973. Reprinted by permission of Prentice-Hall, Inc., Englewood Cliffs, New Jersey.

Now I shall try to present the theory of obligation that seems to me most satisfactory from the moral point of view.

What precedes suggests that perhaps we should recognize two basic principles of obligation, the principle of utility and some principle of justice. The resulting theory would be a deontological one, but it would be much closer to utilitarianism than most deontological theories; we might call it a *mixed deontological theory*. It might maintain that all of our more specific rules of obligation, like that of keeping promises, and all of our judgments about what to do in particular situations can be derived, directly or indirectly, from its two principles. It might even insist that we are to determine what is right or wrong in particular situations, normally at least, by consulting rules such as we usually associate with morality, but add that the way to tell what rules to live by is to see which rules best fulfill the joint requirements of utility and justice (not, as in RU, the requirements of utility alone). This view is still faced with the problem of measuring and balancing amounts of good and evil, and, since it recognizes two basic principles, it must also face the problem of possible conflict between them. This means that it must regard its two principles as principles of prima facie, not of actual duty; and it must, if our above argument is correct, allow that the principle of justice may take precedence over that of utility, at least on some occasions, though perhaps not always. However, it may not be able to provide any formula saying when justice takes precedence and when it does not.

Should we adopt this theory of obligation? To my mind, it is close to the truth but not quite right. Let us begin, however, by asking whether we should recognize the principle of utility at all.

It seems to me we must at least recognize something like it as one of our basic premises. Whether we have even a prima facie obligation to maximize the balance of good over evil depends, in part, on whether it makes sense to talk about good and evil in quantitative terms. Assuming that it makes at least rough sense, it is not easy to deny, as pure deontologists do, that one of the things we ought to do, other things being equal, is to bring about as much of a balance of good over evil as we can, which even Ross, Garritt, and perhaps Butler, allow. I find it hard to believe that any action or rule can be right, wrong, or obligatory in the moral sense, if there is no good or evil connected with it in any way, directly or indirectly. This does not mean that there are no other factors affecting their rightness or wrongness, or that our only duty is to pile up the biggest possible stockpile of what is good, as utilitarians think; but it does imply that we do have, at least as one of our prima facie obligations, that of doing something about the good and evil in the world.

In fact, I wish to contend that we do not have any moral obligations, prima facie or actual, to do anything that does not, directly or indirectly, have some connection with what makes somebody's life good or bad, better or worse. If not our particular actions, then at least our rules must have some bearing on the increase of good or decrease of evil or on their distribution. Morality was made for man, not man for morality. Even justice is concerned about the distribution *of good and evil.* In other words, all of our duties, even that of justice, *presuppose* the existence of good and evil and some kind of concern about their existence and incidence. To this extent, and only to this extent, is the old dictum that love is what underlies and unifies the rules of morality correct. It is the failure to recognize the importance of this point that makes so many deontological systems unsatisfactory.

To say this is to say not only that we have no obligations except when some improvement or impairment of someone's life is involved but also that we have a prima facie obligation *whenever*

this is involved. To quote William James's inimitable way of putting it:

Take any demand, however slight, which any creature, however weak, may make. Ought it not, for its own sole sake, to be satisfied? If not, prove why not.[1]

II. The Principle of Beneficence

If this is so, then we must grant that the utilitarians have hold of an important part of the truth, and that we must recognize something like the principle of utility as one of our basic premises. Still, I do not think that we can regard the principle of utility itself as a basic premise, and my reason is that something more basic underlies it. By the principle of utility I have meant and shall continue to mean, quite strictly, the principle that we ought to do the act or follow the practice or rule that will or probably will bring about *the greatest possible balance of good over evil* in the universe. It seems clear, however, that this principle presupposes another one that is more basic, namely, that we ought to do good and to prevent or avoid doing harm. If we did not have this more basic obligation, we could have no duty to try to realize the greatest balance of good over evil. In fact, the principle of utility represents a compromise with the ideal. The ideal is to do only good and not to do any harm (omitting justice for the moment). But this is often impossible, and then we seem forced to try to bring about the best possible balance of good over evil. If this is so, then the principle of utility presupposes a more basic principle—that of producing good as such and preventing evil. We have a prima facie obligation to maximize the balance of good over evil only if we have a *prior* prima facie obligation to do good and prevent harm. I shall call this prior principle the *principle of beneficence.* The reason I call it the principle of *benificence* and not the principle of *benevolence* is to underline the fact that it asks us actually to do good and not evil, not merely to want or will to do so.

It might be thought that the principle of utility not only presupposes the principle of beneficence but follows from it. This, however, is not the case. The principle of utility is stated in quantitative terms and presupposes that goods and evils can be measured and balanced in some way. The principle of beneficence does not deny this, of course, but neither does it imply this. In applying it in practice one hopes that goods and evils can to a considerable extent at least be measured and balanced, but the principle of beneficence does not itself require that this be always possible; it is, for example, compatible with Mill's insistence that pleasures and pains, and hence goods and evils, differ in quality as well as quantity. I take this to be an advantage of the principle of beneficence over that of utility as I have stated it. There is another advantage. Suppose we have two acts, A and B, and that A produces 99 units of good and no evil, while B produces both good and evil but has a net balance of 100 units of good over evil. In this case, act-utilitarianism requires us to say that B is the right thing to do. But some of us would surely think that act A is the right one, and the principle of beneficence permits one to say this, though it does not require us to do so.

I propose, then, that we take as the basic premises of our theory of right and wrong two principles, that of beneficence and some principle of just distribution. To this proposal it might be objected that, although the principle of justice cannot be derived from that of beneficence, it is possible to derive the principle of beneficence from that of justice. For, if one does not increase the good of others and decrease evil for them when one can do so and when no conflicting obligations are present, then one is being unjust. Hence, justice implies beneficence (when possible and not ruled out by other considerations). In reply, I want to agree that in some sense beneficence is *right* and failure to be beneficent *wrong* under the conditions specified, but I want to deny that they are, respectively, just or unjust, properly speaking. Not everything that is right is just, and not everything that is wrong is unjust. Incest, even if it is

wrong, can hardly be called unjust. Cruelty to children may be unjust, if it involves treating them differently from adults, but it is surely wrong anyway. Giving another person pleasure may be right, without its being properly called just at all. The area of justice is a part of morality but not the whole of it. Beneficence, then, may belong to the other part of morality, and this is just what seems to me to be the case. Even Mill makes a distinction between justice and the other obligations of morality, and puts charity or beneficence among the latter. So does Portia when she says to Shylock,

And earthly power doth then show likest God's
When mercy seasons justice.

It has been contended, nevertheless, that we do not have, properly speaking, a duty or obligation to be beneficent. From this point of view, being beneficent is considered praiseworthy and virtuous, but is beyond the call of moral *duty*. All that morality can demand of us is justice, keeping promises, and the like, not beneficence. There is some truth in this. It is not always strictly wrong not to perform an act of beneficence even when one can, for example, not giving someone else one's concert ticket. Not giving him the ticket is only strictly wrong if he has a *right* to my beneficence, and this he does not always have. It may still be, however, that in some wider sense of "ought," I ought to be beneficent, perhaps even to give my ticket to another who needs it more. Kant made a similar point by saying that beneficence is an "imperfect" duty; one ought to be beneficent, he thought, but one has some choice about the occasions on which to do good. In any case, it is certainly wrong, at least prima facie, to inflict evil or pain on anyone, and to admit this is to admit that the principle of beneficence is partly correct.

A point about our use of terms may help here. The terms "duty," "obligation," and "ought to be done" are often used interchangeably, especially by philosophers, for example, in this book. This is true even to some extent in ordinary discourse. But in our more careful ordinary discourse we tend to use "duty" when we have in mind some rule like "Tell the truth" or some role or office like that of a father or secretary, and to use "obligation" when we have in mind the law or some agreement or promise. In these cases we tend to think that one person has a duty or obligation and another has a correlative right. The expression "ought to do," however, is used in a wider sense to cover things we would not regard as strict duties or obligations or think another person has a right to. Thus, it is natural to say that one ought to go the second mile, not so natural to say one has a duty or obligation to do this, and quite unnatural to say that the other person has a right to expect one to do it. This will help to explain why some assert and others deny that beneficence is a requirement of morality. The matter, it should be observed, is made all the more difficult by two further facts: on the one hand, that "right" sometimes means "ought to be done" and sometimes means only "not wrong," and on the other, that "wrong" is used as the opposite of all the other expressions mentioned, and so has somewhat different forces in different contexts.

One more remark is worth making. Even if one holds that beneficence is not a *requirement* of morality but something supererogatory and morally *good*, one is still regarding beneficence as an important part of morality—as desirable if not required.

What does the principle of beneficence say? Four things, I think:

1. One ought not to inflict evil or harm (what is bad).
2. One ought to prevent evil or harm.
3. One ought to remove evil.
4. One ought to do or promote good.

These four things are different, but they may appropriately be regarded as parts of the principle of beneficence. Of the four, it is most plausible to say that (4) is not a duty in the strict sense. In fact, one is inclined to say that in some sense (1) takes precedence over (2), (2) over (3), and (3) over (4), other things being equal. But all are, at any rate, principles of prima facie duty. By adding "to or for anyone" at the end of each of them one makes the principle of beneficence universalistic, by adding "to or for others" one makes it altruistic. What one does here depends on whether he is willing to say that one has moral duties to oneself or not. For example, does one have a moral duty not to sacrifice any of one's own happiness for that of another? We shall look at this question again later.

It is tempting to think that, since the first four parts of the principle of beneficence may come into conflict with one another in choice situations, say, between actions both of which do some good and some evil, we should regard it as having a fifth part that instructs us, in such cases, to do what will bring about the greatest balance of good over evil. This would, however, presuppose that good and evil can always be measured in some way and lose the advantages ascribed to the principle of beneficence over the principle of utility; in fact, it would make the former equivalent to the latter in practice, since we are always choosing between two courses of action, even if one of them is called "inaction." Even so, we may perhaps follow this instruction—or the principle of utility—as a heuristic maxim in conflict situations involving only the principle of beneficence, at least insofar as the goods and evils involved are susceptible to some kind of measuring and balancing, though remembering its limitations.

There are many rules of prima facie right, wrong, or obligation, to be used in determining our actual duties, which can be derived from the principle of beneficence. Wherever one can form a general statement about what affects the lives of people for better or for worse, there one has a valid principle of prima facie duty, for example, "One ought not to kick people in the shin" or "We ought to promote knowledge." Most of the usual rules—keeping promises, telling the truth, showing gratitude, making reparation, not interfering with liberty, etc.—can be seen on this basis to be valid prima facie rules. For instance, given the principle of beneficence and the fact that knowing the truth is a good (in itself or as a means), it follows that telling the truth is a prima facie duty.

Thus, some of our rules of prima facie duty follow directly from the principle of beneficence. The rule of telling the truth can probably be defended also (perhaps with certain built-in exceptions) on the ground that its adoption makes for the greatest general good—as rule-utilitarians hold.

However, not all of our prima facie obligations can be derived from the principle of beneficence any more than from that of utility. For the principle of beneficence does not tell us how we are to distribute goods and evils; it only tells us to produce the one and prevent the other. When conflicting claims are made upon us, the most it could do (and we saw it cannot strictly even do this) is to instruct us to promote the greatest balance of good over evil and, as we have already seen, we need something more. This is where a principle of justice must come in.

III. The Principle of Justice: Equality

We have seen that we must recognize a basic principle of justice. But which one? What is justice? We cannot go into the whole subject of social justice here, but we must at least complete our outline of a normative theory of moral obligation, in which the principle of justice plays a crucial role. We are talking here about *distributive justice*, justice in the distribution of good and evil. There is also *retributive justice* (punishment, etc.). . . . Distributive justice is a matter of the *comparative treatment* of individuals. The paradigm case of injustice is that in which there are two similar individuals in similar circumstances and one of them is treated better or worse than the other. In this case, the cry of injustice rightly goes up against the responsible agent or group; and unless that agent or group can establish that

there is some relevant dissimilarity after all between the individuals concerned and their circumstances, he or they will be guilty as charged. This is why Sidgwick suggested his formula, according to which justice is the similar and injustice the dissimilar treatment of similar cases. This formula does give a necessary condition of justice; similar cases are to be treated similarly so far as the requirements of justice are concerned, although these requirements may be outweighed by other considerations. But Sidgwick's formula is not sufficient. All it really says is that we must act according to rules if we mean to be just. Although this formula is correct as far as it goes, it tells us nothing about what the rules are to be, and this is what we want to know, since we have already seen that rules themselves may be unjust. If this were not so, there could be no unjust laws or practices, for laws and practices are rules. Much depends, as we shall see, on which similarities and dissimilarities of individuals are taken as the basis for similarity or dissimilarity of treatment.

The question remaining to be answered is how we are to tell what rules of distribution or comparative treatment we are to act on. We have seen that these rules cannot be determined on the basis of beneficence alone (as I think the rules of not injuring anyone and of keeping covenants can be). A number of criteria have been proposed by different thinkers: (1) that justice is dealing with people according to their *deserts* or *merits;* (2) that it is treating human beings as *equals* in the sense of distributing good and evil equally among them, excepting perhaps in the case of punishment; (3) that it is treating people according to their *needs,* their *abilities,* or both. An example of the first is the classical *meritarian* criterion of justice as found in Aristotle and Ross. According to this view, the criterion of desert or merit is virtue, and justice is distributing the good (e.g., happiness) in accordance with virtue. One might, of course, adopt some other criterion of merit, for example, ability, contribution, intelligence, blood, color, social rank, or wealth, and then justice would consist in distributing good and evil in accordance with this criterion. The second criterion is the *equalitarian* one that is characteristic of modern democratic theory. The third is also a modern view, and may take various forms; its most prominent form today is the Marxist dictum, "From each according to his ability, to each according to his needs." I shall argue for the second view.

Some of the criteria of merit mentioned seem to be palpably nonmoral or even unjust, for example, the use of blood, color, intelligence, sex, social rank, or wealth as a basis for one's rules of distribution. Use of ability as a basis would give us a form of the third view. This leaves moral and/or nonmoral virtue as possible criteria of merit. Should we adopt a meritarian theory of this Aristotle-Ross sort? It seems to me that virtue, moral or nonmoral, cannot be our basic criterion in matters of distributive justice, because a recognition of any kind of virtue as a basis of distribution if justified only if every individual has an equal chance of achieving all the virtue of that kind he is capable of (and it must not be assumed that they have all had this chance, for they have not). If the individuals competing for goods, positions, and the like have not had an equal chance to achieve all the virtue they are capable of, then virtue is not a fair basis for distributing such things among them. If this is so, then, before virtue can reasonably be adopted as a basis of distribution, there must first be a prior *equal* distribution of the conditions for achieving virtue, at least insofar as this is within the control of human society. This is where equality of opportunity, equality before the law, and equality of access to the means of education come in. In other words, recognition of virtue as a basis of distribution is reasonable only against the background of an acknowledgment of the principle of equality. The primary criterion of distributive justice, then, is not merit in the form of virtue of some kind or other, but equality.

One might object here that there is another kind of merit, namely, effort, and that effort made should be taken as a basis of distribution in at least certain kinds of cases. This is true, but again, it does seem to me that effort cannot serve as our *basic* criterion of distribution, and that recognition of it in any defensible way presupposes the general notion that we should all be treated equally.

We certainly must consider abilities and needs in determining how we are to treat others. This is required by the principle of beneficence, for it asks us to be concerned about the goodness of their lives, which involves catering to their needs and fostering and making use of their abilities. But is it required by the principle of justice? More particularly, does the principle of justice require us to help people in proportion to their needs or to call on them in proportion to their abilities? It is wrong to ask more of people than they can do or to assign them tasks out of proportion to their ability, but this is because "ought" implies "can." Justice asks us to do something about cases of special need; for example, it asks us to give special attention to people with certain kinds of handicaps, because only with such attention can they have something comparable to an equal chance with others of enjoying a good life. But does it always ask us, at least prima facie, to *proportion* our help to their needs and our demands to their abilities? Are we always prima facie unjust if we help A in proportion to his needs but not B, or if we make demands of C in proportion to his abilities but not of D? It seems to me that the basic question is whether or not in so doing we are showing an equal concern for the goodness of the lives of A and B or of C and D. Whether we should treat them in proportion to their needs and abilities depends, as far as *justice* is concerned, on whether doing so helps or hinders them equally in the achievement of the best lives they are capable of. If helping them in proportion to their needs is necessary for making an equal contribution to the goodness of their lives, then and only then is it unjust to do otherwise. If asking of them in proportion to their abilities is necessary for keeping their chances of a good life equal, then and only then is it unjust to do otherwise. In other words, the basic standard of distributive justice is *equality* of treatment. That, for instance, is why justice calls for giving extra attention to handicapped people.

If this is correct, then we must adopt the equalitarian view of distributive justice. In other words, the principle of justice lays upon us the prima facie obligation of treating people equally. Here we have the answer to our question. This does not mean that it is prima facie unjust to treat people of the same color differently or to treat people of different heights similarly. Color and height are not morally relevant similarities or dissimilarities. Those that are relevant are the ones that bear on the goodness or badness of people's lives, for example, similarities or dissimilarities in ability, interest, or need. Treating people equally does not mean treating them identically; justice is not so monotonous as all that. It means making the same relative contribution to the goodness of their lives (this is equal help or helping according to need) or asking the same relative sacrifice (this is asking in accordance with ability).

Treating people equally in this sense does not mean making their lives equally good or maintaining their lives at the same level of goodness. It would be a mistake to think that justice requires this. For, though people are equally capable of some kind of good life (or least bad one), the kinds of life of which they are capable are not equally good. The lives of which some are capable simply are better, nonmorally as well as morally, than those of which others are capable. In this sense men are not equal, since they are not equal in their capacities. They are equal only in the sense that they ought prima facie to be treated equally, and they ought to be treated equally only in the sense that we ought prima facie to make proportionally the same contribution to the goodness of their lives, once a certain minimum has been achieved by all. This is what is meant by the equal intrinsic dignity or value of the individual that is such an important concept in our culture.

We must remember that this equality of treatment, though it is a basic obligation, is only a prima facie one, and that it may on occasion (and

there is no formula for determining the occasions) be overruled by the principle of beneficence. We may claim, however, that in distributing goods and evils, help, tasks, roles, and so forth, people are to be treated equally in the sense indicated, except when unequal treatment can be justified by considerations of beneficence (including utility) or on the ground that it will promote greater equality in the long run. Unequal treatment always requires justification and only certain kinds of justification suffice.

It is in the light of the preceding discussion, it seems to me, that we must try to solve such social problems as education, economic opportunity, racial integration, and aid to underdeveloped countries, remembering always that the principle of beneficence requires us to respect the liberty of others. Our discussion provides only the most general guidelines for solving such problems, of course, but most of what is needed in addition is good will, clarity of thought, and knowledge of the relevant facts.

Summary of My Theory of Obligation

We have now arrived at a mixed deontological theory of obligation somewhat different from the one tentatively sketched earlier. It takes as basic the principle of beneficence (not that of utility) and the principle of justice, not identified as equal treatment. Must we recognize any other basic principle of right and wrong? It seems to me that we need not. As far as I can see, we can derive all of the things we may wish to recognize as duties from our two principles, either directly as the crow flies or indirectly as the rule-utilitarian does. From the former follow various more specific rules of prima facie obligation, for example those of not injuring anyone, and of not interfering with anyone's liberty. From the latter follow others like equality of consideration and equality before the law. Some, like telling the truth or not being cruel to children, may follow separately from both principles, which may give them a kind of priority they might not otherwise have. Others, like keeping promises and not crossing university lawns, may perhaps be justified in rule-utilitarian fashion on the basis of the two principles taken jointly, as being rules whose general acceptance and obedience is conducive to a state of affairs in which a maximal balance of good over evil is as equally distributed as possible (the greatest good of the greatest number).

The Problem of Conflict

Several problems facing this theory remain to be discussed. One is the problem of possible conflict between its two principles. I see no way out of this. It does seem to me that the two principles may come into conflict, both at the level of individual action and at that of social policy, and I know of no formula that will always tell us how to solve such conflicts or even how to solve conflicts between their corollaries. It is tempting to say that the principle of justice always takes precedence over that of beneficence: do justice though the heavens fall. But is a small injustice never to be preferred to a great evil? Perhaps we should lean over backwards to avoid committing injustice, but are we never justified in treating people unequally? One might contend that the principle of equal treatment always has priority at least over the fourth or positive part of the principle of beneficence, but is it never right to treat people unequally when a considerable good is at stake? The answer to these questions, I regret to say, does not seem to me to be clearly negative, and I

am forced to conclude that the problem of conflict that faced the pluralistic deontological theories discussed earlier is still with us. One can only hope that, if we take the moral point of view, become clearheaded, and come to know all that is relevant, we will also come to agree on ways of acting that are satisfactory to all concerned.

The following reflection may be encouraging in this respect. It seems to me that everyone who takes the moral point of view can agree that the ideal state of affairs is one in which everyone has the best life he or she is capable of. Now, in such a state of affairs, it is clear that the concerns of both the principle of justice or equality and the principle of beneficence will be fulfilled. If so, then we can see that the two principles are in some sense ultimately consistent, and this seems to imply that increasing insight may enable us to know more and more how to solve the conflicts that trouble us now when we know so little about realizing the ideal state of affairs in which the principles are at one. Then, while Ross is right in saying that we must finally appeal to "perception," we can at least give an outline of what that perception is supposed to envision.

Notes

*[Act-Utilitarianism, General Utilitarianism, and Rule-Utilitarianism—Ed.]

1. *Essays in Pragmatism*, A. Castell, ed. (New York: Hafner Publishing Co., 1948), p. 73.

PART VII

Virtue Ethics

Introduction

While most ethical theories have been duty or action oriented, either deontological or teleological, there is a third tradition which goes back to Plato and, especially, Aristotle, and which receives support in the Epicureans, the Stoics, and some sections of the Early Christian Church. I refer to the Virtue-Based Systems, sometimes called *aretaic* (from the Greek word *arete*, "excellence" or 'excellence' or 'virtue'). Rather than seeing the heart of ethics in actions or duties, virtue ethics centers in the heart of the agent, in the character and dispositions of persons. Whereas action-ethics emphasize *doing*, virtue or agent ethics emphasize *being*, being a certain type of person who will no doubt manifest his or her being in actions or non-actions. For traditional duty-based ethics the question is: What should I do? For virtue ethics the question is: What sort of person should I become? Virtue ethics seeks to produce excellent persons who both act well out of spontaneous goodness and serve as examples who inspire others. It seeks to create people like Socrates, Jesus, St. Francis, Gandhi, and Mother Teresa who stand out as "jewels who shine in their own light" (to paraphrase Kant's characterization of the morally good). There is a teleological aspect in virtue ethics, but it is not the kind that is usually found in utilitarianism, which asks what sort of action will maximize happiness or utility. The virtue concept of teleology focuses, rather, on the *goals* of life, living well and achieving excellence.

Our first reading is from the first two books of Aristotle's *Nicomachean Ethics,* the classic work on the virtues, written four centuries before Christ. Virtues are simply those characteristics which enable individuals to live well in communities. In order for one to achieve a state of well-being (*eudaimonia*, often translated as 'happi-

ness'), proper social institutions are necessary. Thus the moral person cannot really exist apart from a flourishing political setting which enables the individual to develop the requisite virtues for the good life. For this reason Aristotle considers ethics to be a branch of politics.

After locating ethics as a part of politics, Aristotle explains that the moral virtues are different from the intellectual ones. While the intellectual virtues may be taught directly, the moral ones, being nonrational, cannot be taught directly but are acquired by training and practice. They must be lived in order to be learned. By living well we acquire the right habits. These habits are in fact the virtues. The virtues are to be sought as the best guarantee of the happy life. But, again, happiness requires that one be lucky enough to live in a flourishing state. The morally virtuous life consists in living according to right reason between excessive extremes. J. O. Urmson correctly notes that for Aristotle "excellence of character is explicitly said to be an intermediate disposition toward action and not a disposition to intermediate action. Extreme action will on some occasions be appropriate and carried out by the man of excellent character."[1]

Bernard Mayo, in our second reading, "Virtue and the Moral Life," provides a contemporary expression of the Aristotelian perspective. Contrasting the ethics of "doing" of the deontologists and teleologists with the ethics of "being" or character, the morality of the saints and heroes, Mayo contends that the saints and heroes show us that it is a living example that is important in ethics, not rigid rules. We learn more about ethics by looking at the lives of such people than by learning a set of principles.

Virtue ethicists are more likely to bring ethics closer to political theory, as Aristotle himself did, and to ask what kinds of upbringing and social institutions are most likely to give rise to the good life and produce good persons. They tend to despair of arguing about objective moral principles or right and wrong action, which is the putting of the cart before the horse. Many modern virtue ethicists (e.g., Alasdair MacIntyre) urge us to go back to the Greeks and center our ethics on the quest for virtue, which is connected with happiness, rather than on questions of right and wrong, which really have their place in custom and law, not humanistic ethics. They believe that duty-based ethics have their origin and justification in religious authority, as divinely given laws which are enforced by the gods or God. Take away that authority and you have only a relativistic morass. The only way to escape chaotic relativism, where everyone does what is right in his or her own eyes, is to return to a virtue-based ethics.

Action or duty-based ethical theorists do not deny the importance of character. But they claim that the nature of the virtues can only be derived from right actions or good consequences. As William Frankena puts it in our third reading, "Traits without principles are blind." Where there is a virtue, there must be some possible action to which the virtue corresponds and from which it derives its virtuosity. For example, the character trait of truthfulness is a virtue because telling the truth, in general, is a moral duty. Likewise, conscientiousness is a virtue because we have a general duty to be morally sensitive. There is a relation of correspondence between principles and virtues, the latter being derived from the former, as the following diagram suggests: the correspondence theory of virtues:

The Virtue		*The Principle*
Truthfulness	which	telling the truth
Conscientiousness	derives	being sensitive to
	from	one's duty
Benevolence		being beneficent
Faithfulness		being loyal or
		faithful

Although derived from the right kind of actions, the virtues are, nonetheless, very important for the moral life. They provide the dispositions which generate right action. In a sense, they are motivationally indispensable. To complete the passage quoted above, "Traits without principles are blind, but principles without traits are impotent." Frankena modifies the above position, distinguishing two types of virtues: (1) the standard moral virtues which correspond to specific kinds of moral principles, and (2) nonmoral virtues, such as natural kindliness or gratefulness (I would suggest that courage fits in here), which are "morality-supporting."

For example, take a situation where you have an obligation to save a drowning child in spite of some risk to your life. The specific rule of 'Always come to the aid of drowning people' is grounded in a foundational principle of general beneficence which in turn generates the foundation virtue of benevolence. In this case, it gives rise to a tendency to try to save the drowning child, but whether or not you actually dive into the lake may depend on the enabling (nonmoral) virtue of courage. Courage itself is not a moral virtue like benevolence or justice, for it is the kind of virtue which enhances and augments both virtues and vices (e.g., the courageous murderer).

In our fourth reading, Alasdair MacIntyre carries on the Aristotelian project of grounding morality in the virtues. He asks whether there is some core conception of the virtues, some vital components that are necessary to any social endeavor or practice. He compares five different conceptions of the virtues as they appear in the works of Homer, Aristotle, Jane Austen and Benjamin Franklin. Five different theories seem to emerge, although MacIntyre finds elements of commonality among them. Without this common core, we are in danger of relapsing into a Hobbesian state of nature. MacIntyre sees his project as carrying on the Aristotelian tradition of virtue ethics.

In our fifth reading, Jonathan Bennett's "The

Conscience of Huckleberry Finn," is a radical challenge to traditional deontic ethics in that Bennett argues that sometimes the moral thing to do is to override one's obligation in favor of one's sympathies. In our final reading, David Norton distinguishes between the ethics of rules and the ethics of character. The ethics of rules is minimalist, largely negative, setting constraints on our actions, whereas the ethics of character challenges us to aspire to excellence.

Note

1. J. O. Urmson, *Aristotle's Ethics* (Oxford: Oxford University Press, 1988).

26

Virtue Ethics

ARISTOTLE

Aristotle (384–322 B.C.), Greek physician, tutor to Alexander the Great, and one of the most important philosophers who ever lived, contributed importantly to virtually every major area of philosophy. This selection is from the first two books of the Nicomachean Ethics. *After a general discussion of the nature of ethics and the nature of the end of human being, Aristotle turns to the nature of virtue. Virtues are simply those characteristics that enable individuals to live well in communities. To achieve a state of well-being (*eudaimonia, *happiness), both proper social institutions and good character are required. Thus, Aristotle considers ethics to be a branch of politics.*

Aristotle holds that the moral virtues are different from the intellectual ones. Whereas the intellectual virtues may be taught directly, the moral ones must be lived in order to be learned. By living well we acquire the right habits. These habits are in fact the virtues. The virtues are to be sought as the best guarantee to the happy life. But, again, happiness

requires that we be lucky enough to live in a flourishing state. The morally virtuous life is a state intermediated between two extremes in which we make wise decisions.

I. The Highest Good: Happiness

Goods Correspond to Ends

Every craft and every investigation, and likewise every action and decision, seems to aim at some good; hence the good has been well described as that at which everything aims.

However, there is an apparent difference among the ends aimed at. For the end is sometimes an activity, sometimes a product beyond the activity; and when there is an end beyond the action, the product is by nature better than the activity.

The Hierarchy of Goods Corresponds to the Hierarchy of Ends

Since there are many actions, crafts, and sciences, the ends turn out to be many as well; for health is the end of medicine, a boat of boat-building, victory of generalship, and wealth of household management.

Reprinted from Aristotle's *Nicomachean Ethics,* trans. Terence Irwin (Indianapolis: Hackett Publishing Company, 1985) by permission of the publisher.

But whenever any of these sciences are sub-ordinate to some one capacity—as e.g., bridle-making and every other science producing equip-ment for horses are subordinate to horsemanship, while this and every action in warfare are in turn subordinate to generalship, and in the same way other sciences are subordinate to further ones—in each of these the end of the ruling science is more choiceworthy than all the ends subordinate to it, since it is the end for which those ends are also pursued. And here it does not matter whether the ends of the actions are the activities them-selves, or some product beyond them, as in the sciences we have mentioned.

The Highest Good

Suppose, then, that (a) there is some end of the things we pursue in our actions which we wish for because of itself, and because of which we wish for the other things; and (b) we do not choose everything because of something else, since (c) if we do, it will go on without limit, making desire empty and futile; then clearly (d) this end will be the good, i.e., the best good.

The Importance of Finding the Science of the Highest Good

Then surely knowledge of this good is also of great importance for the conduct of our lives, and if, like archers, we have a target to aim at, we are more likely to hit the right mark. If so, we should try to grasp, in outline at any rate, what the good is, and which science or capacity is concerned with it. . . .

II. Characteristics of the Good

(1) The Good Is the End of Action

But let us return once again to the good we are looking for, and consider just what it could be, since it is apparently one thing in one action or craft, and another thing in another; for it is one thing in medicine, another in generalship, and so on for the rest.

What, then, is the good in each of these cases? Surely it is that for the sake of which the other things are done; and in medicine this is health, in generalship victory, in housebuilding a house, in another case something else, but in every action and decision it is the end, since it is for the sake of the end that everyone does the other things.

And so, if there is some end of everything that is pursued in action, this will be the good pur-sued in action; and if there are more ends than one, these will be the goods pursued in action.

Our argument has progressed, then, to the same conclusion [as before, that the highest end is the good]; but we must try to clarify this still more.

(2) The Good Is Complete

Though apparently there are many ends, we choose some of them, e.g., wealth, flutes, and, in general, instruments, because of something else; hence it is clear that not all ends are complete. But the best good is apparently something com-plete. Hence, if only one end is complete, this will be what we are looking for; and if more than one are complete, the most complete of these will be what we are looking for.

An end pursued in itself, we say, is more com-plete than an end pursued because of something else; and an end that is never choiceworthy be-cause of something else is more complete than ends that are choiceworthy both in themselves and because of this end; and hence an end that is always [choiceworthy, and also] choiceworthy in itself, never because of something else, is uncon-ditionally complete.

(3) Happiness Meets the Criteria for Completeness, but Other Goods Do Not

Now happiness more than anything else seems unconditionally complete, since we always [choose it, and also] choose it because of itself, never because of something else.

Honor, pleasure, understanding, and every vir-tue we certainly choose because of themselves, since we would choose each of them even if it had no further result, but we also choose them for the sake of happiness, supposing that through them we shall be happy. Happiness, by contrast, no one ever chooses for their sake, or for the sake of anything else at all.

(4) The Good Is Self-sufficient; So Is Happiness

The same conclusion [that happiness is complete] also appears to follow from self-sufficiency, since the complete good seems to be self-sufficient.

Now what we count as self-sufficient is not what suffices for a solitary person by himself, living an isolated life, but what suffices also for parents, children, wife, and in general for friends and fellow-citizens, since a human being is a naturally political [animal]. Here, however, we must impose some limit; for if we extend the good to parents' parents and children's children and to friends of friends, we shall go on without limit; but we must examine this another time.

Anyhow, we regard something as self-sufficient when all by itself it makes a life choiceworthy and lacking nothing; and that is what we think happiness does.

(5) What Is Self-sufficient Is Most Choiceworthy; So Is Happiness

Moreover, we think happiness is most choiceworthy of all goods, since it is not counted as one good among many. If it were counted as one among many, then, clearly, we think that the addition of the smallest of goods would make it more choiceworthy; for [the smallest good] that is added becomes an extra quantity of goods [so creating a good larger than the original good], and the larger of two goods is always more choiceworthy. [But we do not think any addition can make happiness more choiceworthy; hence it is most choiceworthy.]

Happiness, then, is apparently something complete and self-sufficient, since it is the end of the things pursued in action.

III. A Clearer Account of the Good: The Human Soul's Activity Expressing Virtue

But presumably the remark that the best good is happiness is apparently something [generally] agreed, and what we miss is a clearer statement of what the best good is.

(1) If Something Has a Function, Its Good Depends on Its Function

Well, perhaps we shall find the best good if we first find the function of a human being. For just as the good, i.e., [doing] well, for a flautist, a sculptor, and every craftsman, and, in general, for whatever has a function and [characteristic] action, seems to depend on its function, the same seems to be true for a human being, if a human being has some function.

(2) What Sorts of Things Have Functions?

Then do the carpenter and the leatherworker have their functions and actions, while a human being has none, and is by nature idle, without any function? Or, just as eye, hand, foot and, in general, every [bodily] part apparently has its functions, may we likewise ascribe to a human being some function besides all of theirs?

(3) The Human Function

What, then, could this be? For living is apparently shared with plants, but what we are looking for is the special function of a human being; hence we should set aside the life of nutrition and growth. The life next in order is some sort of life of sense-perception; but this too is apparently shared, with horse, ox, and every animal. The remaining possibility, then, is some sort of life of action of the [part of the soul] that has reason.

Now this [part has two parts, which have reason in different ways], one as obeying the reason [in the other part], the other as itself having reason and thinking. [We intend both.] Moreover, life is also spoken of in two ways [as capacity and as activity], and we must take [a human being's special function to be] life as activity, since this seems to be called life to a fuller extent.

(4) The Human Good Is Activity Expressing Virtue

(a) We have found, then, that the human function is the soul's activity that expresses reason [as itself having reason] or requires reason [as obeying reason]. (b) Now the function of F, e.g., of a harpist, is the same kind, so we say, as the function of an excellent F, e.g., an excellent harpist. (c) The same is true unconditionally in every case, when we add to the function the superior achievement that expresses the virtue; for a harpist's function, e.g., is to play the harp, and a good harpist's is to do it well. (d) Now we take the human function to be a certain kind of life, and take this life to be the soul's activity and actions that express reason. (e) [Hence by (c) and (d)] the excellent man's function is to do this finely and well. (f) Each function is completed well when its completion expresses the proper virtue. (g) Therefore [by (d), (e), and (f)] the human good turns out to be the soul's activity that expresses virtue.

(5) The Good Must Also Be Complete

And if there are more virtues than one, the good will express the best and most complete virtue. Moreover, it will be in a complete life. For one swallow does not make a spring, nor does one day; nor, similarly, does one day or a short time make us blessed and happy. . . .

IV. Virtues of Character in General

Virtue, then, is of two sorts, virtue of thought and virtue of character. Virtue of thought arises and grows mostly from teaching, and hence needs experience and time. Virtue of character [i.e., of *ēthos*] results from habit [*ethos*]; hence its name 'ethical', slightly varied from '*ethos*.'

Virtue Comes About, Not by a Process of Nature, but by Habituation

Hence it is also clear that none of the virtues of character arises in us naturally.

(1) What Is Natural Cannot Be Changed by Habituation

For if something is by nature [in one condition], habituation cannot bring it into another condition. A stone, e.g., by nature moves downwards, and habituation could not make it move upwards, not even if you threw it up ten thousand times to habituate it; nor could habituation make fire move downwards, or bring anything that is by nature in one condition into another condition.

Thus the virtues arise in us neither by nature nor against nature. Rather, we are by nature able to acquire them, and reach our complete perfection through habit.

(2) Natural Capacities Are Not Acquired by Habituation

Further, if something arises in us by nature, we first have the capacity for it, and later display the activity. This is clear in the case of the senses; for we did not acquire them by frequent seeing or hearing, but already had them when we exercised them, and did not get them by exercising them.

Virtues, by contrast, we acquire, just as we acquire crafts, by having previously activated them. For we learn a craft by producing the same product that we must produce when we have learned it, becoming builders, e.g., by building and harpists by playing the harp; so also, then, we become just by doing just actions, temperate by doing temperate actions, brave by doing brave actions.

(3) Legislators Concentrate on Habituation

What goes on in cities is evidence for this also. For the legislator makes the citizens good by habituating them, and this is the wish of every legislator; if he fails to do it well he misses his goal. [The right] habituation is what makes the difference between a good political system and a bad one.

(4) Virtue and Vice Are Formed by Good and Bad Actions

Further, just as in the case of a craft, the sources and means that develop each virtue also ruin it. For playing the harp makes both good and bad harpists, and it is analogous in the case of builders and all the rest; for building well makes good builders, building badly, bad ones. If it were not so, no teacher would be needed, but everyone would be born a good or a bad craftsman.

It is the same, then, with the virtues. For actions in dealings with [other] human beings make some people just, some unjust; actions in terrifying situations and the acquired habit of fear or confidence make some brave and others cowardly. The same is true of situations involving appetites and anger; for one or another sort of conduct in these situations makes some people temperate and gentle, others intemperate and irascible.

To sum up, then, in a single account: A state [of character] arises from [the repetition of] similar activities. Hence we must display the right activities, since differences in these imply corresponding differences in the states. It is not unimportant, then, to acquire one sort of habit or another, right from our youth; rather, it is very important, indeed all-important. . . .

V. But Our Claims about Habituation Raise a Puzzle: How Can We Become Good Without Being Good Already?

However, someone might raise this puzzle: 'What do you mean by saying that to become just we must first do just actions and to become temperate we must first do temperate actions? For if we do what is grammatical or musical, we must already be grammarians or musicians. In the same way, then, if we do what is just or temperate, we must already be just or temperate.'

First Reply: Conformity versus Understanding

But surely this is not so even with the crafts, for it is possible to produce something grammatical by chance or by following someone else's instructions. To be a grammarian, then, we must both produce something grammatical and produce it in the way in which the grammarian produces it, i.e., expressing grammatical knowledge that is in us.

Second Reply: Crafts versus Virtues

Moreover, in any case what is true of crafts is not true of virtues. For the products of a craft determine by their own character whether they have been produced well; and so it suffices that they are in the right state when they have been produced. But for actions expressing virtue to be done temperately or justly [and hence well] it does not suffice that they are themselves in the right state. Rather, the agent must also be in the right state when he does them. First, he must know [that he is doing virtuous actions]; second, he must decide on them, and decide on them for themselves; and, third, he must also do them from a firm and unchanging state.

As conditions for having a craft these three do not count, except for the knowing itself. As a condition for having a virtue, however, the knowing counts for nothing, or [rather] for only a little, whereas the other two conditions are very important, indeed all-important. And these other two conditions are achieved by the frequent doing of just and temperate actions.

Hence actions are called just or temperate when they are the sort that a just or temperate person would do. But the just and temperate person is not the one who [merely] does these actions, but the one who also does them in the way in which just or temperate people do them.

It is right, then, to say that a person comes to

be just from doing just actions and temperate from doing temperate actions; for no one has even a prospect of becoming good from failing to do them.

Virtue Requires Habituation, and Therefore Requires Practice, Not Just Theory

The many, however, do not do these actions but take refuge in arguments, thinking that they are doing philosophy, and that this is the way to become excellent people. In this they are like a sick person who listens attentively to the doctor, but acts on none of his instructions. Such a course of treatment will not improve the state of his body; any more than will the many's way of doing philosophy improve the state of their souls.

VI. A Virtue of Character is a State Intermediate between Two Extremes, and Involving Decision

The Genus: Feelings, Capacities, States

Next we must examine what virtue is. Since there are three conditions arising in the soul—feelings, capacities and states—virtue must be one of these.

By feelings I mean appetite, anger, fear, confidence, envy, joy, love, hate, longing, jealousy, pity, in general whatever implies pleasure or pain.

By capacities I mean what we have when we are said to be capable of these feelings—capable of, e.g., being angry or afraid or feeling pity.

By states I mean what we have when we are well or badly off in relation to feelings. If, e.g., our feeling is too intense or slack, we are badly off in relation to anger, but if it is intermediate, we are well off; and the same is true in the other cases.

Virtue Is Not a Feeling . . .

First, then, neither virtues nor vices are feelings. (a) For we are called excellent or base insofar as

we have virtues or vices, not insofar as we have feelings. (b) We are neither praised nor blamed insofar as we have feelings; for we do not praise the angry or the frightened person, and do not blame the person who is simply angry, but only the person who is angry in a particular way. But we are praised or blamed insofar as we have virtues or vices. (c) We are angry and afraid without decision; but the virtues are decisions of some kind, or [rather] require decision. (d) Besides, insofar as we have feelings, we are said to be moved; but insofar as we have virtues or vices, we are said to be in some condition rather than moved.

Or a Capacity . . .

For these reasons the virtues are not capacities either; for we are neither called good nor called bad insofar as we are simply capable of feelings. Further, while we have capacities by nature, we do not become good or bad by nature; we have discussed this before.

But a State

If, then, the virtues are neither feelings nor capacities, the remaining possibility is that they are states. And so we have said what the genus of virtue is.

The Differentia

But we must say not only, as we already have, that it is a state, but also what sort of state it is.

Virtue and the Human Function

It should be said, then, that every virtue causes its possessors to be in a good state and to perform their functions well; the virtue of eyes, e.g., makes the eyes and their functioning excellent, because it makes us see well; and similarly, the virtue of a horse makes the horse excellent, and thereby good at galloping, at carrying its rider and at standing steady in the face of the enemy. If this is true in every case, then the virtue of a human being will likewise be the state that makes a human being good and makes him perform his function well.

We have already said how this will be true, and it will also be evident from our next remarks, if we consider the sort of nature that virtue has.

The Numerical Mean and the Mean Relative to Us

In everything continuous and divisible we can take more, less, and equal, and each of them either in the object itself or relative to us; and the equal is some intermediate between excess and deficiency.

By the intermediate in the object I mean what is equidistant from each extremity; this is one and the same for everyone. But relative to us the intermediate is what is neither superfluous nor deficient; this is not one, and is not the same for everyone.

If, e.g., ten are many and two are few, we take six as intermediate in the object, since it exceeds [two] and is exceeded [by ten] by an equal amount, [four]; this is what is intermediate by numerical proportion. But that is not how we must take the intermediate that is relative to us. For if, e.g., ten pounds [of food] are a lot for someone to eat, and two pounds a little, it does not follow that the trainer will prescribe six, since this might also be either a little or a lot for the person who is to take it—for Milo [the athlete] a little, but for the beginner in gymnastics a lot; and the same is true for running and wrestling. In this way every scientific expert avoids excess and deficiency and seeks and chooses what is intermediate—but intermediate relevant to us, not in the object.

Virtue Seeks the Mean Relative to Us: Argument from Craft to Virtue

This, then, is how each science produces its product well, by focusing on what is intermediate and making the product conform to that. This, indeed, is why people regularly comment on well-made products that nothing could be added or subtracted, since they assume that excess or deficiency ruins a good [result] while the mean preserves it. Good craftsmen also, we say, focus on what is intermediate when they produce their product. And since virtue, like nature, is better and more exact than any craft, it will also aim at what is intermediate.

Arguments from the Nature of Virtue of Character

By virtue I mean virtue of character; for this [pursues the mean because] it is concerned with feelings and actions, and these admit of excess, deficiency and an intermediate condition. We can be afraid, e.g., or be confident, or have appetites, or get angry, or feel pity, in general have pleasure or pain, both too much and too little, and in both ways not well; but [having these feelings] at the right times, about the right things, towards the right people, for the right end, and in the right way, is the intermediate and best condition, and this is proper to virtue. Similarly, actions also admit of excess, deficiency, and the intermediate condition.

Now virtue is concerned with feelings and actions, in which excess and deficiency are in error and incur blame, while the intermediate condition is correct and wins praise, which are both proper features of virtue. Virtue, then, is a mean, insofar as it aims at what is intermediate.

Moreover, there are many ways to be in error, since badness is proper to what is unlimited, as the Pythagoreans pictured it, and good to what is limited; but there is only one way to be correct. That is why error is easy and correctness hard; since it is easy to miss the target and hard to hit it. And so for this reason also excess and deficiency are proper to vice, the mean to virtue; 'for we are noble in only one way, but bad in all sorts of ways.'

Definition of Virtue

Virtue, then, is (a) a state that decides, (b) [consisting] in a mean, (c) the mean relative to us, (d) which is defined by reference to reason, (e) i.e., to the reason by reference to which the intelligent person would define it. It is a mean between two vices, one of excess and one of deficiency.

It is a mean for this reason also: Some vices miss what is right because they are deficient, others because they are excessive, in feelings or in actions, while virtue finds and chooses what is intermediate.

Hence, as far as its substance and the account stating its essence are concerned, virtue is a mean; but as far as the best [condition] and the good [result] are concerned, it is an extremity.

The Definition Must Not Be Misapplied to Cases in Which There Is No Mean

But not every action or feeling admits of the mean. For the names of some automatically include baseness, e.g., spite, shamelessness, envy [among feelings], and adultery, theft, murder, among actions. All of these and similar things are called by these names because they themselves, not their excesses or deficiencies, are base.

Hence in doing these things we can never be correct, but must invariably be in error. We cannot do them well or not well—e.g., by committing adultery with the right woman at the right time in the right way; on the contrary, it is true unconditionally that to do any of them is to be in error.

[To think these admit of a mean], therefore, is like thinking that unjust or cowardly or intemperate action also admits of a mean, an excess and a deficiency. For then there would be a mean of excess, a mean of deficiency, an excess of excess and a deficiency of deficiency.

Rather, just as there is no excess or deficiency of temperance or of bravery, since the intermediate is a sort of extreme [in achieving the good], so also there is no mean of these [vicious actions] either, but whatever way anyone does them, he is in error. For in general there is no mean of excess or of deficiency, and no excess or deficiency of a mean.

VII. The Definition of Virtue as a Mean Applies to the Individual Virtues

However, we must not only state this general account but also apply it to the particular cases. For among accounts concerning actions, though the general ones are common to more cases, the specific ones are truer, since actions are about particular cases, and our account must accord with these. Let us, then, find these from the chart.

Classification of Virtues of Character: Virtues Concerned with Feelings

(1) First, in feelings of fear and confidence the mean is bravery. The excessively fearless person is nameless (and in fact many cases are nameless), while the one who is excessively confident is rash; the one who is excessively afraid and deficient in confidence is cowardly.

(2) In pleasures and pains, though not in all types, and in pains less than in pleasures, the mean is temperance and the excess intemperance. People deficient in pleasure are not often found, which is why they also lack even a name; let us call them insensible.

Virtues Concerned with External Goods

(3) In giving and taking money the mean is generosity, the excess wastefulness and the deficiency ungenerosity. Here the vicious people have contrary excesses and defects; for the wasteful person spends to excess and is deficient in taking, whereas the ungenerous person takes to excess and is deficient in spending. At the moment we are speaking in outline and summary, and that suffices; later we shall define these things more exactly.

(4) In questions of money there are also other conditions. Another mean is magnificence; for the magnificent person differs from the generous by being concerned with large matters, while the generous person is concerned with small. The

excess is ostentation and vulgarity, and the deficiency niggardliness, and these differ from the vices related to generosity in ways we shall describe later.

(5) In honor and dishonor the mean is magnanimity, the excess something called a sort of vanity, and the deficiency pusillanimity.

(6) And just as we said that generosity differs from magnificence in its concern with small matters, similarly there is a virtue concerned with small honors, differing in the same way from magnanimity, which is concerned with great honors. For honor can be desired either in the right way or more or less than is right. If someone desires it to excess, he is called an honor-lover, and if his desire is deficient he is called indifferent to honor, but if he is intermediate he has no name. The corresponding conditions have no name either, except the condition of the honor-lover, which is called honor-loving.

This is why people at the extremes claim that intermediate area. Indeed, we also sometimes call the intermediate person an honor-lover, and sometimes call him indifferent to honor; and sometimes we praise the honor-lover, sometimes the person indifferent to honor. We will mention later the reason we do this; for the moment, let us speak of the other cases in the way we have laid down.

Virtues Concerned with Social Life

(7) Anger also admits of an excess, deficiency, and mean. These are all practically nameless; but since we call the intermediate person mild, let us call the mean mildness. Among the extreme people let the excessive person be irascible, and the vice be irascibility, and let the deficient person be a sort of inirascible person, and the deficiency be inirascibility.

There are three other means, somewhat similar to one another, but different. For they are all concerned with association in conversations and actions, but differ insofar as one is concerned

with truth-telling in these areas, the other two with sources of pleasure, some of which are found in amusement, and the others in daily life in general. Hence we should also discuss these states, so that we can better observe that in every case the man is praiseworthy, while the extremes are neither praiseworthy nor correct, but blameworthy. Most of these cases are also nameless, and we must try, as in the other cases also, to make names ourselves, to make things clear and easy to follow.

(8) In truth-telling, then, let us call the intermediate person truthful, and the mean truthfulness; pretense that overstates will be boastfulness, and the person who has it boastful, pretense that understates will be self-deprecation, and the person who has it self-deprecating.

(9) In sources of pleasure in amusements let us call the intermediate person witty, and the condition wit; the excess buffoonery and the person who has it a buffoon; and the deficient person a sort of boor and the state boorishness.

(10) In the other sources of pleasure, those in daily life, let us call the person who is pleasant in the right way friendly, and the mean state friendliness. If someone goes to excess with no [further] aim he will be ingratiating; if he does it for his own advantage, a flatterer. The deficient person, unpleasant in everything, will be a sort of quarrelsome and ill-tempered person.

Mean States That Are Not Virtues

(11) There are also means in feelings and concerned with feelings: shame, e.g., is not a virtue, but the person prone to shame as well as the virtuous person we have described receives praise. For here also one person is called intermediate, and another—the person excessively prone to shame, who is ashamed about everything—is called excessive; the person who is deficient in shame or never feels shame at all is said to have no sense of disgrace; and the intermediate one is called prone to shame.

(12) Proper indignation is the mean between envy and spite: these conditions are concerned with pleasure and pain at what happens to our neighbors. For the properly indignant person feels pain when someone does well undeservedly; the envious person exceeds him by feeling pain when anyone does well, while the spiteful is so deficient in feeling pain that he actually enjoys [other people's misfortunes]. . . .

VIII. The Relations between Means and Extreme

The Mean Is Opposed to Each Extreme

Among these three conditions, then, two are vices—one of excess, one of deficiency—and one—the mean—is virtue. In a way each of them is opposed to each of the others, since each extreme is contrary both to the intermediate condition and to the other extreme, while the intermediate is contrary to the extremes. For as the equal is greater in comparison to the smaller, and smaller in comparison to the greater, so also the intermediate states are excessive in comparison to the deficiencies and deficient in comparison to the excesses—both in feelings and in actions.

For the brave person, e.g., appears rash in comparison to the coward, and cowardly in comparison to the rash person; similarly, the temperate person appears intemperate in comparison to the insensible person, and insensible in comparison with the intemperate person, and the generous person appears wasteful in comparison to the ungenerous, and ungenerous in comparison to the wasteful person. That is why each of the extreme people tries to push the intermediate person to the other extreme, so that the coward, e.g., calls the brave person rash, and the rash person calls him a coward, and similarly in the other cases.

Extremes Are More Opposed to Each Other Than to the Mean

Because these conditions of soul are opposed to each other in these ways, the extremes are more contrary to each other than to the intermediate. For they are further from each other than from the intermediate, just as the large is further from the small, and the small from the large, than either is from the equal.

Moreover, sometimes one extreme, e.g., rashness or wastefulness, appears somewhat like the intermediate state, e.g., bravery or generosity; but the extremes are most unlike one another; and the things that are furthest apart from each other are defined as contraries. Hence also the things that are further apart are more contrary.

Sometimes One Extreme Is More Opposed Than the Other to the Mean

In some cases the deficiency, in others the excess, is more opposed to the intermediate condition; e.g., it is cowardice, the deficiency, not rashness, the excess, that is more opposed to bravery; on the other hand, it is intemperance, the excess, not insensibility, the deficiency, that is more opposed to temperance. This happens for two reasons.

One reason is derived from the object itself. Since sometimes one extreme is closer and more similar to the intermediate condition, we oppose the contrary extreme, more than this closer one, to the intermediate condition. Since rashness, e.g., seems to be closer and more similar to bravery, and cowardice less similar, we oppose cowardice more than rashness to bravery; for what is further from the intermediate condition seems to be more contrary to it. This, then, is one reason, derived from the object itself.

The other reason is derived from ourselves. For when we ourselves have some natural tendency to one extreme more than the other, this extreme appears more opposed to the intermediate condition; since, e.g., we have more of a natural tendency to pleasure, we drift more easily towards intemperance than towards orderliness. Hence we say that an extreme is more contrary if we naturally develop more in that direction; and this is why intemperance is more contrary to temperance, since it is the excess.

Practical Advice on Ways to Achieve the Mean

We have said enough, then, to show that virtue of character is a mean and what sort of mean it is; that it is a mean between two vices, one of excess and one of deficiency; and that it is a mean because it aims at the intermediate condition in feelings and actions.

Hence it is hard work to be excellent, since in each case it is hard work to find what is intermediate; e.g., not everyone, but only one who knows, finds the midpoint in a circle. So also getting angry, or giving and spending money, is easy and anyone can do it; but doing it to the right person, in the right amount, at the right time, for the right end, and in the right way is no longer easy, nor can everyone do it. Hence [doing these things] well is rare, praiseworthy, and fine.

Avoid the More Opposed Extreme

Hence if we aim at the intermediate condition we must first of all steer clear of the more contrary extreme, following the advice that Calypso also gives—'Hold the ship outside the spray and surge.' For since one extreme is more in error, the other less, and since it is hard to hit the intermediate extremely accurately, the second-best tack, as they say, is to take the lesser of the evils. We shall succeed best in this by the method we describe.

Avoid the Easier Extreme

We must also examine what we ourselves drift into easily. For different people have different natural tendencies towards different goals, and we shall come to know our own tendencies from the pleasure or pain that arises in us. We must drag ourselves off in the contrary direction; for if we pull far away from error, as they do in straight-ening bent wood, we shall reach the intermediate condition.

Be Careful with Pleasures

And in everything we must beware above all of pleasure and its sources; for we are already biased in its favor when we come to judge it. Hence we must react to it as the elders reacted to Helen, and on each occasion repeat what they said; for if we do this, and send it off, we shall be less in error.

These Rules Do Not Give Exact and Detailed Guidance

In summary, then, if we do these things we shall best be able to reach the intermediate condition. But no doubt this is hard, especially in particular cases, since it is not easy to define the way we should be angry, with whom, about what, for how long; for sometimes, indeed, we ourselves praise deficient people and call them mild, and sometimes praise quarrelsome people and call them manly. Still, we are not blamed if we deviate a little in excess or deficiency from doing well, but only if we deviate a long way, since then we are easily noticed.

But how far and how much we must deviate to be blamed is not easy to define in an account; for nothing perceptible is easily defined, and [since] these [circumstances of virtuous and vicious action] are particulars, the judgment about them depends on perception.

All this makes it clear, then, that in every case the intermediate state is praised, but we must sometimes incline towards the excess, sometimes towards the deficiency; for that is the easiest way to succeed in hitting the intermediate condition and [doing] well.

27

Virtue and the Moral Life

BERNARD MAYO

Bernard Mayo taught philosophy at the University of Birmingham in England until his retirement in 1968. He is the author of several works in philosophy, including Ethics and the Moral Life *(1958), from which this selection is taken. Contrasting the ethics of "doing" of the deontologists and teleologists with the ethics of "being" or character, the morality of the saints and heroes, Mayo contends that the saints and heroes show us that it is a living example that is important in ethics, not rigid rules. We learn more about ethics by looking at the lives of such people than by learning a set of principles.*

The philosophy of moral principles, which is characteristic of Kant and the post-Kantian era, is something of which hardly a trace exists in Plato. . . . Plato says nothing about rules or principles or laws, except when he is talking politics. Instead he talks about virtues and vices, and about certain types of human character. The key word in Platonic ethics is Virtue; the key word in Kantian ethics is Duty. And modern ethics is a set of footnotes, not to Plato, but to Kant. . . .

Attention to the novelists can be a welcome correction to a tendency of philosophical ethics of the last generation or two to lose contact with the ordinary life of man, which is just what the novelists, in their own way, are concerned with. Of course there are writers who can be called in to illustrate problems about Duty (Graham Greene is a good example). But there are more who perhaps never mention the words duty, obligation, or principle. Yet they are all concerned—Jane Austen, for instance, entirely and absolutely—with the moral qualities or defects of their heroes and

heroines and other characters. This points to a radical one-sidedness in the philosophers' account of morality in terms of principles: it takes little or no account of qualities, of what people *are*. It is just here that the old-fashioned word Virtue used to have a place; and it is just here that the work of Plato and Aristotle can be instructive. Justice, for Plato, though it is closely connected with acting according to law, does not *mean* acting according to law: it is a quality of character, and a just action is one such as a just man would do. Telling the truth, for Aristotle, is not, as it was for Kant, fulfilling an obligation; again it is a quality of character, or, rather, a whole range of qualities of character, some of which may actually be defects, such as tactlessness, boastfulness, and so on—a point which can be brought out, in terms of principles, only with the greatest complexity and artificiality, but quite simply and naturally in terms of character.

If we wish to enquire about Aristotle's moral views, it is no use looking for a set of principles. Of course we can find *some* principles to which he must have subscribed—for instance, that one ought not to commit adultery. But what we find much more prominently is a set of character-traits, a list of certain types of person—the courageous man, the niggardly man, the boaster, the lavish spender and so on. The basic moral question, for Aristotle, is not, What shall I do? but, What shall I be?

These contrasts between doing and being, negative and positive, and modern as against Greek morality were noted by John Stuart Mill; I quote from the *Essay on Liberty:*

Christian morality (so-called) has all the characters of a reaction; it is, in great part, a protest

Reprinted from *Ethics and the Moral Life* (Macmillan & Co., 1958) by permission of the publisher.

against Paganism. Its ideal is negative rather than positive, passive rather than active; Innocence rather than Nobleness; Abstinence from Evil, rather than energetic Pursuit of the Good; in its precepts (as has been well said) "Thou shalt not" predominates unduly over "Thou shalt . . ." Whatever exists of magnanimity, highmindedness, personal dignity, even the sense of honor, is derived from the purely human, not the religious part of our education, and never could have grown out of a standard of ethics in which the only worth, professedly recognized, is that of obedience.

Of course, there are connections between being and doing. It is obvious that a man cannot just *be;* he can only be what he is by doing what he does; his moral qualities are ascribed to him because of his actions, which are said to manifest those qualities. But the point is that an ethics of Being must include this obvious fact, that Being involves Doing; whereas an ethics of Doing, such as I have been examining, may easily overlook it. As I have suggested, a morality of principles is concerned only with what people do or fail to do, since that is what rules are for. And as far as this sort of ethics goes, people might well have no moral qualities at all except the possession of principles and the will (and capacity) to act accordingly.

When we speak of a moral quality such as courage, and say that a certain action was courageous, we are not merely saying something about the action. We are referring, not so much to what is done, as to the kind of person by whom we take it to have been done. We connect, by means of imputed motives and intentions, with the character of the agent as courageous. This explains, incidentally, why both Kantians and Utilitarians encounter, in their different ways, such difficulties in dealing with motives, which their principles, on the face of it, have no room for. A Utilitarian, for example, can only praise a courageous action in some such way as this: the action is of a sort such as a person of courage is likely to perform, and courage is a quality of character the

cultivation of which is likely to increase rather than diminish the sum total of human happiness. But Aristotelians have no need of such circumlocution. For them a courageous action just is one which proceeds from and manifests a certain type of character, and is praised because such a character trait is good, or better than others, or is a virtue. An evaluative criterion is sufficient: there is no need to look for an imperative criterion as well, or rather instead, according to which it is not the character which is good, but the cultivation of the character which is right. . . .

No doubt the fundamental moral question is just "What ought I to do?" And according to the philosophy of moral principles, the answer (which must be an imperative "Do this") must be derived from a conjunction of premises consisting (in the simplest case) firstly of a rule, or universal imperative, enjoining (or forbidding) all actions of a certain type in situations of a certain type, and, secondly, a statement to the effect that this is a situation of that type, falling under that rule. In practice the emphasis may be on supplying only one of these premises, the other being assumed or taken for granted: one may answer the question "What ought I to do?" either by quoting a rule which I am to adopt, or by showing that my case is legislated for by a rule which I do adopt . . . [I]f I am in doubt whether to tell the truth about his condition to a dying man, my doubt may be resolved by showing that the case comes under a rule about the avoidance of unnecessary suffering, which I am assumed to accept. But if the case is without precedent in my moral career, my problem may be soluble only by adopting a new principle about what I am to do now and in the future about cases of this kind.

This second possibility offers a connection with moral ideas. Suppose my perplexity is not merely an unprecedented situation which I could cope with by adopting a new rule. Suppose the new rule is thoroughly inconsistent with my existing moral code. This may happen, for instance, if the moral code is one to which I only pay lipservice; if . . . its authority is not yet internalized, or if it has ceased to be so; it is ready for rejection, but its final rejection awaits a moral crisis such as we are assuming to occur. What I now need is not a rule for deciding how to act in this situation and others of its kind. I need a whole set of rules, a complete morality, new principles to live by.

Now, according to the philosophy of moral character, there is another way of answering the fundamental question "What ought I to do?" Instead of quoting a rule, we quote a quality of character, a virtue: we say "Be brave," or "Be patient" or "Be lenient." We may even say "Be a man": if I am in doubt, say, whether to take a risk, and someone says "Be a man," meaning a morally sound man, in this case a man of sufficient courage. (Compare the very different ideal invoked in "Be a gentleman." I shall not discuss whether this is a *moral* ideal.) Here, too, we have the extreme cases, where a man's moral perplexity extends not merely to a particular situation but to his whole way of living. And now the question "What ought I to do?" turns into the question "What ought I to be?"—as indeed, it was treated in the first place. ("Be brave.") It is answered, not by quoting a rule or a set of rules, but by describing a quality of character or a type of person. And here the ethics of character gains a practical simplicity which offsets the greater logical simplicity of the ethics of principles. We do not have to give a list of characteristics or virtues, as we might list a set of principles. We can give a unity to our answer.

Of course we can in theory give a unity to our principles: this is implied by speaking of a *set* of principles. But if such a set is to be a system and not merely aggregate, the unity we are looking for is a logical one, namely, the possibility that some principles are deductible from others, and ultimately from one. But the attempt to construct a deductive moral system is notoriously difficult, and in any case ill-founded. Why should we expect that all rules of conduct should be ultimately reducible to a few?

Saints and Heroes

But when we are asked "What shall I be?" we can readily give a unity to our answer, though not a logical unity. It is the unity of character. A person's character is not merely a list of dispositions; it has the organic unity of something that is more than the sum of its parts. And we can say, in answer to our morally perplexed questioner, not only "Be this" and "Be that," but also "Be like So-and-So"—where So-and-So is either an ideal type of character, or else an actual person taken as representative of the ideal, an exemplar. Examples of the first are Plato's "just man" in the *Republic;* Aristotle's man of practical wisdom, in the *Nicomachean Ethics;* Augustine's citizen of the City of God; the good Communist; the American way of life (which is a collective expression for a type of character). Examples of the second kind, the exemplar, are Socrates, Christ, Buddha, St. Francis, the heroes of epic writers and of novelists. Indeed the idea of the Hero, as well as the idea of the Saint, are very much the expression of this attitude to morality. Heroes and saints are not merely people who did things. They are people whom we are expected, and expect ourselves, to imitate. And imitating them means not merely doing what they did; it means being like them. Their status is not in the least like that of legislators whose laws we admire; for the character of a legislator is irrelevant to our judgment about his legislation. The heroes and saints did not merely give us principles to live by (though some of them did that as well): they gave us examples to follow.

Kant, as we should expect, emphatically rejects this attitude as "fatal to morality." According to him, examples serve only to render *visible* an instance of the moral principle, and thereby to demonstrate its practical feasibility. But every exemplar, such as Christ himself, must be judged by the independent criterion of the moral law, before we are entitled to recognize him as worthy of imitation. I am not suggesting that the subordination of exemplars to principles is incorrect, but that it is one-sided and fails to do justice to a large area of moral experience.

Imitation can be more or less successful. And this suggests another defect of the ethics of principles. It has no room for ideals, except the ideal of a perfect set of principles (which, as a matter of fact, is intelligible only in terms of an ideal character or way of life), and the ideal of perfect conscientiousness (which is itself a character-trait). This results, of course, from the "black-or-white" nature of moral verdicts based on rules.

There are no degrees by which we approach or recede from the attainment of a certain quality or virtue; if there were not, the word "ideal" would have no meaning. Heroes and saints are not people whom we try to be *just* like, since we know that is impossible. It is precisely because it is impossible for ordinary human beings to achieve the same qualities as the saints, and in the same degree, that we do set them apart from the rest of humanity. It is enough if we try to be a little like them. . . .

28

A Critique of Virtue-Based Ethics

WILLIAM FRANKENA

William Frankena until his recent retirement was professor of philosophy at the University of Michigan. He is the author of several works in ethical theory. Frankena, a duty-based ethical theorist, agrees with the virtue-ethicist on the importance of character. But he argues that the nature of the virtues can be derived only from right actions or good consequences. "Traits without principles are blind." For every virtue there must be some possible action to which the virtue corresponds and from which it derives its virtuosity. For example, the character trait of truthfulness is a virtue because telling the truth, in general, is a moral duty. Likewise, benevolence is a virtue because we have a general duty to be beneficent. There is a relation of correspondence between principles and virtues.

Morality and Cultivation of Traits

Our present interest, then, is not in moral principles nor in nonmoral values, but in moral values, in what is morally good or bad. Throughout its history morality has been concerned about the cultivation of certain dispositions, or traits, among which are "character" and such "virtues" (an old-fashioned but still useful term) as honesty, kindness, and conscientiousness. Virtues are dispositions or traits that are not wholly innate; they must all be acquired, at least in part, by teaching and practice, or, perhaps, by grace. They are also traits of "character," rather than traits of "personality" like charm or shyness, and they all involve a tendency to do certain kinds of action in certain kinds of situations, not just to think or

From *Ethics*, Second Edition (Prentice-Hall, 1973), pp. 63-71, © 1973. Reprinted by permission of Prentice-Hall, Inc., Englewood Cliffs, New Jersey.

feel in certain ways. They are not just abilities or skills, like intelligence or carpentry, which one may have without using.

In fact, it has been suggested that morality is or should be conceived as primarily concerned, not with rules or principles as we have been supposing so far, but with the cultivation of such dispositions or traits of character. Plato and Aristotle seem to conceive of morality in this way, for they talk mainly in terms of virtues and the virtuous, rather than in terms of what is right or obligatory. Hume uses similar terms, although he mixes in some nonmoral traits like cheerfulness and wit along with moral ones like benevolence and justice. More recently, Leslie Stephen stated the view in these words:

> . . . morality is internal. The moral law . . . has to be expressed in the form, "be this," not in the form, "do this." . . . the true moral law says "hate not," instead of "kill not." . . . the only mode of stating the moral law must be as a rule of character.[1]

Ethics of Virtue

Those who hold this view are advocating an *ethics of virtue* or being, in opposition to an ethics of duty, principle, or doing. . . . The notion of an ethics of virtue is worth looking at here, not only because it has a long history but also because some spokesmen of "the new morality" seem to espouse it. What would an ethics of virtue be like? It would, of course, not take deontic judgments or principles as basic in morality, as we have been doing; instead, it would take as basic aretaic judgments like "That was a courageous deed," "His action was virtuous," or "Courage is a virtue," and it would insist that deontic judgments are either derivative from such aretaic ones or can be dispensed with entirely. Moreover, it would regard aretaic judgments about actions as secondary and as based on aretaic judgments about agents and their motives or traits, as Hume does when he writes:

. . . when we praise any actions, we regard only the motives that produced them. . . . The external performance has no merit. . . . all virtuous actions derive their merit only from virtuous motives.[2]

For an ethics of virtue, then, what is basic in morality is judgments like "Benevolence is a good motive," "Courage is a virtue," "The morally good man is kind to everyone" or, more simply and less accurately, "Be loving!"—not judgments or principles about what our duty is or what we ought to do. But, of course, it thinks that its basic instructions will guide us, not only about what to be, but also about what to do.

It looks as if there would be three kinds of ethics of virtue, corresponding to the three kinds of ethics of duty covered earlier. The question to be answered is: What dispositions or traits are moral virtues? *Trait-egoism* replies that the virtues are the dispositions that are most conducive to one's own good or welfare, or, alternatively, that prudence or a careful concern for one's own good is the cardinal or basic moral virtue, other virtues being derivative from it. *Trait-utilitarianism* asserts that the virtues are those traits that most promote the general good, or, alternatively, that benevolence is the basic or cardinal moral virtue. These views may be called *trait-teleological,* but, of course, there are also *trait-deontological theories,* which will hold that certain traits are morally good or virtuous simply as such, and not just because of the nonmoral value they may have or promote, or, alternatively, that there are other cardinal or basic virtues besides prudence or benevolence, for example, obedience to God, honesty, or justice. If they add that there is only one

such cardinal virtue, they are monistic, otherwise pluralistic.

To avoid confusion, it is necessary to notice here that we must distinguish between *virtues* and *principles of duty* like "We ought to promote the good" and "We ought to treat people equally." A virtue is not a principle of this kind; it is a disposition, habit, quality, or trait of the person or soul, which an individual either has or seeks to have. Hence, I speak of the principle of *beneficence* and the virtue of *benevolence,* since we have two words with which to mark the difference. In the case of justice, we do not have different words, but still we must not confuse the principle of equal treatment with the disposition to treat people equally.

On the basis of our earlier discussions, we may assume at this point that views of the first two kinds are unsatisfactory, and that the most adequate ethics of virtue would be one of the third sort, one that would posit two cardinal virtues, namely, benevolence and justice, considered now as dispositions or traits of character rather than as principles of duty. By a set of cardinal virtues is meant a set of virtues that (1) cannot be derived from one another and (2) all other moral virtues can be derived from or shown to be forms of them. Plato and other Greeks thought there were four cardinal virtues in this sense: wisdom, courage, temperance, and justice. Christianity is traditionally regarded as having seven cardinal virtues: three "theological" virtues—faith, hope, and love; and four "human" virtues—prudence, fortitude, temperance, and justice. This was essentially St. Thomas Aquinas's view; since St. Augustine regarded the last four as forms of love, only the first three were really cardinal for him. However, many moralists, among them Schopenhauer, have taken benevolence and justice to be the cardinal moral virtues, as I would. It seems to me that all of the usual virtues (such as love, courage, temperance, honesty, gratitude, and considerateness), at least insofar as they are *moral* virtues, can be derived from these two. Insofar as a disposition cannot be derived from benevolence and justice, I should try to argue either that it is not a *moral* virtue (e.g., I take faith, hope, and wisdom to be religious or intellectual, not moral, virtues) or that it is not a virtue at all.

On Being and Doing: Morality of Traits vs. Morality of Principles

We may now return to the issue posed by the quotation from Stephen, though we cannot debate it as fully as we should. To be or to do, that is the question. Should we construe morality as primarily a following of certain principles or as primarily a cultivation of certain dispositions and traits? Must we choose? It is hard to see how a morality of principles can get off the ground except through the development of dispositions to act in accordance with its principles, else all motivation to act on them must be of an *ad hoc* kind, either prudential or impulsively altruistic. Moreover, morality can hardly be content with a mere conformity to rules, however willing and self-conscious it may be, unless it has no interest in the spirit of its law but only in the letter. On the other hand, one cannot conceive of traits of character except as including dispositions and tendencies to act in certain ways in certain circumstances. Hating involves being disposed to kill or harm, being just involves tending to do just acts (acts that conform to the principle of justice) when the occasion calls. Again, it is hard to see how we could know what traits to encourage or inculcate if we did not subscribe to principles, for example, to the principle of utility, or to those of benevolence and justice.

I propose therefore that we regard the morality of duty and principles and the morality of virtues or traits of character not as rival kinds of morality between which we must choose, but as two complementary aspects of the same morality. Then, for every principle there will be a morally good trait, often going by the same name, consisting of a disposition or tendency to act according to it; and for every morally good trait there will be a

principle defining the kind of action in which it is to express itself. To parody a famous dictum of Kant's, I am inclined to think that principles without traits are impotent and traits without principles are blind.

Even if we adopt this double-aspect conception of morality, in which principles are basic, we may still agree that morality does and must put a premium on *being* honest, conscientious, and so forth. If its sanctions or sources of motivation are not to be entirely external (for example, the prospect of being praised, blamed, rewarded, or punished by others) or adventitious (for example, a purely instinctive love of others), if it is to have adequate "internal sanctions," as Mill called them, then morality must foster the development of such dispositions and habits as have been mentioned. It could hardly be satisfied with a mere conformity to its principles even if it could provide us with fixed principles of actual duty. For such a conformity might be motivated entirely by extrinsic or nonmoral considerations, and would then be at the mercy of these other considerations. It could not be counted on in a moment of trial. Besides, since morality cannot provide us with fixed principles of actual duty but only with principles of prima facie duty, it cannot be content with the letter of its law, but must foster in us the dispositions that will sustain us in the hour of decision when we are choosing between conflicting principles of prima facie duty or trying to revise our working rules of right and wrong.

There is another reason why we must cultivate certain traits of character in ourselves and others, or why we must be certain sorts of persons. Although morality is concerned that we act in certain ways, it cannot take the hard line of insisting that we act in precisely those ways, even if those ways could be more clearly defined. We cannot praise and blame or apply other sanctions to an agent simply on the ground that he has or has not acted in conformity with certain principles. It would not be right. Through no fault of his own, the agent may not have known all the relevant facts. What action the principles of morality called for in the situation may not have been clear to him, again through no fault of his own, and he may have been honestly mistaken about his duty. Or his doing what he ought to have done might have carried with it an intolerable sacrifice on his part. He may even have been simply incapable of doing it. Morality must therefore recognize various sorts of excuses and extenuating circumstances. All it can really insist on, then, except in certain critical cases, is that we develop and manifest fixed dispositions to find out what the right thing is and to do it if possible. In this sense a person must "be this" rather than "do this." But it must be remembered that "being" involves at least *trying* to "do." Being without doing, like faith without works, is dead.

At least it will be clear from this discussion that an ethics of duty or principles also has an important place for the virtues and must put a premium on their cultivation as a part of moral education and development. The place it has for virtue and/or the virtues is, however, different from that accorded them by an ethics of virtue. Talking in terms of . . . an ethics of duty, we may say that, if we ask for *guidance* about what to do or not do, then the answer is contained, at least primarily, in two deontic principles and their corollaries, namely, the principles of beneficence and equal treatment. Given these two deontic principles, plus the necessary clarity of thought and factual knowledge, we can know what we morally ought to do or not do, except perhaps in cases of conflict between them. We also know that we should cultivate two virtues, a disposition to be beneficial (i.e., benevolence) and a disposition to treat people equally (justice as a trait). But the point of acquiring these virtues is not further guidance or instruction; the function of the virtues in an ethics of duty is not to tell us what to do but to ensure that we will do it willingly in whatever situations we may face. In an ethics of virtue, on the other hand, the virtues play a dual role—they must not only move us to do what we do, they must also tell us what to do. To parody Alfred Lord Tennyson:

Theirs not (only) to do or die,
Theirs (also) to reason why.

Moral Ideals

This is the place to mention ideals again, which are among what we called the ingredients of morality. One may, perhaps, identify moral ideals with moral principles, but, more properly speaking, moral ideals are ways of being rather than of doing. Having a moral ideal is wanting to be a person of a certain sort, wanting to have a certain trait of character rather than others, for example, moral courage or perfect integrity. That is why the use of exemplary persons like Socrates, Jesus, or Martin Luther King has been such an important part of moral education and self-development, and it is one of the reasons for the writing and reading of biographies or of novels and epics in which types of moral personality are portrayed, even if they are not all heroes or saints. Often such moral ideals of personality go beyond what can be demanded or regarded as obligatory, belonging among the things to be praised rather than required, except as one may require them of oneself. It should be remembered, however, that not all personal ideals are moral ones. Achilles, Hercules, Napoleon, and Prince Charming may all be taken as ideals, but the ideals they represent are not moral ones, even though they may not be immoral ones either. Some ideals, e.g., those of chivalry, may be partly moral and partly nonmoral. There is every reason why one should pursue nonmoral as well as moral ideals, but there is no good reason for confusing them.

When one has a moral ideal, wanting to be a certain sort of moral person, one has at least some motivation to live in a certain way, but one also has something to guide him in living. Here the idea of an ethics of virtue may have a point. One may, of course, take as one's ideal that of being a good man who always does his duty from a sense of duty, perhaps gladly, and perhaps even going a second mile on occasion. Then one's guidance clearly comes entirely from one's rules and principles of duty. However, one may also have an ideal that goes beyond anything that can be regarded by others or even oneself as strict duty or obligation, a form or style of personal being that may be morally good or virtuous, but is not morally required of one. An ethics of virtue seems to provide for such an aspiration more naturally than an ethics of duty or principle, and perhaps an adequate morality should at least contain a region in which we can follow such an idea, over and beyond the region in which we are to listen to the call of duty. There certainly should be moral heroes and saints who go beyond the merely good man, if only to serve as an inspiration to others to be better and do more than they would otherwise be or do. Granted all this, however, it still seems to me that, if one's ideal is truly a moral one, there will be nothing in it that is not covered by the principles of beneficence and justice conceived as principles of what we ought to do in the wider sense referred to earlier.

Dispositions to Be Cultivated

Are there any other moral virtues to be cultivated besides benevolence and justice? No cardinal ones, of course. In this sense our answer to Socrates' question whether virtue is one or many is that it is two. We saw, however, that the principles of beneficence and equality have corollaries like telling the truth, keeping promises, etc. It follows that character traits like honesty and fidelity are virtues, though subordinate ones, and should be acquired and fostered. There will then be other such virtues corresponding to other corollaries of our main principles. Let us call all of these virtues, cardinal and noncardinal, first-order moral virtues. Besides first-order virtues like these, there are certain other moral virtues that ought also to be cultivated, which are in a way more abstract and general and may be called second-

order virtues. Conscientiousness is one such virtue; it is not limited to a certain sector of the moral life, as gratitude and honesty are, but is a virtue covering the whole of the moral life. Moral courage, or courage when moral issues are at stake, is another such second-order virtue; it belongs to all sectors of the moral life. Others that overlap with these are integrity and good-will, understanding good-will in Kant's sense of respect for the moral law.

In view of what was said in a previous chapter, we must list two other second-order traits: a disposition to find out and respect the relevant facts and a disposition to think clearly. These are not just abilities but character traits; one might have the ability to think intelligently without having a disposition to use it. They are therefore virtues, though they are intellectual virtues, not moral ones. Still, though their role is not limited to the moral life, they are necessary to it. More generally speaking, we should cultivate the virtue Plato called wisdom and Aristotle practical wisdom, which they thought of as including all of the intellectual abilities and virtues essential to the moral life.

Still other second-order qualities, which may be abilities rather than virtues, but which must be cultivated for moral living, and so may, perhaps, best be mentioned here, are moral autonomy, the ability to make moral decisions and to revise one's principles if necessary, and the ability to realize vividly, in imagination and feeling, the "inner lives" of others. Of these second-order qualities, the first two have been referred to on occasion and will be again, but something should be said about the last.

If our morality is to be more than a conformity to internalized rules and principles, if it is to include and rest on an understanding of the point of these rules and principles, and certainly if it is to involve *being* a certain kind of person and not merely *doing* certain kinds of things, then we must somehow attain and develop an ability to be aware of others as persons, as important to themselves as we are to ourselves, and to have a lively and sympathetic representation in imagination of their interests and of the effects of our actions on their lives. The need for this is particularly stressed by Josiah Royce and William James. Both men point out how we usually go our own busy and self-concerned ways, with only an external awareness of the presence of others, much as if they were things, and without any realization of their inner and peculiar worlds of personal experience; and both emphasize the need and the possibility of a "higher vision of an inner significance" which pierces this "certain blindness in human beings" and enables us to realize the existence of others in a wholly different way, as we do our own.

What then is thy neighbor? He too is a mass of states, of experiences, thoughts and desires, just as concrete, as thou art. . . . Dost thou believe this? Art thou sure what it means? This is for thee the turning-point of thy whole conduct towards him.

These are Royce's quaint old-fashioned words. Here are James's more modern ones.

This higher vision of an inner significance in what, until then, we had realized only in the dead external way, often comes over a person suddenly; and, when it does so, it makes an epoch in his history.

Royce calls this more perfect recognition of our neighbors "the moral insight" and James says that its practical consequence is "the well-known democratic respect for the sacredness of individuality." It is hard to see how either a benevolent (loving) or a just (equalitarian) disposition could come to fruition without it. To quote James again,

We ought, all of us, to realize each other in this intense, pathetic, and important way.

Doing this is part of what is involved in fully taking the moral point of view.

Two Questions

We can now deal with the question, sometimes raised, whether an action is to be judged right or wrong because of its results, because of the principle it exemplifies, or because the motive, intention, or trait of character involved is morally good or bad. The answer . . . is that an action is to be judged *right* or *wrong* by reference to a principle or set of principles. Even if we say it is right or wrong because of its effects, this means that it is right or wrong by the principle of utility or some other teleological principle. But an act may also be said to be *good* or *bad*, praiseworthy or blameworthy, noble or despicable, and so on, and then the moral quality ascribed to it will depend on the agent's motive, intention, or disposition in doing it.

Another important question here is: What is moral goodness? When is a person morally good and when are his actions, dispositions, motives, or intentions morally good? Not just when he does what is actually right, for he may do what is right from bad motives, in which case he is not morally good, or he may fail to do what is right though sincerely trying to do it, in which case he is not morally bad. Whether he and his actions are morally good or not depends, not on the rightness of what he does or on its consequences, but on his character or motives; so far the statement quoted from Hume is certainly correct. But when are his motives and dispositions morally good? Some answer that a person and his actions are morally good if and only if they are motivated wholly by a sense of duty or a desire to do what is right; the Stoics and Kant sometimes seem to take this extreme view. Others hold that a man and his actions are morally good if and only if they are motivated primarily by a sense of duty or desire to do what is right, though other motives may be present too; still others contend, with Aristotle, that they are at any rate not morally good unless they are motivated at least in part by such a sense or desire. A more reasonable view, to my mind, is that a man and his actions are morally good if it is at least true that, whatever his actual motives in acting are, his sense of duty or desire to do the right is so strong in him that it would keep him trying to do his duty anyway.

Actually, I find it hard to believe that no dispositions or motivations are good or virtuous from the moral point of view except those that include a will to do the right as such. It is more plausible to distinguish two kinds of morally good dispositions or traits of character, first, those that are usually called moral virtues and do include a will to do the right, and second, others like purely natural kindliness or gratefulness, which, while they are nonmoral, are still morality-supporting, since they dispose us to do such actions as morality requires and even to perform deeds, for example, in the case of motherly love, which are well beyond the call of duty.

It has even been alleged that conscientiousness or moral goodness in the sense of a disposition to act from a sense of duty alone is not a good thing or not a virtue—that it is more desirable to have people acting from motives like friendship, gratitude, honor, love, and the like, then from a dry or driven sense of obligation. There is something to be said for this view, though it ignores the nobility of great moral courage and of the higher reaches of moral idealism. But even if conscientiousness or good will is not the only thing that is unconditionally good, as Kant believed, or the greatest of intrinsically good things, as Ross thought, it is surely a good thing from the moral point of view. For an ethics of duty, at any rate, it must be desirable that people do what is right for its own sake, especially if they do it gladly, as a gymnast may gladly make the right move just because it is right.

Notes

1. Leslie Stephen, *The Science of Ethics* (New York: G. P. Putnam's Sons, 1882), pp. 155, 158.

2. David Hume, *Treatise of Human Nature* (1739), Book III, Part II, opening of Sec. I.

29

The Nature of the Virtues

ALASDAIR MACINTYRE

Alasdair MacIntyre (b. 1929) is professor of philosophy at Duke University and the author of several works in philosophy of religion, social theory, and ethics. In this selection from his influential work After Virtue, *MacIntyre carries on the Aristotelian project of grounding morality in the virtues. He asks whether there is a core conception of the virtues, some vital components that are necessary to any social endeavor or practice. He compares five different conceptions of the virtues as they appear in the works of Homer, Aristotle, the New Testament, Jane Austen, and Benjamin Franklin.*

MacIntyre argues that in every society there must be practices in which virtues are exhibited and become defined. Even though practices may vary from society to society, so that different virtues will be highlighted differently in different societies, nevertheless a core set of virtues is necessary for the successful functioning of any practice. MacIntyre provides a penetrating description of these core virtues. He ends his essay by comparing his theory of the virtues with Aristotle's project, arguing that his work is within that tradition.

One response to the history [of Greek and medieval thought about the virtues] might well be to suggest that even within the relatively coherent tradition of thought which I have sketched, there are just too many different and incompatible conceptions of a virtue for there to be any real unity to the concept or indeed to the history. Homer, Sophocles, Aristotle, the New Testament, and medieval thinkers differ from each other in too many ways. They offer us different and incompatible lists of the virtues; they give a different rank

Reprinted from *After Virtue* (1981) by permission of the University of Notre Dame Press and the author.

order of importance to different virtues; and they have different and incompatible theories of the virtues. If we were to consider later Western writers on the virtues, the list of differences and incompatibilities would be enlarged still further; and if we extended our enquiry to Japanese, say, or American Indian cultures, the differences would become greater still. It would be all too easy to conclude that there are a number of rival and alternative conceptions of the virtues, but, even within the tradition which I have been delineating, no single core conception.

The case for such a conclusion could not be better constructed than by beginning from a consideration of the very different lists of items which different authors in different times and places have included in their catalogues of virtues. Some of these catalogues—Homer's, Aristotle's and the New Testament's—I have already noticed at greater or lesser length. Let me at the risk of some repetition recall some of their key features and then introduce for further comparison the catalogues of two later Western writers, Benjamin Franklin and Jane Austen.

The first example is that of Homer. At least some of the items in a Homeric list of the *aretai* would clearly not be counted by most of us nowadays as virtues at all, physical strength being the most obvious example. To this it might be replied that perhaps we ought not to translate the word *aretê* in Homer by our word 'virtue,' but instead by our word 'excellence'; and perhaps, if we were so to translate it, the apparently surprising difference between Homer and ourselves would at first sight have been removed. For we could allow without any kind of oddity that the possession of physical strength is the possession of an excellence. But in fact we would not have removed, but instead would merely have relocated, the difference between Homer and ourselves. For we would now seem to be saying that Homer's concept of an *areté*, an excellence, is one thing and that our concept of a virtue is quite another, since a particular quality can be an excellence in Homer's eyes but not a virtue in ours, and *vice versa*.

But of course it is not that Homer's list of virtues differs only from our own; it also notably differs from Aristotle's. And Aristotle's of course also differs from our own. For one thing, as I noticed earlier, some Greek virtue-words are not easily translatable into English or rather out of Greek. Moreover, consider the importance of friendship as a virtue in Aristotle's list—how different from us! Or the place of *phronésis*—how different from Homer and from us! The mind receives from Aristotle the kind of tribute which the body receives from Homer. But it is not just the case that the difference between Aristotle and Homer lies in the inclusion of some items and the omission of others in their respective catalogues. It turns out also in the way in which those catalogues are ordered, in which items are ranked as relatively central to human excellence and which marginal.

Moreover, the relationship of virtues to the social order has changed. For Homer the paradigm of human excellence is the warrior; for Aristotle it is the Athenian gentleman. Indeed according to Aristotle certain virtues are only available to those of great riches and of high social status; there are virtues which are unavailable to the poor man, even if he is a free man. And those virtues are on Aristotle's view ones central to human life; magnanimity—and once again, any translation of *megalopsuchia* is unsatisfactory—and munificence are not just virtues, but important virtues within the Aristotelian scheme.

At once it is impossible to delay the remark that the most striking contrast with Aristotle's catalogue is to be found neither in Homer's nor in our own, but in the New Testament's. For the New Testament not only praises virtues of which Aristotle knows nothing—faith, hope and love—and says nothing about virtues such as *phronêsis*[1] which are crucial for Aristotle, but it praises at least one quality as a virtue which Aristotle seems to count as one of the vices relative to magnanimity, namely humility. Moreover, since the New Testament quite clearly sees the rich as destined for the pains of Hell, it is clear that the key virtues cannot be available to them; yet they *are* available to slaves. And the New Testament of course differs from both Homer and Aristotle not only in the items included in its catalogue, but once again in its rank ordering of the virtues.

Turn now to compare all three lists of virtues considered so far—the Homeric, the Aristotelian, and the New Testament's—with two much later lists, one which can be compiled from Jane Austen's novels and the other which Benjamin Franklin constructed for himself. Two features stand out in Jane Austen's list. The first is the importance that she allots to the virtue which she calls 'constancy,' a virtue about which I shall say more in a later chapter. In some ways constancy plays a role in Jane Austen analogous to that of *phronêsis* in Aristotle; it is a virtue the possession of which is a prerequisite for the possession of other virtues. The second is the fact that what Aristotle treats as the virtue of agreeableness (a virtue for which he says there is no name) she treats as only the simulacrum of a genuine virtue—the genuine virtue in question is the one she calls amiability. For the man who practices agreeableness does so from considerations of honour and expediency, according to Aristotle; whereas Jane Austen thought it possible and necessary for the possessor of that virtue to have a certain real affection for people as such. (It matters here that Jane Austen is a Christian.) Remember that Aristotle himself had treated military courage as a simulacrum of true courage. Thus we find here yet another type of disagreement over the virtues; namely, one as to which human qualities are genuine virtues and which mere simulacra.

In Benjamin Franklin's list we find almost all

the types of differences from at least one of the other catalogues we have considered and one more. Franklin includes virtues which are new to our consideration such as cleanliness, silence and industry; he clearly considers the drive to acquire itself a part of virtue, whereas for most ancient Greeks this is the vice of *pleonexia;* he treats some virtues which earlier ages had considered minor as major; but he also redefines some familiar virtues. In the list of thirteen virtues which Franklin compiled as part of his system of private moral accounting, he elucidates each virtue by citing a maxim obedience to which *is* the virtue in question. In the case of chastity the maxim is 'Rarely use venery but for health or offspring— never to dullness, weakness or the injury of your own or another's peace or reputation.' This is clearly not what earlier writers had meant by 'chastity.'

We have therefore accumulated a startling number of differences and incompatibilities in the five stated and implied accounts of the virtues. So the question which I raised at the outset becomes more urgent. If different writers in different times and places, but all within the history of Western culture, include such different sets and types of items in their lists, what grounds have we for supposing that they do indeed aspire to list items of one and the same kind, that there is any shared concept at all? A second kind of consideration reinforces the presumption of a negative answer to this question. It is not just that each of these five writers lists different and differing kinds of items; it is also that each of these lists embodies, the expression of a different theory about what a virtue is.

In the Homeric poems a virtue is a quality the manifestation of which enables people to do exactly what their well-defined social role requires. The primary role is that of the warrior king, and that Homer lists those virtues which he does becomes intelligible at once when we recognise that the key virtues therefore must be those which enable a man to excel in combat and in the games. It follows that we cannot identify the Homeric virtues until we have first identified the key social roles in Homeric society and the requirements of each of them. The concept of *what anyone filling such-and-such a role ought to do* is prior to the concept of a virtue; the latter concept has application only via the former.

On Aristotle's account matters are very different. Even though some virtues are available only to certain types of people, none the less virtues attach not to men as inhabiting social roles, but to man as such. It is the *telos* of man as a species which determines what human qualities are virtues. We need to remember however that although Aristotle treats the acquisition and exercise of the virtues as means to an end, the relationship of means to end is internal and not external. I call a means internal to a given end when the end cannot be adequately characterised independently of a characterisation of the means. So it is with the virtues and the *telos* which is the good life for man on Aristotle's account. The exercise of the virtues is itself a crucial component of the good life for man. This distinction between internal and external means to an end is not drawn by Aristotle himself in the *Nicomachean Ethics*, as I noticed earlier, but it is an essential distinction to be drawn if we are to understand what Aristotle intended. The distinction *is* drawn explicitly by Aquinas in the course of his defence of St. Augustine's definition of a virtue, and it is clear that Aquinas understood that in drawing it he was maintaining an Aristotelian point of view.

The New Testament's account of the virtues, even if it differs as much as it does in content from Aristotle's—Aristotle would certainly not have admired Jesus Christ and he would have been horrified by St. Paul—does have the same logical and conceptual structure as Aristotle's account. A virtue is, as with Aristotle, a quality the exercise of which leads to the achievement of the human telos. *The* good for man is of course a supernatural and not only a natural good, but supernature redeems and completes nature. Moreover the relationship of virtues as means to the end which is human incorporation in the divine kingdom of the age to come is internal and not external, just as it is in Aristotle. It is of course this parallelism which allows Aquinas to synthesise Aristotle and the New Testament. A key feature of this parallelism is the way in which the concept of *the good life for man* is prior to the concept of a virtue in just the way in which on the Homeric account the concept of a social role was prior. Once again it is the way in which the former concept is applied which determines how the latter is to be applied. In both cases the concept of a virtue is a secondary concept.

The intent of Jane Austen's theory of the virtues is of another kind. C. S. Lewis has rightly emphasised how profoundly Christian her moral vision is and Gilbert Ryle has equally rightly emphasised her inheritance from Shaftesbury and from Aristotle. In fact her views combine elements from Homer as well, since she is concerned with social roles in a way that neither the New Testament nor Aristotle is. She is therefore important for the way in which she finds it possible to combine what are at first sight disparate theoretical accounts of the virtues. But for the moment any attempt to assess the significance of Jane Austen's synthesis must be delayed. Instead we must notice the quite different style of theory articulated in Benjamin Franklin's account of the virtues.

Franklin's account, like Aristotle's, is teleological; but unlike Aristotle's, it is utilitarian. According to Franklin in his *Autobiography* the virtues are means to an end, but he envisages the means-ends relationship as external rather than internal. The end to which the cultivation of the virtues ministers is happiness, but happiness understood as success, prosperity in Philadelphia and ultimately in heaven. The virtues are to be useful, and Franklin's account continuously stresses utility as a criterion in individual cases: 'Make no expence but to do good to others or yourself; i.e., waste nothing,' 'Speak not but what may benefit others or yourself. Avoid trifling conversation,' and, as we have already seen, 'Rarely use venery but for health or offspring. . . .' When Franklin

was in Paris he was horrified by Parisian architecture: 'Marble, porcelain and gilt are squandered without utility.'

We thus have at least three very different conceptions of a virtue to confront: a virtue is a quality which enables an individual to discharge his or her social role (Homer); a virtue is a quality which enables an individual to move toward the achievement of the specifically human *telos*, whether natural or supernatural (Aristotle, the New Testament and Aquinas); a virtue is a quality which has utility in achieving earthly and heavenly success (Franklin). Are we to take these as three rival accounts of the same thing? Or are they instead accounts of three different things? Perhaps the moral structures in archaic Greece, in fourth-century Greece, and in eighteenth-century Pennsylvania were so different from each other that we should treat them as embodying quite different concepts whose difference is initially disguised from us by the historical accident of an inherited vocabulary which misleads us by linguistic resemblance long after conceptual identity and similarity have failed. Our initial question has come back to us with redoubled force.

Yet although I have dwelt upon the *prima facie* case for holding that the differences and incompatibilities between different accounts at least suggest that there is no single, central, core conception of the virtues which might make a claim for universal allegiance, I ought also to point out that each of the five moral accounts which I have sketched so summarily does embody just such a claim. It is indeed just this feature of those accounts that makes them of more than sociological or antiquarian interest. Every one of these accounts claims not only a theoretical but also an institutional hegemony. For Odysseus the Cyclopes stand condemned because they lack agriculture, on *agora* and *themis*. For Aristotle the barbarians stand condemned because they lack the *polis* and are therefore incapable of politics. For New Testament Christians there is no salvation outside the apostolic church. And we know that Benjamin Franklin found the virtues more at home in Philadelphia than in Paris and that for Jane Austen the touchstone of the virtues is a certain kind of marriage and indeed a certain kind of naval officer (that is, a certain kind of *English* naval officer).

The question can therefore now be posed directly: are we or are we not able to disentangle from these rival and various claims a unitary core concept of the virtues of which we can give a more compelling account than any of the other accounts so far? I am going to argue that we can in fact discover such a core concept and that it turns out to provide the tradition of which I have written the history with its conceptual unity. It will indeed enable us to distinguish in a clear way those beliefs about the virtues which genuinely belong to the tradition from those which do not. Unsurprisingly perhaps it is a complex concept, different parts of which derive from different stages in the development of the tradition. Thus the concept itself in some sense embodies the history of which it is the outcome.

One of the features of the concept of a virtue which has emerged with some clarity from the argument so far is that it always requires for its application the acceptance of some prior account of certain features of social and moral life in terms of which it has to be defined and explained. So in the Homeric account the concept of a virtue is secondary to that of *a social role;* in Aristotle's account it is secondary to that of *the good life for man* conceived as the *telos* of human action; and in Franklin's much later account it is secondary to that of utility. What is it in the account which I am about to give which provides in a similar way the necessary background against which the concept of a virtue has to be made intelligible? It is in answering this question that the complex, historical, multilayered character of the core concept of virtue becomes clear. For there are no fewer than three stages in the logical development of the concept which have to be identified in order, if the core conception of a virtue is to be understood, and each of these stages has its own conceptual background. The first stage requires a background account of what I shall call a practice, the

second an account of what I have already characterised as the narrative order of a single human life, and the third an account a good deal fuller than I have given up to now of what constitutes a moral tradition. Each later stage presupposes the earlier, but not *vice versa*. Each earlier stage is both modified by and reinterpreted in the light of, but also provides an essential constituent of each later stage. The progress in the development of the concept is closely related to, although it does not recapitulate in any straightforward way, the history of the tradition of which it forms the core.

In the Homeric account of the virtues—and in heroic societies more generally—the exercise of a virtue exhibits qualities which are required for sustaining a social role and for exhibiting excellence in some well-marked area of social practice: to excel is to excel at war or in the games, as Achilles does; in sustaining a household, as Penelope does; in giving counsel in the assembly, as Nestor does; in the telling of a tale, as Homer himself does. When Aristotle speaks of excellence in human activity, he sometimes, though not always, refers to some well-defined type of human practice: flute-playing, or war, or geometry. I am going to suggest that this notion of a particular type of practice as providing the arena in which the virtues are exhibited and in terms of which they are to receive their primary, if incomplete, definition is crucial to the whole enterprise of identifying a core concept of the virtues. I hasten to add two *caveats* however.

The first is to point out that my argument will not in any way imply that virtues are exercised *only* in the course of what I am calling practices. The second is to warn that I shall be using the word 'practice' in a specially defined way which does not completely agree with current ordinary usage, including my own previous use of that word. What am I going to mean by it?

By a 'practice' I am going to mean any coherent and complex form of socially established cooperative human activity through which goods internal to that form of activity are realised in the course of trying to achieve those standards of excellence which are appropriate to, and partially definitive of, that form of activity, with the result that human powers to achieve excellence, and human conceptions of the ends and goods involved, are systematically extended. Tic-tac-toe is not an example of a practice in this sense, nor is throwing a football with skill; but the game of football is, and so is chess. Bricklaying is not a practice; architecture is. Planting turnips is not a practice; farming is. So are the enquiries of physics, chemistry, and biology, and so is the work of the historian, and so are painting and music. In the ancient and medieval worlds the creation and sustaining of human communities—of households, cities, nations—is generally taken to be a practice in the sense in which I have defined it. Thus the range of practices is wide: arts, sciences, games, politics in the Aristotelian sense, the making and sustaining of family life—all fall under the concept. But the question of the precise range of practices is not at this stage of the first importance. Instead let me explain some of the key terms involved in my definition, beginning with the notion of goods internal to a practice.

Consider the example of a highly intelligent seven-year-old child whom I wish to teach to play chess, although the child has no particular desire to learn the game. The child does however have a very strong desire for candy and little chance of obtaining it. I therefore tell the child that if the child will play chess with me once a week I will give the child 50¢ worth of candy; moreover I tell the child that I will always play in such a way that it will be difficult, but not impossible, for the child to win and that, if the child wins, the child will receive an extra 50¢ worth of candy. Thus motivated the child plays and plays to win. Notice however that, so long as it is the candy alone which provides the child with a good reason for playing chess, the child has no reason not to cheat and every reason to cheat, provided he or she can do so successfully. But, so we may hope, there will come a time when the child will find in those goods specific to chess, in the achievement of a certain highly particular kind of analytical skill,

strategic imagination, and competitive intensity, a new set of reasons, reasons now not just for winning on a particular occasion, but for trying to excel in whatever way the game of chess demands. Now if the child cheats, he or she will be defeating not me but himself or herself.

There are thus two kinds of goods possibly to be gained by playing chess. On the one hand there are those goods externally and contingently attached to chess-playing and to other practices by the accidents of social circumstance—in the case of the imaginary child candy, in the case of real adults such goods as prestige, status, and money. There are always alternative ways for achieving such goods, and their achievement is never to be had *only* by engaging in some particular kind of practice. On the other hand there are the goods internal to the practice of chess which cannot be had in any way but by playing chess or some other game of that specific kind. We call them internal for two reasons: first, as I have already suggested, because we can only specify them in terms of chess or some other game of that specific kind and by means of examples from such games (otherwise the meagerness of our vocabulary for speaking of such goods forces us into such devices as my own resort to writing of 'a certain highly particular kind of'); and secondly because they can only be identified and recognised by the experience of participating in the practice in question. Those who lack the relevant experience are incompetent thereby as judges of internal goods.

This is clearly the case with all the major examples of practices: consider for example—even if briefly and inadequately—the practice of portrait painting as developed in Western Europe from the late middle ages to the eighteenth century. The successful portrait painter is able to achieve many goods which are in the sense just defined external to the practice of portrait painting—fame, wealth, social status, even a measure of power and influence at courts upon occasion. But those external goods are not to be confused with the goods which are internal to the practice. The internal goods are those which result from an extended attempt to show how Wittgenstein's dictum 'The human body is the best picture of the human soul' (*Investigations*, p. 178e) might be made to become true by teaching us 'to regard . . . the picture on our wall as the object itself (the men, landscape, and so on) depicted there' (p. 205e) in a quite new way. What is misleading about Wittgenstein's dictum as it stands is its neglect of the truth in George Orwell's thesis 'At 50 everyone has the face he deserves.' What painters from Giotto to Rembrandt learned to show was how the face at any age may be revealed as the face that the subject of a portrait deserves.

Originally in medieval paintings of the saints the face was an icon; the question of a resemblance between the depicted face of Christ or St. Peter and the face that Jesus or Peter actually possessed at some particular age did not even arise. The antithesis to this iconography was the relative naturalism of certain fifteenth-century Flemish and German painting. The heavy eyelids, the coifed hair, the lines around the mouth undeniably represent some particular woman, either actual or envisaged. Resemblance has usurped the iconic relationship. But with Rembrandt there is, so to speak, synthesis: the naturalistic portrait is now rendered as an icon, but an icon of a new and hitherto inconceivable kind. Similarly in a very different kind of sequence mythological faces in a certain kind of seventeenth-century French painting become aristocratic faces in the eighteenth century. Within each of these sequences at least two different kinds of good internal to the painting of human faces and bodies are achieved.

There is first of all the excellence of the products, both the excellence in performance by the painters and that of each portrait itself. This excellence—the very verb 'excel' suggests it—has to be understood historically. The sequences of development find their point and purpose in a progress toward and beyond a variety of types and modes of excellence. There are of course sequences of decline as well as of progress, and progress is rarely to be understood as straightforwardly linear. But it is in participation in the at-

tempts to sustain progress and to respond creatively to moments that the second kind of good internal to the practices of portrait painting is to be found. For what the artist discovers within the pursuit of excellence in portrait painting—and what is true of portrait painting is true of the practice of the fine arts in general—is the good of a certain kind of life. That life may not constitute the whole of life for someone who is a painter by a very long way, for it may at least for a period, Gauguin-like, absorb him or her at the expense of almost everything else. But it is the painter's living out of a greater or lesser part of his or her life *as a painter* that is the second kind of good internal to painting. And judgment upon these goods requires at the very least the kind of competence that is only to be acquired either as a painter or as someone willing to learn systematically what the portrait painter has to teach.

A practice involves standards of excellence and obedience to rules as well as the achievement of goods. To enter into a practice is to accept the authority of those standards and the inadequacy of my own performance as judged by them. It is to subject my own attitudes, choices, preferences, and tastes to the standards which currently and partially define the practice. Practices of course, as I have just noticed, have a history: games, sciences, and arts all have histories. Thus the standards are not themselves immune from criticism, but none the less we cannot be initiated into a practice without accepting the authority of the best standards realised so far. If, on starting to listen to music, I do not accept my own incapacity to judge correctly, I will never learn to hear, let alone to appreciate, Bartok's last quartets. If, on starting to play baseball, I do not accept that others know better than I when to throw a fast-ball and when not, I will never learn to appreciate good pitching, let alone to pitch. In the realm of practices the authority of both goods and standards operates in such a way as to rule out all subjectivist and emotivist analyses of judgment. De gustibus *est* disputandum.

We are now in a position to notice an important

difference between what I have called internal and what I have called external goods. It is characteristic of what I have called external goods that when achieved they are always some individual's property and possession. Moreover characteristically they are such that the more someone has of them, the less there is for other people. This is sometimes necessarily the case, as with power and fame, and sometimes the case by reason of contingent circumstance, as with money. External goods are therefore characteristically objects of competition in which there must be losers as well as winners. Internal goods are indeed the outcome of competition to excel, but it is characteristic of them that their achievement is a good for the whole community who participate in the practice. So when Turner transformed the seascape in painting or W. G. Grace advanced the art of batting in cricket in a quite new way their achievement enriched the whole relevant community.

But what does all or any of this have to do with the concept of the virtues? It turns out that we are now in a position to formulate a first, even if partial and tentative, definition of a virtue: *A virtue is an acquired human quality the possession and exercise of which tends to enable us to achieve those goods which are internal to practices and the lack of which effectively prevents us from achieving any such goods.* Later this definition will need amplification and amendment. But as a first approximation to an adequate definition it already illuminates the place of the virtues in human life. For it is not difficult to show for a whole range of key virtues that without them the goods internal to practices are barred to us, but not just barred to us generally—barred in a very particular way.

It belongs to the concept of a practice as I have outlined it—and as we are all familiar with it already in our actual lives, whether we are painters or physicists or quarterbacks or indeed just lovers of good painting or first-rate experiments or a well-thrown pass—that its goods can only be achieved by subordinating ourselves to the best standard so far achieved, and that entails subordinating ourselves within the practice in our rela-

tionship to other practitioners. We have to learn to recognise what is due to whom; we have to be prepared to take whatever self-endangering risks are demanded along the way; and we have to listen carefully to what we are told about our own inadequacies and to reply with the same carefulness for the facts. In other words we have to accept as necessary components of any practice with internal goods and standards of excellence the virtues of justice, courage, and honesty. For not to accept these, to be willing to cheat as our imagined child was willing to cheat in his or her early days at chess, so far bars us from achieving the standards of excellence or the goods internal to the practice that it renders the practice pointless except as a device for achieving external goods.

We can put the same point in another way. Every practice requires a certain kind of relationship between those who participate in it. Now the virtues are those goods by reference to which, whether we like it or not, we define our relationships to those other people with whom we share the kind of purposes and standards which inform practices. Consider an example of how reference to the virtues has to be made in certain kinds of human relationship.

A, B, C, and D are friends in that sense of friendship which Aristotle takes to be primary: they share in the pursuit of certain goods. In my terms they share in a practice. D dies in obscure circumstances, A discovers how D died and tells the truth about it to B while lying to C. C discovers the lie. What A cannot then intelligibly claim is that he stands in the same relationship of friendship to both B and C. By telling the truth to one and lying to the other he has partially defined a difference in the relationship. Of course it is open to A to explain this difference in a number of ways; perhaps he was trying to spare C pain or perhaps he is simply cheating C. But some difference in the relationship now exists as a result of the lie. For their allegiance to each other in the pursuit of common goods has been put in question.

Just as, so long as we share the standards and

purposes characteristic of practices, we define our relationships to each other, whether we acknowledge it or not, by reference to standards of truthfulness and trust, as we define them too by reference to standards of justice and of courage. If A, a professor, gives B and C the grades that their papers deserve, but grades D because he is attracted by D's blue eyes or is repelled by D's dandruff, he has defined his relationship to D differently from his relationship to the other members of the class, whether he wishes it or not. Justice requires that we treat others in respect of merit or desert according to uniform and impersonal standards; to depart from the standards of justice in some particular instance defines our relationship with the relevant person as in some way special or distinctive.

The case with courage is a little different. We hold courage to be a virtue because the care and concern for individuals, communities and causes which is so crucial to so much in practices requires the existence of such a virtue. If someone says that he cares for some individual, community or cause, but is unwilling to risk harm or danger on his, her or its own behalf, he puts in question the genuineness of his care and concern. Courage, the capacity to risk harm or danger to oneself, has its role in human life because of this connection with care and concern. This is not to say that a man cannot genuinely care and also be a coward. It is in part to say that a man who genuinely cares and has not the capacity for risking harm or danger has to define himself, both to himself and to others, as a coward.

I take it then that from the standpoint of those types of relationship without which practices cannot be sustained, truthfulness, justice, and courage—and perhaps some others—are genuine excellences, are virtues in the light of which we have to characterise ourselves and others, whatever our private moral standpoint or our society's particular codes may be. For this recognition that we cannot escape the definition of our relationships in terms of such goods is perfectly compatible with the acknowledgment that different societies have and have had different codes of truthfulness, justice, and courage. Lutheran pietists brought up their children to believe that one ought to tell the truth to everybody at all times, whatever the circumstances or consequences, and Kant was one of their children. Traditional Bantu parents brought up their children not to tell the truth to unknown strangers, since they believed that this could render the family vulnerable to witchcraft. In our culture many of us have been brought up not to tell the truth to elderly great-aunts who invite us to admire their new hats. But each of these codes embodies an acknowledgment of the virtue of truthfulness. So it is also with varying codes of justice and of courage.

Practices then might flourish in societies with very different codes; what they could not do is flourish in societies in which the virtues were not valued, although institutions and technical skills serving unified purposes might well continue to flourish. (I shall have more to say about the contrast between institutions and technical skills mobilised for a unified end, on the one hand, and practices on the other, in a moment.) For the kind of cooperation, the kind of recognition of authority and of achievement, the kind of respect for standards and the kind of risk-taking which are characteristically involved in practices demand for example fairness in judging oneself and others—the kind of fairness absent in my example of the professor, a ruthless truthfulness without which fairness cannot find application—the kind of truthfulness absent in my example of A, B, C, and D—and willingness to trust the judgments of those whose achievement in the practice give them an authority to judge which presupposes fairness and truthfulness in those judgments, and from time to time the taking of self-endangering, reputation-endangering and even achievement-endangering risks. It is no part of my thesis that great violinists cannot be vicious or great chess-players mean-spirited. Where the virtues are required, the vices also may flourish. It is just that the vicious and mean-spirited necessarily rely on the virtues of others for the practices in which they engage to flourish and also deny themselves the experience of achieving those internal goods which may reward even not very good chess-players and violinists.

To situate the virtues any further within practices it is necessary now to clarify a little further the nature of a practice by drawing two important contrasts. The discussion so far I hope makes it clear that a practice, in the sense intended, is never just a set of technical skills, even when directed toward some unified purpose and even if the exercise of those skills can on occasion be valued or enjoyed for its own sake. What is distinctive of a practice is in part the way in which conceptions of the relevant goods and ends which the technical skills serve—and every practice does require the exercise of technical skills—are transformed and enriched by these extensions of human powers and by that regard for its own internal goods which are partially definitive of each particular practice or type of practice. Practices never have a goal or goals fixed for all time—painting has no such goal nor has physics—but the goals themselves are transmuted by the history of the activity. It therefore turns out not to be accidental that every practice has its own history and a history which is more and other than that of the improvement of the relevant technical skills. This historical dimension is crucial in relation to the virtues.

To enter into a practice is to enter into a relationship not only with its contemporary practitioners, but also with those who have preceded us in the practice, particularly those whose achievements extended the reach of the practice to its present point. It is thus the achievement, and *a fortiori* the authority, of a tradition which I then confront and from which I have to learn. And for this learning and the relationship to the past which it embodies, the virtues of justice, courage, and truthfulness are prerequisite in precisely the same way and for precisely the same reasons as they are in sustaining present relationships within practices.

It is not only of course with sets of technical skills that practices ought to be contrasted. Practices must not be confused with institutions. Chess, physics, and medicine are practices; chess clubs, laboratories, universities, and hospitals are institutions. Institutions are characteristically and necessarily concerned with what I have called external goods. They are involved in acquiring money and other material goods; they are structured in terms of power and status, and they distribute money, power, and status as rewards. Nor could they do otherwise if they are to sustain not only themselves, but also the practices of which they are the bearers. For no practices can survive for any length of time unsustained by institutions. Indeed so intimate is the relationship of practices to institutions—and consequently of the goods external to the goods internal to the practices in question—that institutions and practices characteristically form a single causal order in which the ideals and the creativity of the practice are always vulnerable to the acquisitiveness of the institution, in which the cooperative care for common goods of the practice is always vulnerable to the competitiveness of the institution. In this context the essential function of the virtues is clear. Without them, without justice, courage, and truthfulness, practices could not resist the corrupting power of institutions.

Yet if institutions do have corrupting power, the making and sustaining of forms of human community—and therefore of institutions—itself has all the characteristics of a practice, and moreover of a practice which stands in a peculiarly close relationship to the exercise of the virtues in two important ways. The exercise of the virtues is itself apt to require a highly determinate attitude to social and political issues; and it is always within some particular community with its own specific institutional forms that we learn or fail to learn to exercise the virtues. There is of course a crucial difference between the way in which the relationship between moral character and political community is envisaged from the standpoint of liberal individualist modernity and the way in which that relationship was envisaged from the standpoint of the type of ancient and medieval tradition of the virtues which I have sketched. For liberal individualism a community is simply an arena in which individuals each pursue their own self-chosen conception of the good life, and political institutions exist to provide that degree of order which makes such self-determined activity possible. Government and law are, or ought to be, neutral between rival conceptions of the good life for man, and hence, although it is the task of government to promote law-abidingness, it is on the liberal view no part of the legitimate function of government to inculcate any one moral outlook.

By contrast, on the particular ancient and medieval view which I have sketched, political community not only requires the exercise of the virtues for its own sustenance, but is one of the tasks of government to make its citizens virtuous, just as it is one of the tasks of parental authority to make children grow up so as to be virtuous adults. The classical statement of this analogy is by Socrates in the *Crito*. It does not of course follow from an acceptance of the Socratic view of political community and political authority that we ought to assign to the modern state the moral function which Socrates assigned to the city and its laws. Indeed the power of the liberal individualist standpoint partly derives from the evident fact that the modern state is indeed totally unfitted to act as moral educator of any community. But the history of how the modern state emerged is of course itself a moral history. If my account of the complex relationship of virtues to practices and to institutions is correct, it follows that we shall be unable to write a true history of practices and institutions unless that history is also one of the virtues and vices. For the ability of a practice to retain its integrity will depend on the way in which the virtues can be and are exercised in sustaining the institutional forms which are the social bearers of the practice. The integrity of a practice causally requires the exercise of the virtues by at least some of the individuals who embody it in their activities; and conversely the corruption of institutions is always in part at least an effect of the vices.

The virtues are of course themselves in turn fostered by certain types of social institution and endangered by others. Thomas Jefferson thought that only in a society of small farmers could the virtues flourish; and Adam Ferguson with a good deal more sophistication saw the institutions of modern commercial society as endangering at least some traditional virtues. It is Ferguson's type of sociology which is the empirical counterpart of the conceptual account of the virtues which I have given, a sociology which aspires to lay bare the empirical, causal connection between virtues, practices, and institutions. For this kind of conceptual account has strong empirical implications; it provides an explanatory scheme which can be tested in particular cases. Moreover my thesis has empirical content in another way, it does entail that without the virtues there could be a recognition only of what I have called external goods and not at all of internal goods in the context of practices. And in any society which recognised only external goods, competitiveness would be the dominant and even exclusive feature. We have a brilliant portrait of such a society in Hobbes's account of the state of nature; and Professor Turnbull's report of the fate of the Ik suggests that social reality does in the most horrifying way confirm both my thesis and Hobbes's.

Virtues then stand in a different relationship to external and to internal goods. The possession of the virtues—and not only of their semblance and simulacra—is necessary to achieve the latter; yet the possession of the virtues may perfectly well hinder us in achieving external goods. I need to emphasise at this point that external goods genuinely are goods. Not only are they characteristic objects of human desire whose allocation is what gives point to the virtues of justice and generosity, but no one can despise them altogether without a certain hypocrisy. Yet notoriously the cultivation of truthfulness, justice, and courage will often, the world being what it contingently is, bar us from being rich or famous or powerful. Thus although we may hope that we can not only achieve the standards of excellence and the internal goods of certain practices by possessing the virtues *and* become rich, famous and powerful, the virtues are always a potential stumbling block to this comfortable ambition. We should therefore expect that, if in a particular society the pursuit of external goods were to become dominant, the concept of the virtues might suffer first attrition and then perhaps something near total effacement, although simulacra might abound.

The time has come to ask the question of how far this partial account of a core conception of the virtues—and I need to emphasise that all that I have offered so far is the first stage of such an account—is faithful to the tradition which I delineated. How far, for example, and in what ways is it Aristotelian? It is—happily—not Aristotelian in two ways in which a good deal of the rest of the tradition also dissents from Aristotle. First, although this account of the virtues is teleological, it does not require the identification of any teleology in nature, and hence it does not require any allegiance to Aristotle's metaphysical biology. And secondly, just because of the multiplicity of human practices and the consequent multiplicity of goods in the pursuit of which the virtues may be exercised—goods which will often be contingently incompatible and which will therefore make rival claims upon our allegiance—conflict will not spring solely from flaws in individual character. But it was just on these two matters that Aristotle's account of the virtues seemed most vulnerable; hence if it turns out to be the case that this socially teleological account can support Aristotle's general account of the virtues as well as does his own biologically teleological account, these differences from Aristotle himself may well be regarded as strengthening rather than weakening the case for a generally Aristotelian standpoint.

There are at least three ways in which the account that I have given *is* clearly Aristotelian. First it requires for its completion a cogent elaboration of just those distinctions and concepts which Aristotle's account requires: voluntariness, the distinction between the intellectual virtues and the virtues of character, the relationship of both to natural abilities and to the passions and the structure of practical reasoning. On every one of these topics something very like Aristotle's view has to be defended, if my own account is to be plausible.

Secondly my account can accommodate an Aristotelian view of pleasure and enjoyment, whereas it is interestingly irreconcilable with any utilitarian view and more particularly with Franklin's account of the virtues. We can approach these questions by considering how to reply to someone who, having considered my account of the differences between goods internal to and goods external to a practice required into which class, if either, does pleasure or enjoyment fall? The answer is, 'Some types of pleasure into one, some into the other.'

Someone who achieves excellence in a practice, who plays chess or football well, or who carries through an enquiry in physics or an experimental mode in painting with success, characteristically enjoys his achievement and his activity in achieving. So does someone who, although not breaking the limit of achievement, plays or thinks or acts in a way that leads toward such a breaking of limit. As Aristotle says, the enjoyment of the activity and the enjoyment of achievement are not the ends at which the agent aims, but the enjoyment supervenes upon the successful activity in such a way that the activity achieved and the activity enjoyed are one and the same state. Hence to aim at the one is to aim at the other; and hence also it is easy to confuse the pursuit of excellence with the pursuit of enjoyment *in this specific sense.* This particular confusion is harmless enough; what is not harmless is the confusion of enjoyment *in this specific sense* with other forms of pleasure.

For certain kinds of pleasure are of course external goods, along with prestige, status, power, and money. Not all pleasure is the enjoyment supervening upon achieved activity; some is the pleasure of psychological or physical states independent of all activity. Such states—for example that produced on a normal palate by the closely successive and thereby blended sensations of Colchester oyster, cayenne pepper and Veuve Cliquot—may be sought as external goods, as external rewards which may be purchased by money or received in virtue of prestige. Hence the pleasures are categorised neatly and appropriately by the classification into internal and external goods.

It is just this classification which can find no place within Franklin's account of the virtues which is formed entirely in terms of external relationships and external goods. Thus although by this stage of the argument it is possible to claim that my account does capture a conception of the virtues which is at the core of the particular ancient and medieval tradition which I have delineated, it is equally clear that there is more than one possible conception of the virtues and that Franklin's standpoint and indeed any utilitarian standpoint is such that to accept it will entail rejecting the tradition and *vice versa*.

One crucial point of incompatibility was noted long ago by D. H. Lawrence. When Franklin asserts, 'Rarely use venery but for health or offspring . . . ,' Lawrence replies, 'Never *use* venery.' It is of the character of a virtue that in order that it be effective in producing the internal goods which are the rewards of the virtues, it should be exercised without regard to consequences. For it turns out to be the case that—and this is in part at least one more empirical factual claim—although the virtues are just those qualities which tend to lead to the achievement of a certain class of goods, none the less unless we practice them irrespective of whether in any particular set of contingent circumstances they will produce those goods or not, we cannot possess them at all. We cannot be genuinely courageous or truthful and be so only on occasion. Moreover, as we have seen, cultivation of the virtues always may and often does hinder the achievement of those external goods which are the mark of worldly success. The road to success in Philadelphia and the road to heaven may not coincide after all.

Furthermore we are now able to specify one crucial difficulty for *any* version of utilitarianism—in addition to those which I noticed earlier.

Utilitarianism cannot accommodate the distinction between goods internal to and goods external to a practice. Not only is that distinction marked by none of the classical utilitarians—it cannot be found in Bentham's writings nor in those of either of the Mills or of Sidgwick—but internal goods and external goods are not commensurable with each other. Hence the notion of summing goods—and *a fortiori* in the light of what I have said about kinds of pleasure and enjoyment the notion of summing happiness—in terms of one single formula or conception of utility, whether it is Franklin's or Bentham's or Mill's, makes no sense. None the less we ought to note that although *this* distinction is alien to J. S. Mill's thought, it is plausible and in no way patronising to suppose that something like this is the distinction which he was trying to make in *Utilitarianism* when he distinguished between 'higher' and 'lower' pleasures. At the most we can say 'something like this'; for J. S. Mill's upbringing had given him a limited view of human life and powers, had unfitted him, for example, for appreciating games just because of the way it had fitted him for appreciating philosophy. None the less the notion that the pursuit of excellence in a way that extends human powers is at the heart of human life is instantly recognisable as at home in not only J. S. Mill's political and social thought but also in his and Mrs. Taylor's life. Were I to choose human exemplars of certain of the virtues as I understand them, there would of course be many names to name, those of St. Benedict and St. Francis of Assisi and St. Theresa *and* those of Frederick Engels and Eleanor Marx and Leon Trotsky among them. But that of John Stuart Mill would have to be there as certainly as any other.

Thirdly my account is Aristotelian in that it links evaluation and explanation in a characteristically Aristotelian way. From an Aristotelian standpoint to identify certain actions as manifesting or failing to manifest a virtue or virtues is never only to evaluate; it is also to take the first step toward explaining why those actions rather than some others were performed. Hence for an

Aristotelian quite as much as for a Platonist the fate of a city or an individual can be explained by citing the injustice of a tyrant or the courage of its defenders. Indeed without allusion to the place that justice and injustice, courage and cowardice play in human life, very little will be genuinely explicable. It follows that many of the explanatory projects of the modern social sciences, a methodological canon of which is the separation of 'the facts' . . . from all evaluation, are bound to fail. For the fact that someone was or failed to be courageous or just cannot be recognised as 'a fact' by those who accept that methodological canon. The account of the virtues which I have given is completely at one with Aristotle's on this point. But now the question may be raised: your account may be in many respects Aristotelian, but is it not in some respects false? Consider the following important objection.

I have defined the virtues partly in terms of their place in practices. But surely, it may be suggested, some practices—that is, some coherent human activities which answer to the description of what I have called a practice—are evil. So in discussions by some moral philosophers of this type of account of the virtues, it has been suggested that torture and sadomasochistic sexual activities might be examples of practices. But how can a disposition be a virtue if it is the kind of disposition which sustains practices and some practices issue in evil? My answer to this objection falls into two parts.

First I want to allow that there *may* be practices—in the sense in which I understand the concept—which simply *are* evil. I am far from convinced that there are, and I do not in fact believe that either torture or sadomasochistic sexuality answers to the description of a practice which my account of the virtues employs. But I do not want to rest my case on this lack of conviction, especially since it is plain that as a matter of contingent fact many types of practice may on particular occasions be productive of evil. For the range of practices includes the arts, the sciences, and certain types of intellectual and athletic games. And it is at once obvious that any of these may under certain conditions be a source of evil: the desire to excel and to win can corrupt; a man may be so engrossed by his painting that he neglects his family; what was initially an honourable resort to war can issue in savage cruelty. But what follows from this?

It certainly is not the case that my account entails *either* that we ought to excuse or condone such evils or that whatever flows from a virtue is right. I do have to allow that courage sometimes sustains injustice, that loyalty has been known to strengthen a murderous aggressor, and that generosity has sometimes weakened the capacity to do good. But to deny this would be to fly in the face of just those empirical facts which I invoked in criticising Aquinas's account of the unity of the virtues. That the virtues need initially to be defined and explained with reference to the notion of a practice thus in no way entails approval of all practices in all circumstances. That the virtues—as the objection itself presupposed—*are* defined not in terms of good and right practices, but of practices, does not entail or imply that practices as actually carried through at particular times and places do not stand in need of moral criticism. And the resources for such criticism are not lacking. There is in the first place no inconsistency in appealing to the requirements of a virtue to criticise a practice. Justice may be initially defined as a disposition which in its particular way is necessary to sustain practices; it does not follow that in pursuing the requirements of a practice violations of justice are not to be condemned. Moreover I already pointed out . . . that a morality of virtues requires as its counterpart a conception of moral law. Its requirements too have to be met by practices. But, it may be asked, does not all this imply that more needs to be said about the place of practices in some larger moral context? Does not this at least suggest that there is more to the core concept of a virtue than can be spelled out in terms of practices? I have after all emphasised that the scope of any virtue in human life extends beyond the practices in terms of which it is initially defined. What then is the place of the virtues in the larger arenas of human life?

I stressed earlier that any account of the virtues in terms of practices could be only a partial and first account. What is required to complement it? The most notable difference so far between my account and any account that could be called Aristotelian is that although I have in no way restricted the exercise of the virtues to the context of practices, it is in terms of practices that I have located their point and function, whereas Aristotle locates that point and function in terms of the notion of a type of whole human life which can be called good. And it does seem that the question 'What would a human being lack who lacked the virtues?' must be given a kind of answer which goes beyond anything which I have said so far. For such an individual would not merely fail *in a variety of particular ways* in respect of the kind of excellence which can be achieved through participation in practices and in respect of the kind of human relationship required to sustain such excellence. His own life *viewed as a whole* would perhaps be defective; it would not be the kind of life which someone would describe in trying to answer the question 'What is the best kind of life for this kind of man or woman to live?' And that question cannot be answered without at least raising Aristotle's own question, 'What is the good life for man?' Consider three ways in which a human life informed only by the conception of the virtues sketched so far would be defective.

It would be pervaded, first of all, by *too many* conflicts and *too much* arbitrariness. I argued earlier that it is a merit of an account of the virtues in terms of a multiplicity of goods that it allows for the possibility of tragic conflict in a way in which Aristotle's does not. But it may also produce even in the life of someone who is virtuous and disciplined too many occasions when one allegiance points in one direction, another in another. The claims of one practice may be incompatible with another in such a way that one may find oneself oscillating in an arbitrary way, rather than making rational choices. So it seems to have been with

T. E. Lawrence. Commitment to sustaining the kind of community in which the virtues can flourish may be incompatible with the devotion which a particular practice—of the arts, for example—requires. So there may be tensions between the claims of family life and those of the arts—the problem that Gauguin solved or failed to solve by fleeing to Polynesia; or between the claims of politics and those of the arts—the problem that Lenin solved or failed to solve by refusing to listen to Beethoven.

If the life of the virtues is continuously fractured by choices in which one allegiance entails the apparently arbitrary renunciation of another, it may seem that the goods internal to practices do after all derive their authority from our individual choices; for when different goods summon in different and in incompatible directions, 'I' have to choose between their rival claims. The modern self with its criterionless choices apparently reappears in the alien context of what was claimed to be an Aristotelian world. This accusation might be rebutted in part by returning to the question of why both goods and virtues do have authority in our lives and repeating what was said earlier in this chapter. But this reply would be only partly successful; the distinctively modern notion of choice would indeed have reappeared, even if with a more limited scope for its exercise than it has usually claimed.

Secondly without an overriding conception of the *telos* of a whole human life, conceived as a unity, our conception of certain individual virtues has to remain partial and incomplete. Consider two examples. Justice, on an Aristotelian view, is defined in terms of giving each person his or her due or desert. To deserve well is to have contributed in some substantial way to the achievement of those goods the sharing of which and the common pursuit of which provide foundations for human community. But the goods internal to practices, including the goods internal to the practice of making and sustaining forms of community, need to be ordered and evaluated in some way if we are to assess relative desert. Thus only substantive application of an Aristotelian concept of justice requires an understanding of goods and of the good that goes beyond the multiplicity of goods which inform practices. As with justice, so also with patience. Patience is the virtue of waiting attentively without complaint, but not of waiting thus for anything at all. To treat patience as a virtue presupposes some adequate answer to the question: waiting for what? Within the context of practices a partial, although for many purposes adequate, answer can be given. The patience of a craftsman with refractory material, of a teacher with a slow pupil, of a politician in negotiations, are all species of patience. But what if the material is just too refractory, the pupil too slow, the negotiations too frustrating? Ought we always at a certain point just to give up in the interests of the practice itself? The medieval exponents of the virtue of patience claimed that there are certain types of situations in which the virtue of patience requires that I do not ever give up on some person or task, situations in which, as they would have put it, I am required to embody in my attitude to that person or task something of the patient attitude of God toward his creation. But this could only be so if patience served some overriding good, some *telos* which warranted putting other goods in a subordinate place. Thus it turns out that the content of the virtue of patience depends on how we order various goods in a hierarchy and *a fortiori* on whether we are able rationally so to order these particular goods.

I have suggested so far that unless there is a *telos* which transcends the limited goods of practices by constituting the good of a whole human life, the good of a human life conceived as a unity, it will be the case *both* that a certain subversive arbitrariness will invade the moral life *and* that we shall be unable to specify the context of certain virtues adequately. These two considerations are reinforced by a third: that there is at least one virtue recognised by the tradition which cannot be specified at all except with reference to the wholeness of a human life—the virtue of integrity or constancy. 'Purity of heart,' said Kierkegaard, 'is to will one thing.' This notion of singleness of purpose in a whole life can have no application unless that of a whole life does.

Note

1. *Phronêsis* is the Greek word standing broadly for practical wisdom. [Editor]

30

The Conscience of Huckleberry Finn

Jonathan Bennett

Jonathan Bennett (b. 1930) is professor of philosophy at Syracuse University. He is the author of several books, including Rationality *(1964),* Linguistic Behaviour *(1976),* A Study of Spinoza's Ethics *(1984) and* Events and Their Names *(1988).*

What is the role of sympathy in moral judgment? Bennett draws our attention to three people who dealt with their sympathies in different ways. Huckleberry Finn allowed himself to be guided by his sympathies, thereby overriding his "obligation" to turn in the runaway slave, Jim. The Nazi leader Heinrich Himmler successfully struggled against his sympathies in doing his "moral duty" in sending Jews to concentration camps. The great Puritan theologian Jonathan Edwards steeled his heart against having any sympathies for the damned, since he believed that their punishment was just. Bennett calls the morality of all three men "bad morality" and argues that sometimes our sympathies are better guides to moral action than our principles. We ought to give our sympathies great weight in deciding on our moral duty.

I

In this paper, I shall present not just the conscience of Huckleberry Finn but those of two others as well. One of them is the conscience of Heinrich Himmler. Himmler became a Nazi in 1923; he served drably and quietly, but well, and was rewarded with increasing responsibility and power. At the peak of his career he held many offices and commands, of which the most powerful was that of leader of the SS—the principal police

Reprinted from "The Conscience of Huckleberry Finn," *Philosophy* 49 (1974), by permission of Cambridge University Press.

force of the Nazi regime. In this capacity Himmler commanded the whole concentration camp system and was responsible for the execution of the so-called final solution of the Jewish problem. It is important for my purposes that this piece of social engineering should be thought of not abstractly but in concrete terms of Jewish families being marched to what they thought were bathhouses, to the accompaniment of loud-speaker renditions of extracts from *The Merry Widow* and *Tales of Hoffmann*, there to be choked to death by poisonous gases. Altogether, Himmler succeeded in murdering about four and a half million of them, as well as several million gentiles, mainly Poles and Russians.

The other conscience to be discussed is that of the Calvinist theologian and philosopher Jonathan Edwards. He lived in the first half of the eighteenth century, and has a good claim to be considered America's first serious and considerable philosophical thinker. He was for many years a widely renowned preacher and Congregationalist minister in New England; in 1748 a dispute with his congregation led him to resign (he couldn't accept their view that unbelievers should be admitted to the Lord's Supper in the hope that it would convert them); for some years after that he worked as a missionary, preaching to Indians through an interpreter; then in 1758 he accepted the presidency of what is now Princeton University, and within two months died from a smallpox inoculation. Along the way he wrote some first-rate philosophy; his book attacking the notion of free will is still sometimes read. Why I should be interested in Edwards's *conscience* will be explained in due course.

I shall use Heinrich Himmler, Jonathan Edwards, and Huckleberry Finn to illustrate different aspects of a single theme, namely the relationship between *sympathy* on the one hand and *bad morality* on the other.

II

All that I can mean by a "bad morality" is a morality whose principles I deeply disapprove of. When I call a morality bad, I cannot prove that mine is better; but when I here call any morality bad, I think you will agree with me that it is bad; and that is all I need.

There could be dispute as to whether the springs of someone's actions constitute a *morality*. I think, though, that we must admit that someone who acts in ways which conflict grossly with our morality may nevertheless have a morality of his own—a set of principles of action which he sincerely assents to, so that for him the problem of acting well or rightly or in obedience to conscience is the problem of conforming to *those* principles. The problem of conscientiousness can arise as acutely for a bad morality as for any other: Rotten principles may be as difficult to keep as decent ones.

As for "sympathy" I use this term to cover every sort of fellow-feeling, as when one feels pity over someone's loneliness, or horrified compassion over his pain, or when one feels a shrinking reluctance to act in a way which will bring misfortune to someone else. These *feelings* must not be confused with *moral judgments*. My sympathy for someone in distress may lead me to help him, or even to think that I ought to help him; but in itself it is not a judgment about what I ought to do but just a *feeling* for him in his plight. We shall get some light on the difference between feelings and moral judgments when we consider Huckleberry Finn.

Obviously, feelings can impel one to action, and so can moral judgments; and in a particular case sympathy and morality may pull in opposite directions. This can happen not just with bad moralities, but also with good ones like yours and mine. For example, a small child, sick and miserable, clings tightly to his mother and screams in terror when she tries to pass him over to the doc-

tor to be examined. If the mother gave way to her sympathy, that is to her feeling for the child's misery and fright, she would hold it close and not let the doctor come near; but don't we agree that it might be wrong for her to act on such a feeling? Quite generally, then, anyone's moral principles may apply to a particular situation in a way which runs contrary to the particular thrusts of fellow-feeling that he has in that situation. My immediate concern is with sympathy in relation to bad morality, but not because such conflicts occur only when the morality is bad.

Now, suppose that someone who accepts a bad morality is struggling to make himself act in accordance with it in a particular situation where his sympathies pull him another way. He sees the struggle as one between doing the right, conscientious thing, and acting wrongly and weakly, like the mother who won't let the doctor come near her sick, frightened baby. Since we don't accept this person's morality, we may see the situation very differently, thoroughly disapproving of the action he regards as the right one, and endorsing the action which from his point of view constitutes weakness and backsliding.

Conflicts between sympathy and bad morality won't always be like this, for we won't disagree with every single dictate of a bad morality. Still, it can happen in the way I have described, with the agent's right action being our wrong one, and vice versa. That is just what happens in a certain episode in Chapter 16 of *The Adventures of Huckleberry Finn*, an episode which brilliantly illustrates how fiction can be instructive about real life.

III

Huck Finn has been helping his slave friend Jim to run away from Miss Watson, who is Jim's owner. In their raft-journey down the Mississippi River, they are near to the place at which Jim will become legally free. Now let Huck take over the story:

Jim said it made him all over trembly and feverish to be so close to freedom. Well I can tell you it made me all over trembly and feverish, too, to hear him, because I begun to get it through my head that he *was* most free—and who was to blame for it? Why, *me.* I couldn't get that out of my conscience, no how nor no way. . . . It hadn't ever come home to me, before, what this thing was that I was doing. But now it did; and it stayed with me, and scorched me more and more. I tried to make out to myself that *I* warn't to blame, because I didn't run Jim off from his rightful owner; but it warn't no use, conscience up and say, every time: "But you knowed he was running for his freedom, and you could a paddled ashore and told somebody." That was so—I couldn't get around that, no way. That was where it pinched. Conscience says to me: "What had poor Miss Watson done to you, that you could see her nigger go off right under your eyes and never say one single word? What did that poor old woman do to you, that you could treat her so mean? . . ." I got to feeling so mean and miserable I most wished I was dead.

Jim speaks his plan to save up to buy his wife, and then his children, out of slavery; and he adds that if the children cannot be bought he will arrange to steal them. Huck is horrified:

Thinks I, this is what comes of my not thinking. Here was this nigger which I had as good as helped to run away, coming right out flat-footed and saying he would steal his children—children that belonged to a man I didn't even know; a man that hadn't ever done me no harm.

I was sorry to hear Jim say that, it was such a lowering of him. My conscience got to stirring me up hotter than ever, until at last I says to it: "Let up on me—it ain't too late, yet—I'll paddle ashore at first light, and tell." I felt easy, and happy, and light as a feather, right off. All my troubles was gone.

This is bad morality all right. In his earliest years Huck wasn't taught any principles, and the only one he has encountered since then are those of

rural Missouri, in which slave-owning is just one kind of ownership and is not subject to critical pressure. It hasn't occurred to Huck to question those principles. So the action, to us abhorrent, of turning Jim in to the authorities presents itself *clearly* to Huck as the right thing to do.

For us, both morality and sympathy would dictate helping Jim to escape. If we felt any conflict, it would have both of these on one side and something else on the other—greed for a reward, or fear of punishment. But Huck's morality conflicts with his sympathy, that is, with his unargued, natural feeling for his friend. The conflict starts when Huck sets off in the canoe toward the shore, pretending that he is going to reconnoiter, but really planning to turn Jim in:

As I shoved off, [Jim] says: "Pooty soon I'll be a-shout'n for joy, en I'll say, it's all on accounts o' Huck I's a free man . . . Jim won't ever forget you, Huck; you's de bes' fren' Jim's ever had; en you's de *only* fren' old Jim's got now."

I was paddling off, all in a sweat to tell on him; but when he says this, it seemed to kind of take the tuck all out of me. I went along slow then, and I warn't right down certain whether I was glad I started or whether I warn't. When I was fifty yards off, Jim says:

"Dah you goes, de ole true Huck; de on'y white genlman dat ever kep' his promise to ole Jim." Well, I just felt sick. But I says, I *got* to do it—I can't get *out* of it.

In the upshot, sympathy wins over morality. Huck hasn't the strength of will to do what he sincerely thinks he ought to do. Two men hunting for runaway slaves ask him whether the man on his raft is black or white:

I didn't answer up prompt. I tried to, but the words wouldn't come. I tried, for a second or two, to brace up and out with it, but I warn't man enough—hadn't the spunk of a rabbit. I see I was weakening; so I just give up trying, and up and says: "He's white."

So Huck enables Jim to escape, thus acting weakly and wickedly—he thinks. In this conflict between sympathy and morality, sympathy wins.

One critic has cited this episode in support of the statement that Huck suffers "excruciating moments of wavering between honesty and respectability." That is hopelessly wrong, and I agree with the perceptive comment on it by another critic, who says:

The conflict waged in Huck is much more serious: He scarcely cares for respectability and never hesitates to relinquish it, but he does care for honesty and gratitude—and both honesty and gratitude require that he should give Jim up. It is not, in Huck, honesty at war with respectability but love and compassion for Jim struggling against his conscience. His decision is for Jim and hell: a right decision made in the mental chains that Huck never breaks. His concern for Jim is and remains *irrational*. Huck finds many reasons for giving Jim up and none for stealing him. To the end Huck sees his compassion for Jim as a weak, ignorant, and wicked felony.[1]

That is precisely correct—and it can have that virtue only because Mark Twain wrote the episode with such unerring precision. The crucial point concerns *reasons,* which all occur on one side of the conflict. On the side of conscience we have principles, arguments, considerations, ways of looking at things:

"It hadn't ever come home to me before what I was doing"
"I tried to make out that I warn't to blame"
"Conscience said 'But you knowed . . .'—I couldn't get around that"
"What had poor Miss Watson done to you?"
"This is what comes of my not thinking"
". . . children that belonged to a man I didn't even know"

On the other side, the side of feeling, we get nothing like that. When Jim rejoices in Huck, as his only friend, Huck doesn't consider the claims of friendship or have the situation "come home" to him in a different light. All that happens is: "When he says this, it seemed to kind of take the tuck all out of me. I went along slow then, and I warn't right down certain whether I was glad I started or whether I warn't." Again, Jim's words about Huck's "promise" to him don't give Huck any *reason* for changing his plan: In his morality promises to slaves probably don't count. Their effect on him is of a different kind: "Well, I just felt sick." And when the moment for final decision comes, Huck doesn't weigh up pros and cons: he simply *fails* to do what he believes to be right—he isn't strong enough, hasn't "the spunk of a rabbit." This passage in the novel is notable not just for its finely wrought irony, with Huck's weakness of will leading him to do the right thing, but also for its masterly handling of the difference between general moral principles and particular unreasoned emotional pulls.

IV

Consider now another case of bad morality in conflict with human sympathy: the case of the odious Himmler. Here, from a speech he made to some SS generals, is an indication of the content of his morality:

What happens to a Russian, to a Czech, does not interest me in the slightest. What the nations can offer in the way of good blood of our type, we will take, if necessary by kidnapping their children and raising them here with us. Whether nations live in prosperity or starve to death like cattle interests me only in so far as we need them as slaves to our *Kultur;* otherwise it is of no interest to me. Whether 10,000 Russian females fall down from exhaustion while digging an antitank ditch interests me only in so far as the antitank ditch for Germany is finished.[2]

But has this a moral basis at all? And if it has, was there in Himmler's own mind any conflict between morality and sympathy? Yes, there was. Here is more from the same speech:

I also want to talk to you quite frankly on a very grave matter . . . I mean . . . the extermination of the Jewish race. . . . Most of you must know what it means when 100 corpses are lying side by side, or 500, or 1,000. To have stuck it out and at the same time—apart from exceptions caused by human weakness—to have remained decent fellows, that is what has made us hard. This is a page of glory in our history which has never been written and is never to be written.

Himmler saw his policies as being hard to implement while still retaining one's human sympathies—while still remaining a "decent fellow." He is saying that only the weak take the easy way out and just squelch their sympathies, and is praising the stronger and more glorious course of retaining one's sympathies while acting in violation of them. In the same spirit, he ordered that when executions were carried out in concentration camps, those responsible "are to be influenced in such a way as to suffer no ill effect in their character and mental attitude." A year later he boasted that the SS had wiped out the Jews

without our leaders and their men suffering any damage in their minds and souls. The danger was considerable, for there was only a narrow path between the Scylla of their becoming heartless ruffians unable any longer to treasure life, and the Charybdis of their becoming soft and suffering nervous breakdowns.

And there really can't be any doubt that the basis of Himmler's policies was a set of principles which constituted his morality—a sick, bad, wicked *morality*. He described himself as caught in "the old tragic conflict between will and obligation." And when his physician Kersten protested at the intention to destroy the Jews, saying that the suffering involved was "not to be contemplated," Kersten reports that Himmler replied that

He knew that it would mean much suffering for the Jews. . . . "It is the curse of greatness that it must step over dead bodies to create new life. Yet we must . . . cleanse the soil or it will never bear fruit. It will be a great burden for me to bear."

This, I submit, is the language of morality.

So in this case, tragically, bad morality won out over sympathy. I am sure that many of Himmler's killers did extinguish their sympathies, becoming "heartless ruffians" rather than "decent fellows"; but not Himmler himself. Although his policies ran against the human grain to a horrible degree, he did not sandpaper down his emotional surfaces so that there was no grain there, allowing his actions to slide along smoothly and easily. He did, after all, bear his hideous burden, and even paid a price for it. He suffered a variety of nervous and physical disabilities, including nausea and stomach-convulsions, and Kersten was doubtless right in saying that these were "the expression of a psychic division which extended over his whole life."

This same division must have been present in some of those officials of the Church who ordered heretics to be tortured so as to change their theological opinions. Along with the brutes and the cold careerists, there must have been some who cared, and who suffered from the conflict between their sympathies and their bad morality.

V

In the conflict between sympathy and bad morality, then, the victory may go to sympathy as in the case of Huck Finn, or to morality as in the case of Himmler.

Another possibility is that the conflict may be avoided by giving up, or not ever having, those sympathies which might interfere with one's principles. That seems to have been the case with Jonathan Edwards. I am afraid that I shall be doing an injustice to Edwards's many virtues, and to his great intellectual energy and inventiveness; for my concern is only with the worst thing about him—namely his morality, which was worse than Himmler's.

According to Edwards, God condemns some men to an eternity of unimaginably awful pain, though he arbitrarily spares others—"arbitrarily" because none deserve to be spared:

Natural men are held in the hand of God over the pit of hell; they have deserved the fiery pit, and are already sentenced to it; and God is dreadfully provoked, his anger is as great toward them as to those that are actually suffering the executions of the fierceness of his wrath in hell . . . ; the devil is waiting for them, hell is gaping for them, the flames gather and flash about them, and would fain lay hold on them . . . ; and . . . there are no means within reach that can be any security to them. . . . All that preserves them is the mere arbitrary will, and unconvenanted unobliged forebearance of an incensed God.[3]

Notice that he says "they have deserved the fiery pit." Edwards insists that men *ought* to be condemned to eternal pain; and his position isn't that this is right because God wants it, but rather that God wants it because it is right. For him, moral standards exist independently of God, and God can be assessed in the light of them (and of course found to be perfect). For example, he says:

They deserve to be cast into hell; so that . . . justice never stands in the way, it makes no objection against God's using his power at any moment to destroy them. Yea, on the contrary, justice calls aloud for an infinite punishment of their sins.

Elsewhere, he gives elaborate arguments to show that God is acting justly in damning sinners. For example, he argues that a punishment should be exactly as bad as the crime being punished; God is infinitely excellent; so any crime against him is infinitely bad; and so eternal damnation is exactly right as a punishment—it is infinite, but, as Edwards is careful also to say, it is "no more than infinite."

Of course, Edwards himself didn't torment the damned; but the question still arises of whether his sympathies didn't conflict with his *approval* of eternal torment. Didn't he find it painful to contemplate any fellow-human's being tortured forever? Apparently not:

The God that holds you over the pit of hell, much as one holds a spider or some loathsome insect over the fire, abhors you, and is dreadfully provoked . . . he is of purer eyes than to bear to have you in his sight; you are ten thousand times so abominable in his eyes as the most hateful venomous serpent is in ours.

When God is presented as being as misanthropic as that, one suspects misanthropy in the theologian. This suspicion is increased when Edwards claims that "the saints in glory will . . . understand how terrible the sufferings of the damned are; yet . . . will not be sorry for [them]."[4] He bases this partly on a view of human nature whose ugliness he seems not to notice:

The seeing of the calamities of others tends to heighten the sense of our own enjoyments. When the saints in glory, therefore, shall see the doleful state of the damned, how will this heighten their sense of the blessedness of their own state. . . . When they shall see how miserable others of their fellow-creatures are . . . when they shall see the smoke of their torment . . . and hear their dolorous shrieks and cries, and consider that they in the mean time are in the most blissful state, and shall surely be in it to all eternity; how they will rejoice!

I hope this is less than the whole truth! His other main point about why the saints will rejoice to see the torments of the damned is that it is *right* that they should do so:

The heavenly inhabitants . . . will have no love nor pity to the damned. . . . [This will not show] a want of spirit of love in them for the heavenly inhabitants will know that it is not fit that they should love [the damned] because they will know then, that God has no love to them, nor pity for them.

The implication that *of course* one can adjust one's feelings of pity so that they conform to the dictates of some authority—doesn't this suggest that ordinary human sympathies played only a small part in Edwards's life?

VI

Huck Finn, whose sympathies are wide and deep, could never avoid the conflict in that way; but he is determined to avoid it, and so he opts for the only other alternative he can see—to give up morality altogether. After he has tricked the slave-hunters, he returns to the raft and undergoes a peculiar crisis:

I got aboard the raft, feeling bad and low, because I knowed very well I had done wrong, and I see it warn't no use for me to try to learn to do right; a body that don't get *started* right when he's little, ain't got no show—when the pinch comes there ain't nothing to back him up and keep him to his work, and so he gets beat. Then I thought a minute, and says to myself, hold on—s'pose you'd a done right and give Jim up; would you feel better than what you do now? No, says I, I'd feel bad—I'd feel just the same way I do now. Well, then, says I, what's the use you learning to do right, when it's troublesome to do right and ain't no trouble to do wrong, and the wages is just the same? I was stuck. I couldn't answer that. So I reckoned I wouldn't bother no more about it, but after this always do whichever come handiest at the time.

Huck clearly cannot conceive of having any morality except the one he has learned—too late, he thinks—from his society. He is not entirely a prisoner of that morality, because he does after all reject it; but for him that is a decision to relinquish morality as such; he cannot envisage revising his morality, altering its content in the face of

the various pressures to which it is subject, including pressures from his sympathies. For example, he does not begin to approach the thought that slavery should be rejected on moral grounds, or the thought that what he is doing is not theft because a person cannot be owned and therefore cannot be stolen.

The basic trouble is that he cannot or will not engage in abstract intellectual operations of any sort. In Chapter 33 he finds himself "feeling to blame, somehow" for something he knows he had no hand in; he assumes that this feeling is a deliverance of conscience; and this confirms him in his belief that conscience shouldn't be listened to:

It don't make no difference whether you do right or wrong, a person's conscience ain't got no sense, and just goes for him *anyway*. If I had a yaller dog that didn't know no more than a person's conscience does, I would poison him. It takes up more than all of a person's insides, and yet ain't no good, nohow.

That brisk, incurious dismissiveness fits well with the comprehensive rejection of morality back on the raft. But this is a digression.

On the raft, Huck decides not to live by principles, but just to do whatever "comes handiest at the time"—always acting according to the mood of the moment. Since the morality he is rejecting is narrow and cruel, and his sympathies are broad and kind, the results will be good. But moral principles are good to have, because they help to protect one from acting badly at moments when one's sympathies happen to be in abeyance. On the highest possible estimate of the role one's sympathies should have, one can still allow for principles as embodiments of one's best feelings, one's broadest and keenest sympathies. On that view, principles can help one across intervals when one's feelings are at less than their best, i.e. through periods of misanthropy or meanness or self-centeredness or depression or anger.

What Huck didn't see is that one can live by principles and yet have ultimate control over their content. And one way such control can be exercised is by checking one's principles in the light of one's sympathies. This is sometimes a pretty straightforward matter. It can happen that a certain moral principle becomes untenable—meaning literally that one cannot hold it any longer—because it conflicts intolerably with the pity or revulsion or whatever that one feels when one sees what the principle leads to. One's experience may play a large part here: Experiences evoke feelings, and feelings force one to modify principles. Something like this happened to the English poet Wilfred Owen, whose experiences in the First World War transformed him from an enthusiastic soldier into a virtual pacifist. I can't document his change of conscience in detail; but I want to present something which he wrote about the way experience can put pressure on morality.

The Latin poet Horace wrote that it is sweet and fitting (or right) to die for one's country—*dulce et decorum est pro patria mori*—and Owen wrote a fine poem about how experience could lead one to relinquish that particular moral principle.[5] He describes a man who is too slow donning his gas mask during a gas attack—"As under a green sea I saw him drowning," Owen says. The poem ends like this:

In all my dreams before my helpless sight
He plunges at me, guttering, choking, drowning.
If in some smothering dreams, you too could pace
Behind the wagon that we flung him in,
And watch the white eyes writhing in his face,
His hanging face, like a devil's sick of sin;
If you could hear, at every jolt, the blood
Come gargling from the froth-corrupted lungs.
Bitter as the end
Of vile, incurable sores on innocent tongues,—
My friend, you would not tell with such high zest
To children ardent for some desperate glory,
The old Lie; Dulce et decorum est
Pro patria mori.

There is a difficulty about drawing from all this

a moral for ourselves. I imagine that we agree in our rejection of slavery, eternal damnation, genocide, and uncritical patriotic self-abnegation; so we shall agree that Huck Finn, Jonathan Edwards, Heinrich Himmler, and the poet Horace would all have done well to bring certain of their principles under severe pressure from ordinary human sympathies. But then we can say this because we can say that all those are bad moralities, whereas we cannot look at our own moralities and declare them bad. This is not arrogance; It is obviously incoherent for someone to declare the system of moral principles that he *accepts* to be *bad*, just as one cannot coherently say of anything that one *believes* it but it is *false*.

Still, although I can't point to any of my beliefs and say "That is false," I don't doubt that some of my beliefs *are* false; and so I should try to remain open to correction. Similarly, I accept every single item in my morality—that is inevitable—but I am sure that my morality could be improved, which is to say that it could undergo changes which I should be glad of once I had made them. So I must try to keep my morality open to revision, exposing it to whatever valid pressures there are—including pressures from my sympathies.

I don't give my sympathies a blank check in advance. In a conflict between principle and sympathy, principles ought sometimes to win. For example, I think it was right to take part in the Second World War on the allied side; there were many ghastly individual incidents which might have led someone to doubt the rightness of his participation in that war; and I think it would have been right for such a person to keep his sympathies in a subordinate place on those occasions, not allowing them to modify his principles in such a way as to make a pacifist of him.

Still, one's sympathies should be kept as sharp and sensitive and aware as possible, and not only because they can sometimes affect one's principles or one's conduct or both. Owen, at any rate, says that feelings and sympathies are vital even when they can do nothing but bring pain and distress.

In another poem he speaks of the blessings of being numb in one's feelings: "Happy are the men who yet before they are killed/Can let their veins run cold," he says. These are the ones who do not suffer from any compassion which, as Owen puts it, "makes their feet/Sore on the alleys cobbled with their brothers." He contrasts these "happy" ones, who "lose all imagination," with himself and others "who with a thought besmirch/Blood over all our soul." Yet the poem's verdict goes against the "happy" ones. Owen does not say that they will act worse than the others whose souls are besmirched with blood because of their keen awareness of human suffering. He merely says that they are the losers because they have cut themselves off from the human condition:

By choice they made themselves immune
To pity and whatever moans in man
Before the last sea and the hapless stars;
Whatever mourns when many leave these shores;
Whatever shares
The eternal reciprocity of tears.

Notes

1. M. J. Sidnell, "Huck Finn and Jim," *The Cambridge Quarterly*, vol. 2, pp. 205–6.

2. Quoted in William L. Shirer, *The Rise and Fall of the Third Reich* (New York, 1960), pp. 937–38. Next quotation: ibid., p. 966. All further quotations relating to Himmler are from Roger Manwell and Heinrich Fraenkel, *Heinrich Himmler* (London, 1965), pp. 132, 197, 184 (twice), 187.

3. Vergilius Ferm (ed.), *Puritan Sage: Collected Writings of Jonathan Edwards* (New York, 1953), p. 370. Next three quotations: ibid., p. 366, p. 294 ("no more than infinite"), p. 372.

4. This and the next two quotations are from "The End of the Wicked Contemplated by the Righteous: Or, The Torments of the Wicked in Hell, No Occasion of Grief to the Saints in Heaven," from *The Works of President Edwards* (London, 1817), vol. 4, pp. 507–8, 511–12, and 509 respectively.

5. We are grateful to the Executors of the Estate of Harold Owen, and to Chatto and Windus Ltd. for permission to quote from Wilfred Owen's "Dulce et Decorum Est" and "Insensibility."

31

Moral Minimalism and the Development of Moral Character

David L. Norton

David L. Norton is Professor of Philosophy at the University of Delaware. In this article Norton contrasts two profoundly different emphases in ethics: the ethics of rules, which characterizes modern ethics, and the ethics of character, which characterizes classical ethics. Whereas modern duty-centered ethics is minimalist, cutting off morality from much of life, classical ethics is comprehensive, encompassing all of life ("coterminous with human life"). In the last section of his essay Norton gives an appreciative critique of Urmson's attempt to rectify the class between normative rules and supererogatory acts.

Three recent books in ethics—Alasdair MacIntyre's *After Virtue,* Richard Taylor's *Ethics, Faith, and Reason,* and Edmund L. Pincoffs's *Quandaries and Virtues*[1]—have, each in its own way, contrasted modern ethics and classical ethics as very disparate modes of ethical theorizing, and each has offered arguments for the superiority of the classical mode. It is my intent in what follows to contribute to their theses, both of the radical disparity of the two modes, and of the superiority of the classical mode in important respects. Specifically I will argue that modern ethics is typically minimalist (a) with respect to the kinds of situations and choices that count as moral, and (b) in its conception of moral character, and that its minimalism in these respects removes from moral consideration factors that cannot be disregarded without the dilution of moral thought and moral life. I will begin by attempting my own characterizations of modern and classical ethics. . . .

Reprinted from *Midwest Studies in Philosophy,* vol. 13. *Ethical Theory: Character and Virtue,* eds. Peter A. French, Theodore E. Uehling, Jr., and Howard K. Wettseing, (Notre Dame, Ind.: University of Notre Dame Press, 1988) by permission.

We will begin the study in contrast by observing that "rules ethics" and "character ethics" start with different primary questions. For modern moral philosophy the primary question is: "What is the right thing to do in particular (moral) situations?" and it is answered by finding the rule that applies to the given situation and acting in accordance with it. Thus if I am driving my car and collide with another vehicle, I am obligated by law to describe the event, and morality (here backed by law) holds me to the rule, "always tell the truth." Within this framework what we refer to as "contemporary moral problems"—e.g., abortion, euthanasia, compensatory preferential hiring—are problems for which the covering rule(s) is unsettled and in dispute. The point, however, is the unquestioned assumption that such problems are to be solved by arriving at the covering rule.

The accepted agenda of modern ethics is to formulate (discover; devise and contractually agree upon) a supreme and universally applicable moral principle—Hobbes's natural right of self-preservation, Kant's categorical imperative, Bentham's "greatest happiness of the greatest number," and Rawls's two principles of justice are famous examples—together with criteria for distinguishing moral from nonmoral situations, criteria for recognizing relevantly different kinds of moral situations, and, as far as practicable, a complete list of rules representing the application of the supreme principle to all possible types of moral situations, or a set of rules for applying the supreme principle to particular situations. Then moral conduct is the conduct that best accords with the applicable rules in given moral situations. What is meant by a "prima facie duty" is a duty to obey a rule that is held to prevail in appropriate moral situations unless contravened by a higher rule.

By contrast, classical morality begins with the question, "What is a good life for a human being?" (Socrates: "But we ought to consider more carefully, for this is no light matter: it is the question, what is the right way to live"[2]) It leads directly to the problem of the development of moral character, because any adequate description of a good human life will necessarily include attributes that are not manifest in persons in the beginning of their lives, but are developmental outcomes. The attributes on which classical ethics focuses are the moral virtues, and here it is enough to name the famous four of Plato's *Republic*—wisdom, courage, temperance, and justice—to recognize that none of them can be expected of children, but only in persons in later life, and only in the later life of persons in whom the requisite moral development occurs.

In this classical understanding the virtues are excellences of character that are objective goods, of worth to others as well as to the virtues-bearer (for example, the courage of our friend enhances the assistance he or she renders to us, just as it strengthens his or her pursuit of independent ends). Second, the manifestation of a virtue is understood to be the actualization of what was theretofore not totally absent in the person, but present in the form of a potentiality.[3] In other words, to be a human being is to be capable of manifesting virtues, and the problem of moral development is the problem of discovering the conditions for the actualization of qualities that are originally within persons as potentialities.

Classical ethics endeavors to answer the question, "What is a good life for a human being?" but to deepen our understanding it is important to consider first the prior question, "What sort of a being is it to which the question of the good life is posed?" The eudaimonistic answer is famously expressed by Plato in his image of the human soul as chariot, charioteer, and two contrary-minded horses *(Phaedrus):* distinctively, human being is problematic being; to be a human is in the deep-

est sense to be a problem to oneself, specifically an identity problem. It is the problem of deciding what to become and endeavoring to become it. The problem of deciding what to become is the problem of learning to recognize ideal goods and choosing among them which good to aim at as the goal of one's self-fulfilling and objectively worthy life. The problem of endeavoring to become the person one chooses to become is the problem of acquiring the resourcefulness and force of character to overcome external and internal obstacles. In the eudaimonistic view, human freedom has its ground in the absence in human beings of the metaphysical necessity that characterizes all other kinds of being, and in virtue of which they cannot be other than they are. But the absence of metaphysical necessity in the individual human being must be compensated for if his or her chosen end is to be achievable, and the compensatory necessity, because it must itself be chosen, is termed moral necessity. Here is the "fire" that Prometheus steals from the gods to equip man—left naked and helpless in the world by the negligence of Epimetheus—for survival. Despite conventional misinterpretation it is not physical fire but spiritual fire. In the myth we are told that it is the god's most precious possession, and, indeed, it is nothing less than the power of creation *(Eros)* by which man is equipped to carry out the unfinished work of making himself. Persons in whom moral necessity is lacking are described by Thoreau as "thrown off the track by every nutshell and mosquito's wing that falls on the rails."[4] Moral necessity is the "I must" of the dedicated and resourceful person. As against "I wish to," "I hope to," and even "I will," it bespeaks the strength of character to overcome the inevitable obstacles in the world, as well as vagrant impulses and ordinary apprehensions within the self.

Deciding what to become requires knowledge of the good, which is wisdom, and endeavoring to become it requires moral necessity. Connecting these two sides of the problem that every person is to him- or herself is the virtue of integrity, consisting in integration of the separable and initially disordered aspects of the self-faculties, desires, interests, roles—such that they complement rather than contradict one another, and each contributes to the realization of the chosen good.

It will be evident that the classical themes briefly touched upon above have taken us a good distance into the development of moral character, for alike, moral necessity, wisdom, and integrity are developmental outcomes, possessed *ab initio* by persons not as manifest capacities but as unactualized potentialities. What now requires to be noticed is that modern ethics, in its dominant mode that I have termed "rule" ethics, is notable for its relative disregard of the problems pertaining to the development of moral character. This is an important respect in which modern morality is "minimalist" in comparison to classical morality—it makes minimal demands upon the intelligence and developed moral character of moral agents, requiring little or nothing of them in the way of wisdom, courage, or integrity. It is also minimalist in a second sense, namely, that it delimits the arena of moral choice to but a small sector of human experience. We shall say something about each of these instances of minimalism, beginning with the delimitation of moral choice.

It has often been observed that modern ethical theory typically works with a threefold classification of actions from the standpoint of moral meaning—right actions, wrong actions, and morally indifferent actions. This classification is coupled with a distinction between moral and nonmoral situations, which accounts for the restrictive stipulation in what we earlier offered as the foundational question of modern ethics, "What is the right thing to do in particular *moral situations?*" The restriction is not to be found in classical ethics because the distinction does not exist. For classical ethics nothing in human experience is without moral meaning, and "the moral situation" is the life of each person in its entirety. If these contentions appear extreme, support for them will be offered shortly. Meanwhile it can

readily be recognized that some situations typically adjudged nonmoral in modern terms are importantly moral in classical terms.

An example of a situation that is generally understood to be nonmoral by modern standards is the situation of vocational choice. Suppose, for instance, that my supreme moral principle is Kant's categorical imperative, and I decide to become a chemical engineer. I obviously cannot will that everyone in my situation, i.e., the situation of vocational choice, decide to become a chemical engineer, yet it is entirely conceivable that this choice is the right choice for me. This problem might be handled in a number of ways, but modern ethics is typified by the simple expedient of agreeing to regard the situation of vocational choice as normally a nonmoral situation. Then to say that my choice is the "right" choice for me is to use the word "right" in one of its nonmoral senses.

The same categorial distinction expels from the domain of the moral countless other types of choice that human beings characteristically make, e.g., of what friends to cultivate, what avocations to pursue, what books to read. Indeed, John Stuart Mill, in his utilitarian voice, says that "ninety-nine hundredths of all our actions are done from other [than moral] motives, and rightly so done if the rule of duty does not condemn them."[5] He is obliged to thus delimit the workings of the utilitarian principle in order to preserve any vestige of individual autonomy under utilitarianism. Were we at all times obliged to seek to produce the greatest happiness of the greatest number (with its correlative rule on diminishing pain), we would be morally culpable in reading a book, writing a poem, or attending to the needs of our children, for in these cases there are many things we might do instead that would better serve to alleviate human misery in the world. . . .

The distinction of moral from nonmoral situations affords to persons, institutions, and practices the opportunity to pitch their tents on nonmoral turf, and it is difficult to find arguments or incentives that will induce them to move to moral ground. One class of arguments to this end is conspicuously circular, resting on premises that the outlander is under no obligation to accept, while another, by offering nonmoral incentives to moral conduct (e.g., prudence, happiness), appears to "degrade and prostitute virtue,"[6] setting it in the service of nonmoral ends.

Two such nonmoral campouts that have decisively shaped modern history are science and business management. Modern science gained its immunity on the ground of the supposed gulf between facts and values, description and prescription; its devotion to facts was thus at the same time its claim to be "value-free." And for approximately the past hundred years, business management has sought to claim for itself the status of applied social science on the bridge of economics, availing itself of moral exemption (except with respect to the "my station and its duties" type of code that no practice can be without) on the fact-value distinction. The prevailing spirit of management theory and practice is succinctly captured by management scholar Neil W. Chamberlain: "Employees are being paid to produce, not to make themselves into better people. Corporations are purchasing employee time to make a return on it, not investing in employees to enrich their lives. Employees are human capital, and when capital is hired or leased, the objective is not to embellish it for its own sake but to use it for financial advantage."[7]

The proliferation of nonmoral domains of refuge from morality comes home to roost when the so-called private sector, which Mill (in his eudaimonistic voice) fought for as a sanctuary for the self-development of moral character, becomes regarded instead as an arena for the gratification of desires that are relieved of any obligation to answer for their worth. Self-development is arduous (albeit deeply rewarding) work, and private life has become, for many, the playground for mindless diversions from the public workplace. The modern rise to predominance of both science and business appears to be accounted for on the basis of powerful a priori human incentives—

the love of truth on one side, and the desire for material gain on the other. But to this I believe the following consideration should be added. On any viable conception of human nature, *aspiration* is a definitive human characteristic. (I mean nothing heroic by this, but only that in order to understand any human being's present conduct, we must know the sought-for future toward which present conduct is meant to be contributory.) The effect of modern moral minimalism is to afford to moral life little space for aspiration; it is a small room with a low ceiling and not much of a view. In particular, it calls for little in the way of developed moral character—our second sense of modernity's moral minimalism. I believe an important consequence of this has been to redirect human aspirations away from the confines of morality and toward the apparently limitless horizons afforded by the laboratory and the market.

By contrast to modern ethics, classical ethics gives a central place to ideals, and it is characteristic of ideals that they are capable of enlisting the full measure of human aspiration. The function of ideals in classical ethical theory and moral life is to guide moral development, transforming random change in the lives of individuals and societies into the directed change that deserves to be called moral growth. Central to the development of moral character that constitutes moral growth is the achievement of integrity, by which all of an individual's faculties, desires, choices, dispositions, courses of conduct, and roles are alike expressive of him or her, and contribute to the chosen end. . . .

It will be immediately obvious that choices which were earlier cited as typically nonmoral in the modern understanding of morality are moral choices in the classical understanding. This is because choices of vocation, of avocations, of friends to cultivate and books to read (our previous examples), have a direct bearing on the development of moral character. In the matter of vocation, for example: if it is the fundamental moral responsibility of every person to discover his or her innate potential worth and progressively actualize it in the world, then vocational choice is clearly one of the important means for such actualization, and *vocation* has thematic moral meaning beneath the periodic "moral situations" that arise in it. This is why Socrates, Plato, and Aristotle refused to categorically divorce vocational skills from moral virtues (and not, as some modern commentators have hastily assumed, because they failed analytically to recognize the difference). Indeed, classical thought integrates the vocation and the life of the individual by the understanding that the true work of each person is his or her life, to which vocation and all other dimensions should be contributory. Were it possible here to pursue the implications of vocation as moral choice, I would argue for vocation as a foundational form of generosity, for by identifying with, and investing themselves in their vocations, persons are endeavoring to give the best of themselves to others in the products of their work, including their own developed traits of character.

Similarly friendship is inseparable from the moral work of self-discovery and self-actualization, and the long section given to it by Aristotle in the *Nicomachean Ethics* is not, as many modern moral philosophers have supposed, a diversionary ramble. According to Socrates in the *Lysis* and Aristotle in the *Nicomachean Ethics,* true friends, willing the best for one another, furnish reciprocal aid toward worthy living. Socrates says that friends, to be of such use to one another, must be alike in pursuing the good, but different and complementary in the kind of good that each pursues, each contributing something of worth to the other that the other cannot self-supply. Though I cannot develop the point, it is worth noting that Socrates is here working out a conception of individual autonomy that is compatible with interdependence, rather than implying a total self-sufficiency that would belie the social nature of humankind.

We have cited key instances of choices that are typically nonmoral by modern parameters but moral in classical understanding. However, our earlier contention that for classical ethics nothing

in human experience is without moral meaning requires that we go further. Specifically, we must speak to the trivial desires, choices, and acts which fill a considerable portion of our days. The answer, however, is the same: even our trivial desires, choices, and acts have moral meaning because they have some effect—no matter how small—on the person we are in process of becoming. To modern moral theory they appear to be devoid of moral meaning because they have no direct effect upon others, but classical morality is concerned with their effect upon the self, and quite clearly the kind of person one is in process of becoming has its effects upon others. But suppose that it did not and could not affect others? An individual marooned upon a desert island with no prospect of rescue would be relieved of all moral responsibility under the sort of theory that restricts moral meaning to the effects of a person's conduct on others. By contrast, under eudaimonistic theory such an individual would be nonetheless responsible for doing the utmost that circumstances allowed to manifest his or her potential worth. Because this worth is objective it is meant to be appreciated and utilized by (some) others, but the fact that in the desert island situation this is impossible is a contingency that does not abolish the moral responsibility to (as far as possible) actualize one's potential worth.

It is common in modern theory to distinguish prudential conduct from a moral conduct (Kant is a notable example), but eudaimonism recognizes prudence as a necessary condition of worthy living and therefore a moral responsibility.

Returning to our trivial desires, choices, and acts—the virtue of integrity represents the integration of all dimensions of the self, such that each complements all others, and all contribute to the end of the worthy life that is one's own to live. It is an inclusive virtue, leaving nothing out, and an extraneous desire, choice, or act, however minor, is an inner disorder and in some degree (however small) an impediment. Granted, integrity as thus described is an ideal that, as such, cannot be fully realized. Granted also, our very finitude obliges us to adopt measures of economy, included among which is the measure of disregarding truly minor desires, choices, and acts in order to attend to larger ones (as, if asked to describe the features of the room in which I now sit, I would confine myself to conspicuous ones while recognizing that description in infinite detail literally could not be concluded in a lifetime). But notice that this policy of economy is but a plea *de minimus,* ignoring moral meaning that it acknowledges to exist.

If morality is coterminous with human life and unrestrictedly pervasive within it, then individuals are afforded no nonmoral domain of refuge, and no human institution, practice, or discipline can claim exemption from morality's ultimate concern—the good life for human beings. Plato expresses this for state government when he says *(The Republic),* "Can anything be better for a commonwealth than to produce in it men and women of the best type?"[8] Mill is a modern spokesman for this view when he says, "The most important point of excellence which any form of government can possess is to promote the virtue and intelligence of the people themselves."[9] And John Dewey puts the same principle by saying, "Democracy has many meanings, but if it has a moral meaning, it is found in resolving that the supreme test of all political institutions and industrial arrangements shall be the contribution they make to the all-around growth of every member of society"[10]. . . .

The other "minimalist" delimitation of modern morality that we have identified is the limited demands it makes upon developed moral character. The reason for this delimitation is that modern morality is built upon what Edmund Pincoffs terms the "Hobbesian truism" that in absence of recognized rules and generally rule-abiding conduct, the lives of persons would be unbearable. On this foundation morality is paired with law in the interest of the preservation of social order. This interest requires the observance by (almost) everyone of rules that are understood and acknowledged as authoritative by (almost) everyone.

For this to be the case, the rules must be very simple and straightforward, and acting in accordance with them must require very little in the way of developed moral character. This accounts for the tendency of modern modes of normative ethics—contractarianism, deontology, utilitarianism, intuitionism, ideal observer theory, agent theory—to devolve (from their ultimate and far from simple principles) upon simple rules of the sort as, "Do not lie," "Do not steal," "Keep your promises," "Do not commit murder," etc., and to introduce exceptions and complications with great reluctance.

One consequence of directing morality to the preservation of social order is that morality becomes very difficult to distinguish from law; moral requirements are framed as rules, moral rules serve the same basic purpose as civil and criminal statutes, and moral judgments are modeled on judicial decisions in terms of impartiality and impersonality. Impartiality and impersonality mean that rightly made moral judgments will be made identically by whomever is called upon to judge, and will be applied identically to different persons in relevantly similar circumstances. We say of such judgments that they are "universalizable," typically meaning that what is right for any person in given circumstances is right for every person in relevantly similar circumstances. But there is an internal disparity here, for of the two principal factors in the formula—circumstances and persons—only the former is qualified by "relevantly similar." The reason that differences among persons typically are disregarded or disallowed is that universalizability is intended to thwart the inherent propensity of individuals to regard themselves as the exception to any rule. The effect of this disregard is to preclude recognition of differences among persons in respect to levels of the development of moral character, and this in turn means that only such moral rules can be recognized as make no demands upon moral capacities that (almost) everyone cannot be expected to possess. In sum, the universalizability criterion, by the internal disparity just noted, is obliged to confine its demands upon moral character to the barest minimum. . . .

To be sure, this bare minimum is not nothing; it includes the ability to understand simple moral rules and recognize the situations to which they apply, together with the ability to act in accordance with them and the will to do so. Edmund Pincoffs gathers these abilities under the terms "conscientiousness" and "rule responsibility." He extends the requisite minimum capacities by using an analogy between rule-morality demands and military imperatives. Among the latter a distinction is recognized between "commands" and "orders." "A command tells us what to do or refrain from doing in such explicit terms that there is either no or very little room for variation in the way in which it is obeyed or disobeyed. An order, on the other hand, does not so much specifically tell us what to do as what to accomplish or at what we should aim. 'Report at 10:00' is a command; 'Provide protective screen for the convoy' is an order. There can, of course, be general and standing orders and commands. A general command would be 'All hands report at 10:00 tomorrow morning', and a general standing command would require all hands to report every morning at 10:00. 'Exercise extreme caution when in enemy waters' can serve as a general standing order." On this analogy, Pincoffs notes that moral rules that resemble general standing orders require for compliance more in the way of developed individual capacities than do rules resembling general standing commands. Nevertheless what is required remains characterizable under "conscientiousness" or "rule responsibility," which, as the single virtue (or closely interrelated set of virtues) implicated by the modern mode of ethical theorizing, neglects most of the developed moral capacities recognized as moral virtues in classical thought. This prompts Pincoffs's comment that "The attempt to reduce moral character to any given trait by philosophical fiat is open to suspicion."

The question of what "rule responsibility" requires in the way of developed moral character has not often been addressed by modern ethical theorists, but an attempt at adequate description would have something to gain, for example, from John Rawls's "Two Concepts of Rules" and R. M. Hare's "Universalizability,"[11] among other contributions. (Hare points out that by the universalizability criterion we are not told what to do, but must propose hypothetical acts and submit them to the touchstone of the criterion.) What makes an attempt at adequate description unnecessary for our purposes is that by assigning responsibility for preserving social order to morality, modern ethics (as noted earlier) has been obliged to make minimal demands on developed moral character, whatever the precise description of the requisite character may prove to be. Urmson captures this decisively when he says in his essay, "Saints and Heroes": "If we are to exact basic duties like debts, and censure failure, such duties must be, in ordinary circumstances, within the capacity of the ordinary man. It would be silly for us to say to ourselves, our children, and our fellow men, 'This and that you and everyone else must do,' if the acts in question are such that manifestly but few could bring themselves to do them, though we may ourselves resolve to try to be of that few."

To summarize what has here been said about modernity's moral minimalism in the second of the two respects we have identified: modern ethics either disregards, or treats inadequately, "good" or "right" acts that make large demands upon developed moral character in individuals.

It may be supposed that Mill and Kant, as dominant figures in modern ethical theory, furnish decisive counterexamples to our thesis that modern ethics makes minimal demands upon developed moral character, and I will speak briefly to each case. It is true that Mill gives great importance to the "sympathetic feelings" in chapter 3 of *Utilitarianism*, and calls for their deliberate cultivation by the "influences of education." But his reason for this is that it is through sympathetic feelings that human beings are induced to act on the principle of "the greatest happiness of the greatest number." This is to say that character development is here conceived by Mill as instrumental to rule-adherence, which subsumes it under Pincoffs's "conscientiousness," and fits our description of "rules morality" offered at the outset.

Similarly Kant's preoccupation with "the good will," which is dutiful solely for duty's sake, is a "conscientiousness" that considers character development only insofar as it procures "rule responsibility." Otherwise he treats moral virtues, not as developed traits of character, but as "a matter of temperament," and of no moral importance. Kant does indeed (in his monograph *Education)* treat "moral culture" as the part of education intended to develop moral character, but for Kant moral character is the "readiness to act in accord with 'maxims'" which precisely subsumes it under Pincoffs's "conscientiousness."

[A Critique of Urmson's "Saints and Heroes"]

In the matter of conduct that makes large demands upon developed moral character we can effectively contrast the modern and classical perspectives by means of Urmson's "Saints and Heroes," which calls attention to the deficiency of modern moral theory in this respect, but then tries to rectify it in a distinctly modern—and, I believe, unsatisfactory—manner.

Urmson criticizes the three-part classification of actions by most ethical theorists—acts that are morally obligatory, acts that are morally forbidden, and acts that are morally indifferent—for its inability to handle supererogation, understood as the class of acts that are good to do but not wrong not to do. Using "saintly" and "heroic" acts as his paradigms, he says "It would be absurd to suggest that moral philosophers have hitherto been unaware of the existence of saints and heroes and have never even alluded to them in their work. But it does seem that these facts have been neglected in their general, systematic accounts of morality." He thinks it possible to revise the theories he specifically considers (Kantianism, utili-

tarianism, and intuitionism) "to accommodate the facts," but adds that "until so modified successfully they must surely be treated as unacceptable, and the modifications required might well detract from their plausibility."

A saint acts for the good in contexts in which inclination, desire, or self-interest would prevent most people from so acting; a hero acts for the good in contexts in which terror, fear, or a drive to self-preservation would prevent such action by most people. Both the saint and the hero act "far beyond the limits of [their] duty," but Urmson indicates that the class of acts that ethical theory must be rectified to include begins with acts that exceed the limits of duty in the least measure, e.g., acts that are even "a little more generous, forbearing, helpful, or forgiving than fair dealing demands," and all cases of "going the second mile." Because "basic duties" are uniformly obligatory for everyone they must make minimal demands on developed moral character, and Urmson (as we have seen in a previous citation) argues for retention of their minimalist character. The case he makes is for the revision of ethical theory to include the category of supererogation as "higher flights of morality [to be] regarded as more positive contributions that go beyond what is universally to be exacted." He says of these "higher flights" that while they are not to be "exacted publicly," they are "clearly equally pressing *in foro interno* on those who are not content merely to avoid the intolerable."

The problems in Urmson's position to which I want to call attention are two. In the first place he has acknowledged a continuum of what might be called "degrees of difficulty" between basic duties and the "higher flights" of morality, which means that wherever the line is drawn between basic duties and acts that exceed basic duties (acts of supererogation), it will be prone to the appearance of arbitrariness. Second, Urmson acknowledges that saints and heroes regard their saintly and heroic deeds as their duty ("There is indeed no degree of saintliness that a suitable person may not come to consider it to be his duty to achieve"), yet Urmson is in the position of contending that their deeds are in truth "far beyond the limits of [their] duty," and it is unclear by what authority Urmson contradicts the saint or hero.

At bottom, Urmson is beset by the same dilemma that is responsible for the deficiency he calls attention to in the ethical theories he cites. If impartiality precludes consideration of relevant differences among persons, then either moral heroism is obligatory for everyone, or moral duties are confined to what Urmson terms the "rock-bottom" minimum, and moral conduct that exceeds the minimum is the duty of no one. In the latter case there will be nothing *admirable* in moral conduct; ("the admirable" is what deserves to be "looked up to," whereas minimal moral demands are groundlevel); in the former case everyone will be morally responsible for conduct that lies beyond the developed capacities of most, and which it is therefore unreasonable to expect of them. To avoid this consequence, Urmson opts for restriction of duties to "rock-bottom" minimum, to which he adds the category of supererogation. The supererogatory is what is morally good to do but not morally obligatory. The problem here is that by his fidelity to impartiality and universality, Urmson is obliged to conclude that whatever is supererogatory, i.e., whatever is in the least beyond minimum "rock-bottom" duties, is not morally obligatory for anyone. But he acknowledges that heroes perceive their heroic conduct as their duty.

Urmson's key mistake, I think, lies in minimizing the significance of the hero's or saint's own conception of his or her moral duty. Noting that only the saint or hero can thus identify his or her duty, and that he or she characteristically attributes this duty to no one else, Urmson says it is *not* "a piece of objective reporting." This propensity to minimize the saint's or hero's own sense of moral responsibility is widespread in modern ethics. Thus Michael W. Jackson says it is "modesty" or "genuine confusion" when Dr. Bernard Rieux, in Albert Camus's *The Plague,* or Corneille's El

Cid, refer to their heroic conduct as their duty.[12] But on the contrary, I think that both Camus and Corneille are astute in the matter of the psychology of heroism, and that this psychology accurately reflects the facts. The seeming warrant of Urmson's denial of objectivity to the hero's self-judgment is the equation of objective human responsibilities with universally distributed human responsibilities, but this ignores the objective fact of moral development—a morally developed individual possesses greater capabilities than does an individual of lesser development, as a skilled swimmer can accomplish a deep-water rescue that would be beyond the capabilities of a novice swimmer. The recognition that the moral life of individuals is a development is the recognition that moral demands continually increase, and this is corroborated by the testimony of "heroes" (Corneille's, Camus's, Urmson's) that they demand more of themselves than they expect of most persons, and more than they expected of themselves at prior levels of development. Drawing upon eudaimonistic ethical theory, what we must add to this is the inalienable moral responsibility of every human being for continuous moral development. This cuts off the populist resort of contending that a handful of persons are "born heroes," while nothing but moral mediocrity is to be expected of the rest of us.

In sum, eudaimonism's thesis is that some of what is obligatory at later stages of moral development is supererogatory with respect to prior stages of moral development. This is a continuity-thesis concerning what exceeds or is included within the moral obligations of persons at given times. But the distinction between duty and supererogation is not arbitrary—it is grounded in the objective fact of moral development.

We have referred to the "Hobbesian truism" that for life to be tolerable (almost) everyone must conform to basic moral rules, which entails that demands upon developed moral character must be minimal. To this I will counterpose what I will term the "Socratic truism." It is the proposition that any person may in the course of his or her life encounter one or more ultimate tests in which to pursue the course of life that he or she has chosen to live is at the risk of life or well-being (Socrates, *Apology:* "This is the truth of the matter, gentlemen of the jury: wherever a man has taken a position that he believes to be best, or has been placed by his commander, there he must I think remain and face danger, without a thought for death or anything else, rather than disgrace"). My leave to call this a truism rests in well-recognized cases, for example, when citizens are called upon to risk their lives in defense of their country; or again, when a parent is called upon to risk his or her life to save his or her child. Similarly we recognize, I think, that were we residents of a Nazi-occupied country in WW II, our humanitarian principles would demand of us that we attempt to shelter Jews from Nazi genocide. In general, we know that we cannot live lives that are worthy in our own estimation if we abandon our commitments at the first sign of trouble. Our supreme test may or may not come, but because it may, we must prepare ourselves for it. The Hobbesian truism tells us that minimally acceptable conduct is required of everyone; the Socratic truism tells us that moral heroism may be required of anyone. The demands implicit in the Socratic truism are universalizable because the opportunity of moral growth is in principle universalizable. On the question of universality this is to say that eudaimonism holds the demand for moral growth in individuals to be universal, but holds that morally obligatory conduct in "relevantly similar" situations will differ among persons by virtue of differences in the levels of moral development that they have achieved.

Urmson is surely correct in holding as a paramount criterion of normative ethical philosophy that "our morality must be one that will work," (this follows from the definition of normative ethics as "practical reason") but modern ethical philosophy is mistaken in supposing this to entail moral minimalism. Large moral demands are practicable when they are proportional to moral development, and when moral development of indi-

viduals is a social undertaking. And until morality is understood to include the higher reaches of moral development (as represented by the classical virtues), it is so impoverished as to be unable to enlist human aspiration. The following, by mountaineer Reinhold Messner, will do metaphoric service here: "Striding along, my body becomes so highly-charged it would be quite impossible for me to stop. It feels as if something wants to break free, to burst from my breast. It is a surge of longing that carries me forward as if I were possessed."[13] It is a reflection recorded by Messner during his ascent of K-2 in the Karakoram Himalaya, and would not be likely to have visited him in the flatlands. Moral thought and moral life require their upper reaches if they are to enlist human aspiration lifelong, and ethical theory is bound to accommodate them. But we must recognize that, like the mountain, the upper reaches of moral character can only be attained by starting from where one is, and ascending in steps, and for this one must know how to climb. What happens when lofty goals are posed but nothing is done about learning to climb is illustrated by "strong" utilitarianism, which I earlier referred to as in some respects an anomaly in modern ethical theory, and which I will speak to briefly in conclusion.

Urmson judges utilitarianism to be the (modern) normative ethical theory that is most amenable to the inclusion of the category of the supererogatory. He says that this is because "Utilitarians, when attempting to justify the main rules of duty in terms of a *summum bonum,* have surely invoked many different types of utilitarian justification, ranging from the avoidance of the intolerable to the fulfillment of the last detail of a most rarified ideal." In other words, utilitarianism can be formulated in such a way as to include the "higher flights" of morality. The trouble is that when it is so formulated, it results in making out "the most heroic self-sacrifice or saintly self-forgetfulness [to] be duties on all fours with truth telling and promise keeping." And Urmson concludes that because the saintly and heroic are "too far beyond the capacity of the ordinary men or ordinary occasions . . . a general breakdown of compliance with the moral code would be an inevitable consequence."

It is "strong" versions of utilitarianism that Urmson has in mind, as distinguished from "weak." The latter seek to obviate the problem that Urmson cites by placing limits of one kind or another on utilitarian responsibility. Accordingly, in our earlier citation Mill contended that "ninety-nine hundredths of all our actions are done from other [than moral] motives, and rightly so done if the rule of duty does not condemn them." What Mill may safely be supposed to have in mind as the principal category of the "ninety-nine hundredths" is conduct in the private sector that he maps in *On Liberty*, consisting in conduct that either does not affect others, or does not affect others directly. But the problem here is that identification of a private sector does not, as Mill supposes, deactivate the utilitarian principle and its derivative responsibilities. The reason for this is that human beings can exchange their situations. It is true enough that if I am alone in my apartment, my decision whether for the next hour to read a book, watch TV, or develop photographic film in my darkroom is unlikely to have direct effect upon others—but why am I not, say, out on the street finding shelter for the homeless? The utilitarian principle mandates that I *always* act for the greatest good of the greatest number. To be sure, the qualification "within the limits of human possibilities" is to be understood (e.g., I must eat and sleep), but it cannot grant exemption to Mill's private sector of individual experience for the reason just given.

This leaves us with "strong" utilitarianisms, e.g., Bentham's version and the formulation by Moore that Urmson brands unworkable. But the most interesting in this category is that of Peter Singer. With Mill, Singer perceives that on the face of it the utilitarian principle makes moral demands upon persons that most are going to perceive as extravagant, and by the touchstone of which almost all human lives must be judged

morally wanting. But unlike Mill, Singer's response is unequivocal acceptance—indeed, insistence—upon these entailments. In his words, "if it is in our power to prevent something bad from happening, without thereby sacrificing anything of comparable moral importance, we ought, morally, to do it."[14] He contends that considerations of distance and proximity are disallowed, and argues that it is irrelevant whether we are the only person who could possibly help, or one among millions. The effect is that suffering anywhere in the world is every person's moral problem, and because suffering in its concrete forms (starvation, malnutrition, disease, etc.) is the exigent moral problem, the only way any of us is at any time relieved of responsibility to be contributing to the alleviation of suffering in, say, Bengal (the best publicized example when Singer wrote), is by contributing to the limit of his or her ability to the alleviation of suffering elsewhere. The amount of resources (energy, money, skill, etc.) each is to contribute is "at least up to the point at which by giving more one would begin to cause serious suffering for oneself and one's dependents— perhaps even beyond this point to the point of marginal utility, at which by giving more one would cause oneself and one's dependents as much suffering as one would prevent in Bengal."

[For] persons who accept the utilitarian principle as the supreme moral principle Singer is, I think, difficult and perhaps impossible to refute. Moreover from the standpoint of classical ethics, Singer is to be commended for reintroducing the moral mountain without which ethical theory becomes an arid flatland. But how can it be other than futile to present a mountaineering demand to flatlands-dwellers without reckoning with the problem that they are devoid of climbing skills? It is precisely in its recognition that learning to climb must come first that the classical mode of ethical theorizing demonstrates its superiority to prevailing modern modes. Supposing that Singer's argument for the preemptive status of the moral problem of physical suffering is decisive and irrefutable, it is nevertheless a fallacy of anachronism to suppose that it will be recognized and responded to if prior attention is not given to the discovery and establishment of the conditions that conduce to generalization of moral development in individuals. To distill the thesis of the present essay, it is by giving priority not to one contemporary moral ill or another, but to the neglected problem of the development of moral character, that we gain prospect of generalizing the dedication of persons in substantial numbers to the realization of moral ends.

Notes

For critical comments on earlier drafts of this essay, I am grateful to John Kekes, Edmund L. Pincoffs, William G. Scott, and Mary K. Norton. This should not be understood to imply their unqualified or qualified endorsement of the present version.

1. Alasdair MacIntyre, *After Virtue: A Study in Moral Theory* (Notre Dame, Ind.: University of Notre Dame Press, 1981); Richard Taylor, *Ethics, Faith, and Reason* (Englewood Cliffs, N.J.: Prentice-Hall, 1985); Edmund L. Pincoffs, *Quandaries and Virtues: Against Reductivism in Ethics* (Lawrence, Kans.: University Press of Kansas, 1986). My *Personal Destinies* (Princeton, 1976) attempted to outfit classical eudaimonism for current service. Bernard Williams shows some favor for the classical model of ethical theorizing in *Ethics and the Limits of Philosophy* (Cambridge, Mass.: Harvard University Press, 1985). In addition it will be recognized that interest in "the virtues" has been mounting rapidly among ethical theorists for a decade or more, e.g., Philippa Foot, *Virtues and Vices* (Berkeley: University of California Press, 1978); James D. Wallace, *Virtues and Vices* (Ithaca, N.Y.: Cornell University Press, 1978). First-rate work on virtues, coupled with the recognition that this emphasis is at home in the classical mode of ethical theorizing, is to be found in essays by Lester H. Hunt, John Kekes, Lawrence C. Becker, and R. W. Hepburn.

2. Plato, *Republic,* translated by F. M. Cornford (New York, 1945), p. 37.

3. A recent and thorough consideration of the concept of potentiality is Israel Scheffler, *Of Human Potential* (Boston: Routledge & Kegan Paul, 1985).

4. Henry D. Thoreau, *Walden,* edited by J. Lyndon Shanley (Princeton, 1971), p. 97.

5. John Stuart Mill, *Utilitarianism* (Indianapolis: Bobbs-Merrill, 1957), p. 23.

6. F. H. Bradley, *Ethical Studies,* cited in Peter Singer, *Practical Ethics* (Cambridge: Cambridge University Press, 1979), p. 209.

7. Neil W. Chamberlain, *The Limits of Corporate Responsibility* (New York, 1973), p. 92. I am indebted to Prof. David K. Hart for this reference.

8. Plato, *Republic,* p. 154.

9. John Stuart Mill, *Considerations on Representative Government* (Indianapolis: Bobbs-Merrill, 1958), p. 25.

10. John Dewey, *Reconstruction in Philosophy* (Boston: Beacon Press, 1957), p. 186.

11. John Rawls, "Two Concepts of Rules," in *An Introduction to Ethics,* edited by Robert E. Dewey and Robert H. Hurlbutt III (New York, 1977), pp. 259–66. R. M. Hare, "Universalizability," in *Essays on the Moral Concepts* (Berkeley: University of California Press, 1972), pp. 13–28, esp. pp. 19–20.

12. Michael W. Jackson, *Matters of Justice* (London, 1986), pp. 126, 122.

13. Reinhold Messner and Alessandro Gogna, *K-2, Mountain of Mountains* (New York, 1980), p. 78.

14. Peter Singer, "Famine, Affluence, and Morality," in *Reason and Responsibility,* edited by Joel Feinberg (Belmont, Calif.: Wadsworth, 1985), p. 523. I here neglect Singer's weakened version of his principle—"If it is in our power to prevent something very bad from happening, without thereby sacrificing anything morally significant, we ought, morally, to do it"—as less interesting and more problematic than his strong version.

PART VIII

Morality and Religion

Introduction

Whether it be the impoverished Calcutta harijan accepting his degradation as his karma, the Shiite Moslem fighting a jihad in the name of Allah, the Jew circumspectly striving to keep kosher, or the Christian giving to charity in the name of Christ, religion has traditionally so dominated the moral landscape as to be virtually indistinguishable from it.

There have been exceptions to be sure. Confucianism in China is essentially a secular system; there are nontheist versions of Buddhism; and the philosophers of Greece thought of morality independently from religion; but for the most part, throughout most of our history most people have identified morality with religion, with the commands of God.

The question is whether the equation is a valid one. Is morality essentially tied to religion so that the term 'secular ethic' is an oxymoron, a contradiction? Can morality survive without religion? Is it the case, as Tolstoy thought, that separating morality from religion is like cutting a flower from its roots and transplanting it rootless into the ground? Is Dostoevsky's character Ivan Karamazov correct when he proclaims that "If God doesn't exist, everything is permissible"?

Essentially, our inquiry comes down to addressing two questions: Does morality depend on religion? and Are religious ethics essentially different from secular ethics?

Does Morality Depend on Religion?

The first question is whether moral standards themselves depend on God for their validity or whether there is an autonomy of ethics, so that even God is subject to the moral order. The question first arises in Plato's dialogue the *Euthyphro*

(our first reading) where Socrates asks the pious Euthyphro, "Do the gods love holiness because it is holy, or is it holy because the gods love it?" Changing the terms but still preserving the meaning, we want to know whether God commands what is Good because it is good or whether the Good is good because God commands it? According to one theory, called the *divine command theory*, ethical principles are simply the commands of God. They derive their validity from God's commanding them, and they *mean* 'commanded by God.' Without God, there would be no universally valid morality. Here is how the theologian, Carl F. H. Henry states this view:

Biblical ethics discredits an autonomous morality. It gives theonomous ethics its classic form—the identification of the moral law with the Divine will. In Hebrew-Christian revelation, distinctions in ethics reduce to what is good or what is pleasing, and to what is wicked or displeasing to the Creator-God alone. The biblical view maintains always a dynamic statement of values, refusing to sever the elements of morality from the will of God. . . . The good is what the Creator-Lord does and commands. He is the creator of the moral law, and defines its very nature.[1]

Morality not only originates with God, but "moral rightness" simply means "willed by God" and "moral wrongness" means "being against the will of God." Since, essentially, morality is based on divine will, not on independently existing reasons for action, no further reasons for action are necessary. As Ivan Karamazov asserts, "If God doesn't exist, everything is permissible." Nothing is forbidden or required. Without God we have moral nihilism.

The opposing viewpoint, call it the *autonomy thesis* (standing for the independence of ethics), denies the theses of the divine command theory, asserting, to the contrary, that: (1) morality does not originate with God (though the way God created us may affect the specific nature of morality); (2) rightness and wrongness are not based simply on God's will; and (3) essentially, there are reasons for acting one way or the other, which may be known independently of God's will. In sum, ethics are autonomous, and even God must obey the moral law, which exists independently of himself—as the laws of mathematics and logic do. Just as even God cannot make a three-sided square or make it the case that he never existed, so even God cannot make what is intrinsically evil good or make what is good, evil.

Theists who espouse the autonomy thesis may well admit some epistemological advantage to God. God *knows* what is right—better than we do. And since he is good, we can always learn from consulting him, but in principle, we act morally for the same reasons that God does. We both follow moral reasons that are independent of God. We are against torturing the innocent because it is cruel and unjust, just as God is against torturing the innocent because it is cruel and unjust. If there is no God, on this account, nothing is changed. Morality is left intact, and both theists and nontheists have the very same moral duties.

The attractiveness of the divine command theory lies in the fact that it seems to do justice to the omnipotence or sovereignty of God. God somehow is thought to be less sovereign or necessary to our lives if he is not the source of morality. It seems inconceivable to many believers that anything having to do with goodness or duty could be "higher" than or independent of God. He is the supreme Lord of the believer's life, and what the believer means by "morally right" is that "the Lord commands it—even if I do not fully understand it." When the believer asks what the will of God is, it is a direct appeal to a personal will, not to an independently existing rule.

There are two problems with the divine com-

mand theory that need to be faced by those who hold it. One problem is that the divine command theory would seem to make the attribution of 'goodness' to God redundant. When we say 'God is good,' we think that we are ascribing a property to God, but if 'good' simply means 'what God commands or wills,' then we are not attributing any property to God. Our statement 'God is good' merely means 'God does whatever he wills to do' or 'God practices what he preaches,' and the statement 'God commands us to do what is good' merely is the tautology 'God commands us to do what God commands us to do.'

A second problem with the divine command theory is that it seems to make morality into something arbitrary. If God's fiat is the sole arbiter of right and wrong, it would seem to be logically possible for such 'heinous' acts as rape, killing of the innocent for the fun of it, and gratuitous cruelty to become morally good actions—if God suddenly decided to command us to do these things. The radicality of the divine command theory is set forth by a classic statement of Occam:

The hatred of God, theft, adultery, and actions similar to these actions according to common law, may have an evil quality annexed, insofar as they are done by a divine command to perform the opposite act. But as far as the sheer being in the actions is concerned, they can be performed by God without any evil condition annexed; and they can even be performed meritoriously by an earthly pilgrim if they should come under divine precepts, just as now the opposite of these in fact fall under the divine command.[2]

The implications of this sort of reasoning seem far-reaching. If there are no constraints on what God can command, no independent measure or reason for moral action, then anything can become a moral duty, and our moral duties can change from moment to moment. Could there be any moral stability? The proponent of the divine command theory may object that God has revealed what is his will in his word, sacred Scriptures. But, the fitting response is, how do you know that God is not lying? For if there is no independent criterion of right and wrong except what God happens to will, how do we know God is not willing to make lying into a duty?—in which case believers have no reason to believe the Bible!

If God could make morally good what seems morally heinous simply by willing it, wouldn't morality be reduced to the right of the powerful? Nietzsche's 'Might makes Right'? Indeed, what would be the difference between the devil and God, if morality were simply an arbitrary command?

Suppose we had two sets of commands, one from the devil and one from God. How would we know which set was which? Could they be identical? What would make them different? If there is no independent criterion by which to judge right and wrong, it is difficult to see how we could know which was which. The only basis for comparison would be who won. God is simply the biggest bully on the block (granted it is a pretty big block—covering the entire universe).

There is a second question with regard to the relationship of ethics and religion: "Does morality need the sanctions of a divine being to inspire adequate motivation for compliance?" Although Immanuel Kant (VI.18) held to the autonomy thesis, he argued that morality would not be justified if there were not a God to enforce the moral law, rewarding and punishing rational agents in the next life. Whereas Kant did not think that this ultimate sanction should play any role in motivating us (we should be moral for its own sake), others have argued that without God there is insufficient reason to be moral. Why be moral when no one will punish us for being selfish or profiting from immoral behavior?

In our second reading, "A Free Man's Worship," Bertrand Russell argues that morality does not need God or an afterlife. Reason alone provides the adequate basis for morality.

In our third reading, "Religion and the Queerness of Morality," George Mavrodes criticizes Russell's view of morality as "queer," arguing that it is shallow, fails to account for our depth of feeling about moral values, and is uninspiring in that it fails to give an adequate answer to the question, "Why should I be moral?"

In our final reading, Kai Nielsen's "Ethics without Religion," we have a secular response to Mavrodes' arguments. Even if "God is dead," as Nielsen believes, nothing vital is lost, for there are intrinsically good things that make life worth living and provide the basis for morality.

Notes

1. Carl F. Henry, *Christian Personal Ethics* (Grand Rapids, Mich.: Eerdmans, 1957), p. 210.

2. William of Occam, quoted in *Divine Command Morality*, ed. J. M. Idziak (Toronto: Mellon, 1979).

32

The Euthyphro Problem

PLATO

Socrates is questioning the ardently religious Euthy-phro, who, believing it to be his religious and moral duty, is going to court to report his father for having killed a slave, who himself had committed murder. In the course of the dialogue Socrates raises the question that has come to be known as "The Euthyphro Problem," of whether the Good is good because God loves or chooses it or whether God loves or chooses the Good because it is good.

SOCRATES: Come now, my dear Euthyphro, tell me, too, that I may become wiser, what proof you have that all the gods consider that man to have been killed unjustly who became a murderer while in your service . . . and that it is right for a son to denounce and to prosecute his father on behalf of such a man. Come, try to show me a clear sign that all the gods definitely believe this action to be right. If you can give me adequate proof of this, I shall never cease to extol your wisdom.

EUTHYPHRO: This is perhaps no light task, Soc-rates, though I could show you very clearly. . . .

S: Let us assume, if you will, that all the gods consider this [act of killing the servant] unjust and that they all hate it. However, is this the correction we are making in our discussion, that what all the gods hate is impious, and what they all love is pious, and that what some gods love and others hate is neither or both? Is that how you now wish us to define piety and impiety?

E: What prevents us from doing so, Socrates?

Reprinted from Plato, *The Trial and Death of Socrates,* trans. G.M.A. Grube, as revised by Richard Hogan and Donald J. Zeyl (Indianapolis: Hackett Publishing Company), by permission of the publisher.

S: For my part nothing, Euthyphro, but you look whether on your part this proposal will enable you to teach me most easily what you promised.

E: I would certainly say that the pious is what all the gods love, and the opposite, what all the gods hate, is the impious.

S: Then let us again examine whether that is a sound statement, or do we let it pass, and if one of us, or someone else, merely says that something is so, do we accept that it is so? Or should we examine what the speaker means?

E: We must examine it, but I certainly think that this is now a fine statement.

S: We shall soon know better whether it is. Consider this: Is the pious loved by the gods because it is pious, or is it pious because it is loved by the gods?

E: I don't know what you mean, Socrates.

S: I shall try to explain more clearly: we speak of something being carried and something carrying, of something being led and something leading, of something being seen and something seeing, and you understand that these things are all different from one another and how they differ?

E: I think I do.

S: So there is something being loved and something loving, and the loving is a different thing.

E: Of course.

S: Tell me then whether that which is being carried is being carried because someone carries it or for some other reason.

E: No, that is the reason.

S: And that which is being led is so because someone leads it, and that which is being seen because someone sees it?

E: Certainly.

S: It is not seen by someone because it is being seen but on the contrary it is being seen because someone sees it, nor is it because it is being led that someone leads it but because someone leads it that it is being led; nor does someone carry an object because it is being carried, but it is being carried because someone carries it. Is what I want to say clear, Euthyphro? I want to say this, namely, that if anything comes to be, or is affected, it does not come to be because it is coming to be, but it is coming to be because it comes to be; nor is it affected because it is being affected but because something affects it. Or do you not agree?

E: I do.

S: What is being loved is either something that comes to be or something that is affected by something?

E: Certainly.

S: So it is in the same case as the things just mentioned; it is not loved by those who love it because it is being loved, but it is being loved because they love it?

E: Necessarily.

S: What then do we say about the pious, Euthyphro? Surely that it is loved by all the gods, according to what you say?

E: Yes.

S: Is it loved because it is pious, or for some other reason?

E: For no other reason.

S: It is loved then because it is pious, but it is not pious because it is loved?

E: Apparently.

S: And because it is loved by the gods it is being loved and is dear to the gods?

E: Of course.

S: The god-beloved is then not the same as the pious, Euthyphro, nor the pious the same as the god-beloved, as you say it is, but one differs from the other.

E: How so, Socrates?

S: Because we agree that the pious is beloved for the reason that it is pious, but it is not pious because it is loved. Is that not so?

E: Yes.

S: And that the god-beloved, on the other hand, is so because it is loved by the gods, by the very fact of being loved, but it is not loved because it is god-beloved.

E: True.

S: But if the god-beloved and the pious were the same, my dear Euthyphro, and the pious were loved because it was pious, then the god-beloved would be loved because it was god-beloved, and if the god-beloved was god-beloved because it was loved by the gods, then the pious would also be pious because it was loved by the gods; but now you see that they are in opposite cases as being altogether different from each other: the one is of a nature to be loved because it is loved, the other is loved because it is of nature to be loved. I'm afraid, Euthyphro, that when you were asked what piety is, you did not wish to make its nature clear to me, but you told me an affect or quality of it, that the pious has the quality of being loved by all the gods, but you have not yet told me what the pious is. Now, if you will, do not hide things from me but tell me again from the beginning what piety is, whether loved by the gods or having some other quality—we shall not quarrel about—but be keen to tell me what the pious and the impious are.

33

A Free Man's Worship

Bertrand Russell

Bertrand Russell (1872–1970) was educated at Cambridge University, where he later taught philosophy. A writer of more than a hundred books and articles on almost every major area in philosophy, he is one of the most significant philosophers of the twentieth century. In this essay written in 1903 Russell rejects the idea that religion is necessary for morality. We can be both moral and happy without God. The world is absurd, a godless tragedy in which "Nature, omnipotent but blind, in the revolutions of her secular hurryings through the abysses of space, has brought forth at last a child, subject still to her power, but gifted with sight, with knowledge of good and evil, with the capacity of judging all the works of his unthinking Mother." It is this conscious power of moral evaluation that makes the child superior to his omnipotent Mother. He is free to think, to evaluate, to create, and to live committed to ideals. So in spite of suffering, despair, and death, humans are free and life may be meaningful.

To Dr Faustus in his study Mephistopheles told the history of the Creation, saying:

"The endless praises of the choirs of angels had begun to grow wearisome; for, after all, did he not deserve their praise? Had he not given them endless joy? Would it not be more amusing to obtain undeserved praise, to be worshiped by beings whom he tortured? He smiled inwardly, and resolved that the great drama should be performed.

"For countless ages the hot nebula whirled aimlessly through space. At length it began to take shape, the central mass threw off planets, the planets cooled, boiling seas and burning mountains heaved and tossed, from black masses of

cloud hot sheets of rain deluged the barely solid crust. And now the first germ of life grew in the depths of the ocean, and developed rapidly in the fructifying warmth into vast forest trees, huge ferns springing from the damp mold, sea monsters breeding, fighting, devouring, and passing away. And from the monsters, as the play unfolded itself, Man was born, with the power of thought, the knowledge of good and evil, and the cruel thirst for worship. And Man saw that all is passing in this mad, monstrous world, that all is struggling to snatch, at any cost, a few brief moments of life before Death's inexorable decree. And Man said: 'There is a hidden purpose, could we but fathom it, and the purpose is good; for we must reverence something, and in the visible world there is nothing worthy of reverence.' And Man stood aside from the struggle, resolving that God intended harmony to come out of chaos by human efforts. And when he followed the instincts which God had transmitted to him from his ancestry of beasts of prey, he called it Sin, and asked God to forgive him. But he doubted whether he could be justly forgiven, until he invented a divine Plan by which God's wrath was to have been appeased. And seeing the present was bad, he made it yet worse, that thereby the future might be better. And he gave God thanks for the strength that enabled him to forgo even the joys that were possible. And God smiled; and when he saw that Man had become perfect in renunciation and worship, he sent another sun through the sky, which crashed into Man's sun; and all returned again to nebula.

"'Yes,' he murmured, 'it was a good play; I will have it performed again.'"

Such, in outline, but even more purposeless, more void of meaning, is the world which Science presents for our belief. Amid such a world, if anywhere, our ideals henceforward must find a home. That Man is the product of causes which had no prevision of the end they were achieving; that his origin, his growth, his hopes and fears, his loves and his beliefs, are but the outcome of accidental collocations of atoms; that no fire, no heroism, no intensity of thought and feeling, can preserve an individual life beyond the grave; that all the labors of the ages, all the devotion, all the inspiration, all the noonday brightness of human genius, are destined to extinction in the vast death of the solar system, and that the whole temple of Man's achievement must inevitably be buried beneath the debris of a universe in ruins—all these things, if not quite beyond dispute, are yet so nearly certain, that no philosophy which rejects them can hope to stand. Only within the scaffolding of these truths, only on the firm foundation of unyielding despair, can the soul's habitation henceforth be safely built.

How, in such an alien and inhuman world, can so powerless a creature as Man preserve his aspirations untarnished? A strange mystery it is that Nature, omnipotent but blind, in the revolutions of her secular hurryings through the abysses of space, has brought forth at last a child, subject still to her power, but gifted with sight, with knowledge of good and evil, with the capacity of judging all the works of his unthinking Mother. In spite of Death, the mark and seal of the parental control, Man is yet free, during his brief years, to examine, to criticize, to know, and in imagination to create. To him alone, in the world with which he is acquainted, this freedom belongs; and in this lies his superiority to the resistless forces that control his outward life.

The savage, like ourselves, feels the oppression of his impotence before the powers of Nature; but having in himself nothing that he respects more than Power, he is willing to prostrate himself before his gods, without inquiring whether they are worthy of his worship. Pathetic and very terrible is the long history of cruelty and torture, of degradation and human sacrifice, endured in the hope of placating the jealous gods: surely, the trembling believer thinks, when what is most pre-cious has been freely given, their lust for blood must be appeased, and more will not be required. The religion of Moloch—as such creeds may be generically called—is in essence the cringing submission of the slave, who dare not, even in his heart, allow the thought that his master deserves no adulation. Since the independence of ideals is not yet acknowledged, Power may be freely worshiped, and receive an unlimited respect, despite its wanton infliction of pain.

But gradually, as morality grows bolder, the claim of the ideal world begins to be felt; and worship, if it is not to cease, must be given to gods of another kind than those created by the savage. Some, though they feel the demands of the ideal, will still consciously reject them, still urging that naked Power is worthy of worship. Such is the attitude inculcated in God's answer to Job out of the whirlwind: the divine power and knowledge are paraded, but of the divine goodness there is no hint. Such also is the attitude of those who, in our own day, base their morality upon the struggle for survival, maintaining that the survivors are necessarily the fittest. But others, not content with an answer so repugnant to the moral sense, will adopt the position which we have become accustomed to regard as specially religious, maintaining that, in some hidden manner, the world of fact is really harmonious with the world of ideals. Thus Man creates God, all-powerful and all-good, the mystic unity of what is and what should be.

But the world of fact, after all, is not good; and, in submitting our judgment to it, there is an element of slavishness from which our thoughts must be purged. For all things it is well to exalt the dignity of Man, by freeing him as far as possible from the tyranny of nonhuman Power. When we have realized that Power is largely bad, that Man, with his knowledge of good and evil, is but a helpless atom in a world which has no such knowledge, the choice is again presented to us: Shall we worship Force, or shall we worship Goodness? Shall our God exist and be evil, or shall he be recognized as the creation of our own conscience?

The answer to this question is very momentous, and effects profoundly our whole morality. The worship of Force, to which Carlyle and Nietzsche and the creed of Militarism have accustomed us, is the result of failure to maintain our own ideals against a hostile universe: it is itself a prostrate submission to evil, a sacrifice of our best to Moloch. If strength indeed is to be respected, let us respect rather the strength of those who refuse that false 'recognition of facts' which fails to recognize that facts are often bad. Let us admit that, in the world we know, there are many things that would be better otherwise, and that the ideals to which we do and must adhere are not realized in the realm of matter. Let us preserve our respect for truth, for beauty, for the ideal of perfection which life does not permit us to attain, though none of these things meet with the approval of the unconscious universe. If Power is bad, as it seems to be, let us reject it from our hearts. In this lies Man's true freedom: in determination to worship only the God created by our own love of the good, to respect only the heaven which inspires the insight of our best moments. In action, in desire, we must submit perpetually to the tyranny of outside forces; but in thought, in aspiration, we are free, free from our fellow men, free from the petty planet on which our bodies impotently crawl, free even, while we live, from the tyranny of death. Let us learn, then, that energy of faith which enables us to live constantly in the vision of the good; and let us descend, in action, into the world of fact, with that vision always before us.

When first the opposition of fact and ideal grows fully visible, a spirit of fiery revolt, of fierce hatred of the gods, seems necessary to the assertion of freedom. To defy with Promethean constancy a hostile universe, to keep its evil always in view, always actively hated, to refuse no pain that the malice of Power can invent, appears to be the duty of all who will not bow before the inevitable. But indignation is still a bondage, for it compels our thoughts to be occupied with an evil world; and in the fierceness of desire from which rebellion springs there is a kind of self-assertion which it is necessary for the wise to overcome.

Indignation is a submission of our thoughts, but not of our desires; the Stoic freedom in which wisdom consists is found in the submission of our desires, but not of our thoughts. From the submission of our desires springs the virtue of resignation; from the freedom of our thoughts springs the whole world of art and philosophy, and the vision of beauty by which, at last, we half reconquer the reluctant world. But the vision of beauty is possible only to unfettered contemplation, to thoughts not weighted by the load of eager wishes; and thus Freedom comes only to those who no longer ask of life that it shall yield them any of those personal goods that are subject to the mutations of Time.

Although the necessity of renunciation is evidence of the existence of evil, yet Christianity, in preaching it, has shown a wisdom exceeding that of the Promethean philosophy of rebellion. It must be admitted that, of the things we desire, some, though they prove impossible, are yet real goods; others, however, as ardently longed for, do not form part of a fully purified ideal. The belief that what must be renounced is bad, though sometimes false, is far less often false than untamed passion supposes; and the creed of religion, by providing a reason for proving that it is never false, has been the means of purifying our hopes by the discovery of many austere truths.

But there is in resignation a further good element: even real goods, when they are unattainable, ought not to be fretfully desired. To every man comes, sooner or later, the great renunciation. For the young, there is nothing unattainable; a good thing desired with the whole force of a passionate will, and yet impossible, is to them not credible. Yet, by death, by illness, by poverty, or by the voice of duty, we must learn, each one of us, that the world was not made for us, and that, however beautiful may be the things we crave, Fate may nevertheless forbid them. It is the part of courage, when misfortune comes, to bear without repining the ruin of our hopes, to turn away our thoughts from vain regrets. This degree of submission to Power is not only just and right: it is the very gate of wisdom.

But passive renunciation is not the whole of wisdom; for not by renunciation alone can we build a temple for the worship of our own ideals. Haunting foreshadowings of the temple appear in the realm of imagination, in music, in architecture, in the untroubled kingdom of reason, and in the golden sunset magic of lyrics, where beauty shines and glows, remote from the touch of sorrow, remote from the fear of change, remote from the failures and disenchantments of the world of fact. In the contemplation of these things the vision of heaven will shape itself in our hearts, giving at once a touchstone to judge the world about us, and an inspiration by which to fashion to our needs whatever is not incapable of serving as a stone in the sacred temple.

Except for those rare spirits that are born without sin, there is a cavern of darkness to be traversed before that temple can be entered. The gate of the cavern is despair, and its floor is paved with the gravestones of abandoned hopes. There Self must die; there the eagerness, the greed of untamed desire must be slain, for only so can the soul be free from the empire of Fate. But out of the cavern the Gate of Renunciation leads again to the daylight of wisdom, by whose radiance a new insight, a new joy, a new tenderness, shine forth to gladden the pilgrim's heart.

When, without the bitterness of impotent rebellion, we have learnt both to resign ourselves to the outward rule of Fate and to recognize that the nonhuman world is unworthy of our worship, it becomes possible at last so to transform and refashion the unconscious universe, so to transmute it in the crucible of imagination, that a new image of shining gold replaces the old idol of clay. In all the multiform facts of the world—in the visual shapes of trees and mountains and clouds, in the events of the life of Man, even in the very omnipotence of Death—the insight of creative idealism can find the reflection of a beauty which its own thoughts first made. In this way mind asserts its subtle mastery over the thoughtless forces of Nature. The more evil the material with which it deals, the more thwarting to untrained desire, the greater is its achievement in inducing the reluctant rock to yield up its hidden treasures, the prouder its victory in compelling the opposing forces to swell the pageant of its triumph. Of all the arts, Tragedy is the proudest, the most triumphant; for it builds its shining citadel in the very center of the enemy's country, on the very summit of his highest mountain; from its impregnable watchtowers, his camps and arsenals, his columns and forts, are all revealed; within its walls the free life continues, while the legions of Death and Pain and Despair, and all the servile captains of tyrant Fate, afford the burghers of that dauntless city new spectacles of beauty. Happy those sacred ramparts, thrice happy the dwellers on that all-seeing eminence. Honor to those brave warriors who, through countless ages of warfare, have preserved for us the priceless heritage of liberty, and have kept undefiled by sacrilegious invaders the home of the unsubdued.

But the beauty of Tragedy does but make visible a quality which, in more or less obvious shapes, is present always and everywhere in life. In the spectacle of Death, in the endurance of intolerable pain, and in the irrevocableness of a vanished past, there is a sacredness, an overpowering awe, a feeling of the vastness, the depth, the inexhaustible mystery of existence, in which, as by some strange marriage of pain, the sufferer is bound to the world by bonds of sorrow. In these moments of insight, we lose all eagerness of temporary desire, all struggling and striving for petty ends, all care for the little trivial things that, to a superficial view, make up the common life of day by day; we see, surrounding the narrow raft illumined by the flickering light of human comradeship, the dark ocean on whose rolling waves we toss for a brief hour; from the great night without, a chill blast breaks in upon our refuge; all the loneliness of humanity amid hostile forces is concentrated upon the individual soul, which must struggle alone, with what of courage it can command, against the whole weight of a universe that cares nothing for its hopes and fears. Victory, in this struggle with the powers of darkness, is the true baptism into the glorious company of heroes, the true initiation into the overmastering beauty of human existence. From that awful encounter of the soul with the outer world, renunciation, wisdom, and charity are born; and with their birth a new life begins. To take into the inmost shrine of the soul the irresistible forces whose puppets we seem to be—Death and change, the irrevocableness of the past, and the powerlessness of Man before the blind hurry of the universe from vanity to vanity—to feel these things and know them is to conquer them.

This is the reason why the Past has such magical power. The beauty of its motionless and silent pictures is like the enchanted purity of late autumn, when the leaves, though one breath would make them fall, still glow against the sky in golden glory. The Past does not change or strive; like Duncan, after life's fitful fever it sleeps well; what was eager and grasping, what was petty and transitory, has faded away, the things that were beautiful and eternal shine out of it like stars in the night. Its beauty, to a soul not worthy of it, is unendurable; but to a soul which has conquered Fate it is the key of religion.

The life of Man, viewed outwardly, is but a small thing in comparison with the forces of Nature. The slave is doomed to worship Time and Fate and Death, because they are greater than anything he finds in himself, and because all his thoughts are of things which they devour. But, great as they are, to think of them greatly, to feel their passionless splendor, is greater still. And such thought makes us free men; we no longer bow before the inevitable in Oriental subjection, but we absorb it, and make it a part of ourselves. To abandon the struggle for private happiness, to expel all eagerness of temporary desire, to burn with passion for eternal things—this is emancipation, and this is the free man's worship. And this liberation is effected by a contemplation of Fate; for Fate itself is subdued by the mind which leaves nothing to be purged by the purifying fire of Time.

United with his fellow men by the strongest of all ties, the tie of a common doom, the free man finds that a new vision is with him always, shedding over every daily task the light of love. The life of Man is a long march through the night, surrounded by invisible foes, tortured by weariness and pain, toward a goal that few can hope to reach, and where none may tarry long. One by one, as they march, our comrades vanish from our sight, seized by the silent orders of omnipotent Death. Very brief is the time in which we can help them, in which their happiness or misery is decided. Be it ours to shed sunshine on their path, to lighten their sorrows by the balm of sympathy, to give them the pure joy of a never-tiring affection, to strengthen failing courage, to instill faith in hours of despair. Let us not weigh in grudging scales their merits and demerits, but let us think only of their need—of the sorrows, the difficulties, perhaps the blindnesses, that make the misery of their lives; let us remember that they are fellow sufferers in the same darkness, actors in the same tragedy with ourselves. And so, when their day is over, when their good and their evil have become eternal by the immortality of the past, be it ours to feel that, where they suffered, where they failed, no deed of ours was the cause; but wherever a spark of the divine fire kindled in their hearts, we were ready with encouragement, with sympathy, with brave words in which high courage glowed.

Brief and powerless is Man's life; on him and all his race the slow, sure doom falls pitiless and dark. Blind to good and evil, reckless of destruction, omnipotent matter rolls on its relentless way; for Man, condemned today to lose his dearest, tomorrow himself to pass through the gate of darkness, it remains only to cherish, ere yet the blow fall, the lofty thoughts that ennoble his little day; disdaining the coward terrors of the slave of Fate, to worship at the shrine that his own hands have built; undismayed by the empire of chance, to preserve a mind free from the wanton tyranny that rules his outward life; proudly defiant of the irresistible forces that tolerate, for a moment, his knowledge and his condemnation, to sustain alone, a weary but unyielding Atlas, the world that his own ideals have fashioned despite the trampling march of unconscious power.

34

Religion and the Queerness of Morality

GEORGE MAVRODES

George Mavrodes is professor of philosophy at the University of Michigan. In this essay he argues that if ethics is to be completely justified, a religious or deep metaphysical grounding is necessary. He criticizes Russell's secular view as puzzling, for if there is no God, secular ethics suffers from a certain inadequacy. Mavrodes argues that the Russellian world of secular morality can not satisfactorily answer the question, Why should I be moral? For, on its account, the common goods, which morality in general aims at, are often just those that we sacrifice in carrying out our moral obligations. Why should we sacrifice our welfare for our moral duty?

The second oddity about secular ethics is that it is superficial and not deeply rooted. It seems to lack that metaphysical basis that a Platonic or Judeo-Christian world view affords. Values and obligations are not as deep in a secular world. Mavrodes outlines how a religious morality can meet these desiderata, and, if we are inclined to believe that morality is not queer, provide some evidence for the religious world view.

Many arguments for the existence of God may be construed as claiming that there is some feature of the world that would somehow make no sense unless there was something else that had a stronger version of that feature or some analogue of it. So, for example, the cosmological line of argument may be thought of as centering upon the claim that the way in which the world exists (called "contingent" existence) would be incomprehensible unless there were something else—

From *Rationality, Religious Belief and Moral Commitment: New Essays in the Philosophy of Religion*, eds. R. Audi and W. Wainwright (Cornell University Press, 1986). Copyright © 1986 by Cornell University. Reprinted by permission of the publisher and author.

that is, God—that had a stronger grip upon existence (that is, "necessary" existence).

Now, a number of thinkers have held a view something like this with respect to morality. They have claimed that in some important way morality is dependent upon religion—dependent, that is, in such a way that if religion were to fail, morality would fail also. And they have held that the dependence was more than psychological, that is, if religion were to fail, it would somehow be *proper* (perhaps logically or perhaps in some other way) for morality to fail also. One way of expressing this theme is by Dostoevsky's "If there is no God, then everything is permitted," a sentiment that in this century has been prominently echoed by Sartre. But perhaps the most substantial philosophical thinker of the modern period to espouse this view, though in a rather idiosyncratic way, was Immanual Kant, who held that the existence of God was a necessary postulate of 'practical' (that is, moral) reason.

On the other hand, it has recently been popular for moral philosophers to deny this theme and to maintain that the dependence of morality on religion is, at best, merely psychological. Were religion to fail, so they apparently hold, this would grant no sanction for the failure of morality. For morality stands on its own feet, whatever those feet may turn out to be.

Now, the suggestion that morality somehow depends on religion is rather attractive to me. It is this suggestion that I wish to explore in this paper, even though it seems unusually difficult to formulate clearly the features of this suggestion that make it attractive. I will begin by mentioning briefly some aspects that I will not discuss.

First, beyond this paragraph I will not discuss the claim that morality cannot survive psychologically without the support of religious belief. At least in the short run, this proposal seems to me false. For there certainly seem to be people who reject religious belief, at least in the ordinary sense, but who apparently have a concern with morality and who try to live a moral life. Whether the proposal may have more force if it is understood in a broader way, as applying to whole cultures, epochs, and so forth, I do not know.

Second, I will not discuss the attempt to define some or all moral terms by the use of religious terms, or vice versa. But this should not be taken as implying any judgment about this project.

Third, beyond this paragraph I shall not discuss the suggestion that moral statements may be entailed by religious statements and so may be "justified" by religious doctrines or beliefs. It is popular now to hold that no such alleged entailment can be valid. But the reason usually cited for this view is the more general doctrine that moral statements cannot be validly deduced from nonmoral statements, a doctrine usually traced to Hume. Now, to my mind the most important problem raised by this general doctrine is that of finding some interpretation of it that is both significant and not plainly false. If it is taken to mean merely that there is *some* set of statements that entails no moral statement, then it strikes me as probably true, but trivial. At any rate, we should then need another reason to suppose that religious statements fall in this category. If, on the other hand, it is taken to mean that one can divide the domain of statements into two classes, the moral and the nonmoral, and that none of the latter entail any of the former, then it is false. I, at any rate, do not know a version of this doctrine that seems relevant to the religious case and that has any reasonable likelihood of being true. But I am not concerned on this occasion with the possibly useful project of deducing morality from religion, and so I will not pursue it further. My interest is closer to a move in the other direction, that of deducing religion from morality. (I am not quite satisfied with this way of putting it and will try to explain this dissatisfaction later on.)

For the remainder of this discussion, then, my project is as follows. I will outline one rather common nonreligious view of the world, calling attention to what I take to be its most relevant features. Then I shall try to portray some sense of the odd status that morality would have in a world of that sort. I shall be hoping, of course, that you will notice that this odd status is not the one that you recognize morality to have in the actual world. But it will perhaps be obvious that the "world-view" amendments required would move substantially toward a religious position.

First, then, the nonreligious view. I take a short and powerful statement of it from a 1903 essay by Bertrand Russell, "A Free Man's Worship."

That man is the product of causes which had no prevision of the end they were achieving; that his origin, his growth, his hopes and fears, his loves and his beliefs are but the outcome of accidental collocations of atoms; that no fire, no heroism, no intensity of thought and feeling, can preserve an individual life beyond the grave; that all the labors of the ages, all the devotion, all the inspiration, all the noonday brightness of human genius, are destined to extinction in the vast death of the solar system, and that the whole temple of man's achievement must inevitably be buried beneath the debris of a universe in ruins—all these things, if not quite beyond dispute, are yet so nearly certain that no philosophy which rejects them can hope to stand. Only within the scaffolding of these truths, only on the firm foundation of unyielding despair, can the soul's habitation henceforth be safely built.[1]

For convenience, I will call a world that satisfies the description given here a "Russellian world." But we are primarily interested in what the status of morality would be in the actual world if that world should turn out to be Russellian. I shall therefore sometimes augment the description of a Russellian world with obvious features of the actual world.

What are the most relevant features of a Russellian world? The following strike me as especially important: (1) Such phenomena as minds, mental activities, consciousness, and so forth are the products of entities and causes that give no indication of being mental themselves. In Russell's words, the causes are "accidental collocations of atoms" with "no prevision of the end they were achieving." Though not stated explicitly by Russell, we might add the doctrine, a commonplace in modern science, that mental phenomena—and indeed life itself—are comparative latecomers in the long history of the earth. (2) Human life is bounded by physical death and each individual comes to a permanent end at his physical death. We might add to this the observation that the span of human life is comparatively short, enough so that in some cases we can, with fair confidence, predict the major consequences of certain actions insofar as they will affect a given individual throughout his whole remaining life. (3) Not only each individual but also the human race as a species is doomed to extinction "beneath the debris of a universe in ruins."

So much, then, for the main features of a Russellian world. Because the notion of benefits and goods plays an important part in the remainder of my discussion, I want to introduce one further technical expression—"Russellian benefit." A Russellian benefit is one that could accrue to a person in a Russellian world. A contented old age would be, I suppose, a Russellian benefit, as would a thrill of sexual pleasure or a good reputation. Going to heaven when one dies, though a benefit, is not a Russellian benefit. Russellian benefits are only the benefits possible in a Russellian world. But one can have Russellian benefits even if the world is not Russellian. In such a case there might, however, also be other benefits, such as going to heaven.

Could the actual world be Russellian? Well, I take it to be an important feature of the actual world that human beings exist in it and that in it their actions fall, at least sometimes, within the sphere of morality—that is, they have moral obligations to act (or to refrain from acting) in certain ways. And if they do not act in those ways, then they are properly subject to a special and peculiar sort of adverse judgment (unless it happens that there are special circumstances that serve to excuse their failure to fulfill the obligations). People who do not fulfill their obligations are not merely stupid or weak or unlucky; they are morally reprehensible.

Now, I do not have much to say in an illuminating manner about the notion of moral obligation, but I could perhaps make a few preliminary observations about how I understand this notion. First, I take it that morality includes, or results in, judgments of the form "*N* ought to do (or to avoid doing) _____" or "It is *N*'s duty to do (or to avoid doing) _____." That is, morality ascribes to particular people an obligation to do a certain thing on a certain occasion. No doubt morality includes others things as well—general moral rules, for example. I shall, however, focus on judgments of the sort just mentioned, and when I speak without further qualification of someone's having an obligation I intend it to be understood in terms of such a judgment.

Second, many authors distinguish prima facie obligations from obligations "all things considered." Probably this is a useful distinction. For the most part, however, I intend to ignore prima facie obligations and to focus upon our obligations all things considered, what we might call our "final obligations." These are the obligations that a particular person has in some concrete circumstance at a particular place and time, when all the aspects of the situation have been taken into account. It identifies the action that, if not done, will properly subject the person to the special adverse judgment.

Finally, it is, I think, a striking feature of moral obligations that a person's being unwilling to fulfill the obligation is irrelevant to having the obligation and is also irrelevant to the adverse judgment in case the obligation is not fulfilled. Perhaps even more important is the fact that, at least for some obligations, it is also irrelevant in both these ways for one to point out that he does not see how fulfilling the obligations can do him any good. In fact, unless we are greatly mistaken about our obligations, it seems clear that in a Russellian world there are an appreciable number of cases in which fulfilling an obligation would result in a loss of good to ourselves. On the most prosaic level, this must be true of some cases of repaying a debt, keeping a promise, refraining from stealing, and so on. And it must also be true of those rarer but more striking cases of obligation to risk death or serious injury in the performance of a duty. People have, of course, differed as to what is good for humans. But so far as I can see, the point I have been making will hold for any candidate that is plausible in a Russellian world. Pleasure, happiness, esteem, contentment, self-realization, knowledge—all of these can suffer from the fulfillment of a moral obligation.

It is not, however, a *necessary* truth that some of our obligations are such that their fulfillment will yield no net benefit, within Russellian limits, to their fulfiller. It is not contradictory to maintain that, for every obligation that I have, a corresponding benefit awaits me within the confines of this world and this life. While such a contention would not be contradictory, however, it would nevertheless be false. I discuss below one version of this contention. At present it must suffice to say that a person who accepts this claim will probably find the remainder of what I have to say correspondingly less plausible.

Well, where are are now? I claim that in the actual world we have some obligations that, when we fulfill them, will confer on us no net Russellian benefit—in fact, they will result in a Russellian loss. If the world is Russellian, then Russellian benefits and losses are the only benefits and losses, and also then we have moral obligations whose fulfillment will result in a net loss of good to the one who fulfills them. I suggest, however, that it would be very strange to have such obligations—strange not simply in the sense of being unexpected or surprising but in some deeper way. I do not suggest that it is strange in the sense of having a straightforward logical defect, of being self-contradictory to claim that we have

such obligations. Perhaps the best thing to say is that were it a fact that we had such obligations, then the world that included such a fact would be absurd—we would be living in a crazy world.

Now, whatever success I may have in this paper will in large part be a function of my success (or lack thereof) in getting across a sense of that absurdity, that queerness. On some accounts of morality, in a Russellian world there would not be the strangeness that I allege. Perhaps, then, I can convey some of that strangeness by mentioning those views of morality that would eliminate it. In fact, I believe that a good bit of their appeal is just the fact that they do get rid of this queerness.

First, I suspect that morality will not be queer in the way I suggest, even in a Russellian world, if judgments about obligations are properly to be analyzed in terms of the speaker rather than in terms of the subject of the judgment. And I more than suspect that this will be the case if such judgments are analyzed in terms of the speaker's attitude or feeling toward some action, and/or his attempt or inclination to incite a similar attitude in someone else. It may be, of course, that there is something odd about the supposition that human beings, consciousness, and so forth, could arise at all in a Russellian world. A person who was impressed by that oddity might be attracted toward some "teleological" line of reasoning in the direction of a more religious view. But I think that this oddity is not the one I am touching on here. Once given the existence of human beings with capacities for feelings and attitudes, there does not seem to be anything further that is queer in the supposition that a speaker might have an attitude toward some action, might express that attitude, and might attempt (or succeed) in inciting someone else to have a similar attitude. Anyone, therefore, who can be satisfied with such an analysis will probably not be troubled by the queerness that I allege.

Second, for similar reasons, this queerness will also be dissipated by any account that understands judgments about obligation purely in terms of the feelings, attitudes, and so forth of the subject of the judgment. For, given again that there are human beings with consciousness, it does not seem to be any additional oddity that the subject of a moral judgment might have feelings or attitudes about an actual or prospective action of his own. The assumption that morality is to be understood in this way takes many forms. In a closely related area, for example, it appears as the assumption—so common now that it can pass almost unnoticed—that guilt could not be anything other than guilt *feelings,* and that the "problem" of guilt is just the problem generated by such feelings.

In connection with our topic here, however, we might look at the way in which this sort of analysis enters into one plausible-sounding explanation of morality in a Russellian world, an explanation that has a scientific flavor. The existence of morality in a Russellian world, it may be said, is not at all absurd because its existence there can be given a perfectly straightforward explanation: morality has a survival value for a species such as ours because it makes possible continued cooperation and things of that sort. So it is no more absurd that people have moral obligations than it is absurd that they have opposable thumbs.

I think that this line of explanation will work only if one analyzes obligations into feelings, or beliefs. I think it is plausible (though I am not sure it is correct) to suppose that everyone's having feelings of moral obligation might have survival value for a species such as Man, given of course that these feelings were attached to patterns of action that contributed to such survival. And if that is so, then it is not implausible to suppose that there may be a survival value for the species even in a moral feeling that leads to the death of the individual who has it. So far so good. But this observation, even if true, is not relevant to the queerness with which I am here concerned. For I have not suggested that the existence of moral feelings would be absurd in a Russellian world; it is rather the existence of moral *obligations* that is absurd, and I think it important to make the distinction. It is quite possible, it seems to me, for one to feel (or to believe) that he has a

certain obligation without actually having it, and also vice versa. Now, beliefs and feelings will presumably have some effect upon actions, and this effect may possibly contribute to the survival of the species. But, so far as I can see, the addition of actual moral obligations to these moral beliefs and feelings will make no further contribution to action nor will the actual obligations have an effect upon action in the absence of the corresponding feelings and beliefs. So it seems that neither with nor without the appropriate feelings will moral obligations contribute to the survival of the species. Consequently, an "evolutionary" approach such as this cannot serve to explain the existence of moral obligations, unless one rejects my distinction and equates the obligations with the feelings.

And finally, I think that morality will not be queer in the way I allege, or at least it will not be as queer as I think, if it should be the case that every obligation yields a Russellian benefit to the one who fulfills it. Given the caveat expressed earlier, one can perhaps make some sense out of the notion of a Russellian good or benefit for a sentient organism in a Russellian world. And one could, I suppose, without further queerness imagine that such an organism might aim toward achieving such goods. And we could further suppose that there were certain actions—those that were "obligations"—that would, in contrast with other actions, actually yield such benefits to the organism that performed them. And finally, it might not be too implausible to claim that an organism that failed to perform such an action was defective in some way and that some adverse judgment was appropriate.

Morality, however, seems to require us to hold that certain organisms (namely, human beings) have in addition to their ordinary properties and relations another special relation to certain actions. This relation is that of being "obligated" to perform those actions. And some of those actions are pretty clearly such that they will yield only Russellian losses to the one who performs them. Nevertheless, we are supposed to hold that a person who does not perform an action to which he is thus related is defective in some serious and important way and an adverse judgment is appropriate against him. And that certainly does seem odd.

The recognition of this oddity—or perhaps better, this absurdity—is not simply a resolution to concern ourselves only with what "pays." Here the position of Kant is especially suggestive. He held that a truly moral action is undertaken purely out of respect for the moral law and with no concern at all for reward. There seems to be no room at all here for any worry about what will "pay." But he also held that the moral enterprise needs, in a deep and radical way, the postulate of a God who can, and will, make happiness correspond to virtue. This postulate is "necessary" for practical reason. Perhaps we could put this Kantian demand in the language I have been using here, saying that the moral enterprise would make no sense in a world in which that correspondence ultimately failed.

I suspect that what we have in Kant is the recognition that there cannot be, in any "reasonable" way, a moral demand upon me, unless reality itself is committed to morality in some deep way. It makes sense only if there is a moral demand on the world too and only if reality will in the end satisfy that demand. This theme of the deep grounding of morality is one to which I return briefly near the end of this paper.

The oddity we have been considering is, I suspect, the most important root of the celebrated and somewhat confused question, "Why should I be moral?" Characteristically, I think, the person who asks that question is asking to have the queerness of that situation illuminated. From time to time there are philosophers who make an attempt to argue—perhaps only a halfhearted attempt—that being moral really is in one's interest after all. Kurt Baier, it seems to me, proposes a reply of this sort. He says:

Moralities are systems of principles whose acceptance by everyone as overruling the dictates of self-interest is in the interest of everyone alike though following the rules of a morality is not of course identical with following self-interest. . . .

The answer to our question 'Why should we be moral?' is therefore as follows. We should be moral because being moral is following rules designed to overrule self-interest whenever it is in the interest of everyone alike that everyone should set aside his interest.[2]

As I say, this seems to be an argument to the effect that it really is in everyone's interest to be moral. I suppose that Baier is here probably talking about Russellian interests. At least, we must interpret him in that way if his argument is to be applicable in this context, and I will proceed on that assumption. But how exactly is the argument to be made out?

It appears here to begin with a premise something like

(A) It is in everyone's best interest (including mine, presumably) for everyone (including me) to be moral.

This premise itself appears to be supported earlier by reference to Hobbes. As I understand it, the idea is that without morality people will live in a "state of nature," and life will be nasty, brutish, and short. Well, perhaps so. At any rate, let us accept (A) for the moment. From (A) we can derive

(B) It is in my best interest for everyone (including me) to be moral.

And from (B) perhaps one derives

(C) It is in my best interest for me to be moral.

And (C) may be taken to answer the question, "Why should I be moral?" Furthermore, if (C) is true, then moral obligation will at least not have the sort of queerness that I have been alleging.

Unfortunately, however, the argument outlined above is invalid. The derivation of (B) from (A) *may* be all right, but the derivation of (C) from (B) is invalid. What does follow from (B) is

(C′) It is in my best interest for me to be moral *if everyone else is moral.*

The argument thus serves to show that it is in a given person's interest to be moral only on the assumption that everyone else in the world is moral. It might, of course, be difficult to find someone ready to make that assumption.

There is, however, something more of interest in this argument. I said that the derivation of (B) from (A) may be all right. But in fact is it? If it is not all right, then this argument would fail even if everyone else in the world were moral. Now (A) can be interpreted as referring to "everyone's best interest" ("the interest of everyone alike," in Baier's own words) either collectively or distributively; that is, it may be taken as referring to the best interest of the whole group considered as a single unit, or as referring to the best interest of each individual in the group. But if (A) is interpreted in the collective sense, then (B) does not follow from it. It may not be in *my* best interest for everyone to act morally, even if it is in the best interest of the group as a whole, for the interest of the group as a whole may be advanced by the sacrificing of my interest. On this interpretation of (A), then, the argument will not answer the question "Why should I be moral?" even on the supposition that everyone else is moral.

If (A) is interpreted in the distributive sense, on the other hand, then (B) does follow from it, and the foregoing objection is not applicable. But another objection arises. Though (A) in the collective sense has some plausibility, it is hard to imagine that it is true in the distributive sense. Hobbes may have been right in supposing that life in the state of nature would be short, etc. But some lives are short anyway. In fact, some lives are short just because the demands of morality are observed. Such a life is not bound to have been shorter in the state of nature. Nor is it bound to have been less happy, less pleasurable, and so forth. In fact, does it not seem obvious that *my* best Russellian interest will be further advanced in a situation in which everyone else acts morally but I act immorally (in selected cases) than it will be

in case everyone, including me, acts morally? It certainly seems so. It can, of course, be observed that if I act immorally then so will other people, perhaps reducing my benefits. In the present state of the world that is certainly true. But in the present state of the world it is also true, as I observed earlier, that many other people will act immorally *anyway*, regardless of what I do.

A more realistic approach is taken by Richard Brandt.[3] He asks, "Is it *reasonable* for me to do my duty if it conflicts seriously with my personal welfare?" After distinguishing several possible senses of this question, he chooses a single one to discuss further, presumably a sense that he thinks important. As reformulated, the question is now: "Given that doing *x* is my duty and that doing some conflicting act *y* will maximize my personal welfare, will the performance of *x* instead of *y* satisfy my reflective preferences better?" And the conclusion to which he comes is that "the correct answer may vary from one person to another. It depends on what kind of person one is, what one cares about." And within Russellian limits Brandt must surely be right in this. But he goes on to say, "It is, of course, no defense of one's failure to do one's duty, before others or society, to say that doing so is not 'reasonable' for one in this sense." And this is just to bring the queer element back in. It is to suppose that besides "the kind of person" I am and my particular pattern of "cares" and interests there is something else, my duty, which may go against these and in any case properly overrides them. And one feels that there must be some sense of "reasonable" in which one can ask whether a world in which that is true is a reasonable world, whether such a world makes any sense.

This completes my survey of some ethical or metaethical views that would eliminate or minimize this sort of queerness of morality. I turn now to another sort of view, stronger I think than any of these others, which accepts that queerness but goes no further. And one who holds this view will also hold, I think, that the question "Why should I be moral?" must be rejected in one way or another. A person who holds this view will say that it is simply a fact that we have the moral obligations that we do have, and that is all there is to it. If they sometimes result in a loss of good, then that too is just a fact. These may be puzzling or surprising facts, but there are lots of puzzling and surprising things about the world. In a Russellian world, morality will be, I suppose, an "emergent" phenomenon; it will be a feature of certain effects though it is not a feature of their causes. But the wetness of water is an emergent feature, too. It is not a property of either hydrogen or oxygen. And there is really nothing more to be said; somewhere we must come to an end of reasons and explanations. We have our duties. We can fulfill them and be moral, or we can ignore them and be immoral. If all that is crazy and absurd—well, so be it. Who are we to say that the world is not crazy and absurd?

Such a view was once suggested by William Alston in a criticism of Hasting Rashdall's moral argument for God's existence. Alston attributed to Rashdall the view that "God is required as a locus for the moral law." But Alston then went on to ask, "Why could it not just be an ultimate fact about the universe that kindness is good and cruelty bad? This seems to have been Plato's view." And if we rephrase Alston's query slightly to refer to obligations, we might be tempted to say, "Why not indeed?"

I say that this is perhaps the strongest reply against me. Since it involves no argument, there is no argument to be refuted. And I have already said that, so far as I can see, its central contention is not self-contradictory. Nor do I think of any other useful argument to the effect that the world is not absurd and crazy in this way. The reference to Plato, however, might be worth following for a moment. Perhaps Plato did think that goodness, or some such thing related to morality, was an ultimate fact about the world. But a Platonic world is not very close to a Russellian world. Plato was not a Christian, of course, but his world view has very often been taken to be congenial (especially congenial compared to some other philosophical views) to a religious understanding of the world. He would not have been satisfied, I think, with

Russell's "accidental collocations of atoms," nor would he have taken the force of the grave to be "so nearly certain." The idea of the Good seems to play a metaphysical role in his thought. It is somehow fundamental to what *is* as well as to what ought to be, much more fundamental to reality than are the atoms. A Platonic man, therefore, who sets himself to live in accordance with the Good aligns himself with what is deepest and most basic in existence. Or to put it another way, we might say that whatever values a Platonic world imposes on a man are values to which the Platonic world itself is committed, through and through.

Not so, of course, for a Russellian world. Values and obligations cannot be deep in such a world. They have a grip only upon surface phenomena, probably only upon man. What is deep in a Russellian world must be such things as matter and energy, or perhaps natural law, chance, or chaos. If it really were a fact that one had obligations in a Russellian world, then something would be laid upon man that might cost a man everything but that went no further than man. And that difference from a Platonic world seems to make all the difference.

This discussion suggests, I think, that there are two related ways in which morality is queer in a Russellian world. Or maybe they are better construed as two aspects of the queerness we have been exploring. In most of the preceding discussion I have been focusing on the strangeness of an overriding demand that does not seem to conduce to the *good* of the person on whom it is laid. (In fact, it does not even promise his good.) Here, however, we focus on the fact that this demand—radical enough in the human life on which it is laid—is *superficial* in a Russellian world. Something that reaches close to the heart of my own life, perhaps even demanding the sacrifice of that life, is not deep at all in the world in which (on a Russellian view) that life is lived. And that, too, seems absurd.

This brings to an end the major part of my discussion. If I have been successful at all you will have shared with me to some extent in the sense of the queerness of morality, its absurdity in a Russellian world. If you also share the conviction that it cannot in the end be absurd in that way, then perhaps you will also be attracted to some religious view of the world. Perhaps you also will say that morality must have some deeper grip upon the world than a Russellian view allows. And, consequently, things like mind and purpose must also be deeper in the real world than they would be in a Russellian world. They must be more original, more controlling. The accidental collocation of atoms cannot be either primeval or final, nor can the grave be an end. But of course that would be only a beginning, a sketch waiting to be filled in.

We cannot here do much to fill it in further. But I should like to close with a final, and rather tentative suggestion, as to a direction in which one might move in thinking about the place of morality in the world. It is suggested to me by certain elements in my own religion, Christianity.

I come more and more to think that morality, while a fact, is a twisted and distorted fact. Or perhaps better, that it is a barely recognizable version of another fact, a version adapted to a twisted and distorted world. It is something like, I suppose, the way in which the pine that grows at timberline, wind blasted and twisted low against the rock, is a version of the tall and symmetrical tree that grows lower on the slopes. I think it may be that the related notions of sacrifice and gift represent (or come close to representing) the fact, that is, the pattern of life, whose distorted version we know here as morality. Imagine a situation, an "economy" if you will, in which no one ever buys or trades for or seizes any good thing. But whatever good he enjoys it is either one which he himself has created or else one which he receives as a free and unconditional gift. And as soon as he has tasted it and seen that it is good he stands ready to give it away in his turn as soon as the opportunity arises. In such a place, if one were to speak either of his rights or his duties, his remark might be met with puzzled laughter as his hearers struggled to recall an ancient world in which those terms referred to something important.

We have, of course, even now some occasions

that tend in this direction. Within some families perhaps, or even in a regiment in desperate battle, people may for a time pass largely beyond morality and live lives of gift and sacrifice. On those occasions nothing would be lost if the moral concepts and the moral language were to disappear. But it is probably not possible that such situations and occasions should be more than rare exceptions in the daily life of the present world. Christianity, however, which tells us that the present world is "fallen" and hence leads us to expect a distortion in its important features, also tells us that one day the redemption of the world will be complete and that then all things shall be made new. And it seems to me to suggest an "economy" more akin to that of gift and sacrifice than to that of rights and duties. If something like that should be true, then perhaps morality, like the Marxist state, is destined to wither away (unless perchance it should happen to survive in hell).

Christianity, then, I think is related to the queerness or morality in one way and perhaps in two. In the first instance, it provides a view of the world in which morality is not an absurdity. It gives morality a deeper place in the world than does a Russellian view and thus permits it to "make sense." But in the second instance, it perhaps suggests that morality is not the deepest thing, that it is provisional and transitory, that it is due to serve its use and then to pass away in favor of something richer and deeper. Perhaps we can say that it begins by inverting the quotation with which I began and by telling us that, since God exists, not everything is permitted; but it may also go on to tell us that, since God exists, in the end there shall be no occasion for any prohibition.

Notes

1. Bertrand Russell, *Mysticism and Logic* (New York: Barnes & Noble, 1917), pp. 47–48.

2. Kurt Baier, *The Moral Point of View* (Ithaca: Cornell University Press, 1958), p. 314.

3. Richard Brandt, *Ethical Theory* (Englewood Cliffs, N.J.: Prentice-Hall, 1959), pp. 375–78.

35

Ethics without Religion

KAI NIELSEN

Kai Nielsen is professor of philosophy at Calgary University in Canada. This article was written twenty years before Mavrodes' paper on the queerness of morality, but it anticipates some of Mavrodes' arguments. Nielsen's thesis is that even if "God is dead," it really doesn't matter—as far as our morality is concerned. First, with the loss of faith all our essential moral values are left intact. We still can be happy, find security and emotional peace, experience love and friendship, enjoy creative work and a rich variety of experiences. Second, both the secular basis and the religious basis of ethics involve an objective rationale involving central principles such as respect for persons and justice, and benevolence. Our common nature and quest for the good life is all the grounding that ethics needs. It is true that morality sometimes calls for sacrifice of nonmoral goods. It would be nice if this were not the case, but life is sometimes hard. Nielsen notes that both secular ethics and religion have a difficult time with evil because it is the central hindrance to religious belief for many.

There certainly are fundamental difficulties and perhaps even elements of incoherence in Christian ethics, but what can a secular moralist offer in its stead? Religious morality—and Christian morality in particular—may have its difficulties, but secular morality, religious apologists argue, has still greater difficulties. It leads they claim, to ethical scepticism, nihilism, or, at best, to a pure conventionalism. Such apologists could point out that if we look at morality with the cold eye of an anthropologist we will—assuming we are clear

From "Ethics Without Religion," *Ohio University Review* 6, 1964, 48–51, 57–62. Reprinted by permission of the publisher and author.

headed—find morality to be nothing more than the often conflicting *mores* of the various tribes spread around the globe. If we eschew the kind of insight that religion can give us, we will have no Archimedean point in accordance with which we can decide how it is that we ought to live and die. If we look at ethics from such a purely secular point of view, we will discover that it is constituted by tribal conventions, conventions which we are free to reject if we are sufficiently free from ethnocentrism. We can continue to act in accordance with them or we can reject them and adopt a different set of conventions; but whether we act in accordance with the old conventions or forge "new tablets," we are still acting in accordance with certain conventions. Relative to them certain acts are right or wrong, reasonable or unreasonable, but we cannot justify these fundamental moral conventions themselves or the ways of life which they partially codify.

When these points are conceded, theologians are in a position to press home a powerful apologetic point. When we become keenly aware, they argue, of the true nature of such conventionalism and when we become aware that there is no overarching purpose that men were destined to fulfill, the myriad purposes, the aims and goals humans create for themselves, will be seen not to be enough. When we realize that life does not have a meaning—that is, a significance—which is there to be found, but that we human beings must by our deliberate decisions give it whatever meaning it has, we will (as Sartre so well understood) undergo estrangement and despair. We will drain our cup to its last bitter drop and feel our alienation to the full. Perhaps there are human purposes, purposes to be found *in* life, and we can and do have them even in a Godless world, but without God there can be no one overarching purpose, no one basic scheme of human existence, in virtue of which we could find a meaning for our grubby lives. It is this overall sense of meaning that man so ardently strives for, but it is not to be found in a purely secular worldview. You secularists, a new Pascal might argue, must realize, if you really want to be clearheaded, that no purely human purposes are ultimately worth striving for. What you humanists can give us by way of a scheme of human existence will always be a poor second-best and not what the human heart most ardently longs for.

The considerations for and against an ethics not rooted in a religion are complex and involuted; a fruitful discussion of them is difficult, for in considering the matter our passions, our anxieties, our (if you will) ultimate concerns are involved, and they tend to blur our vision, enfeeble our understanding, of what exactly is at stake. But we must not forget that what is at stake here is just what kind of ultimate commitments or obligations a man could have without evading any issue, without self-deception or without delusion. I shall be concerned to display and assess, to make plain but also to weigh, some of the most crucial considerations for and against a purely secular ethic. While I shall in an objective fashion try to make clear what the central issues are, I shall also give voice to my reflective convictions on this matter. I shall try to make evident my reasons for believing that we do not need God or any religious conception to support our moral convictions. I shall do this, as I think one should in philosophy, by making apparent the dialectic of the problem (by bringing to the fore the conflicting and evolving considerations for and against) and by arguing for what I take to be their proper resolution.

I am aware that Crisis Theologians would claim that I am being naive, but I do not see why purposes of purely human devising are not ultimately worth striving for. There is much that we humans prize and would continue to prize even in a Godless world. Many things would remain to give our

lives meaning and point even after "the death of God."

Take a simple example. All of us *want* to be happy. But in certain bitter or sceptical moods we question what happiness is or we despairingly ask ourselves whether anyone can really be happy. Is this, however, a sober, sane view of the situation? I do not think that it is. Indeed we cannot adequately define "happiness" in the way that we can "bachelor," but neither can we in that way define "chair," "wind," "pain," and the vast majority of words in everyday discourse. For words like "bachelor," "triangle," or "father" we can specify a consistent set of properties that all the things and only the things denoted by these words have, but we cannot do this for "happiness," "chair," "pain," and the like. In fact, we cannot do it for the great majority of our words. Yet there is no greater loss here. Modern philosophical analysis has taught us that such an essentially Platonic conception of definition is unrealistic and unnecessary.[1] I may not be able to define "chair" in the way that I can define "bachelor," but I understand the meaning of "chair" perfectly well. In normal circumstances, at least, I know what to sit on when someone tells me to take a chair. I may not be able to define "pain," but I know what it is like to be in pain, and sometimes I can know when others are in pain. Similarly, though I cannot define "happiness" in the same way that I can define "bachelor," I know what it is like to be happy, and I sometimes can judge with considerable reliability whether others are happy or sad. "Happiness" is a slippery word, but it is not so slippery that we are justified in saying that nobody knows what happiness is.

A man could be said to have lived a happy life if he had found lasting sources of satisfaction in his life and if he had been able to find certain goals worthwhile and to achieve at least some of them. He could indeed have suffered some pain and anxiety, but his life must, for the most part, have been free from pain, estrangement, and despair, and must, on balance, have been a life which he has liked and found worthwhile. But surely we have no good grounds for saying that no one achieves such a balance or that no one is ever happy even for a time. We all have some idea of what would make us happy and of what would make us unhappy; many people, at least, can remain happy even after "the death of God." At any rate, we need not strike Pascalian attitudes, for even in a purely secular world there are permanent sources of human happiness for anyone to avail himself of.

What are they? What are these relatively permanent sources of human happiness that we all want or need? What is it which, if we have it, will give us the basis for a life that could properly be said to be happy? We all desire to be free from pain and want. Even masochists do not seek pain for its own sake; they endure pain because this is the only psychologically acceptable way of achieving something else (usually sexual satisfaction) that is so gratifying to them that they will put up with the pain to achieve it. We all want a life in which sometimes we can enjoy ourselves in which we can attain our fair share of some of the simple pleasures that we all desire. They are not everything in life, but they are important, and our lives would be impoverished without them.

We also need security and emotional peace. We need and want a life in which we will not be constantly threatened with physical or emotional harassment. Again this is not the only thing worth seeking, but it is an essential ingredient in any adequate picture of the good life.

Human love and companionship are also central to a significant or happy life. We prize them, and a life which is without them is most surely an impoverished life, a life that no man, if he would take the matter to heart, would desire. But I would most emphatically assert that human love and companionship are quite possible in a Godless world, and the fact that life will some day inexorably come to an end and cut off love and companionship altogether enhances rather than diminishes their present value.

Furthermore, we all need some sort of creative employment or meaningful work to give our lives point, to save them from boredom, drudgery, and futility. A man who can find no way to use the talents he has or a man who can find no work which is meaningful to him will indeed be a miserable man. But again there is work—whether it be as a surgeon, a farmer, or a fisherman—that has a rationale even in a world without God. And poetry, music, and art retain their beauty and enrich our lives even in the complete absence of God or the gods.

We want and need art, music, and the dance. We find pleasure in travel and conversation and in a rich variety of experiences. The sources of human enjoyment are obviously too numerous to detail. But all of them are achievable in a Godless universe. If some can be ours, we can attain a reasonable measure of happiness. Only a Steppenwolfish personality beguiled by impossible expectations and warped by irrational guilts and fears can fail to find happiness in the realization of such ends. But to be free of impossible expectations people must clearly recognize that there is no "one big thing" or, for that matter, "small thing" which would make them permanently happy; almost anything permanently and exclusively pursued will lead to that nausea that Sartre has so forcefully brought to our attention. But we can, if we are not too sick and if our situation is not too precarious, find lasting sources of human happiness in a purely secular world.

It is not only happiness for ourselves that can give us something of value, but there is the need to do what we can to diminish the awful sum of human misery in the world. I have never understood those who say that they find contemporary life meaningless because they find nothing worthy of devoting their energies to. Throughout the world there is an immense amount of human suffering, suffering that can, through a variety of human efforts, be partially alleviated. Why can we not find a meaningful life in devoting ourselves, as did Doctor Rieux in Albert Camus's *The Plague*, to relieving somewhat the sum total of human suffering? Why cannot this give our lives point, and for that matter an overall rationale? It is childish to think that by human effort we will someday totally rid the world of suffering and hate, of deprivation and sadness. This is a permanent part of the human condition. But specific bits of human suffering can be alleviated. The plague is always potentially with us, but we can destroy the Nazis and we can fight for racial and social equality throughout the world. And as isolated people, as individuals in a mass society, we find people turning to us in dire need, in suffering and in emotional deprivation, and we can as individuals respond to those people and alleviate or at least acknowledge that suffering and deprivation. A man who says, "If God is dead, nothing matters," is a spoilt child who has never looked as his fellow men with compassion.

Yet, it might be objected, if we abandon a Judaeo-Christian *Weltanschauung*, there can, in a secular world, be no "one big thing" to give our lives an overall rationale. We will not be able to see written in the stars the final significance of human effort. There will be no architectonic purpose to give our lives such a rationale. Like Tolstoy's Pierre in *War and Peace*, we desire *somehow* to gather the sorry scheme of things entire into one intelligible explanation so that we can finally crack the riddle of human destiny. We long to understand why it is that men suffer and die. If it is a factual answer that is wanted when such a question is asked, it is plain enough. Ask any physician. But clearly this is not what people who seek such answers are after. They want some *justification* for suffering; they want some way of showing that suffering is after all for a good purpose. It can, of course, be argued that suffering sometimes is a good thing, for it occasionally gives us insight and at times even brings about in the man who suffers a capacity to love and to be kind. But there is plainly an excessive amount of human suffering—the suffering of children in childrens' hospitals, the suffering of people devoured by cancer, and the sufferings of millions of Jews under the Nazis—for which there simply is no justification. Neither the religious man nor the secularist can explain, that is justify, such suffer-

ing and find some overall "scheme of life" in which it has some place, but only the religious man needs to do so. The secularist understands that suffering is not something to be justified but simply to be struggled against with courage and dignity. And in this fight, even the man who has been deprived of that which could give him some measure of happiness can still find or make for himself a meaningful human existence. . . .

The dialectic of our problem has not ended. The religious moralist might acknowledge that human happiness is indeed plainly a good thing while contending that secular morality, where it is consistent and reflective, will inevitably lead to some variety of egoism. An individual who recognized the value of happiness and self-consciousness might, if he were free of religious restraints, ask himself why he should be concerned with the happiness and self-awareness of *others*, except where their happiness and self-awareness would contribute to his own good. We must face the fact that sometimes, as the world goes, people's interests clash. Sometimes the common good is served only at the expense of some individual's interest. An individual must therefore, in such a circumstance, sacrifice what will make him happy for the common good. Morality requires this sacrifice of us, *when it is necessary* for the common good; morality, any morality, exists in part at least to adjudicate between the conflicting interests and demands of people. It is plainly evident that everyone cannot be happy all the time and that sometimes one person's happiness or the happiness of a group is at the expense of another person's happiness. Morality requires that we attempt to distribute happiness as evenly as possible. We must be fair: each person is to count for one and none is to count for more than one. Whether we like a person or not, whether he is useful to his society or not, his interests, and what will make him happy, must also be considered in any final decision as to what ought to be done. The requirements of justice make it necessary that each person be given equal consideration. I cannot justify my neglect of another person in some matter of morality simply on the grounds that I do not like him, that he is *not* a member of my set, or that he is *not* a productive member of society. The religious apologist will argue that behind these requirements of justice as fairness there lurks the ancient religious principle that men are creatures of God, each with an infinite worth, and thus men are never to be treated only as means but as persons deserving of respect in their own right. They have an infinite worth simply as persons.

My religious critic, following out the dialectic of the problem, should query: why should you respect someone, why should you treat all people equally, if doing this is not in your interest or not in the interests of your group? No purely secular justification can be given for so behaving. My critic now serves his *coup de grâce:* the secularist, as well as the "knight of faith," acknowledges that the principle of respect for persons is a precious one—a principle that he is unequivocally committed to, but the religious man alone can *justify* adherence to this principle. The secularist is surreptitiously drawing on Christian inspiration when he insists that all men should be considered equal and that people's rights must be respected. For a secular morality to say all it wants and needs to say, it must, at this crucial point, be parasitical upon a God-centered morality. Without such a dependence on religion, secular morality collapses into egoism.

It may well be the case that, as a historical fact, our moral concern for persons came from our religious conceptions, but it is a well known principle of logic that the validity of a belief is independent of its origin. What the religious moralist must do is to show that only on religious grounds could such a principle of respect for persons be justifiably asserted. But he has not shown that this is so; and there are good reasons for thinking that it is not so. Even if the secularist must simply subscribe to the Kantian principle, "Treat every man as an end and never as a means only," as he must subscribe to the claim, "Happiness is good," it does not follow that he is on worse ground than

the religious moralist, for the religious moralist too, as we have seen, must simply subscribe to his ultimate moral principle, "Always do what God wills." *In a way*, the religious moralist's position here is simpler than the secularist's, for he needs only the fundamental moral principle that he ought to do what God wills. The secularist appears to need at least two fundamental principles. But in another and more important way the religious moralist's position is more complex, for he must subscribe to the extraordinarily obscure notion that man is a creature of God and as such has infinite worth. The Kantian principle may in the last analysis simply require subscription, but it is not inherently mysterious. To accept it does not require a crucifixion of the intellect. And if we are prepared simply to commit ourselves to one principle, why not to two principles, neither of which involves any appeal to conceptions whose very intelligibility is seriously in question?

The above argument is enough to destroy the believer's case here. But need we even make those concessions? I do not think so. There is a purely secular rationale for treating people fairly, for regarding them as persons. Let me show how this is so. We have no evidence that men ever lived in a presocial state of nature. Man, as we know him, is an animal with a culture; he is part of a community, and the very *concept* of community implies binding principles and regulations—duties, obligations, and rights. Yet, by an exercise in imagination, we could conceive, in broad outline at any rate, what it would be like to live in such a presocial state. In such a state no one would have any laws or principles to direct his behavior. In that sense man would be completely free. But such a life, as Hobbes graphically depicted, would be a clash of rival egoisms. Life in that state of nature would, in his celebrated phrase, "be nasty, brutish and short." Now if men were in such a state and if they were perfectly rational egoists, what kind of community life would they choose, given the fact that they were, very roughly speaking, nearly equal in strength and ability? (That in communities as we find them men are not so nearly equal in power is beside the point, for our *hypothetical* situation.) Given that they all start from scratch and have roughly equal abilities, it seems to me that it would be most reasonable, even for rational egoists, to band together into a community where each man's interests were given equal consideration, where each person was treated as deserving of respect. Each rational egoist would want others to treat him with respect, for his very happiness is contingent upon that; and he would recognize, if he were rational, that he could attain the fullest cooperation of others only if other rational egoists knew or had good grounds for believing that their interests and their persons would also be respected. Such cooperation is essential for each egoist if all are to have the type of community life which would give them the best chance of satisfying their own interests to the fullest degree. Thus, even if men were thorough egoists, we would still have rational grounds for subscribing to a principle of respect for persons. That men are not thoroughly rational, do not live in a state of nature, and are not thorough egoists, does not gainsay the fact that we have rational grounds for regarding social life, organized in accordance with such a principle, as being objectively better than a social life which ignored this principle. The point here is that even rational egoists could see that this is the best possible social organization where men are nearly equal in ability.

Yet what about the world we live in—a world in which, given certain extant social relationships, men are not equal or even nearly equal in power and opportunity? What reason is there for an egoist who is powerfully placed to respect the rights of others, when they cannot hurt him? We can say that his position, no matter how strong, might change and he might be in a position where he would need his rights protected, but this is surely not a strong enough reason for respecting those rights. To be moral involves respecting those rights, but our rational egoist may not propose to be moral. In considering such questions we reach a point in reasoning at which

we must simply *decide* what sort of person we shall strive to become. But, as I have said, the religious moralist reaches the same point. He too must make a decision of principle, but the principle he adopts is a fundamentally incoherent one. He not only must decide, but his decision must involve the acceptance of an absurdity.

It is sometimes argued by religious apologists that only if there is a God who can punish men will we be assured that naturally selfish men will be fair and considerate of others. Without this punitive sanction of threat men would go wild. Men will respect the rights of others only if they fear a wrathful and angry God. Yet it hardly seems to be the case that Christians, with their fear of hell, have been any better at respecting the rights of others than non-Christians. A study of the Middle Ages or the conquest of the non-Christian world makes this plain enough. And even if it were true (as it is not) that Christians were better in this respect than non-Christians, it would not show that they had a superior moral reason for their behavior, for in so acting and in so reasoning, they are not giving a morally relevant reason at all but are simply acting out of fear for their own hides. Yet Christian morality supposedly takes us beyond the clash of the rival egoisms of secular life.

In short, Christian ethics has not been able to give us a sounder ground for respecting persons than we have with a purely secular morality. The Kantian principle of respect for persons is actually bound up in the very idea of morality, either secular or religious, and there are good reasons, of a perfectly mundane sort, why we should have the institution of morality as we now have it, namely, that our individual welfare is dependent on having a device which equitably resolves social and individual conflicts. Morality has an objective rationale in complete independence of religion. Even if God is dead, it doesn't really matter.

It is in just this last thrust, it might be objected, that you reveal your true colors and show your own inability to face a patent social reality. At this point the heart of your rationalism is very irrational. For millions of people "the death of God" means very much. It really does matter. In your somewhat technical sense, the concept of God may be chaotic or unintelligible, but this concept, embedded in our languages—embedded in "the stream of life"—has an enormous social significance for many people. Jews and Christians, if they take their religion to heart, could not but feel a great rift in their lives with the loss of God, for they have indeed organized a good bit of their lives around their religion. Their very life-ideals have grown out of these, if you will, myth-eaten concepts. What should have been said is that if "God is dead" it matters a lot, but we should stand up like men and face this loss and learn to live in the Post-Christian era. As Nietzsche so well knew, to do this involves a basic reorientation of one's life and not just an intellectual dissent to a few statements of doctrine.

There is truth in this and a kind of "empiricism about man" that philosophers are prone to neglect. Of course it does matter when one recognizes that one's religion is illusory. For a devout Jew or Christian to give up his God most certainly is important and does take him into the abyss of a spiritual crisis. But in saying that it doesn't *really* matter I was implying what I have argued for in this essay, namely, that if a believer loses his God but can keep his nerve, think the matter over, and thoroughly take it to heart, life can still be meaningful and morality yet have an objective rationale. Surely, for good psychological reasons, the believer is prone to doubt this argument, but if he will only "hold on to his brains" and keep his courage, he will come to see that it is so. In this crucial sense it remains true that if "God is dead" it doesn't really matter.

Notes

1. This is convincingly argued in Michael Scriven's essay "Definitions, Explanations, and Theories," in Herbert Feigl, Michael Scriven, and Grover Maxwell, eds. *Minnesota Studies in the Philosophy of Science,* III (Minneapolis, 1958), pp. 99–195.

PART IX

Applied Ethics

Introduction

Several moral issues are tearing our society apart; among the most prominent of these are abortion, euthanasia, racism, reverse discrimination, the death penalty, and our obligation to people dying of AIDS and hunger in Africa and Asia. Can philosophical analysis throw light on these issues? Can philosophy have practical implications?

For this section I have chosen two articles on the issue of helping the poor of other nations, two on the ethics of abortion, one on war and the possibility of channeling aggressivity for peaceful purposes, and one on the question of keeping oneself pure from evil or whether morality requires that we get our hands dirty in trying to do good.

What are our obligations to people suffering of starvation and disease in poor countries? Ten thousand people starve to death every day, another two billion (out of a global population of six billion) are malnourished, and millions more are dying of AIDS and other diseases. On the other hand, another third of the world lives in affluence. Imagine ten children eating at a table. The three healthiest eat the best food and throw much of it away or give it to their pets. Two other children get just enough food to get by on. The other five do not get enough food. Three of them manage to stave off hunger pangs by eating bread and rice, but the other two are unable to do even that and die of hunger-related diseases.

In the United States enough food is thrown into the garbage each day to feed an entire nation, more money is spent on pet food than aid to developing and poor countries, and many people are grossly overweight.

What should we do about the problem of world hunger, malnourishment, and disease? In our first reading, "Lifeboat Ethics," Garrett Hardin argues that affluent societies, like passengers on lifeboats, ought above all to conserve resources for their own survival. To give away resources to needy nations or admit immigrants is like taking on additional passengers who threaten to capsize the lifeboat. We end up helping neither the poor, who must learn to deal with their population and economic problems, nor ourselves, who need to make provisions to our children and grandchildren. In our second reading, "Famine, Affluence, and Morality," Peter Singer argues from a utilitarian perspective that we do have a stringent duty to come to the aid of those in dire need. He offers a strong and a weak principle of moral responsibility for aid. The *strong principle* is "If it is in our power to prevent something bad from happening, without thereby sacrificing anything of *comparable* moral importance, we ought, morally, to do it." The *weak principle* is "If it is in our power to prevent something bad from happening, without thereby sacrificing anything morally significant, we ought, morally, to do it." Singer believes that the strong principle is valid, but even if the weak principle is correct, we would have to make substantial changes in our lives to comply with it.

The next two readings concern the problem of abortion, a moral issue that often is debated with heated passion. Why is abortion a moral issue? Take a fertilized egg, a zygote, a tiny sphere of cells. By itself, it is hard to see what is so important about such an inconspicuous piece of matter. It is virtually indistinguishable from other clusters of cells or the zygotes of other animals. On the other hand, take an adult human being, a class of beings that we all intuitively feel to be worthy of high respect, having rights, including the right to life. To kill an innocent human being is an act of murder and universally condemned. However, no obvious line of division separates that single-cell zygote from the adult it will become. Hence, the problem of abortion. In our third reading, "Abortion Is Morally Wrong," John T. Noonan Jr. writes that failure to locate a cutoff point between conception and childhood is a presumption for finding conception as the morally significant cutoff point of moral rights. He argues that since it is always wrong to kill innocent human beings, and since fetuses are innocent human beings, it is wrong to kill fetuses. He makes an exception when the mother's life is in danger, since something of comparable worth is at stake. Noonan argues that conception is the only nonarbitrary cut-off place between nonpersonhood and personhood. In the fourth reading, "The Personhood Argument in Favor of Abortion," Mary Anne Warren argues against Noonan that fetuses are not persons, since persons must have such characteristics as self-consciousness and rationality and fetuses do not have these.

In our fifth reading, "The Moral Equivalent of War," William James argues that we must find a moral alternative to war, channeling the aggressivity to peaceful purposes. The military does cultivate admirable virtues—courage, honor, discipline, dedication to duty—often lacking in civilian society. We must find a way of promoting these virtues without the deadly violence.

In our final reading, "Political Action: The Problem of Dirty Hands," Michael Walzer argues that military and political leaders often find themselves forced to choose between accomplishing morally worthwhile goals by compromising their principles, and not accomplishing those worthy goals. They must, if they would succeed, follow Machiavelli's advice and "learn how not to be good." Walzer's perceptive essay should provoke much discussion. Act-utilitarians, as he notes, will probably reject the dilemma, arguing that whatever course maximizes utility is the right thing to do, but rule-utilitarians and deontologists will find the situation Walzer describes a burning issue, one which haunts morally concerned leaders.

36

Lifeboat Ethics: The Case Against Helping the Poor

GARRETT HARDIN

Garrett Hardin was for many years Professor of Biology at the University of California at Santa Barbara. He is the author of many books and articles on environmental ethics. In this essay Hardin, using the metaphor of a lifeboat adrift at sea, argues that our first obligation is to ourselves and our posterity. For that reason it would be unwise and a dereliction of duty to share our surplus with poor nations, whether through a world food bank, the exporting of technology, or unrestricted immigration. In view of the growing population and improvident behavior of poor nations, such sharing would be counterproductive, doing more harm than good. It would overload and sink the environmental lifeboat.

From "the Case Against Helping the Poor," *Psychology Today* (1974), pp. 38–43, 123–26. Reprinted with permission from *Psychology Today* magazine. Copyright © 1974 Sussex Publishers, Inc. Addendum 1989. Reprinted by permission of the author.

Environmentalists use the metaphor of the earth as a "spaceship" in trying to persuade countries, industries, and people to stop wasting and polluting our natural resources. Since we all share life on this planet, they argue, no single person or institution has the right to destroy, waste, or use more than a fair share of its resources.

But does everyone on earth have an equal right to an equal share of its resources? The spaceship metaphor can be dangerous when used by misguided idealists to justify suicidal policies for sharing our resources through uncontrolled immigration and foreign aid. In their enthusiastic but unrealistic generosity, they confuse the ethics of a spaceship with those of a lifeboat.

A true spaceship would have to be under the control of a captain, since no ship could possibly survive if its course were determined by committee. Spaceship Earth certainly has no captain; the United Nations is merely a toothless tiger, with little power to enforce any policy upon its bickering members.

If we divide the world crudely into rich nations and poor nations, two thirds of them are desperately poor, and only one third comparatively rich, with the United States the wealthiest of all. Metaphorically each rich nation can be seen as a lifeboat full of comparatively rich people. In the ocean outside each lifeboat swim the poor of the world, who would like to get in, or at least to share some of the wealth. What should the lifeboat passengers do?

First, we must recognize the limited capacity of any lifeboat. For example, a nation's land has a limited capacity to support a population and as the current energy crisis has shown us, in some ways we have already exceeded the carrying capacity of our land.

Adrift in a Moral Sea

So here we sit, say fifty people in our lifeboat. To be generous, let us assume it has room for ten more, making a total capacity of sixty. Suppose the fifty of us in the lifeboat see one hundred others swimming in the water outside, begging for admission to our boat or for handouts. We have several options: We may be tempted to try to live by the Christian ideal of being "our brother's keeper," or by the Marxist ideal of "to each according to his needs." Since the needs of all in the water are the same, and since they can all be seen as "our brothers, " we could take them all into our boat, making a total of 150 in a boat designed for sixty. The boat swamps, everyone drowns. Complete justice, complete catastrophe.

Since the boat has an unused excess capacity of ten more passengers, we could admit just ten more to it. But which ten do we let in? How do we choose? Do we pick the best ten, the neediest ten, "first come, first served"? And what do we say to the ninety we exclude? If we do let an extra ten into our lifeboat, we will have lost our "safety factor," an engineering principle of critical importance. For example, if we don't leave room for excess capacity as a safety factor in our country's agriculture, a new plant disease or a bad change in the weather could have disastrous consequences.

Suppose we decide to preserve our small safety factor and admit no more to the lifeboat. Our survival is then possible, although we shall have to be constantly on guard against boarding parties.

While this last solution clearly offers the only means of our survival, it is morally abhorrent to many people. Some say they feel guilty about their good luck. My reply is simple: "get out and yield your place to others." This may solve the problem of the guilt-ridden person's conscience, but it does not change the ethics of the lifeboat. The needy person to whom the guilt-ridden person yields his place will not himself feel guilty about his good luck. If he did, he would not climb aboard. The net result of conscience-stricken people giving up their unjustly held seats is the elimination of that sort of conscience from the lifeboat.

This is the basic metaphor within which we must work out our solutions. Let us now enrich the image, step by step, with substantive additions from the real world, a world that must solve real and pressing problems of overpopulation and hunger.

The harsh ethics of the lifeboat become even harsher when we consider the reproductive differences between the rich nations and the poor nations. The people inside the lifeboats are doubling in numbers every eighty-seven years; those swimming around outside are doubling, on the average, every thirty-five years, more than twice as fast as the rich. And since the world's resources are dwindling, the difference in prosperity between the rich and the poor can only increase.

As of 1973, the United States had a population of 210 million people, who were increasing by 0.8 percent per year. Outside our lifeboat, let us imagine another 210 million people (say the combined populations of Colombia, Ecuador, Venezuela, Morocco, Pakistan, Thailand, and the Philippines), who are increasing at a rate of 3.3 percent per year. Put differently, the doubling time for this aggregate population is twenty-one years, compared to eighty-seven years for the United States.

Multiplying the Rich and the Poor

Now suppose the United States agreed to pool its resources with those seven countries, with everyone receiving an equal share. Initially the ratio of Americans to non-Americans in this model would be one-to-one. But consider what the ratio would be after eight-seven years, by which time the Americans would have doubled to a population of 420 million. By then, doubling every twenty-one years, the other group would have swollen to 354 billion. Each American would have to share the available resources with more than eight people.

But, one could argue, this discussion assumes that current population trends will continue, and they may not. Quite so. Most likely the rate of population increase will decline much faster in the United States than it will in the other countries, and there does not seem to be much we can do about it. In sharing with "each according to his needs," we must recognize that needs are determined by population size, which is determined by the rate of reproduction, which at present is regarded as a sovereign right of every nation, poor or not. This being so, the philanthropic load created by the sharing ethic of the spaceship can only increase.

The Tragedy of the Commons

The fundamental error of spaceship ethics, and the sharing it requires, is that it leads to what I call "the tragedy of the commons." Under a system of private property, the men who own property recognize their responsibility to care for it, for if they don't they will eventually suffer. A farmer, for instance, will allow no more cattle in a pasture than its carrying capacity justifies. If he overloads it, erosion sets in, weeds take over, and he loses the use of the pasture.

If a pasture becomes a commons open to all, the right of each to use it may not be matched by a corresponding responsibility to protect it. Asking everyone to use it with discretion will hardly do, for the considerate hersdman who refrains from overloading the commons suffers more than a selfish one who says his needs are greater. If everyone would restrain himself, all would be well; but it takes only one less than everyone to ruin a system of voluntary restraint. In a crowded world of less than perfect human beings, mutual ruin is inevitable if there are no controls. This is the tragedy of the commons.

One of the major tasks of education today should be the creation of such an acute awareness of the dangers of the commons that people will recognize its many varieties. For example, the air and water have become polluted because they are treated as commons. Further growth in the population or per-capita conversion of natural resources into pollutants will only make the problem worse. The same holds true for the fish of the oceans. Fishing fleets have nearly disappeared in many parts of the world; technological improvements in the art of fishing are hastening the day of complete ruin. Only replacement of the system of the commons with a responsible system of control will save the land, air, water, and oceanic fisheries.

The World Food Bank

In recent years there has been a push to create a new commons called a World Food Bank, an international depository of food reserves to which nations would contribute according to their abilities and from which they would draw according to their needs. This humanitarian proposal has received support from many liberal international groups, and from such prominent citizens as Margaret Mead, U.N. Secretary General Kurt Waldheim, and Senators Edward Kennedy and George McGovern.

A World Food Bank appeals powerfully to our humanitarian impulses. But before we rush ahead with such a plan, let us recognize where the greatest political push comes from, lest we be disillusioned later. Our experience with the "Food for Peace program," or Public Law 480, gives us the answer. This program moved billions of dollars worth of U.S. surplus grain to food-short, population-long countries during the past two decades. But when P.L. 480 first became law, a headline in the business magazine *Forbes* revealed the real power behind it: "Feeding the World's Hungry Million: How It Will Mean Billions for U.S. Business."

And indeed it did. In the years 1960 to 1970, U.S. taxpayers spent a total of $7.9 billion on the Food for Peace program. Between 1948 and 1970, they also paid an additional $50 billion for other economic-aid programs, some of which went for food and food-producing machinery and technology. Though all U.S. taxpayers were forced to contribute to the cost of P.L. 480, certain special interest groups gained handsomely under the program. Farmers did not have to contribute the grain; the government, or rather the taxpayers, bought it from them at full market prices. The increased demand raised prices of farm products generally. The manufacturers of farm machinery, fertilizers, and pesticides benefited by the farmers' extra efforts to grow more food. Grain elevators profited from storing the surplus until it could be shipped. Railroads made money hauling it to ports, and shipping lines profited from carrying it overseas. The implementation of P.L. 480 required the creation of a vast government bureaucracy, which then acquired its own vested interest in continuing the program regardless of its merits.

Extracting Dollars

Those who proposed and defended the Food for Peace program in public rarely mentioned its importance to any of these special interests. The public emphasis was always on its humanitarian effects. The combination of silent selfish interests and highly vocal humanitarian apologists made a powerful and successful lobby for extracting money from taxpayers. We can expect the same lobby to push now for the creation of a World Food Bank.

However great the potential benefit to selfish interests, it should not be a decisive argument against a truly humanitarian program. We must ask if such a program would actually do more good than harm, not only momentarily but also in the long run. Those who propose the food bank usually refer to a current "emergency" or "crisis" in terms of world food supply. But what is an emergency? Although they may be infrequent and sudden, everyone knows that emergencies will occur from time to time. A well-run family, company, organization, or country prepares for the likelihood of accidents and emergencies. It expects them, it budgets for them, it saves for them.

Learning the Hard Way

What happens if some organizations or countries budget for accidents and others do not? If each country is solely responsible for its own well-being, poorly managed ones will suffer. But they can learn from experience. They may mend their ways and learn to budget for infrequent but certain emergencies. For example, the weather varies from year to year, and periodic crop failures are certain. A wise and competent government saves out of the production of the good years in anticipation of bad years to come. Joseph taught this policy to Pharaoh in Egypt more than 2,000 years ago. Yet the great majority of the governments in the world today do not follow such a policy. They lack either the wisdom or the competence, or both. Should those nations that do manage to put something aside be forced to come to the rescue each time an emergency occurs among the poor nations?

"But it isn't their fault!" some kindhearted liberals argue. "How can we blame the poor people who are caught in an emergency? Why must they suffer for the sins of their government? The concept of blame is simply not relevant here. The real question is, what are the operational consequences of establishing a World Food Bank? If it is open to every country every time a need develops, slovenly rulers will not be motivated to take Joseph's advice. Someone will always come to their aid. Some countries will deposit food in the World Food Bank, and others will withdraw it. There will be almost no overlap. As a result of such solutions to food shortage emergencies, the poor countries will not learn to mend their ways and will suffer progressively greater emergencies as their populations grow.

Population Control the Crude Way

On the average, poor countries undergo a 2.5 percent increase in population each year; rich countries, about 0.8 percent. Only rich countries have anything in the way of food reserves set aside, and even they do not have as much as they should. Poor countries have none. If poor countries received no food from the outside, the rate of their population growth would be periodically checked by crop failures and famines. But if they can always draw on a World Food Bank in time of need, their population can continue to grow unchecked, and so will their "need" for aid. In the short run, a World Food Bank may diminish that need, but in the long run it actually increases the need without limit.

Without some system of worldwide food sharing, the proportion of people in the rich and poor nations might eventually stabilize. The overpopulated poor countries would decrease in numbers, while the rich countries that had room for more people would increase. But with a well-meaning system of sharing, such as a World Food Bank, the growth differential between the rich and the poor countries will not only persist, it will increase. Because of the higher rate of population growth in the poor countries of the world, 88 percent of today's children are born poor, and only 12 percent rich. Year by year the ratio becomes worse, as the fast-reproducing poor outnumber the slow-reproducing rich.

A World Food Bank is thus a commons in disguise. People will have more motivation to draw from it than to add to any common store. The less provident and less able will multiply at the expense of the abler and more provident, bringing eventual ruin upon all who share in the commons. Besides, any system of "sharing" that amounts to foreign aid from rich nations to the poor nations will carry the taint of charity, which will contribute little to the world peace so devoutly desired by those who support the idea of a World Food Bank.

As past U.S. foreign-aid programs have amply and depressingly demonstrated, international charity frequently inspires mistrust and antagonism rather than gratitude on the part of the recipient nation.

Chinese Fish and Miracle Rice

The modern approach to foreign aid stresses the export of technology and advice, rather than money and food. As an ancient Chinese proverb goes: "Give a man a fish and he will eat for a day; teach him how to fish and he will eat for the rest of his days." Acting on this advice, the Rockefeller and Ford Foundations have financed a number of programs for improving agriculture in the hungry nations. Known as the "Green Revolution," these programs have led to the development of "miracle rice" and "miracle wheat," new strains that offer bigger harvests and greater resistance to crop damage. Norman Borlaug, the Nobel Prize–winning agronomist who, supported by the Rockerfeller Foundation, developed "miracle wheat," is one of the most prominent advocates of a World Food Bank.

Whether or not the Green Revolution can increase food production as much as its champions claim is a debatable but possibly irrelevant point. Those who support this well-intended humanitarian effort should first consider some of the fundamentals of human ecology. Ironically, one man who did was the late Alan Gregg, a vice-president of the Rockefeller Foundation. Two decades ago he expressed strong doubts about the wisdom of such attempts to increase food production. He likened the growth and spread of humanity over the surface of the earth to the spread of cancer in the human body, remarking that "cancerous growths demand food; but, as far as I know, they have never been cured by getting it."

Overloading the Environment

Every human born constitutes a draft on all aspects of the environment: food, air, water, forests, beaches, wildlife, scenery, and solitude. Food can, perhaps, be significantly increased to meet a growing demand. But what about clean beaches, unspoiled forests, and solitude? If we satisfy a growing population's need for food, we necessarily decrease its per capita supply of the other resources needed by men.

India, for example, now has a population of 600 million, which increases by 15 million per year. This population already puts a huge load on a relatively impoverished environment. The country's forests are now only a small fraction of what they were three centuries ago, and floods and erosion continually destroy the insufficient farmland that remains. Every one of the 15 million new lives added to India's population puts an additional burden on the environment and increases the economic and social costs of crowding. However humanitarian our intent, every Indian life saved through

medical or nutritional assistance from abroad diminishes the quality of life for those who remain, and for subsequent generations. If rich countries make it possible, through foreign aid, for 600 million Indians to swell to 1.2 billion in a mere twenty-eight years, as their current growth rate threatens, will future generations of Indians thank us for hastening the destruction of their environment? Will our good intentions be sufficient excuse for the consequences of our actions?

My final example of a commons in action is one for which the public has the least desire for rational discussion—immigration. Anyone who publicly questions the wisdom of current U.S. immigration policy is promptly charged with bigotry, prejudice, ethnocentrism, chauvinism, isolationism, or selfishness. Rather than encounter such accusations, one would rather talk about other matters, leaving immigration policy to wallow in the crosscurents of special interests that take no account of the good of the whole, or the interests of posterity.

Perhaps we still feel guilty about things we said in the past. Two generations ago the popular press frequently referred to Dagos, Wops, Polacks, Chinks, and Krauts, in articles about how America was being "overrun" by foreigners of supposedly inferior genetic stock. But because the implied inferiority of foreigners was used then as justification for keeping them out, people now assume that restrictive policies could only be based on such misguided notions. There are other grounds.

A Nation of Immigrants

Just consider the numbers involved. Our government acknowledges a net inflow of 400,000 immigrants a year. While we have no hard data on the extent of illegal entries, educated guesses put the figure at about 600,000 a year. Since the natural increase (excess of births over deaths) of the resident population runs about 1.7 million per year, the yearly gain from immigration amounts to at least 19 percent of the total annual increase, and may be as much as 37 percent if we include the estimate for illegal immigrants. Considering the growing use of birth-control devices, the potential effect of educational campaigns by such organizations as Planned Parenthood Federation of America and Zero Population Growth, and the influence of inflation and the housing shortage, the fertility rate of American women may decline so much that immigration could account for all the yearly increase in population. Should we not at least ask if that is what we want?

For the sake of those who worry about whether the "quality" of the average immigrant compares favorably with the quality of the average resident, let us assume that immigrants and native-born citizens are of exactly equal quality, however one defines that term. We will focus here only on quantity; and since our conclusions will depend on nothing else, all charges of bigotry and chauvinism become irrelevant.

Immigration versus Food Supply

World food banks *move food to the people*, hastening the exhaustion of the environment of poor countries. Unrestricted immigration, on the other hand, *moves people to the food*, thus speeding up the destruction of the environment of the rich countries. We can easily understand why poor people should want to make this latter transfer, but why should rich hosts encourage it?

As in the case of foreign-aid programs, immigration receives support from selfish interests and humanitarian impulses. The primary selfish interest in unimpeded immigration is the desire of employers for cheap labor, particularly in industries and trades that offer degrading work. In the past, one wave of foreigners after another was brought into the United States to work at wretched jobs for wretched wages. In recent years the Cubans, Puerto Ricans, and Mexicans have had this dubious honor. The interests of the employers of cheap labor mesh well with the guilty silence

of the country's liberal intelligentsia. White Anglo-Saxon Protestants are particularly reluctant to call for a closing of the doors to immigration for fear of being called bigots.

But not all countries have such reluctant leadership. Most educated Hawaiians, for example, are keenly aware of the limits of their environment, particularly in terms of population growth. There is only so much room on the islands, and the islanders know it. To Hawaiians, immigrants from the other forty-nine states present as great a threat as those from other nations. At a recent meeting of Hawaiian government officials in Honolulu, I had the ironic delight of hearing a speaker, who like most of his audience was of Japanese ancestry, ask how the country might practically and constitutionally close its doors to further immigration. One member of the audience countered: "How can we shut the doors now? We have many friends and relatives in Japan that we'd like to bring here some day so that they can enjoy Hawaii too." The Japanese-American speaker smiled sympathetically and answered: "Yes, but we have children now, and someday we'll have grandchildren too. We can bring more people here from Japan only by giving away some of the land that we hope to pass on to our grandchildren some day. What right do we have to do that?"

At this point, I can hear U.S. liberals asking: "How can you justify slamming the door once you're inside? You say that immigrants should be kept out. But aren't we all immigrants, or the descendants of immigrants? If we insist on staying, must we not admit all others?" Our craving for intellectual order leads us to seek and prefer symmetrical rules and morals: a single rule for me and everybody else; the same rule yesterday, today, and tomorrow. Justice, we feel, should not change with time and place.

We Americans of non-Indian ancestry can look upon ourselves as the descendants of thieves who are guilty morally, if not legally, of stealing this land from its Indian owners. Should we then give back the land to the now living American descendants of those Indians? However morally or logically sound this proposal may be, I, for one, am unwilling to live by it and I know no one else who is. Besides, the logical consequence would be absurd. Suppose that, intoxicated with a sense of pure justice, we should decide to turn our land over to the Indians. Since all our wealth has also been derived from the land, wouldn't we be morally obliged to give that back to the Indians too?

Pure Justice versus Reality

Clearly, the concept of pure justice produces an infinite regression to absurdity. Centuries ago, wise men invented statutes of limitation to justify rejection of such pure justice, in the interest of preventing continual disorder. The law zealously defends property rights, but only relatively recent property rights. Drawing a line after an arbitrary time has elapsed may be unjust, but the alternatives are worse.

We are all descendants of thieves, and the world's resources are inequitably distributed. But we must begin the journey to tomorrow from the point where we are today. We cannot remake the past. We cannot safely divide the wealth equitably among peoples so long as people reproduce at different rates. To do so would guarantee that our grandchildren, and everyone else's grandchildren, would have only a ruined world to inhabit.

To be generous with one's own possessions is quite different from being generous with those of posterity. We should call this point to the attention of those who, from a commendable love of justice and equality, would institute a system of the commons, either in the form of a world food bank, or of unrestricted immigration. We must convince them if we wish to save at least some parts of the world from environmental ruin.

Without a true world government to control reproduction and the use of available resources, the sharing ethic of the spaceship is impossible. For the foreseeable future, our survival demands that we govern our actions by the ethics of a lifeboat, harsh though they may be. Posterity will be satisfied with nothing less.

Addendum 1989

Can anyone watch children starve on television without wanting to help? Naturally sympathetic, a normal human being thinks that he can imagine what it is like to be starving. We all want to do unto others as we would have them do unto us.

But wanting is not doing. Forty years of activity by the U.S. Agency for International Development, as well as episodic nongovernmental attempts to feed the world's starving, have produced mixed results. Before we respond to the next appeal we should ask, "Does what we call 'aid' really help?"

Some of the shortcomings of food aid can be dealt with briefly. Waste is unavoidable: Because most poor countries have wretched transportation systems, food may sit on a dock until it rots. Then there are the corrupt politicians who take donated food away from the poor and give it to their political supporters. In Somalia in the 1980s, fully 70 percent of the donated food went to the army.

We can school ourselves to accept such losses. Panicky projects are always inefficient: Waste and corruption are par for the course. But there is another kind of loss that we cannot—in fact, we should not—accept, and that is the loss caused by the boomerang effects of philanthropy. Before we jump onto the next "feed-the-starving" bandwagon we need to understand how well-intentioned efforts can be counterproductive.

Briefly put, it is a mistake to focus only on starving people while ignoring their surroundings. Where there is great starvation there is usually an impoverished environment: poor soil, scarce water, and wildly fluctuating weather. As a result, the "carrying capacity" of the environment is low. The territory simply cannot support the population that is trying to live on it. Yet if the population were much smaller, and if it would stay smaller, the people would not need to starve.

Let us look at a particular example. Nigeria, like all the central African countries, has increased greatly in population in the last quarter-century. Over many generations, Nigerians learned that their farmlands would be most productive if crop-growing alternated with "fallow years"—years in which the land was left untilled to recover its fertility.

When modern medicine reduced the death rate, the population began to grow. More food was demanded from the same land. Responding to that need, Nigerians shortened the fallow periods. The result was counterproductive. In one carefully studied village, the average fallow period was shortened from 5.3 to 1.4 years. As a result, the yearly production (averaged over both fallow and crop years) fell by 30 percent.

Are Nigerian farmers stupid? Not at all! They know perfectly well what they are doing. But a farmer whose family has grown too large for his farm has to take care of next year's need before he can provide for the future. To fallow or not to fallow translates into this choice: zero production in a fallow year or a 30 percent shortfall over the long run. Starvation cannot wait. Long-term policies have to give way to short-term ones. So the farmer plows up his overstressed fields, thus diminishing long-term productivity.

Once the carrying capacity of a territory has been transgressed, its capacity goes down, year after year. Transgression is a one-way road to ruin. Ecologists memorialize this reality with an Eleventh Commandment: "Thou shalt not transgress the carrying capacity."

Transgression takes many forms. Poor people are poor in energy resources. They need energy to cook their food. Where do they get it? Typically, from animal dung or trees and bushes. Burning dung deprives the soil of nitrogen. Cutting down trees and bushes deprives the land of protection against eroding rain. Soil-poor slopes cannot support a crop of fuel-plants. Once the soil is gone, water runs off the slopes faster and floods the valleys below. First

poor people deforest their land, and then deforestation makes them poorer.

When Americans send food to a starving population that has already grown beyond the environment's carrying capacity, we become a partner in the devastation of their land. Food from the outside keeps more natives alive; these demand more food and fuel; greater demand causes the community to transgress the carrying capacity more, and transgression results in lowering the carrying capacity. The deficit grows exponentially. Gifts of food to an overpopulated country boomerang, increasing starvation over the long run. Our choice is really between letting some die this year and letting more die in the following years.

You may protest, "That's easy enough for a well-fed American to say, but do citizens of poor countries agree?" Well, wisdom is not restricted to the wealthy. The Somali novelist Nuruddin Farrah has courageously condemned foreign gifts as being not truly aid, but a poison, because (if continued) such gifts will make Africans permanently dependent on outside aid.

The ethicist Joseph Fletcher has given a simple directive to would-be philanthropists: "Give if it helps, but not if it hurts." We can grant that giving makes the donor feel good at first—but how will he feel later when he realizes that he has harmed the receiver?

Only one thing can really help a poor country: population control. Having accepted disease control the people must now accept population control.

What the philosopher–economist Kenneth Boulding has called "lovey-dovey charity" is not enough. "It is well to remember," he said, "that the symbol of Christian love is a cross and not a Teddy bear." A good Christian should obey the Eleventh Commandment, refusing to send gifts that help poor people destroy the environment that must support the next generation.

37

Famine, Affluence, and Morality

PETER SINGER

Peter Singer is DeCamp Professor of Bioethics, University Center for Human Values, Princeton University. His book Animal Liberation *(1975) is one of the most influential books ever written on animal rights and has converted many to the animal rights movement.*

Singer argues that we have a duty to provide aid to famine victims and others who are suffering from hunger and poverty. He proposes two principles, a strong and a moderate one, which show that we have a duty to give substantial aid to those who are starving. The strong principle is "If it is in our power to prevent something bad from happening, without thereby sacrificing anything of comparable moral importance, we ought, morally, to do it." The moderate (or weak) principle is "If it is in our power to prevent something very bad from happening, without thereby sacrificing anything morally significant, we ought, morally, to do it."

As I write this, in November, 1971, people are dying in East Bengal from lack of food, shelter, and medical care. The suffering and death that are occurring there now are not inevitable, not unavoidable in any fatalistic sense of the term. Constant poverty, a cyclone, and a civil war have turned at least nine million people into destitute refugees; nevertheless, it is not beyond the capacity of the richer nations to give enough assistance to reduce any further suffering to very small proportions. The decisions and actions of human beings can prevent this kind of suffering. Unfortunately, human beings have not made the necessary decisions. At the

individual level, people have, with very few exceptions, not responded to the situation in any significant way. Generally speaking, people have not given large sums to relief funds; they have not written to their parliamentary representatives demanding increased government assistance; they have not demonstrated in the streets, held symbolic fasts, or done anything else directed toward providing the refugees with the means to satisfy their essential needs. At the government level, no government has given the sort of massive aid that would enable the refugees to survive for more than a few days. Britain, for instance, has given rather more than most countries. It has, to date, given £14,750,000. For comparative purposes, Britain's share of the nonrecover-able development costs of the Anglo-French Concorde project is already in excess of £275,000,000, and on present estimates will reach £440,000,000. The implication is that the British government values a supersonic transport more than thirty times as highly as it values the lives of the nine million refugees. Australia is another country which, on a per capita basis, is well up in the "aid to Bengal" table. Australia's aid, however, amounts to less than one-twentieth of the cost of Sydney's new opera house. The total amount given, from all sources, now stands at about £65,000,000. The estimated cost of keeping the refugees alive for one year is £464,000,000. Most of the refugees have now been in the camps for more than six months. The World Bank has said that India needs a minimum of £300,000,000 in assistance from other countries before the end of the year. It seems obvious that assistance on this scale will not be forthcoming. India will be forced to choose between letting the refugees starve or diverting funds from her own development program, which will mean that more of her own people will starve in the future.[1]

These are the essential facts about the present situation in Bengal. So far as it concerns us here, there is nothing unique about this situation except its magnitude. The Bengal emergency is just the latest and most acute of a series of major emergencies in various parts of the world, arising both from natural and from man-made causes. There are also many parts of the world in which people die from malnutrition and lack of food independent of any special emergency. I take Bengal as my example only because it is the present concern, and because the size of the problem has ensured that it has been given adequate publicity. Neither individuals nor governments can claim to be unaware of what is happening there.

What are the moral implications of a situation like this? In what follows, I shall argue that the way people in relatively affluent countries react to a situation like that in Bengal cannot be justified; indeed, the whole way we look at moral issues—our moral conceptual scheme—needs to be altered, and with it, the way of life that has come to be taken for granted in our society.

In arguing for this conclusion I will not, of course, claim to be morally neutral. I shall, however, try to argue for the moral position that I take, so that anyone who accepts certain assumptions, to be made explicit, will, I hope, accept my conclusion.

I begin with the assumption that suffering and death from lack of food, shelter, and medical care are bad. I think most people will agree about this, although one may reach the same view by different routes. I shall not argue for this view. People can hold all sorts of eccentric positions, and perhaps from some of them it would not follow that death by starvation is in itself bad. It is difficult, perhaps impossible, to refute such positions, and so for brevity I will henceforth take this assumption as accepted. Those who disagree need read no further.

My next point is this: If it is in our power to prevent something bad from happening, without thereby sacrificing anything of comparable moral importance, we ought, morally, to do it. By "without sacrificing anything of comparable moral importance" I mean without causing anything else comparably bad to happen, or doing something that is wrong in itself, or failing to promote some moral good, comparable in significance to the bad thing that we can prevent. This principle seems almost as uncontroversial as the last one. It requires us only to prevent what is bad, and not to promote what is good, and it requires this of us only when we can do it without sacrificing anything that is, from the moral point of view, comparably important. I could even, as far as the application of my argument to the Bengal emergency is concerned, qualify the point so as to make it: if it is in our power to prevent something very bad from happening, without thereby sacrificing anything morally significant, we ought, morally, to do it. An application of this principle would be as follows: if I am walking past a shallow pond and see a child drowning in it, I ought to wade in and pull the child out. This will mean getting my clothes muddy, but this is insignificant, while the death of the child would presumably be a very bad thing.

The uncontroversial appearance of the principle just stated is deceptive. If it were acted upon, even in its qualified form, our lives, our society, and our world would be fundamentally changed. For the principle takes, firstly, no account of proximity or distance. It makes no moral difference whether the person I can help is a neighbor's child ten yards from me or a Bengali whose name I shall never know, ten thousand miles away. Secondly, the principle makes no distinction between cases in which I am the only person who could possibly do anything and cases in which I am just one among millions in the same position.

I do not think I need to say much in defense of the refusal to take proximity and distance into account. The fact that a person is physically near to us, so that we have personal contact with him, may make it more likely that we shall assist him, but this does not show that we ought to help him rather than another who happens to be further away. If we accept any principle of impartiality, universalizability, equality, or whatever, we cannot discriminate against someone merely because he is far away from us (or we are far away from him). Admittedly, it is possible that we are in a better position to judge what needs to be done to help a person near to us than one far away, and perhaps also to provide the assistance we judge to be necessary. If this were the case, it would be a reason for helping those near to us first. This may once have been a justification for being more concerned with the poor in one's town than with famine victims in India. Unfortunately for those who like to keep their moral responsibilities limited, instant communication and swift transportation have changed the situation. From the moral point of view, the development of the world into a "global village" has made an important, though still unrecognized, difference to our moral situation. Expert observers and supervisors, sent out by famine relief organizations or permanently stationed in famine-prone areas, can direct our aid to a refugee in Bengal almost as effectively as we could get it to someone in our own block. There would seem, therefore, to be no possible justification for discriminating on geographical grounds.

There may be a greater need to defend the second implication of my principle—that the fact that there are millions of other people in the same position, in respect to the Bengali refugees, as I am, does not make the situation significantly different from a situation in which I am the only person who can prevent something very bad from occurring. Again, of course, I admit that there is a psychological difference between the cases; one feels less guilty about doing nothing if one can point to others, similarly placed, who have also done

nothing. Yet this can make no real difference to our moral obligations.[2] Should I consider that I am less obliged to pull the drowning child out of the pond if on looking around I see other people, no further away than I am, who have also noticed the child but are doing nothing? One has only to ask this question to see the absurdity of the view that numbers lessen obligation. It is a view that is an ideal excuse for inactivity; unfortunately most of the major evils—poverty, overpopulation, pollution—are problems in which everyone is almost equally involved.

The view that numbers do make a difference can be made plausible if stated in this way: if everyone in circumstances like mine gave £5 to the Bengal Relief Fund, there would be enough to provide food, shelter, and medical care for the refugees; there is no reason why I should give more than anyone else in the same circumstances as I am; therefore I have no obligation to give more than £5. Each premise in this argument is true, and the argument looks sound. It may convince us, unless we notice that it is based on a hypothetical premise, although the conclusion is not stated hypothetically. The argument would be sound if the conclusion were: if everyone in circumstances like mine were to give £5, I would have no obligation to give more than £5. If the conclusion were so stated, however, it would be obvious that the argument has no bearing on a situation in which it is not the case that everyone else gives £5. This, of course, is the actual situation. It is more or less certain that not everyone in circumstances like mine will give £5. So there will not be enough to provide the needed food, shelter, and medical care. Therefore by giving more than £5 I will prevent more suffering than I would if I gave just £5.

It might be thought that this argument has an absurd consequence. Since the situation appears to be that very few people are likely to give substantial amounts, it follows that I and everyone else in similar circumstances ought to give as much as possible, that is, at least up to the point at which by giving more one would begin to cause serious suffering for oneself and one's dependents—perhaps even beyond this point to the point of marginal utility, at which by giving more one would cause oneself and one's dependents as much suffering as one would prevent in Bengal. If everyone does this, however, there will be more than can be used for the benefit of the refugees, and some of the sacrifice will have been unnecessary. Thus, if everyone does what he ought to do, the result will not be as good as it would be if everyone did a little less than he ought to do, or if only some do all that they ought to do.

The paradox here arises only if we assume that the actions in question—sending money to the relief funds—are performed more or less simultaneously, and are also unexpected. For if it is to be expected that everyone is going to contribute something, then clearly each is not obliged to give as much as he would have been obliged to had others not been giving too. And if everyone is not acting more or less simultaneously, then those giving later will know how much more is needed, and will have no obligation to give more than is necessary to reach this amount. To say this is not to deny the principle that people in the same circumstances have the same obligations, but to point out that the fact that others have given, or may be expected to give, is a relevant circumstance: those giving after it has become known that many others are giving and those giving before are not in the same circumstances. So the seemingly absurd consequence of the principle I have put forward can occur only if people are in error about the actual circumstances—that is, if they think they are giving even when others are not, but in fact they are giving when others are. The result of everyone doing what he really ought to do cannot be worse than the result of everyone doing less than he ought to do, although the result of everyone doing what he reasonably believes he ought to do could be.

If my argument so far has been sound, neither our distance from a preventable evil nor the number of other people who, in respect to that evil, are in the same situation as we are, lessens our obligation to mitigate or prevent that evil. I shall therefore take as established the principle I asserted earlier. As I have already said, I need to assert it only in its qualified form: if it is in our power to prevent something very bad from happening, without thereby sacrificing anything else morally significant, we ought, morally, to do it.

The outcome of this argument is that our traditional moral categories are upset. The traditional distinction between duty and charity cannot be drawn, or at least, not in the place we normally draw it. Giving money to the Bengal Relief Fund is regarded as an act of charity in our society. The bodies which collect money are known as "charities." These organizations see themselves in this way—if you send them a check, you will be thanked for your "generosity." Because giving money is regarded as an act of charity, it is not thought that there is anything wrong with not giving. The charitable man may be praised, but the man who is not charitable is not condemned. People do not feel in any way ashamed or guilty about spending money on new clothes or a new car instead of giving it to famine relief. (Indeed, the alternative does not occur to them.) This way of looking at the matter cannot be justified. When we buy new clothes not to keep ourselves warm but to look "well-dressed" we are not providing for any important need. We would not be sacrificing anything significant if we were to continue to wear our old clothes, and give the money to famine relief. By doing so, we would be preventing another person from starving. It follows from what I have said earlier that we ought to give money away, rather than spend it on clothes which we do not need to keep us warm. To do so is not charitable, or generous. Nor is it the kind of act which philosophers and theologians have called "supererogatory"—an act which it would be good to do, but not wrong not to do. On the contrary, we ought to give money away, and it is wrong not to do so.

I am not maintaining that there are no acts which are charitable, or that there are no acts which it would be good to do but not wrong not to do. It may be possible to redraw the distinction between duty and charity in some other place. All I am arguing here is that the present way of drawing the distinction, which makes it an act of charity for a man living at the level of affluence which most people in the "developed nations" enjoy to give money to save someone else from starvation, cannot be supported. It is beyond the scope of my argument to consider whether the distinction should be redrawn or abolished altogether. There would be many other possible ways of drawing the distinction—for instance, one might decide that it is good to make other people as happy as possible, but not wrong not to do so.

Despite the limited nature of the revision in our moral conceptual scheme which I am proposing, the revision would, given the extent of both affluence and famine in the world today, have radical implications. These implications may lead to further objections, distinct from those I have already considered. l shall discuss two of these.

One objection to the position I have taken might be simply that it is too drastic a revision of our moral scheme. People do not ordinarily judge in the way I have suggested they should. Most people reserve their moral condemnation for those who violate some moral norm, such as the norm against taking another person's property. They do not condemn those who indulge in luxury instead of giving to famine relief. But given that I did not set out to present a morally neutral description of the way people make moral judgments, the way people do in fact judge has nothing to do with the validity of my conclusion. My conclusion follows from the principle which I advanced earlier, and unless that principle is rejected, or the arguments shown to be unsound, I think the conclusion must stand, however strange it appears.

It might, nevertheless, be interesting to consider why our society, and most other societies, do judge differently from the way I have suggested they should. In a well-known article, J. O. Urmson suggests that the imperatives of duty, which tell us what we must do, as distinct from what it would be good to do but not wrong not to do, function so as to prohibit behavior that is intolerable if men are to live together in society.[3] This may explain the origin and continued existence of the present division between acts of duty and acts of charity. Moral attitudes are shaped by the needs of society, and no doubt society needs people who will observe the rules that make social existence tolerable. From the point of view of a particular society, it is essential to prevent violations of norms against killing, stealing, and so on. It is quite inessential, however, to help people outside one's own society.

If this is an explanation of our common distinction between duty and supererogation, however, it is not a justification of it. The moral point of view requires us to look beyond the interests of our own society. Previously, as I have already mentioned, this may hardly have been feasible, but it is quite feasible now. From the moral point of view, the prevention of the starvation of millions of people outside our society must be considered at least as pressing as the upholding of property norms within our society.

It has been argued by some writers, among them Sidgwick and Urmson, that we need to have a basic moral code which is not too far beyond the capacities of the ordinary man, for otherwise there will be a general breakdown of compliance with the moral code. Crudely stated, this argument suggests that if we tell people that they ought to refrain from murder and give everything they do not really need to famine relief, they will do neither, whereas if we tell them that they ought to refrain from murder and that it is good to give to famine relief but not wrong not to do so, they will at least refrain from murder. The issue here is: Where should we draw the line between conduct that is required and conduct that is good although not required, so as to get the best possible result? This would seem to be an empirical question, although a very difficult one. One objection to the Sidgwick-Urmson line of argument is that it takes insufficient account of the effect that moral standards can have on the decisions we make. Given a society in which a wealthy man who gives 5 percent of his income to famine relief is regarded as most generous, it is not surprising that a proposal that we all ought to give away half our incomes will be thought to be absurdly unrealistic. In a society which held that no man should have more than enough while others have less than they need, such a proposal might seem narrow-minded. What it is possible for a man to do and what he is likely to do are both, I think, very greatly influenced by what people around him are doing and expecting him to do. In any case, the possibility that by spreading the idea that we ought to be doing very much more than we are to relieve famine we shall bring about a general breakdown of moral behavior seems remote. If the stakes are an end to widespread starvation, it is worth the risk. Finally, it should be emphasized that these considerations are relevant only to the issue of what we should require from others, and not to what we ourselves ought to do.

The second objection to my attack on the present distinction between duty and charity is one which has from time to time been made against utilitarianism. It follows from some forms of utilitarian theory that we all ought, morally, to be working full time to increase the balance of happiness over misery. The position I have taken here would not lead to this conclusion in all circumstances, for if there were no bad occurrences that we could prevent without sacrificing something of comparable moral importance, my argument would have no application. Given the present conditions in many parts of the world, however, it does follow from my argument that we ought, morally, to be working full time to relieve great suffering of the sort that occurs as a result of famine or other disasters. Of course, mitigating circum-

stances can be adduced—for instance, that if we wear ourselves out through overwork, we shall be less effective than we would otherwise have been. Nevertheless, when all considerations of this sort have been taken into account, the conclusion remains: we ought to be preventing as much suffering as we can without sacrificing something else of comparable moral importance. This conclusion is one which we may be reluctant to face. I cannot see, though, why it should be regarded as a criticism of the position for which I have argued, rather than a criticism of our ordinary standards of behavior. Since most people are self-interested to some degree, very few of us are likely to do everything that we ought to do. It would, however, hardly be honest to take this as evidence that it is not the case that we ought to do it.

It may still be thought that my conclusions are so wildly out of line with what everyone else thinks and has always thought that there must be something wrong with the argument somewhere. In order to show that my conclusions, while certainly contrary to contemporary Western moral standards, would not have seemed so extraordinary at other times and in other places, I would like to quote a passage from a writer not normally thought of as a way-out radical, Thomas Aquinas.

Now, according to the natural order instituted by divine providence, material goods are provided for the satisfaction of human needs. Therefore the division and appropriation of property, which proceeds from human law, must not hinder the satisfaction of man's necessity from such goods. Equally, whatever a man has in superabundance is owed, of natural right, to the poor for their sustenance. So Ambrosius says, and it is also to be found in the *Decretum Gratiana*: "The bread which you withhold belongs to the hungry; the clothing you shut away, to the naked; and the money you bury in the earth is the redemption and freedom of the penniless."[4]

I now want to consider a number of points, more practical than philosophical, which are relevant to the application of the moral conclusion we have reached. These points challenge not the idea that we ought to be doing all we can to prevent starvation, but the idea that giving away a great deal of money is the best means to this end.

It is sometimes said that overseas aid should be a government responsibility, and that therefore one ought not to give to privately run charities. Giving privately, it is said, allows the government and the noncontributing members of society to escape their responsibilities.

This argument seems to assume that the more people there are who give to privately organized famine relief funds, the less likely it is that the government will take over full responsibility for such aid. This assumption is unsupported, and does not strike me as at all plausible. The opposite view—that if no one gives voluntarily, a government will assume that its citizens are uninterested in famine relief and would not wish to be forced into giving aid— seems more plausible. In any case, unless there were a definite probability that by refusing to give one would be helping to bring about massive government assistance, people who do refuse to make voluntary contributions are refusing to prevent a certain amount of suffering without being able to point to any tangible beneficial consequence of their refusal. So the onus of showing how their refusal will bring about government action is on those who refuse to give.

I do not, of course, want to dispute the contention that governments of affluent nations should be giving many times the amount of genuine, no-strings-attached aid that they are giving now. I agree, too, that giving privately is not enough, and that we ought to be campaigning actively for entirely new standards for both public and private contributions to famine relief. Indeed, I would sympathize with someone who thought that campaigning was more important than giving oneself, although I doubt whether preaching what one does not practice would be very effective. Unfortunately, for many people the idea that "it's the government's responsibility" is a reason for not giving which does not appear to entail any political action either.

Another, more serious reason for not giving to famine relief funds is that until there is effective population control, relieving famine merely postpones starvation. If we save the Bengal refugees now, others, perhaps the children of these refugees, will face starvation in a few years' time. In support of this, one may cite the now well-known facts about the population explosion and the relatively limited scope for expanded production.

This point, like the previous one, is an argument against relieving suffering that is happening now, because of a belief about what might happen in the future; it is unlike the previous point in that very good evidence can be adduced in support of this belief about the future. I will not go into the evidence here. I accept that the earth cannot support indefinitely a population rising at the present rate. This certainly poses a problem for anyone who thinks it important to prevent famine. Again, however, one could accept the argument without drawing the conclusion that it absolves one from any obligation to do anything to prevent famine. The conclusion that should be drawn is that the best means of preventing famine, in the long run, is population control. It would then follow from the position reached earlier that one ought to be doing all one can to promote population control (unless one held that all forms of population control were wrong in themselves, or would have significantly bad consequences). Since there are organizations working specifically for population control, one would then support them rather than more orthodox methods of preventing famine.

A third point raised by the conclusion reached earlier relates to the question of just how much we all ought to be giving away. One possibility, which has already been mentioned, is that we ought to give until we reach the level of marginal utility—that is, the level at which, by giving more, I would cause as much suffering to myself or my dependents as I would relieve by my gift. This would mean, of course, that one would reduce oneself to very near the material circumstances of a Bengali refugee. It will be recalled that earlier I put forward both a strong and a moderate version of the principle of preventing bad occurrences. The strong version, which required us to prevent bad things from happening unless in doing so we would be sacrificing something of comparable moral significance, does seem to require reducing ourselves to the level of marginal utility. I should also say that the strong version seems to me to be the correct one. I proposed the more moderate version—that we should prevent bad occurrences unless, to do so, we had to sacrifice something morally significant—only in order to show that even on this surely undeniable principle a great change in our way of life is required. On the more moderate principle, it may not follow that we ought to reduce ourselves to the level of marginal utility, for one might hold that to reduce oneself and one's family to this level is to cause something significantly bad to happen. Whether this is so I shall not discuss, since, as I have said, I can see no good reason for holding the moderate version of the principle rather than the strong version. Even if we accepted the principle only in its moderate form, however, it should be clear that we would have to give away enough to ensure that the consumer society, dependent as it is on people spending on trivia rather than giving to famine relief, would slow down and perhaps disappear entirely. There are several reasons why this would be desirable in itself. The value and necessity of economic growth are now being questioned not only by conservationists, but by economists as well.[5] There is no doubt, too, that the consumer society has had a distorting effect on the goals and purposes of its members. Yet looking at the matter purely from the point of view of overseas aid, there must be

a limit to the extent to which we should deliberately slow down our economy; for it might be the case that if we gave away, say, 40 percent of our Gross National Product, we would slow down the economy so much that in absolute terms we would be giving less than if we gave 25 percent of the much larger GNP that we would have if we limited our contribution to this smaller percentage.

I mention this only as an indication of the sort of factor that one would have to take into account in working out an ideal. Since Western societies generally consider one percent of the GNP an acceptable level for overseas aid, the matter is entirely academic. Nor does it affect the question of how much an individual should give in a society in which very few are giving substantial amounts.

It is sometimes said, though less often now than it used to be, that philosophers have no special role to play in public affairs, since most public issues depend primarily on an assessment of facts. On questions of fact, it is said, philosophers as such have no special expertise, and so it has been possible to engage in philosophy without committing oneself to any position on major public issues. No doubt there are some issues of social policy and foreign policy about which it can truly be said that a really expert assessment of the facts is required before taking sides or acting, but the issue of famine is surely not one of these. The facts about the existence of suffering are beyond dispute. Nor, I think, is it disputed that we can do something about it, either through orthodox methods of famine relief or through population control or both. This is therefore an issue on which philosophers are competent to take a position. The issue is one which faces everyone who has more money than he needs to support himself and his dependents, or who is in a position to take some sort of political action. These categories must include practically every teacher and student of philosophy in the universities of the Western world. If philosophy is to deal with matters that are relevant to both teachers and students, this is an issue that philosophers should discuss.

Discussion, though, is not enough. What is the point of relating philosophy to public (and personal) affairs if we do not take our conclusions seriously? In this instance, taking our conclusion seriously means acting upon it. The philosopher will not find it any easier than anyone else to alter his attitudes and way of life to the extent that, if I am right, is involved in doing everything that we ought to be doing. At the very least, though, one can make a start. The philosopher who does so will have to sacrifice some of the benefits of the consumer society, but he can find compensation in the satisfaction of a way of life in which theory and practice, if not yet in harmony, are at least coming together.

Notes

1. There was also a third possibility: that India would go to war to enable the refugees to return to their lands. Since I wrote this paper, India has taken this way out. The situation is no longer that described above, but this does not affect my argument, as the next paragraph indicates.

2. In view of the special sense philosophers often give to the term, I should say that I use "obligation" simply as the abstract noun derived from "ought," so that "I have an obligation to" means no more, and no less, than "I ought to." This usage is in accordance with the definition of "ought" given by the *Shorter Oxford English Dictionary*: "the general verb to express duty or obligation." I do not think any issue of substance hangs on the way the term is used; sentences in which I use "obligation" could all be rewritten, although somewhat clumsily, as sentences in which a clause containing "ought" replaces the term "obligation."

3. J. O. Urmson, "Saints and Heroes," in *Essays in Moral Philosophy*, ed. Abraham L. Melden (Seattle: University of Washington Press, 1958), p. 214. For a related but significantly different view see also Henry Sidgwick, *The Methods of Ethics*, 7th ed. (London: Dover Press, 1907), pp. 220–21, 492–93.

4. *Summa Theologica*, II–II, Question 66, Article 7, in Aquinas, *Selected Political Writings*, ed. A. P.

d'Entreves, trans. J. G. Dawson (Oxford: Basil Blackwell, 1948), p. 171.

5. See, for instance, John Kenneth Galbraith, *The New Industrial State* (Boston: Houghton-Mifflin, 1967); and E. J. Mishan, *The Costs of Economic Growth* (New York: Praeger, 1967).

38

Abortion is Morally Wrong

JOHN T. NOONAN JR.

John T. Noonan Jr is Professor of Law Emeritus at the University of California, Berkeley. He has written several works on moral issues, including Contraception: A History of Its Treatment by the Catholic Theologians and Canonists *and* The Morality of Abortion, *from which this selection is taken. Noonan defends the view that an entity becomes a person at conception and that abortion, except to save the mother's life, is morally wrong. He uses an argument from probabilities to show that his criterion of humanity is objectively valid.*

The most fundamental question involved in the long history of thought on abortion is: How do you determine the humanity of a being? To phrase the question that way is to put in comprehensive humanistic terms what the theologians either dealt with as an explicitly theological question under the heading of "ensoulment" or dealt with implicitly in their treatment of abortion. The Christian position as it originated did not depend on a narrow theological or philosophical concept. It had no relation to theories of infant baptism. It appealed to no special theory of instantaneous ensoulment. It took the world's view on ensoulment as that view changed from Aristotle to Zacchia. There was, indeed, theological influence affecting the theory of ensoulment finally adopted, and, of course, ensoulment itself was a theological concept, so that the position was always explained

in theological terms. But the theological notion of ensoulment could easily be translated into humanistic language by substituting "human" for "rational soul"; the problem of knowing when a man is a man is common to theology and humanism.

If one steps outside the specific categories used by the theologians, the answer they gave can be analyzed as a refusal to discriminate among human beings on the basis of their varying potentialities. Once conceived, the being was recognized as man because he had man's potential. The criterion for humanity, thus, was simple and all-embracing: if you are conceived by human parents, you are human.

The strength of this position may be tested by a review of some of the other distinctions offered in the contemporary controversy over legalizing abortion. Perhaps the most popular distinction is in terms of viability. Before an age of some many months, the fetus is not viable, that is, it cannot be removed from the mother's womb and live apart from her. To that extent, the life of the fetus is absolutely dependent on the life of the mother. This dependence is made the basis of denying recognition to its humanity.

There are difficulties with this distinction. One is that the perfection of artificial incubation may make the fetus viable at any time: it may be removed and artificially sustained. Experiments with animals already show that such a procedure is possible. This hypothetical extreme case relates to an actual difficulty: there is considerable elasticity to the idea of viability. Mere length of life is not an exact measure. The viability of the fetus depends on the extent of its anatomical and functional development. The weight and length of the fetus are better guides to the state of its development than age, but weight and length vary. Moreover, different racial groups have different ages at which their fetuses are viable. Some evidence, for example, suggests that Negro fetuses mature more quickly than white fetuses. If viability is the norm, the standard would vary with race and with many individual circumstances.

The most important objection to this approach is that dependence is not ended by viability. The fetus is still absolutely dependent on someone's care in order to continue existence; indeed a child of one or three or even five years of age is absolutely dependent on another's care for existence; uncared for, the older fetus or the younger child will die as surely as the early fetus detached from the mother. The unsubstantial lessening in dependence at viability does not seem to signify any special acquisition of humanity.

A second distinction has been attempted in terms of experience. A being who has had experience, has lived and suffered, who possesses memories, is more human than one who has not. Humanity depends on formation by experience. The fetus is thus "unformed" in the most basic human sense.

This distinction is not serviceable for the embryo which is already experiencing and reacting. The embryo is responsive to touch after eight weeks and at least at that point is experiencing. At an earlier stage the zygote is certainly alive and responding to its environment. The distinction may also be challenged by the rare case where aphasia has erased adult memory: has it erased humanity? More fundamentally, this distinction leaves even the older fetus or the younger child to be treated as an unformed inhuman thing. Finally, it is not clear why experience as such confers humanity. It could be argued that certain central experiences such as loving or learning are necessary to make a man human. But then human beings who have failed to love or to learn might be

excluded from the class called man.

A third distinction is made by appeal to the sentiments of adults. If a fetus dies, the grief of the parents is not the grief they would have for a living child. The fetus is an unnamed "it" till birth, and is not perceived as personality until at least the fourth month of existence when movements in the womb manifest a vigorous presence demanding joyful recognition by the parents.

Yet feeling is notoriously an unsure guide to the humanity of others. Many groups of humans have had difficulty in feeling that persons of another tongue, color, religion, sex, are as human as they. Apart from reactions to alien groups, we mourn the loss of a ten-year-old boy more than the loss of his one-day-old brother or his 90-year-old grandfather. The difference felt and the grief expressed vary with the potentialities extinguished, or the experience wiped out; they do not seem to point to any substantial difference in the humanity of baby, boy, or grandfather.

Distinctions are also made in terms of sensations by the parents. The embryo is felt within the womb only after about the fourth month. The embryo is seen only at birth. What can be neither seen nor felt is different from what is tangible. If the fetus cannot be seen or touched at all, it cannot be perceived as man.

Yet experience shows that sight is even more untrustworthy than feeling in determining humanity. By sight, color became an appropriate index for saying who was a man, and the evil of racial discrimination was given foundation. Nor can touch provide the test; a being confined by sickness, "out of touch" with others, does not thereby seem to lose his humanity. To the extent that touch still has appeal as a criterion, it appears to be a survival of the old English idea of "quickening"—a possible mistranslation of the Latin *animatus* used in the canon law. To that extent touch as a criterion seems to be dependent on the Aristotelian notion of ensoulment, and to fall when this notion is discarded.

Finally, a distinction is sought in social visibility. The fetus is not socially perceived as human. It cannot communicate with others. Thus, both subjectively and objectively, it is not a member of society. As moral rules are rules for the behavior of members of society to each other, they cannot be made for behavior toward what is not yet a member. Excluded from the society of men, the fetus is excluded from the humanity of men.

By force of the argument from the consequences, this distinction is to be rejected. It is more subtle than that founded on an appeal to physical sensation, but it is equally dangerous in its implications. If humanity depends on social recognition, individuals or whole groups may be dehumanized by being denied any status in their society. Such a fate is fictionally portrayed in *1984* and has actually been the lot of many men in many societies. In the Roman empire, for example, condemnation to slavery meant the practical denial of most human rights; in the Chinese Communist world, landlords have been classified as enemies of the people and so treated as nonpersons by the state. Humanity does not depend on social recognition, though often the failure of society to recognize the prisoner, the alien, the heterodox as human has led to the destruction of human beings. Anyone conceived by a man and a woman is human. Recognition of this condition by society follows a real event in the objective order, however imperfect and halting the recognition. Any attempt to limit humanity to exclude some group runs the risk of furnishing authority and precedent for excluding other groups in the name of the consciousness or perception of the controlling group in the society.

A philosopher may reject the appeal to the humanity of the fetus because he views "humanity" as a secular view of the soul and because he doubts the existence of anything real and objective which can be identified as humanity. One answer to such a philosopher is to ask how he reasons about moral questions without supposing that there is a sense in which he and the others of whom he speaks are human. Whatever group is taken as the society which determines who may be killed is thereby taken as human. A second answer is to ask if he does not believe that there is a right and wrong way of deciding moral questions. If there is such a difference, experience may be appealed to: to decide who is human on the basis of the sentiment of a given society has led to consequences which rational men would characterize as monstrous.

The rejection of the attempted distinctions based on viability and visibility, experience and feeling, may be buttressed by the following considerations: Moral judgments often rest on distinctions, but if the distinctions are not to appear arbitrary fiat, they should relate to some real difference in probabilities. There is a kind of continuity in all life, but the earlier stages of the elements of human life possess tiny probabilities of development. Consider for example, the spermatozoa in any normal ejaculate: there are about 200,000,000 in any single ejaculate, of which one has a chance of developing into a zygote. Consider the oocytes which may become ova: there are 100,000 to 1,000,000 oocytes in a female infant, of which a maximum of 390 are ovulated. But once spermatozoon and ovum meet and the conceptus is formed, such studies as have been made show that roughly in only 20 percent of the cases will spontaneous abortion occur. In other words, the chances are about 4 out of 5 that this new being will develop. At this stage in the life of the being there is a sharp shift in probabilities, an immense jump in potentialities. To make a distinction between the rights of spermatozoa and the rights of the fertilized ovum is to respond to an enormous shift in possibilities. For about twenty days after conception the egg may split to form twins or combine with another egg to form a chimera, but the probability of either even happening is very small.

It may be asked, What does a change in biological probabilities have to do with establishing humanity? The argument from probabilities is not aimed at establishing humanity but at establishing an objective discontinuity which may be taken into account in moral discourse. As life itself is a matter of probabilities, as most moral reasoning is an estimate of probabilities, so it seems in accord with the structure of reality and the nature of moral thought to found a moral judgment on the change in probabilities at conception. The appeal to probabilities is the most commonsensical of arguments, to a greater or smaller degree all of us base our actions on probabilities, and in morals, as in law, prudence and negligence are often measured by the account one has taken of the probabilities. If the chance is 200,000,000 to 1 that the movement in the bushes into which you shoot is a man's, I doubt if many persons would hold you careless in shooting; but if the chances are 4 out of 5 that the movement is a human being's, few would acquit you of blame. Would the argument be different if only one out of ten children conceived came to term? Of course this argument would be different. This argument is an appeal to probabilities that actually exist, not to any and all states of affairs which may be imagined.

The probabilities as they do exist do not show the humanity of the embryo in the sense of a demonstration in logic any more than the probabilities of the movement in the bush being a man demonstrate beyond all doubt that the being is a man. The appeal is a "buttressing" consideration, showing the plausibility of the standard adopted. The argument focuses on the decisional factor in any moral judgment and assumes that part of the business of a moralist is drawing lines. One evidence of the nonarbitrary character of the line drawn is the difference of probabilities on either side of it. If a spermatozoon is destroyed, one destroys a being which had a chance of far less than 1 in 200 million of developing into a reasoning being, possessed of the genetic code, a heart and other organs, and capable of pain. If a fetus is destroyed, one destroys a being already pos-

sessed of the genetic code, organs, and sensitivity to pain, and one which had an 80 percent chance of developing further into a baby outside the womb who, in time, would reason.

The positive argument for conception as the decisive moment of humanization is that at conception the new being receives the genetic code. It is this genetic information which determines his characteristics, which is the biological carrier of the possibility of human wisdom, which makes him a self-evolving being. A being with a human genetic code is man.

This review of current controversy over the humanity of the fetus emphasizes what a fundamental question the theologians resolved in asserting the inviolability of the fetus. To regard the fetus as possessed of equal rights with other humans was not, however, to decide every case where abortion might be employed. It did decide the case where the argument was that the fetus should be aborted for its own good. To say a being was human was to say it had a destiny to decide for itself which could not be taken from it by another man's decision. But human beings with equal rights often come in conflict with each other, and some decision must be made as whose claims are to prevail. Cases of conflict involving the fetus are different only in two respects: the total inability of the fetus to speak for itself and the fact that the right of the fetus regularly at stake is the right to life itself.

The approach taken by the theologians to these conflicts was articulated in terms of "direct" and "indirect." Again, to look at what they were doing from outside their categories, they may be said to have been drawing lines or "balancing values." "Direct" and "indirect" are spatial metaphors: "line-drawing" is another. "To weigh" or "to balance" values is a metaphor of a more complicated mathematical sort hinting at the process which goes on in moral judgments. All the metaphors suggest that, in the moral judgments made, comparisons were necessary, that no value completely controlled. The principle of double effect was no doctrine fallen from heaven, but a method of analysis appropriate where two relative values were being compared. In Catholic moral theology, as it developed, life even of the innocent was not taken as an absolute. Judgments on acts affecting life issued from a process of weighing. In the weighing, the fetus was always given a value greater than zero, always a value separate and independent from its parents. This valuation was crucial and fundamental in all Christian thought on the subject and marked it off from any approach which considered that only the parents' interests needed to be considered.

Even with the fetus weighed as human, one interest could be weighed as equal or superior: that of the mother in her own life. The casuists between 1450 and 1895 were willing to weigh this interest as superior. Since 1895, that interest was given decisive weight only in the two special cases of the cancerous uterus and the ectopic pregnancy. In both of these cases the fetus itself had little chance of survival even if the abortion were not performed. As the balance was once struck in favor of the mother whenever her life was endangered, it could be so struck again. The balance reached between 1895 and 1930 attempted prudentially and pastorally to forestall a multitude of exceptions for interests less than life.

The perception of the humanity of the fetus and the weighing of fetal rights against other human rights constituted the work of the moral analysts. But what spirit animated their abstract judgments? For the Christian community it was the injunction of Scripture to love your neighbor as yourself. The fetus as human was a neighbor; his life had parity with one's own. The commandment gave life to what otherwise would have been only rational calculation.

The commandment could be put in humanistic as well as theological terms: Do not injure your fellow man without reason. In these terms, once the humanity of the fetus is perceived, abortion is never right except in self-defense. When life must be taken to save life, reason alone cannot say that a mother must prefer a child's life to her own. With this exception, now of great rarity, abortion violates the rational humanist tenet of the equality of human lives.

For Christians the commandment to love had received a special imprint in that the exemplar proposed of love was the love of the Lord for his disciples. In the light given by this example, self-sacrifice carried to the point of death seemed in the extreme situations not without meaning. In the less extreme cases, preference for one's own interests to the life of another seemed to express cruelty or selfishness irreconcilable with the demands of love.

39

The Personhood Argument in Favor of Abortion

MARY ANNE WARREN

Mary Anne Warren is Associate Professor of Philosophy at San Francisco State University and has written widely on feminism, including The Nature of Woman: An Encyclopedia and Guide to the Literature *(1980). In this selection she defends the view that abortion is always morally permissible. She attacks Noonan's argument on the basis of an ambiguity in the use of the term* human being, *showing that the term has both a biological and moral sense. What is important is the moral sense, which presupposes certain characteristics, such as self-consciousness and rationality, which a fetus does not have. At the end of her article (not included here), she addresses the issue of infanticide.*

The question which we must answer in order to produce a satisfactory solution to the problem of the moral status of abortion is this: How are we to define the moral community, the set of beings with full and equal moral rights, such that we can decide whether a human fetus is a member of his community or not? What sort of entity, exactly, has the inalienable rights to life, liberty, and the pursuit of happiness? Jefferson attributed these rights to all *men*, and it may or may not be fair to suggest that he intended to attribute them *only* to men. Perhaps he ought to have attributed them to all human beings. If so, then we arrive, first, at Noonan's problem of defining what makes a being human, and, second, at the equally vital question which Noonan does not consider, namely, What reason is there for identifying the moral community with the set of all human beings, in whatever way we have chosen to define that term?

Reprinted by permission from *The Monist* 57: 1 (1973).

1. On the Definition of "Human"

One reason why this vital second question is so frequently overlooked in the debate over the moral status of abortion is that the term "human" has two distinct, but not often distinguished, senses. This fact results in a slide of meaning, which serves to conceal the fallaciousness of the traditional argument that since (1) it is wrong to kill innocent human beings, and (2) fetuses are innocent human beings, then (3) it is wrong to kill fetuses. For if "human" is used in the same sense in both (1) and (2) then, whichever of the two senses is meant, one of these premises is question-begging. And if it is used in two different senses then of course the conclusion doesn't follow.

Thus, (1) is a self-evident moral truth, and avoids begging the question about abortion, only if "human being" is used to mean something like "a full-fledged member of the moral community." (It may or may not also be meant to refer exclusively to members of the species *Homo sapiens*.) We may call this the *moral* sense of "human." It is not to be confused with what we will call the *genetic* sense, i.e., the sense in which any member of the species is a human being, and no member of any other species could be. If (1) is acceptable only if the moral sense is intended, (2) is non-question-begging only if what is intended is the genetic sense.

In "Deciding Who Is Human," Noonan argues for the classification of fetuses with human beings by pointing to the presence of the full genetic code, and the potential capacity for rational thought. It is clear that what he needs to show, for his version of the traditional argument to be valid, is that fetuses are human in the moral sense, the sense in which it is analytically true that all human beings have full moral rights. But, in the absence of any argument showing that whatever is genetically human is also morally human, and he gives none, nothing more than genetic humanity can be demonstrated by the presence of the human genetic code. And, as we will see, the *potential* capacity for rational thought can at most show that an entity has the potential for *becoming* human in the moral sense.

2. Defining the Moral Community

Can it be established that genetic humanity is sufficient for moral humanity? I think that there are very good reasons for not defining the moral community in this way. I would like to suggest an alternative way of defining the moral community, which I will argue for only to the extent of explaining why it is, or should be, self-evident. The suggestion is simply that the moral community consists of all and only *people*, rather than all and only human beings; and probably the best way of demonstrating its self-evidence is by considering the concept of personhood, to see what sorts of entities are and are not persons, and what the decision that a being is or is not a person implies about its moral rights.

What characteristics entitle an entity to be considered a person? This is obviously not the place to attempt a complete analysis of the concept of personhood, but we do not need such a fully adequate analysis just to determine whether and why a fetus is or isn't a person. All we need is a rough and approximate list of the most basic criteria of personhood, and some idea of which, or how many, of these an entity must satisfy in order to properly be considered a person.

In searching for such criteria, it is useful to look beyond the set of people with whom we are acquainted, and ask how we would decide whether a totally alien being was a person or not. (For we have no right to assume that genetic humanity is necessary for personhood.) Imagine a space traveler who lands on an unknown planet and encounters a race of beings utterly unlike any he has ever seen or heard of. If he wants to be sure of behaving morally toward these beings, he has to somehow decide whether they are peo-

ple, and hence have full moral rights, or whether they are the sort of thing which he need not feel guilty about treating as, for example, a source of food.

How should he go about making this decision? If he has some anthropological background, he might look for such things as religion, art, and the manufacturing of tools, weapons, or shelters, since these factors have been used to distinguish our human from our prehuman ancestors, in what seems to be closer to the moral than the genetic sense of "human." And no doubt he would be right to consider the presence of such factors as good evidence that the alien beings were people, and morally human. It would, however, be overly anthropocentric of him to take the absence of these things as adequate evidence that they were not, since we can imagine people who have progressed beyond, or evolved without ever developing, these cultural characteristics.

I suggest that the traits which are most central to the concept of personhood, or humanity in the moral sense, are, very roughly, the following:

1. consciousness (of objects and events external and/or internal to the being), and in particular the capacity to feel pain;
2. reasoning (the *developed* capacity to solve new and relatively complex problems);
3. self-motivated activity (activity which is relatively independent of either genetic or direct external control);
4. the capacity to communicate, by whatever means, messages of an indefinite variety of types, that is, not just with an indefinite number of possible contents, but on indefinitely many possible topics;
5. the presence of self-concepts, and self-awareness, either individual or racial, or both.

Admittedly, there are apt to be a great many problems involved in formulating precise definitions of these criteria, let alone in developing universally valid behavioral criteria for deciding when they apply. But I will assume that both we and our explorer know approximately what (1)–(5) mean, and that he is also able to determine whether or not they apply. How, then, should he use his findings to decide whether or not the alien beings are people? We needn't suppose that an entity must have *all* of these attributes to be properly considered a person; (1) and (2) alone may well be sufficient for personhood, and quite probably (1)–(3) are sufficient. Neither do we need to insist that any one of these criteria is *necessary* for personhood, although once again (1) and (2) look like fairly good candidates for necessary conditions, as does (3), if "activity" is construed so as to include the activity of reasoning.

All we need to claim, to demonstrate that a fetus is not a person, is that any being which satisfies *none* of (1)–(5) is certainly not a person. I consider this claim to be so obvious that I think anyone who denied it, and claimed that a being which satisfied none of (1)–(5) was a person all the same, would thereby demonstrate that he had no notion at all of what a person is—perhaps because he had confused the concept of a person with that of genetic humanity. If the opponents of abortion were to deny the appropriateness of these five criteria, I do not know what further arguments would convince them. We would probably have to admit that our conceptual schemes were indeed irreconcilably different, and that our dispute could not be settled objectively.

I do not expect this to happen, however, since I think that the concept of a person is one which is very nearly universal (to people), and that it is common to both proabortionists and antiabortionists, even though neither group has fully realized the relevance of this concept to the resolution of their dispute. Furthermore, I think that on reflection even the antiabortionists ought to agree that (1)–(5) are central to the concept of personhood, but also that it is a part of this concept that all and only people have full moral rights. The concept of a person is in part a moral concept; once we have admitted that *x* is a person we have recognized, even if we have not agreed to respect, *x*'s right to be treated as a member of the moral community. It is true that the claim that *x is a human being* is more commonly voiced as part of an appeal to treat *x* decently than is the claim that *x* is a person, but this is either because "human being" is here used in the sense which implies personhood, or because the genetic and moral senses of "human" have been confused.

Now if (1)–(5) are indeed the primary criteria of personhood, then it is clear that genetic humanity is neither necessary nor sufficient for establishing that an entity is a person. Some human beings are not people, and there may well be people who are not human beings. A man or woman whose consciousness has been permanently obliterated but who remains alive is a human being which is no longer a person; defective human beings, with no appreciable mental capacity, are not and presumably never will be people; and a fetus is a human being which is not yet a person, and which therefore cannot coherently be said to have full moral rights. Citizens of the next century should be prepared to recognize highly advanced, self-aware robots or computers, should such be developed, and intelligent inhabitants of other worlds, should such be found, as people in the fullest sense, and to respect their moral rights. But to ascribe full moral rights to an entity which is not a person is as absurd as to ascribe moral obligations and responsibilities to such an entity.

3. Fetal Development and the Right to Life

Two problems arise in the application of these suggestions for the definition of the moral community to the determination of the precise moral status of a human fetus. Given that the paradigm example of a person is a normal adult human being, then (1) How like this paradigm, in particular how far advanced since conception, does a human being need to be before it begins to have a right to life by virtue, not of being fully a person as of yet, but of being *like* a person? and (2) To what extent, if any, does the fact that a fetus has the *potential* for becoming a person endow it with some of the same rights? Each of these questions requires some comment.

In answering the first question, we need not attempt a detailed consideration of the moral rights of organisms which are not developed enough, aware enough, intelligent enough, etc., to be considered people, but which resemble people in some respects. It does seem reasonable to suggest that the more like a person, in the relevant respects, a being is, the stronger is the case for regarding it as having a right to life, and indeed the stronger its right to life is. Thus we ought to take seriously the suggestion that, insofar as "the human individual develops biologically in a continuous fashion . . . the rights of a human person might develop in the same way." But we must keep in mind that the attributes which are relevant in determining whether or not an entity is enough like a person to be regarded as having some of the same moral rights are no different from those which are relevant to determining whether or not it is fully a person—i.e., are no different from (1)–(5) — and that being genetically human, or having recognizably human facial and other physical features, or detectable brain activity, or the capacity to survive outside the uterus, are simply not among these relevant attributes.

Thus it is clear that even though a seven- or eight-month fetus has features which make it apt to arouse in us almost the same powerful protective instinct as is commonly aroused by a small infant, nevertheless it is not significantly more personlike than is a very small embryo. It is *somewhat* more personlike; it can apparently feel and respond to pain, and it may even have a rudimentary form of consciousness, insofar as its brain is quite active. Nevertheless, it seems safe to say that it is not fully conscious, in the way that an infant of a few months is, and that it cannot reason, or communicate messages of indefinitely many sorts, does not engage in self-motivated activity, and has no self-awareness. Thus, in the *relevant* respects, a fetus, even a fully developed one, is considerably less personlike than is the average mature mammal, indeed the average fish.

And I think that a rational person must conclude that if the right to life of a fetus is to be based upon its resemblance to a person, then it cannot be said to have any more right to life than, let us say, a newborn guppy (which also seems to be capable of feeling pain), and that a right of that magnitude could never override a woman's right to obtain an abortion, at any stage of her pregnancy.

There may, of course, be other arguments in favor of placing legal limits upon the stage of pregnancy in which an abortion may be performed. Given the relative safety of the new techniques of artificially inducing labor during the third trimester, the danger to the woman's life or health is no longer such an argument. Neither is the fact that people tend to respond to the thought of abortion in the later stages of pregnancy with emotional repulsion, since mere emotional responses cannot take the place of moral reasoning in determining what ought to be permitted. Nor, finally, is the frequently heard argument that legalizing abortion, especially late in the pregnancy, may erode the level of respect for human life, leading, perhaps, to an increase in unjustified euthanasia and other crimes. For this threat, if it is a threat, can be better met by educating people to the kinds of moral distinctions which we are making here than by limiting access to abortion (which limitation may, in its disregard for the rights of women, be just as damaging to the level of respect for human rights).

Thus, since the fact that even a fully developed fetus is not personlike enough to have any significant right to life on the basis of its personlikeness shows that no legal restrictions upon the stage of pregnancy in which an abortion may be performed can be justified on the grounds that we should protect the rights of the older fetus, and since there is no apparent justification for such restrictions, we may conclude that they are entirely unjustified. Whether or not it would be *indecent* (whatever that means) for a woman in her seventh month to obtain an abortion just to avoid having to postpone a trip to Europe, it would not, in itself, be *immoral*, and therefore it ought to be permitted.

4. Potential Personhood and the
Right to Life

We have seen that a fetus does not resemble a person in any way which can support the claim that it has even some of the same rights. But what about its *potential*, the fact that if nurtured and allowed to develop naturally it will very probably become a person? Doesn't that alone give it at least some right to life? It is hard to deny that the fact that an entity is a potential person is a strong prima facie reason for not destroying it; but we need not conclude from this that a potential person has a right to life, by virtue of that potential. It may be that our feeling that it is better, other things being equal, not to destroy a potential person is better explained by the fact that potential people are still (felt to be) an invaluable resource, not to be lightly squandered. Surely, if every speck of dust were a potential person, we would be much less apt to conclude that every potential person has a right to become actual.

Still, we do not need to insist that a potential person has no right to life whatever. There may well be something immoral, and not just imprudent, about wantonly destroying potential people, when doing so isn't necessary to protect anyone's rights. But even if a potential person does have some prima facie right to life, such a right could not possibly outweigh the right of a woman to obtain an abortion, since the rights of any actual person invariably outweigh those of any potential person, whenever the two conflict. Since this may not be immediately obvious in the case of a human fetus, let us look at another case.

Suppose that our space explorer falls into the hands of an alien culture, whose scientists decide to create a few hundred thousand or more human beings, by breaking his body into its component cells, and using these to create fully developed human beings, with, of course, his genetic code. We may imagine that each of these newly created men will have all of the original man's abilities, skills, knowledge, and so on, and also have an individual self-concept, in short that each of them will be a bona fide (though hardly unique)

person. Imagine that the whole project will take only seconds, and that its chances of success are extremely high, and that our explorer knows all of this, and also knows that these people will be treated fairly. I maintain that in such a situation he would have every right to escape if he could, and thus to deprive all of these potential people of their potential lives; for his right to life outweighs all of theirs together, in spite of the fact that they are all genetically human, all innocent, and all have a very high probability of becoming people very soon if only he refrains from acting.

Indeed, I think he would have a right to escape even if it were not his life which the alien scientists planned to take, but only a year of his freedom, or, indeed, only a day. Nor would he be obligated to stay if he had gotten captured (thus bringing all these people-potentials into existence) because of his own carelessness, or even if he had done so deliberately, knowing the consequences. Regardless of how he got captured, he is not morally obligated to remain in captivity for *any* period of time for the sake of permitting any number of potential people to come into actuality, so great is the margin by which one actual person's right to liberty outweighs whatever right to life even a hundred thousand potential people have. And it seems reasonable to conclude that the rights of a woman will outweigh by a similar margin whatever right to life a fetus may have by virtue of its potential personhood.

Thus, neither a fetus's resemblance to a person, nor its potential for becoming a person provides any basis whatever for the claim that it has any significant right to life. Consequently, a woman's right to protect her health, happiness, freedom, and even her life, by terminating an unwanted pregnancy, will always override whatever right to life it may be appropriate to ascribe to a fetus, even a fully developed one. And thus, in the absence of any overwhelming social need for every possible child, the laws which restrict the right to obtain an abortion, or limit the period of pregnancy during which an abortion may be performed, are a wholly unjustified violation of a woman's most basic moral and constitutional rights.

40

The Moral Equivalent of War

WILLIAM JAMES

William James (1842–1910), philosopher and psychologist, taught psychology at Harvard University and is one of the founders of philosophical pragmatism. In this essay James first laments the tragic history of humankind, marked by war and violence. But he then notes something salutary in the military tradition, worth extracting from the negative aspects: ideals such as courage and discipline, obedience to legitimate commands, endurance, and honor. Unless we can transpose these virtues into a peaceful context, we will not take the desire for war from humanity. James calls for a peace army to combat nature, into which every male should be conscripted. Had James lived in our day, he might have supported the Peace Corps or AmeriCorps. The essay is noteworthy for its plea that militaristic sentiment be channeled for moral, nonmilitary purposes.

The war against war is going to be no holiday excursion or camping party. The military feelings are too deeply grounded to abdicate their place among our ideals until better substitutes are offered than the glory and shame that come to nations as well as to individuals from the ups and downs of politics and the vicissitudes of trade. There is smething highly paradoxical in the modern man's relation to war. Ask all our millions, north and south, whether they would vote now (were such a thing possible) to have our war for the Union expunged from history, and the record of a peaceful transition to the present time substituted for that of its marches

This essay was printed in 1910 as a tract, and 30,000 copies were distributed. It can be found in *The Writings of William James*, edited by John McDermott (New York: Random House, 1967).

and battles, and probably hardly a handful of eccentrics would say yes. Those ancestors, those efforts, those memories and legends, are the most ideal part of what we now own together, a sacred spiritual possession worth more than all the blood poured out. Yet ask those same people whether they would be willing in cold blood to start another civil war now to gain another similar possession, and not one man or woman would vote for the proposition. In modern eyes, precious though wars may be, they must not be waged solely for the sake of the ideal harvest. Only when forced upon one, only when an enemy's injustice leaves us no alternative, is a war now thought permissable.

It was not thus in ancient times. The earlier men were hunting men, and to hunt a neighboring tribe, kill the males, loot the village and possess the females, was the most profitable, as well as the most exciting, way of living. Thus were the more martial tribes selected, and in chiefs and peoples a pure pugnacity and love of glory came to mingle with the more fundamental appetite for plunder.

Modern war is so expensive that we feel trade to be a better avenue to plunder; but modern man inherits all the innate pugnacity and all the love of glory of his ancestors. Showing war's irrationality and horror is of no effect upon him. The horrors make the fascination. War is the *strong* life; it is life *in extremis;* war-taxes are the only ones men never hesitate to pay, as the budgets of all nations show us.

History is a bath of blood. The *Iliad* is one long recital of how Diomedes and Ajax, Sarpedon and Hector *killed*. No detail of the wounds they made is spared us, and the Greek mind fed upon the story. Greek history is a panorama of jingoism and imperialism—war for war's sake, all the citizens being warriors. It is horrible reading, because of the irrationality of it all—save for the purpose of making "history"—and the history is that of the utter ruin of a civilization in intellectual respects perhaps the highest the earth has ever seen.

Those wars were purely piratical. Pride, gold, women, slaves, excitement, were their only motives. In the Peloponnesian war, for example, the Athenians ask the inhabitants of Melos (the island where the "Venus of Milo" was found), hitherto neutral, to own their lordship. The envoys meet, and hold a debate which Thucydides gives in full, and which, for sweet reasonableness of form, would have satisfied Matthew Arnold. "The powerful exact what they can," said the Athenians, "and the weak grant what they must." When the Meleans say that sooner than be slaves they will appeal to the gods, the Athenians reply: "Of the gods we believe and of men we know that, by a law of their nature, wherever they can rule they will. This law was not made by us, and we are not the first to have acted upon it; we did but inherit it, and we know that you and all mankind, if you were as strong as we are, would do as we do. So much for the gods; we have told you why we expect to stand as high in their good opinion as you." Well, the Meleans still refused, and their town was taken. "The Athenians," Thucydides quietly says "thereupon put to death all who were of military age and made slaves of the women and children. They then colonized the island, sending thither five hundred settlers of their own."

Alexander's career was piracy pure and simple, nothing but an orgy of power and plunder, made romantic by the character of the hero. There was no rational principle in it, and the moment he died his generals and governors attacked one another. The cruelty of those times is incredible. When Rome finally conquered Greece, Paulus Aemilius was told by the Roman Senate to reward his soldiers for their toil by "giving" them the old kingdom of Epirus. They sacked seventy cities and carried off a hundred and fifty thousand inhabitants as slaves. How many they killed I know not; but in Etolia they killed all the senators, five hundred and fifty in number. Brutus was "the noblest Roman of them all," but to reanimate his soldiers on the eve of Philippi he similarly promises to give them the cities of Sparta and Thessalonica to ravage, if they win the fight.

Such was the gory nurse that trained societies to cohesiveness. We inherit the warlike type; and for most of the capacities of heroism that the human race is full of we have to thank this cruel history. Dead men tell no tales, and if there were any tribes of other type than this they have left no survivors. Our ancestors have bred pugnacity into our bone and marrow, and thousands of years of peace won't breed it out of us. The popular imagination fairly fattens on the thought of wars. Let public opinion once reach a certain fighting pitch, and no ruler can withstand it. In the Boer War both governments began with bluff but couldn't stay there, the military tension was too much for them. In 1898 our people had read the word "war" in letters three inches high for three months in ever newspaper. The pliant politician McKinley was swept away by their eagerness, and our squalid war with Spain became a necessity.

At the present day, civilized opinion is a curious mental mixture. The military instincts and ideals are as strong as ever, but are confronted by reflective criticisms which sorely curb their ancient freedom. Innumerable writers are showing up the bestial side of military service. Pure loot and mastery seem no longer morally avowable motives, and pretexts must be found for attributing them solely to the enemy. England and we, our army and navy authorities repeat without ceasing, arm solely for "peace," Germany and Japan it is who are bent on loot and glory. "Peace" in military mouths today is a synonym for "war expected." The word has become a pure provocative, and no government wishing peace sincerely should allow it ever to be printed in a newspaper. Every up-to-date dictionary should say that "peace" and "war" mean the same thing, now *in posse*, now *in actu:* It may even reasonably be said that the intensely sharp competitive *preparation* for war by the nation *is the real war,* permanent, unceasing; and that the battles are only a sort of public verification of the mastery gained during the "peace" interval.

It is plain that on this subject civilized man has developed a sort of double personality. If we take European nations, no legitimate interest of any one of them would seem to justify the tremendous destructions which a war to compass it would necessarily entail. It would seem as though common sense and reason ought to find a way to reach agreement in every conflict of honest interests. I myself think it our bounden duty to believe in such international rationality as possible. But, as things stand, I see how desperately hard it is to bring the peace-party and the war-party together, and I believe that the difficulty is due to certain deficiencies in the program of pacifism which set the militarist imagination strongly, and to a certain extent justifiably, against it. In the whole discussion both sides are on imaginative and sentimental ground. It is but one utopia against another, and everything one says must be abstract and hypothetical. Subject to this criticism and caution, I will try to characterize in abstract strokes the opposite imaginative forces, and point out what to my own very fallible mind seems the best utopian hypothesis, the most promising line of conciliation.

In my remarks, pacificist though I am, I will refuse to speak of the bestial side of the war *regime* (already done justice to by many writers) and consider only the higher aspects of militaristic sentiment. Patriotism no one thinks discreditable; nor does any one deny that war is the romance of history. But inordinate ambitions are the soul of every patriotism, and the possibility of violent death the soul of all romance. The military patriotic and romantic-minded everywhere, and especially the professional military class, refuse to admit for a

moment that war may be a transitory phenomenon in social evolution. The notion of a sheep's paradise like that revolts, they say, our higher imagination. Where then would be the steeps of life? If war had ever stopped, we should have to re-invent it, on this view, to redeem life from flat degeneration.

Reflective apologists for war at the present day all take it religiously. It is a sort of sacrament. Its profits are to the vanquished as well as to the victor; and quite apart from any question of profit, it is an absolute good, we are told, for it is human nature at its highest dynamic. Its "horrors" are a cheap price to pay for rescue from the only alternative supposed, of a world of clerks and teachers, of coeducation and zoophily, of "consumer's leagues" and "associated charities," of industrialism unlimited, and feminism unabashed. No scorn, no hardness, no valor any more! Fie upon such a cattleyard of a planet!

So far as the central essence of this feeling goes, no healthy minded person, it seems to me, can help to some degree partaking of it. Militarism is the great preserver of our ideals of hardihood, and human life with no use for hardihood would be contemptible. Without risks or prizes for the darer, history would be insipid indeed; and there is a type of military character which everyone feels that the race should never cease to breed, for every one is sensitive to its superiority. The duty is incumbent on mankind, of keeping military characters in stock—of keeping them, if not of use, then as ends in themselves and as pure pieces of perfection,—so that Roosevelt's weaklings and mollycoddles may not end by making everything else disappear from the face of nature.

This natural sort of feeling forms, I think, the innermost soul of army-writings. Without any exception known to me, militarist authors take a highly mystical view of their subject, and regard war as a biological or sociological necessity, uncontrolled by ordinary psychological checks and motives. When the time of development is ripe the war must come, reason or no reason, for the justifications pleaded are invariably fictitious. War is, in short, a permanent human *obligation*. General Homer Lea, in his recent book "The Valor of Ignorance," plants himself squarely on this ground. Readiness for war is for him the essence of nationality, and ability in it the supreme measure of the health of nations.

Nations, General Lea says, are never stationary—they must necessarily expand or shrink, according to their vitality or decrepitude. Japan now is culminating; and by the fatal law in question it is now impossible that her statesmen should not long since have entered, with extraordinary foresight, upon the vast policy of conquest—the game in which the first moves were her wars with China and Russia and her treaty with England, and of which the final objective is the capture of the Philippines, the Hawaiian Islands, Alaska, and the whole of our Coast west of the Sierra Passes. This will give Japan what her ineluctable vocation as a state absolutely forces her to claim, the possession of the entire Pacific Ocean; and to oppose these deep designs we Americans have according to our author, nothing but our conceit, our ignorance, our commercialism, our corruption, and our feminism. General Lea makes a minute technical comparison of the military strength which we at present could oppose to the strength of Japan, and concludes that the islands, Alaska, Oregon, and Southern California, would fall almost without resistance, that San Francisco must surrender in a fortnight to a Japanese investment, that in three or four months the war would be over, and our republic, unable to regain what it had heedlessly neglected to protect sufficiently, would then "disintegrate," until perhaps some Caesar should arise to weld us again into a nation.

A dismal forecast indeed! Yet not unplausible, if the mentality of Japan's statesmen be of the Caesarian type of which history shows so many examples, and which is all that General Lea seems able to imagine. But there is no reason to think that women can no longer be the mothers of Napoleonic or Alexandrian characters; and if these come in Japan and find their opportunity, just such surprises as "The Valor of Ignorance" paints may lurk in ambush for us. Ignorant as we still are of the innermost recesses of Japanese mentality, we may be foolhardy to disregard such possibilities.

Other militarists are more complex and more moral in their considerations. The "Philosophie des Krieges," by S. R. Steinmetz is a good example. War, according to this author, is an ordeal instituted by God, who weighs the nation in its balance. It is the essential form of the State, and the only function in which peoples can employ all their powers at once and convergently. No victory is possible save as the resultant of a totality of virtues, no defeat for which some vice or weakness is not responsible. Fidelity, cohesiveness, tenacity, heroism, conscience, education, inventiveness, economy, wealth, physical health and vigor—there isn't a moral or intellectual point of superiority that doesn't tell, when God holds his assizes and hurls the peoples upon one another. *Die Weltgeschichte ist das Weltgericht;*[1] and Dr. Steinmetz does not believe that in the long run chance and luck play any part in apportioning the issues.

The virtues that prevail, it must be noted, are virtues anyhow, superiorities that count in peaceful as well as in military competition; but the strain on them, being infinitely intenser in the latter case, makes war infinitely more searching as a trial. No ordeal is comparable to its winnowings. Its dread hammer is the welder of men into cohesive states, and nowhere but in such states can human nature adequately develop its capacity. The only alternative is "degeneration."

Dr. Steinmetz is a conscientious thinker, and his book, short as it is, takes much into account. Its upshot can, it seems to me, be summed up in Simon Patten's word, that mankind was nursed in pain and fear, and that the transition to a "pleasure-economy" may be fatal to a being wielding no powers of defense against its disintegrative influences. If we speak of the *fear of emancipation from the fear-regime*, we put the whole situation into a single phrase; fear regarding ourselves now taking the place of the ancient fear of the enemy.

Turn the fear over as I will in my mind, it all seems to lead back to two unwillingnesses of the imagination, one aesthetic, and the other moral; unwillingness, first to envisage a future in which army-life, with its many elements of charm, shall be forever impossible, and in which the destinies of peoples shall nevermore be decided quickly, thrillingly and tragically, by force, but only gradually and insipidly by "evolution"; and, secondly, unwillingness to see the supreme theatre of human strenuousness closed, and the splendid military aptitudes of men doomed to keep always in a state of latency and never show themselves in action. These insistent unwillingnesses, no less than other aesthetic and ethical insistencies, have, it seems to me, to be listened to and respected. One cannot meet them effectively by mere counter-insistency on war's expensiveness and horror. The horror makes the thrill; and when the question is of getting the extremest and supremest out of human nature, talk of expense sounds ignominious. The weakness of so much merely negative criticism is evident—pacificism makes no converts from the military party. The military party denies neither the bestiality nor the horror, nor the expense; it only says that these things tell but half the story. It only says that war is *worth* them; that, taking human nature as a whole, its wars are its best protection against its weaker and more cowardly self, and that mankind cannot *afford* to adopt a peace-economy.

Pacificists ought to enter more deeply into the aesthetical and ethical point of view of their opponents. Do that first in any controversy, says J. J. Chapman, *then move the point*, and your opponent will follow. So long as anti-militarists propose no substitute for war's disciplinary function, no *moral equivalent* of war, analogous, as one might say, to the mechanical

equivalent of heat, so long they fail to realize the full inwardness of the situation. And as a rule they do fail. The duties, penalties, and sanctions pictured in the utopias they paint are all too weak and tame to touch the military-minded. Tolstoi's pacificism is the only exception to this rule, for it is profoundly pessimistic as regards all this world's values, and makes the fear of the Lord furnish the moral spur provided elsewhere by the fear of the enemy. But our socialistic peace-advocates all believe absolutely in this world's values; and instead of the fear of the Lord and the fear of the enemy, the only fear they reckon with is the fear of poverty if one be lazy, this weakness pervades all the socialistic literature with which I am acquainted. Even in Lowes Dickinson's exquisite dialogue,[2] high wages and short hours are the only forces invoked for overcoming man's distaste for repulsive kinds of labor. Meanwhile men at large still live as they always have lived, under a pain-and-fear economy—for those of us who live in an ease-economy are but an island in the stormy ocean—and the whole atmosphere of present-day utopian literature tastes mawkish and dishwatery to people who still keep a sense for life's more bitter flavors. It suggests, in truth, ubiquitous inferiority.

Inferiority is always with us, and merciless scorn of it is the keynote of the military temper. "Dogs, would you live forever?" shouted Frederick the Great. "Yes," say our utopians, "let us live forever, and raise our level gradually. The best thing about our "inferiors" to-day is that they are as tough as nails, and physically and morally almost as insensitive. Utopianism would see them soft and squeamish, while militarism would keep their callousness, but transfigure it into a meritorious characteristic, needed by "the service," and redeemed by that from the suspicion of inferiority. All the qualities of a man acquire dignity when he knows that the service of the collectivity that owns him needs them. If proud of the collectivity, his own pride rises in proportion. No collectivity is like an army for nourishing such pride; but it has to be confessed that the only sentiment which the image of pacific cosmopolitan industrialism is capable of arousing in countless worthy breasts is shame at the idea of belonging to such a collectivity. It is obvious that the United States of America as they exist to-day impress a mind like General Lea's as so much human blubber. Where is the savage "yes" and "no," the unconditional duty? Where is the conscription? Where is the blood-tax? Where is anything that one feels honored by belonging to?

Having said thus much in preparation, I will now confess my own utopia. I devoutly believe in the reign of peace and in the gradual advent of some sort of a socialistic equilibrium. The fatalistic view of the war-function is to me nonsense, for I know that war-making is due to definite motives and subject to prudential checks and reasonable criticisms, just like any other form of enterprise. And when whole nations are the armies, and the science of destruction vies in intellectual refinement with the sciences of production, I see that war becomes absurd and impossible from its own monstrosity. Extravagant ambitions will have to be replaced by reasonable claims, and nations must make common cause against them. I see no reason why all this should not apply to yellow as well as to white countries, and I look forward to a future when acts of war shall be formally outlawed as between civilized peoples.

All these beliefs of mine put me squarely into the anti-militarist party. But I do not believe that peace either ought to be or will be permanent on this globe, unless the states pacifically organized preserve some of the old elements of army-discipline. A permanently successful peace-economy cannot be a simple pleasure-economy. In the more or less socialistic future towards which mankind seems drifting, we must still subject ourselves collectively to those severities which answer to our real position upon this only partly hospitable globe. We must make new energies and hardihoods continue the manliness to which the military mind so faithfully clings. Martial virtues must

be the enduring cement; intrepidity, contempt of softness, surrender of private interest, obedience to command, must still remain the rock upon which states are built—unless, indeed, we wish for dangerous reactions against commonwealth fit only for contempt, and liable to invite attack whenever a center of crystallization for military-minded enterprise gets formed anywhere in their neighborhood.

The war-party is assuredly right in affirming and reaffirming that the martial virtues, although originally gained by the race though war, are absolute and permanent human goods. Patriotic pride and ambition in their military form are, after all, only specifications of a more general competitive passion. They are its first form, but that is no reason for supposing them to be its last form. Men now are proud of belonging to a conquering nation, and without a murmur they lay down their persons and their wealth, if by so doing they may fend off subjection. But who can be sure that *other aspects of one country* may not, with time and education and suggestion enough, come to be regarded with similarly effective feelings of pride and shame? Why should men not some day feel that it is worth a blood-tax to belong to a collectivity superior in *any* ideal respect? Why should they not blush with indignant shame if the community that owns them is vile in any way whatsoever? Individuals, daily more numerous, now feel this civic passion. It is only a question of blowing on the spark till the whole population gets incandescent, and on the ruins of the old morals of military honor, a stable system of morals of civic honor builds itself up. What the whole community comes to believe in grasps the individual as in a vise. The war-function has grasped us so far; but constructive interests may some day seem no less imperative, and impose on the individual a hardly lighter burden.

Let me illustrate my idea more concretely. There is nothing to make one indignant in the mere fact that life is hard, that men should toil and suffer pain. The planetary conditions once for all are such, and we can stand it. But that so many men, by mere accidents of birth and opportunity, should have a life of *nothing else* but toil and pain and hardness and inferiority imposed upon them, should have *no* vacation, while others natively no more deserving never get any taste of this campaigning life at all,— *this* is capable of arousing indignation in reflective minds. It may end by seeming shameful to all of us that some of us have nothing but campaigning, and others nothing but unmanly ease. If now—and this is my idea—there were, instead of military conscription a conscription of the whole youthful population to form a certain number of years a part of the army enlisted against *Nature,* the injustice would tend to be evened out, and numerous other goods to the commonwealth would follow. The military ideals of hardihood and discipline would be wrought into the growing fiber of the people; no one would remain blind as the luxurious classes now are blind, to man's relations to the globe he lives on, and to the permanently sour and hard foundations of his higher life. To coal and iron mines, to freight trains, to fishing fleets in December, to dish-washing, clothes-washing, and window-washing, to road-building and tunnel-making, to foundries and stoke-holes, and to the frames of skyscrapers, would our gilded youths be drafted off, according to their choice, to get the childishness knocked out of them, and to come back into society with healthier sympathies and soberer ideas. They would have paid their blood–tax, done their own part in the immemorial human warfare against nature; they would tread the earth more proudly, the women would value them more highly, they would be better fathers and teachers of the following generation.

Such a conscription, with the state of public opinion that would have required it, and the many moral fruits it would bear, would preserve in the midst of a pacific civilization the manly virtues which the military party is so afraid of seeing disappear in peace. We should get toughness without callousness, authority

with as little criminal cruelty as possible, and painful work done cheerily because the duty is temporary, and threatens not, as now, to degrade the whole remainder of one's life. I spoke of the "moral equivalent" of war. So far, war has been the only force that can discipline a whole community, and until an equivalent discipline is organized, I believe that war must have its way. But I have no serious doubt that the ordinary prides and shames of social man, once developed to a certain intensity, are capable of organizing such a moral equivalent as I have sketched, or some other just as effective for preserving manliness of type. It is but a question of time, of skillful propagandism, and of opinion-making men seizing historic opportunities.

The martial type of character can be bred without war. Strenuous honor and disinterestedness abound elsewhere. Priests and medical men are in a fashion educated to it, and we should all feel some degree of it imperative if we were conscious of our work as an obligatory service to the state. We should be *owned,* as soldiers are by the army, and our pride would rise accordingly. We could be poor, then, without humiliation, as army officers now are. The only thing needed henceforward is to inflame the civic temper as past history has inflamed the military temper. H. G. Wells, as usual, sees the center of the situation. "In many ways," he says,

Military organization is the most peaceful of activities. When the contemporary man steps from the street, of clamorous insincere advertisement, push, adulteration, underselling and intermittent employment into the barrack-yard, he steps on to a higher social plane, into an atmosphere of service and cooperation and of infinitely more honorable emulations. Here at least men are not flung out of employment to degenerate because there is no immediate work for them to do. They are fed and drilled and trained for better services. Here at least a man is supposed to win promotion by self-forgetfulness and not by self-seeking. And beside the feeble and irregular endowment of research by commericalism, its little short-sighted snatches at profit by innovation and scientific economy, see how remarkable is the steady and rapid development of method and appliances in naval and military affairs! Nothing is more striking than to compare the progress of civil conveniences which has been left almost entirely to the trader, to the progress in military apparatus during the last few decades. The house-appliances of to-day, for example, are little better than they were fifty years ago. A house of to-day is still almost as ill-ventilated, badly heated by wasteful fires, clumsily arranged and furnished as the house of 1858. Houses a couple hundred years old are still satisfactory places of residence, so little have our standards risen. But the rifle or battleship of fifty years ago was beyond all comparison inferior to those we posses,—in power, in speed, in convenience alike. No one has a use now for such superannuated things.[3]

Wells adds that he thinks that the conceptions of order and discipline, the tradition of service and devotion, of physical fitness, unstinted exertion, and universal responsibility, which universal military duty is now teaching European nations, will remain a permanent acquisition, when the last ammunition has been used in the fireworks that celebrate the final peace. I believe as he does. It would be simply preposterous if the only force that could work ideals of honor and standards of efficiency into English or American natures should be the fear of being killed by the Germans or the Japanese. Great indeed is Fear; but it is not, as our military enthusiasts believe and try to make us believe, the only stimulus known for awakening the higher ranges of men's spiritual energy. The amount of alteration in public opinion which my utopia postulates is vastly less than the difference between the mentality of those black warriors who pursued Stanley's party on the Congo with their cannibal war-cry of "Meat! Meat!" and that of the "general-staff" of any civilized nation. History has seen the latter interval bridged over: the former one can be bridged over much more easily.

Notes

1. [Schiller, "The history of the world is the judgment of the world."—Ed.]
2. "Justice and Liberty," New York, 1909.
3. "First and Last Things, 1908, p. 215.

41

Political Action: The Problem of Dirty Hands[1]

MICHAEL WALZER

Michael Walzer (b. 1935) is a Senior Fellow at the Institute for Advanced Studies in Princeton, New Jersey, and the author of several books and articles on moral and political philosophy. In this essay Walzer considers the problem of moral dilemmas. Sometimes our options put us in situations in which we seem to have no choice but to do wrong. An officer fighting on the side of righteousness may have to choose between losing a battle and violating a moral principle in order to win. A politician dedicated to a moral cause may not be able to realize that goal without making a "deal" or compromising his or her integrity. Good political leaders may have no choice but to dirty their hands in carrying out their legitimate and admirable goals. Act-utilitarians would reject such a situation as a misperception. According to them, the moral action is simply the one with the best cost-benefit ratio, the one that maximizes utility. But Walzer rejects such a solution and argues that in politics we face dilemmas regularly.

At the end of the essay he considers three traditional responses to the problem of dirty hands; the neoclassical, the Protestant Weberian response, and Camus' quasi-Catholic response.

In an earlier issue of *Philosophy & Public Affairs* there appeared a symposium on the rules of war which was actually (or at least more importantly) a symposium on another topic.[2] The actual topic was whether or not a man can ever face, or ever has to face, a moral dilemma, a situation where he must choose between two courses of action both of which it would be wrong for him to undertake. Thomas Nagel worriedly suggested that this could happen and that it did happen whenever someone was forced to choose between upholding an important moral principle and avoiding some looming disaster.[3] R. B. Brandt argued that it could not possibly happen, for there were guidelines we might follow and calculations we might go through which would necessarily yield the conclusion that one or the other course of action was the right one to undertake in the circumstances (or that it did not matter which we undertook). R. M. Hare explained how it was that someone might wrongly suppose that he was faced with a moral dilemma: sometimes, he suggested, the precepts and principles of an ordinary man, the products of his moral education, come into conflict with injunctions developed at a higher level of moral discourse. But this conflict is, or ought to be, resolved at the higher level; there is no real dilemma.

I am not sure that Hare's explanation is at all comforting, but the question is important even if no such explanation is possible, perhaps especially so if this is the case. The argument relates not only to the coherence and harmony of the moral universe, but also to the relative ease or difficulty—or impossibility—of living a moral life. It is not, therefore, merely a philosopher's question. If such a dilemma can arise, whether frequently or very rarely, any of us might one day face it. Indeed, many men have faced it, or think they have, especially men involved in political activity or war. The dilemma, exactly as Nagel describes it, is frequently discussed in the literature of political action—in novels and plays dealing with politics and in the work of theorists too.

In modern times the dilemma appears most often as the problem of "dirty hands," and it is typically stated by the Communist leader Hoerderer in Sartre's play of that name: "I have dirty hands right up to the elbows. I've plunged them in filth and blood. Do you think you can govern innocently?"[4] My own answer is no, I don't think I could govern innocently; nor do most of us believe that those who govern us are innocent—as I shall argue below—even the best of them. But this does not mean that it isn't possible to do the right thing while governing. It means that a particular act of government (in a political party or in the state) may be exactly the right thing to do in utilitarian terms and yet leave the man who does it guilty of a moral wrong. The innocent man, afterwards, is no longer innocent. If on the other hand he remains innocent, chooses, that is, the "absolutist" side of Nagel's dilemma, he not only fails to do the right thing (in utilitarian terms), he may also fail to measure up to the duties of his office (which imposes on him a considerable responsibility for consequences and outcomes). Most often, of course, political leaders accept the utilitarian calculations; they try to measure up. One might offer a number of sardonic comments on this fact, the most obvious being that by the calculations they usually make they demonstrate the great virtues of the "absolutist" position. Nevertheless, we would not want to be governed by men who consistently adopted that position.

The notion of dirty hands derives from an effort to refuse "absolutism" without denying the reality of the moral dilemma. Though this may appear to utilitarian philosophers to pile confusion upon confusion, I propose to take it very seriously. For the literature I shall examine is the work of serious and often wise men, and it reflects, though it may also have helped to shape, popular thinking about politics. It is important to pay attention to that too. I shall do so without assuming, as Hare suggests one might, that everyday moral and political discourse constitutes a distinct level of argument,

where content is largely a matter of pedagogic expediency.[5] If popular views are resistant (as they are) to utilitarianism, there may be something to learn from that and not merely something to explain about it.

I

Let me begin, then, with a piece of conventional wisdom to the effect that politicians are a good deal worse, morally worse, than the rest of us (it is the wisdom of the rest of us). Without either endorsing it or pretending to disbelieve it, I am going to expound this convention. For it suggests that the dilemma of dirty hands is a central feature of political life, that it arises not merely as an occasional crisis in the career of this or that unlucky politician but systematically and frequently.

Why is the politician singled out? Isn't he like the other entrepreneurs in an open society, who hustle, lie, intrigue, wear masks, smile and are villains? He is not, no doubt for may reasons, three of which I need to consider. First of all, the politician claims to play a different part than other entrepreneurs. He doesn't merely cater to our interests; he acts on our behalf, even in our name. He has purposes in mind, causes and projects that require the support and redound to the benefit, not of each of us individually, but of all of us together. He hustles, lies, and intrigues *for us*—or so he claims. Perhaps he is right, or at least sincere, but we suspect that he acts for himself also. Indeed, he cannot serve us without serving himself, for success brings him power and glory, the greatest rewards that men can win from their fellows. The competition for these two is fierce; the risks are often great, but the temptations are greater. We imagine ourselves succumbing. Why should our representatives act differently? Even if they would like to act differently, they probably can not: for other men are all too ready to hustle and lie for power and glory, and it is the others who set the terms of the competition. Hustling and lying are necessary because power and glory are so desirable—that is, so widely desired. And so the men who act for us and in our name are necessarily hustlers and liars.

Politicians are also thought to be worse than the rest of us because they rule over us, and the pleasures of ruling are much greater than the pleasures of being ruled. The successful politician becomes the visible architect of our restraint. He taxes us, licenses us, forbids and permits us, directs us to this or that distant goal—all for our greater good. Moreover, he takes chances for our greater good that put us, or some of us, in danger. Sometimes he puts himself in danger too, but politics, after all, is his adventure. It is not always ours. There are undoubtedly times when it is good or necessary to direct the affairs of other people and to put them in danger. But we are a little frightened of the man who seeks, ordinarily and every day, the power to do so. And the fear is reasonable enough. The politician has, or pretends to have, a kind of confidence in his own judgment that the rest of us know to be presumptuous in any man.

The presumption is especially great because the victorious politician uses violence and the threat of violence—not only against foreign nations in our defense but also against us, and again ostensibly for our greater good. This is a point emphasized and perhaps overemphasized by Max Weber in his essay "Politics as a Vocation."[6] It has not, so far as I can tell, played an overt or obvious part in the development of the convention I am examining. The stock figure is the lying, not the murderous, politician—though the murderer lurks in the background, appearing most often in the form of the revolutionary or terrorist, very rarely as an ordinary magistrate or official. Nevertheless, the sheer weight of official violence in human history does suggest the kind of power to which politicians aspire, the kind of power they want to wield, and it may point to the roots of our half-conscious dislike and unease. The men who act for us and in our name are often killers, or seem to become killers too quickly and too easily.

Knowing all this or most of it, good and decent people still enter political life, aiming at some specific reform or seeking a general reformation. They are then required to learn the lesson Machiavelli first set out to teach: "how not to be good."[7] Some of them are incapable of learning; many more profess to be incapable. But they will not succeed unless they learn, for they have joined the terrible competition for power and glory; they have chosen to work and struggle as Machiavelli says, among "so many who are not good." They can do no good themselves unless they win the struggle, which they are unlikely to do unless they are willing and able to use the necessary means. So we are suspicious even of the best of winners. It is not a sign of our perversity if we think them only more clever than the rest. They have not won, after all, because they were good or not only because of that, but also because they were not good. No one succeeds in politics without getting his hands dirty. This is conventional wisdom again, and again I don't mean to insist that it is true without qualification. I repeat it only to disclose the moral dilemma inherent in the convention. For sometimes it is right to try to succeed, and then it must also be right to get one's hands dirty. But one's hands get dirty from doing what it is wrong to do. And how can it be wrong to do what is right? Or, how can we get our hands dirty by doing what we ought to do?

II

It will be best to turn quickly to some examples. I have chosen two, one relating to the struggle for power and one to its exercise. I should stress that in both these cases the men who face the dilemma of dirty hands have in an important sense chosen to do so; the cases tell us nothing about what it would be like, so to speak, to fall into the dilemma; nor shall I say anything about that here. Politicians often argue that they have no right to keep their hands clean, and that may well be true of them, but it is not so clearly true of the rest of us. Probably we do have a right to avoid, if we possibly can, those positions in which we might be forced to do terrible things. This might be regarded as the moral equivalent of our legal right not to incriminate ourselves. Good men will be in no hurry to surrender it, though there are reasons for doing so sometimes, and among these are or might be the reasons good men have for entering politics. But let us imagine a politician who does not agree to that: he wants to do good only by doing good, or a least he is certain that he can stop short of the most corrupting and brutal uses of political power. Very quickly that certainty is tested. What do we think of him then?

He wants to win the election, someone says, but he doesn't want to get his hands dirty. This is meant as a disparagement, even though it also means that the man being criticized is the sort of man who will not lie, cheat, bargain behind the backs of his supporters, shout absurdities at public meetings, or manipulate other men and women. Assuming that this particular election ought to be won, it is clear, I think, that the disparagement is justified. If the candidate didn't want to get his hands dirty, he should have stayed at home; if he can't stand the heat, he should get out of the kitchen, and so on. His decision to run was a commitment (to all of us who think the election important) to try to win, that is, to do within rational limits whatever is necessary to win. But the candidate is a moral man. He has principles and a history of adherence to those principles. That is why we are supporting him. Perhaps when he refuses to dirty his hands, he is simply insisting on being the sort of man he is. And isn't that the sort of man we want?

Let us look more closely at this case. In order to win the election the candidate must make a deal with a dishonest ward boss, involving the granting of contracts for school construction over the next four years. Should he make the deal? Well, at least he shouldn't be surprised by the offer, most of us would probably say (a conventional piece of sarcasm). And he should

accept it or not, depending on exactly what is at stake in the election. But that is not the candidate's view. He is extremely reluctant even to consider the deal, puts off his aides when they remind him of it, refuses to calculate its possible effects upon the campaign. Now, if he is acting this way because the very thought of bargaining with that particular ward boss makes him feel unclean, his reluctance isn't very interesting. His feelings by themselves are not important. But he may also have reasons for his reluctance. He may know, for example, that some of his supporters support him precisely because they believe he is a good man, and this means to them a man who won't make such deals. Or he may doubt his own motives for considering the deal, wondering whether it is the political campaign or his own candidacy that makes the bargain at all tempting. Or he may believe that if he makes deals of this sort now he may not be able later on to achieve those ends that make the campaign worthwhile, and he may not feel entitled to take such risks with a future that is not only his own future. Or he may simply think that the deal is dishonest and therefore wrong, corrupting not only himself but all those human relations in which he is involved.

Because he has scruples of this sort, we know him to be a good man. But we view the campaign in a certain light, estimate its importance in a certain way, and hope that he will overcome his scruples and make the deal. It is important to stress that we don't want just *anyone* to make the deal; we want *him* to make it, precisely because he has scruples about it. We know he is doing right when he makes the deal because he knows he is doing wrong. I don't mean merely that he will feel badly or even very badly after he makes the deal. If he is the good man I am imagining him to be, he will feel guilty, that is, he will believe himself to be guilty. That is what it means to have dirty hands.

All this may become clearer if we look at a more dramatic example, for we are, perhaps, a little blasé about political deals and disinclined to worry much about the man who makes one. So consider a politician who has seized upon a national crisis—a prolonged colonial war—to reach for power. He and his friends win office pledged to decolonization and peace; they are honestly committed to both, though not without some sense of the advantages of the commitment. In any case, they have no responsibility for the war; they have steadfastly opposed it. Immediately, the politician goes off to the colonial capital to open negotiations with the rebels. But the capital is in the grip of a terrorist campaign, and the first decision the new leader faces is this: he is asked to authorize the torture of a captured rebel leader who knows or probably knows the location of a number of bombs hidden in apartment buildings around the city, set to go off within the next twenty-four hours. He orders the man tortured, convinced that he must do so for the sake of the people who might otherwise die in the explosions—even though he believes that torture is wrong, indeed abominable, not just sometimes, but always.[8] He had expressed this belief often and angrily during his own campaign; the rest of us took it as a sign of his goodness. How should we regard him now? (How should he regard himself?)

Once again, it does not seem enough to say that he should feel very badly. But why not? why shouldn't he have feelings like those of St. Augustine's melancholy soldier, who understood both that his war was just and that killing, even in a just war, is a terrible thing to do?[9] The difference is that Augustine did not believe that it was wrong to kill in a just war; it was just sad, or the sort of thing a good man would be saddened by. But he might have thought it wrong to torture in a just war, and later Catholic theorists have certainly thought it wrong. Moreover, the politician I am imagining thinks it wrong, as do many of us who supported him. Surely we have a right to expect more than melancholy from him now. When he ordered the prisoner tortured, he

committed a moral crime and he accepted a moral burden. Now he is a guilty man. His willingness to acknowledge and bear (and perhaps to repent and do penance for) his guilt is evidence, and it is the only evidence he can offer us, both that he is not too good for politics and that he is good enough. Here is the moral politician: it is by his dirty hands that we know him. If he were a moral man and nothing else, his hands would not be dirty; if he were a politician and nothing else, he would pretend that they were clean.

III

Machiavelli's argument about the need to learn how not to be good clearly implies that there are acts known to be bad quite apart from the immediate circumstances in which they are performed or not performed. He points to a distinct set of political methods and stratagems which good men must study (by reading his books), not only because their use does not come naturally, but also because they are explicitly condemned by the moral teachings good men accept—and whose acceptance serves in turn to mark men as good. These methods may be condemned because they are thought contrary to divine law or to the order of nature or to our moral sense, or because in prescribing the law to ourselves we have individually or collectively prohibited them. Machiavelli does not commit himself on such issues, and I shall not do so either if I can avoid it. The effects of these different views are, at least in one crucial sense, the same. They take out of our hands the constant business of attaching moral labels to such Machiavellian methods as deceit and betrayal. Such methods are simply bad. They are the sort of thing that good men avoid, at least until they have learned how not to be good.

Now, if there is no such class of actions, there is no dilemma of dirty hands, and the Machiavellian teaching loses what Machiavelli surely intended it to have, its disturbing and paradoxical character. He can then be understood to be saying that political actors must sometimes overcome their moral inhibitions, but not that they must sometimes commit crimes. I take it that utilitarian philosophers also want to make the first of these statements and to deny the second. From their point of view, the candidate who makes a corrupt deal and the official who authorizes the torture of a prisoner must be described as good men (given the cases as I have specified them), who ought, perhaps, to be honored for making the right decision when it was a hard decision to make. There are three ways of developing this argument. First, it might be said that every political choice ought to be made solely in terms of its particular and immediate circumstances—in terms, that is, of the reasonable alternatives, available knowledge, likely consequences, and so on. Then the good man will face difficult choices (when his knowledge of options and outcomes is radically uncertain), but it cannot happen that he will face a moral dilemma. Indeed, if he always makes decisions in this way, and has been taught from childhood to do so, he will never have to overcome his inhibitions, whatever he does, for how could he have acquired inhibitions? Assuming further that he weighs the alternatives and calculates the consequences seriously and in good faith, he cannot commit a crime, though he can certainly make a mistake, even a very serious mistake. Even when he lies and tortures, his hands will be clean, for he has done what he should do as best he can, standing alone in a moment of time, forced to choose.

This is in some ways an attractive description of moral decision-making, but it also a very improbable one. For while any one of us may stand alone, and so on, when we make this or that decision, we are not isolated or solitary in our moral lives. Moral life is a social phenomenon, and it is constituted at least in part by rules, the knowing of which (and perhaps the making of which) we share with our fellows. The experience of coming up against these rules, challenging their prohibitions, and explaining ourselves to other men and women is so common and so obviously important that no account of moral decision-making can possibly fail to come to grips with it. Hence the second utilitarian argument: such rules do indeed exist, but they are not really prohibitions of wrongful actions (though they do, perhaps for pedagogic reasons, have that form). They are moral guidelines, summaries of previous calculations. They ease our choices in ordinary cases, for we can simply follow their injunctions and do what has been found useful in the past; in exceptional cases they serve as signals warning us against doing too quickly or without the most careful calculations what has not been found useful in the past. But they do no more than that; they have no other purpose, and so it cannot be the case that it is or even might be a crime to override them.[10] Nor is it necessary to feel guilty when one does so. Once again, if it is right to break the rule in some hard case, after conscientiously worrying about it, the man who acts (especially if he knows that many of his fellows would simply worry rather than act) may properly feel pride in his achievement.

But this view, it seems to me, captures the reality of our moral life no better than the last. It may well be right to say that moral rules ought to have the character of guidelines, but it seems that in fact they do not. Or at least, we defend ourselves when we break the rules as if they had some status entirely independent of their previous utility (and we rarely feel proud of ourselves). The defenses we normally offer are not simply justifications; they are also excuses. Now, as Austin says, these two can *seem* to come very close together—indeed, I shall suggest that they can appear side by side in the same sentence—but they are conceptually distinct, differentiated in this crucial respect: an excuse is typically an admission of fault; a justification is typically a denial of fault and an assertion of innocence.[11] Consider a well-known defense from Shakespeare's *Hamlet* that has often reappeared in political literature: "I must be cruel only to be kind."[12] The words are spoken on an occasion when Hamlet is actually being cruel to his mother. I will leave aside the possibility that she deserves to hear (to be forced to listen to) every harsh word he utters, for Hamlet himself makes no such claim—and if she did indeed deserve that, his words might not be cruel or he might not be cruel for speaking them. "I must be cruel" contains the excuse, since it both admits a fault and suggests that Hamlet has no choice but to commit it. He is doing what he has to do; he can't help himself (given the ghost's command, the rotten state of Denmark, and so on). The rest of the sentence is a justification, for it suggests that Hamlet intends and expects kindness to be the outcome of his actions—we must assume that he means greater kindness, kindness to the right persons, or some such. It is not, however, so complete a justification that Hamlet is able to say that he is not *really* being cruel. "Cruel" and "kind" have exactly the same status; they both follow the verb "to be," and so they perfectly reveal the moral dilemma.

When rules are overridden, we do not talk or act as if they had been set aside, canceled, or annulled. They still stand and have this much effect at least: that we know we have done something wrong even if what we have done was also the best thing to do on the whole in the circumstances. Or at least we feel that way, and this feeling is itself a crucial feature of our moral life. Hence the third utilitarian argument, which recognizes the usefulness of guilt and seeks to explain it. There are, it appears, good reasons for "overvaluing" as well as for overriding the rules. For the consequences might be very bad indeed if the rules were overridden every time the moral calculation seemed to go against them. Indeed, if he did not feel guilty, "he would not be such a good man."[13] It is by his feelings that we know him. Because of those feeling he will never be in a hurry to override the rules, but will wait until there is no choice, acting only to avoid consequences that

are both imminent and almost certainly disastrous.

The obvious difficulty with this argument is that the feeling whose usefulness is being explained is most unlikely to be felt by someone who is convinced only of its usefulness. He breaks a utilitarian rule (guideline), let us say, for good utilitarian reasons: but can he then feel guilty, also for good utilitarian reasons, when he has no reason for believing that he is guilty? Imagine a moral philosopher expounding the third argument to a man who actually does feel guilty or to the sort of man who is likely to feel guilty. Either the man won't accept the utilitarian explanation as an account of his feelings about the rules (probably the best outcome from a utilitarian point of view) or he will accept it and then cease to feel that (useful) feeling. But I do not want to exclude the possibility of a kind of superstitious anxiety, the possibility, that is, that some men will continue to feel guilty even after they have been taught, and have agreed, that they cannot possibly be guilty. It is best to say only that the more fully they accept the utilitarian account, the less likely they are to feel that (useful) feeling. The utilitarian account is not at all useful, then, if political actors accept it, and that may help us to understand why it plays, as Hare has pointed out, so small a part in our moral education.

IV

One further comment on the third argument: it is worth stressing that to feel guilty is to suffer, and that the men whose guilt feelings are here called useful are themselves innocent according to the utilitarian account. So we seem to have come upon another case where the suffering of the innocent is permitted and even encouraged by utilitarian calculation. But surely an innocent man who has done something painful or hard (but justified) should be helped to avoid or escape the sense of guilt; he might reasonably expect the assistance of his fellow men, even of moral philosophers, at such a time. On the other hand, if we intuitively think it true of some other man that he *should* feel guilty, then we ought to be able to specify the nature of his guilt (and if he is a good man, win his agreement). I think I can construct a case which, with only small variation, highlights what is different in these two situations.

Consider the common practice of distributing rifles loaded with blanks to some of the members of a firing squad. The individual men are not told whether their own weapons are lethal, and so though all of them look like executioners to the victim in front of them, none of them know whether they are really executioners or not. The purpose of this stratagem is to relieve each man of the sense that he is a killer. It can hardly relieve him of whatever moral responsibility he incurs by serving on a firing squad, and that is not its purpose, for the execution is not thought to be (and let us grant this to be the case) an immoral or wrongful act. But the inhibition against killing another human being is so strong that even if the men believe that what they are doing is right, they will still feel guilty. Uncertainty as to their actual role apparently reduces the intensity of these feelings. If this is so, the stratagem is perfectly justifiable, and one can only rejoice in every case where it succeeds—for every success subtracts one from the number of innocent men who suffer.

But we would feel differently, I think, if we imagine a man who believes (and let us assume here that we believe also) either that capital punishment is wrong or that this particular victim is innocent, but who nevertheless agrees to participate in the firing squad for some overriding political or moral reason—I won't try to suggest what that reason might be. If he is comforted by the trick with the rifles, then we can be reasonably certain that his opposition to capital punishment or his belief in the victim's innocence is not morally serious. And if it is serious, he will not merely feel guilty, he will know that he is guilty (and we will know it too), though he may also believe (and we may agree)

that he has good reasons for incurring the guilt. Our guilt feelings can be tricked away when they are isolated from our moral beliefs, as in the first case, but not when they are allied with them, as in the second. The beliefs themselves and the rules which are believed in can only be *overridden*, a painful process which forces a man to weigh the wrong he is willing to do in order to do right, and which leaves pain behind, and should do so, even after the decision has been made.

V

That is the dilemma of dirty hands as it has been experienced by political actors and written about in the literature of political action. I don't want to argue that it is only a political dilemma. No doubt we can get our hands dirty in private life also, and sometimes, no doubt we should. But the issue is posed most dramatically in politics for the three reasons that make political life the kind of life it is, because we claim to act for others but also serve ourselves, rule over others, and use violence against them. It is easy to get one's hands dirty in politics and it is often right to do so. But it is not easy to teach a good man how not to be good, nor is it easy to explain such a man to himself once he has committed whatever crimes are required of him. At least, it is not easy once we have agreed to use the word "crimes" and to live with (because we have no choice) the dilemma of dirty hands. Still, the agreement is common enough, and on its basis there have developed three broad traditions of explanation, three ways of thinking about dirty hands, which derive in some very general fashion from neoclassical, Protestant, and Catholic perspectives on politics and morality. I want to try to say something very briefly about each of them, or rather about a representative example of each of them, for each seems to me partly right. But I don't think I can put together the compound view that might be wholly right.

The first tradition is best represented by Machiavelli, the first man, so far as I know, to state the paradox that I am examining. The good man who aims to found or reform a republic must, Machiavelli tells us, do terrible things to reach his goal. Like Romulus, he must murder his brother; like Numa, he must lie to the people. Sometimes, however, "when the act accuses, the result excuses."[14] This sentence from *The Discourses* is often taken to mean that the politician's deceit and cruelty are justified by the good results he brings about. But if they were justified, it wouldn't be necessary to learn what Machiavelli claims to teach: how not to be good. It would only be necessary to learn how to be good in a new, more difficult, perhaps roundabout way. That is not Machiavelli's argument. His political judgments are indeed consequentialist in character, but not his moral judgments. We know whether cruelty is used well or badly by its effect over time. But that it is bad to use cruelty we know in some other way. The deceitful and cruel politician is excused (if he succeeds) only in the sense that the rest of us come to agree that the results were "worth it" or, more likely, that we simply forget his crimes when we praise his success.

It is important to stress Machiavelli's own commitment to the existence of moral standards. His paradox depends upon that commitment as it depends upon the general stability of the standards—which he upholds in his consistent use of words like good and bad. If he wants the standards to be disregarded by good men more often than they are, he has nothing with which to replace them and no other way of recognizing the good men except by their allegiance to those same standards. It is exceedingly rare, he writes, that a good man is willing to employ bad means to become prince.[15] Machiavelli's purpose is to persuade such a person to make the attempt, and he holds out the supreme political rewards, power and glory, to the man who does so and succeeds. The good man is not rewarded (or excused), however, merely for his willingness to get his hands dirty. He must do bad things well. There is no reward for doing bad things badly, though they are

done with the best of intentions. And so political action necessarily involves taking risk. But it should be clear that what is risked is not personal goodness—*that is thrown away*—but power and glory. If the politician succeeds, he is a hero; external praise is the supreme reward for not being good.

What the penalties are for not being good, Machiavelli doesn't say, and it is probably for this reason above all that his moral sensitivity has so often been questioned. He is suspect not because he tells political actors they must get their hands dirty, but because he does not specify the state of mind appropriate to a man with dirty hands. A Machiavellian hero has no inwardness. What he thinks of himself we don't know. I would guess, along with most other readers of Machiavelli, that he basks in his glory. But then it is difficult to account for the strength of his original reluctance to learn how not to be good. In any case, he is the sort of man who is unlikely to keep a diary and so we cannot find out what he thinks. Yet we do want to know; above all, we want a record of his anguish. That is a sign of our own conscientiousness and of the impact on us of the second tradition of thought that I want to examine, in which personal anguish sometimes seems the only acceptable excuse for political crimes.

The second tradition is best represented, I think, by Max Weber, who outlines its essential features with great power at the very end of his essay "Politics as a Vocation." For Weber, the good man with dirty hands is a hero still, but he is a tragic hero. In part, his tragedy is that though politics is his vocation, he has not been called by God and so cannot be justified by Him. Weber's hero is alone in a world that seems to belong to Satan, and his vocation is entirely his own choice. He still wants what Christian magistrates have always wanted, both to do good in the world and to save his soul, but now these two ends have come into sharp contradiction. They are contradictory because of the necessity for violence in a world where God has not instituted the sword. The politician takes the sword himself, and only by doing so does he measure up to his vocation. With full consciousness of what he is doing, he does bad in order to do good, and surrenders his soul. He "lets himself in," Weber says, "for the diabolic forces lurking in all violence." Perhaps Machiavelli also meant to suggest that his hero surrenders salvation in exchange for glory, but he does not explicitly say so. Weber is absolutely clear: "the genius or demon of politics lives in an inner tension with the god of love . . . [which] can at any time lead to an irreconcilable conflict."[16] His politician views this conflict when it comes with a tough realism, never pretends that it might be solved by compromise, chooses politics once again, and turns decisively away from love. Weber writes about this choice with a passionate high-mindedness that makes a concern for one's soul seem no more elevated than a concern for one's flesh. Yet the reader never doubts that his mature, superbly trained, relentless, objective, responsible, and disciplined political leader is also a suffering servant. His choices are hard and painful, and he pays the price not only while making them but forever after. A man doesn't lose his soul one day and find it the next.

The difficulties with this view will be clear to anyone who has ever met a suffering servant. Here is a man who lies, intrigues, sends other men to their death—and suffers. He does what he must do with a heavy heart. None of us can know, he tells us, how much it costs him to do his duty. Indeed, we cannot, for he himself fixes the price he pays. And that is the trouble with this view of political crime. We suspect the suffering servant of either masochism or hypocrisy or both, and while we are often wrong, we are not always wrong. Weber attempts to resolve the problem of dirty hands entirely within the confines of the individual conscience, but I am inclined to think that this is neither possible nor desirable. The self-awareness of the tragic hero is obviously of great value. We want the politician to have an inner life at least something like that which Weber describes. But sometimes the

hero's suffering needs to be socially expressed (for like punishment, it confirms and reinforces our sense that certain acts are wrong). And equally important, it sometimes needs to be socially limited. We don't want to be ruled by men who have lost their souls. A politician with dirty hands needs a soul, and it is best for us all if he has some hope of personal salvation, however that is conceived. It is not the case that when he does bad in order to do good he surrenders himself forever to the demon of politics. He commits a determinate crime, and he must pay a determinate penalty. When he has done so, his hands will be clean again, or as clean as human hands can ever be. So the Catholic Church has always taught, and this teaching is central to the third tradition that I want to examine.

Once again I will take a latter-day and a lapsed representative of the tradition and consider Albert Camus' *The Just Assasins*. The heroes of this play are terrorists at work in nineteenth-century Russia. The dirt on their hands is human blood. And yet Camus' admiration for them, he tells us, is complete. We consent to being criminals, one of them says, but there is nothing with which anyone can reproach us. Here is the dilemma of dirty hands in a new form. The heroes are innocent criminals, just assassins, because, having killed, they are prepared to die—*and will die*. Only their execution, by the same despotic authorities they are attacking, will complete the action in which they are engaged: dying, they need make no excuses. That is the end of their guilt and pain. The execution is not so much punishment as self-punishment and expiation. On the scaffold they wash their hands clean and, unlike the suffering servant, they die happy.

Now the argument of the play when presented in so radically simplified a form may seem a little bizarre, and perhaps it is marred by the moral extremism of Camus' politics. "Political action has limits," he says in a preface to the volume containing *The Just Assassins*, "and there is no good and just action but what recognizes those limits and if it must go beyond them, at least accepts death."[17] I am less interested here in the violence of that "at least" — what else does he have in mind?—than in the sensible doctrine that it exaggerates. That doctrine might best be described by an analogy: just assassination, I want to suggest, is like civil disobedience. In both men violate a set of rules, go beyond a moral or legal limit, in order to do what they believe they should do. At the same time, they acknowledge their responsibility for the violation by accepting punishment or doing penance. But there is also a difference between the two, which has to do with the difference between law and morality. In most cases of civil disobedience the laws of the state are broken for moral reasons, and the state provides the punishment. In most cases of dirty hands moral rules are broken for reasons of state, and no one provides the punishment. There is rarely a Czarist executioner waiting in the wings for politicians with dirty hands, even the most deserving among them. Moral rules are not usually enforced against the sort of actor I am considering, largely because he acts in an official capacity. If they were enforced, dirty hands would be no problem. We would simply honor the man who did bad in order to do good, and at the same time we would punish him. We would honor him for the good he has done, and we would punish him for the bad he has done. We would punish him, that is, for the same reasons we punish anyone else; it is not my purpose here to defend any particular view of punishment. In any case, there seems no way to establish or enforce the punishment. Short of the priest and the confessional there are no authorities to whom we might entrust the task.

I am nevertheless inclined to think Camus' view the most attractive of the three, if only because it requires us at least to imagine a punishment or a penance that fits the crime and so to examine closely the nature of the crime. The others do not require that. Once he has launched his career, the crimes of Machiavelli's prince seem subject only to prudential control.

And the crimes of Weber's tragic hero are limited only by *his* capacity for suffering and not, as they should be, by *our* capacity for suffering. In neither case is there any explicit reference back to the moral code, once it has, at great personal cost to be sure, been set aside. The question posed by Sartre's Hoerderer (whom I suspect of being a suffering servant) is rhetorical, and the answer is obvious (I have already given it), but the characteristic sweep of both is disturbing. Since it is concerned only with those crimes that ought to be committed, the dilemma of dirty hands seems to exclude questions of degree. Wanton or excessive cruelty is not at issue, any more than is cruelty directed at bad ends. But political action is so uncertain that politicians necessarily take moral as well as political risks, committing crimes that they only think ought to be committed. They override the rules without ever being certain that they have found the best way to the results they hope to achieve, and we don't want them to do that too quickly or too often. So it is important that the moral stakes be very high—which is to say, that the rules be rightly valued. That, I suppose, is the reason for Camus' extremism. Without the executioner, however, there is no one to set the stakes or maintain the values except ourselves, and probably no way to do either except through philosophic reiteration and political activity.

"We shall not abolish lying by refusing to tell lies," says Hoerderer, "but by using every means at hand to abolish social classes."[18] I suspect we shall not abolish lying at all, but we might see to it that fewer lies were told if we contrived to deny power and glory to the greatest liars—except of course, in the case of those lucky few whose extraordinary achievements make us forget the lies they told. If Hoerderer succeeds in abolishing social classes, perhaps he will join the lucky few. Meanwhile, he lies, manipulates, and kills, and we must make sure he pays the price. We won't be able to do that, however, without getting our own hands dirty, and then we must find some way of paying the price ourselves.

Notes

1. An earlier version of this paper was read at the annual meeting of the Conference for the Study of Political Thought in New York, April 1971. I am indebted to Charles Taylor, who served as commentator at that time and encouraged me to think that its arguments might be right.

2. *Philosophy Public Affairs* 1, no. 2 (Winter 1971/72): Thomas Nagel, "War and Massacre," pp. 123–44; R. B. Brandt, "Utilitarianism and the Rules of War," pp. 145–65; and R. M. Hare, "Rules of War and Moral Reasoning," pp. 166–81.

3. For Nagel's description of a possible "moral blind alley," see "War and Massacre," pp. 142–44. Bernard Williams has made a similar suggestion though without quite acknowledging it as his own: "many people can recognize the thought that a certain course of action is, indeed, the best thing to do on the whole in the circumstances, but that doing it involves doing something wrong" (*Morality: An Introduction to Ethics* [New York, 1972], p. 93).

4. Jean-Paul Sartre, *Dirty Hands*, in *No Exit and Three Other Plays*, trans. Lionel Abel (New York, n.d.), p. 224.

5. Hare, "Rules of War and Moral Reasoning," pp. 173–78, esp. p. 174: "the simple principles of the deontologist . . . have their place at the level of character-formation (moral education and self-education)."

6. In *From Max Weber: Essays in Sociology*, trans. and ed. Hans H. Gerth and C. Wright Mills (New York, 1946), pp. 77–128.

7. See *The Prince*, chap. XV; cf. *The Discourses*, bk. I, chaps. IX and XVIII. I quote from the Modern Library edition of the two works (New York, 1950), p. 57.

8. I leave aside the question of whether the prisoner is himself responsible for the terrorist campaign. Perhaps he opposed it in meetings of the rebel organization. In any case, whether he deserves to be punished or not, he does not deserve to be tortured.

9. Other writers argued that Christians must never kill, even in a just war; and there was also an intermediate position which suggests the origins of the idea of dirty hands. Thus Basil The Great (Bishop of Caesarea in the fourth century A.D.): "Killing in war was differentiated by our fathers from murder . . . nevertheless, perhaps it would be well that those whose hands are unclean abstain from communion for three years." Here dirty hands are a kind of impurity or unworthiness, which is not the same as guilt, though closely related to it. For a general survey of these and other Christian views, see Roland H. Bainton, *Christian Attitudes Toward War and Peace* (New York, 1960), esp. chaps. 5–7.

10. Brandt's rules do not appear to be of the sort that can be overridden—except perhaps by a soldier who decides that he just *won't* kill any more civilians, no matter what cause is served—since all they require is careful calculation. But I take it that rules of a different sort, which have the form of ordinary injunctions and prohibitions, can and often do figure in what is called "rule-utilitarianism."

11. J. L. Austin, "A Plea for Excuses," in *Philosophical Papers*, ed. J. O. Urmson and G. J. Warnock (Oxford, 1961), pp. 123–52.

12. *Hamlet* 3.4.178.

13. Hare, "Rules of War and Moral Reasoning," p. 179.

14. *The Discourses*, bk. I, chap. IX (p. 139).

15. *The Discourses*, bk. I, chap. XVIII (p. 171).

16. "Politics as a Vocation," pp. 125–26. But sometimes a political leader does choose the "absolutist" side of the conflict, and Weber writes (p. 127) that it is "immensely moving when a *mature* man . . . aware of a responsibility for the consequences of his conduct . . . reaches a point where he says: 'Here I stand; I can do no other.' " Unfortunately, he does not suggest just where that point is or even where it might be.

17. *Caligula and Three Other Plays* (New York, 1958), p. x. (The preface is translated by Justin O'Brian, the plays by Stuart Gilbert.)

18. *Dirty Hands*, p. 223.

Selected Bibliography

Part 1

Ethical Theory (General)

Baier, Kurt. *The Moral Point of View.* Ithaca, N.Y.: Cornell University Press, 1958. This influential work sees morality primarily in terms of social control.

Frankena, William K. *Ethics.* 2d ed. Englewood Cliffs, N.J.: Prentice-Hall, 1973. A succinct, reliable guide.

Gert, Bernard. *Morality: A New Justification of the Moral Rules.* 2d ed. Oxford: Oxford University Press, 1988. A clear and comprehensive discussion of the nature of morality.

MacIntyre, Alasdair. *A Short History of Ethics.* New York: Macmillan, 1966. A lucid, if uneven, survey of the history of Western ethics.

Mackie, J. L. *Ethics: Inventing Right and Wrong.* New York: Penguin, 1976. This book takes a very different view of ethics from mine, viewing ethics from a skeptical perspective.

Pojman, Louis. *Ethics: Discovering Right and Wrong.* Belmont, Calif.: Wadsworth Publishing Company, 1990. An objectivist perspective.

Singer, Peter. *The Expanding Circle: Ethics and Sociobiology.* Oxford: Oxford University Press, 1983. A fascinating attempt to relate ethics to sociobiology.

Taylor, Paul. *Principles of Ethics.* Evanston, Ill.: Dickerson, 1975. This work covers many of the same topics as my book, usually from a different perspective. His discussion of the principle of universalizabiltiy (pp. 95–105) is especially useful.

Taylor, Richard. *Good and Evil.* Buffalo, N.Y.: Prometheus, 1970. A lively, easy-to-read work that sees the main role of morality to be the resolution of conflicts of interest.

Turnbull, Colin. *The Mountain People.* New York: Simon & Schuster, 1972. An excellent anthropological study of a people living on the edge of morality.

Van Wyk, Robert. *Introduction to Ethics.* New York: St. Martin's Press, 1990. A clearly written recent introduction to the subject.

Warnock, G. J. *The Object of Morality.* London: Methuen, 1971. A clearly written, well-argued analysis of the nature of morality.

Part II

Ethical Relativism and Objectivism

Brink, David. *Moral Realism and the Foundation of Ethics.* Cambridge: Cambridge University Press, 1989.

Fishkin, James. *Beyond Subjective Morality.* New Haven: Yale University Press, 1984.

Harman, Gilbert. "Moral Relativism Defended." *Philosophical Review* 84 (1975).

Ladd, John, ed. *Ethical Relativism.* Belmont, Calif.: Wads-worth Publishing Company, 1973. A good collection of basic readings.

Westermarck, Edward. *Ethical Relativity.* Atlantic Highlands, N.J.: Humanities Press, 1960.

Williams, Bernard. *Morality.* New York: Harper Torchbooks, 1972.

Wong, David Berkeley and Los Angeles: University of California Press, 1985.

Part III

Morality, Self-Interest, and Egoism

Axelrod, Robert M. *The Evolution of Cooperation.* New York: Basic Books, 1984. A brilliant study on the rationality of cooperation.

Dawkins, Richard. *The Selfish Gene.* 2d ed. Oxford: Oxford University Press, 1989. One of the most fascinating studies on the subject, defending limited altruism.

Gauthier, David. *Morality by Agreement.* Oxford: Clarendon Press, 1986.

Gauthier, David, ed. *Morality and Rational Self-Interest.* Englewood Cliffs, N.J.: Prentice-Hall, 1970.

Hospers, John. *Human Conduct: An Introduction to the Problems of Ethics.* New York: Harcourt Brace Jovanovich, 1961.

MacIntyre, Alasdair, "Egoism and Altruism." In *The Encyclopedia of Philosophy,* edited by Paul Edwards. New York: Macmillan, 1967.

Nielsen, Kai. "Why Should I be Moral?" *Methodos* 15, no. 59–60 (1963). This comprehensive article appears in several anthologies.

Olen, Jeffrey. *Moral Freedom.* Philadelphia: Temple University Press, 1988.

Rachels, James. *The Elements of Moral Philosophy.* New York: Random House, 1986. Chapters 5 and 6.

Singer, Peter. *The Expanding Circle: Ethics and Sociobiology.* N.Y.: Farrar, Straus & Giroux, 1981.

Taylor, Richard. *Good and Evil.* New York: Macmillan, 1970. Especially Chapter 5.

Part IV

Value

Aristotle. *Nicomachean Ethics.* Books I and X. There are several good translations, including those of T. E. Irwin, Martin Ostwald, W. D. Ross, and J. A. K. Thomson.

Bond, E. J. *Reason and Value.* Cambridge: Cambridge University Press, 1983. A thoughtful defense of objectivism in values.

Brandt, Richard B. "Happiness." In *Encyclopedia of Philosophy,* edited by Paul Edwards. New York: Macmillan, 1969.

Hospers, John. *Human Conduct: Problem of Ethics.* New York: Harcourt Brace Jovanovich, 1972. Chapters 2–8. An accessible introduction.

Nagel, Thomas. *The View from Nowhere.* Oxford: Oxford University Press, 1986.

Nietzsche, Friedrich. *Beyond Good and Evil.* Translated by Walter Kaufmann. New York: Random House, 1966.

Rescher, Nicholas. *Introduction to Value Theory.* Englewood Cliffs, N.J.: Prentice-Hall, 1982.

Ross, W. D. *The Right and the Good.* Oxford: Oxford University Press, 1930. Chapters 3–7 for a seminal discussion of the nature of Good.

Taylor, Richard. *Good and Evil.* New York: Macmillan, 1970.

Part V

Utilitarianism

Bentham, Jeremy. *Introduction to the Principles of Morals and Legislation.* Edited by W. Harrison. Oxford: Oxford University Press, 1948.

Hardin, Russell. *Morality within the Limits of Reason.* Chicago: University of Chicago Press, 1988. A cogent contemporary defense of utilitarianism.

Hare, R. M. *Moral Thinking.* Oxford: Oxford University Press, 1981.

Mill, John Stuart. *Utilitarianism.* Indianapolis: Bobbs-Merrill, 1957.

Quinton, Anthony. *Utilitarian Ethics.* New York: Macmillan, 1973. A clear exposition of classical utilitarianism.

Smart, J. J. C., and Bernard Williams. *Utilitarianism For and Against.* Cambridge: Cambridge University Press, 1973. A classic debate on the subject.

Part VI

Deontological Ethics

Acton, Harry. *Kant's Moral Philosophy.* New York: Macmillan, 1970.

Broad, C. D. *Five Types of Ethical Theory.* London: Routledge and Kegan Paul, 1930.

Donagan, Alan. *The Theory of Morality.* Chicago: University of Chicago Press, 1977.

Feldman, Fred. *Introductory Ethics.* Englewood Cliffs, N.J.: Prentice-Hall, 1978. Chapters 7 and 8. A clear and critical exposition.

Harris, C. E. *Applying Moral Theories.* Belmont, Calif.: Wadsworth, 1986. Chapter 7. An excellent exposition of contemporary deontological theories, especially of Gewirth's work.

Kant, Immanuel. *Critique of Practical Reason.* Translated by Lewis White Beck. Indianapolis: Bobbs-Merrill, 1956.

———. *Grounding for the Metaphysics of Morals.* Translated by James Ellington. Indianapolis: Hackett Publishing Company, 1981.

———. *Lectures on Ethics.* Translated by Louis Infield. Indianapolis: Hackett Publishing Company, 1963.

Raphael, D. D. *Moral Philosophy.* Oxford: Oxford University Press, 1981. Chapter 6.

Ross, W. D. *Kant's Ethical Theory.* Oxford: Clarendon Press, 1954.

———. *The Right and the Good.* Oxford: Clarendon Press, 1930.

Ward, Keith. *The Development of Kant's Views of Ethics.* Oxford: Blackwell, 1972.

Wolff, Robert P. *The Autonomy of Reason: A Commentary on Kant's* Groundwork of the Metaphysics of Morals. New York: Harper & Row, 1973.

Part VII

Virtue Ethics

Anscombe, Elizabeth. "Modern Moral Philosophy." *Philosophy* 33 (1958).

Blum, Lawrence A. *Friendship, Altruism and Morality.* London: Routledge & Kegan Paul, 1980.

Foot, Philippa. *Virtues and Vices.* Oxford: Blackwell, 1978. A collection of articles by one of the foremost virtue ethicists.

French, Peter, T. Uehling, and H. K. Wettstein, eds. *Midwest Studies in Philosophy.* Vol. 13, *Ethical Theory: Character and Virtue.* South Bend, Ind.: University of Notre Dame Press, 1988. This book contains several important recent articles on the virtues, including David Norton's "Moral Minimalism and the Development of Moral Character."

Kruschwitz, Robert, and Robert Roberts, eds. *The Virtues.* Belmont, Calif.: Wadsworth, 1987. Contains excellent readings and bibliography.

Loudan, Robert. "Some Vices of Virtue Ethics." *American Philosophical Quarterly* 21 (1984). Reprinted in Kruschwitz and Roberts, *The Virtues.*

MacIntyre, Alasdair. *After Virtue.* South Bend, Ind.: University of Notre Dame Press, 1981.

Murdoch, Iris. *The Sovereignty of Good.* New York: Schocken Books, 1971.

Taylor, Richard. *Ethics, Faith and Reason.* Englewood Cliffs, N.J.: Prentice-Hall, 1985.

Wallace, James. *Virtues and Vices.* Ithaca, N.Y.: Cornell University Press, 1978.

Part VIII

Morality and Religion

Adams, Robert M. *The Virtue of Faith.* Oxford: Oxford University Press, 1987. Especially Part III.

Helm, Paul, ed. *The Divine Command Theory of Ethics.* Oxford: Oxford University Press, 1979. Contains valuable articles by Frankena, Rachels, Quinn, Adams, and Young.

Kant, Immanuel. *Religion within the Bounds of Reason Alone.* Translated by T. M. Greene and H. H. Hudson. New York: Harper and Row, 1960.

Kierkegaard, Søren. *Fear and Trembling.* Translated by Howard and Edna Hong. Princeton, N.J.: Princeton University Press, 1983.

Mitchell, Basil. *Morality: Religious and Secular.* Oxford: Oxford University Press, 1980.

Nielsen, Kai. *Ethics without a God.* San Angelo, Tx.: Pemberton Books, 1973. A very accessible defense of secular morality.

Ward, Keith. *Ethics and Christianity.* London: George Allen & Unwin, 1970.

Part IX

Applied Ethics

Aiken, William, and Hugh LaFollette, eds. *World Hunger and Moral Obligation.* Englewood Cliffs, N.J.: Prentice-Hall, 1977.

Christopher, Paul. *The Ethics of War and Peace.* Englewood Cliffs, N.J.: Prentice-Hall, 1994.

Divine, Philip. *The Ethics of Homicide.* Ithaca, N.Y.: Cornell University Press, 1978.

Norman, Richard. *Ethics, Killing and War.* Cambridge: Cambridge University Press, 1995.

Pojman, Louis, and Frank Beckwith, eds. *The Abortion Controversy.* 2d ed. Belmont, Calif.: Wadsworth, 1998.

Sartre, Jean-Paul. *Dirty Hands,* in *No Exit and Three Other Plays,* translated by Lionel Abel. New York: Vintage, 1949.

Singer, Peter. *Practical Ethics.* 2d ed. Cambridge: Cambridge University Press, 1993.

Walzer, Michael. *Just and Unjust Wars.* New York: Basic Books, 1977.